MAPI, SAPI, and TAPI
Developer's Guide

Michael C. Amundsen

SAMS
PUBLISHING

201 West 103rd Street
Indianapolis, Indiana 46290

SAMS Developer's Guide

This book is dedicated to Joe and Ida LaSala in thanks for their love, support, and generosity over the last twenty years.

President and Publisher	Richard K. Swadley
Publishing Team Leader	Greg Wiegand
Managing Editor	Cindy Morrow
Director of Marketing	John Pierce
Assistant Marketing Managers	Kristina Perry
	Rachel Wolfe

Acquisitions Editor
Sharon Cox

Development Editor
Tony Amico
Andrew Fritzinger

Software Development Specialist
Steve Straiger

Production Editor
Mary Ann Faughnan

Indexer
Chris Barrick

Technical Reviewer
John Charlesworth

Editorial Coordinator
Bill Whitmer

Technical Edit Coordinator
Lynette Quinn

Resource Coordinator
Deborah Frisby

Editorial Assistants
Carol Ackerman
Andi Richter
Rhonda Tinch-Mize

Cover Designer
Tim Amrhein

Book Designer
Alyssa Yesh

Copy Writer
Peter Fuller

Production Team Supervisor
Brad Chinn

Production
Stephen Adams, Debra Bolhuis,
Mona Brown, Michael Dietsch,
Jason Hand, Daniel Harris,
Susan Knose, Casey Price,
Laura Robbins, Susan Van Ness

Overview

	Introduction	xxii

Part I Introduction

1	Windows Communications Overview	3
2	Introduction to Windows Open Services Architecture (WOSA)	11

Part II The Messaging API (MAPI)

3	What Is MAPI?	25
4	MAPI Architecture	37
5	Using the Microsoft Exchange Forms Designer	57
6	Creating MAPI-Aware Applications	91
7	Creating a Simple MAPI Client with the MAPI Controls	129
8	The OLE Messaging Library	161
9	Creating a MAPI Mailing List Manager with the OLE Messaging Library	221
10	Building a MAPI-Enabled Forum Tool	259
11	Creating a MAPI E-Mail Agent	311
12	Creating Windows Messaging Client Extensions	373
13	Part II Summary—The Messaging API	411

Part III The Speech API (SAPI)

14	What Is SAPI?	423
15	SAPI Architecture	435
16	SAPI Basics	455
17	SAPI Tools—Using SAPI Objects with Visual Basic 4.0	469
18	SAPI Behind the Scenes	505
19	Creating SAPI Applications with C++	533
20	Building the Voice-Activated Text Reader	563
21	Part III Summary—The Speech API	583

Part IV The Telephony API (TAPI)

22	What Is TAPI?	593
23	TAPI Architecture	607
24	TAPI Basics	633
25	TAPI Hardware Considerations	653
26	TAPI Tools—Using the TAPILine Control	663
27	TAPI Behind the Scenes—The TELEPHON.INI File	703
28	Using TAPI to Handle Incoming Calls	725
29	Writing TAPI-Assisted Applications	745
30	Creating TAPI-Enabled Applications	779
31	Third-Party TAPI Tools	841
32	Part IV Summary—The Telephony API	875

Part V Creating Integrated Applications

33	Design Considerations for Integrated Communications Applications	885
34	Building the FaxBack Application	895
35	Creating the Voice Phone Application	923
36	The Talk Mail Project	959
37	Integration Summary	1009

Part VI Appendixes

A	MAPI Resources	1017
B	SAPI Resources	1027
C	TAPI Resources	1041
D	The CD-ROM Contents	1063
	Index	1065

Contents

Introduction   **xxii**

I Introduction

1   Windows Communications Overview   3

MAPI Message Services 4
TAPI Telephony Services 4
SAPI Speech Services 5
MCI Multimedia Services 5
Applications Covered in This Book 5
Development Tools 6
Hardware and Software Tools 7
What's Not Covered in This Book 8
How to Use This Book 9

2   Introduction to Windows Open Services Architecture (WOSA)   11

What Is WOSA? 12
The WOSA Model 13
   The Client API Makes Requests 13
   The Server SPI Responds to Requests 14
   The Interface DLL Talks to Both the API and SPI 15
WOSA Services 16
   Common Application Services 16
   Communication Services 17
   Vertical Market Services 17
Benefits of WOSA 18
   Isolated Development 18
   Multivendor Support 19
   Upgrade Protection 19
   Leveraging WOSA in Your Own Applications 19
Summary 20

II The Messaging API (MAPI)

3   What Is MAPI?   25

MAPI Services and Windows 26
   Flexibility 27
   Consistency 28
   Portability 28

Messages 29
    Text Messages 30
    Formatted Documents and Binary Files 30
    Control Messages 30
  MAPI Applications 31
    Electronic Mail Clients 31
    Message-Aware Applications 32
    Message-Enabled Applications 32
    Other Types of Message Applications 33
  Summary 35

4   MAPI Architecture   37
  The MAPI Client 39
    Messages and Attachments 39
    Storage Folders 45
    Addresses 47
  The MAPI Server 48
    Message Transport 50
    Message Stores 51
    Address Books 52
  The MAPI Spooler 54
  Summary 55

5   Using the Microsoft Exchange Forms Designer   57
  Introduction 58
  What Is the Microsoft Exchange Forms Designer? 58
    EFD Design Wizards 59
    The QuickHelp Feature 59
    Extending EFD with Visual Basic 59
  Using the Microsoft Exchange Forms Designer to Create
    a Custom Form 60
    Using the Microsoft Exchange Forms Designer Wizard 60
    Modifying the Job Request Form 65
    Completing the Job Request Form Fields 67
    Setting Form and Window Properties of the Job Request Form 68
    Adding Online Help to the Job Request Form 75
    Installing the Job Request Form 77
    Testing the Job Request Form 78
    More Forms Designing Techniques 80
  Designing Microsoft Exchange Folders 80
    Creating and Managing Folder Views 81
    Installing Forms in Folders 87
  Summary 89

6   Creating MAPI-Aware Applications   91

The Simple MAPI API Calls 92

The User-Defined Types 93

The API Functions 97

Creating Mail-Aware Applications 121

Creating `QIKMAIL.XLS` with Excel 121

Adding MAPI Services to Existing Visual Basic 4.0 Programs 123

Summary 127

7   Creating a Simple MAPI Client with the MAPI Controls   129

The Visual Basic MAPI Controls 130

The `MAPISession` Control 131

The `MAPIMessage` Control 134

Building a Simple MAPI Client Application 143

Laying Out the Forms 143

Coding the Main Support Routines 148

Coding the `MAPIMAIN.FRM` Events 151

Coding the Main Button Bar 153

Coding the Reader Form 155

Running the Simple Mail Client 157

Additional Features 158

Summary 159

8   The OLE Messaging Library   161

Introduction 162

The `Session` Object 162

The `Session` Object Methods 162

The `Session` Object Properties 168

The `InfoStore` Objects and Collections 170

The `InfoStores` Collection 170

The `InfoStore` Object 173

The `Folder` Objects and Collections 175

The `Folders` Collection Object 175

The `Folder` Object 177

The `Inbox` and `OutBox` Folders 180

The `Message` Objects and Collections 180

The `Messages` Collection Object 180

The `Message` Object 184

The `Recipient` Objects and Collections and the `Address` Object 194

The `Recipients` Collection Object 194

The `Recipient` Object 198

The `AddressEntry` Object 203

The `Attachment` Objects and Collections 209

The `Attachments` Collection Object 209

The `Attachment` Object 212

Summary 219

**9   Creating a MAPI Mailing List Manager with
the OLE Messaging Library   221**

Introduction 222

Laying Out the MLM Form 222

Coding the Support Routines 228

Coding the Edit Routines 230

Coding the `MAPIStart` and `MAPIEnd` routines 235

Coding the `SendMail` Routines 236

Coding the `Inbox` Routines 240

Adding New Subscribers 243

Dropping Subscribers 247

Listing Archives 249

Sending Requested Archives 251

Running the MLM Application 254

Testing the MLM Application 255

Summary 258

10   Building a MAPI-Enabled Forum Tool   259

Discussion Groups versus E-Mail 260

Folders as Destinations 261

Using the `ConversationTopic` and `ConversationIndex` Properties 261

`Update` versus `Send` 263

The Discuss Project 265

The `MAPIPost` Code Library 266

The Discuss and Msgs Forms 279

Laying Out the Discuss Form 279

Coding the Discuss Form 285

Laying Out and Coding the Msgs Form 289

Building the Other Forms 291

The Note Form 291

The Options Form 298

The About Dialog Box 305

Testing the Discuss Forum Tool 307

Summary 309

11   Creating a MAPI Email Agent   311

Designing the Email Agent 312

Features of the MAPI Email Agent 313

Storing the Rules in a Control File 314

Coding the MAPI Email Agent Forms 315
   The Main Form 316
   The Add Rule Form 327
   The Setup Form 332
Coding the Support Routines 341
   The Initialization Routines 341
   The List-Handling Routines 351
   The Message Processing Routines 358
Installing and Testing the MAPI Email Agent 369
   Setting Up Your Email Folders 369
   Building MAPI Email Agent Actions, Tests, and Rules 370
   Running the MAPI Email Agent 371
Summary 371

12   Creating Windows Messaging Client Extensions   373

What Are Exchange Client Extensions? 374
   How Microsoft Exchange Client Extensions Work 375
   Advantages of Microsoft Exchange Client Extensions 376
   The Microsoft Exchange Client Contexts 376
   The Microsoft Exchange COM Interface 378
   Mapping Contexts to COM Interfaces 379
   Message Event Extensions 381
   Property Extensions 382
   Registering Extensions 383
Creating the Message Signing Extension 386
   Building the Initial Header File 387
   Coding the Main DLL Routines 390
   Laying Out and Coding the Property Sheet Dialog Box 405
Installing and Testing the Message Signing Extension 408
   Running the Message Signing Extension 409
Summary 410

13   Part II Summary—The Messaging API   411

Chapter 3, "What Is MAPI?" 412
Chapter 4, "MAPI Architecture" 414
Chapter 5, "Using the Microsoft Exchange Forms Designer" 414
Chapter 6, "Creating MAPI-Aware Applications" 415
Chapter 7, "Creating a Simple MAPI Client with
   the MAPI Controls" 416
Chapter 8, "The OLE Messaging Library" 416
Chapter 9, "Creating a MAPI Mailing List Manager with
   the OLE Messaging Library" 417

Chapter 10, "Building a MAPI-Enabled Forum Tool" 417
Chapter 11, "Creating a MAPI E-Mail Agent" 418
Chapter 12, "Creating Microsoft Exchange Client Extensions" 418

III   The Speech API (SAPI)

14   What Is SAPI?   **423**

Speech Recognition 424
    Word Separation 425
    Speaker Dependence 426
    Word Matching 427
    Vocabulary 428
    Text-to-Speech 428
    Voice Quality 429
    Phonemes 430
    TTS Synthesis 430
    TTS Diphone Concatenation 431
Grammar Rules 431
    Context-Free Grammars 432
    Dictation Grammars 433
    Limited Domain Grammars 434
Summary 434

15   SAPI Architecture   **435**

Introduction 436
High-Level SAPI 436
    Voice Command 437
    Voice Text 439
Low-Level SAPI 440
    Speech Recognition 441
    Text-to-Speech 445
Speech Objects and OLE Automation 446
    OLE Automation Speech Recognition Services 447
    OLE Automation Text-to-Speech Services 451
Summary 453

16   SAPI Basics   **455**

SAPI Hardware 456
    General Hardware Requirements 457
    Software Requirements—Operating Systems
        and Speech Engines 458
    Special Hardware Requirements—Sound Cards, Microphones,
        and Speakers 459

Technology Issues 460

SR Techniques.. 460

SR Limits... 462

TTS Techniques 463

TTS Limits 463

General SR Design Issues 464

Voice Command Menu Design 465

TTS Design Issues 466

Summary 467

17 SAPI Tools—Using SAPI Objects with Visual Basic 4.0   469

OLE Voice Text Object 470

Using the Visual Basic Object Browser 470

Using the Register Method to Connect to the TTS Engine 472

Using the Enable Property to Start and Stop the TTS Engine 473

Using the Speak Method to Play Text 474

Adjusting the Speed of Voice Playback 480

Adding Playback Controls for TTS Services 483

Getting TTS Status Reports with the IsSpeaking Property 485

Establishing a TTS Callback in Visual Basic 4.0 486

OLE Voice Command Objects.. 489

Creating the Voice Command Menu Object................................... 489

Using the Register Method to Connect to the SR Engine 490

Using the Awake Property to Start and Stop SR Processing 491

Creating the Menu Object 491

Adding Commands to the Voice Menu Object................................. 494

Using the CommandSpoken Property to Respond

to Menu Commands 497

Establishing an SR Callback in Visual Basic 4.0 499

Creating List Commands for the Voice Menu Object 500

Removing Commands from the Voice Menu Object 502

Summary 503

18 SAPI Behind the Scenes   505

Control Tags 506

The Voice Character Control Tags 509

The Phrase Modification Control Tags 512

The Low-Level TTS Control Tags 514

Grammar Rules 516

General Rules for the SAPI Context-Free Grammar 516

Creating and Compiling a SAPI Context-Free Grammar 521

Loading and Testing SAPI Context-Free Grammars 526

International Phonetic Alphabet.. 528

Summary 530

19   Creating SAPI Applications with C++   533

The TTS Demo Project 534

The VCMD Demo Project 541

Summary 561

20   Building the Voice-Activated Text Reader   563

Designing the Application 564

Adding TTS Services 564

Adding SR Services 565

Coding the MDISpeech Module 565

Declaring the Global Variables 566

Coding the InitSAPI and UnInitSAPI Routines 566

Coding the InitVoice Routine 568

Coding the InitVText Routine 569

Coding the VTextAction Routine 569

Modifying the MDINote Forms 571

Modifying the MDI Form 572

Modifying the NotePad Form 577

Testing the SAPI-Enabled MDI NotePad 579

Summary 581

21   Part III Summary—The Speech API   583

Chapter 14, "What Is SAPI?" 584

Chapter 15, "SAPI Architecture" 584

Chapter 16, "SAPI Basics" 584

Chapter 17, "SAPI Tools—Using SAPI Objects
with Visual Basic 4.0" 586

Chapter 18, "SAPI Behind the Scenes" 586

Chapter 19, "Creating SAPI Applications with C++" 587

Chapter 20, "Building the Voice-Activated Text Reader" 587

The Future of SAPI 587

IV   The Telephony API (TAPI)

22   What Is TAPI?   593

The Telephony API Model 594

Lines 595

Phones 596

TAPI and the WOSA Model 596

Typical Configurations 597

Phone-Based Configurations 598

PC-Based Configurations 598

Shared or Unified Line Configurations 600
Multiline Configurations 601
Telephone Line Services 602
The Telephone Switching Network 602
Plain Old Telephone Service (POTS) 603
Digital T1 Lines 604
Integrated Services Digital Network (ISDN) 604
Private Branch Exchange (PBX) 605
Summary 605

23   TAPI Architecture   607

Assisted Telephony Services 608
Basic Telephony Services 610
The Basic Telephony Line Device API Set 611
The Basic Telephony Line Device Structures 614
Basic Telephony Line Device Messages 616
Supplemental Telephony Services 620
Supplemental Telephony API for Line Devices 621
Supplemental Telephony API for Phone Devices 624
The Supplemental Telephony Phone Device Structures ... 627
The Supplemental Telephony Phone Device Messages 628
Extended Telephony Services 630
Summary 631

24   TAPI Basics   633

Using TAPI to Place Outbound Calls 634
Calling lineInitialize to Start the TAPI Session 634
Calling lineNegotiateAPIVersion to Check TAPI Services 635
Using lineOpen to Locate an Appropriate TAPI Line Device 635
Setting Call Parameters with the LINECALLPARAMS Structure 635
Using lineMakeCall to Place the Call 636
The TAPIOut Project 636
The Initial Declarations 637
The User Dialog Box and the WinMain Procedure 638
The PlaceCall Function 644
The ShowProgress and SetVarProps Procedures 646
The lineCallBackProc Procedure 647
Testing the TAPIOut Project 651
Summary 651

25   TAPI Hardware Considerations   653

Modems and the UniModem Drivers for Win95 and WinNT 654
A Quick Review of How Modems Work 655
The Universal Modem Drivers and TAPI Service Providers............. 655

Basic Data Modems 656
Data Modems with Voice... 657
Telephony Cards 659
Summary 660

26   TAPI Tools—Using the TAPILINE Control   663

The TAPILINE Control 664
  Installing the TAPILINE Control 664
  The TAPI Control's TapiCallBack Event 666
  The TAPILINE.OCX Properties... 667
  The TAPILINE.OCX Methods 668
  The TAPILINE DLL Functions 669
The TAPILINE Test Project 670
  The DLL Declarations and General TAPI Constants........................ 671
  The Line Structures and Constants 673
The TAPILine Function Module 675
  The TAPICallBackHandler Function 676
  A Sample CallState Message Function 677
  The Clean and OffSet Functions 678
Laying Out the TAPILine Form 680
Coding the TAPILine Form... 685
  Adding the Support Routines 685
  Adding the Form Event Code 688
  Adding the Button Event Code 689
  Displaying Call Information and Address Status 696
  Displaying TAPI Dialog Boxes 697
Summary.. 701

27   TAPI Behind the Scenes—The TELEPHON.INI File   703

Building the TAPI Dialog Utility Program...................................... 704
  Laying Out the TAPI Dialog Utility Form 704
  Coding the TAPI Dialog Utility Project 707
The TELEPHON.INI File 711
TAPI Service Provider Information 712
  The Providers Section 712
  The Provider-Specific Section 713
Handoff Priorities Information 714
Dialing Location Information 716
  Modifying the Location Values with the
    lineTranslateDialog Method 718
Credit Card Dialing Instructions.. 720
  Understanding the TAPI Dialing Rules 721
  Testing the Calling Card Settings of TAPIDLG.EXE 722
Summary.. 723

28 Using TAPI to Handle Incoming Calls   725

Process Flow for Inbound Calls 726
The TAPIANS Project 728
   Creating the TAPIANS Form 729
   Coding the TAPIANS Form 731
   Testing TAPIANS 741
Summary 744

29 Writing TAPI-Assisted Applications   745

The Assisted Telephony API Calls 746
   Testing the Assisted TAPI Functions 747
Creating the QikDial Application Using Excel 95 749
Writing the TeleBook Application Using Visual Basic 4.0 752
   Creating the TeleBook Class Module 753
   Coding the TeleBook Main Form 756
   Coding the TeleBook Phone Entry Form 766
   Coding the Phone Log Form for TeleBook 772
   Coding the Support Routines for the TeleBook Application 774
   Running the TeleBook TAPI Application 776
Summary 777

30 Creating TAPI-Enabled Applications   779

Designing the TAPIFONE Application 780
The libTAPI Module 782
frmTAPI—The Main Form 788
   Laying Out the frmTAPI Form 788
   The frmTAPI Menu 810
   Coding the frmTAPI Form 812
The Call and About Dialog Boxes 828
   Laying Out and Coding the Call Dialog Box 828
   Laying Out and Coding the About Dialog Box 834
Testing TAPIFONE 836
Summary 838

31 Third-Party TAPI Tools   841

The Visual Voice Telephony Toolkit for Windows 842
   The Voice Control 844
   The Test Control 851
   The Vlink Control 854
   The Voice Workbench 857
   The Voice Monitor 859
   The TAPI Examiner and the Stylus Trace Applications 861

Pronexus' VBVoice Development Kit 862
    The VBFrame Control 863
    The VBVoice Controls 863
    The Process of Building a VBVoice Application 866
    VBVoice and Voice Files 867
    VBVoice Test Mode 868
Microsoft Phone 869
    Adding Announcement, Message, and AutoFax Mailboxes 871
    Configuring the Microsoft Phone Answering Machine 872
Summary 873

32   Part IV Summary—The Telephony API   875
Chapter 22, "What Is TAPI?" 876
Chapter 23, "TAPI Architecture" 876
Chapter 24, "TAPI Basics" 877
Chapter 25, "TAPI Hardware Considerations" 877
Chapter 26, "TAPI Tools—Using the TAPILINE Control" 878
Chapter 27, "TAPI Behind the Scenes—
    The TELEPHON.INI File" 879
Chapter 28, "Using TAPI to Handle Incoming Calls" 879
Chapter 29, "Writing TAPI-Assisted Applications" 880
Chapter 30, "Creating TAPI-Enabled Applications" 880
Chapter 31, "Third-Party TAPI Tools" 881
The Future of Telephony and TAPI 882

V Creating Integrated Applications

**33   Design Considerations for Integrated
Communications Applications   885**
Introduction 886
General Considerations 886
    Rules of Complexity 887
    Native API versus High-Level Tools 888
    Standalone versus Extensions and Add-ins 888
MAPI versus Comm API 889
Assisted TAPI versus Full TAPI 890
When to Use the Speech API 891
Summary 892

34 Building the FaxBack Application **895**

Introduction 896
Project Resources 896
   The VBVoice Controls 897
   The FAX.VAP Voice Prompt File 897
   The SMAPI Support Modules 898
Starting the FaxBack Project 899
Coding the FaxBack Support Module 900
The FaxBack Form 904
   Laying Out the FaxBack Form 904
   Setting the VBVoice Control Properties 911
   Coding the FaxBack Form 914
The About Dialog Box 918
Testing the FaxBack Application 920
Summary 921

35 Creating the Voice Phone Application **923**

Project Resources 924
Coding the Library Modules 925
   The AssistedTAPI Module 925
   The CallBack Modules 928
Building the LibVPhone Module 930
   Adding the Voice Command Routines 931
   Adding the Voice Text Routines 933
   Adding the Database Engine Routines 934
   Adding the TAPI and Form Support routines 938
Laying Out the VPhone Form 939
Coding the VPhone Form 944
Laying Out the Support Forms 949
   The VRec Form 949
   The VHelp Form 953
   The VAbout Form 954
Testing Voice Phone 957
Summary 958

36 The Talk Mail Project **959**

Design Considerations 960
   Project Forms and Resources 961
Coding the LibTalkMail Module 962

The tmView Form 969
    Laying Out tmView 969
    Coding tmView 973
    Coding the Form Events 974
    The Control Building Code 975
    The Menu Support Routines 978
    Coding the Control Events 981
The tmNew and tmRead Forms 983
    Laying Out tmNew 983
    Coding tmNew 989
    Laying Out tmRead 995
    Coding tmRead 1000
The tmAbout Box 1003
Testing Talk Mail 1005
Summary 1008

37   Integration Summary   1009
Design Issues 1010
The FaxBack Application 1011
The Voice Phone Application 1011
The Talk Mail Project 1012
Some Final Remarks 1012

VI Appendixes

A   MAPI Resources   1017
Books 1018
Web Links 1022
Other Online Resources 1024

B   SAPI Resources   1027
Books 1028
Web Links 1029
Other Online Resources 1034
Software and Hardware Resources 1034

C   TAPI Resources   1041
Books 1042
Web Links 1044
Other Online Resources 1054
Software and Hardware Resources 1054

D   The CD-ROM Contents   1063

Index   1065

Acknowledgments

Putting this book together took lots of help from many talented people. Although I can't list them all, I want to take a moment to single out a few of the individuals who made this work possible.

First, I want to thank Jefferson Schuler and Bill Zembrodt of Pioneer Solutions. They accepted my challenge to build a simple TAPI OCX tool that would allow Visual Basic programmers virtually the same access to Microsoft's Telephony API services as C++ programmers. The result is the TAPILINE.OCX that is included on the CD-ROM that accompanies this book. They spent several long days and late nights developing this handy tool and I thank them for all their work and assistance.

Next, I must thank all those in cyberspace who answered my queries about telephony, speech systems, and electronic mail. Many of the concepts that appear in this book were hashed out in extensive messages over the Internet, and I thank all those who assisted me in my efforts. I could name many who helped, but I will refrain from doing so lest they be blamed for any of my mistakes within these pages.

I also want to thank the people at Sams Publishing. It takes a great number of talented individuals to get a book from the idea stage to the store shelves, and I consider it a privilege to be able to work with the folks at Sams. Completing this book took more time and effort than any of us originally suspected and more than once it seemed like the book would never be done. I am especially indebted to Sharon Cox for her continued help and support. I doubt this book would be in your hands today were it not for her assistance.

Finally, I need to acknowledge the special contributions made by my family. Without their support, patience, and understanding, I could not have completed this book. (And now that I *have* completed it, I have a long list of promises that I must live up to!)

About the Author

Mike Amundsen works as an IS consulting and training specialist for Design-Synergy Corporation, a consulting and project management firm specializing in information technology services. He has earned Microsoft certifications for Windows operating systems, Visual Basic, SQL Server, and Microsoft Exchange Server. Mike's work takes him to various locations in the U.S. and Europe where he teaches Windows programming and helps companies develop and manage Windows-based client/server solutions.

He is co-author of *Teach Yourself Database Programming with Visual Basic 4 in 21 Days*, published by Sams, and was a contributing author for *Visual Basic 4 Unleashed* and *Visual Basic 4 Developer's Guide* from Sams Publishing. Mike is the contributing editor for Cobb's "Inside Visual Basic for Windows" newsletter, and his work has been published in "Visual Basic Programmer's Journal" magazine, "VB Tech" magazine, and "Access Developer's Journal."

When he's not busy writing or traveling to client sites, Mike spends time with his family at his home in Kentucky. You may write to Mike at his CompuServe address 102461,1267, at MikeAmundsen@msn.com on the Internet, or you can visit his Web site at www.iac.net/~mamund/.

Tell Us What You Think!

As a reader, you are the most important critic and commentator of our books. We value your opinion and want to know what we're doing right, what we could do better, what areas you'd like to see us publish in, and any other words of wisdom you're willing to pass our way. You can help us make strong books that meet your needs and give you the computer guidance you require.

Do you have access to CompuServe or the World Wide Web? Then check out our CompuServe forum by typing GO SAMS at any prompt. If you prefer the World Wide Web, check out our site at http://www.mcp.com.

> **NOTE**
>
> If you have a technical question about this book, call the technical support line at (800) 571-5840, ext. 3668.

As the team leader of the group that created this book, I welcome your comments. You can fax, e-mail, or write me directly to let me know what you did or didn't like about this book—as well as what we can do to make our books stronger. Here's the information:

FAX:	317/581-4669
E-mail:	Greg Wiegand programming_mgr@sams.mcp.com
Mail:	Greg Wiegand
	Comments Department
	Sams Publishing
	201 W. 103rd Street
	Indianapolis, IN 46290

Introduction to *MAPI, SAPI, and TAPI Developer's Guide*

This book covers the three most exciting programming services available on the Microsoft Windows platform—messaging (MAPI), speech (SAPI), and telephony (TAPI). Each of these APIs provides a specialized set of services that expand the reach of the Windows operating system in a way that makes it easier to write programs that work without having to deal with the differences between hardware provided from third parties.

The addition of these services as part of the basic operating system not only is a boon to programmers—it is of great interest to users, too. Computers that can handle messages and telephones, and that can generate and understand simple speech, are computers that, ultimately, are easier to use. Learning how you add these vital features to your applications will give your software a greater reach and appeal that can make a real difference to your target audience.

This book is arranged in the following parts:

- **Part I—Introduction** covers some preliminary issues regarding the Windows Open Services Architecture (WOSA) upon which all three of the API sets are based.

- **Part II—The Messaging API (MAPI)** contains chapters that describe the MAPI service model, review existing client and server software that implements the MAPI model, and show you how to use common developer tools for building MAPI-compliant applications. There are also several chapters devoted to creating commonly used MAPI-based programs, including e-mail clients, a broadcast mailing list manager, an e-mail-based discussion forum tool, and an e-mail agent. You'll also learn how to use the Microsoft Exchange Forms designer and discover how you can use C++ to create built-in extensions to the Windows Messaging client interface.

- **Part III—The Speech API (SAPI)** covers the Microsoft Voice product available for Windows 95. You'll learn the details of the API model and how you can use it to create applications that use Text-to-Speech (TTS) and Speech Recognition (SR) engines to add a voice to your PC applications. You'll use both C++ and Visual Basic to build programs that respond to voice commands and read printed text back to users.

- **Part IV—The Telephony API (TAPI)** outlines the API set that allows Windows programmers to add inbound and outbound telephony features to their applications. You'll learn about the telephony object model, and how to build simple dialing applications and basic inbound call handlers. Along the way you'll learn how to select telephony hardware and third-party TAPI development tools that will make it easier to build and maintain TAPI-compliant applications.

- **Part V—Creating Integrated Applications** covers design issues you need to keep in mind when designing Windows applications that combine messaging, telephony, and speech services. You'll learn how to build a FaxBack service using MAPI and TAPI; an integrated voice response system that uses TAPI to allow users to call in and request data from the computer and have the results spoken over the phone; and an application that combines all three extension services to create an integrated voice and telephony application that uses voice commands to place outbound telephone calls.

- **Part VI—Appendixes** contains lists of third-party vendors for each of the three API sets and pointers to printed and online documentation sources, along with a handful of e-mail and Web addresses that you can use to keep current on these three technologies.

I encourage you to contact me via the Internet or through my Web site. I hope you enjoy this book, and I look forward to hearing from you soon.

Mike Amundsen

MikeAmundsen@msn.com

www.iac.net/~mamund/

I

Introduction

The first part of this book gives you a quick tour of communications development issues using messaging (MAPI), speech (SAPI), and telephony (TAPI) in the Windows environment and describes where these technologies fit in the overall Windows world.

In Chapter 1, "Windows Communications Overview," you'll learn about the common hardware and software tools you'll need to start developing desktop applications that use these powerful extensions of the Windows 95 and Windows NT operating systems. Chapter 2, "Introduction to Windows Open Services Architecture (WOSA)," gives you a basic introduction to WOSA. This is the primary design model used to develop Windows extensions like MAPI, SAPI, and TAPI.

Once you have a grounding in these foundation topics, you'll be ready to start tackling the discussions of each of the API sets in the subsequent parts of the book.

1

Windows Communications Overview

This developer's guide is designed to show you how to design, develop, and deploy applications that use messaging, telephony, and speech services available within the Windows 95 operating system. The primary focus is on developing client-side applications. Several chapters in this book cover the server-side aspects of these APIs, too. However, the emphasis is on the client or desktop.

> **NOTE**
>
> The primary focus of this book is Windows 95, and all examples are therefore in 32 bits. The same examples will work for Windows NT. The ideas can be applied to 16-bit Win31, but no 16-bit examples are given in this book.

One book cannot begin to cover all the possible development tools and API sets that provide message, telephony, and speech services for desktop PCs. The approach taken here is to concentrate on the Microsoft API sets. This offers several advantages: First, by using all Microsoft API models, the programmer gets to work with a consistent set of interfaces that work well together. Second, there is no denying that Microsoft's presence in the marketplace adds strength to any service model they develop. The time you invest in learning a set of API calls to provide advanced Windows services is usually time well spent. Using Microsoft API models assures you that your knowledge will not be useless in a year or so when some other API model is abandoned due to lack of use. And third, the Microsoft approach to service models is designed to allow third-party vendors to contribute to the growth and development of the service model. This open approach means you're really learning how to create programs that work with a variety of hardware/software combinations and not tying your efforts to a single hardware or software system.

MAPI Message Services

The messaging system explored in this book is the Microsoft Messaging API (MAPI). The MAPI system is one of the most widely used message models available for the PC environment. While there are other message models in use today, they are not covered here just because one book can't cover everything. If you are familiar with other message models, your knowledge will help you gain a greater understanding of the MAPI system.

TAPI Telephony Services

The telephony model covered here is the Microsoft Telephony API (TAPI). Just as with message services, there are competing telephony service models, too. The primary advantage of TAPI to the programmer is that Microsoft has committed to providing the TAPI model as part of the basic operating system for all future versions of Windows. For example, TAPI is shipped as part of every Windows 95 operating system. Version 4.0 of Windows NT is also designed to contain TAPI services as a fundamental part of the operating system.

Another major advantage of the TAPI model is that it is designed to work with multiple hardware products. Programmers who use TAPI can be assured that their programs will work the same from one installation to the next as long as TAPI-compliant hardware is used at all locations.

SAPI Speech Services

The speech service discussed here is Microsoft's Speech API (SAPI). There are several vendor-specific speech APIs. As in the TAPI model, the real advantage of Microsoft's SAPI is that it is designed to support multiple third-party vendor products. By writing to the SAPI model, you can potentially increase the reach of your speech-enabled software to all SAPI-compliant hardware.

MCI Multimedia Services

Some of the examples in this book also use the Microsoft Multimedia Communications Interface (MCI) to add audio and video services. This is a well-established interface that is supported by almost all existing audio and video hardware.

Applications Covered in This Book

The programming examples in this book move from simple, high-level examples and progress to more complex, full-featured applications. Each section of the book has four basic parts:

- General theory
- Creating simple service-aware applications
- Building full-featured service implementation examples
- Designing applications that use the service in unique ways

Each section starts with the general theory of the API service. This includes coverage of the general design of the service model and its objects, methods, and properties. You'll also get information about the various developer tools available for building programs that use the target service.

You'll then learn how to create service-aware applications. This usually involves adding the target service to existing applications, such as adding Send, Dial, or Speak buttons to a form. Service-aware applications use the target service as an added feature instead of as a basic part of the program. You'll see how you can add service features using high-level code routines.

The next level of programming examples shows you how to build applications that take advantage of the target service as a basic part of the program design. Examples would be an e-mail message reader, an online address book that can dial the selected address at the push of a button, or a program that allows users to drag and drop text documents onto a palette and then reads a selected document aloud.

Lastly, you'll learn how to create applications that use the service in unique ways. For example, you could use the message service to send data between two programs running on different machines on the same network, or use TAPI services to create an answering machine application.

The final section of the book contains examples of applications that provide integrated services: using MAPI and TAPI to build a dial-up FAX-back application; building a program that allows users to dial in, request information from a database, and hear the results spoken to them over the phone; and creating a single application that combines messaging, telephony, and speech into a single voice-mail system.

While the examples in this book don't cover every possible use of the target APIs, you'll find enough examples here to give you the techniques and skills you'll need to build your own Windows applications to exploit the features of the MAPI, TAPI, and SAPI services.

Development Tools

In the past, if you wanted to access advanced Windows services like MAPI, SAPI, and TAPI, you had to use C or C++ developer tools. But now, with the introduction of OLE libraries and the Microsoft OCX add-in control specification, Microsoft has made it possible to access these advanced services from high-level developer tools like Visual Basic 4.0 and Microsoft FoxPro. You can even complete a number of the programming examples included in this book using the VBA-compatible Microsoft Office tools like Excel, Access, Word, and others.

Most of the programming examples presented in this book are done in the 32-bit version of Microsoft Visual Basic 4.0 Professional Edition. Several examples are done using Microsoft's Excel 95 and Microsoft Access 95. However, a few of the services are only available via C++ programming. You'll therefore see some short programming examples here using Microsoft's Visual C++ 4.0. If you do not own a copy of Visual C++, you can still get a lot out of the C++ examples simply by reading them to get the general concepts. None of the major projects in this book require coding in C++. In the cases where C++ code is needed to gain access to a specific feature in the Windows service, you'll find compiled OLE libraries and/or OCX tools included on the accompanying CD-ROM. You can use these compiled tools as part of your high-level language projects.

All of the programming concepts described here are applicable to non-Microsoft programming environments, too. If you are using products such as Borland's Delphi, dBASE, Borland C++, and so on, you can still get a lot out of this book. You'll need to re-create the detail of the code examples in code usable in your programming environment, but the Windows API calls will be exactly the same.

Hardware and Software Tools

The programming examples in this book cover a wide range of hardware and software requirements, and it's no small matter to equip your workstation with all the tools necessary to access all the Windows services described within these pages. The following list summarizes the tools used in developing the programs presented here:

■ *Windows 95 operating system*—Most of the examples require Windows 95. Some of the examples will run under Windows 3.1 and most will run without problems under Windows NT (WinNT). However, all of the programming examples in this book were developed under Windows 95. You'll avoid lots of difficulty by sticking with Windows 95.

■ *Messaging API tools*—MAPI services are accessed via the MAPI OCX controls, the OLE Message Library, and the MAPI 1.0 API set. The MAPI OCXs ship with the Professional Edition of Visual Basic 4.0. The OLE Message Library and the MAPI 1.0 API developer tools can be found on the Microsoft Developer's Network (MSDN) Level II CD-ROMs. You'll need access to MSDN CD-ROMs to complete the advanced examples in this book.

■ *Telephony API tools*—The examples in this book were written using TAPI v1.4 for Windows 95. The v1.4 run-time files are shipped as part of the Windows 95 operating system. TAPI services are accessed via a custom OCX that comes on the CD-ROM shipped with this book and via calls directly through the API set. TAPI developer tools are found on the MSDN Professional Level CD-ROMs, too. It is important to note that all the examples in this book were developed as 32-bit applications for Windows 95. There is a 16-bit version of TAPI (v1.3), and a new version of TAPI (v2.0) for WinNT will be released with NT v4.0. To keep frustration to a minimum, stick with Win95 and TAPI 1.4.

■ *Speech API tools*—The release version of SAPI developer tools and run-time modules are available from Microsoft and are included on the CD-ROM that ships with this book. However, a major piece of the SAPI kit is not included automatically as part of the SAPI developer kit. You'll need a text-to-speech engine supplied by a third-party vendor in order to run the SAPI examples in this book. Check the accompanying CD-ROM for demo versions of Text-to-Speech (TTS) engines. You'll also find a list of vendors of SAPI tools in Appendix B, "SAPI Resources."

■ *Microsoft Exchange E-Mail*—Almost all the examples in this book that involve e-mail clients were created using the Microsoft Exchange client for Windows 95. Some were created using the Microsoft Exchange Server or Microsoft Mail Server clients. MAPI services are pretty much the same regardless of the client installed on your workstation. Where the differences are important, they are noted in the text of the book.

■ *Sound cards, speakers, and microphones*—Some of the examples here require the use of a PC audio system. Just about any WAV-compatible audio card will work fine. Some examples use voice input and playback. You can accomplish this with an attached microphone and speakers. In some cases, you can even use an attached telephone handset, too.

■ *Data modems*—You'll need at least a basic data/fax modem to run the examples in this book. Both the TAPI and the MAPI examples require a data modem. For some of the TAPI examples, you can perform all the functions using a simple data modem. For others, you'll need a data modem that supports the Unimodem/V communications driver. Not all modems support Unimodem/V even though they offer voice-mail or telephony features. Consult the appendix at the back of the book and the accompanying CD-ROM for a list of vendors who offer data modems that support TAPI and the Unimodem/V standard.

■ *Telephony cards*—While you can get through almost all the TAPI examples in this book without a telephony card in your workstation, you'll get a lot more out of the TAPI section if you have access to one. Telephony cards provide a much more advanced set of telephony features than do TAPI-compliant data modems. The CD-ROM that comes with this book contains some demo tools that can be used to mimic the presence of a telephony card. These demo tools can be used during development and testing, but they will not work in a production setting. Consult Appendix C, "TAPI Resources," and the CD-ROM for information on third-party developers who offer full-featured TAPI-compliant telephony hardware. When shopping for telephony cards, be sure to confirm that they are TAPI-compliant and that there are TAPI drivers (service providers) available for your telephony card.

■ *Access to live phone service*—You'll need access to a live phone line to run most of the programs in this book. All the examples will work with a simple analog phone line like the line available to most U.S. households. The nature of the TAPI services makes it very easy to use digital lines such as T1 and ISDN to run these examples, too. However, if you use digital lines, be sure your hardware (data modem and/or telephony card) is compatible with the type of phone service you're using.

What's Not Covered in This Book

Even though this book covers a lot of territory, it leaves a lot out, too. The main focus of this book is the client desktop. However, there's another set of APIs designed for building server-side applications for Windows. Microsoft provides developer kits for the creation of MAPI message servers like transport providers, address books, and message storage systems. Every TAPI client depends on a server-side interface that talks directly to the vendor hardware to translate the requests from the client into something the hardware understands. Microsoft publishes the Telephony Service Provider Interface (TSPI) as a set of API calls for handling the server-side aspects of Windows telephony. Finally, the Speech API is designed to allow third-party vendors to create separate text-to-speech and speech recognition engines that work within the SAPI system.

Covering the details of each of these server-side models could fill an entire book. For our purposes, you'll learn the general facts about how the clients and servers relate to each other, but you'll need to look elsewhere if you want to learn how to build server-side components.

It is also important to keep in mind that all the material here was built for the Windows 95 platform. Even though many of the examples will run on other Windows platforms, not much will be said about Windows 3.1 or even Windows NT. This is mainly to keep the book clear of confusing exceptions and special notations for cases where the platforms behave in different ways. If you're unlucky enough to have the responsibility of deploying advanced Windows services on multiple platforms, you'll need to supplement this text with copious experimenting and tweaking.

How to Use This Book

Since this book is divided into very clear sections, you can use it in a number of ways:

- *Start from the beginning*—The chapters of the book are arranged to start with relatively simple issues and progress through more complex topics toward the end of the book. If you're new to programming with WOSA and APIs, you'll get the most out of the book by following along in chapter order.

- *Focus on a target service*—If you have a good understanding of WOSA and the use of Windows services, you can jump right into the API sections that interest you most. The three service sections (MAPI, SAPI, and TAPI) are each self-contained. You can read these sections in any order without missing any vital material.

- *Focus on integrating services*—If you already know one or more of the APIs and are mainly interested in building advanced integration applications, you can skip the API sections you have had previous experience with and move directly to the section on building integrated applications. If you take this approach, you may run into areas of the book that refer to previous programming examples or concepts discussed in previous sections of the book. Be prepared to do a bit of skipping around at times to follow some of these threads back to their source. In this way, you can use this book as more of a reference guide than a tutorial.

No matter how you use this book, by the time you complete the examples and absorb the basic concepts explained here, you'll have a solid understanding of some of the most advanced Windows extension services available.

That's about it for the preliminaries—now it's time to get started!

2

Introduction to Windows Open Services Architecture (WOSA)

Before we jump into the details of the three API sets covered in this book, it is a good idea to spend some time reviewing the overall architecture upon which these APIs are built. Although these API sets are only slightly related in their function, they are all closely related in their construction and implementation. It is the construction and implementation of the APIs that is the topic of this chapter.

All of the API sets covered in this book are part of the Windows Open Services Architecture (WOSA). This chapter offers a brief overview of the WOSA model and describes how it works and the benefits of the WOSA model for developers. Once you understand the general notions behind the creation and deployment of API services via the WOSA model, you will also have a good understanding of how to build well-designed end-user applications that use WOSA-based API services. The WOSA model APIs offer clear benefits to developers who understand the model. Those who fail to grasp the basic theories behind WOSA may end up using the APIs incorrectly, thus ruining their chances of taking advantage of the real benefits of the WOSA model.

What Is WOSA?

The Windows Open Services Architecture was developed by Microsoft to "...provide a single, open-ended interface to enterprise computing environments." The concept of WOSA is to design a way to access extended services from the Windows operating system that require having only a minimum amount of information about the services. For example, the MAPI (Message API) model is designed to allow programmers to develop applications that use the message services without having to understand the complexities of the hardware and software routines that implement messaging on various Windows platforms. The same is true for the Speech (SAPI) and Telephony (TAPI) services we will discuss in this book.

The WOSA model goes beyond the idea of exposing services in a uniform way across Windows operating systems. WOSA is also designed to work in a mixed operating system environment. For example, the Microsoft RPC (Remote Procedure Call) interface is a WOSA service that is designed to work with the Open Software Foundation's DCE (Distributed Computing Environment) RPC model. The design of Microsoft RPC allows programmers to design software that will safely interface with any product that uses the DCE model, regardless of the operating system with which the software must interact.

In order to attain this flexibility, the WOSA model defines two distinct interfaces—the Client API and the Server SPI. These interfaces are linked by a single interface module that can talk to both API and SPI applications. As a result, all client applications need to do is conform to the API rules and then to the universal interface. All server applications need to do is conform to the SPI rules and then to the universal interface. No matter what changes are made to the client or server applications, both software modules (client and server) will be compatible as long as they both continue to conform to the API/SPI model and use the universal interface.

The next two sections of this chapter outline the WOSA model in detail and give several examples of WOSA services currently available.

The WOSA Model

The WOSA model consists of three distinct pieces. Each of these pieces plays an important, and independent, role in providing programming services to your applications. The three WOSA components are

- The Client API—the application programming interface used by the program requesting the service.
- The Server SPI—the service provider interface used by the program that provides the extended service (for example, e-mail, telephony, speech services, and so on).
- The API/SPI Interface—the single module that links the API and SPI calls. This is usually implemented as a separate DLL in the Windows environment.

Figure 2.1 shows the relationship between the three WOSA components.

FIGURE 2.1.
The three components of the WOSA model.

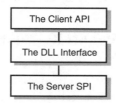

Each of the components has an important job to do. Even though they perform their tasks independently, the components work together to complete the service interface. This is the key to the success of the WOSA model—distinct, independent roles that together provide the whole interface.

The Client API Makes Requests

The Client API is the interface for the application requesting the service. API sets are usually implemented at the Windows desktop. The Message API (MAPI) is a good example of a WOSA client API. Each client API defines a stable set of routines for accessing services from the back-end service provider. For example, the operations of logging into an e-mail server, creating an e-mail message, addressing it, and sending it to another e-mail client are all defined in the MAPI set. These services are requested by the client. The actual services are provided by the server-side application.

The key point is that the client application interface allows programs to *request* services from the server-side service provider but does not allow the client software to access the underlying services directly. In fact, the request is not even sent directly to the server-side application. It is sent to the DLL interface that sits between the API and SPI (see Figure 2.2).

FIGURE 2.2.
Client APIs talk directly to the DLL interface.

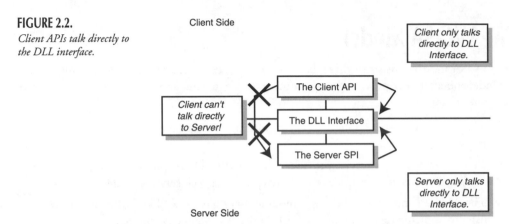

This isolates API calls from the SPI and limits the possibility that future changes to one or the other component will adversely affect the interface.

The Server SPI Responds to Requests

The Server SPI (Service Provider Interface) accepts requests for services and acts upon those requests. The SPI is not designed to interface directly with a client application. Most SPI programs are implemented on network servers or as independent services running on desktop PCs. Users rarely interact with these service providers, except through the client API requests.

A good example of an SPI implementation is the Open Database Connectivity (ODBC) interface. Even though programmers use API calls (or some other method of requesting ODBC services) in their programs, these calls merely request services from an external program. ODBC calls to Microsoft's SQL Server, for example, are simply requests to SQL Server to perform certain database operations and to return the results to the client application. When making an ODBC request to SQL Server, the client actually performs very few (if any) database operations. It is SQL Server that performs the real database work.

As mentioned earlier, service providers rarely display interfaces directly to client applications. Their job is to respond to requests. These requests do not even come directly from the client program. In the WOSA model, all requests come directly from the interface DLL. The SPI talks only to the interface DLL. Any information that the SPI needs to supply as a part of the response to the request is sent directly to the interface DLL. It is the DLL's job to send the information on to the client that made the initial request.

Another important point should be highlighted here. The service provider portion of the WOSA model allows for multiple clients to request services (see Figure 2.3).

FIGURE 2.3.
*SPIs must handle requests
from multiple clients.*

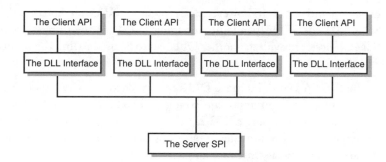

The DLL interface tells the SPI which client is making the request. It is the SPI's responsibility to keep the various clients straight. SPIs must have the ability to handle multiple requests from the same client and from multiple clients.

The Interface DLL Talks to Both the API and SPI

Since a key design aspect of WOSA is the isolation of the client API and the server SPI, a single interface between the two components is required. This single interface is usually implemented as a Windows dynamic link library (DLL) that allows programs to link to existing services at run-time instead of at compile time. The advantage of using DLLs is that programs need not know everything about an interface at compile time. Thus, programmers can upgrade DLL modules without having to recompile the applications that access the interface.

The primary role of the DLL is to broker the requests of the client API and the responses of the server SPI. The DLL does not actually perform any real services for the client and makes no requests to the SPI.

> **NOTE**
>
> Actually, the interface DLL may request basic information from the SPI at startup about the underlying SPI services, their availability, and other information that may be needed to support requests from clients.

The interface DLL is the only application in the Windows environment that actually "speaks" both API and SPI. It is the DLL's job to act as translator between the client and server applications.

In the past (before WOSA), these DLLs were written as translators from the client API directly to a specific back-end product. In other words, each DLL interface understood how to talk to only one back-end version of the service. For example, early implementations of the MAPI interface involved different DLLs for each type of MAPI service provider. If a program needed to talk to a Microsoft MAPI service provider, the MAPI.DLL was used as an interface between the client and server. If, however, the program needed to talk to another message server [such as Lotus Vendor Independent Messaging (VIM) or the universal Common Message Calls (CMC) service provider], another DLL had to be used to link the client request with the back-end provider.

In the WOSA world, interface DLLs can speak to any service provider that understands the SPI call set. This is an important concept. Now, a single interface DLL can be used for each distinct service. This single DLL is capable of linking the client application with any vendor's version of the service provider. This is possible because the service provider speaks SPI rather than some proprietary interface language (see Figure 2.4).

FIGURE 2.4.
Interface DLLs can talk to multiple service providers.

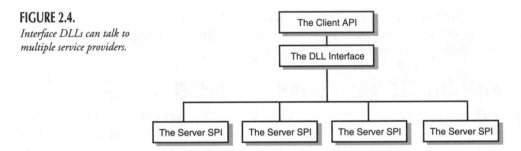

WOSA Services

Microsoft has been championing the WOSA model for several years and promotes three types of WOSA services:

■ Common Application Services

■ Communication Services

■ Vertical Market Services

Each type has its own purpose and its own core of services. The following sections describe the WOSA service types and give examples of services currently available for each.

Common Application Services

Common Application Services allow applications to access services provided by more than one vendor. This implementation of WOSA focuses on providing a uniform interface for all Windows applications while allowing programmers and/or users to select the vendor that provides the best service option for the requirement. In this way, Microsoft can encourage multiple (even competing) vendors to provide their own versions of key service components for the Windows operating system.

By defining a single set of APIs to access the service, all third-party vendors are assured equal access to the Windows operating environments. Since the interface is stable, vendors can concentrate on building service providers that expose the services that customers request most often. These vendors can also be confident that, as Windows operating systems change and evolve, the basic model for service access (the WOSA model) will not change.

The list of Common Application Services available for Windows operating systems is constantly growing and changing. Here is a list of some of the services provided under the WOSA model:

- *License Service Application Program Interface* (LSAPI) provides access to software license management services.
- *Messaging Application Program Interface* (MAPI) provides access to e-mail and other message services.
- *Open Database Connectivity* (ODBC) provides access to database services.
- *Speech Application Program Interface* (SAPI) provides access to speech and speech recognition services.
- *Telephony Application Program Interface* (TAPI) provides access to telephone services.

Communication Services

Communication Services provide access to network services. This set of WOSA services focuses on gaining uniform access to the underlying network on which the Windows PC is running. The Communications Services also provide uniform access to all the network resources exposed by the underlying network. By defining a universal interface between the PC and the network, Windows applications are able to interact with any network operating system that conforms to the WOSA model.

The following list shows some examples of WOSA implementations of Communication Services:

- *Windows SNA Application Program Interface* provides access to IBM SNA services.
- *Windows Sockets* provide access to network services across multiple protocols, including TCP/IP, IPX/SPX, and AppleTalk.
- *Microsoft RPC* provides access to a common set of remote procedure call services. The Microsoft RPC set is compatible with the Open Software Foundation Distributed Computing Environment (DCE) model.

Vertical Market Services

The last category of WOSA services defined by Microsoft is Vertical Market Services. These are sets of API/SPI calls that define an interface for commonly used resources in a particular vertical market. By defining the interfaces in this way, Microsoft is able to work with selected vertical markets (banking, health care, and so on) to develop a standard method for providing the services and functions most commonly used by a market segment. In effect, this allows users and programmers to invent Windows-based solutions for an entire market segment without having to know the particular requirements of back-end service provider applications.

As of this writing, Microsoft has defined two Vertical Market Services under the WOSA umbrella:

- *WOSA Extensions for Financial Services* provide access to common services used in the banking industry.
- *WOSA Extensions for Real-Time Market Data* provide access to live stock, bond, and commodity tracking data for Windows applications.

Benefits of WOSA

There are several benefits for both users and programmers in the WOSA model. The three key benefits worth mentioning here are

- Isolated development
- Multivendor support
- Upgrade protection

The next three sections describe the details of the benefits of the WOSA model as it relates to both client and server programmers and application users.

Isolated Development

In one way or another, all WOSA benefits are a direct result of the model's ability to separate the details of service providers from the application running on users' desktops. By keeping the details of hardware and software interface locked away in the SPI-side, programmers can concentrate on providing a consistent interface to the services, rather than concerning themselves with the low-level coding needed to supply the actual services.

The isolation of services from user applications has several other benefits. With WOSA services, developers can limit their investment in understanding the details of a service technology, where appropriate. Those focused on developing client-side applications can leave the details of server-side development to others. They can concentrate their efforts on developing quality client-side software knowing that, as long as the service providers maintain WOSA compatibility, the client software will be able to take advantage of new services as they become available.

Of course, this works the same for developers of server-side software. They can concentrate their efforts on providing the most efficient and effective means for exposing and supporting requested services and leave the client interface details to others. Service provider developers are assured equal access to all Windows clients because the WOSA model ensures that all links to the services are the same, regardless of the client software used.

Multivendor Support

In addition to allowing programmers to focus on the client-side of the equation instead of the server-side, WOSA implementations provide benefits to application programmers. With a common interface for the service, application programmers can build software solutions that are independent of vendor-specific implementations. The WOSA model allows programmers to build programs that interact with any vendor's service implementation as long as that vendor adheres to the WOSA model.

This is a key benefit for both client-side and provider-side developers. Now service provider vendors can be assured that, as client-side applications change, the interface to their services will remain the same. At the same time, client-side developers can be assured that as service providers upgrade their software, client applications need not be rewritten except to take advantage of new services. This feature allows client-side and service-side development to go forward independently. The result is greater freedom to advance the technology on both sides of the interface.

Upgrade Protection

Another benefit of WOSA-compliant systems is the protection it provides during service or application upgrades or platform migrations. Users can more easily plan and implement software and hardware upgrades when the service access to uniform calls is isolated to a single DLL. Since the WOSA model ensures that service provision and access is standardized across vendors and platforms, changing software and hardware has a minimal effect on users who access services from WOSA-compliant applications.

Thus, when users decide to move their primary database services from an IBM VSAM system to a DB2 or SQL Server environment, the client applications see minimal change as long as the WOSA model was implemented for database access. This protects users' software investment and allows greater flexibility when selecting client and server software.

At the same time, this approach provides protection for commercial software providers because a single application can be designed to work with multiple service providers. Developers can focus on creating full-featured applications without tying their software to a single service provider. As the market grows and changes, and service providers come and go, client-side applications can remain the same when the WOSA model is used as the route for service access.

Leveraging WOSA in Your Own Applications

Now that you understand the concepts behind the WOSA model, you can use this information in your own development efforts. For example, when accessing WOSA services from your client applications, isolate those calls in your code. This will make it easier to modify and enhance your application's WOSA interface in the future. As the services available change and grow, you'll need only to make changes in a limited set of your code.

Also, when designing your application, plan for the future from the start. Assume that the various program services will be provided via WOSA-compliant tools—even if they are not currently available as true WOSA components. This approach will make it much easier to add true WOSA components to your client application once they become available and will increase the life and flexibility of your software.

The same holds true for back-end service provider developers. If there is a WOSA SPI defined for the services you are providing, use it. This will make your software client-ready for virtually all Windows desktops. If no WOSA interface is yet defined for your service, code as if there is one. Limit the code that talks directly to hardware to a single area in your program. If you are using vendor-specific calls, isolate these, too. This way, when a WOSA model *is* defined for your service, you'll have an easier time converting your software to comply with the WOSA model.

As you work through the book, you learn about the specific API calls that are used to access extension services. You'll see a consistent pattern throughout all three extensions. Each of the extension services is divided into layers. The first layer provides a simple interface—sometimes as simple as a single function call—to the target service. The second level provides a more extensive access to a complete feature set. Finally, you'll find a third level of service that allows sophisticated programmers access to all the nifty little details of the extension service. When you're coding your own applications, it is a good idea to use this same approach. Where possible, give users a single function or subroutine that provides access to the extension service. For more advanced applications, create a function library or class object that encapsulates all the extension service calls. By doing this, you'll make it easier to make modifications to your program logic without touching the extension routines. It will also be easier to update the extension routines in the future without damaging your local program logic.

Summary

In this chapter, you learned that the WOSA model was developed by Microsoft to "... provide a single, open-ended interface to enterprise computing environments." You learned that the WOSA model has three key components:

- The *Client API* usually resides on the desktop workstation and makes service requests.
- The *Server SPI* usually resides on a network server and receives and responds to service requests made by clients.
- The *interface DLL* acts as a broker between the client API and the server SPI. The API and SPI never talk directly to each other. They both talk only to the interface DLL.

You learned that there are three types of WOSA implementations. Each of these implementations focuses on a different aspect of service implementation. The three WOSA types are

■ *Common Application Services* provide common access to system-level services, independent of vendor implementations. Examples of WOSA Common Application Services are ODBC, MAPI, SAPI, TAPI, and LSAPI.

■ *Communication Services* provide standard access to network services, independent of the underlying network available to the workstation. Examples of Communication Services are Windows SNA API, Windows Sockets API, and the Microsoft RPC interface.

■ *Vertical Market Services* provide access to common services used in a particular vertical market, such as banking, health care, and so on. Examples of this type of WOSA service are the WOSA Extensions for Financial Services and the WOSA Extensions for Real-Time Market Data.

We also covered some of the key benefits of using WOSA-defined services in developing Windows applications. The benefits mentioned are

■ *Isolated development*—Using WOSA-compliant services isolates access to external services. As these services change, the impact on your application is limited.

■ *Multivendor support*—WOSA-compliant services are vendor neutral. If your application uses WOSA-defined service calls, they can be provided by any vendor's service provider if it is also WOSA-compliant.

■ *Upgrade protection*—When you use WOSA components, you can easily plan and implement software and hardware upgrades because the WOSA model is consistent across platforms and operating systems.

Finally, you learned how you will use the concepts behind the WOSA model in your own software development to improve compatibility and ensure easy future upgrades.

II

The Messaging API (MAPI)

The *Messaging Application Programming Interface*, known as MAPI, is the heart of the Windows operating system message service. Microsoft introduced the MAPI model when it released the MS Mail server API several years ago and the model has grown in complexity and functionality ever since. The release of the Microsoft Exchange Server in 1996 marks a major move forward for Windows message technology. This section of the book introduces the MAPI programming model, reviews various MAPI-compliant client- and server-side software packages available from Microsoft, and illustrates how to use the most common programming tools to build your own MAPI-compliant applications for all the current Windows operating systems, including

- Windows 3.1
- Windows for Workgroups 3.11
- Windows NT 3.51
- Windows 95

Let's take a quick tour of the MAPI section of this book.

The first three chapters in this section cover the general theory and design of MAPI. In Chapter 3, "What Is MAPI?," you'll get a general overview of the MAPI model and the most common types of MAPI applications (MAPI clients, MAPI-aware applications, and MAPI-enabled applications). In Chapter 4, "MAPI Architecture," you'll learn more about the basic pieces of the MAPI client-side service model, including messages, addresses, attachments, and storage folders. Chapter 4 also covers the server-side MAPI services: storage, transport, and address books. In Chapter 5, "Using the Microsoft Exchange Forms Designer," you'll get a look at the development tool that ships with Microsoft Exchange Server.

The next five chapters in this section cover programming techniques using Microsoft's MAPI programming tools: Simple MAPI custom controls, the OLE Messaging Library, the Common Message Controls (CMC) API, and Extended MAPI (MAPI 1.0). Chapter 6, "Creating MAPI-Aware Applications," shows you how to build MAPI features into existing Windows applications. You'll learn to build a full-featured MAPI-client application in Chapter 7, "Creating a Simple MAPI Client with the MAPI Controls." You'll learn the details of the OLE Messaging Library in Chapter 8, "The OLE Messaging Library," and you'll learn to use the OLE Messaging Library to create an automated mailing list manager and a MAPI-enabled remote job server in Chapter 9, "Creating a MAPI Mailing List Manager with the OLE Messaging Library." In Chapter 10, "Building a MAPI-Enabled Forum Tool," you'll learn how to create your own discussion forum tool, and in Chapter 11, "Creating a MAPI E-Mail Agent," you'll learn how to use MAPI services to create your own MAPI inbox agent.

Chapter 12, "Creating Windows Messaging Client Extensions," shows you how to use C++ to create custom extensions to the Microsoft Exchange client interface.

Finally, Chapter 13, "Part II Summary—The Messaging API," provides a complete summary of all the material covered in Part II.

3

What Is MAPI?

Before getting into the details of how the Messaging Application Programming Interface (MAPI) works and how to write MAPI applications, we'll take a moment to review the general architecture of Microsoft's messaging API and how this set of message services fits into the overall Windows operating system. As you will see a bit later in this chapter, MAPI is more than a handful of e-mail APIs—it is a defined set of message services available to all programs that run in the Windows operating environment.

We'll also discuss the various kinds of applications and message types commonly used under MAPI services. In this chapter, you'll learn about the three general types of MAPI messages: text messages, formatted documents and binary files, and control messages. Each of these message types has a distinct set of properties and uses within the MAPI framework. This chapter describes each of the message types and shows how you can use them within the MAPI architecture.

There are also three common types of MAPI applications: electronic mail clients, message-aware applications, and message-enabled applications. Each of these application types is defined and illustrated in this chapter. You'll also learn the relative strengths of each type of MAPI application.

MAPI Services and Windows

The MAPI service set is more than a set of API commands and functions that you can use to send e-mail from point to point. The MAPI interface is actually a carefully defined set of messaging services available to all Windows programs. This pre-defined set has three key attributes:

- Flexibility
- Consistency
- Portability

Because the MAPI service set contains these three characteristics, it has become the *de facto* messaging interface standard for Windows applications.

Access to MAPI services is the same for all versions of the Windows operating system. But even though your Windows programs use the same methods for accessing MAPI services, MAPI services can vary from system to system. Also, MAPI architecture allows software designers to create their own service providers (SPs) to support the MAPI service set.

These services are also available within all existing flavors of the Windows operating system. Even more important, the methods of access to these message services is the same, regardless of the version of Windows you are working with. This means that programs using MAPI services that were written under Windows 3.1 will still be able to access those same MAPI services under Windows 95.

Flexibility

Probably the most important aspect of the MAPI service architecture is its flexibility. Microsoft has implemented MAPI within the Windows Open Systems Architecture (WOSA). This architecture is designed to allow customization at both the client (user) side and the server (provider) side. In other words, you can use MAPI not only to create your own end-user software to read, write, create, and send messages, but also to construct custom server-side software to store and transport those same messages. As part of the WOSA model, MAPI services are implemented in a tiered format (see Figure 3.1).

FIGURE 3.1.

The tiered implementation of MAPI services.

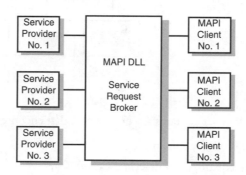

The first layer is the *client* layer. This is what the end-user most often sees. At this level a set of well-defined services are available. These services are accessed when the client layer makes a service request to the second layer—the *MAPI DLL*. The MAPI DLL takes the service request from the client and forwards it on to the third layer in the tier—the *service provider*. The service provider is responsible for fulfilling the client request and sending the results of that request back to the DLL where it is then forwarded to the client that made the initial request. Throughout the process, the DLL layer acts as a broker between the client side and the server side.

The primary advantage of this layered implementation is the ease with which users can interchange client and server components. Since the only constant required in the mix is the DLL layer, any client can be matched with any server component to provide a working message service. It is very common to switch client-side components in a messaging service. Each e-mail reader is a MAPI client application. Any application that sports a send button is actually a MAPI client. Any specialized program written to manipulate messages at the end-user level is a MAPI client.

While interchanging MAPI clients is rather commonplace, interchanging MAPI service providers is not. In a network environment, a single service provider will usually be designated as the default provider of MAPI services. It is no longer rare to have several MAPI service providers available at the same time, however. In fact, the Microsoft Mail Exchange client that ships with Windows 95 is specifically designed to be able to access more than one service provider. It is possible to use the Windows Exchange client to access messages via Microsoft Mail Server, Microsoft FAX, or through the Microsoft Network (MSN). You can even install third-party service providers into the Exchange client (such as the one provided by CompuServe) to access messages stored in other mail systems (see Figure 3.2).

FIGURE 3.2.
Microsoft Exchange can link to multiple service providers.

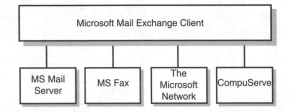

Consistency

The MAPI service set contains a set of services that encompasses all the basic messaging tasks:

- Message service logon and logoff
- Reading, creating, and deleting text messages
- Adding and deleting message binary file attachments
- Addressing and transporting the completed messages

The exact behavior and properties of each of these services are defined as part of MAPI. All vendors who supply a MAPI-compliant set of tools provide these services in the exact same manner. This way, any program that uses MAPI services can be assured that there are no special API variations to deal with when moving from one vendor's MAPI product to another. This means the programs you write today using your current implementation of MAPI services will function under other implementations of the MAPI service set (see Figure 3.3).

FIGURE 3.3.
Consistency of MAPI services across vendor implementations.

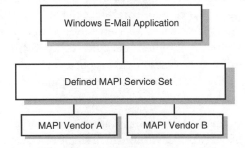

Portability

This leads to the second strength of Microsoft's MAPI service set—portability. Microsoft supports MAPI services on all versions of its Windows operating systems. If you write a program for the Windows 3.1 version of MAPI services, that same program can still access the MAPI services under any other version of Windows that supports your executable program. This is a key issue when you consider how many versions of Windows are currently in use and how quickly new versions of the operating system are developed and deployed.

Not only will you be able to move your MAPI-related programs to various Windows platforms, you can also allow programs to access MAPI services from more than one platform at once. In other words, users of more than one version of Windows can all be accessing MAPI services from a central location at the same time (see Figure 3.4).

FIGURE 3.4.
Portability of MAPI across Windows platforms.

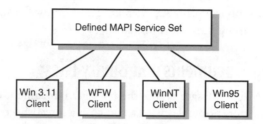

Microsoft has announced plans to move several of its service sets (MAPI included) beyond the Windows operating environment, too. As this happens, Microsoft has pledged that the same set of functions and routines used under the Windows environment will be available in other operating systems.

Messages

The primary role of the MAPI service is to transport and store messages. This section identifies three common message types supported by MAPI services:

- Text messages
- Formatted documents or binary files
- Control messages

The most basic message form is the text message, commonly thought of as e-mail. Most electronic message systems also support the second type of message—formatted documents or binary files. These are usually included as attachments to a text message.

The third message type is a *control message*. Control messages are usually used by the operating system to pass vital information such as system faults, potential failure conditions, or some other type of status information. Control messages can also be passed between programs in order to implement a level of distributed processing in a computer network.

The following sections review each message type in more detail.

Text Messages

The text message is the most common MAPI message. In fact, all MAPI messages have a default text message component. A text message contains the letters and words composed by users to communicate with other message system users.

All MAPI service providers must supply a simple text message editor as part of their MAPI implementation. All MAPI message providers support plain ASCII text characters as a message body. Many also support rich-text messages that contain formatting characters such as font and color. The Microsoft Mail client supplied for Windows 3.11 and Windows for Workgroups supports plain ASCII text. The Microsoft Mail Exchange client supplied for Windows 95 supports rich-text formatting.

Formatted Documents and Binary Files

The second MAPI message type is the formatted document or binary file, which is usually a file containing non-printable characters such as a spreadsheet, a word-processing file, graphics, or even an executable program. Binary files are supported by MAPI services as attachments to text messages. The MAPI service set allows multiple attachments to a single text message. This means you can send several binary files to the same e-mail address using a single message body.

All MAPI service providers support the use of binary attachments to a message body. However, the transport of binary attachments across multiple message servers may not be supported. For example, if you compose a message that contains attached binary files, address it to an associate at a distant location, and attempt to send the message using a service provider that supports only Simple Mail Transfer Protocol (SMTP) format, your attached binary files will not be successfully transported to the recipient.

Control Messages

The third type of MAPI message is the control message. Control messages are usually used by the operating system to deliver system status information, such as a component failure or other system-related problem. These messages are usually addressed directly to the system administrator.

Control messages can also be used to pass data or other control information between programs. Control messages of this type can contain requests for information that is to be collected by one program and returned to another for further processing. Or the control message can contain actual data to be manipulated by another program. Since MAPI services can stretch across the LAN or across the globe, control messages can be passed to systems halfway around the globe as easily as to systems across the room.

It is possible to designate one or more workstations on a network as *batch job* computers. These machines wait for control messages that direct them to perform time-consuming tasks, such as extended database searches or generating long reports, thus freeing up users' workstations for more immediate business. Once the task is complete, the batch job machine can send a completion notice via e-mail to the user who sent the original request. While it is true that OLE Automation servers are beginning to replace batch job computers that are controlled by MAPI messages, MAPI services are still a very powerful alternative.

MAPI Applications

Just as there are three types of MAPI messages, there are three general types of MAPI applications:

■ Electronic mail clients
■ Message-aware applications
■ Message-enabled applications

Electronic Mail Clients

Electronic mail (e-mail) clients are the most common form of MAPI application. An e-mail client allows end-users direct access to the MAPI services supported by the back-end service provider. Figure 3.5 shows the Microsoft Exchange electronic mail client.

FIGURE 3.5.
The Microsoft Exchange Mail Client.

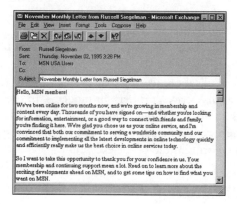

Typical services provided by a MAPI e-mail client include

■ Message service logon and logoff
■ Reading, creating, and deleting text messages
■ Adding and deleting binary file message attachments
■ Addressing and transporting completed messages

Electronic mail clients can also provide additional services to make it easy to manipulate, store, and retrieve text messages and binary file attachments. Electronic mail clients may also have additional features for addressing and transporting messages, including the use of defined mailing lists and the capability to address messages as CC (courtesy copies) or BCC (blind courtesy copies).

Message-Aware Applications

Message-aware applications are non-MAPI programs that allow users access to MAPI services. Typically, this access is implemented through the addition of a send option in a menu or button bar. Figure 3.6 shows the Microsoft Word 95 main menu with the Send menu item highlighted.

FIGURE 3.6.

Microsoft Word 95 is a message-aware application.

Message-aware applications usually treat e-mail services just like any other storage or output location, such as disk drives, printers, or modems. In these cases, the ability to send the standard output as an electronic mail message is an added feature for the application. As MAPI services become a standard part of the Windows operating system, message-aware applications will become the norm instead of the exception.

Message-Enabled Applications

The last category of MAPI applications is message-enabled applications. Message-enabled applications are programs that offer message services as a fundamental feature. While message-aware applications provide message services as an additional feature and can operate well without them, message-enabled applications are specifically designed to use message services and most will not run properly unless message services are available on the workstation.

Here are some examples of message-enabled applications:

■ *Computerized service dispatch*—Customer calls are handled by representatives at PC workstations where they fill out data entry forms outlining the repair needs and the location of the service call. When the data entry is complete, the program analyzes the information and, based on the parts needed and the service location, routes an instant electronic message containing the service request and a list of needed parts to the repair office nearest to the customer.

■ *Online software registration*—When a user installs a new software package, part of the installation process includes an online registration form that already contains the unique software registration code along with a data entry form for the user to complete. Once the form is completed, the results are placed in the user's e-mail outbox to be sent directly to the software company to confirm the user's software registration.

■ *End-user support services*—When network end-users have a question about a software package or need to report a problem with their workstation or the network, they call up a data entry form prompting them to state the nature of the problem. This program will also automatically load the user's system control files and add them as attachments to the incident report. Once the form is complete, it is sent (along with the attachments) to the appropriate network administrator for prompt action.

It is important to note that, in some cases, users of message-enabled applications may not even be aware that they are using the e-mail system as part of their application. MAPI services define properties and methods for logging users in and out of the message server without using on-screen prompts. MAPI also provides options for addressing and sending messages without the use of on-screen prompts or user confirmation. By using these features of MAPI services, you can design a program that starts a message session, reads mail, composes replies, addresses the new mail, and sends it to the addressee without ever asking the user for input.

Other Types of Message Applications

There are two more types of message-enabled applications that deserve comment here. These two application types are

■ Electronic forms applications

■ Message-driven applications

Electronic forms applications display a data entry screen that contains one or more data fields for the user to complete. These data fields act as full-fledged windows controls and can support all the events normally supported by Windows data entry forms. Once the form is completed, the data, along with additional control information, is sent to the addressee through MAPI services. When the addressee opens the new mail, the same formatted data entry form appears with the fields filled in (see Figure 3.7).

The *message-driven* application looks for data contained in a message and acts based on the data it finds. Message-driven applications can use any aspect of the message as control information for taking action. Message-driven applications can inspect the message body or subject line for important words or phrases, check the sender's name or the date and time the message was sent, or even scan attachments for important data. These applications can then use the data to forward messages to another person automatically, to set alerts to notify the user of important messages, or to start other programs or processes at the workstation.

FIGURE 3.7.

The filled-in electronic form.

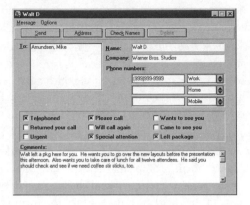

Below are some examples of message-driven applications:

- *Message filtering agent*—Users can enter a list of important keywords into a list box. This list is used to scan all incoming text messages automatically. If the message contains one or more of the keywords, the user is notified immediately that an important message has arrived. Users could also set values to scan for the message sender's name. For example, if the message came from the user's boss, an alert could sound to warn the user that an urgent message has arrived. The same technique can be used to automatically forward specific messages when the user is away on a trip.

- *File transfer database update application*—This program could be used by outlying sales offices to update a central database automatically. Each day the remote offices would enter sales figures in a database, then attach the binary database file to an e-mail message, and send the message to the corporate headquarters. There, a special work-station (logged in as the addressee for all sales database updates) would receive the message and automatically run a program that takes the binary database file and merges it into the central database. This same program could then provide summary data back to the remote offices to keep them up to date on their progress.

- *Electronic database search tool*—Many companies have large libraries of information on clients, products, company regulations, policies and procedures, and so on. Often users would like to run a search of the information but don't have time to physically visit the library and pour through thousands of pages in search of related items. If the information is kept in online databases, users at any location around the world could formulate a set of search criteria to apply against the databases and then submit these queries, via MAPI messages, to one or more workstations dedicated to performing searches. After the search is completed, the resulting data set could be returned to the user who requested the data.

Filtering agents, remote update routines, and long-distance search tools are all examples of how MAPI services can be used to extend the reach of the local workstation to resources at far-away locations. The Windows MAPI services provide excellent tools for building programs that enable users to collect and/or disseminate data over long distances or to multiple locations. The next several chapters will explore the details of MAPI architecture, teach you how to incorporate MAPI services into your programs, and show you examples of real-life programs that take advantage of Windows MAPI services.

Summary

In this chapter, you learned that the Messaging Application Programming Interface (MAPI) is a part of the Windows Open Systems Architecture (WOSA) model. MAPI is designed to offer three key benefits over other messaging services:

■ *Flexibility*—Since MAPI is implemented within the WOSA model, there are three distinct layers:

   ■ The client layer (the end-user software)
   ■ The MAPI DLL layer (the MAPI service broker)
   ■ The service layer (the actual message service provider)

   Because the MAPI DLL layer acts as the service request broker between the MAPI client and the MAPI server, you can interchange servers and clients without having to modify your MAPI software modules.

■ *Consistency*—MAPI services and the methods for accessing them are the same no matter what vendor you are using to provide the message services.

■ *Portability*—MAPI services are available on all supported versions of Windows (Win3.11, WFW, WinNT, and Win95). As Microsoft moves WOSA services to non-Windows platforms, MAPI services will be available within those operating systems, too.

You also learned the three general types of MAPI messages:

■ *Text messages*—These are the standard plain ASCII text messages commonly known as e-mail. Some MAPI service providers support the use of rich-text formatted messages (for example, the Microsoft Exchange Mail client).

■ *Formatted documents and binary files*—These are word-processing documents, graphics files, databases, and so on. MAPI enables you to send these binary files as attachments to the body of a text message.

■ *Control messages*—These are used by operating systems and specialized batch programs to send information about the operating system, or send commands to tell remote machines how to process attached data or run special jobs.

Finally, you learned about the various types of MAPI applications. These application types are

■ *Electronic mail clients*—The sole purpose of these programs is to give users direct access to the available MAPI services (for example, the Microsoft Mail Exchange client that ships with Windows 95).

■ *Message-aware applications*—These are programs that provide MAPI services as an added feature. These programs usually offer users a send button or menu option. The standard output of the program can then be routed to another location through MAPI. The Send menu option of Microsoft Word 95 is an example of a message-aware application.

■ *Message-enabled applications*—These programs offer MAPI services as a basic part of their functionality. Usually, message-enabled applications will not operate properly unless MAPI services are available to the workstation. Examples of message-enabled applications include data entry forms that collect data and automatically route the information to the appropriate e-mail address, sometimes without asking the user for MAPI logons or addresses.

Two more application types reviewed in this chapter are

■ *Electronic forms applications*—These programs are fully functional data entry forms that are MAPI-enabled. Users treat the form like any Windows program. Once the data entry is completed and the form sent, the addressee can open the message and see the same data form.

■ *Message-driven applications*—These are programs that can inspect portions of the message (body, header, attachments) and perform requested actions based on the contents of the message parts. Examples of message-driven applications include e-mail filtering agents, file transfer and update routines, and long-distance data search and retrieval programs.

Now that you know the common types of MAPI messages and applications, it's time to review the details of MAPI architecture. That is the subject of the next chapter.

4

MAPI Architecture

In Chapter 3, "What Is MAPI?," you learned the general outline of the messaging API and how MAPI fits into Microsoft's Windows Open Systems Architecture (WOSA) scheme. You also learned about the three most common types of MAPI messages (ASCII text, formatted documents or binary files, and control messages). Lastly, Chapter 3 described the three major categories of MAPI applications (e-mail, message-aware, and message-enabled).

In this chapter, you'll learn about the basic conceptual components of MAPI—the MAPI Client and the MAPI Server. These two components work together to create, transport, and store messages within the MAPI system.

MAPI clients deal with three main objects:

- Messages and attachments
- Storage folders
- Addresses

Each of these objects is represented slightly differently in the various versions of MAPI implementations you'll learn about in this book. For example, the MAPI OCX tools that ship with Visual Basic allow only limited access to folders and address information. The Messaging OLE layer (provided through the MAPI 1.0 SDK) provides increased access to folders and addresses, but only the full MAPI 1.0 functions allow programmers to add, edit, and delete folders and addresses at the client level. This chapter will cover all three objects in a general sense. Later chapters will provide detailed programming examples.

MAPI servers also deal with three main objects:

- Message transport
- Message stores
- Addresses books

As you can see, the server side of MAPI is quite similar to the client side (see Figure 4.1).

FIGURE 4.1.

Client and server aspects of the MAPI system.

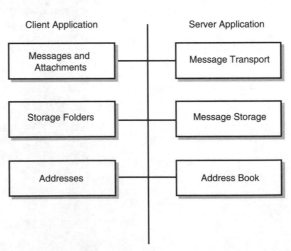

Where the client is concerned with creating and manipulating messages, the server component is concerned with the transporting of those same messages. Where the client side is accessing storage folders, the server side is dealing with message storage, and both client and server must deal with message addresses. However, the MAPI server has the responsibility of managing the transport, storage, and addressing of messages from any number of client applications.

In addition to maintaining the message base for all local clients, MAPI servers also have the task of moving messages to and from remote servers and clients. The final section of this chapter talks briefly about a special MAPI component that handles this task—the MAPI Spooler.

When you complete this chapter, you'll understand the fundamental tasks that must be performed by all MAPI clients and MAPI servers and the basic objects maintained and manipulated by both client and server applications. Once you have a grasp of the general operations of a MAPI system, you'll be ready to explore MAPI functions from a Windows programming perspective in the coming chapters.

The MAPI Client

The MAPI Client is the application that runs on the user's workstation. This is the application that requests services from the MAPI Server. As mentioned in the preceding chapter, client applications can be generic e-mail tools such as Microsoft's Microsoft Mail or Exchange Mail Client for Windows 95. Client applications can also be message-aware applications like the Microsoft Office Suite of applications. Each of these applications provides access to the message server via a send menu option or command button. Lastly, message-enabled applications, ones that use MAPI services as a primary part of their functionality, can be built to meet a specific need. These programs usually hide the MAPI services behind data entry screens that request message-related information and then format and send messages using the available message server.

All MAPI clients must, at some level, deal with three basic objects:

- Messages and attachments
- Storage folders
- Addresses

Depending on the type of client application, one or more of these MAPI objects may be hidden from the client interface. However, even though they may not be visible to the application user, all three objects are present as part of the MAPI architecture. The next three sections describe each of the MAPI client objects and their functions in the MAPI model.

Messages and Attachments

The MAPI system exists in order to move messages from one location to another. Therefore, the heart of the system is the MAPI message object. All message objects must have two components—a message header and a message body. The message header contains information used by MAPI to route and track the movement of the message object. The message body contains the actual text message portion of the message object. Even though every message object must have a message body, the body can be left blank. In addition to the two required components, message objects can also have one or more attachments. Attachments can be any valid operating system file such as an ASCII text file, a binary image, or an executable program.

The Message Header

The Message Header contains all the information needed to deliver the associated message body and attachments. Data stored in the message header varies, depending on the messaging service provider. While the exact items and their names and values differ between messaging systems (CMC, MAPI, OLE Messaging), there is a basic core set that appears in all message headers. Examples of basic data items that can be found in a message header are listed in Table 4.1.

> **NOTE**
>
> The item names given in Table 4.1 do not necessarily correspond to a valid property or variable name in programming code. The actual property names for each item can vary from one code set to another. Also, the order in which these properties appear differs greatly for each MAPI implementation. The chapters following this one focus on different code sets (CMC API, MAPI Controls, OLE Messaging) and detail the exact keywords and property names used to access the items described here.

Table 4.1. Basic data items found in a message header.

Property Name	Type	Description
Recipients	Recipients object	E-mail address of the person who will receive the message. This could be a single name, a list of names, or a group name.
Sender	AddressEntry object	E-mail address of the person who sent the message.
Subject	String	A short text line describing the message.
TimeReceived	Variant (Date/Time)	The date and time the message was received.
TimeSent	Variant (Date/Time)	The date and time the message was sent.

Along with this basic set, additional data items may appear or be available to the programmer. These additional items add functionality to the MAPI interface, but because they are not part of the core set, you cannot expect them to be available to you when you write your programs. Table 4.2 contains a list of additional header data items.

Table 4.2. Optional items that may be found in the message header.

Property Name	Type	Description
DeliveryReceipt	Boolean	Flag that indicates the sender asked for a return receipt message upon either delivery of the message to the recipient or the reading of the message by the recipient.
Importance	Long	A value that indicates the relative importance of the message. Currently, Microsoft Mail clients recognize three priorities: High, Medium, and Low.
Submitted	Boolean	Flag that indicates the item has been sent to the recipient.
Sent	Boolean	Read/write.
Signed	Boolean	Read/write.
Type	String	Value that identifies this message as one of a class of messages. Currently, Microsoft Mail systems recognize the IPM (Interpersonal Message) type for sending messages read by persons. Microsoft has defined the IPC (Interprocess Communication) type for use between program processes. Other types can be defined and used by other programs.
Unread	Boolean	Flag that indicates whether the message has been received and/or read by the recipient.

The Message Body

The message body contains the text data sent to the recipient from the sender. For most systems, this is a pure ASCII text message. However, some service providers can handle rich-text format message bodies, which allows for additional information such as font, color, and format codes to be included in the message body (see Figure 4.2).

FIGURE 4.2.

*Using Microsoft Exchange
to send a rich-text message.*

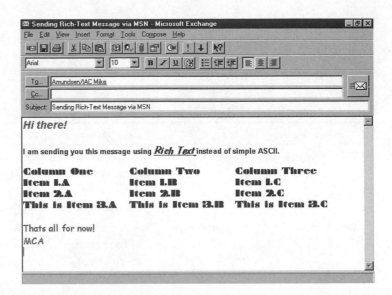

The availability and support of rich-text message bodies vary between service providers. Some service providers allow you to create rich-text message bodies but translate the information into simple ASCII upon delivery. For example, Microsoft Exchange allows users to build rich-text message bodies but translates that message into simple ASCII text when using the SMTP service provider. All messages received by the Microsoft Mail system are converted into simple text as well. This behavior ensures that the message will be delivered but may result in surprise or even unreadable material at the recipient's end (see Figure 4.3).

FIGURE 4.3.

*Receiving a rich-text
message that has been
changed to simple ASCII.*

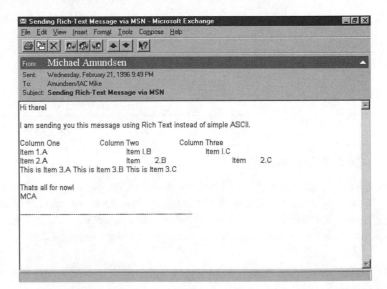

Other transport providers may transmit the rich-text and allow the receiving message provider to handle the translation to simple ASCII, if needed. This option allows for the most flexibility but can result in undeliverable messages. For example, Microsoft Exchange users have the option of sending rich-text messages through the CompuServe message transport. The CompuServe transport supports rich-text messages. Rich-text messages sent from one Windows Messaging Client to another by way of the CompuServe transport retain their original layout and look. However, recipients using something other than Microsoft Exchange may see something different. For example, the WinCIM client provided by CompuServe treats rich-text messages as binary attachments to a simple ASCII text message. WinCIM clients would receive the message shown in Figure 4.2 as an attachment to view with Microsoft Word or some other viewer.

If, however, the CompuServe recipient is defined as an Internet user through the CompuServe address (for example, 102461.1267@compuserve.com), the CompuServe message transport reports the message as undeliverable when it is discovered that the message body contains anything other than simple ASCII text (see Figure 4.4).

FIGURE 4.4.

Reporting an undeliverable rich-text message.

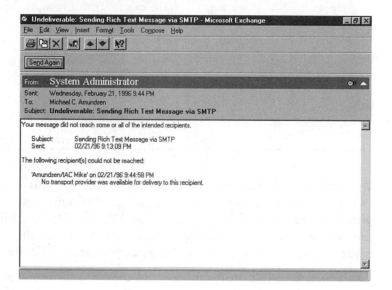

Message Attachments

Message attachments are supported by all forms of Microsoft MAPI. A MAPI attachment can be any data file, of any type (text, binary programs, graphics, and so on). These attachments are sent to the recipient along with the message header and body. Upon receipt of the message, the recipient can, depending on the features of the message client software, view, manipulate, and store the attachments on the local workstation. The MAPI system keeps track of attachments with a set of properties. Table 4.3 lists an example set of attachment properties. The actual properties and their names can differ between program code sets.

Table 4.3. Example MAPI attachment properties.

Property Name	Type	Description
Index	Long	Each message object can contain more than one attachment. Attachments are numbered starting with 0.
Name	String	The name to display in a list box or in the client message area (for example, "June Sales Report").
Position	Long	A value that indicates where in the message body the attachment is to be displayed. Microsoft Mail and Windows Messaging clients display an icon representing the attachment within the message body. Other clients may ignore this information, show an icon, or show ASCII text that represents the attachment.
Source	String	The exact filename used by the operating system to locate and identify the attachment (for example, "\\Server1\Data\Accounting\JuneSales.xls").
Type	Long	A value that indicates the type of attachment. Microsoft defines three attachment types: *Data*—A direct file attachment *Embedded OLE*—An embedded OLE object *Static OLE*—A static OLE object

Attachments can be handled differently by the message transport provider. Microsoft Mail and Windows Messaging clients display attachments within the message body and transport the attachments as part of the message body, too. Microsoft Mail and Microsoft Exchange recipients see the attachment within the message body and can use the mouse to select, view, and save the attachment when desired. Other transports may handle the attachment differently.

SMTP transports will report a message that contains attachments as undeliverable unless the transport supports MIME or some other binary transfer protocol. The Internet transport that ships with the Windows Messaging Client does support MIME protocol.

The CompuServe service provider for Microsoft Exchange will transport the attachments as additional messages addressed to the same recipient. For example, a single ASCII text message with one attachment would be received as two messages when sent via the CompuServe transport.

Storage Folders

MAPI messages can be saved in storage folders. The MAPI model defines several storage folders. Figure 4.5 shows a set of folders as viewed from the Windows Messaging Client.

FIGURE 4.5.

Viewing the folders from the Windows Messaging Client.

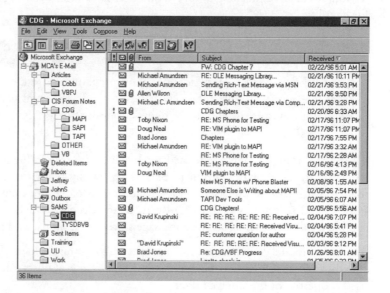

The defined storage folders within MAPI are

■ *Inbox*—This is the place where all incoming messages first appear.

■ *Outbox*—This is the place where all outgoing messages are placed before they are sent to their destination.

■ *Sent*—This is the place where all outgoing messages are placed after they are sent to their destination. This is, in effect, a set of message copies that can be referenced after the original has been sent.

■ *Deleted*—This is the place where all messages are placed once they have been marked for deletion.

■ *User-defined folders*—This can be one or more folders defined by the user. Each folder can hold messages that have been received and copies of messages that have been sent.

Not all implementations of MAPI support all of the folders listed above. For example, the Simple MAPI interface allows access to the Inbox (by way of the .Fetch method of the MAPISession Control) and the Outbox (by way of the .Send method of the MAPISession Control). Simple MAPI allows no other folder access. Programmers cannot inspect the contents of the Sent folder or move messages from the Inbox to other user-defined storage folders.

The OLE Messaging library offers a more complete access to the MAPI storage system. The Inbox and Outbox folders are accessible by name (that is, Session.Inbox and Session.OutBox). The Sent and Deleted folders are available. The OLE MAPI implementation allows access to all folders through the InfoStore object. An Infostore object contains all folder and message objects. All MAPI service providers can implement their own message stores, and a single client can have access to more than one message store at the same time. Therefore, a single MAPI session can involve attaching to several message stores and presenting their contents to the user for handling.

> **NOTE**
>
> The OLE Messaging library does not allow programmers to create or delete folders from the InfoStore collection. Only the MAPI 1.0 API set available from C++ allows programmers to create and delete folders from the storage set.

The MAPI storage folders are defined as a hierarchy (as seen in Figure 4.5). The MAPI model allows for the creation of multiple levels of the hierarchy at any time. The MAPI model allows for the creation of subfolders at any level and on any folder. For example, the Inbox folder can have several subfolders such as UnRead, Read, Urgent, and Unknown. The addition of subfolders allows users to organize message stores based on use and preference.

The MAPI model defines a handful of properties for storage folders. These properties are available through the OLE Messaging library and C++. Table 4.4 lists some of the more commonly used properties of the storage folder.

Table 4.4. Example MAPI storage folder properties.

Property Name	Type	Description
FolderID	String	This is a string value that uniquely identifies this folder.
Folders	Folders collection object	This is the set of folder objects contained by the current folder. Any folder can contain one or more sublevel folders.
Messages	Messages collection object	This is the set of messages stored in this folder.

Property Name	Type	Description
Name	String	A unique user-defined string that identifies the storage folder.
Parent	Object	This contains the name of the parent folder or InfoStore to which the current folder belongs.

> **NOTE**
>
> You can find additional information on Folder and InfoStore objects, their properties, and their methods in Chapter 8, "The OLE Messaging Library," and Chapter 9, "Creating a MAPI Mailing List Manager with the OLE Messaging Library."

Physical organization of the storage folders can differ greatly depending on the service provider. For example, the Microsoft Mail Server storage arrangement involves a single directory on the disk that identifies the post office and subsequent directories underneath that correspond to an individual user's InfoStores (and subfolders within the storage). However, the physical organization of storage folders for the Windows Messaging Client that ships with Windows 95 involves a single data file (usually found in \Exchange\mailbox.pst). This single file is used to store all the personal messages maintained on the user's workstation. It is up to the service provider to establish the storage details and to support access to the physical storage using the pre-defined InfoStore, Folder, and Message objects.

Addresses

Addresses are the last class of objects dealt with at the client level. Every electronic message has at least two address objects: the sender object and the recipient object. MAPI allows you to add several recipient address objects to the same message. Each address object has several properties. Table 4.5 shows a set of sample properties for the MAPI Address object.

Table 4.5. MAPI Address object properties.

Property Name	Type	Description
Address	String	This is the unique electronic address for this address object. The combination of the Type property (see below) and the Address property creates the complete MAPI address. Sample address properties are MikeA@isp.net—Internet address /MailNet1/PostOfc9/MCA—MS Mail address

continues

Table 4.5. continued

Property Name	Type	Description
DisplayType	Long	The MAPI service allows programmers to define addresses by type. This means you can sort or filter messages using the DisplayType property. Sample address types are
		mapiUser—Local user
		mapiDistList—Distribution list
		mapiForum—Public folder
		mapiRemoteUser—Remote user
Name	String	This is the name used in the Address book. Usually, this is an easy-to-remember name such as "Fred Smith" or "Mary in Home Office."
Type	String	This value contains the name of the message transport type. This allows MAPI to support the use of external message transport services. Sample address types are
		MS:—Microsoft Mail transport
		SMTP:—Simple Mail Transport Protocol
		MSN:—Microsoft Network transport

MAPI address objects are a part of every MAPI message and are stored in the MAPI address book. You'll learn more about the address book in the following section on MAPI Server objects.

The MAPI Server

The MAPI Server handles all the message traffic generated by MAPI clients. The MAPI Server usually runs on a standalone workstation connected to the network, but this is not a requirement. There are versions of user-level MAPI servers that can be used to handle message services.

Microsoft supports two standalone MAPI servers:

■ Microsoft Mail Server (for both PCs and Apple workstations)

■ Microsoft Exchange Server (for NT Server workstations)

The Microsoft Mail Server runs standalone on both Intel PCs or Apple workstations. It provides direct MAPI services for all connected MAPI users and also provides gateway MAPI services for remote users. The Microsoft Mail Server has, until recently, been Microsoft's primary electronic mail server. Even though Microsoft is stressing the early adoption of the new Microsoft Exchange Server for NT, the Microsoft Mail Server will continue to be the primary mail server for thousands of users. All MAPI Clients can share information with connected Microsoft Mail Servers regardless of the client platform (Win31, WinNT, or Win95).

The Microsoft Exchange Server runs as a service on an NT Server workstation. It provides MAPI services to all MAPI users. Unlike the Microsoft Mail Server, which distinguishes between local and remote users, the Microsoft Exchange Server treats all MAPI users as remote users. This simplifies several aspects of MAPI administration. Unlike the Microsoft Mail Server, which only supports Microsoft Mail format messages, the Microsoft Exchange Server supports multiple message formats and services, including Microsoft Mail. This also means that the administration of gateways and remote transports is quite different for Microsoft Exchange.

Microsoft also supports two peer-to-peer message servers. These servers run on the user's workstation, usually as a part of the MAPI client software. The two client-level MAPI servers provided by Microsoft are

■ WorkGroup Post Office for Windows for WorkGroups
■ Windows Messaging Client for Windows 95

The WorkGroup Post Office runs as a limited version of the Microsoft Mail Server. Clients that use Microsoft's peer-to-peer networking are able to establish a post office on a single workstation and then share the post office directories with other peers on the network. The design and operation are very much like the Microsoft Mail Server system, but it runs on an individual PC. The primary advantage of the peer-to-peer version is that a single user can set up a WorkGroup Post Office and use that as a base for adding remote mail connections and fax support. The main disadvantage of the peer-to-peer client is that users were not able to attach to both the WorkGroup Post Office and an existing Microsoft Mail Server post office.

With the introduction of Windows 95, Microsoft introduced a client version of Microsoft Exchange that provides the same features as the Microsoft Exchange Server version. Users are able to install and share a WorkGroup Post Office and are also able to attach to existing Microsoft Mail post offices. In addition, users can connect using other mail transports as they become available.

Regardless of the actual server application used, the same basic processes must occur for all MAPI server systems. The three main tasks of all MAPI servers are

■ *Message transport*—Moving the message from location to location.
■ *Message storage*—Providing a filing system for the storage and retrieval of received messages.
■ *Address book services*—Providing centralized addressing and verification services that can be used by all MAPI clients.

The next three sections discuss each of these processes in greater detail.

Message Transport

Message Transport is the process of moving messages from one place to another. Under the MAPI model, message transport is a distinct, and often separate, process. MAPI 1.0 allows for the use of *external message transports*. In other words, programmers can write software that knows how to handle a particular type or types of message formats and register this transport mechanism as part of the MAPI system. This allows third-party vendors to create format-specific transports that can be seamlessly integrated into the MAPI system.

It is the message transport that knows just how to format and, if necessary, pre-process messages for a particular messaging format. The message transport knows exactly what information must be supplied as part of the message header and how it needs to be arranged. The message transport also knows what types of message bodies are supported. For example, SMTP format allows only text message bodies. However, the Microsoft Network message format allows rich-text message bodies. It is the job of the message transport to keep track of these differences, modify the message where appropriate, or reject the message if modification or pre-processing is not possible.

One of the key features of the MAPI model is the provision for multiple message transports within the MAPI system. Once message transports are installed (or registered) with a MAPI client application, they are called into action whenever the pre-defined message type is received by the MAPI client software. Since MAPI is designed to accept the registration of multiple transports, the MAPI Client is potentially capable of handling an unlimited number of vendor-specific message formats.

NOTE

Message types are stored as part of the address. These types were discussed earlier in this chapter in the "Addresses" section.

Figure 4.6 shows how the multiple message transports are used when messages are received by the MAPI Client.

Under the MAPI system, message transports provide another vital service. It is the responsibility of the message transport to enforce any security features required by the message format. For example, the MSN mail transport is responsible for prompting the user for a username and password before attempting to link with the MSN mail system.

It is important to note that the message transport is not responsible for storing the messages that have been received. The transport is only in charge of moving messages from one location to another. Message storage is discussed in the next section.

FIGURE 4.6.
Handling incoming messages with multiple message transports.

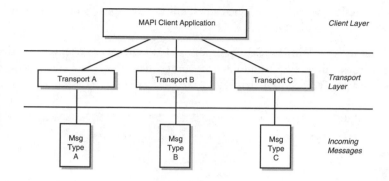

Message Stores

Message stores are responsible for providing the filing system for the messages received via the message transport. The MAPI model dictates that the message store must be in a hierarchical format that allows multilevel storage. In other words, the system must allow users to create folders to hold messages, and these folders must also be able to hold other folders that hold messages. Under the MAPI model, there is no limit to the number of folder levels that can be defined for a message store (see Figure 4.7).

FIGURE 4.7.
MAPI message stores are hierarchical filing systems.

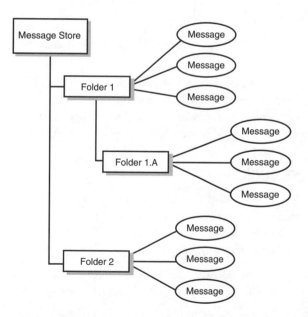

Under the MAPI model, storage folders can have properties that control how they are used and how they behave. For example, storage folders can be public or private. Folders can have properties that make the contained messages read-only to prevent modification. The options available depend on the implementation of the message store. In other words, the programmer who designs the message store can establish the scope of storage options and the MAPI Client will comply with those rules.

As in the case with message transports, MAPI clients can access more than one message store. Figure 4.8 shows the Windows Messaging Client that is currently accessing two different message stores. You can see that each store has its own set of folders and its own set of messages.

FIGURE 4.8.

Accessing multiple message stores at the same time.

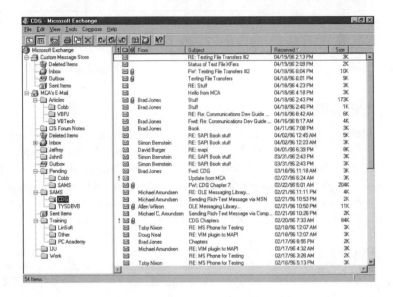

The Windows Messaging Client that ships with Microsoft Exchange Server also allows you to create folder column, grouping, sort, and filter rules for personal and public folders. By doing this, you can create storage views that reflect the course of an ongoing discussion and allow for easy search and retrieval of data kept in the message store (see Figure 4.9).

Address Books

The last of the main MAPI server objects is the *address book*. The MAPI address book contains all the directory information about a particular addressee. The book can contain data for individual users or groups of users (a distribution list). The minimum data stored in the address book is the user's display name, the transport type, and the user's e-mail address.

Additional information such as mailing address, telephone number, and other data may be available depending on the design of the address book.

Address books, like the other objects described in this chapter, work independently under the MAPI model. Also, the MAPI client can access more than one address book at a time. This means that several address books of various formats can all be viewed (and used) at the same time when composing messages (see Figure 4.10).

FIGURE 4.9.

A Microsoft Exchange folder with discussion properties.

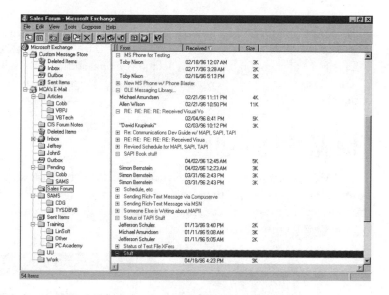

FIGURE 4.10.

Accessing multiple address books at the same time.

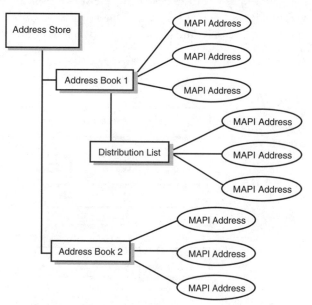

Along with storing addresses, the address book interface also acts to resolve display names used in the MAPI interface with the actual e-mail addresses and transport types for those display names. To do this, MAPI offers a ResolveName service that performs lookups upon request. The ResolveName service is able to look at all address books (regardless of their storage format) in order to locate the proper e-mail address.

Users are also able to designate one of the address books as the default or *personal* address book. This is the first address book in which new addresses are stored and the first address book that is checked when resolving a display name. The Windows Messaging Client and the Microsoft Mail client both ship with default personal address books. The Windows Messaging Client allows users to add new address books and designate their own personal address book container.

The MAPI Spooler

The MAPI Spooler is a special process that interacts with both message stores and message transports. It is the spooler's job to route messages from the client to the proper transport and from the transport to the client. The spooler is the direct link between the client and the transport. All messages go through the MAPI Spooler.

NOTE

Actually there are some cases in which a message moves directly from the message store to the message transport. This occurs when service providers offer both message store and message transport. E-mail service providers that offer these features are known as *tightly coupled* service providers.

FIGURE 4.11.
The MAPI Spooler passes messages between the message store and the message transport.

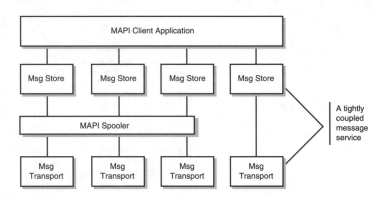

Figure 4.11 illustrates the different paths messages can take when the MAPI Spooler is used.

As each message is moved from the message store (the "outbox") to the transport, the MAPI

Spooler checks the address type to see which transport should be used. Once this is determined, the spooler notifies the transport and attempts to pass the message from the message store to the message transport. If the transport is not currently available, the MAPI Spooler holds onto the message until the transport is free to accept messages. This allows transport providers to act as remote connections without any additional programming or addressing on the client side.

> **NOTE**
>
> In fact, the implementation used in the Microsoft Exchange version of MAPI treats all connections as if they were remote—even when the message is moved from one user's Microsoft Exchange outbox to another Microsoft Exchange user's inbox on the same network.

In the case of messages that move along a constantly connected transport (that is, between two addresses on the same Microsoft Exchange Server), the spooler notifies the transport (Microsoft Exchange) and the transport accepts the message almost immediately. Often the user is not aware of any delay in the handling of the message.

In the case of messages that move from the Windows Messaging Client by way of an SMTP transport through a dial-up connection to the Internet, the MAPI Spooler holds onto the message until the user connects to the Internet account through Win95 Dial-Up Networking. Once the connection is made, the MAPI Spooler sends all local messages on to the Internet mail server, retrieves any waiting mail from the mail server, and passes these new messages to the appropriate message store.

The MAPI Spooler is also able to move a single message to several recipients when some of those recipients are not using the same message transport. For example, users can build distribution lists that contain names of users on the local Microsoft Exchange Server, users who have addresses on a local Microsoft Mail Server, and users who can only be contacted through a fax address. When the message is sent, it moves from the message store to the spooler, which then sorts out all the transports needed and passes the messages on to the correct transports at the first available moment.

The MAPI Spooler is also responsible for marking messages as read or unread, notifying the sender when a message has been successfully passed to the transport, and, when requested, notifying the sender when the recipient has received (or read) the message. The MAPI Spooler also reports when messages cannot be sent due to unavailable transports or other problems.

Summary

In this chapter, you learned about the general architecture of the MAPI system. You learned that there are two main components to the system:

- The MAPI Client
- The MAPI Server

You learned that the MAPI Client resides on the user's desktop and handles three main MAPI objects:

- Messages and attachments
- Storage folders
- MAPI addresses

This chapter also reviewed the basic properties and features of MAPI messages, including message headers, folders, and address objects.

You learned that the MAPI Server usually resides on a standalone workstation connected to the network (although not always). Like the MAPI Client, the MAPI Server handles three main objects:

- Message transports
- Message stores
- Address books

You learned that the MAPI model allows users to use multiple versions of message transports (such as Microsoft Exchange Server messages and SMTP Internet messages), message storage, and address books. You also learned about the MAPI Spooler. The MAPI Spooler is the process that moves items from the message store to the appropriate provider.

Now that you know the basic architecture of the MAPI system, it's time to build some applications that use the system. In the next chapter, you'll learn how to use the Microsoft Exchange Forms Designer to build MAPI-enabled applications that work within the Microsoft Exchange interface.

5

Using the Microsoft
Exchange Forms Designer

Introduction

One of the quickest ways to develop MAPI applications is to use the Microsoft Exchange Forms Designer kit. This tool ships with the Microsoft Exchange Server and includes a GUI form designer tool, sample templates, design wizards, and an installation wizard. The Microsoft Exchange Forms Designer (called the *EFD*) generates Visual Basic 4.0 code. Once the forms are generated, you can also use Visual Basic 4.0 to modify and enhance the forms.

> **NOTE**
>
> For those who do not own a copy of Visual Basic 4.0, the Microsoft Exchange Forms Designer includes a version of the Visual Basic 4.0 16-bit compiler.

To get the most out of this chapter, you should have access to a copy of the Microsoft Exchange Forms Designer on your machine. You do not have to be linked to a Microsoft Exchange Server to complete the project in this chapter. If you do not have a copy of the Microsoft Exchange Forms Designer, you can still get a lot out of this chapter. The concepts and techniques discussed here apply to any project that uses Microsoft Exchange as a message platform. The last section of the chapter focuses on folder views. You do not need the Microsoft Exchange Forms Designer to complete the exercises in that section of the chapter.

You can use the EFD to develop two different types of forms:

- *Send forms*—These are forms used to send information from one location to the next. This is, in effect, a formatted e-mail message.
- *Post forms*—These are forms used to place information into a particular folder. This is an application designed to control the content of bulletin board messages to be viewed by several people.

You can also use the EFD to design folder views. Folder views are rules that control just how a folder appears to the users. By setting values such as `Sort Order`, `Message Grouping`, and `Message Filtering`, you can present folder contents in ways that reflect users' needs and highlight the most important aspects of the message collection.

When you complete this chapter, you'll know how to design, code, test, and install customized forms and folders using the Microsoft Exchange Forms Designer. You'll learn how to use the EFD to create a Send form and a Post form. You'll also create several new folders with custom views. Finally, you'll learn how to link customer forms to folders.

What Is the Microsoft Exchange Forms Designer?

The Microsoft Exchange Forms Designer is a development tool that is a part of Microsoft Exchange Server. The EFD is a complete design tool for the creation and management of customized electronic message applications. You can design forms that perform various tasks, including forms that

- Originate new messages
- Respond to existing messages
- Are read-only
- Are pre-addressed to one or more users
- Are posted for public viewing
- Allow for anonymous postings (no Sender address)

The Microsoft Exchange Forms Designer uses the Visual Basic development environment. If you are familiar with Visual Basic or Microsoft Access, you'll have no trouble learning to use the Microsoft Exchange Forms Designer. Even if you have not had a lot of experience with Visual Basic or Access, you'll find the EFD environment easy to work with.

EFD Design Wizards

Most of the form design work involves drag-and-drop operations to add fields to a form. When you use the EFD wizards, toolbars, and menus, most of the basic message fields (To, Cc, Subject, and so on) are automatically added to your forms. You can add custom controls such as labels, text boxes, list and combo boxes, check boxes and radio buttons, and even tabs, frames, and picture boxes. One of the controls available with the Microsoft Exchange Forms Designer is a 16-bit version of the rich-text control. This allows users to select fonts, type sizes, and colors within an editable text box.

The QuickHelp Feature

Another very handy feature of the Microsoft Exchange Forms Designer is the ability to add field-level and form-level help to the project without having to create a WinHelp file. The EFD's QuickHelp allows you to enter help information for each control on the form and for the form itself. You can create a message that appears on the status bar at the bottom of the form. You can also create a message window that acts as context-sensitive help whenever the user presses the F1 key. And if you are really serious, the EFD allows you to enter help context IDs that link to standard WinHelp files.

Extending EFD with Visual Basic

It is also possible to use the Microsoft Exchange Forms Designer to generate an initial form and then use Visual Basic to modify the form, for example, by

- Adding new controls
- Modifying the form layout or backgrounds

- Linking the form to existing databases
- Adding calculation fields to the form
- Adding the capability to launch executable programs from the form
- Linking the form to an existing WinHelp file

Although it is possible to use Visual Basic alone to design and implement Microsoft Exchange forms, the EFD provides several advantages over "pure" Visual Basic. With the Microsoft Exchange Forms Designer, you get a tool that handles most of the drudgery of linking message fields to form controls. The EFD helps you establish a consistent look and feel for all your forms. The EFD also walks you through the installation process, which involves creating a custom message type, registering that message type with Microsoft Exchange, and creating a configuration file to link the form to Microsoft Exchange.

Using the Microsoft Exchange Forms Designer to Create a Custom Form

In this section, you'll use the Microsoft Exchange Forms Designer to create a job request form to initiate requests to have maintenance jobs completed in a workplace. This will be a single-window Send form (addressed to a user). After you build the form, you'll install it into your personal forms library for use at any time.

Using the Microsoft Exchange Forms Designer Wizard

The easiest way to start developing forms with the Microsoft Exchange Forms Designer is to use the Forms Designer wizard. The wizard will take you through the initial steps in creating an electronic form. Once you answer all the wizard's questions, you'll see the EFD build a basic form for your use. You can then use the EFD to modify the project before saving and installing the new application.

If you haven't already done so, start up the Microsoft Exchange Forms Designer. You can do this from the Microsoft Exchange program group. To do this, press the `Start` button on the Windows 95 task bar. Then select `Programs | Microsoft Exchange | Microsoft Exchange Forms Designer`. You can also start the EFD directly from Microsoft Exchange. To do this, start Microsoft Exchange and log in to your e-mail system. Then select `Tools | Application Design | Forms Designer...` (see Figure 5.1).

TIP

Starting the EFD from the Microsoft Exchange menu takes more memory. On some systems, it may seem a bit slower than starting EFD from the program menu.

However, when you're developing an EFD form, it's really handy to have Microsoft Exchange up and running at the same time. That way you can easily switch between design and test mode while you debug your EFD application.

FIGURE 5.1.
Selecting the EFD from the Windows Messaging client.

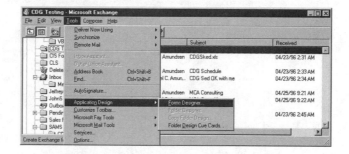

Creating Your Form

The first screen you'll see is the Forms Designer Wizard. It asks whether you want to begin a new project using the wizard, load a template form, or open an existing form (see Figure 5.2).

FIGURE 5.2.
Starting the Microsoft Exchange Forms Designer Wizard.

For now, select the Form Template Wizard option and press Next to continue.

Where Will Your Information Go?

The wizard asks whether you are designing a Send form or a Post form (see Figure 5.3).

Send forms are used to send messages directly to one or more users. Send forms have a field on the form for the "To" and "Cc" fields of a message. Post messages are sent to a folder, not a person, and therefore do not have a "To" or a "Cc" field on them. For our example job request form, you want to use a Send form. This will make sure that the form is sent directly to a person. Select Send and press Next.

FIGURE 5.3.

Creating a Send form or a Post form.

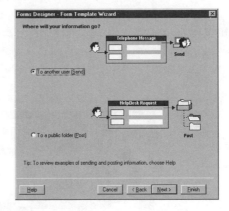

How Will Your Form Be Used?

The wizard next asks whether you are creating a form to send information to someone or a form to respond to an existing EFD form (see Figure 5.4).

FIGURE 5.4.

Creating a Send- or Response-type form.

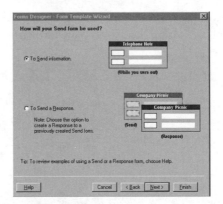

The first option allows you to create an "initiating" form. The second option allows you to create a response form. For now, select the Send option and press the Next button.

WARNING

Don't confuse the Send option on this screen with the previous screen where you were asked if you wanted to create a Send or a Post form. This screen is really asking you to describe the action of your form—send or respond. The previous screen asked about the destination of your form—a person or a group.

One Window or Two?

The wizard now asks whether you want your form to have one or two windows (see Figure 5.5).

FIGURE 5.5.
Specify a one-window or two-window form.

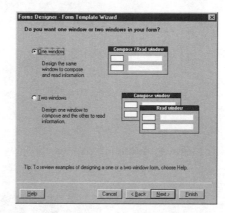

You use single-window forms when you want to allow the reader to be able to edit the same fields filled out by the sender. A good example would be a form that you send to people with information for their editing and final approval.

You use the two-window form when you do not want to allow readers to alter the data on the form that they read. When you select a two-window option, the EFD creates a compose form and a read form. The compose form appears when a user first creates a form to send to someone. When the recipient opens the two-window form, only the read form appears. This form has the same controls as the compose form, but the fields are all read-only.

For this example, select the one-window option and then press Next.

Setting the Form Name and Description

Finally, the Forms Designer Wizard asks you to supply the name and general description of your form (see Figure 5.6).

The name you enter appears in list boxes (and in some cases on menus) within the Windows Messaging client. The description you enter appears in information dialog boxes that users can view when selecting Microsoft Exchange forms from their client interface. For now, enter the information contained in Table 5.1.

Table 5.1. Job request form name and description.

Property	Setting
Name	Job Request Form
Description	Use this form to initiate a job request to the maintenance department.

FIGURE 5.6.
Setting the form name and description.

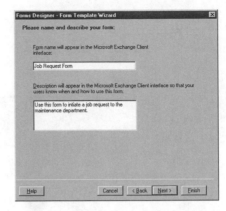

After you supply the form name and description, press Next. The wizard displays a final screen telling you that you have completed the wizard steps (see Figure 5.7).

FIGURE 5.7.
The final screen of the Forms Designer Wizard.

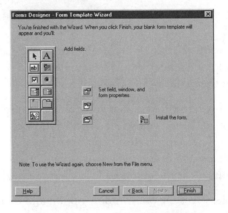

At this point you could press the Back button to return to previous screens and make any changes needed. When you are sure that all screens have been completed properly, select Finish to close the wizard.

Your form should look like the one in Figure 5.8.

You now have a basic electronic form ready for final modification and use. You can see that the top part of the form has been filled in with the Date and From fields. These will be filled in automatically when you first execute the completed form. You'll also see the To, Cc, and Subject fields. These fields will be filled in by the person executing the form.

The rest of the form has been left blank. It will contain application-specific controls and information. In the next few sections, you'll add labels, input boxes, list controls, and a picture control to the form.

Before going further, save this project as JOBREQ.EFP.

FIGURE 5.8.

The results of the Forms Designer Wizard.

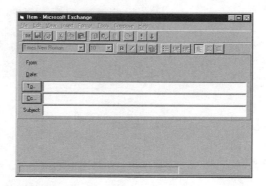

Modifying the Job Request Form

Now that you have the basic electronic form built, it's time to add the fields needed to collect and display specific data. To do this, you add controls for new fields and set the field properties. After adding all the needed fields, you set a few form-level properties, add some help, and you're ready to install and test your form.

Adding a Field to the Job Request Form

It's very easy to add fields to the form. All you do is click once on the toolbox object you want to use, then move your mouse to the desired location on the form, and click once again to drop the object onto the form.

> **WARNING**
>
> If you're used to Visual Basic, you'll discover that the method for dragging and dropping form objects is slightly different here. You do not paint the objects onto the EFD form as you do in Visual Basic. Here you just click, point, and click.

As a test, select the Entry Field object (called a text box in Visual Basic) and drop it onto the body of the form.

> **NOTE**
>
> You'll notice that you cannot use the EFD to place standard form objects in the header area of the form. You can, however, place one of the MAPI fields (From, Date, To, Cc, Bcc, and Subject) on the header.

Notice that the control is placed on the form along with an associated label control (see Figure 5.9).

FIGURE 5.9.
Adding an Entry Field
object to the form.

You can click on the label in design mode to edit the contents. You can also use the anchors on the object to move or resize it as needed. It is also possible to "unlink" the caption and input control by selecting the large square on the upper left of the input control and moving it independently of the caption.

> **TIP**
>
> Deleting the caption from the input form will also delete the input control itself. You can use the General tab of the Field Properties dialog box (double-click the control) to remove the caption. Locate the Position drop-down list and set its value to None.

Now that you've added a field to the form, you need to adjust several of the field's properties. In the next section, you'll learn how to do this using the Field Properties dialog box.

Using the Field Properties Dialog Box

The Field Properties dialog box gives you access to several properties of the field object (see Figure 5.10).

This dialog has three tabs:

- ■ *General*—Use this tab to set the name, caption, and position of the control on the form. You can also use the tab to establish the control's locked, hidden, and required status and to enter the field-level help.

- ■ *Format*—Use this tab to set the font, size, color, alignment, and other formatting properties of the control. Note that you must use this same tab to set properties for both input control and the caption.

FIGURE 5.10.
Viewing the Field
Properties dialog box.

■ *Initial Value*—Use this tab to enter the default value for this control. The contents of this tab depend on the type of control. List and combo boxes allow you to enter multiple items, text boxes allow you to enter straight text, picture boxes allow you to load a graphic image from the disk, and so on.

Use Table 5.2 as a guide in setting the field properties of the text box field on your job request form.

Table 5.2. Setting field properties of the text box control.

Tab	*Property*	*Setting*
General	Reference Name	ContactPhone
	Column Name	Contact Phone
	Field Caption	Contact Phone:
	Required	(Checked)
Format	Maximum Characters	(Checked) 80
Initial Value	Initial Text	XXX-XXXX

After setting the properties on the three tabs, select Close to save the information.

Completing the Job Request Form Fields

You need to add several fields to the job request form before it is complete. Now that you have an idea of how to add fields and set their properties, use the information in Table 5.3 and Figure 5.11 to add, size, and locate the remaining fields on the form.

The area of the EFD form where you place your controls is scrollable. It is very easy to lose one or more fields due to unexpected scrolling when you place a control on the form. To make it easy to see where things are on the form, you need to turn on the scroll bars. Select View ¦ Show Scroll Bars from the main menu. If you do not want users to see these at runtime, turn them off before you install the form.

FIGURE 5.11.

Laying out the job request form.

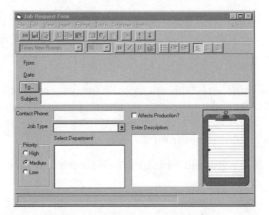

Be sure to use a complete path/directory name for the Picture Field control in Table 5.3. You can find the Chap05 directory under the main directory created when you installed the source code from the CD-ROM that ships with the book.

After adding all the fields and setting their properties, save the project (JOBREQ.EFP) before continuing with the next step.

Setting Form and Window Properties of the Job Request Form

There are several form- and window-level properties that you can set for Microsoft Exchange forms. These settings affect the way your form looks and behaves once it's up and running under Microsoft Exchange.

First, select View ¦ Window Properties from the main menu. Then set the properties using the information in Table 5.4.

continues

Table 5.3. Control properties for the job request form.

Control	Property Tab	Property	Setting
Entry Field	General	Reference Name	ContactPhone
		Column Name	Contact Phone
		Field Caption	Contact Phone:
		Required	(Checked)
		Left	1290
		Top	90
		Width	2400
		Height	300
	Format	Maximum Characters	(Checked) 80
	Initial Value	Initial Text	XXX-XXXX
ComboBox Field	General	Reference Name	JobType
		Column Name	Job Type
		Field Caption	Job Type:
		Required	(Checked)
		Left	1290
		Top	545
		Width	2400
		Height	300
		Style	DropDown List
	Format	List Values	Cleaning
	Initial Value		Construction
			General

Table 5.3. continued

Control	Property Tab	Property	Setting
			Electrical Plumbing
Frame Control	General	Reference Name	Priority
		Column Name	Priority
		Field Caption	Priority:
		Required	(Checked)
		Left	120
		Top	1155
		Width	1050
		Height	1545
OptionButton Field	General	Reference Name	Priority_1
		Field Caption	High
		Left	120
		Top	240
		Width	900
		Height	300
	Initial Value	Unselected	(checked)
OptionButton Field	General	Reference Name	Priority_2
		Field Caption	Medium
		Left	120
		Top	560
		Width	900

continues

Control	Property Tab	Property	Setting
	Initial Value	Height	300
		Selected	(checked)
OptionButton Field	General	Reference Name	Priority_3
		Field Caption	Low
		Left	120
		Top	880
		Width	900
		Height	300
	Initial Value	Unselected	(checked)
OptionButton Field	General	Reference Name	Department
		Column Name	Department
		Field Caption	Department:
		Caption Position	Top
		Left	1350
		Top	1260
		Width	2415
		Height	1570
		Required	(checked)
	Initial Value	List Values	Administration
			Customer Service
			Production
			Repairs
			Sales

Table 5.3. continued

Control	Property Tab	Property	Setting
Check Box Field	General	Reference Name	Affects Production
		Column Name	Affects Production
		Left	3945
		Top	120
		Width	1770
		Height	300
		Caption:	Affects Production?
	Initial Value	Unchecked	(checked)
Entry Field	General	Reference Name	Description
		Column Name	Description
		Left	3945
		Top	900
		Width	2265
		Height	1785
		Caption	Description:
		Caption Position	Top
		Required	(checked)
	Format	Allow Multiple Lines	(checked)
		Vertical Scroll Bars	(checked)
	Initial Values	Initial Text	Describe the nature of the problem

Control	Property Tab	Property	Setting
Picture Field	General	Reference Name	Logo
		Omit this field	(checked)
		Left	6360
		Top	60
		Width	1620
		Height	2640
	Format	Stretch Picture	(checked)
	Initial Value	Picture	chap05\efd\clipbord.wmf

Table 5.4. Setting the window properties of the job request form.

Dialog Tab	Property	Setting
General	Window Name	JobRequestWindow
	Window Caption	Job Request Form
	Fields in Tab Order	MAPI_To
		MAPI_Subject
		ContactPhone
		JobType
		Priority_1
		Priority_2
		Priority_3
		Department
		AffectsProduction
		Description
Format	Maximize Button	(off)
	Minimize Button	(off)
	ToolBar	(off)
	Formatting Toolbar	(off)
	Status Bar	(on)
	Window Sizing Options	Fixed Size

Next you need to set the form-level properties. Select View ¦ Form Properties from the main menu. Refer to Table 5.5 for the proper settings.

Table 5.5. Setting the form properties of the job request form.

Tab	Property	Setting
General	Form Display Name	Job Request Form
	Version	1
	Number	1
	Item Type	IPM.JobRequest

You will note that the first time you bring up a new form, the Item Type property is set to a long string of letters and numbers. This is a *GUID* (*guaranteed unique ID*). Microsoft Exchange uses this ID value internally to identify the form. The value you enter here does not have to be this cryptic. It is a good idea to enter a value that will mean something to you and others in your organization. It is, however, important that you keep this name unique.

Save this project again (JOBREQ.EFP) before you go on to your last development step—adding help.

Adding Online Help to the Job Request Form

It is very easy to add online help to your electronic forms. The Microsoft Exchange Forms Designer has a built-in QuickHelp feature that lets you build tooltips and pop-up help boxes at the field, window, and form levels. You can even add notes to the design-time version of the form for tracking development issues.

Adding Designer Notes

First, let's add a few notes to the design-time form. Select Help ¦ Designer Notes... from the main menu to bring up the Designer Notes screen (see Figure 5.12).

FIGURE 5.12.

Viewing the Designer Notes screen.

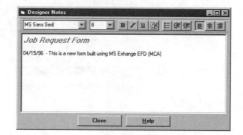

Enter a short comment about the form, the date, and the author. The information you enter here is stored with the project and will be available each time you load the project into the Microsoft Exchange Forms Designer. Notice that this is a rich-text box. You can set the font type, size, and color at any time.

Adding Form-Level Help

You can also have a help pop-up at the form level. To do this, bring up the Form Properties page (select View ¦ Form Properties ¦ General Tab) and press the Form Help... button. You'll see a dialog box like the one in Figure 5.13.

Notice that you can select No Help, QuickHelp, or enter a context ID for a standard WinHelp file. For now, enter a short comment into the QuickHelp pop-up box and press Close to save the form. You can also set the Windows Caption by moving the cursor up into the title bar of the sample help window and typing a caption.

Adding Window-Level Help

You can enter help at the window level, too. This is most useful when you have a project with multiple windows. For now, select the Window Properties dialog box (View ¦ Window Properties ¦ General) and press the Window Help... button. Your screen will look like the one in Figure 5.14.

FIGURE 5.13.
Adding form-level help.

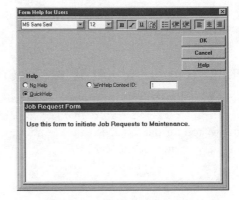

FIGURE 5.14.
Viewing the window-level help dialog box.

Notice that you have an additional control on this dialog box. If you have multiple windows in your project, you can use the drop-down list control to select each window and enter unique help information.

Adding Field-Level Help

Finally, you can also enter help information at the field level. Double-click a field object or select View ¦ Field Properties ¦ General Tab to bring up the Field Properties dialog box. Then press the Field Help... button to view the help dialog box (see Figure 5.15).

Notice that there are now two controls at the top of the help dialog box. The drop-down list can be used to select the field for which you want to create a help topic. The Status Bar control lets you enter a short help line that will appear at the bottom of the form as you select each field. Of course, the QuickHelp box contains the help information that will appear in a pop-up box if you press F1 at run-time while a field is in focus.

Enter QuickHelp information for several fields and then save the project. Save your project as JOBREQ.EFP before continuing with the last step—installing and testing your new form.

FIGURE 5.15.
Viewing the Field Help for Users dialog box.

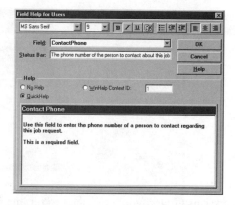

Installing the Job Request Form

After you have completed the development phase of your Microsoft Exchange form, you need to run the Install routine from the Microsoft Exchange Forms Designer. This routine

■ Saves the project

■ Generates Visual Basic 4.0 code from the project

■ Loads Visual Basic 4.0 (16-bit version) and compiles the form

■ Prompts you for a Microsoft Exchange forms library in which to install the new form

■ Prompts you for a final set of Form Properties to help Microsoft Exchange categorize your form

■ Registers the form with Microsoft Exchange and closes Microsoft Exchange

■ Returns you to the Microsoft Exchange Forms Designer

This entire process may take awhile, depending on the size of your project and your hardware configuration. If you do not have the project loaded now, open the Microsoft Exchange Forms Designer and load the JOBREQ.EFP project.

Select File ¦ Install... from the main menu. You'll see a small dialog box telling you that the Microsoft Exchange Forms Designer is generating Visual Basic code. Then you'll see Visual Basic 4.0 load and compile the project.

After Visual Basic finishes, you'll see a dialog box that asks you where you want to install the form (see Figure 5.16).

Select Personal Forms Library for now. This will install the form on your workstation. Once you have tested it thoroughly, you can re-install the form on a network location to allow others to use the form.

FIGURE 5.16.
Selecting a forms library for installation.

After selecting a forms library, you'll be asked to fill in a few more questions about the form (see Figure 5.17). The information in these fields is used by Microsoft Exchange to categorize your form. Forms are sorted and grouped to make them easier to locate and use.

FIGURE 5.17.
Supplying the form properties for Microsoft Exchange.

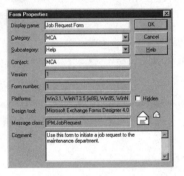

For now, enter your initials for the first category and Help for the second category. Enter your initials again as the contact person. Notice that several of the fields you set in design mode appear here, too.

Your new Microsoft Exchange form is now installed. Exit the Microsoft Exchange Forms Designer and switch to your Windows Messaging client so that you can start testing your new form.

Testing the Job Request Form

Once you have installed the form, you can switch to Microsoft Exchange and run it. In the previous step, you installed the form in your personal forms library. In order to start an instance of the form, you need to launch your Windows Messaging client and select Compose ¦ New Forms... from the main menu. You'll see a dialog box that lists all the forms you have in your personal library (see Figure 5.18).

FIGURE 5.18.

Viewing your personal forms library.

Select the job request form from the list to launch an instance of the form. You'll see the form appear with several fields already filled in with suggested entries (see Figure 5.19).

FIGURE 5.19.

Viewing the job request form at run-time.

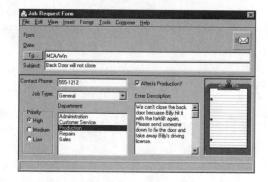

Complete the form and send it to yourself. Then check your inbox for the arrival of the message.

TIP

If your server is slow in returning your form to you, select Tools ¦ Deliver Now Using... ¦ Microsoft Exchange or Tools ¦ Deliver Now Using... ¦ Microsoft Mail if you are running a standalone version of Microsoft Exchange for Windows 95.

When you open the message, you'll see that it appears in the same electronic form that it was sent in. If you select Compose ¦ Reply from the main menu of the form, you'll see your form automatically convert the data on the application into a text message (see Figure 5.20).

FIGURE 5.20.

The reply gets converted into a text message.

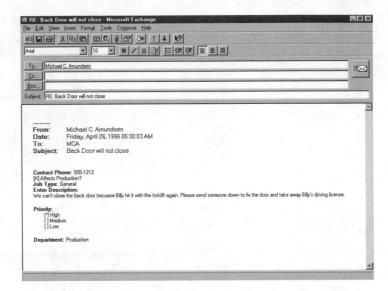

You can now fill out a response to the request and return it to the person who sent you the note (in this case, yourself!).

More Forms Designing Techniques

You can use the Microsoft Exchange Forms Designer to create a response form that reads information from the job request form and includes that data automatically on the response form. You can also create Post forms that are not addressed to users, but to folders. These Post forms help you control discussion groups and other public data sharing in your organization.

The Microsoft Exchange Forms Designer ships with several example projects that illustrate using multiwindow forms and using several forms together to create a set of send/respond forms. Check out the Templates folder and the Samples folder for more examples of Microsoft Exchange forms development.

In the next section, you'll learn how to create folder views and then how to install an electronic form in a folder.

Designing Microsoft Exchange Folders

Another very easy and powerful way to create custom MAPI interfaces is to use the Windows Messaging client's capabilities to create and control folder views. Folder views are an excellent way to set up customized views of the message base. You can create folder views that show and group messages according to their subject. You can also create views that show only selected items in the folder based on subject, sender, or several other criteria.

In effect, you can use folder views to narrow the scope of your incoming messages. This is especially handy in large organizations where you get a lot of information and must focus on the most important messages first.

In this section, you'll learn how to create a new discussion folder and establish its view properties. You'll then write several messages to test the folder view. Finally, you'll install a form in the folder. This way every time someone wants to post a message to the folder, he or she can use the custom form.

> **NOTE**
>
> You need to have access to the Windows Messaging client that ships with the Microsoft Exchange Server. That version has the capability to create folder views. You do not, however, have to be connected to the Microsoft Exchange Server to create folders and views. This example uses personal folders and views.

Creating and Managing Folder Views

Creating folder views is the easiest way to build custom discussion applications using Microsoft Exchange. You can create a specialized view, test it on your personal system, and then publish it for others to use. You can even use the Microsoft Exchange Forms Designer to create custom posting forms for use in the discussion forum. These forms can be installed in the folder itself and will be available to anyone who enters the forum.

There are just a few steps to creating a custom folder and view:

- Select a message store and add a new folder.
- Create a folder view by setting the Sort, Group, and Filter options.
- Test the view by sending/posting messages to the folder.
- Install a new or existing form in the folder.
- Test the form by using it to send messages.
- Share the folder and place the form in the folder library.

Creating a New Folder

The first step is to create a new folder. If you haven't done so yet, start the Windows Messaging client and select your personal message store. Point to the top level of the message store and add a new folder called "MAPI Discussion Group" (see Figure 5.21).

Once the folder is created, it is a good idea to set its Description property. This description will help everyone know what kind of information is supposed to be in the folder. It is also a good idea to add the name of the person who created the folder and the date it was first created. To set the `Description` property of a new folder, select the folder, and then select `File | Properties` from the main menu. Enter a general description of the folder along with a creation date and the author's initials (see Figure 5.22).

FIGURE 5.21.
*Adding the MAPI
Discussion Group Folder.*

FIGURE 5.22.
Setting the folder's
`Description` *property.*

Once you fill in the description, press the `Apply` button or the `OK` button to update the folder properties.

Setting the Folder View

The folder view controls just which messages are seen by the user, along with the order in which they are seen and what message columns appear in the summary listing. There are four main steps to setting a folder view:

- Select the columns to be displayed in the listing window.
- Select the grouping rules.
- Select the sorting rules.
- Set the filtering rules.

Once you have set all the view properties, you can test the folder view by posting messages to the folder.

First, highlight the MAPI Discussion Group folder again and select `File | Properties` to bring up the Folder Properties page. This time select the `View` tab. Be sure the `Folder Views` radio button is selected and then press the `New` button to create a new view.

The first step is to name the folder view. Enter "Group By Conversation Topic."

It is a good habit to name views based on grouping and sorting criteria. That way, as you build up a library of folder views, it is easy to remember how the view affects the message displays.

The next step is to select the columns to be displayed in the list window. Press the Columns button to bring up the Columns dialog box (see Figure 5.23).

FIGURE 5.23.
Selecting the columns for the list window.

Locate and select the Conversation Topic column from the list box on the left. Add this column to the very top of the list box on the right. Now delete the From column from the list box on the right. You can save this selection by pressing OK.

You may have noticed that there is a small input box at the lower right-hand side of the dialog box. This input box allows you to set the display width of each column in the list. The Conversation Topic column defaults to one character. You do not need to change this. When messages are grouped together, their topic will appear as a header within the listing. Adding the conversation topic to the listing would only clutter the display.

Next you need to set the grouping value. Press the Group By button to bring up the Group By dialog box (see Figure 5.24).

In the topmost combo box, select Conversation Topic and select the Ascending radio button. Notice that you can set the sort order by activating the combo box at the bottom of the Group By dialog box. It should be set to Received, Ascending. If it is not, set it now, and then press OK to update the grouping and sorting properties.

Now select the Filter button from the Views dialog box. This calls up the first of two filter dialogs boxes (see Figure 5.25).

FIGURE 5.24.
Setting the grouping criteria.

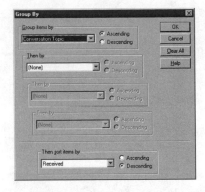

FIGURE 5.25.
The first Filter dialog box.

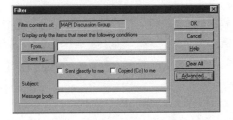

Through this dialog box, you can set criteria for limiting the display of messages:

- *From*—Use this to limit the view to only those messages that are from a specified user or distribution list (defined in the MAPI Address Book). Notice that you can list more than one address on this line.

- *Sent To*—Use this to limit the view to only those messages that you sent to a specified user or distribution list. You can include more than one address on this line.

- *Sent directly to me*—Check this box if you want to see only messages addressed directly to you.

- *Copied (Cc) to me*—Check this box if you want to see only messages that have you on the Cc: line.

- *Subject*—When you enter text here, the Windows Messaging client displays only messages that have that text in the Subject line. You cannot use wildcards.

- *Message body*—When you enter text here, the Windows Messaging client displays only messages that have that text somewhere in the message body.

You can also set additional filter criteria by pressing the Advanced button on the Filter dialog box (see Figure 5.26).

A second form appears through which you can set filters based on file size, date ranges, read/unread flags, and level of importance. You can also set filters based on forms ("show me only Job Request Forms") or document statistics ("show me only Word documents").

FIGURE 5.26.

*Viewing the Advanced
Filter dialog box.*

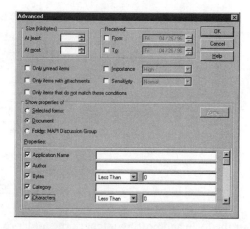

For now, select Cancel from the Advanced Filter dialog box and select Clear All at the main Filter dialog box to turn off all filtering.

> **WARNING**
>
> It is important to remember that setting message filters affects only the *display* of message folders, not their *content.* If you have a folder that filters all but a few messages, you should keep in mind that there may actually be hundreds of messages in the folder, it's just that you can see only a few. Message filtering will not remove messages from a folder; it just hides them.

Under the Views tab of the Folder Properties dialog box, press Apply to update the properties and then select OK to exit the dialog box. You have created a custom view for your folder. Now it's time to test the view.

Testing the Folder View

To test the new folder view you just created, you need to add a few messages. For now, you can add these messages and replies yourself. Once you are sure the view is working properly, you can place this view in a new or existing public folder and share it with other users.

Since this view was built as a discussion forum, you'll use a Post form instead of the standard Send form. To create a new post in the MAPI Discussion Group, highlight the folder and select Compose ¦ New Post in this Folder... from the main menu. This will bring up the default posting form (see Figure 5.27).

FIGURE 5.27.

Using the default posting form.

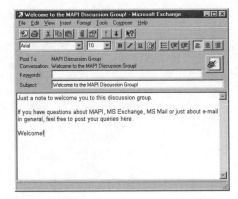

After filling out the form and posting it, check the folder to see how the view works. You'll see that a conversation topic has been started and that your first message appears underneath the topic. You can click on the topic to expand the message listing and then select the message to read it. When you create a reply to the message, it is added to the folder, under the same topic. Figure 5.28 shows you how an extended set of messages appears in a discussion folder.

FIGURE 5.28.

Viewing multiple messages in a discussion folder.

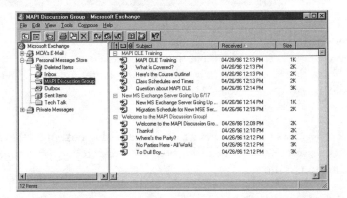

> **NOTE**
>
> Although the folder we created is a discussion folder, you are not restricted to using Post messages while you are in the folder. If you wish, you can use Send forms to reply directly to a user's inbox. This is a way to start private conversations with people you first meet in a public discussion group.

Although there's a lot more to creating and managing folders and views, you should now have a pretty good idea of the possibilities. If you are interested in learning more about Microsoft Exchange folders and views, check out the documentation that ships with the Microsoft Exchange Server.

Installing Forms in Folders

The final step in this chapter is to install a custom form in a folder. You can install forms in personal forms libraries or folder forms libraries. The advantage of installing forms in the personal forms library is that it is available to the users no matter what other folder they are looking in. All they need to do is select Compose ¦ New Forms... to locate the form installed on the local workstation.

The advantage of installing forms in a folder form library is that each time the user enters the folder, that custom form appears on the Compose menu. This makes it easier to find and more likely that it will be used.

For this example, you'll install the job request form in the MAPI Discussion Group folder.

> **NOTE**
>
> It actually doesn't matter what folder you use for this exercise.

First, start up the Windows Messaging client and select the target folder (the MAPI Discussion Group folder). Then select File ¦ Properties and select the Forms tab. This brings up the Forms page. Press the Manage button to display the Forms Manager dialog box, and press the Set button above the list box on the left to bring up the Set Library To dialog box (see Figure 5.29).

FIGURE 5.29.
Setting the forms library.

You've seen this dialog box before. It's the same one you used when you used the Microsoft Exchange Forms Designer to install the job request form. Select the Personal Forms Library radio button; then press OK to return to the Forms Manager.

You'll now see one or more topics and forms in the list box on the left side of the form (see Figure 5.30).

FIGURE 5.30.
Selecting a form to install.

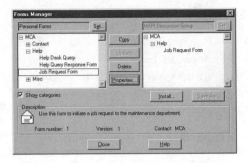

Locate and select the job request form in the list box on the left. Then press Copy to copy the form to the list box on the right. You have just associated the job request form with the MAPI Discussion Group folder. Now it's time to install the form in the folder's library.

When you press Install..., Microsoft Exchange asks you for the location of the configuration file (.CFG) for the form. This is stored in the subfolder in which you created the job request form. Locate the folder where you saved the JOBREQ.EFP file. You'll see a subfolder called JOBREQ.VB. This is the folder that has the Visual Basic source code and the JOBREQ.CFG file (see Figure 5.31).

FIGURE 5.31.
Locating and selecting the
JOBREQ.CFG *file.*

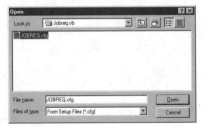

After locating and selecting the JOBREQ.CFG file, click OK to load the configuration file. Microsoft Exchange will then show you the Form Properties dialog box from the Microsoft Exchange Forms Designer. Select a category and a subcategory, and enter your initials as the contact name for the form (see Figure 5.32).

FIGURE 5.32.
Filling out the Form
Properties dialog box.

Now you can press Close on the Forms Manager dialog box and press OK on the Form Properties tab page. You have just installed your form into the MAPI Discussion Group folder.

Select Compose from the main menu, and you'll see an item at the bottom of the menu list called "New Job Request Form" (see Figure 5.33).

FIGURE 5.33.

Selecting the new job request form from the menu.

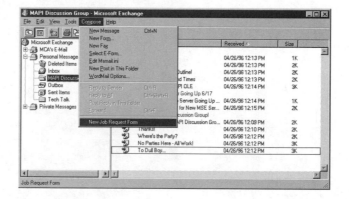

You can start from here and run the job request form just like any other form. If you move to another folder, however, you will not see the form on the menu. It appears on a folder's menu only if it has been installed in that folder's form library.

Summary

In this chapter, you learned how to use the Microsoft Exchange Forms Designer kit that ships with Microsoft Exchange Server. You learned how to design, code, test, and install custom message forms for use at individual workstations or over a large network.

The Microsoft Exchange Forms Designer discussion in this chapter covered

- Using the Microsoft Exchange Forms Designer
- Creating custom forms
- Testing and compiling custom forms
- Installing custom forms

You also learned how to set up Microsoft Exchange folders for use with custom forms, including

- Creating new folders
- Setting folder views including sorting, filtering, and grouping messages
- Installing custom forms in folders

In the next chapter, you'll learn how to use the Messaging API to create MAPI-aware windows applications that can read and write MAPI messages from outside Windows Messaging clients.

6

Creating MAPI-Aware Applications

The most basic MAPI service is the ability to provide a send feature to a program. Almost all Windows programs have a print feature to send output to a print device. The send feature works basically the same way. It provides the user a way to send output to some other e-mail address. Adding this most basic form of MAPI service to your Windows applications makes it "MAPI-aware." MAPI-aware applications do not have e-mail services as a basic part of their functionality (that is, an e-mail client) but provide it as an added feature. For example, most office suite applications (word processing, spreadsheet, and so on) provide a send feature on the main menu of all their programs. Basically, whatever documents you can create with the program can be sent to other locations using the mail services available on the network.

In this chapter, you'll learn how to make your programs MAPI-aware using the Simple MAPI API call set. This API set provides very easy, very quick access to the most needed MAPI services. Another advantage of using the API set is that it is available to any program that supports DLL calls. This means it is quite easy to add MAPI services to most any Windows application.

In the first half of this chapter, you'll get a quick overview of the API calls themselves. You'll learn about the eleven API calls and three user-defined types that comprise the Simple MAPI interface, and you'll build a set of examples that illustrate the use of Simple MAPI services.

In the second half of the chapter, you'll create some real-world examples of Windows applications that have MAPI-aware features. You'll create a quick spreadsheet routine that can send its results using MAPI. You'll also modify an existing Visual Basic 4.0 program to add MAPI capabilities.

When you complete this chapter, you'll have a good understanding of the Microsoft MAPI API calls. You will also be able to design and build applications that can use the MAPI interface to provide mail services from within your Visual Basic programs.

The Simple MAPI API Calls

The Simple MAPI (SMAPI) calls allow you to add MAPI services to virtually any Windows program. While these calls offer only the smallest set of MAPI services, they are still quite useful. In the next few sections, you'll learn about the three user-defined structures needed to provide MAPI via the API calls, and you'll experiment with each of the API calls themselves.

> **NOTE**
>
> All the SMAPI services for Visual Basic and VBA applications are provided through the dynamic link library (DLL) called VBAMAP32.DLL (or VBAMAPI.DLL for 16-bit platforms). If you do not already have this DLL on your system, you can find it on the CD-ROM that ships with this book.

Before you begin this part of the chapter, start Visual Basic 4.0 and begin a new project. Locate the VBAMAP32.BAS module in the Chap06 folder and add that module to your project. This has all the API calls and structures defined along with several constants and a helper error function.

The User-Defined Types

Simple MAPI defines three structures for passing information

- *MAPIMessage*—Contains all the information about a message packet, including originator, subject, text, recipients, and attachments.
- *MAPIRecip*—Contains all the information about a message recipient, including name, address type, full address, and unique entry ID.
- *MAPIFile*—Contains all the information about an attached file, including display name, operating system name, and position in the message packet.

MAPIMessage

The MAPIMessage structure is used to hold all the vital information about a message packet. You will use this structure to pass message data from your programs to the DLL and back. Table 6.1 shows the structure of the MAPIMessage along with short descriptions for each element.

Table 6.1. The MAPIMessage structure.

Field	Type	Description
Reserved	Long	Reserved for future use. This field must be 0.
Subject	String	The subject text, limited to 256 characters or fewer. (Messages saved using MAPISaveMail are not limited to 256 characters.) An empty string indicates no subject text.

continues

Table 6.1. continued

Field	Type	Description
NoteText	String	A string containing text in the message. An empty string indicates no text. For inbound messages, each paragraph is terminated with a carriage return-line feed pair (0x0d0a). For outbound messages, paragraphs can be delimited with a carriage return, a line feed, or a carriage return-line feed pair (0x0d, 0x0a, or 0x0d0a, respectively).
MessageType	String	A message type string used by applications other than interpersonal electronic mail. An empty string indicates an interpersonal message (IPM) type.
DateReceived	String	A string indicating the date a message is received. The format is YYYY/MM/DD HH:MM; hours are measured on a 24-hour clock.
ConversationID	String	A string indicating the conversation thread ID to which this message belongs.
Flags	Long	A bitmask of flags. Unused flags are reserved. Unused flags must be 0 for outbound messages and are ignored for inbound messages. The following flags are defined: MAPI_RECEIPT_REQUESTED MAPI_SENT MAPI_UNREAD
RecipCount	Long	A count of the recipient descriptor types pointed to by Recips. A value of 0 indicates that no recipients are included.
FileCount	Long	A count of the file attachment descriptor types pointed to by Files. A value of 0 indicates that no file attachments are included.

Listing 6.1 shows how the MAPIMessage structure is built using Visual Basic 4.0.

NOTE

The user-defined types and API calls are all contained in the VBAMAP32.BAS and VBAMAPI16.BAS modules on the CD-ROM. You do not have to type these structures and API calls into your projects.

Listing 6.1. The `MAPIMessage` user-defined type.

```
'*****************************************************
'   MAPI Message holds information about a message
'*****************************************************

Type MapiMessage
    Reserved As Long
    Subject As String
    NoteText As String
    MessageType As String
    DateReceived As String
    ConversationID As String
    Flags As Long
    RecipCount As Long
    FileCount As Long
End Type
```

MAPIRecip

The `MAPIRecip` structure holds all the important data related to a message recipient. Table 6.2 describes the structure, and Listing 6.2 shows how it looks in VBA code.

Table 6.2. The `MAPIRecip` structure.

Field	Type	Description
Reserved	Long	Reserved for future use. This field must be 0.
RecipClass	Long	Classifies the recipient of the message. (Different classes can be used to sort messages by the recipient class.) It can also contain information about the originator of an inbound message.
Name	String	The name of the recipient that is displayed by Mail.
Address	String	Provider-specific message delivery data. This can be used by the message system to identify recipients who are not in an address list (one-off addresses).
EIDSize	Long	The size (in bytes) of the opaque binary data in `EntryID`.
EntryID	String	A binary string used by Mail to efficiently specify the recipient. Unlike the Address field, this data is opaque and is not printable. Mail returns valid `EntryID`s for recipients or originators included in the address list.

Listing 6.2. The MAPIRecip user-defined type.

```
'***************************************************
'   MAPIRecip holds information about a message
'   originator or recipient
'***************************************************

Type MapiRecip
    Reserved As Long
    RecipClass As Long
    Name As String
    Address As String
    EIDSize As Long
    EntryID As String
End Type
```

MAPIFile

The last structure used by SMAPI is the MAPIFile structure. This user-defined type holds all the information about a message attachment. Table 6.3 describes the structure, and Listing 6.3 shows the UDT definition.

Table 6.3. The MAPIFile structure.

Field	Type	Description
Reserved	Long	Reserved for future use. This field must be 0.
Flags	Long	A bitmask of flags. Unused flags are reserved and must be 0. The following flags are defined: MAPI_OLE MAPI_OLE_STATIC MAPI_OLE is set if the attachment is an OLE object. If MAPI_OLE_STATIC is also set, the attachment is a static OLE object rather than an embedded OLE object.
Position	Long	An integer describing where the attachment should be placed in the message body. Attachments replace the character found at a certain position in the message body; in other words, attachments replace the MapiMessage type field NoteText[Position]. Applications may not place two attachments in the same location within a message, and attachments may not be placed beyond the end of the message body.

Field	Type	Description
PathName	String	The full pathname of the attached file. The file should be closed before this call is made.
FileName	String	The filename seen by the recipient. This name may differ from the filename in PathName if temporary files are being used. If FileName is empty, the filename from PathName is used. If the attachment is an OLE object, FileName contains the class name of the object; for example, "Microsoft Excel Worksheet."
FileType	Long	A reserved descriptor that is used to indicate to the recipient the type of the attached file. An empty string indicates an unknown or operating system-determined file type. Use 0 for this parameter at all times.

Listing 6.3. The MAPIFile user-defined type.

```
'*******************************************************
'   MapiFile holds information about file attachments
'*******************************************************

Type MapiFile
    Reserved As Long
    Flags As Long
    Position As Long
    PathName As String
    FileName As String
    FileType As Long
End Type
```

These are the only three structures needed to establish MAPI services with the VBAMAPI DLLs. The next section describes each of the API calls and constants and shows you examples of how to use them.

The API Functions

There are eleven SMAPI API calls. This set of calls provides access to the core MAPI services including

■ Logging on and logging off MAPI sessions
■ Gaining access to the MAPI address book
■ Reading, sending, saving, and deleting MAPI Messages

■ Performing address validations and lookups

■ Handling binary message attachments

The next several sections describe each of the API calls and provide Visual Basic 4.0 examples of how to use them.

If you haven't already done so, start Visual Basic 4.0 and load the VBAMAP32.BAS module into your project. Listing 6.4 shows the complete set of API calls for SMAPI. You do not have to type this information into your project. You can find this module in the Chap06 directory that was created when you installed the source code from the CD-ROM.

Listing 6.4. The Simple MAPI API call declarations.

```
'****************************
'   FUNCTION Declarations
'****************************

Declare Function MAPILogon Lib "VBAMAP32.DLL" Alias "BMAPILogon" (ByVal UIParam&,
➡ByVal User$, ByVal Password$, ByVal Flags&, ByVal Reserved&, Session&) As Long

Declare Function MAPILogoff Lib "VBAMAP32.DLL" Alias "BMAPILogoff" (ByVal Session&,
➡ByVal UIParam&, ByVal Flags&, ByVal Reserved&) As Long

Declare Function MAPIDetails Lib "VBAMAP32.DLL" Alias "BMAPIDetails" (ByVal
➡Session&, ByVal UIParam&, Recipient As MapiRecip, ByVal Flags&, ByVal Reserved&)
➡As Long

Declare Function MAPIResolveName Lib "VBAMAP32.DLL" Alias "BMAPIResolveName" (ByVal
➡Session&, ByVal UIParam&, ByVal UserName$, ByVal Flags&, ByVal Reserved&,
➡Recipient As MapiRecip) As Long

Declare Function MAPISendDocuments Lib "VBAMAP32.DLL" Alias "BMAPISendDocuments"
➡(ByVal UIParam&, ByVal DelimStr$, ByVal FilePaths$, ByVal FileNames$, ByVal
➡Reserved&) As Long

Declare Function MAPIFindNext Lib "VBAMAP32.DLL" Alias "BMAPIFindNext" (ByVal
➡Session&, ByVal UIParam&, ByVal MsgType$, ByVal SeedMsgID$, ByVal Flag&, ByVal
➡Reserved&, MsgID$) As Long

Declare Function MAPIDeleteMail Lib "VBAMAP32.DLL" Alias "BMAPIDeleteMail" (ByVal
➡Session&, ByVal UIParam&, ByVal MsgID$, ByVal Flags&, ByVal Reserved&) As Long

Declare Function MAPIAddress Lib "VBAMAP32.DLL" Alias "BMAPIAddress" (ByVal
➡Session&, ByVal UIParam&, ByVal Caption$, ByVal EditFields&, ByVal Label$,
➡RecipCount&, Recipients() As MapiRecip, ByVal Flags&, ByVal Reserved&) As Long

Declare Function MAPISaveMail Lib "VBAMAP32.DLL" Alias "BMAPISaveMail" (ByVal
➡Session&, ByVal UIParam&, Message As MapiMessage, Recipient As MapiRecip, File As
➡MapiFile, ByVal Reserved&, MsgID$) As Long

Declare Function MAPISendMail Lib "VBAMAP32.DLL" Alias "BMAPISendMail" (ByVal
➡Session&, ByVal UIParam&, Message As MapiMessage, Recipient As MapiRecip, File As
➡MapiFile, ByVal Flags&, ByVal Reserved&) As Long
```

```
Declare Function MAPIReadMail Lib "VBAMAP32.DLL" Alias "BMAPIReadMail" (ByVal
➡Session&, ByVal UIParam&, ByVal MsgID$, ByVal Flags&, ByVal Reserved&, Message As
➡MapiMessage, Originator As MapiRecip, recips() As MapiRecip, files() As MapiFile)
➡As Long
```

There are also a number of CONSTANT declarations needed to make the API calls easier to work with. Listing 6.5 shows the error constants and flag declarations used for SMAPI.

Listing 6.5. The SMAPI constants.

```
'**************************
'   CONSTANT Declarations
'**************************
'

Global Const SUCCESS_SUCCESS = 0
Global Const MAPI_USER_ABORT = 1
Global Const MAPI_E_FAILURE = 2
Global Const MAPI_E_LOGIN_FAILURE = 3
Global Const MAPI_E_DISK_FULL = 4
Global Const MAPI_E_INSUFFICIENT_MEMORY = 5
Global Const MAPI_E_BLK_TOO_SMALL = 6
Global Const MAPI_E_TOO_MANY_SESSIONS = 8
Global Const MAPI_E_TOO_MANY_FILES = 9
Global Const MAPI_E_TOO_MANY_RECIPIENTS = 10
Global Const MAPI_E_ATTACHMENT_NOT_FOUND = 11
Global Const MAPI_E_ATTACHMENT_OPEN_FAILURE = 12
Global Const MAPI_E_ATTACHMENT_WRITE_FAILURE = 13
Global Const MAPI_E_UNKNOWN_RECIPIENT = 14
Global Const MAPI_E_BAD_RECIPTYPE = 15
Global Const MAPI_E_NO_MESSAGES = 16
Global Const MAPI_E_INVALID_MESSAGE = 17
Global Const MAPI_E_TEXT_TOO_LARGE = 18
Global Const MAPI_E_INVALID_SESSION = 19
Global Const MAPI_E_TYPE_NOT_SUPPORTED = 20
Global Const MAPI_E_AMBIGUOUS_RECIPIENT = 21
Global Const MAPI_E_MESSAGE_IN_USE = 22
Global Const MAPI_E_NETWORK_FAILURE = 23
Global Const MAPI_E_INVALID_EDITFIELDS = 24
Global Const MAPI_E_INVALID_RECIPS = 25
Global Const MAPI_E_NOT_SUPPORTED = 26

Global Const MAPI_E_NO_LIBRARY = 999
Global Const MAPI_E_INVALID_PARAMETER = 998

Global Const MAPI_ORIG = 0
Global Const MAPI_TO = 1
Global Const MAPI_CC = 2
Global Const MAPI_BCC = 3

Global Const MAPI_UNREAD = 1
Global Const MAPI_RECEIPT_REQUESTED = 2
Global Const MAPI_SENT = 4
```

continues

Listing 6.5. continued

```
'***********************
'   FLAG Declarations
'***********************

Global Const MAPI_LOGON_UI = &H1
Global Const MAPI_NEW_SESSION = &H2
Global Const MAPI_DIALOG = &H8
Global Const MAPI_UNREAD_ONLY = &H20
Global Const MAPI_ENVELOPE_ONLY = &H40
Global Const MAPI_PEEK = &H80
Global Const MAPI_GUARANTEE_FIFO = &H100
Global Const MAPI_BODY_AS_FILE = &H200
Global Const MAPI_AB_NOMODIFY = &H400
Global Const MAPI_SUPPRESS_ATTACH = &H800
Global Const MAPI_FORCE_DOWNLOAD = &H1000

Global Const MAPI_OLE = &H1
Global Const MAPI_OLE_STATIC = &H2
```

These are all the basic tools needed to begin to write MAPI applications. The next section reviews each API call in greater depth, including at least one coding example for each call.

> **WARNING**
>
> In order for the 32-bit API calls to work, you must have the VBAMAP32.DLL in your WINDOWS\SYSTEM folder. If you are using Visual Basic 4.0 on a 16-bit platform, you can load the VBAMAPI.BAS module and make sure that the VBAMAPI.DLL is in your WINDOWS\SYSTEM folder.

MAPIErr—An Added Helper Function

All SMAPI calls return a status code (either SUCCESS or some error). You should always check this value before continuing on with your program. In order to make it easier to work with the SMAPI calls, you can add a helper function that returns meaningful error messages for the established MAPI errors. Add a BAS module to your Visual Basic project called MAPIERR.BAS and enter the code in Listing 6.6.

Listing 6.6. Adding the MAPIErr function.

```
Public Function MapiErr(lError) As String
    '
    ' return displayable string for error
    '
    Dim cRtn As String
    '
    Select Case lError
        Case MAPI_USER_ABORT  ' 1
```

```
            cRtn = "MAPI User Cancel"
        Case MAPI_E_FAILURE  ' 2
            cRtn = "MAPI Failure"
        Case MAPI_E_LOGIN_FAILURE ' 3
            cRtn = "MAPI Login failure"
        Case MAPI_E_DISK_FULL ' 4
            cRtn = "MAPI Disk full"
        Case MAPI_E_INSUFFICIENT_MEMORY ' 5
            cRtn = "MAPI Insufficient memory"
        Case MAPI_E_BLK_TOO_SMALL ' 6
            cRtn = "MAPI Block too small"
        Case MAPI_E_TOO_MANY_SESSIONS ' 8
            cRtn = "MAPI Too many sessions"
        Case MAPI_E_TOO_MANY_FILES ' 9
            cRtn = "MAPI too many files"
        Case MAPI_E_TOO_MANY_RECIPIENTS ' 10
            cRtn = "MAPI Too many attachments"
        Case MAPI_E_ATTACHMENT_NOT_FOUND ' 11
            cRtn = "MAPI Attachment not found"
        Case MAPI_E_ATTACHMENT_OPEN_FAILURE ' 12
            cRtn = "MAPI Attachment open failure"
        Case MAPI_E_ATTACHMENT_WRITE_FAILURE ' 13
            cRtn = "MAPI Attachment Write Failure"
        Case MAPI_E_UNKNOWN_RECIPIENT ' 14
            cRtn = "MAPI Unknown recipient"
        Case MAPI_E_BAD_RECIPTYPE ' 15
            cRtn = "MAPI Bad recipient type"
        Case MAPI_E_NO_MESSAGES ' 16
            cRtn = "MAPI No messages"
        Case MAPI_E_INVALID_MESSAGE ' 17
            cRtn = "MAPI Invalid message"
        Case MAPI_E_TEXT_TOO_LARGE ' 18
            cRtn = "MAPI Text too large"
        Case MAPI_E_INVALID_SESSION ' 19
            cRtn = "MAPI Invalid session"
        Case MAPI_E_TYPE_NOT_SUPPORTED ' 20
            cRtn = "MAPI Type not supported"
        Case MAPI_E_AMBIGUOUS_RECIPIENT ' 21
            cRtn = "MAPI Ambiguous recipient"
        Case MAPI_E_MESSAGE_IN_USE ' 22
            cRtn = "MAPI Message in use"
        Case MAPI_E_NETWORK_FAILURE ' 23
            cRtn = "MAPI Network failure"
        Case MAPI_E_INVALID_EDITFIELDS ' 24
            cRtn = "MAPI Invalid edit fields"
        Case MAPI_E_INVALID_RECIPS ' 25
            cRtn = "MAPI Invalid Recipients"
        Case MAPI_E_NOT_SUPPORTED ' 26
            cRtn = "MAPI Not supported"
        Case MAPI_E_NO_LIBRARY ' 999
            cRtn = "MAPI No Library"
        Case MAPI_E_INVALID_PARAMETER ' 998
            cRtn = "MAPI Invalid parameter"
    End Select
    '
    MapiErr = cRtn & " [" & CStr(lError) & "]"
    '
End Function
```

Now you're ready to start coding your SMAPI examples.

MAPILogon and MAPILogOff

The MAPILogon and MAPILogOff functions are used to start and stop MAPI sessions.

> **NOTE**
>
> It is always a good idea to log off a session when you no longer need MAPI services. Leaving an unused session open can slow your program and, if it's left open after you exit, can lead to unexpected problems.

Table 6.4 shows the MAPILogon parameters along with their type and description.

Table 6.4. The MAPILogon parameters.

Parameter	Type	Description
UIParam	Long	The parent window handle for the dialog box. A value of 0 specifies that any dialog box displayed is application modal.
User	String	A user account name. An empty string indicates that a sign-in dialog box with an empty name field should be generated (if the appropriate flag is set).
Password	String	The user's MAPI password. An empty string indicates that a sign-in dialog box with an empty password field should be generated (if the appropriate flag is set) or that MAPI does not expect a password.
Flags	Long	A bitmask of flags. The following flags are defined: MAPI_LOGON_UI=&H1 MAPI_NEW_SESSION=&H2 MAPI_FORCE-DOWNLOAD=&H1000
Reserved	Long	Reserved for future use. This parameter must be 0.
Session	Long	A unique session handle whose value is set by MAPI when the MAPILogon call is successful. The session handle can then be used in subsequent MAPI calls.

Table 6.5 shows the MAPILogOff parameters along with their type and description.

Table 6.5. The MAPILogOff parameters.

Parameter	Type	Description
Session	Long	A unique MAPI-assigned session handle whose value represents an already existing MAPI session.
UIParam	Long	The parent window handle for the dialog box. A value of 0 specifies that any dialog box displayed is application modal.
Flags	Long	Reserved for future use. This parameter must be 0.
Reserved	Long	Reserved for future use. This parameter must be 0.

Add a new command button to your Visual Basic form. Set its Caption property to LogOn. Use Edit¦Copy, Edit¦Paste to add a second command button as part of a control array. Set the second command button's caption to LogOff. Then add the code in Listing 6.7 to the Command1_Click event.

Listing 6.7. Adding code to the Command1_Click event.

```
Private Sub Command1_Click(Index As Integer)
    '
    ' handle button press
    '
    Select Case Index
        Case 0 ' log on session
            SMAPIStart
        Case 1 ' log off session
            SMAPIEnd
    End Select
    '
End Sub
```

Next add the following form-level declarations to the general declaration area of your form. You'll use these throughout the project.

```
Option Explicit
'
Dim lReturn As Long ' return flag
Dim lSession As Long ' session handle
Dim udtMessage As MapiMessage ' message object
Dim udtRecip As MapiRecip ' recipient object
Dim udtRecips() As MapiRecip ' recipient collection
Dim udtFile As MapiFile ' attachment object
Dim udtFiles() As MapiFile ' attachment collection
```

Now add a new subroutine called SMAPIStart to the project, and enter the code shown in Listing 6.8.

Listing 6.8. Adding the SMAPIStart routine.

```
Public Sub SMAPIStart()
    '
    ' start an SMAPI session
    '
    lReturn = MAPILogon(Me.hWnd, "", "", MAPI_LOGON_UI, 0, lSession)
    If lReturn <> SUCCESS_SUCCESS Then
        MAPIErr (lReturn)
    End If
    '
End Sub
```

Finally, add the SMAPIEnd routine, and enter the code shown in Listing 6.9.

Listing 6.9. Adding the SMAPIEnd routine.

```
Public Sub SMAPIEnd()
    '
    ' end an SMAPI session
    '
    lReturn = MAPILogoff(lSession, Me.hWnd, 0, 0)
    If lReturn <> SUCCESS_SUCCESS Then
        MAPIErr (lReturn)
    Else
        MsgBox "MAPI Session Closed", vbInformation, "SMAPI LogOff"
    End If
    '
End Sub
```

Now save the form as SMAPI.FRM and the project as SMAPI.VBP. When you run the project, click the LogOn button to bring up the logon dialog box (see Figure 6.1).

FIGURE 6.1.

The logon dialog box.

MAPIAddress

The MAPIAddress call produces the address book dialog box and allows users to add, edit, and delete records from the address book. There are several flags you can use to control the address book dialog box behavior. Table 6.6 shows the MAPIAddress call parameters and their type and description.

Table 6.6. The MAPIAddress parameters.

Parameter	Type	Description
Session	Long	A unique MAPI-assigned session handle whose value represents a session with the messaging subsystem. The session handle is returned by MAPILogon and invalidated by MAPILogoff. If the value is 0, MAPI initiates a session from a system default session (if one exists) or presents a sign-in dialog box.
UIParam	Long	The parent window handle for the dialog box. A value of 0 specifies that any dialog box displayed is application modal.
Caption	String	The caption of the address list dialog box. If this parameter is an empty string, the default value "Address Book" is used.
EditFields	String	The number of edit controls that should be present in the address list. The values 0 to 4 are valid. The edit values are defined as: ReadOnly(0) To(1) CC(2) BCC(3) If EditFields is 1 and more than one kind of entry exists in Recips, Label is ignored.
Label	String	A string used as an edit control label in the address list dialog box. This argument is ignored and should be an empty string except when EditFields is 1.
RecipCount	Long	The number of entries in Recipients. If RecipCount is 0, Recipients is ignored.

continues

Table 6.6. continued

Parameter	Type	Description
Recipients()	MAPIRecip	The initial array of recipient entries to be used to populate edit controls in the address list dialog box. This array is re-dimensioned as necessary to accommodate the entries made by the user in the address list dialog box.
Flags	Long	A bitmask of flags. Unspecified flags should always be passed as 0. Undocumented flags are reserved. The following flags are defined: MAPI_LOGON_UI=&H1 MAPI_NEW_SESSION=&H2
Reserved	Long	Reserved for future use. This parameter must be 0.

Now add a new button to the control array and set its caption to AddressBook. Then modify the Command1_Click event to match the code in Listing 6.10.

Listing 6.10. Modifying the Command1_Click event.

```
Private Sub Command1_Click(Index As Integer)
    '
    ' handle button press
    '
    Select Case Index
        Case 0 ' log on session
            SMAPIStart
        Case 1 ' log off session
            SMAPIEnd
        Case 2 ' addressbook
            AddressBook
    End Select
    '
End Sub
```

Next add the AddressBook subroutine and enter the code shown in Listing 6.11.

Listing 6.11. Adding the AddressBook routine.

```
Public Sub AddressBook()
    '
    ' call up the address book
    '
    On Error Resume Next
    '
    lReturn = MAPIAddress(lSession, Me.hWnd, "SMAPI Address Book", 3, "", 0,
➥udtRecips(), 0, 0)
```

```
    If lReturn <> SUCCESS_SUCCESS Then
        MsgBox MAPIErr(lReturn)
    End If
    '
    MsgBox "Selected Recipients: " & CStr(UBound(udtRecips) + 1), vbInformation,
➥"AddressBook"
    '
End Sub
```

The AddressBook routine calls up the MAPI address book, passing a new dialog title, and enabling all possible recipient class buttons (TO:, CC:, and BCC:). The AddressBook function returns a collection of recipients.

Save and run the project. After clicking the AddressBook, you should see something like the screen in Figure 6.2.

FIGURE 6.2.
Viewing the address book.

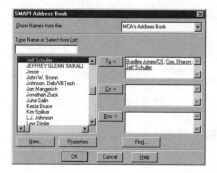

MAPIResolveName

The MAPIResolveName function is used to look up and/or validate a recipient object. You can use this to retrieve the complete e-mail address of a recipient and to present a dialog box to the user to resolve any unknown or ambiguous names. The MAPIResolveName parameters are described in Table 6.7.

Table 6.7. The MAPIResolveName parameters.

Parameter	Type	Description
Session	Long	A unique, MAPI-assigned session handle whose value represents a session with the messaging subsystem. The session handle is returned by MAPILogon and invalidated by MAPILogoff. If the value is 0, MAPI initiates a session from a system default session (if one exists) or by presenting a sign-in dialog box.

continues

Table 6.7. continued

Parameter	Type	Description
UIParam	Long	The parent window handle for the dialog box. A value of 0 specifies that any dialog box displayed is application modal.
UserName	String	A string containing the name to be resolved.
Flags	Long	A bitmask of flags. The following flags are defined: MAPI_LOGON_UI=&H1 (display logon dialog) MAPI_NEW_SESSION=&H2 (start new session) MAPI_DIALOG=&H8 (show resolve dialog) MAPI_AB_NOMODIFY=&H400 (no modify address book)
Reserved	Long	Reserved for future use. This parameter must be 0.
Recipient	MapiRecip	A recipient type set by MAPIResolveName if the resolution results in a single match. The type contains the recipient information of the resolved name. The descriptor can then be used in calls to MAPISendMail, MAPISaveMail, and MAPIAddress.

To test MAPIResolve, add a new button to the control array and set its caption to ResolveName. Then modify the Command1_Click event to match the one in Listing 6.12.

Listing 6.12. Modifying the Command1_Click event.

```
Private Sub Command1_Click(Index As Integer)
    '
    ' handle button press
    '
    Select Case Index
        Case 0 ' log on session
            SMAPIStart
        Case 1 ' log off session
            SMAPIEnd
        Case 2 ' addressbook
            AddressBook
        Case 3 ' resolve name
            ResolveName
    End Select
    '
End Sub
```

Now add the new ResolveName subroutine and enter the code in Listing 6.13.

Listing 6.13. Adding the `ResolveName` routine.

```
Public Sub ResolveName()
    '
    ' test resolvename service
    '
    lReturn = MAPIResolveName(lSession, Me.hWnd, "MCA", MAPI_DIALOG, 0, udtRecip)
    If lReturn <> SUCCESS_SUCCESS Then
        MsgBox MAPIErr(lReturn)
    End If
    '
End Sub
```

If you run this routine and supply an ambiguous name, MAPI returns a dialog box asking you to resolve the differences (see Figure 6.3).

FIGURE 6.3.

Viewing the `ResolveName` *dialog box.*

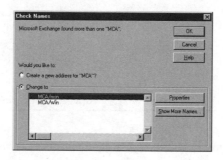

You can avoid viewing the dialog box (and just trap any error) by setting the `Flag` value to 0.

MAPIDetails

The `MAPIDetails` function returns a special dialog box that allows users to inspect and edit information about a single recipient. You can use this in your programs to give users direct access to an address entry edit form. Table 6.8 shows the `MAPIDetails` parameter list.

Table 6.8. The `MAPIDetails` parameters.

Parameter	Type	Description
Session	Long	A unique session handle whose value represents a session with the messaging subsystem. Session handles are returned by `MAPILogon` and invalidated by `MAPILogoff`. If the value is 0, MAPI sets up a session from a system default session (if one exists) or by presenting a sign-in dialog box.

continues

Table 6.8. continued

Parameter	Type	Description
UIParam	Long	The parent window handle for the dialog box. A value of 0 specifies that any dialog box displayed is application modal.
Recipient	MAPIRecip	A recipient descriptor containing the entry whose details are to be displayed. All fields of the MapiRecip type except EIDSize and EntryID are ignored. If the field EIDSize is zero, MAPI_E_AMBIG_RECIP is returned.
Flags	Long	A bitmask of flags. Unspecified flags should always be passed as 0. Undocumented flags are reserved. The following flags are defined: MAPI_LOGON_UI=&H1 (force log on) MAPI_NEW_SESSION=&H2 (force new session) MAPI_AB_NOMODIFY=&H400 (no addrbook changes)
Reserved	Long	Reserved for future use. This parameter must be 0.

Add a new button to the control array and set its caption to MAPIDetails. Then modify the Command1_Click event to match the code in Listing 6.14.

Listing 6.14. Modifying the Command1_Click event.

```
Private Sub Command1_Click(Index As Integer)
    '
    ' handle button press
    '
    Select Case Index
        Case 0 ' log on session
            SMAPIStart
        Case 1 ' log off session
            SMAPIEnd
        Case 2 ' addressbook
            AddressBook
        Case 3 ' resolve name
            ResolveName
        Case 4 ' addr details
            AddrDetails
    End Select
    '
End Sub
```

Now add the `AddrDetails` subroutine and fill it in with the code from Listing 6.15.

Listing 6.15. Adding the `AddrDetails` routine.

```
Public Sub AddrDetails()
    '
    ' show the details of a valid address
    '
    lReturn = MAPIResolveName(lSession, Me.hWnd, "MCA/Win", 0, 0, udtRecip)
    If lReturn <> SUCCESS_SUCCESS Then
        MsgBox MAPIErr(lReturn)
        Exit Sub
    End If
    '
    lReturn = MAPIDetails(lSession, Me.hWnd, udtRecip, MAPI_LOGON_UI, 0)
    If lReturn <> SUCCESS_SUCCESS Then
        MsgBox MAPIErr(lReturn)
    End If
    '
End Sub
```

When you save and run the project, you will see an address entry dialog box appear when you press the `AddrDetails` button (see Figure 6.4).

FIGURE 6.4.
Viewing the Address Book Details dialog box.

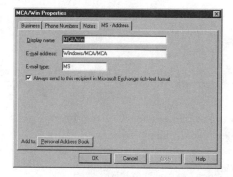

MAPISendDocuments

The `MAPISendDocuments` function is unique. You do not need to log in to MAPI before you call this function. As an option, you can fill simple test strings with information for attachments and pass them in the call, too. When the call is used, it brings up a full-featured compose dialog box that you can use to create and send an e-mail message. Table 6.9 shows the parameters for `MAPISendDocuments`.

Table 6.9. The `MAPISendDocuments` parameters.

Parameter	Type	Description
UIParam	Long	The parent window handle for the dialog box. A value of 0 specifies that the Send Note dialog box is application modal.
DelimChar	String	A string containing the character used to delimit the names in the `FilePaths` and `FileNames` parameters. This character should not be used in filenames on your operating system.
FilePaths	String	A string containing the list of full paths (including drive letters) for the attached files. The list is formed by concatenating correctly formed file paths separated by the character specified in the `DelimChar` parameter. The files specified in this parameter are added to the message as file attachments.
FileNames	String	A string containing the list of the original filenames (in 8.3 format) as they should be displayed in the message. When multiple names are specified, the list is formed by concatenating the filenames separated by the character specified in the `DelimChar` parameter.
Reserved	Long	Reserved for future use. This parameter must be 0.

Add another button to the control array and set its caption to `SendDocs`. Make sure your `Command1_Click` event matches the one in Listing 6.16.

Listing 6.16. Modifying the `Command1_Click` event.

```
Private Sub Command1_Click(Index As Integer)
    '
    ' handle button press
    '
    Select Case Index
        Case 0 ' log on session
            SMAPIStart
        Case 1 ' log off session
            SMAPIEnd
        Case 2 ' addressbook
            AddressBook
        Case 3 ' resolve name
            ResolveName
        Case 4 ' addr details
            AddrDetails
```

```
        Case 5 ' send documents
            SendDocs
    End Select
    '
End Sub
```

Now add the SendDocs subroutine and enter the code in Listing 6.17.

Listing 6.17. Adding the SendDocs routine.

```
Public Sub SendDocs()
    '
    ' start senddocuments
    '
    Dim cFiles As String
    Dim cNames As String
    Dim cDelim As String
    '
    cDelim = ";"
    cFiles = "C:\WINDOWS\WIN.INI;C:\CONFIG.SYS"
    cNames = "WIN.INI;CONFIG.SYS"
    '
    lReturn = MAPISendDocuments(Me.hWnd, cDelim, cFiles, cNames, 0)
    If lReturn <> SUCCESS_SUCCESS Then
        MsgBox MAPIErr(lReturn)
    End If
    '
End Sub
```

NOTE

The code in Listing 6.17 refers to documents in the C:\WINDOWS directory. If your Windows directory is not found at C:\WINDOWS, make the needed changes to the code example.

Save and run the project. Remember that you do not have to press LogOn before you press the SendDocs button. The MAPISendDocuments API will log you in automatically. Your screen should look similar to the one in Figure 6.5.

MAPISendMail

The MAPISendMail function is similar to MAPISendDocuments. The difference is that MAPISendMail uses the MAPIRecip and MAPIFile structures to pass data to MAPI. The MAPISendMail function also allows you to compose, address, and send a message without the use of any dialog boxes. Table 6.10 shows the MAPISendMail parameters.

FIGURE 6.5.
The results of the
SendDocs *routine.*

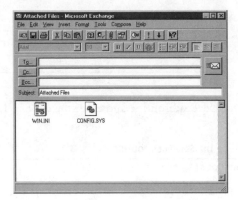

Table 6.10. The MAPISendMail **parameters.**

Parameter	Type	Description
Session	Long	An opaque session handle whose value represents a session with the messaging subsystem. If the value is 0, Mail sets up a session either from a system default session (if one exists) or by presenting a sign-in dialog box. In all cases, Mail returns to its state before the call.
UIParam	Long	The parent window handle for the dialog box. A value of 0 specifies that any dialog box displayed is application modal.
Message	MapiMessage	
	Subject	An empty string indicates no subject text. Some implementations may truncate subject lines that are too long or that contain carriage returns, line feeds, or other control characters.
	Note Text	An empty string indicates no text. Each paragraph should be terminated with either a carriage return (0x0d), a line feed (0x0a), or a carriage return-line feed pair (0x0d0a). The implementation wraps lines as appropriate.
	Message Type	A pointer to a string that is the message type. This field is for use by applications other than interpersonal mail (electronic forms, game message transmittal, and so on). For an interpersonal mail message (IPM), specify an empty string for this field.

Parameter	Type	Description
Recips	MapiRecips	The first element of an array of recipients. When RecipCount is zero, this parameter is ignored.
Files	MapiFiles	The first element of an array of attachment files written when the message is read. The number of attachments per message may be limited in some systems. If the limit is exceeded, the error MAPI_E_TOO_MANY_FILES is returned. When FileCount is 0, this parameter is ignored.
Flags	Long	A bitmask of flags. The following flags are defined: MAPI_LOGON_UI=&H1 (force logon) MAPI_NEW_SESSION=&H2 (use a new session) MAPI_DIALOG=&H8 (show send dialog box)
Reserved	Long	Reserved for future use. This parameter must be 0.

Add another button to the control array and set its caption to SendDialog. Update the Command1_Click event to match the code in Listing 6.18.

Listing 6.18. Updated Command1_Click event.

```
Private Sub Command1_Click(Index As Integer)
    '
    ' handle button press
    '
    Select Case Index
        Case 0 ' log on session
            SMAPIStart
        Case 1 ' log off session
            SMAPIEnd
        Case 2 ' addressbook
            AddressBook
        Case 3 ' resolve name
            ResolveName
        Case 4 ' addr details
            AddrDetails
        Case 5 ' send documents
            SendDocs
        Case 6 ' sendmail w/ dialog
            SendDialog
    End Select
    '
End Sub
```

Now add the `SendDialog` subroutine and enter the code from Listing 6.19.

Listing 6.19. Adding the `SendDialog` routine.

```
Public Sub SendDialog()
    '
    ' use sendmail w/ dialog
    '
    ' first build message
    udtMessage.Subject = "My Subject"
    udtMessage.NoteText = "This was written using VB Code"
    '
    ' next get valid recipient
    lReturn = MAPIResolveName(lSession, Me.hWnd, "MCA/Win", 0, 0, udtRecip)
    If lReturn <> SUCCESS_SUCCESS Then
        MsgBox MAPIErr(lReturn)
        Exit Sub
    End If
    '
    ' now add recipient to the message
    udtMessage.RecipCount = 1
    udtMessage.FilesCount = 0
    '
    ' now call sendmail w/ dialog
    lReturn = MAPISendMail(lSession, Me.hWnd, udtMessage, udtRecip, udtFile,
➡MAPI_DIALOG, 0)
    If lReturn <> SUCCESS_SUCCESS Then
        MsgBox MAPIErr(lReturn)
    End If
    '
End Sub
```

Save and run the project and press `SendMail`. You should see the Send Note dialog box on your screen, already filled out and ready to go (see Figure 6.6).

You can use `MAPISendMail` to send a message without invoking the Send Note dialog box. To do this, modify the `MAPISendMail` line by removing the `MAPI_DIALOG` constant and replacing it with `0`.

MAPIFindNext **and** MAPIReadMail

The `MAPIFindNext` and `MAPIReadMail` functions are used to read messages that have been placed in the user's InBox. The `MAPIFindNext` function is used to point to the next (or first) unread message in the InBox. The `MAPIReadMail` function takes information received during the `MAPIFindNext` operation and retrieves the message for viewing or other processing. Table 6.11 contains a list of `MAPIFindNext` parameters.

FIGURE 6.6.

The completed Send Note dialog box.

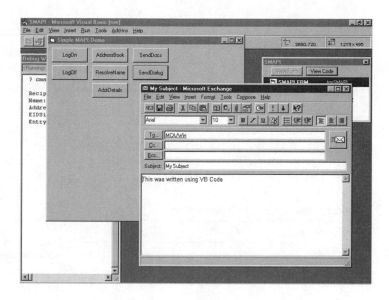

Table 6.11. The `MAPIFindNext` **parameters.**

Parameter	Type	Description
Session	Long	A unique session handle whose value represents a session with the messaging subsystem. Session handles are returned by `MAPILogon` and invalidated by `MAPILogoff`. If the value is 0, `MAPIFindNext` returns `MAPI_E_INVALID_SESSION`.
UIParam	Long	The parent window handle for the dialog box. A value of 0 specifies that any dialog box displayed is application modal.
MessageType	String	A pointer to a string that is the message type. To specify an interpersonal mail message, use an empty string, "".
SeedMessageID	String	A string that is the message identifier seed for the request. If the identifier is an empty string, the first message matching the type specified in the `MessageType` parameter is returned.
Flags	Long	A bitmask of flags. Unspecified flags should always be passed as 0. Undocumented flags are reserved. The following flags are defined: $\quad$`MAPI_UNREAD_ONLY=&H20` (new messages only) $\quad$`MAPI_GUARANTEE_FIFO=&H100` (get oldest first)

continues

Table 6.11. continued

Parameter	Type	Description
Reserved	long	Reserved for future use. This parameter must be 0.
MessageID	String	A unique variable-length string that is the message identifier.

The MAPIReadMail function reads a message from the MAPI InBox and places it into the MAPIMessage structure. You use MAPIReadMail to retrieve messages from the Inbox for review and subsequent action. Table 6.12 shows the MAPIReadMail parameters.

Table 6.12. The MAPIReadMail parameters.

Parameter	Type	Description
Session	Long	A unique session handle whose value represents a session with the messaging subsystem. If the value is 0, MAPIReadMail returns MAPI_E_INVALID_SESSION.
UIParam	Long	The parent window handle for the dialog box. A value of 0 specifies that any dialog box displayed is application modal.
MessageID	String	A variable-length string that is the message identifier of the message to be read. Message IDs can be obtained from the MAPIFindNext and MAPISaveMail functions.
Flags	Long	A bitmask of flags. Undocumented flags are reserved. The following flags are defined: MAPI_ENVELOPE_ONLY=&H40 (only get headers) MAPI_SUPPRESS_ATTACH=&H800 (no attachments) MAPI_BODY_AS_FILE=&H200 (save body as an attachment) MAPI_PEEK=&H80 (don't mark message as read).
Reserved	Long	Reserved for future use. This parameter must be 0.
Message	MAPIMessage	A type set by MAPIReadMail to a message containing the message contents.
Originator	MAPIRecip	The originator of the message.
Recips ()	MAPIRecip	An array of recipients. This array is redimensioned as necessary to accommodate the number of recipients chosen by the user.
Files ()	MAPIFiles	An array of attachment files written when the message is read. When MAPIReadMail is called, all

Parameter	Type	Description
		message attachments are written to temporary files. It is the caller's responsibility to delete these files when no longer needed. When MAPI_ENVELOPE_ONLY or MAPI_SUPPRESS_ATTACH is set, no temporary files are written and no temporary names are filled into the file attachment descriptors. This array is re-dimensioned as necessary to accommodate the number of files attached by the user.

Now add another button to the control array and set its caption to ReadMail. Update the Command1_click event to match Listing 6.20.

Listing 6.20. Updated Command1_Click event.

```
Private Sub Command1_Click(Index As Integer)
    '
    ' handle button press
    '
    Select Case Index
        Case 0 ' log on session
            SMAPIStart
        Case 1 ' log off session
            SMAPIEnd
        Case 2 ' addressbook
            AddressBook
        Case 3 ' resolve name
            ResolveName
        Case 4 ' addr details
            AddrDetails
        Case 5 ' send documents
            SendDocs
        Case 6 ' sendmail w/ dialog
            SendDialog
        Case 7 ' read mail
            ReadMail
    End Select
    '
End Sub
```

Now add the ReadMail subroutine and enter the code from Listing 6.21.

Listing 6.21. Adding the ReadMail routine.

```
Public Sub ReadMail()
    '
    ' read the first message in the Inbox
    '
    Dim cMsgID As String
```

continues

Listing 6.21. continued

```
    Dim udtOrig As MapiRecip
    Dim cMsg As String
    Dim cMsgType As String
    '
    cMsgID = Space(256)
    cMsgType = ""
    '
    lReturn = MAPIFindNext(lSession, Me.hWnd, cMsgType, cMsgID,
➥MAPI_GUARANTEE_FIFO, 0, cMsgID)
    If lReturn <> SUCCESS_SUCCESS Then
        MsgBox MAPIErr(lReturn)
        Exit Sub
    End If
    '
    lReturn = MAPIReadMail(lSession, Me.hWnd, cMsgID, MAPI_PEEK, 0, udtMessage,
➥udtOrig, udtRecips, udtFiles)
    If lReturn <> SUCCESS_SUCCESS Then
        MsgBox MAPIErr(lReturn)
        Exit Sub
    End If
    '
    cMsg = cMsg & "Message.Subject: " & udtMessage.Subject & Chr(13)
    cMsg = cMsg & "Originator.Name: " & udtOrig.Name & Chr(13)
    MsgBox cMsg, vbInformation, "ReadMail"
    '
End Sub
```

Save and run the project. After you press the ReadMail button, you'll see a message box that shows the subject and sender name (see Figure 6.7).

FIGURE 6.7.
The results of
MAPIReadMail.

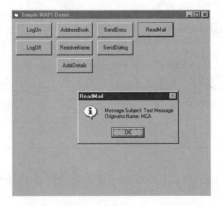

Even though MAPI services provide a built-in compose form (see SendMail), there is no built-in read form. You must provide that through Visual Basic code.

Creating Mail-Aware Applications

The most basic form of MAPI applications is the mail-aware application. This is a program that offers mail services as an added feature. A good example of this is the send option in Word, Excel, Access, and the other Microsoft Office programs.

Making your programs mail-aware is about the same as making them aware of a printer. Usually, you can add a send option to the main menu and treat mail output the same way you treat printer output. It is possible that you may have to create an interim ASCII text file that you can then import into the message text using the clipboard or a few lines of Visual Basic code. All in all, it's quite easy.

In this section, you'll develop a send feature for an Excel spreadsheet and then modify a Visual Basic project to add MAPI-aware features to its menu.

Creating QIKMAIL.XLS with Excel

One of the quickest ways to add MAPI services to existing applications is through the use of the MAPISendDocuments API call. This API requires no user-defined types and does not even require that you perform a MAPI logon before attempting the send operation. All you need to do is add a MAPISendDocuments API declaration and write a short routine to handle the selection of files for the send.

All the Microsoft Office applications allow you to build this kind of MAPI service into your spreadsheets, input forms, and other projects. As an illustration, let's build a quick Excel spreadsheet that allows users to select from a friendly list of accounting reports and then route those reports to someone else in the company.

> **NOTE**
>
> This example uses Excel 95 and requires the VBAMAP32.DLL be present in the WINDOWS\SYSTEM folder. If you are running a 16-bit version of Excel, you need to have the VBAMAPI.DLL installed in your WINDOWS\SYSTEM folder, and you need to change the code referenced DLL to match your version.

First, bring up Excel and start a new worksheet. Insert a code module (Insert ¦ Macro ¦ Module) and enter the code shown in Listing 6.22.

Listing 6.22. Building a MAPI-aware Excel worksheet.

```
'
' declare API call for MAPI service
Declare Function MAPISendDocuments Lib "VBAMAP32.DLL" Alias "BMAPISendDocuments"
(ByVal UIParam&, ByVal DelimStr$, ByVal FilePaths$, ByVal FileNames$, ByVal
Reserved&) As Long

'
' send file in active cell
'
Sub MAPIAware()
    '
    ' send the selected file as attachments
    '
    Dim x As Long ' for return
    Dim cFile As String
    Dim cName As String
    '
    If ActiveCell = "" Then
        MsgBox "Select a Report to Send"
        Exit Sub
    End If
    '
    cName = ActiveCell & ";"
    cFile = ActiveCell.Offset(0, 1) & ";"
    '
    x = MAPISendDocuments(0, ";", cFile, cName, 0)
    '
    If x <> 0 Then
        MsgBox "SendDocuments Error [" & Str(x) & "]"
    End If
    '
End Sub
```

Now select a new worksheet page and, using Figure 6.8 as a guide, enter the columns of information shown in Table 6.13.

FIGURE 6.8.

Laying out the
QIKSEND.XLS worksheet.

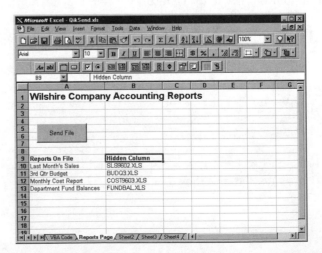

Table 6.13. Column data for `QIKSEND.XLS`.

Column A	Column B
Reports On File	Hidden Column
Last Month's Sales	`SLS9602.XLS`
3rd Qtr Budget	`BUDQ3.XLS`
Monthly Cost Report	`COST9603.XLS`
Department Fund Balances	`FUNDBAL.XLS`

Add a button to the worksheet (selected from the Forms Toolbar) and connect the button to the `MAPIAware` routine you built earlier. Set its caption to `Send Report`. Now hide column B so that users cannot see the exact operating system filenames. To do this, click the column header, click the right mouse button, and select `Hide`. Finally, add a title to the worksheet and save it as `QIKSEND.XLS`.

Now press `Send Report`. You'll be asked to log into the MAPI service; then MAPI will collect the file you selected and present you with the Send Note dialog box with the attachment already in place (see Figure 6.9).

FIGURE 6.9.

Sending attachments from Excel.

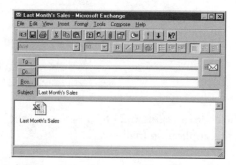

That's all there is to it! You can create much more sophisticated forms and options, though—including building the entire message, attaching the selected file, even routing directly to the person who is authorized to see the report. And all this can be done without ever asking the user to do more than select the report and click `Send`!

Next you'll add MAPI services to a Visual Basic project.

Adding MAPI Services to Existing Visual Basic 4.0 Programs

For this example, you'll borrow the code from a sample program that ships with Visual Basic 4.0 Standard Edition: the MDI sample application. This can be found in the `SAMPLES\MDI` folder within the main Visual Basic folder. If you do not have this application or if you want to leave your copy alone, you can find another copy of it on the CD-ROM shipped with this book.

This MDI application is a simple project that creates a multidocument editor that can save documents as ASCII files. To make this system mail-aware will require a few lines of code behind a Send... menu item in one form.

> **NOTE**
>
> This project uses the MAPI controls that ship with Visual Basic 4.0. You'll cover the MAPI controls in detail in the next chapter. For now, just remember that the MAPI controls offer the same level of access to MAPI services that the SMAPI API offers.

Load the MDI project and open the NOTEPAD form. First, add the MAPI Session and MAPI Message controls to the bottom of the form. Next, add a separator line and a Send... menu item just after the Save As... menu item (see Figure 6.10).

FIGURE 6.10.

Modifying the NOTEPAD *form.*

Finally, add the code in Listing 6.23 to the mnuFileSend_Click event. This is all the code you need to make this application mail-aware.

Listing 6.23. MAPI Send routine for NOTEPAD.

```
Private Sub mnuFileSend_Click()
    '
    ' log onto mail server
    ' start mail compose session
    ' log off mail server
    '
    On Error GoTo mnuFileSendErr
    '
    '
    MAPISession1.DownloadMail = False    ' dont check box
    MAPISession1.SignOn    ' start mail session
    MAPIMessages1.SessionID = MAPISession1.SessionID
    '
    ' handle sending msg
    MAPIMessages1.Compose    ' clear buffer
    MAPIMessages1.MsgNoteText=Me.Text1 ' move text to message
```

```
    MAPIMessages1.MsgSubject = Me.Caption ' get subject
    MAPIMessages1.Send True ' show server dialog
    '
    MAPISession1.SignOff      ' end mail session
    '
    Exit Sub
    '
mnuFileSendErr:
    MsgBox Error$, vbCritical, "Mail Send Error " + Str(Err)
    On Error Resume Next
    MAPISession1.SignOff
    '
End Sub
```

Notice that the `DownloadMail` property is set to skip over checking the `Inbox`. The `Inbox` isn't important here; you just want to send this document to someone via the mail server. The message text and message subject are set using data from the input form.

Now save and run the project. Begin to edit a new document (see Figure 6.11).

FIGURE 6.11.

Using the MDI application.

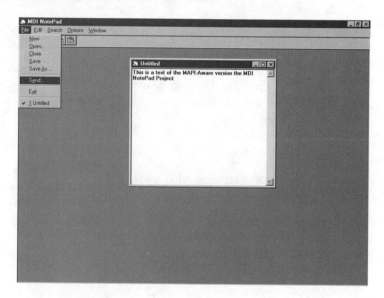

When you are done editing the text, select the Send... menu item to send the document out. You'll see the default compose form appear with the text and subject already supplied (see Figure 6.12).

There is a way to "bury" the mail features even deeper into this application. You really only need a way to tack on an address to this document. Listing 6.24 shows a modified routine that calls only the address dialog box and then sends the document out.

FIGURE 6.12.
*The MDI text ready to
address and send.*

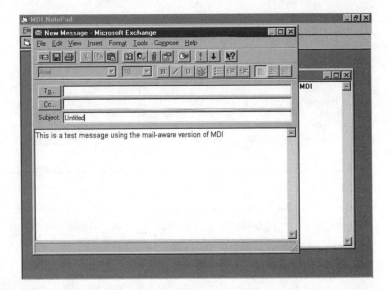

In Listing 6.24, it is possible for the user to call the address book and exit it without
selecting a valid address. This will be reported as an error when the Send method is
invoked. To prevent the error, you could check the RecipAddress property before
invoking the Send method.

Listing 6.24. Sending NOTEPAD using Address Book.

```
Private Sub mnuFileSend_Click()
    '
    ' log onto mail server
    ' start mail compose session
    ' log off mail server
    '
    On Error GoTo mnuFileSendErr
    '
    '
    MAPISession1.DownloadMail = False    ' dont check box
    MAPISession1.SignOn       ' start mail session
    MAPIMessages1.SessionID = MAPISession1.SessionID
    '
    ' handle sending msg
    MAPIMessages1.Compose    ' clear buffer
    MAPIMessages1.MsgNoteText = Me.Text1    ' get text
    MAPIMessages1.MsgSubject = Me.Caption   ' get subject
    MAPIMessages1.Show       ' get address
    MAPIMessages1.Send       ' send without dialog
    '
```

```
        MAPISession1.SignOff     ' end mail session
        '
        Exit Sub
        '
mnuFileSendErr:
        MsgBox Error$, vbCritical, "Mail Send Error " + Str(Err)
        On Error Resume Next
        MAPISession1.SignOff
        '
End Sub
```

Save and run this project. When you select the Send... menu option, you now will see only the address dialog box before the program sends your document out to the server.

As you can see, it's not at all difficult to add mail features to your existing applications. This technique of adding a send option to the menu will work with just about any Windows application.

Summary

In this chapter, you learned how to make your programs MAPI-aware using the Simple MAPI API call set. This API set provides very easy, very quick access to the most-needed MAPI services.

You learned that there are three user-defined types required to provide full SMAPI services:

■ *MAPIMessage*—Contains all the information about a message packet, including originator, subject, text, recipients, and attachments.

■ *MAPIRecip*—Contains all the information about a message recipient, including name, address type, full address, and unique entry ID.

■ *MAPIFile*—Contains all the information about an attached file, including display name, operating system name, and position in the message packet.

You also learned that there are eleven API calls in the SMAPI set. This set of calls provides access to the core MAPI services, including

■ Logging on and logging off MAPI sessions

■ Gaining access to the MAPI address book

■ Reading, sending, saving, and deleting MAPI messages

■ Performing address validations and lookups

■ Handling binary message attachments

You also discovered that the MAPISendDocuments API call is the only MAPI call that requires no use of user-defined types to pass data via MAPI. This API call is very useful for adding quick MAPI support to existing applications.

In the second half of the chapter, you used SMAPI to add send features to an Excel worksheet (using the MAPISendDocuments API). You also modified an existing Visual Basic 4.0 project by adding a Send... menu option to the form.

In the next chapter, you'll get an in-depth look at the Visual Basic MAPI controls, and in the process you'll build a fully functional e-mail client application that you can use to read and write all your MAPI messages.

7

Creating a Simple MAPI Client with the MAPI Controls

In this chapter, you'll learn how to use the MAPI controls from Visual Basic to create a simple program that can read and reply to all e-mail sent to the logon ID. You'll also learn how to write routines to access all the electronic mail services available to a basic MAPI client application on a desktop workstation. This includes creating new e-mail messages, checking the inbox for new mail, and accessing and updating the e-mail address book. When you complete this chapter, you will have a fully functional e-mail client application.

You'll also learn the details of using the MAPISession and MAPIMessage controls with Visual Basic 4.0. The Visual Basic MAPI controls offer a quick way to build Simple MAPI applications. The MAPI controls allow you full access to the Inbox object, to the MAPI Compose, Fetch, Read, Delete, and Send services, and limited access to the address book.

> **NOTE**
>
> Simple MAPI is sometimes called MAPI 0 to indicate that it precedes the MAPI 1.0 release that matches Microsoft Exchange Server. Throughout this book, you'll see Simple MAPI instead of MAPI 0.

When you complete the coding examples in this chapter, you will understand the basics of Simple MAPI, and you'll know how to use Visual Basic and the MAPI controls to read, compose, address, send, and delete MAPI messages.

The Visual Basic MAPI Controls

> **NOTE**
>
> Throughout the rest of this chapter, there are sample programs that illustrate the use of the MAPI controls to create mail-aware applications with Visual Basic 4.0. These programs must be run on a workstation that has access to simple MAPI services through a MAPI-compliant mail server. MAPI-compatible servers from Microsoft include the Microsoft Mail Server for DOS, Microsoft Exchange Server for NT, Microsoft Mail for Windows for Workgroups, Windows 95 Exchange Mail, or any other fully MAPI-compliant system (such as WordPerfect Office).

Visual Basic 4.0 Professional Edition ships with two OCX controls that provide access to all the MAPI services you'll need to create fully functional electronic mail applications using Visual Basic. The MAPISession control provides access to everything you'll need to sign on and sign off any MAPI-compliant server. The MAPIMessage control provides access to the MAPI routines that allow you to read, compose, address, and send messages using the session established with the MAPISession control. This section of the chapter will review the MAPI-related properties and methods of each of these controls.

The MAPISession Control

The MAPISession control is used to establish a link between your Visual Basic program (the mail client) and the electronic mail server. The MAPI-compliant mail server must be installed and available to the Visual Basic client program. If your program will run on a traditional network server, the mail server may be Microsoft Mail installed on a network workstation. If you are running Windows for Workgroups or Windows 95, Microsoft Mail or Microsoft Exchange can act as a mail server. There are other mail servers available for both file server and peer-to-peer networks.

There are two methods and seven properties for the MAPISession control that are directly MAPI related. The two following sections identify these components of the MAPISession control, and describe their meaning and their use in Visual Basic programs.

Methods of the MAPISession Control

There are only two MAPISession methods: SignOn and SignOff. The SignOn method is used to begin a MAPI session. By default, the SignOn method provides a logon dialog box that prompts the user for valid logon information. The exact nature of the logon dialog box depends on the mail server. The Microsoft Mail logon dialog box prompts the user for a valid username and password (see Figure 7.1).

FIGURE 7.1.
Default logon dialog box for Microsoft Mail.

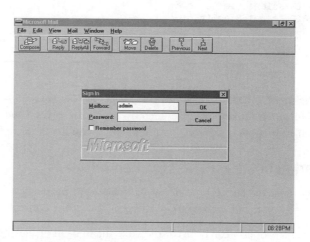

The default logon dialog box for the Microsoft Exchange Mail product simply asks the user to select the desired mail services profile (see Figure 7.2).

If a valid username and password are supplied by way of the SignOn method, the MAPISession control returns a unique value in the SessionID property. This unique value is used in all message transactions to identify the link between the client application and the mail server. We'll talk more about the SessionID property in the next section of this chapter.

FIGURE 7.2.
Default logon dialog box
for Microsoft Exchange
Mail.

The `SignOff` method of the `MAPISession` control does just what you'd expect—it safely ends your link to the mail server. There is no dialog box associated with the `SignOff` method.

In order to use the `MAPISession` control methods, you must first place the `MAPISession` control on a Visual Basic form. The form is invisible at run-time and is only used to provide the methods and properties needed to establish a MAPI session between your Visual Basic program and the mail server.

As an example of the `MAPISession` control, start a Visual Basic project. Use the `Tools ¦ Custom Controls` menu item to add the Microsoft MAPI controls to your project. Place a `MAPISession` control on the form and add the three lines of code in Listing 7.1 to the `Form_Load` event.

Listing 7.1. A tiny e-mail client.

```
Private Sub Form_Load()
    '
    MAPISession1.SignOn
    MAPISession1.SignOff
    End
    '
End Sub
```

Save the form as `CDG0701.FRM` and the project as `CDG0701.VBP`, and run the project. You'll see the default logon dialog box provided by your mail server. Once you sign in, the Visual Basic program immediately signs you out and ends. You'll add more features as we go along.

Properties of the `MAPISession` Control

The `MAPISession` control has seven MAPI-related properties. These properties all deal with options that you can set to control the behavior of the control at logon time.

The `Action` property can be used to invoke the sign-on or sign-off methods. This property was present in Visual Basic 3.0 and has been replaced by the `SignOn` and `SignOff` methods discussed earlier.

The `DownloadMail` property is used to control whether new messages are downloaded from the mail server at logon time. By default, all new messages are forced into the user's mailbox at logon time. You can set this property to `False` to prevent this from happening. In the code example in Listing 7.2, the `DownloadMail` property has be set to `False` before invoking the `SignOn` method.

Listing 7.2. Setting the `DownloadMail` property of the `MAPISession` control.

```
Private Sub Form_Load()
    '
    MAPISession1.DownloadMail = False ' don't get new mail
    MAPISession1.SignOn
    MAPISession1.SignOff
    End
    '
End Sub
```

The `LogonUI` property can be used to turn off the default logon screen provided by the mail server. You can set this property to `False` to suppress the mail server from presenting the logon screen when you invoke the `SignOn` method. If you set this property to `False`, you must supply valid data in the `UserName` and `Password` properties, or an error will be reported.

You can use the `NewSession` property to force the creation of a new MAPI session, even if a MAPI session already exists for this workstation. By default, the `SignOn` method will attempt to locate any current MAPI interface sessions before attempting to log on to the mail server. When you set the `NewSession` parameter to `True`, the `SignOn` method will create a second MAPI session link with the mail server. The code in Listing 7.3 shows how this is done.

Listing 7.3. Setting the `NewSession` property of the `MAPISession` control.

```
Private Sub Form_Load()
    '
MAPISession1.DownloadMail = False    ' dont get new mail
    MAPISession1.NewSession = True   ' force a new session
    MAPISession1.SignOn
    MAPISession1.SignOff
    End
    '
End Sub
```

The `Password` and `UserName` properties should be set to valid values if you want to bypass the default logon screen. If you supply a `UserName` but leave the `Password` property blank, the `SignOn` method will force the logon dialog box to appear and prompt for the missing information. If, however, the `LogonUI` property is set to `False`, no dialog box will appear, and an error will be returned.

If you are using the Microsoft Exchange Mail Client, you only need to provide a valid Profile Name. Microsoft Exchange Mail will ignore any value in the `Password` property. If you are using the Microsoft Mail client (network or workgroup version), you will need to supply both the `UserName` and the `Password` properties if you want to bypass the default logon dialog box. Refer to Listing 7.4 for an example.

Listing 7.4. Getting the username and password at sign-on.

```
Private Sub Form_Load()
    '
    MAPISession1.DownloadMail = False    ' don't get new mail
    MAPISession1.NewSession = True       ' force a new session
    MAPISession1.UserName = "MCA"        ' username for mail
    MAPISession1.Password = "PASSWORD"   ' users password
    MAPISession1.SignOn
    MAPISession1.SignOff
    End
    '
End Sub
```

The `SessionID` property is a read-only property available only at run-time that contains the unique session ID number of a completed link between your Visual Basic program and the mail server. This session ID value must be used in all transactions to the mail server. Its value is used to set the `SessionID` of the `MAPIMessage` control before attempting to access the message services provided by the mail server. The code in Listing 7.5 displays the value of the `SessionID` after a successful logon of the user.

Listing 7.5. Displaying the `SessionID` property.

```
Private Sub Form_Load()
    '
    MAPISession1.DownloadMail = False      ' dont get new mail
    MAPISession1.NewSession = True         ' force a new session
    MAPISession1.UserName = "VBU Profile"  ' username for mail
    MAPISession1.Password = ""             ' user password
    MAPISession1.SignOn
    MsgBox Str(MAPISession1.SessionID)     ' show unique session handle
    MAPISession1.SignOff
    End
    '
End Sub
```

Modify the `UserName` and, if needed, the `Password` properties to contain valid logon data for your mail server. Then save and run the project. You will see a message box that shows the unique session handle for the MAPI session (see Figure 7.3).

FIGURE 7.3.
Displaying the `SessionID`
of a MAPI session.

The `MAPIMessage` Control

The `MAPIMessage` control gives your Visual Basic program access to all the message services available from the mail server with which your program has established a session. The

MAPIMessage control provides services for reading, composing, addressing, and sending mail messages. You can perform all major mail operations by requesting the service from the server.

The MAPIMessage control has four primary functions:

- Creating and sending messages
- Reading any new messages
- Deleting any old messages
- Maintaining the address list

There are 11 methods and over 30 properties of the MAPIMessage control that are MAPI-related. We'll review these methods and properties briefly. You can find additional documentation on each of the MAPIMessage properties in the Visual Basic online help files.

Methods

There are 11 methods for the MAPIMessage control:

- To create and send messages, the control uses the Compose, Copy, Forward, Reply, ReplyAll, and Send methods.
- To read messages, the control uses the Fetch method.
- To manage old messages, the control uses the Save and Delete methods.
- To maintain the address list, the control uses the Show and ResolveName methods.

The message-creation methods account for six of the eleven methods. Of these six, you only need to know two before you can create a functional e-mail application. The Compose method clears out the edit buffer area and prepares a clean slate for the creation of a new message. The Send method attempts to send the new message to the address supplied. If an address or message is not supplied, the Send method forces the mail server to present the default message compose form to the user.

In other words, you can create a complete e-mail composer by adding only two lines to the code we started earlier in this chapter. The code shown in the following listing is all you need to create a Visual Basic application that can compose and send e-mail messages. Start a new Visual Basic project and add the MAPISession and the MAPIMessage controls to the form. Then add the code shown in Listing 7.6 to the Form_Load event.

Listing 7.6. Creating a MAPIMessage.

```
Private Sub Form_Load()
    '
    MAPISession1.SignOn      ' log into MAPI server
    MAPIMessages1.SessionID = MAPISession1.SessionID
    '
    MAPIMessages1.Compose    ' clear buffers
```

continues

Listing 7.6. continued

```
    MAPIMessages1.Send True ' show default form
    '
    MAPISession1.SignOff    ' exit MAPI server
    End
    '
End Sub
```

Now save the form as CDG0702.FRM and the project as CDG0702.VBP, and run the program. You'll be prompted for a logon, and then you'll see the default compose form. Figure 7.4 shows what comes up if you are using Microsoft Exchange Mail.

FIGURE 7.4.

The default compose form for Microsoft Exchange.

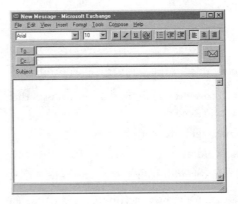

Notice that you have a highly functional e-mail program with very little coding. Use this form to send yourself a message. We'll use other Visual Basic code to read the message later in this chapter.

You can use the other message creation methods (Copy, Forward, Reply, and ReplyAll) to load the compose buffer with messages that have been sent to you by others. You can then use the default compose dialog box to edit the old message and send it just as you would a new message you created from scratch. The Forward, Reply, and ReplyAll methods also alter the subject line to reflect the action. For example, when you use the Forward method, the mail server will add "FW:" to the beginning of the subject line. The Reply methods place "RE:" at the start of the subject line.

The code example in Listing 7.7 takes the first message in the user's inbox and copies it to the compose buffer with "FW:" on the subject line.

Listing 7.7. Forwarding a message.

```
Private Sub Form_Load()
    '
    MAPISession1.SignOn      ' log into MAPI server
    MAPIMessages1.SessionID = MAPISession1.SessionID
```

```
        '
        MAPIMessages1.Fetch        ' get messages
        MAPIMessages1.Forward      ' forward the current message
        MAPIMessages1.Send True    ' send it
        '
        MAPISession1.SignOff       ' exit MAPI server
        End
        '
End Sub
```

You can use the `Fetch` method to tell the mail server to send your Visual Basic program all the messages that are currently on file in the inbox for the logged-on user. The code example shown in Listing 7.8 fetches all the messages for the user and then uses the `MsgCount` property to find out how many messages are actually on file.

Listing 7.8. Displaying the `MsgCount` property.

```
Private Sub Form_Load()
    '
    MAPISession1.SignOn        ' log into MAPI server
    MAPIMessages1.SessionID = MAPISession1.SessionID
    '
    MAPIMessages1.Fetch        ' get all messages into inbox
    MsgBox Str(MAPIMessages1.MsgCount)  ' show number of msgs
    '
    MAPISession1.SignOff       ' exit MAPI server
    End
    '
End Sub
```

You can use the `Delete` method to remove messages from the user's collection. The `Delete` method can also be used to remove a single recipient from a list of addresses or to remove a single attachment from a list of currently attached files. The code in Listing 7.9 removes the current message from the user's collection.

Listing 7.9. Deleting a message from the user's storage.

```
Private Sub Form_Load()
    '
    MAPISession1.SignOn        ' log into MAPI server
    MAPIMessages1.SessionID = MAPISession1.SessionID
    '
    MAPIMessages1.Fetch        ' get all messages into inbox
    MsgBox Str(MAPIMessages1.MsgCount)
    MAPIMessages1.Delete       ' get rid of first message
    MsgBox Str(MAPIMessages1.MsgCount)
    '
    MAPISession1.SignOff       ' exit MAPI server
    End
    '
End Sub
```

Finally, you can tell the mail server to show you a list of all the mail server addresses on file by invoking the Show method. The Show method can also be used to display details of the current message recipient (if this is supported by the MAPI mail server). The example code shown in Listing 7.10 will display the current mail server address list.

Listing 7.10. Showing the MAPI address book.

```
Private Sub Form_Load()
    '
    MAPISession1.SignOn       ' log into MAPI server
    MAPIMessages1.SessionID = MAPISession1.SessionID
    '
    MAPIMessages1.Show        ' show the addresss list
    '
    MAPISession1.SignOff      ' exit MAPI server
    End
    '
End Sub
```

Properties

The MAPIMessage control has more than thirty MAPI-related properties. We will quickly review them here. You can find more detailed information on each of the MAPIMessage control properties by consulting the topic "MAPIMessage Control" in the Visual Basic online help file.

The MAPIMessage control properties can be divided into several groups. Each group contains a set of properties that all deal with the same aspect of the message services provided by the mail server. Table 7.1 shows the MAPI-related properties, divided by service group.

Table 7.1. MAPI-related properties of the MAPIMessage control.

Group	Property	Description
Address	AddressCaption	Allows you to set the caption of the Address Book dialog box.
	AddressEditFieldCount	Use this property to set the number of edit buttons available on the Address Book dialog box.
	AddressLabel	If you use only one edit button (To:), you can set the button label with this property.
	AddressModifiable	When set to True, allows user to modify the contents of the address book; the default is False.

Group	Property	Description
	AddressResolveUI	When set to `True`, presents a dialog box to help users resolve rejected addresses. Use this property in conjunction with the `ResolveName` method. The default is `False`.
Attachment	AttachmentCount	Contains the number of attachments for the current message.
	AttachmentIndex	Pointer to the current attachment in the list.
	AttachmentName	Filename of the attachment pointed to by the `AttachmentIndex` property.
	AttachmentPathName	Contains full pathname of the current attachment.
	AttachmentPosition	Position (in characters) where the attachment is located within the message body.
	AttachmentType	Indicates the type of the current attachment. Valid values are `DATA` (data file), `EOLE` (embedded OLE object), and `SOLE` (static OLE object).
Fetch	FetchMsgType	Contains the type of message to look for when executing the `Fetch` method. Not commonly used by current products.
	FetchSorted	Controls sort order when building message collection. Set to `True` for First In, First Out sort order. Set to `False` to sort by user's `InBox` setting. The default is `False`.
	FetchUnreadOnly	Set to `True` to get only the unread messages into the user's collection. If `False`, all messages for the user's ID are loaded into the local set. The default is `True`.
Message	MsgConversationID	Contains internally generated ID that keeps track of all messages in a related "thread." You can use this value to collect all related messages into a single group.
	MsgCount	Contains the total number of messages in the set.
	MsgDateReceived	Date the current message was received.
	MsgID	Internally generated unique ID value.

continues

Table 7.1. continued

Group	Property	Description
	MsgIndex	Pointer to the current message in the message collection.
	MsgNoteText	This is the actual body of the message (less any attachments).
	MsgOrigAddress	Address of the originator (sender) of the current message.
	MsgOrigDisplayName	Contains the display name associated with the MsgOrigAddress property.
	MsgRead	Flag to indicate that the message has been read by the user to whom it was addressed. When set to True, the user has read the message.
	MsgReceiptRequested	Flag to indicate that a return receipt has been requested by the sender. When set to True, the sender wants a confirmation that the message has been successfully delivered.
	MsgSent	Flag to show that the message has been sent to the mail server for delivery. This flag is updated by the server, not the client.
	MsgSubject	The text line that identifies the subject of the message.
	MsgType	Contains the message type code. Currently, all MsgType codes are left null or empty to indicate an Interpersonal Message (IPM).
Recipient	RecipAddress	Address of the current recipient (could be a list).
	RecipCount	Contains the number of recipients for the current piece of mail.
	RecipDisplayName	The display name associated with an address in the address book.
	RecipIndex	Points to the current recipient in the list.
	RecipType	Shows what type of recipient is currently pointed to by the RecipIndex property. A value of 0 = OrigList (used only by the message editor); 1 = ToList (a person in a "To" address list); 2 = CcList (a person on the courtesy copy list); 3 = BccList (a person on the blind courtesy copy list).

Group	Property	Description
Other	Action	Carryover from Visual Basic 3.0—use the new methods instead.
	SessionID	Contains the value of the SessionID generated by the MAPISession control. You must update this property before you can perform any Message operations.

You can use these properties to modify the behavior of the MAPI dialog boxes supplied by the mail server. For example, you can change the caption of the address list, change the number of buttons that appear on the list, even change the caption of the To: button. You can also use these properties to add increased functionality to your Visual Basic mail applications by honoring attached documents, allowing the use of blind courtesy copy recipients, and so on.

While there are a number of things you can do with the numerous properties of the MAPIMessage control, one of the most useful is the ability to create e-mail attachments. That is the subject of the next section.

Creating E-Mail Attachments

Creating e-mail attachments is very useful and very easy to do with the MAPIMessage control and Visual Basic. Attachments can be simple text files, word processing documents, or even databases. For the next example, you'll attach a system file from a user's workstation and prepare a message to send to the help desk at a large corporation.

There are four property values you need to set in order to successfully create an e-mail attachment:

- ■ *AttachmentPathName*—This contains the complete filename as it is used by the operating system (for example, c:\config.sys or \\server\directory1\file.ext).
- ■ *AttachmentName*—This is a text string that appears underneath the attachment icon in the message.
- ■ *AttachmentType*—This flag tells the server what type of attachment you are using. Visual Basic constants for this property are mapData (a data file), mapEOLE (an embedded OLE object), and mapSOLE (a static OLE object).
- ■ *AttachmentPosition*—This is an integer value that contains the exact character position where the attachment icon is to appear in the message text.

If you plan on adding multiple attachments to the message, you'll also need to use the `AttachmentCount` and `AttachmentIndex` properties to fetch the attachments when you read the message.

You can add an attachment to any valid message in the compose buffer. The code example below creates a new message and adds the workstation's `CONFIG.SYS` file as an attachment. Modify the `Form_Load` event of `CDG0702.FRM` to match the code in Listing 7.11.

Listing 7.11. Creating an e-mail attachment.

```
Private Sub Form_Load()
    '
    MAPISession1.SignOn      ' log into MAPI server
    MAPIMessages1.SessionID = MAPISession1.SessionID
    '
    MAPIMessages1.Compose    ' clear buffer
    MAPIMessages1.MsgSubject = "User's CONFIG.SYS File"
    MAPIMessages1.MsgNoteText = "Here is the CONFIG.SYS File" + Chr(13) + " "
    '
    MAPIMessages1.AttachmentPosition = Len(MAPIMessages1.MsgNoteText)
    MAPIMessages1.AttachmentType = mapData
    MAPIMessages1.AttachmentName = "System Configuration File"
    MAPIMessages1.AttachmentPathName = "C:\CONFIG.SYS"
    '
    MAPIMessages1.Send True ' send it
    '
    MAPISession1.SignOff     ' exit MAPI server
    End
    '
End Sub
```

Now save and run the `CDG0702.VBP` project. After logging onto the mail server, you'll see a form appear with the `C:\CONFIG.SYS` file already attached to the message (see Figure 7.5).

FIGURE 7.5.

Viewing an added attachment to the message.

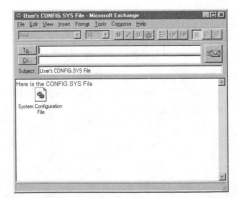

Building a Simple MAPI Client Application

The rest of this chapter covers the creation of a complete e-mail client for Simple MAPI access. This example uses all of the default MAPI services supplied by the installed MAPI service provider. The look and feel of the sign-in dialog box, the compose form, and the address book are completely controlled by the underlying MAPI engine running on the workstation. As you saw earlier in the chapter, each of these forms looks different depending on whether you are running Microsoft Mail, Microsoft Exchange, or any other MAPI-compliant messaging provider (such as Perfect Office). By using the services already available on the workstation, you can reduce your coding and maintain a familiar look and feel for your users' e-mail applications.

You will notice that one of the services unavailable within this client is the ability to store and retrieve old messages within the existing private and public mail folders. Simple MAPI services do not include access to the message store. You can only read information from the inbox using Simple MAPI. The Send method automatically writes messages to the outbox, but the Simple MAPI client cannot view messages in the outbox once they are placed there.

> **NOTE**
>
> The ability to access mail folders is available through MAPI OLE Messaging. You'll learn how to use OLE Messaging in Chapter 8, "The OLE Messaging Library."

Laying Out the Forms

The simple mail client project requires two forms. The first form (MAPIMAIN.FRM) is the main form in the application. This form will consist of a single list box that shows all the messages in the user's e-mail inbox and a set of command buttons that can be used to perform e-mail activities such as creating new messages, reading e-mail, deleting old messages, saving messages to text files, and replying to existing messages. This form will also hold the MAPI controls and a common dialog box control that will be used to save e-mail messages as text files. Refer to Figure 7.6 when laying out the form.

Listing 7.12 shows the Visual Basic form code for MAPIMAIN.FRM. When you build the MAPIMAIN.FRM, be sure to add the picture control first; then add a single command button to the form by selecting the command button from the toolbox and *drawing* it onto the picture control rather than double-clicking the command button from the toolbox. By drawing it on the picture control, you establish the command button as a child control of the picture box. Now, whenever you move the picture box, the command button will move with it.

FIGURE 7.6.

Laying out the e-mail forms.

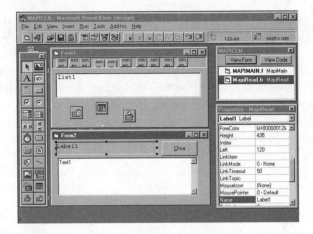

Listing 7.12. The MAPIMAIN.FRM layout code.

```
VERSION 4.00
Begin VB.Form MapiMain
    Caption         =   "Form1"
    ClientHeight    =   1710
    ClientLeft      =   1875
    ClientTop       =   1725
    ClientWidth     =   6345
    Height          =   2115
    Left            =   1815
    LinkTopic       =   "Form1"
    ScaleHeight     =   1710
    ScaleWidth      =   6345
    Top             =   1380
    Width           =   6465
    Begin VB.ListBox List1
        BeginProperty Font
            name            =   "Courier"
            charset         =   0
            weight          =   400
            size            =   9.75
            underline       =   0   'False
            italic          =   0   'False
            strikethrough   =   0   'False
        EndProperty
        Height          =   840
        Left            =   120
        TabIndex        =   1
        Top             =   540
        Width           =   4695
    End
    Begin VB.PictureBox Picture1
        Align           =   1   'Align Top
        Height          =   375
        Left            =   0
        ScaleHeight     =   315
        ScaleWidth      =   6285
        TabIndex        =   0
```

```
Top            =    0
Width          =    6345
Begin VB.CommandButton Command1
    Caption        =    "Command1"
    Height         =    315
    Index          =    9
    Left           =    900
    TabIndex       =    11
    Top            =    0
    Width          =    375
End
Begin VB.CommandButton Command1
    Caption        =    "Command1"
    Height         =    315
    Index          =    8
    Left           =    1380
    TabIndex       =    10
    Top            =    60
    Width          =    375
End
Begin VB.CommandButton Command1
    Caption        =    "Command1"
    Height         =    315
    Index          =    7
    Left           =    1800
    TabIndex       =    9
    Top            =    60
    Width          =    375
End
Begin VB.CommandButton Command1
    Caption        =    "Command1"
    Height         =    315
    Index          =    6
    Left           =    2280
    TabIndex       =    8
    Top            =    0
    Width          =    375
End
Begin VB.CommandButton Command1
    Caption        =    "Command1"
    Height         =    315
    Index          =    5
    Left           =    2820
    TabIndex       =    7
    Top            =    0
    Width          =    375
End
Begin VB.CommandButton Command1
    Caption        =    "Command1"
    Height         =    315
    Index          =    4
    Left           =    540
    TabIndex       =    6
    Top            =    0
    Width          =    375
End
```

continues

Listing 7.12. continued

```
         Begin VB.CommandButton Command1
            Caption         =   "Command1"
            Height          =   315
            Index           =   3
            Left            =   3240
            TabIndex        =   5
            Top             =   0
            Width           =   375
         End
         Begin VB.CommandButton Command1
            Caption         =   "Command1"
            Height          =   315
            Index           =   2
            Left            =   3720
            TabIndex        =   4
            Top             =   0
            Width           =   375
         End
         Begin VB.CommandButton Command1
            Caption         =   "Command1"
            Height          =   315
            Index           =   1
            Left            =   4200
            TabIndex        =   3
            Top             =   0
            Width           =   375
         End
         Begin VB.CommandButton Command1
            Caption         =   "Command1"
            Height          =   315
            Index           =   0
            Left            =   120
            TabIndex        =   2
            Top             =   0
            Width           =   375
         End
      End
      Begin MSComDlg.CommonDialog CommonDialog1
         Left            =   5280
         Top             =   900
         _Version        =   65536
         _ExtentX        =   847
         _ExtentY        =   847
         _StockProps     =   0
      End
      Begin MSMAPI.MAPISession MAPISession1
         Left            =   5880
         Top             =   540
         _Version        =   65536
         _ExtentX        =   741
         _ExtentY        =   741
         _StockProps     =   0
      End
      Begin MSMAPI.MAPIMessages MAPIMessages1
         Left            =   5100
         Top             =   480
         _Version        =   65536
```

```
        _ExtentX        =    741
        _ExtentY        =    741
        _StockProps     =    0
    End
End
```

Also, you'll notice that the command buttons are in the form of a control array. Control arrays are easier to work with than a set of individually named controls. Control arrays also consume fewer Windows resources than a set of individually named controls. You create the array by clicking on the first command button and setting its Index property to 0. Then highlight the control and select Edit ¦ Copy from the Visual Basic main menu. Select Edit ¦ Paste from the same menu. You'll see a dialog box asking you to confirm that you want to create a control array—click Yes. Visual Basic will then place a copy of the control on the form. Continue cutting and pasting until you have ten command buttons in the picture control.

The second form (MAPIREAD.FRM) will be used to display messages sent to you by other users. This form will have a label control to display the e-mail header information, a text box control to display the actual body of the message, and a single command button to close the form. Use the Visual Basic form code in Listing 7.13 and Figure 7.6 as a reference when building the MAPIREAD.FRM.

Listing 7.13. The MAPIREAD.FRM control table.

```
Begin VB.Form MapiRead
    Caption          =    "Form2"
    ClientHeight     =    4575
    ClientLeft       =    1140
    ClientTop        =    1515
    ClientWidth      =    6690
    Height           =    4980
    Left             =    1080
    LinkTopic        =    "Form2"
    ScaleHeight      =    4575
    ScaleWidth       =    6690
    Top              =    1170
    Width            =    6810
    Begin VB.CommandButton cmdClose
        Caption      =    "&Close"
        Height       =    495
        Left         =    5340
        TabIndex     =    2
        Top          =    3900
        Width        =    1215
    End
    Begin VB.TextBox Text1
        Height       =    2415
        Left         =    120
        MultiLine    =    -1   'True
        ScrollBars   =    2    'Vertical
        TabIndex     =    1
```

continues

Listing 7.13. continued

```
    Text            =    "MapiRead.frx":0000
    Top             =    1320
    Width           =    6435
End
Begin VB.Label Label1
    BorderStyle     =    1    'Fixed Single
    Caption         =    "Label1"
    BeginProperty Font
        name            =    "MS LineDraw"
        charset         =    2
        weight          =    400
        size            =    9.75
        underline       =    0    'False
        italic          =    0    'False
        strikethrough   =    0    'False
    EndProperty
    Height          =    1215
    Left            =    120
    TabIndex        =    0
    Top             =    60
    Width           =    6435
End
End
```

Coding the Main Support Routines

There are four support routines that you need to add to the MAPIMAIN.FRM form. The first routine, AdjustForm (see Listing 7.14), will do all the work to set the proper size and location for all the controls on the form, including the ten command buttons.

Listing 7.14. Coding the AdjustForm routine.

```
Public Sub AdjustForm()
    '
    ' set tool bar buttons
    '
    Dim x As Integer
    Dim cBtnCaption(9) As String
    '
    cBtnCaption(0) = "&Read"
    cBtnCaption(1) = "&New"
    cBtnCaption(2) = "&Save"
    cBtnCaption(3) = "&Del"
    cBtnCaption(4) = "&Addr"
    cBtnCaption(5) = "&Fwd"
    cBtnCaption(6) = "&Reply"
    cBtnCaption(7) = "A&ll"
    cBtnCaption(8) = "&InBox"
    cBtnCaption(9) = "E&xit"
    '
    For x = 0 To 9
        Command1(x).Caption = cBtnCaption(x)
```

```
        Command1(x).Width = (Picture1.Width / 10) * 0.9
        Command1(x).Height = 300
        Command1(x).Top = 0
        Command1(x).Left = (x * (Picture1.Width / 10))
    Next x
    '
    Picture1.Height = 360
    '
    ' set list box dimensions
    '
    List1.Left = 120
    List1.Width = Me.Width - 360
    List1.Top = Picture1.Height + 120
    List1.Height = Me.Height - (List1.Top + 600)

End Sub
```

This routine is called at the very start of the program and also each time the user resizes the form during run-time. When you add this routine to the `Form_Resize` event, all controls will be adjusted automatically each time the user changes the size of the form.

The next support routine you need to add is the `MAPIStart` routine (see Listing 7.15). This is the routine that attempts to log the user onto the mail server. Calling the `MAPISession1.Signon` method forces the mail server to display the default logon screen for the e-mail system.

Listing 7.15. Coding the `MAPIStart` routine.

```
Public Sub MAPIStart()
    '
    ' attempt to start a mapi session
    '
    On Error GoTo MAPIStartErr  ' error trap
    '
    MAPISession1.SignOn ' start session
    MAPIMessages1.SessionID = MAPISession1.SessionID ' pass ID
    '
    Exit Sub
    '
MAPIStartErr:
    MsgBox Error$, vbCritical, "Error " + Str(Err)
    '
End Sub
```

TIP

Notice the use of the error-handling routine. You'll see these throughout the application. Adding error handlers is always a good idea. Error handlers are even more critical whenever your programs are calling for system services like e-mail, since unexpected errors in the e-mail system can affect your Visual Basic program, too.

Once your user has successfully logged onto the mail server, you need to check for any messages in the user's inbox. The MAPIFetch routine (see Listing 7.16) does this. The MAPIMessages1.Fetch method brings all messages from the inbox into the MAPI read buffer. You can then use a For...Next loop to "walk" through this buffer and read each message. This program pulls the messages into the read buffer and then copies the message header information (message subject, the sender's name, and the date and time the message was received) into a list box on the main form.

Listing 7.16. Coding the MAPIFetch routine.

```
Public Sub MAPIFetch()
    '
    ' load all messages from 'inbox'
    '
    On Error GoTo MAPIFetchErr  ' error trap
    '
    Dim x As Integer
    Dim cLine As String
    '
    MAPIMessages1.Fetch ' get stuff from mail server
    '
    ' now load into list box
    '
    List1.Clear
    For x = 0 To MAPIMessages1.MsgCount - 1
        MAPIMessages1.MsgIndex = x
        cLine = MAPIMessages1.MsgSubject
        cLine = cLine + Space(30)
        cLine = Left(cLine, 30) + Space(2)
        cLine = cLine + MAPIMessages1.MsgOrigDisplayName
        cLine = cLine + Space(20)
        cLine = Left(cLine, 52) + Space(2)
        cLine = cLine + MAPIMessages1.MsgDateReceived
        List1.AddItem cLine
    Next x
    '
    Exit Sub
    '
MAPIFetchErr:
    MsgBox Error$, vbCritical, "Error " + Str(Err)
    '
End Sub
```

The last support routine you need to add to the MAPIMAIN.FRM form is MAPISave (see Listing 7.17). This routine is used to save selected messages to your local workstation for later use. The common dialog box control is used to provide the standard save file dialog box. Once a valid name is given for the file, the routine writes out the message header information followed by the actual message text. This is saved as an ASCII file that can be loaded by Notepad or any standard text editor.

Listing 7.17. Coding the MAPISave routine.

```
Public Sub MAPISave()
    '
    ' save the selected message as a text file
    '
    On Error GoTo MAPISaveErr ' error trap
    '
    ' set dialog parms and show SaveAs box
    '
    CommonDialog1.Filter = "Text File¦*.txt" ' file types to view/save
    CommonDialog1.DialogTitle = "Save Mail Message" ' dialog caption
    CommonDialog1.filename = "mailmsg.txt" ' suggest savename
    CommonDialog1.Flags = &H2 ' force overwrite confirmation
    CommonDialog1.ShowSave ' pop up the dialog
    '
    ' if user picked a real name, save the message
    '
    If Len(CommonDialog1.filename) > 0 Then
        Open CommonDialog1.filename For Output As 1
        Print #1, "DATE:" + Chr(9) + MAPIMessages1.MsgDateReceived
        Print #1, "FROM:" + Chr(9) + MAPIMessages1.MsgOrigDisplayName
        Print #1, "TO:" + Chr(9) + MAPIMessages1.RecipDisplayName
        Print #1, "SUBJ:" + Chr(9) + MAPIMessages1.MsgSubject
        Print #1, "" ' blank line
        Print #1, MAPIMessages1.MsgNoteText
        Close #1
    End If
    '
    Exit Sub
    '
MAPISaveErr:
    MsgBox Error$, vbCritical, "Error " + Str(Err)
    '
End Sub
```

Now that you have coded the support routines, you need to add code for four Visual Basic events on the MAPIMAIN.FRM form.

Coding the MAPIMAIN.FRM Events

The MAPIMAIN.FRM form has only five events that require code. Four of them are described here. The last event is described in the next section. The four events covered here are

■ Form_Load

■ Form_Unload

■ Form_Resize

■ List1_DblClick

The code for these events can be found in Listing 7.18.

Listing 7.18. Code for the Form and List1 events.

```
Private Sub Form_Load()
    '
    On Error GoTo FormLoadErr ' error trap
    '
    Me.Width = 9000 ' set starting width
    Me.Height = 4500 ' set starting height
    Me.Left = (Screen.Width - Me.Width) / 2
    Me.Top = (Screen.Height - Me.Height) / 2
    Me.Caption = "Simple Mail Client"
    '
    AdjustForm   ' fix up display form
    MAPIStart    ' start MAPI Session
    MAPIFetch    ' get any new messages
    '
    Exit Sub
    '
FormLoadErr:
    MsgBox Error$, vbCritical, "Error " + Str(Err)
    Unload Me
End Sub

Private Sub Form_Resize()
    AdjustForm ' resize all controls as needed
End Sub

Private Sub Form_Unload(Cancel As Integer)
    '
    On Error Resume Next     ' ignore error
    MAPISession1.SignOff     ' end mapi session
    '
End Sub


Private Sub List1_DblClick()
    '
    ' read the selected message
    MAPIMessages1.MsgIndex = List1.ListIndex
    MapiRead.Show vbModal
    '
End Sub
```

The Form_Load event first sets the form size and location and then calls the support routines AdjustForm, MAPIStart, and MAPIFetch. If any of these routines returns an error, the program is halted. The Form_Resize event calls the AdjustForm routine. This automatically resizes all controls each time the user changes the size of the form during run-time. The Form_Unload event invokes the MAPISession1.SignOff method to end the e-mail session and log the user out of the message server. The List1_DblClick event gets the currently selected message and calls the MAPIREAD.FRM form to display the e-mail note. You'll code the MAPIREAD.FRM form later on.

Coding the Main Button Bar

The last code routine needed for the MAPIMAIN.FRM form is the code used for the Command1_Click event (see Listing 7.19). Since you built a command button array, all button clicks are sent to the same routine. The program will be able to tell which button was pressed by checking the Index parameter passed to the Click routine.

Listing 7.19. Coding the Command1_Click event.

```
Private Sub Command1_Click(Index As Integer)
    '
    ' main command loop
    '
    On Error GoTo CommandErr  ' error trap
    '
    Dim nTemp As Integer
    '
    Select Case Index
        Case Is = 0
            ' open the selected message
            If List1.ListIndex <> -1 Then
                MAPIMessages1.MsgIndex = List1.ListIndex
                MapiRead.Show vbModal
            Else
                MsgBox "No Message Selected", vbCritical, "Read Message"
            End If
        Case Is = 1
            ' start a new message
            MAPIMessages1.Compose   ' point to compose buffer
            MAPIMessages1.Send True ' start new message dialog
        Case Is = 2
            ' save the selected message
            If List1.ListIndex <> -1 Then
                MAPIMessages1.MsgIndex = List1.ListIndex
                MAPISave
            Else
                MsgBox "No Message Selected", vbCritical, "Save Message"
            End If
        Case Is = 3
            ' delete the selected message
            If List1.ListIndex <> -1 Then
                nTemp = MsgBox("Delete Selected Message?", vbInformation + vbYesNo,
➥"Delete Message")
                If nTemp = vbYes Then
                    MAPIMessages1.MsgIndex = List1.ListIndex
                    MAPIMessages1.Delete
                    MAPIFetch
                End If
            Else
                MsgBox "No Message Selected", vbCritical, "Delete Message"
            End If
        Case Is = 4
            ' open the address book
            MAPIMessages1.Show   ' show address book
        Case Is = 5
```

continues

Listing 7.19. continued

```
                ' forward the selected message
                If List1.ListIndex <> -1 Then
                    MAPIMessages1.MsgIndex = List1.ListIndex
                    MAPIMessages1.Forward
                    MAPIMessages1.Send True
                Else
                    MsgBox "No Message Selected", vbCritical, "Forward Message"
                End If
            Case Is = 6
                ' reply to the originator of selected message
                If List1.ListIndex <> -1 Then
                    MAPIMessages1.MsgIndex = List1.ListIndex
                    MAPIMessages1.Reply
                    MAPIMessages1.Send True
                Else
                    MsgBox "No Message Selected", vbCritical, "Reply Message"
                End If
            Case Is = 7
                ' reply to all of selected message
                If List1.ListIndex <> -1 Then
                    MAPIMessages1.MsgIndex = List1.ListIndex
                    MAPIMessages1.ReplyAll
                    MAPIMessages1.Send True
                Else
                    MsgBox "No Message Selected", vbCritical, "Reply All Message"
                End If
            Case Is = 8
                ' check inbox for new messages
                MAPIFetch    ' call fetch routine
            Case Is = 9
                ' exit program
                nTemp = MsgBox("Exit Program?", vbInformation + vbYesNo, "Exit")
                If nTemp = vbYes Then
                    Unload Me
                End If
    End Select
    '
    Exit Sub
    '
CommandErr:
    MsgBox Error$, vbCritical, "Error " + Str(Err)
    '
End Sub
```

Each time a user presses one of the command buttons, this routine will execute the desired function. For most routines, the user must first select one of the messages in the inbox. If no message is selected, a dialog box pops up. Notice also that the only function that will require much code is the message-reading routine. You need to provide your own MAPI message reader (you'll use the MAPIREAD.FRM for that). All other e-mail services (New, Delete, Forward, Reply, ReplyAll, and AddressBook) are all provided by the message server your user logged onto at the start of the program.

> **NOTE**
>
> There is, of course, a downside to this "easy-code" access to MAPI services. Simple MAPI does not allow you to read, write, or search the MAPI address book via code. You can only gain access to the address book by starting the address book dialog box with the MAPIMessages.Show method. Also, you cannot see any existing MAPI storage folders except the inbox. This means you cannot save messages to an existing folder, and you cannot read old messages stored in other folders in the past. These limitations make the Simple MAPI interface less than ideal for building robust MAPI clients. However, Simple MAPI is very good for general access to MAPI messages and for creating very simple e-mail interfaces.

Coding the Reader Form

You need to code the MAPIREAD.FRM form to complete the project. This form has two support routines and four events that require code. The first support routine, AdjustReader, handles the resizing and locating of controls on the reader form. The second support routine, LoadReader, loads the message from the read buffer onto the form for display. This routine also creates a message header to display in the label control of the form. The code for these two support routines is shown in Listing 7.20.

Listing 7.20. Code for the MAPIREAD.FRM support routines.

```
Public Sub AdjustReader()
    '
    ' arrange controls on the form
    '
    On Error Resume Next ' ignore any errors
    '
    ' locate & size header label
    Label1.Top = 120
    Label1.Left = 120
    Label1.Width = Me.Width - 360
    Label1.Height = Me.Height * 0.3
    '
    ' locate & size close button
    cmdClose.Top = Me.Height - 840
    cmdClose.Left = Me.Width - 1440
    cmdClose.Width = 1200
    cmdClose.Height = 300
    '
    ' locate & size message text box
    Text1.Top = Label1.Height + 240
    Text1.Left = 120
    Text1.Width = Me.Width - 360
    Text1.Height = cmdClose.Top - (Text1.Top + 120)
    '
End Sub
```

continues

Listing 7.20. continued

```
Public Sub LoadReader()
    '
    ' fill in message header and body
    '
    Label1.Caption = ""
    Label1.Caption = "DATE:   " + MapiMain.MAPIMessages1.MsgDateReceived + Chr(13)
    Label1.Caption = Label1.Caption + "FROM:   " +
➥MapiMain.MAPIMessages1.MsgOrigDisplayName + Chr(13)
    Label1.Caption = Label1.Caption + "TO:     " +
➥MapiMain.MAPIMessages1.RecipDisplayName + Chr(13)
    Label1.Caption = Label1.Caption + "SUBJ:   " + MapiMain.MAPIMessages1.MsgSubject
    '
    Text1.Text = MapiMain.MAPIMessages1.MsgNoteText
End Sub
```

The `Form_Load` event contains code to set the form size and then call the `AdjustReader` and `LoadReader` routines. The `Form_Resize` event calls the `AdjustReader` routine to resize the controls. The `cmdClose_Click` event unloads the `MAPIREAD.FRM` form, and the `Text1_KeyPress` event contains a single line of code that tells Visual Basic to ignore any key presses that occur within the text box control. This is a simple way to make a text box control read-only. Each time a user presses a key, the `KeyPress` event will zero out the ASCII key value before it gets typed to the screen. Listing 7.21 contains the code for the `MAPIREAD.FRM` form events.

Listing 7.21. Code for the `MAPIREAD.FRM` events.

```
Private Sub Form_Load()
    '
    Me.Width = 7500
    Me.Height = 3750
    Me.Left = (Screen.Width - Me.Width) / 2
    Me.Top = (Screen.Height - Me.Height) / 2
    Me.Caption = "Read Mail [" + MapiMain.MAPIMessages1.MsgSubject + "]"
    '
    AdjustReader ' arrange controls on form
    LoadReader   ' fill in header and body
    '
End Sub

Private Sub Form_Resize()
    AdjustReader ' arrange controls on form
End Sub

Private Sub Text1_KeyPress(KeyAscii As Integer)
    KeyAscii = 0 ' ignore all key presses
End Sub

Private Sub cmdClose_Click()
    Unload Me
End Sub
```

Running the Simple Mail Client

After you add all the code, save the project (MAPICLN.VBP) and run it. When the program first starts, you'll see a prompt to log onto your e-mail server. After you log on, you'll see the main form of the application (see Figure 7.7).

FIGURE 7.7.

The main form of the simple e-mail client.

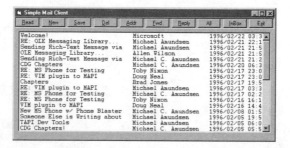

This form shows all the e-mail messages that are currently in your inbox. Notice that you can resize the form, and all the controls will adjust to the new form dimensions. If you double-click an item in the list box or select an item with a single click and press the Read button, you'll see the MAPIREAD.FRM form with the message header and selected e-mail message (see Figure 7.8).

FIGURE 7.8.

Displaying the message reader form.

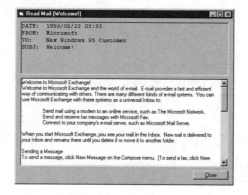

If you press the New button, you'll see the default message compose dialog box. This box will look different depending on the e-mail system you are using. Figure 7.9 shows how the Microsoft Exchange compose dialog box looks in Windows 95.

You can get direct access to the e-mail address book by clicking the Addr command button on the MAPIMAIN.FRM form. Figure 7.10 shows what the Microsoft Exchange address book looks like in Windows 95.

FIGURE 7.9.
The Microsoft Exchange compose dialog box.

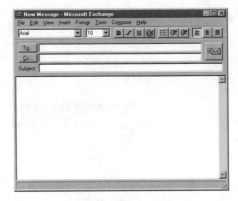

FIGURE 7.10.
The Microsoft Exchange address book.

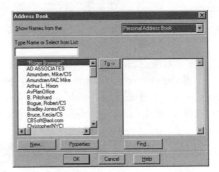

You can test the application by sending yourself e-mail and then using the various command buttons to forward, reply, save, and delete e-mail messages. You now have a completed e-mail client application!

Additional Features

Even though this project is fairly complete, there are a few features you might consider adding to improve the program. Some possible enhancements are

- Adding a print button to print the selected message. This involves adding a print button to the control button array and setting up the common dialog box properties to access the printer.

- Adding the ability to read and save e-mail attachments. This involves adding the ability to collect and list attachments to the MAPIREAD.FRM form. The Visual Basic text box will not allow you to render an icon within the message body as is done by the Microsoft Mail and Windows Messaging clients. However, VB4-32bit does contain a rich-text edit box that will allow you to render icons. If you wish, you can collect the attachment properties and add them to a list box at the end of the MAPIREAD form, or to a list on another form launched from MAPIREAD.FRM. After viewing the attachment list, you'll need to offer the user the chance to save the attachments via the file options of the Visual Basic common dialog box control.

■ Replacing the command buttons with icon buttons using the Sheridan 3-D command button that ships with the Professional Edition of Visual Basic. If you are working in the 32-bit version of Visual Basic, use the new `Toolbar` control instead.

■ Adding a set of menu items to the forms to match the functions of the command buttons.

Summary

This chapter covered two main topics:

■ The Visual Basic MAPI controls
■ Building a Simple MAPI client application

You learned the properties and methods of the two Visual Basic MAPI controls. The `MAPISession` control is used to gain access to MAPI service providers through the `SignOn` and `SignOff` methods. The `MAPIMessages` control is used to read, create, delete, address, and send MAPI messages.

The Simple MAPI client detailed in this chapter showed you how to build a complete MAPI-enabled application with a minimum of coding. This sample application shows how you can use the Visual Basic MAPI controls to create a fully functional e-mail client that can read and delete incoming messages, compose new messages, address them, and send them to their recipients.

You also learned that Simple MAPI services allow only limited access to the MAPI address book. You can search and edit the address book only through the pre-defined `MAPI.Show` method. You cannot directly search for existing addresses or add, edit, or delete addresses without using the address dialog box supplied by the MAPI service provider.

You also learned that Simple MAPI does not allow you to access any of the existing mail folders. You can only see the inbox folder and its contents.

Now that you know how to use the Visual Basic MAPI controls to create a simple e-mail client, you're ready to tackle OLE messaging. In the next chapter, you'll learn how to build a mailing list server application that is capable of managing large mailing lists.

8

The OLE Messaging Library

Introduction

One of the new features of Microsoft Exchange is the creation of the *OLE Messaging library.* This set of OLE objects, properties, and methods allows any VBA-compliant development tool to gain access to MAPI services and incorporate them into desktop applications. This chapter shows you how the OLE Messaging library works and how you can use the OLE objects to create MAPI-enabled programs.

This chapter provides an overview of all the OLE Messaging library objects and gives examples of their use. You'll learn about the following objects:

- The `Session` object
- The `InfoStore` objects and collections
- The `Folder` objects and collections
- The `Message` objects and collections
- The `Recipient` objects and collections
- The `Address` objects
- The `Attachment` objects and collections

You'll also learn how these objects interact with each other and how to use them to perform several advanced MAPI tasks, including:

- Moving messages from one folder to another
- Renaming existing folders
- Modifying and deleting address entries
- Switching between message stores

When you complete this chapter, you'll understand the OLE Messaging library objects and how to use them to build MAPI-compliant e-mail applications with any VBA-compatible development tool.

The `Session` Object

The `Session` object of the OLE Messaging library is the top-most object in the hierarchy. You must create an instance of a MAPI `Session` object before you can gain access to any other aspects of the MAPI system. The `Session` object has several properties (including subordinate objects) and a handful of methods that you can invoke.

The `Session` Object Methods

Table 8.1 shows the `Session` Object Methods along with a list of parameters and short descriptions.

Table 8.1. Session object methods.

Methods	Parameters	Description
AddressBook	(opt) title as String, (opt) oneAddress as Boolean, (opt) forceResolution as Boolean, (opt) recipLists as long, (opt) toLabel as String, (opt) ccLabel as String, (opt) bccLabel as String, (opt) parentWindow as Long	Access to session address book.
GetAddressEntry	entryID as String	Direct access to a single entry in the address book.
GetInfoStore	storeID as String	Direct access to one of the Message storage objects.
GetFolder	folderID as String, storeID as String	Direct access to a single folder object in the folders collection.
GetMessage	messageID as String, storeID as String	Direct access to a single message in the Messages collection.
Logoff	(none)	End the current MAPI Session.
Logon	(opt) profileName as String, (opt) profilePassword as String, (opt) showDialog as Boolean, (opt) newSession as Boolean, (opt) parentWindow as Long	Start new MAPI Session.

The most used of these methods are the Logon and Logoff methods. You use these to start and end MAPI sessions. You will also use the AddressBook and GetInfoStore methods frequently in your programs.

Using the MAPI Logon and Logoff Methods

If you have not done so yet, load Visual Basic 4.0 and start a new project. Place a single button on the form. Set its index property to 0 and its caption to MAPI &Start. Copy and paste a second command button onto the form and set its caption property to MAPI &End. Now add the code in Listing 8.1 to the Command1_Click event of the buttons.

Listing 8.1. Adding Code to the Command1_Click event.

```
Private Sub Command1_Click(Index As Integer)
    '
    ' handle user selections
    Select Case Index
        Case 0 ' mapi start
            MAPIStart
        Case 1 ' mapi end
            MAPIEnd
    End Select
    '
End Sub
```

The code in Listing 8.1 calls two subroutines—MAPIStart and MAPIEnd. They each use a form-level variable called objSession. Add this variable to the general declarations section of the form.

```
Option Explicit
'
Dim objSession As Object ' for mapi session
```

Now create a new subroutine called MAPIStart and add the code shown in Listing 8.2. This routine initializes the session object and calls the MAPI logon dialog box.

Listing 8.2. Adding the MAPIStart routine.

```
Public Sub MAPIStart()
    '
    ' start a mapi session
    '
    On Error GoTo MAPIStartErr
    '
    Set objSession = CreateObject("MAPI.Session")
    objSession.logon
    Exit Sub
    '
MAPIStartErr:
    MsgBox Error$, vbCritical, "MAPIStartErr [" & CStr(Err) & "]"
    '
End Sub
```

It is important that you formally end each MAPI session you begin. This will ensure that you do not have any stray sessions running in the background.

By default, the MAPI Logon method will attempt to connect you to the first available active session currently running on your workstation. For example, if you have started a MAPI session with your e-mail client and you then run this sample code, MAPI will attach this program to the same MAPI session started by the MAPI client. This could give you unexpected results. That is another reason why you should always close your MAPI sessions when you are exiting your programs.

Now add a new subroutine to the project called MAPIEnd and add the code shown in Listing 8.3. Notice that this routine sets the objSession variable to Nothing. This is done to clear Visual Basic's memory storage and conserve RAM space.

Listing 8.3. Adding the MAPIEnd routine.

```
Public Sub MAPIEnd()
    '
    ' end the current session
    '
    On Error Resume Next
    '
    objSession.logoff
    Set objSession = Nothing
    '
End Sub
```

Save the form as OML.FRM and the project as OML.VBP. You can now run the project and log into and out of a MAPI session. You won't see much, but it works!

Accessing the MAPI Address Book

You will often need to give your users access to the MAPI Address Book. This is achieved with the AddressBook method of the Session object. Access to the address book gives users the ability to look up names in the address book; add, edit, and delete names from the book; and select one or more addresses as recipients of a message.

Add another command button to the array (Edit | Copy, Edit | Paste) and modify the Command1_Click event to match the code in Listing 8.4. This will call up the MAPI address book.

Listing 8.4. Modifying the Command1_Click event to call the address book.

```
Private Sub Command1_Click(Index As Integer)
    ' handle user selections
```

continues

Listing 8.4. continued

```
    Select Case Index
        Case 0 ' mapi start
            MAPIStart
        Case 1 ' mapi end
            MAPIEnd
        Case 2 ' call address book
            MAPIAddrBook
    End Select
    '
End Sub
```

Now add the MAPIAddrBook routine to the form and enter the code in Listing 8.5.

Listing 8.5. Adding the MAPIAddrBook routine.

```
Public Sub MAPIAddrBook()
    '
    ' call the address book
    '
    On Error Resume Next
    '
    objSession.AddressBook
    '
End Sub
```

Save and run the project. After clicking the MAPI Start button, press the Address Book button. Your screen should look like the one in Figure 8.1.

FIGURE 8.1.

Displaying the address book.

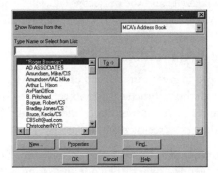

You can set several parameters when you call the Address Book method. For example, you can set the title of the address book using the Title property. You can also control the number and caption of the recipient selection buttons that appear on the address book. You can even set the address book dialog so that the user can review the addresses but cannot select one.

Listing 8.6 shows you how to modify the code in the MAPIAddrBook routine to set the title and remove all recipient selection buttons.

Listing 8.6. Controlling the appearance of the MAPI address book.

```
Public Sub MAPIAddrBook()
    '
    ' call the address book
    '
    On Error Resume Next
    '
    objSession.AddressBook recipLists:=0, Title:="For Viewing Only"
    '
End Sub
```

When you run the project, your address book will look something like the one in Figure 8.2.

FIGURE 8.2.

Modified Address Book dialog box.

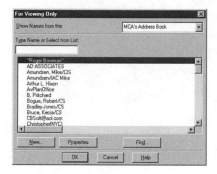

Automating the Session Logon

You can also control the Logon method behavior by passing selected parameters. The most common use for this is automatically logging a user into MAPI without the use of the Logon dialog box. To do this you need to pass the user profile and password and set the ShowDialog flag to false.

Listing 8.7 shows you how to modify the MAPIStart routine to perform an automatic logon. You should change the ProfileName parameter to match your personal Microsoft Exchange logon.

Listing 8.8. Creating an automatic MAPI session logon.

```
Public Sub MAPIStart()
    '
    ' start a mapi session
    '
    On Error GoTo MAPIStartErr
    '
    Set objSession = CreateObject("MAPI.Session")
    objSession.logon ProfileName:="MCA", ShowDialog:=False
    Exit Sub
```

continues

Listing 8.8. continued

```
MAPIStartErr:
    MsgBox Error$, vbCritical, "MAPIStartErr [" & CStr(Err) & "]"

End Sub
```

The Session **Object Properties**

Now let's look at some of the Session object properties. After reviewing the properties, you can add another button to the form to display the properties of your MAPI session. Table 8.2 has a list of the Session object properties, their type, and a short description.

Table 8.2. Session object properties.

Properties	Type	Description
Application	String	Name of the library. Always set to OLE/ Messaging.
Class	Long	Internal identifying code for all MAPI objects. Always set to 0 for Session objects.
CurrentUser	AddressEntry object	Address object of current user (see "Address Objects" later in this chapter).
Inbox	Folder object	Folder object where all new unread messages are placed (see "Folder Objects" later in this chapter).
InfoStores	InfoStores object	InfoStores object collection for this session (see "InfoStore Objects" later in this chapter).
Name	String	Session name. Always set to the current profile name on Microsoft Exchange system.
OperatingSystem	String	Name of operating system in use.
Outbox	Folder object	Folder object where all outgoing messages are placed (see "Folder Objects" later in this chapter).
Version	String	Version number of OLE Messaging library. Current version is 1.00.

The Session object has several properties, many of them objects themselves. Using these object properties allows you to gain access to more complex data than standard strings or numbers. You'll inspect the object properties later in the chapter.

Now add another button to the control array (use Edit ǀ Copy, Edit ǀ Paste), set its Caption to "MapiProps" and modify the code in the Command1_Click event to look like the code in Listing 8.9.

Listing 8.9. Updated Command1_Click event.

```
Private Sub Command1_Click(Index As Integer)
    '
    ' handle user selections
    Select Case Index
        Case 0 ' mapi start
            MAPIStart
        Case 1 ' mapi end
            MAPIEnd
        Case 2 ' call address book
            MAPIAddrBook
        Case 3 ' session properties
            SessionProps
    End Select
    '
End Sub
```

Now create a new subroutine called SessionProps and enter the code that appears in Listing 8.10. This routine creates a message box that displays several of the Session object's properties.

Listing 8.10. Adding the SessionProps code.

```
Public Sub SessionProps()
    '
    ' get basic session properties
    '
    On Error GoTo SessionPropsErr
    '
    Dim cMsg As String
    '
    cMsg = "Application: " & objSession.Application & Chr(13)
    cMsg = cMsg & "Operating System: " & objSession.OperatingSystem & Chr(13)
    cMsg = cMsg & "Session Name: " & objSession.Name & Chr(13)
    cMsg = cMsg & "Version: " & objSession.Version & Chr(13)
    cMsg = cMsg & "Object Class: " & CStr(objSession.Class)
    '
    MsgBox cMsg
    '
    Exit Sub
    '
SessionPropsErr:
    MsgBox Error$, vbCritical, "SessionPropsErr [" & CStr(Err) & "]"
    '
End Sub
```

Save the project again and run it. After clicking on the MAPI Start button, click on the MapiProps button. Your screen should look like the one in Figure 8.3.

FIGURE 8.3.
Displaying the Session
properties.

Now it's time to start inspecting the subordinate objects in the OLE Messaging library.

The InfoStore Objects and Collections

The first-level subordinate object of the Session object is the InfoStore object. Each InfoStore object represents a separate message store. The MAPI model allows clients to access more than one message storage system at the same time. For example, the Microsoft Exchange shared folders are a separate message store (represented by a separate InfoStore object). The Microsoft Exchange Personal Folders are another separate message store. Users can have any number of message stores connected to their MAPI client.

The InfoStores collection object is an OLE Messaging library object that allows you to view all the connected message stores for the logged-in user. You can use the InfoStores object to locate a particular message store and then access that message store using the InfoStore object.

> **NOTE**
>
> Be sure not to confuse the InfoStore object with the InfoStores object. The InfoStore object is the OLE Messaging library object that you use to gain access to the contents of a single message store. The InfoStores object is the OLE Messaging library object you use to gain access to the *collection* of message stores. In Microsoft OLE naming rules, collection objects are plural (InfoStores) and single objects are not (InfoStore).

The InfoStores Collection

The InfoStores collection has only a few properties and no methods at all. You cannot add, modify, or delete InfoStore objects using the OLE Messaging library interface. Table 8.3 shows the InfoStores properties with their type and a short description.

Table 8.3. The InfoStores collection object properties.

Property name	Type	Description
Application	String	Name of the library. Always set to OLE/Messaging.
Class	Long	Internal identifying code for all MAPI objects. Always set to 17 for InfoStores objects.
Count	Long	The total number of InfoStore objects in the collection. The count starts at 1.
Item	InfoStore object	Allows access to one of the member InfoStore objects. The Item property accepts an Index value between 1 and the value of Count.

To test the InfoStores object, add another button to the control array on the form with the caption of InfoStoreColl and modify the Command1_Click event as shown in Listing 8.11.

Listing 8.11. Updated Command1_Click event.

```
Private Sub Command1_Click(Index As Integer)
    '
    ' handle user selections
    '
    Select Case Index
        Case 0 ' mapi start
            MAPIStart
        Case 1 ' mapi end
            MAPIEnd
        Case 2 ' call address book
            MAPIAddrBook
        Case 3 ' session properties
            SessionProps
        Case 4 ' show infostores collection
            SessionInfoStoreColl
    End Select
    '
End Sub
```

Next you'll need to add two new form-level variables to the general declaration section of the form. Your general declaration section should now look like this:

```
Option Explicit
'
Dim objSession As Object ' for mapi session
Dim objInfoStoreColl As Object ' collection of stores
Dim objInfoStore As Object ' single info store
```

Now add the SessionInfoStoreColl routine shown in Listing 8.12. This routine gets the InfoStores properties and displays the names of all the message stores in the collection.

Listing 8.12. Adding the `SessionInfoStoreColl` routine.

```
Public Sub SessionInfoStoreColl()
    '
    ' show list of available infostores
    '
    Dim cMsg As String
    Dim nCount As Integer
    Dim x As Integer
    Dim cStoresList As String
    '
    Set objInfoStoreColl = objSession.InfoStores
    cMsg = "Application: " & objInfoStoreColl.Application & Chr(13)
    cMsg = cMsg & "Class: " & CStr(objInfoStoreColl.Class) & Chr(13)
    cMsg = cMsg & "Count: " & CStr(objInfoStoreColl.Count) & Chr(13)
    '
    nCount = objSession.InfoStores.Count
    cStoresList = "List:" & Chr(13)
    For x = 1 To nCount
        cStoresList = cStoresList & "  " & objSession.InfoStores.Item(x).Name
        cStoresList = cStoresList & Chr(13)
    Next x
    '
    MsgBox cMsg & Chr(13) & cStoresList, vbInformation, "InfoStores Collection
    ➥Object"
    '
End Sub
```

> **WARNING**
>
> The OLE Messaging library does not require message stores to have unique names. If you are using the `InfoStores` collection object to locate a particular message store, you must be sure that there is not more than one store with that name in the collection! `InfoStore` objects are assigned a unique unchanging ID value. Once you know the ID value of an `InfoStore` object, you can locate it using the `GetInfoStore` method of the `Session` object.

Save and run this project. After logging in, press the `InfoStoreColl` button. Your screen should look similar to the one in Figure 8.4.

FIGURE 8.4.

Viewing the `InfoStores`
object properties.

Now that you know how to review the `InfoStore` collection, it's time to learn more about the individual `InfoStore` objects.

The `InfoStore` Object

The `InfoStore` object contains all the folders and messages defined for a single message store. `InfoStore` objects have several properties and no methods. You cannot use the OLE Messaging library to add, modify, or delete `InfoStore` objects. Table 8.4 shows the important `InfoStore` object properties, their types, and their descriptions.

Table 8.4. The `InfoStore` object properties.

Property name	Type	Description
Application	String	Name of the library. Always set to OLE/Messaging.
Class	Long	Internal identifying code for all MAPI objects. Always set to 1 for InfoStore objects.
ID	String	A unique value that never changes. It is assigned by MAPI when the store is created.
Index	Long	The count position of the InfoStore in the InfoStores collection. This can be used with the Item property of the InfoStores object.
Name	String	The display name of the message store.
ProviderName	String	The name of the message store vendor or programmer.
RootFolder	Folder object	The starting folder of the message store.

Now add some code to view the properties of an `InfoStore` object. First, add another command button to the control array and set its caption to `InfoStore`. Then modify the `Command1_Click` routine so that it matches the one in Listing 8.13.

Listing 8.13. Updated `Command1_Click` event.

```
Private Sub Command1_Click(Index As Integer)
    '
    ' handle user selections
    '
    Select Case Index
        Case 0 ' mapi start
            MAPIStart
        Case 1 ' mapi end
            MAPIEnd
        Case 2 ' call address book
            MAPIAddrBook
        Case 3 ' session properties
            SessionProps
```

continues

Listing 8.13. continued

```
    Case 4 ' show infostores collection
        SessionInfoStoreColl
    Case 5 ' show infostore properties
        InfoStoreProps
End Select
'
End Sub
```

Now add the `InfoStoreProps` subroutine and enter the code shown in Listing 8.14.

Listing 8.14. Adding the `InfoStoreProps` routine.

```
Public Sub InfoStoreProps()
    '
    ' show the infostore object properties
    '
    Dim cMsg As String
    '
    Set objInfoStoreColl = objSession.InfoStores
    For Each objInfoStore In objInfoStoreColl
        cMsg = "Application: " & objInfoStore.Application & Chr(13)
        cMsg = cMsg & "Class: " & CStr(objInfoStore.Class) & Chr(13)
        cMsg = cMsg & "ID: " & objInfoStore.ID & Chr(13)
        cMsg = cMsg & "Name: " & objInfoStore.Name & Chr(13)
        cMsg = cMsg & "ProviderName: " & objInfoStore.ProviderName & Chr(13)
        cMsg = cMsg & "RootFolder: " & objInfoStore.RootFolder.Name
        '
        MsgBox cMsg, vbInformation, "InfoStore Object Properties"
    Next
    '
End Sub
```

Note that the `InfoStore` object is part of what is called a *small collection*. OLE object collections that are considered to have a limited number of members are called *small collections*. All small collection objects have an `Index` property and a `Count` property. Most of them also have an `Item` property. Small collection objects support the use of the `For Each...Next` programming construct.

Save and run the project. After clicking the `InfoStore` button, you should see a series of dialog boxes showing the properties of each message store available to your client (see Figure 8.5).

FIGURE 8.5.

Viewing the InfoStore *properties.*

The next object to review is the `Folder` object and the `Folders` collection object.

The `Folder` Objects and Collections

One of the first level objects below the `InfoStore` object is the `Folder` object. The `Folder` object can hold messages and other folders. Each `InfoStore` object also has a `Folders` collection object that contains a list of all the `Folder` objects in the message store.

There is no limit to the number of messages or folders a `Folder` object can have. For this reason it is called a `large collection` object. `large collection` objects do not have an `Index` property or a `Count` property. The only way you can locate all the folders in a message store is to "walk through" the store using a set of methods to get each item. All `large collection` objects support the use of the `GetFirst`, `GetNext`, `GetPrevious`, and `GetLast` methods to provide a way to navigate through the collection. You'll use these methods in the next few examples.

The `Folders` Collection Object

The `Folders` collection object has only a few properties and methods. Table 8.5 shows the important `Folders` collection object properties and Table 8.6 shows the `Folders` collection object methods.

Table 8.5. The `Folders` collection object properties.

Property name	Type	Description
Application	String	Name of the library. Always set to `OLE/Messaging`.
Class	Long	Internal identifying code for all MAPI objects. Always set to `18` for `Folders` objects.

Table 8.6. The `Folders` collection object methods.

Method name	Parameters	Description
GetFirst	(none)	Points to the first `Folder` object in the collection.
GetLast	(none)	Points to the last `Folder` object in the collection.
GetNext	(none)	Points to the next `Folder` object in the collection.
GetPrevious	(none)	Points to the previous `Folder` object in the collection.

To test the `Folders` object, add two new variables to the general declaration area of the form. Your form-level variable list should now look like this:

```
Option Explicit
'
Dim objSession As Object ' for mapi session
Dim objInfoStoreColl As Object ' collection of stores
Dim objInfoStore As Object ' single info store
Dim objFolderColl As Object ' collection of folders
Dim objFolder As Object ' single folder
```

Now add another command button to the control array and set its Caption property to FolderColl. Then modify the Command1_Click event so that it matches the code in Listing 8.15.

Listing 8.15. Updated Command1_Click event.

```
Private Sub Command1_Click(Index As Integer)
    '
    ' handle user selections
    '
    Select Case Index
        Case 0 ' mapi start
            MAPIStart
        Case 1 ' mapi end
            MAPIEnd
        Case 2 ' call address book
            MAPIAddrBook
        Case 3 ' session properties
            SessionProps
        Case 4 ' show infostores collection
            SessionInfoStoreColl
        Case 5 ' show infostore properties
            InfoStoreProps
        Case 6 ' folders collection
            FoldersColl
    End Select
    '
End Sub
```

Now add the new subroutine called FoldersColl and enter the code from Listing 8.16.

Listing 8.16. Adding the FoldersColl routine.

```
Public Sub FoldersColl()
    '
    ' show the folders collection
    '
    Dim cMsg As String
    '
    Set objFolderColl = objSession.InfoStores.Item(1).RootFolder.Folders
    '
    cMsg = "Application: " & objFolderColl.Application & Chr(13)
    cMsg = cMsg & "Class: " & CStr(objFolderColl.Class) & Chr(13)
    '
    cMsg = cMsg & Chr(13) & "Folders:" & Chr(13)
    Set objFolder = objFolderColl.GetFirst
    Do Until objFolder Is Nothing
        cMsg = cMsg & objFolder.Name & Chr(13)
        Set objFolder = objFolderColl.GetNext
```

```
    Loop
    '
    MsgBox cMsg, vbInformation, "Folders Collection Object"
    '
End Sub
```

The `FoldersColl` routine shows the application and class property of the object and then lists all the folder names in the collection. Note that you cannot determine the folder hierarchy from the list returned by the `Get` methods. The `Get` methods traverse the folder collection in the order the folders were created, not in the order they are displayed or arranged within the MAPI client.

Save and run the program. Clicking the `FoldersColl` button should give you a display similar to the one in Figure 8.6.

FIGURE 8.6.

Viewing the Folders *collection object properties.*

The Folder Object

The `Folder` object has several properties and one method. The OLE Messaging library allows you to modify the `Name` property of a `Folder` object, but you cannot add or delete a `Folder` object from the message store. Table 8.7 contains the list of important `Folder` object properties.

Table 8.7. The Folder object properties.

Property name	Type	Description
Application	String	Name of the library. Always set to OLE/ Messaging.
Class	Long	Internal identifying code for all MAPI objects. Always set to 2 for Folder objects.

continues

Table 8.7. continued

Property name	Type	Description
Fields	Fields collection object	A collection of user-defined fields added to the folder object.
FolderID	String	A unique and permanent value that identifies the Folder object in the message store. This value is set by MAPI when the folder is created.
Folders	Folders collection object	A collection of subfolders that are members of this folder object.
ID	String	The same as the FolderID property.
Messages	Messages collection object	A collection of messages that are members of this Folder object.
Name	String	Display name of the folder. This name does not have to be unique and can be modified through the OLE Messaging library using the Update method of the Folder object.
StoreID	String	A unique and permanent value that is the same as the ID value of the InfoStore object in which this folder resides.

Add a new button to the command array and set its Caption property to Fo&lder Object. Then modify the Command1_Click event to match the one in Listing 8.17.

Listing 8.17. Updated Command1_Click event.

```
Private Sub Command1_Click(Index As Integer)
    '
    ' handle user selections
    '
    Select Case Index
        Case 0 ' mapi start
            MAPIStart
        Case 1 ' mapi end
            MAPIEnd
        Case 2 ' call address book
            MAPIAddrBook
        Case 3 ' session properties
            SessionProps
        Case 4 ' show infostores collection
            SessionInfoStoreColl
        Case 5 ' show infostore properties
            InfoStoreProps
```

```
        Case 6 ' folders collection
            FoldersColl
        Case 7 ' folder object
            FolderProps
    End Select
    '
End Sub
```

Now create a new subroutine called `FolderProps` and add the code shown in Listing 8.18.

Listing 8.18. Adding the `FolderProps` routine.

```
Public Sub FolderProps()
    '
    ' inspect the folder object properties
    '
    Dim cMsg As String
    '
    Set objFolder = objSession.InfoStores.Item(1).RootFolder
    '
    cMsg = "Application: " & objFolder.Application & Chr(13)
    cMsg = cMsg & "Class: " & CStr(objFolder.Class) & Chr(13)
    cMsg = cMsg & "FolderID: " & objFolder.folderID & Chr(13)
    cMsg = cMsg & "ID: " & objFolder.ID & Chr(13)
    cMsg = cMsg & "Name: " & objFolder.Name & Chr(13)
    cMsg = cMsg & "StoreID: " & objFolder.storeID
    '
    MsgBox cMsg, vbInformation, "Folder Object Properties"
    '
End Sub
```

Save and run the project. Then click the `Folder Object` button and compare your results with those shown in Figure 8.7.

FIGURE 8.7.
Viewing the Folder *object properties.*

The only method available for `Folder` objects is the `Update` method. You can use this method to save changes made to the `Folder` object properties. The only property you can modify is the `Name` property. If you wish to change the name of an existing folder you can use the following line of code:

```
objFolder.Name = "New Name" ' modify name
objFolder.Update ' save changes
```

> **NOTE**
>
> The MAPI system will not let you modify the name of the Inbox, Outbox, Sent Items, or Deleted Items folders. Attempting to do this will cause MAPI to return an error to your program.

The Inbox and OutBox Folders

There are two folders that are used for almost every MAPI message transaction:

■ The InBox, where new messages are received;

■ The OutBox, where composed messages are placed when they are to be sent out.

Because these two folders are used so often, the OLE Messaging library has defined them as a property of the InfoStore object. This means you can access the InBox and OutBox folders directly from the InfoStore object.

> **NOTE**
>
> The InfoStore object was discussed in the earlier section of this chapter titled "The InfoStore Objects and Collections."

You can modify the FolderProp routine to access the properties of the Inbox by changing the line that sets the objFolder object.

```
'Set objFolder = objSession.InfoStores.Item(1).RootFolder
Set objFolder = objSession.Inbox
'
```

Now when you click the Folder Object button, you'll get data on the Inbox folder in message store #1. This works the same way for the Outbox.

The Message Objects and Collections

The Message object and Messages collection object are the heart of the OLE Messaging library. These objects hold the actual messages composed and received by the MAPI client. You will use the Message objects to read, modify, create, and delete messages from the message store.

The Messages Collection Object

The Messages collection object has very few properties and a number of methods. Because the Message collection is a large collection (that is, it has an unlimited number of members), you must use the GetFirst, GetNext, GetPrevious, and GetLast methods to retrieve messages from the collection. You can also add and delete messages within the collection.

Table 8.8 shows the properties for the Messages collection object.

Table 8.8. The Messages collection object properties.

Property name	Type	Description
Application	String	Name of the library. Always set to OLE/Messaging.
Class	Long	Internal identifying code for all MAPI objects. Always set to 19 for Messages objects.

Table 8.9 shows the list of methods for the Messages collection object.

Table 8.9. The Messages collection object methods.

Method name	Parameters	Description
Add	(optional) subject as String, (optional) text as String, (optional) type as String, (optional) importance as Long	Adds a new, null, message to the collection.
Delete	(none)	Deletes *all* messages from the collection.
GetFirst	(optional) filter as Variant	Returns the first message in the collection. The filter value allows you to collect only messages with a specified Type value.
GetLast	(optional) filter as Variant	Returns the last message in the collection. The filter value allows you to collect only messages with a specified Type value.
GetNext	(none)	Returns the next message in the collection.
GetPrevious	(none)	Returns the previous message in the collection.
Sort	sortOrder as Long	Sorts the message collection based on the following values: None = 0, Ascending = 1 Descending = 2

To test the Messages collection object, you first need to add two new variables to the general declaration area of the form. Make sure your variables match the ones in Listing 8.19.

Listing 8.19. Declaring the form-level variables.

```
Option Explicit
'
Dim objSession As Object ' for mapi session
Dim objInfoStoreColl As Object ' collection of stores
Dim objInfoStore As Object ' single info store
Dim objFolderColl As Object ' collection of folders
Dim objFolder As Object ' single folder
Dim objMessageColl As Object ' messages collection
Dim objMessage As Object ' single message
```

Next add a new button to the control array and set its caption to M&essageColl. Then modify the Command1_Click event to match the code shown in Listing 8.20.

Listing 8.20. The updated Command1_Click event.

```
Private Sub Command1_Click(Index As Integer)
    '
    ' handle user selections
    '
    Select Case Index
        Case 0 ' mapi start
            MAPIStart
        Case 1 ' mapi end
            MAPIEnd
        Case 2 ' call address book
            MAPIAddrBook
        Case 3 ' session properties
            SessionProps
        Case 4 ' show infostores collection
            SessionInfoStoreColl
        Case 5 ' show infostore properties
            InfoStoreProps
        Case 6 ' folders collection
            FoldersColl
        Case 7 ' folder object
            FolderProps
        Case 8 ' messsage collection
            MessagesColl
    End Select
    '
End Sub
```

Then add the new MessagesColl subroutine to the project and enter the code from Listing 8.22.

Listing 8.22. Adding the MessagesColl routine.

```
Public Sub MessagesColl()
    '
    ' inspect the messages collection
    '
    Dim cMsg As String
    Dim nCount As Integer
    '
    Set objMessageColl = objSession.Inbox.Messages ' get inbox messages
    '
    cMsg = "Application: " & objMessageColl.Application & Chr(13)
    cMsg = cMsg & "Class: " & CStr(objMessageColl.Class) & Chr(13)
    '
    cMsg = cMsg & Chr(13) & "Inbox Messages:" & Chr(13)
    Set objMessage = objMessageColl.GetFirst
    Do Until objMessage Is Nothing
        nCount = nCount + 1
        cMsg = cMsg & CStr(nCount) & " - " & objMessage.subject & Chr(13)
        Set objMessage = objMessageColl.GetNext
    Loop
    '
    MsgBox cMsg, vbInformation, "Messages Collection Object"
End Sub
```

The MessagesColl routine reads the Application and Class properties of the object and then uses the Get methods to build a list of messages currently in the message store inbox.

Save and run the project. Your screen should look similar to the one in Figure 8.8.

FIGURE 8.8.

Viewing the Messages *collection object properties.*

You can sort the messages in the collection using the Sort method. Setting the sort order affects how the Get methods access the messages in the collection. The sort order is based on the TimeReceived property of the messages. The sort method can be set for None(0), Ascending(1), or Descending(2). The default SortOrder is None(0). If there is no sort order specified, the Get methods access the messages in the order in which they were added to the message collection.

TIP

Because the sort order affects the way in which the Get methods access the file, setting the SortOrder to Ascending(1) and performing the GetFirst method on the messages collection will return the same message as setting the SortOrder to Descending(2) and performing the GetLast method on the messages collection.

Modify the `MessageColl` routine to ask you for a sort order. Add the lines of code to the routine as indicated in Listing 8.23.

Listing 8.23. Adding the `SortOrder` lines to the `MessageColl` routine.

```
cMsg = cMsg & "Class: " & CStr(objMessageColl.Class) & Chr(13)
' *** add these lines to the routine ***************
nCount = InputBox("Enter Sort Order (0=None, 1=Ascending, 2=Descending):",
➥"Message Collection Sort")
objMessageColl.Sort nCount
cMsg = cMsg & "Sort Order: " & CStr(nCount) & Chr(13)
nCount = 0 ' clear value
' *** end of added lines ***************************
cMsg = cMsg & Chr(13) & "Inbox Messages:" & Chr(13)
```

Now when you press the `MessageColl` button you'll be asked to supply a sort order and then be presented with a different view of the message collection list.

You can delete all the messages in a message collection by invoking the `Delete` method followed by the `Update` method on the parent object to save the change. The code below shows how this is done.

```
Set objMessageColl = objSession.Inbox.Messages ' get inbox messages
   objMessageColl.Delete ' dump all messages in the inbox
objSession.Inbox.Update ' make the modification permanent
```

You'll learn about the `Add` method in the section on the `Message` object.

The `Message` Object

The `Message` object is the richest object in the OLE Messaging library system. It has only a few methods, but they are all quite powerful. They allow you to delete the message from the collection (`Delete`), display a message option dialog box (`Options`), display a send dialog box (`Send`), and save the modified message properties (`Update`). These properties range from handling attachments to flagging a message as read or unread. Table 8.10 shows the `Message` object methods with their parameters and a short description.

Table 8.10. The `Message` object methods.

Method name	Parameters	Description
Delete	(none)	Removes a message from the collection. This is a non-recoverable delete.
Options	(optional) parentWindow as Long	Displays a dialog box that allows users to modify message properties. Not all properties may appear on the dialog box.

Method name	Parameters	Description
Send	(optional) `saveCopy` as Boolean, (optional) `showDialog` as Boolean, (optional) `parentWindow` as Long	Sends the message to the recipient(s). Optionally displays a dialog box for the composition and ending of the message.
Update	(none)	Saves all changes to message properties. Any modifications to properties are not permanent until the `Update` method is invoked.

The `Message` object properties are extensive and powerful. The properties range from simple Boolean flags to indicate the importance of a message, to the actual text body of the message, to the list of binary attachments to the message. Table 8.11 shows the important Message object properties, their type, and a short description.

Table 8.11. The `Message` object properties.

Property name	Type	Description
Application	String	Name of the library. Always set to `OLE/Messaging`.
Attachments	`Attachments` collection object	The collection of binary attachments to the message.
Class	Long	Internal identifying code for all MAPI objects. Always set to `3` for `Message` objects.
ConversationIndex	String	This is a value that shows the order of the message within the conversation topic. Microsoft Exchange uses an eight-byte value that expresses the time stamp of the message.

continues

Table 8.11. continued

Property name	Type	Description
ConversationTopic	String	An identifying string. All messages with the same ConversationTopic value can be grouped together to show relationships. The Windows Messaging client supports the ConversationTopic property in its Folder Views options.
DeliveryReceipt	Boolean	A flag that indicates the sender wants to receive notification when the message is delivered to the recipient. The default value is False.
Encrypted	Boolean	A flag to indicate the message has been encrypted. The support of encrypted messages is dependent on the message store. MAPI does not perform message encryption.
Fields	Fields collection object	A collection of custom, user-defined fields added to the message. You can add any number of fields to your messages.
FolderID	String	The unique MAPI-assigned value that identifies the folder in which this message resides.
ID	String	The unique MAPI-assigned value that identifies this message in the message store. This value is assigned when the message is first created and cannot be changed.

Property name	Type	Description
Importance	Long	A flag to indicate the relative importance of this message. Microsoft Exchange supports the following values for this property: `Low(0)` `Normal(1)`—the default `High(2)`
ReadReceipt	Boolean	Flag to indicate that the sender wants to be notified when the recipient reads (opens) the message.
Recipients	Recipients object	A collection of recipient objects. Each recipient object represents one e-mail address to which this message has been sent. A message can have any number of recipients. These recipients do not have to be found in the MAPI address book.
Sender	AddressEntry object	The AddressEntry object of the user that sent this message. This points to an entry in the Microsoft Exchange address book.
Sent	Boolean	A flag that indicates that the message has been sent to the recipient(s). When sending a message, this flag is set by MAPI. However, under some cases the programmer can set this value as part of an Update operation on messages sent to shared folders or saved in the message store in some other way.

continues

Table 8.11. continued

Property name	Type	Description
Signed	Boolean	A flag indicating that the message has been marked with a digital signature. Message signing is not supplied by MAPI, but is provided by the message store.
Size	Long	The approximate size of the message (in bytes).
StoreID	String	The unique MAPI-assigned value that indicates the message store to which this message belongs.
Subject	String	The subject line of the message.
Submitted	Boolean	A flag that indicates this message has been submitted for viewing. This property is related to (but not the same as) the Sent property. The submitted property must be set to True for messages sent to shared folders in order for some clients to be able to see them.
Text	String	The actual body of the message.
TimeReceived	Variant (Date/Time)	The date and time the message was received.
TimeSent	Variant (Date/Time)	The date and time the message was sent. These values must be set by the programmer for messages placed in public folders.
Type	String	Microsoft message type in the form "XXX.?" There are two main message types:

Property name	Type	Description
		IPM—Interpersonal messages. These are recognized by the MAPI client and displayed in the Inbox when received.
		IPC—Interprocess communications. These are not recognized by the MAPI client, but can be processed behind the scenes.
Unread	Boolean	Flag indicating whether the message has been read.

Now add another button to the control array and set its caption to MessageProps. Then modify the Command1_Click event as shown in Listing 8.24.

Listing 8.24. Modifying the Command1_Click event.

```
Private Sub Command1_Click(Index As Integer)
    '
    ' handle user selections
    '
    Select Case Index
        Case 0 ' mapi start
            MAPIStart
        Case 1 ' mapi end
            MAPIEnd
        Case 2 ' call address book
            MAPIAddrBook
        Case 3 ' session properties
            SessionProps
        Case 4 ' show infostores collection
            SessionInfoStoreColl
        Case 5 ' show infostore properties
            InfoStoreProps
        Case 6 ' folders collection
            FoldersColl
        Case 7 ' folder object
            FolderProps
        Case 8 ' messsage collection
            MessagesColl
        Case 9 ' message properties
            MessageProps
    End Select
    '
End Sub
```

Next add a new subroutine called MessageProps to the form and enter the code from Listing 8.25.

Listing 8.25. Adding the MessageProps routine.

```
Public Sub MessageProps()
    '
    ' display message properties
    '
    Dim cMsg As String
    '
    ' get the inbox message collection
    Set objMessageColl = objSession.Inbox.Messages
    ' get the first message in the inbox
    Set objMessage = objMessageColl.GetFirst
    '
    On Error Resume Next ' when property is missing
    '
    cMsg = "Application: " & objMessage.Application & Chr(13)
    cMsg = cMsg & "Class: " & objMessage.Class & Chr(13)
    cMsg = cMsg & "ConversationIndex: " & objMessage.ConversationIndex & Chr(13)
    cMsg = cMsg & "ConversationTopic: " & objMessage.conversationtopic & Chr(13)
    cMsg = cMsg & "DeliveryReceipt: " & objMessage.DeliveryReceipt & Chr(13)
    cMsg = cMsg & "Encrypted: " & objMessage.Encrypted & Chr(13)
    cMsg = cMsg & "FolderID: " & objMessage.folderID & Chr(13)
    cMsg = cMsg & "ID: " & objMessage.ID & Chr(13)
    cMsg = cMsg & "Importance: " & CStr(objMessage.importance) & Chr(13)
    cMsg = cMsg & "ReadReceipt: " & objMessage.ReadReceipt & Chr(13)
    cMsg = cMsg & "Sent: " & objMessage.Sent & Chr(13)
    cMsg = cMsg & "Signed: " & objMessage.Signed & Chr(13)
    cMsg = cMsg & "Size: " & CStr(objMessage.Size) & Chr(13)
    cMsg = cMsg & "StoreID: " & objMessage.storeID & Chr(13)
    cMsg = cMsg & "Subject: " & objMessage.subject & Chr(13)
    cMsg = cMsg & "Submitted: " & objMessage.Submitted & Chr(13)
'   cMsg = cMsg & "Text: " & objMessage.Text & Chr(13)
    cMsg = cMsg & "TimeReceived: " & Format(objMessage.TimeReceived, "general
►date") & Chr(13)
    cMsg = cMsg & "TimeSent: " & Format(objMessage.TimeSent, "general date") &
►Chr(13)
    cMsg = cMsg & "Type: " & objMessage.Type & Chr(13)
    cMsg = cMsg & "Unread: " & objMessage.Unread
    '
    MsgBox cMsg, vbInformation, "Message Object Properties"
    '
End Sub
```

The MessageProps routine first selects the session's Inbox message collection and then selects the first message in the collection.

> **WARNING**
>
> This routine crashes with an error if no message is present in the Inbox. If you do not currently have at least one message in the Inbox, fire up an e-mail client and place one there before running this routine. In production applications, you should make sure you trap for such an error to prevent needless (and annoying) crashes.

Notice the addition of the On Error Resume Next just before the series of statements that retrieve the message properties. This is done in case one or more properties are missing in the selected message. Since MAPI supports messages from several different providers, it is quite likely that some of the properties will contain garbage or nothing at all. You should keep this in mind when writing routines that read Message object properties.

Save and run the project. After starting MAPI and pressing the MessageProps button, you'll see something like the data shown in Figure 8.9. Of course, the actual values of the properties will vary depending on the message you are reading.

FIGURE 8.9.

Viewing the Message *object properties.*

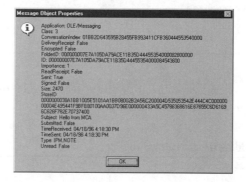

Adding a New Message

It's easy to add new messages to the message collection. The simplest method is to use the Send method of the Message object to invoke the MAPI Send dialog box. From this dialog box, the user can compose, address, and send the message without any additional coding.

Add a new button to the control array and set its caption property to MessageAdd. Then update the Command1_Click event so that it matches the one in Listing 8.26.

Listing 8.26. Updating the Command1_Click event.

```
Private Sub Command1_Click(Index As Integer)
'
' handle user selections
'
```

continues

Listing 8.26. continued

```
    Select Case Index
        Case 0 ' mapi start
            MAPIStart
        Case 1 ' mapi end
            MAPIEnd
        Case 2 ' call address book
           MAPIAddrBook
        Case 3 ' session properties
            SessionProps
        Case 4 ' show infostores collection
            SessionInfoStoreColl
        Case 5 ' show infostore properties
            InfoStoreProps
        Case 6 ' folders collection
            FoldersColl
        Case 7 ' folder object
            FolderProps
        Case 8 ' messsage collection
            MessagesColl
        Case 9 ' message properties
            MessageProps
        Case 10 ' add a message w/ dialogs
            MessageAdd
    End Select
    '
End Sub
```

Now add the MessageAdd subroutine and enter the code from Listing 8.27. This will create a new Message object in the message collection and then bring up the MAPI Send dialog box.

Listing 8.27. Adding the MessageAdd routine.

```
Public Sub MessageAdd()
    '
    ' add a message w/ dialog
    '
    On Error Resume Next ' skip errors
    '
    Set objMessageColl = objSession.Outbox.Messages
    Set objMessage = objMessageColl.Add
    objMessage.Send showdialog:=True
    '
End Sub
```

You can also build the message using Visual Basic code and then call the Send method to address and ship the message. Listing 8.28 shows a new routine MessageMake that codes this.

Listing 8.28. Adding the `MessageMake` routine.

```
Public Sub MessageMake()
    '
    ' make a message from code
    ' then show send dialog
    '
    On Error Resume Next
    '
    Set objMessageColl = objSession.Outbox.Messages
    Set objMessage = objMessageColl.Add ' add a new message
    objMessage.subject = "Creating a Message in Code"
    objMessage.Text = "This message was written with VB code."
    objMessage.Update ' save the message properties
    objMessage.Send showdialog:=True ' show dialog
    '
End Sub
```

After adding this routine, add a new button to the array and set its caption property to
`MessageMake`. Also add another line to the `Select Case` structure to handle the button selection
(see Listing 8.29).

Listing 8.29. Updating the `Command1_Click` event.

```
Private Sub Command1_Click(Index As Integer)
    '
    ' handle user selections
    '
    Select Case Index
        Case 0 ' mapi start
            MAPIStart
        Case 1 ' mapi end
            MAPIEnd
        Case 2 ' call address book
            MAPIAddrBook
        Case 3 ' session properties
            SessionProps
        Case 4 ' show infostores collection
            SessionInfoStoreColl
        Case 5 ' show infostore properties
            InfoStoreProps
        Case 6 ' folders collection
            FoldersColl
        Case 7 ' folder object
            FolderProps
        Case 8 ' messsage collection
            MessagesColl
        Case 9 ' message properties
            MessageProps
        Case 10 ' add a message w/ dialogs
            MessageAdd
        Case 11 ' make a message in code
            MessageMake
    End Select
    '
End Sub
```

You can also set several message options by calling the `Options` method to bring up the Options dialog box. Modify the code in the `MessageMake` routine to call the `Options` method before the `Send` method. Insert the line shown below into the code just *before* the `objMessage.Send` line.

```
objMessage.Options ' call options dialog
```

When you save and run the project, press the `MessageMake` button. You'll see the Options dialog box before you see the Send dialog box. The exact layout and contents of the Options dialog box depend on the type of message you are working with and the available message transports at your workstation (see Figure 8.10).

FIGURE 8.10.

Viewing the Options dialog box.

You can also compose a complete message, address it, and send it without the use of dialog boxes. However, to do that you need to create at least one recipient object. You learn how to do that in the next section.

The `Recipient` Objects and Collections and the `Address` Object

The OLE Messaging library defines two address objects—the `Recipient` object and the `AddressEntry` object. The two objects are related, but serve different purposes. The purpose of the `Recipient` object is to provide valid addressing information for the message. The purpose of the `AddressEntry` object is to gain access to individual records in the MAPI address book.

The next several sections outline the properties and methods of both the `Recipient` and `AddressEntry` objects.

The `Recipients` Collection Object

The `Recipients` collection object holds a list of all recipients for a message. Every message has a recipients collection—even if the message has only one recipient in the collection. There are three methods for the collection and a handful of properties. Because the `Recipients` collection is a small collection, it has `Count` and `Item` properties. This also means that the `Recipient` object supports an `Index` property.

Table 8.12 shows the `Recipients` object methods and Table 8.13 shows the object's properties.

Table 8.12. The `Recipients` collection object methods.

Method name	Parameters	Description
Add	(optional) name as String, (optional) address as String, (optional) type as Long, (optional) entryID as String	Used to add a new recipient to the collection.
Delete	(none)	Used to delete *all* recipients from the collection.
Resolve	(optional) showDialog as Boolean	Used to validate *all* Recipient objects in the collection. Can optionally show a dialog box to help resolve ambiguous entries.

Table 8.13. The `Recipients` collection object properties.

Property name	Type	Description
Application	String	Name of the library. Always set to OLE/ Messaging.
Class	Long	Internal identifying code for all MAPI objects. Always set to 20 for Recipients objects.
Count	Long	Total number of Recipient objects in the collection.
Item	Recipient object	Used to gain access to a particular Recipient object in the collection (using the Recipient Index property).
Resolved	Boolean	Flag to indicate that all Recipient objects in the collection contain valid addressing information. Set when you call the Resolve method of the object.

To test the properties of the `Recipients` collection object, add a new button to the control array and set its caption to `RecipColl`. Then add a new line in the `Command1_Click` event to match the code in Listing 8.30.

Listing 8.30. Updating the `Command1_Click` event.

```
Private Sub Command1_Click(Index As Integer)
    '
    ' handle user selections
    '
    Select Case Index
        Case 0 ' mapi start
            MAPIStart
        Case 1 ' mapi end
            MAPIEnd
        Case 2 ' call address book
            MAPIAddrBook
        Case 3 ' session properties
            SessionProps
        Case 4 ' show infostores collection
            SessionInfoStoreColl
        Case 5 ' show infostore properties
            InfoStoreProps
        Case 6 ' folders collection
            FoldersColl
        Case 7 ' folder object
            FolderProps
        Case 8 ' messsage collection
            MessagesColl
        Case 9 ' message properties
            MessageProps
        Case 10 ' add a message w/ dialogs
            MessageAdd
        Case 11 ' make a message in code
            MessageMake
        Case 12 ' recipients collection
            RecipColl
    End Select
    '
End Sub
```

Before coding the collection routine, you must first add three new variables to the general declaration area of the form. Modify the declaration list to match the code in Listing 8.31.

Listing 8.31. Modifying the form-level declarations.

```
Option Explicit
'
Dim objSession As Object ' for mapi session
Dim objInfoStoreColl As Object ' collection of stores
Dim objInfoStore As Object ' single info store
Dim objFolderColl As Object ' collection of folders
Dim objFolder As Object ' single folder
Dim objMessageColl As Object ' messages collection
```

```
Dim objMessage As Object ' single message
Dim objRecipColl As Object ' recipient collection
Dim objRecipient As Object ' single recipient
Dim objAddrEntry As Object ' addressentry object
```

Next add the `RecipColl` subroutine to the project and enter the code in Listing 8.32.

Listing 8.32. Adding the `RecipColl` routine.

```
Public Sub RecipColl()
    '
    ' show the recipient collection properties
    '
    Dim cMsg As String
    '
    ' get the recipient collection
    ' from the first message in the inbox
    Set objMessageColl = objSession.Inbox.Messages
    Set objMessage = objMessageColl.GetFirst
    '
    ' get its recipient collection
    Set objRecipColl = objMessage.Recipients
    '
    ' get the properties
    cMsg = "Application: " & objRecipColl.Application & Chr(13)
    cMsg = cMsg & "Class: " & CStr(objRecipColl.Class) & Chr(13)
    cMsg = cMsg & "Count: " & CStr(objRecipColl.Count) & Chr(13)
    cMsg = cMsg & "Item (Name): " & objRecipColl.Item(1).Name & Chr(13)
    cMsg = cMsg & "Resolved: " & objRecipColl.Resolved

    MsgBox cMsg, vbInformation, "Recipients Collection Object"
    '
End Sub
```

The `RecipColl` routine locates the first message in the `Inbox` collection and then displays the `Recipients` collection object properties. Notice that the routine calls the `Name` property of the `Item` object in the collection. The `Item(1)` property points to the first `recipient` object in the collection.

In Figure 8.11 you can see the results of a message with three recipients. Your exact results will vary based on the message you select.

FIGURE 8.11.

Viewing the Recipients *collection object properties.*

Using the `Delete` method will remove all the `Recipient` objects from the collection. After calling the `Delete` method, you must call the `Update` method on the `Message` object to make the changes permanent. Once the recipients are deleted, they cannot be recovered. The following code sample illustrates how to remove all recipients from a collection:

```
objMessage.Recipients.Delete
objMessage.Update
```

You can use the `Add` method to add a new recipient to a message, as explained in the next section.

The `Recipient` Object

The `Recipient` object holds all the information needed to address a message to its destination. Along with the usual properties, the `Recipient` object has an `AddressEntry` property. This property points to a valid `AddressEntry` object. You'll learn more about the `AddressEntry` object in the next section. The methods for the `Recipient` object allow you to delete the recipient from the collection and validate the address before attempting to send the message.

Table 8.14 shows the `Recipient` object methods, and Table 8.15 shows the `Recipient` object properties.

Table 8.14. The `Recipient` object methods.

Method name	Parameters	Description
Delete	(none)	Used to delete the selected recipient from the collection.
Resolve	(optional) showDialog as Boolean	Used to validate the recipient entry against the MAPI address book. Can optionally show a dialog box to help resolve ambiguous entries.

Table 8.15. The `Recipient` object properties.

Property name	Type	Description
Address	String	The complete routing address for the target recipient. In the format: *TransportType:EmailAddress*. The *TransportType* is taken from the `Type` property of the child `AddressEntry` object. The *EmailAddress* is taken from the `Address` property of the `AddressEntry` object.

Property name	Type	Description
AddressEntry	AddressEntry object	The underlying object that contains detailed information on the recipient, including the exact address and message transport type.
Application	String	Name of the library. Always set to OLE/ Messaging.
Class	Long	Internal identifying code for all MAPI objects. Always set to 4 for Recipient objects.

DisplayType	Long	A value that indicates the type of recipient. This is used to control how the message is displayed by client applications. Valid display types are
		
		    Local User
		    Distribution List
		    Shared Folder
		    Agent
		    Organization
		    Private Distribution List
		    Remote User
		
		MAPI performs no special processing based on the DisplayType property. It is up to the programmer to use this property where appropriate.

Index	Long	A value that indicates the position of the Recipient object in the collection.
Name	String	The displayable Name property of the underlying AddressEntry object. This is the value shown in the MAPI address book.

Type	Long	A value indicating the type of recipient for this message. Valid types are
		    To—Primary addressee
		    CC—Courtesy copy addressee
		    BC—Blind courtesy copy addressee

To view the properties of a Recipient object, add another button to the control array and set its caption property to RecipProps. Then modify the Command1_Click event as shown in Listing 8.33.

Listing 8.33. Updating the `Command1_Click` event.

```
Private Sub Command1_Click(Index As Integer)
    '
    ' handle user selections
    '
    Select Case Index
        Case 0 ' mapi start
            MAPIStart
        Case 1 ' mapi end
            MAPIEnd
        Case 2 ' call address book
            MAPIAddrBook
        Case 3 ' session properties
            SessionProps
        Case 4 ' show infostores collection
            SessionInfoStoreColl
        Case 5 ' show infostore properties
            InfoStoreProps
        Case 6 ' folders collection
            FoldersColl
        Case 7 ' folder object
            FolderProps
        Case 8 ' messsage collection
            MessagesColl
        Case 9 ' message properties
            MessageProps
        Case 10 ' add a message w/ dialogs
            MessageAdd
        Case 11 ' make a message in code
            MessageMake
        Case 12 ' recipients collection
            RecipColl
        Case 13 ' recipient object
            RecipProps
    End Select
    '
End Sub
```

Now add the `RecipProps` subroutine to the form and enter the code from Listing 8.34.

Listing 8.34. Adding the `RecipProps` routine.

```
Public Sub RecipProps()
    '
    ' show the recipient object properties
    '
    Dim cMsg As String
    '
    ' select a message and recipient
    Set objMessageColl = objSession.Inbox.Messages
    Set objMessage = objMessageColl.GetFirst
    Set objRecipient = objMessage.Recipients.Item(1)
    '
    ' now get properties
    cMsg = "Address: " & objRecipient.address & Chr(13)
```

```
    cMsg = cMsg & "Application: " & objRecipient.Application & Chr(13)
    cMsg = cMsg & "Class: " & CStr(objRecipient.Class) & Chr(13)
    cMsg = cMsg & "DisplayType: " & CStr(objRecipient.DisplayType) & Chr(13)
    cMsg = cMsg & "Index: " & CStr(objRecipient.Index) & Chr(13)
    cMsg = cMsg & "Name: " & objRecipient.Name & Chr(13)
    cMsg = cMsg & "Type: " & CStr(objRecipient.Type)
    '
    MsgBox cMsg, vbInformation, "Recipient Object Properties"
    '
End Sub
```

Adding a Recipient Object to a Collection

You can use the Add method of the Recipients collection object to add a valid recipient to a message. To do this you must have a Message object, access the recipients collection for that message, execute the Add method, and then populate the new Recipient object properties. Once that is done, you must execute the Update method of the message to save all changes.

Add a new button to the control array and set its caption property to RecipAdd. Be sure to modify the Command1_Click event to match the code in Listing 8.35.

Listing 8.35. Modifying the Command1_Click event.

```
Private Sub Command1_Click(Index As Integer)
    '
    ' handle user selections
    '
    Select Case Index
        Case 0 ' mapi start
            MAPIStart
        Case 1 ' mapi end
            MAPIEnd
        Case 2 ' call address book
            MAPIAddrBook
        Case 3 ' session properties
            SessionProps
        Case 4 ' show infostores collection
            SessionInfoStoreColl
        Case 5 ' show infostore properties
            InfoStoreProps
        Case 6 ' folders collection
            FoldersColl
        Case 7 ' folder object
            FolderProps
        Case 8 ' messsage collection
            MessagesColl
        Case 9 ' message properties
            MessageProps
        Case 10 ' add a message w/ dialogs
            MessageAdd
        Case 11 ' make a message in code
            MessageMake
```

continues

Listing 8.35. continued

```
        Case 12 ' recipients collection
            RecipColl
        Case 13 ' recipient object
            RecipProps
        Case 14 ' add a recipient to a message
            RecipAdd
    End Select
    '
End Sub
```

Now add the RecipAdd subroutine to the form and enter the code from Listing 8.36.

Listing 8.36. Adding the RecipAdd routine.

```
Public Sub RecipAdd()
    '
    ' adding a new recipient to a message
    '
    ' add a new message first
    Set objMessageColl = objSession.Outbox.Messages
    Set objMessage = objMessageColl.Add
    objMessage.subject = "New Message"
    objMessage.Text = "Added this using VB code"
    '
    ' now add a recipient
    Set objRecipColl = objMessage.Recipients
    Set objRecipient = objRecipColl.Add
    objRecipient.Name = "MCA" ' select a good name
    objRecipient.Resolve ' force validation
    '
    ' update and send
    objMessage.Update
    objMessage.Send showdialog:=True
    '
End Sub
```

The RecipAdd routine first creates a new message in the outbox and then adds a new recipient to the message. Finally, after validating the Recipient object, the routine updates all the changes and calls the Send dialog box (see Figure 8.12).

FIGURE 8.12.

Viewing the results of adding a recipient to a message.

This routine could easily be modified to complete the send operation without presenting any dialog boxes. If you change the ShowDialog parameter to False, the OLE Messaging library will post the message without interfacing with the user.

The AddressEntry Object

The AddressEntry object is a child object of the Recipient object. The AddressEntry object contains all the valid addressing information for a message system. The AddressEntry object is also the object that represents an entry in the MAPI address book. In this way, the AddressEntry object provides a link between the MAPI address book and MAPI messages.

The OLE Messaging library interface allows you to modify or delete AddressEntry objects from the MAPI address book. However, there is no Add method for the AddressEntry object. You cannot use the OLE Messaging library to create new entries in the MAPI address book. Table 8.16 shows the AddressEntry object methods, their parameters, and brief descriptions.

Table 8.16. The AddressEntry object methods.

Method name	Parameters	Description
Delete	(none)	Removes the AddressEntry object from the MAPI address book.
Details	(opt) parentWindow as Long	Displays a dialog box that allows the user to modify published properties of the AddressEntry.
Update	(opt) makePermanent as Boolean, (opt) refreshObject as Boolean	Make changes to the object's properties permanent.

The AddressEntry object has a handful of properties. These properties identify the message transport used to send messages to this location, the actual address, and other internal properties. Table 8.17 shows the properties of the AddressEntry object.

Table 8.17. The AddressEntry object properties.

Property name	Type	Description
Address	String	The electronic mail address of the record.
Application	String	Name of the library. Always set to OLE/ Messaging.

continues

Table 8.17. continued

Property name	Type	Description
Class	Long	Internal identifying code for all MAPI objects. Always set to 8 for AddressEntry objects.
DisplayType	Long	A value that indicates the type of recipient. This is used to control how the message is displayed by client applications. Valid display types are Local User Distribution List Shared Folder Agent Organization Private Distribution List Remote User MAPI performs no special processing based on the DisplayType property. It is up to the programmer to use this property where appropriate.
Fields	Fields collection object	A collection of user-defined properties. This is used by programmers to add additional unique information to AddressEntry objects.
ID	String	A MAPI-assigned unique value that identifies this address object.
Name	String	The displayable Name property of the AddressEntry object. This is the value shown in the MAPI address book.
Type	Long	A value indicating the type of recipient for this message. Valid types are To—Primary addressee CC—Courtesy copy addressee BC—Blind courtesy copy addressee

Add a new button to the control array and set its caption to AddrProps. Then modify the Command1_Click event to match the code in Listing 8.37.

Listing 8.37. Modifying the `Command1_Click` event.

```
Private Sub Command1_Click(Index As Integer)
    '
    ' handle user selections
    '
    Select Case Index
        Case 0 ' mapi start
            MAPIStart
        Case 1 ' mapi end
            MAPIEnd
        Case 2 ' call address book
            MAPIAddrBook
        Case 3 ' session properties
            SessionProps
        Case 4 ' show infostores collection
            SessionInfoStoreColl
        Case 5 ' show infostore properties
            InfoStoreProps
        Case 6 ' folders collection
            FoldersColl
        Case 7 ' folder object
            FolderProps
        Case 8 ' messsage collection
            MessagesColl
        Case 9 ' message properties
            MessageProps
        Case 10 ' add a message w/ dialogs
            MessageAdd
        Case 11 ' make a message in code
            MessageMake
        Case 12 ' recipients collection
            RecipColl
        Case 13 ' recipient object
            RecipProps
        Case 14 ' add a recipient to a message
            RecipAdd
        Case 15 ' address entry object
            AddrProps
    End Select
    '
End Sub
```

Now add the AddrProps subroutine and enter the code in Listing 8.38.

Listing 8.38. Adding the `AddrProps` routine.

```
Public Sub AddrProps()
    '
    ' show address entry properties
    '
    Dim cMsg As String
    '
    ' start a new message
    Set objMessageColl = objSession.Outbox.Messages
    Set objMessage = objMessageColl.Add
```

continues

Listing 8.38. continued

```
        objMessage.subject = "Testing AddressEntry Objects"
        objMessage.Text = "Testing the AddrProps routine"
        '
        ' add a recipient
        Set objRecipient = objMessage.Recipients.Add
        objRecipient.Name = "MCA"
        objRecipient.Resolve ' validate it
        '
        ' set addressentry object
        Set objAddrEntry = objRecipient.AddressEntry
        '
        ' now get properties of address entry object
        cMsg = "Address: " & objAddrEntry.address & Chr(13)
        cMsg = cMsg & "Application: " & objAddrEntry.Application & Chr(13)
        cMsg = cMsg & "Class: " & CStr(objAddrEntry.Class) & Chr(13)
        cMsg = cMsg & "DisplayType: " & CStr(objAddrEntry.DisplayType) & Chr(13)
        cMsg = cMsg & "ID: " & objAddrEntry.ID & Chr(13)
        cMsg = cMsg & "Name: " & objAddrEntry.Name & Chr(13)
        cMsg = cMsg & "Type: " & objAddrEntry.Type
        '
        MsgBox cMsg, vbInformation, "Address Entry Object Properties"
        '
End Sub
```

When you save and run the project, then click AddrProps, you'll see a set of property information for the message recipient. Although the details will vary, your screen should look like the one in Figure 8.13.

FIGURE 8.13.
Viewing the
AddressEntry *properties.*

Accessing the AddressEntry **Details Dialog Box**

You can use the Details method to invoke a Details dialog box for an AddressEntry object. This is handy for looking up additional information on a known AddressEntry object. Add another button to the control array and set its caption to AddrDetails. Modify the Command1_Click event as shown in Listing 8.39.

Listing 8.39. Updated Command1_Click event.

```
Private Sub Command1_Click(Index As Integer)
    '
    ' handle user selections
    '
```

```
     Select Case Index
         Case 0 ' mapi start
             MAPIStart
         Case 1 ' mapi end
             MAPIEnd
         Case 2 ' call address book
             MAPIAddrBook
         Case 3 ' session properties
             SessionProps
         Case 4 ' show infostores collection
             SessionInfoStoreColl
         Case 5 ' show infostore properties
             InfoStoreProps
         Case 6 ' folders collection
             FoldersColl
         Case 7 ' folder object
             FolderProps
         Case 8 ' messsage collection
             MessagesColl
         Case 9 ' message properties
             MessageProps
         Case 10 ' add a message w/ dialogs
             MessageAdd
         Case 11 ' make a message in code
             MessageMake
         Case 12 ' recipients collection
             RecipColl
         Case 13 ' recipient object
             RecipProps
         Case 14 ' add a recipient to a message
             RecipAdd
         Case 15 ' address entry object
             AddrProps
         Case 16 ' address entry details dialog
             AddrDetails
     End Select

     '

End Sub
```

Now add the AddrDetails subroutine and enter the code from Listing 8.40.

Listing 8.40. Adding the AddrDetails routine.

```
Public Sub AddrDetails()
    '
    ' show the details of an address entry
    '
    ' first get an existing message
    Set objMessageColl = objSession.Inbox.Messages
    Set objMessage = objMessageColl.GetFirst
    '
    ' now get the recipient/address entry objects
    Set objRecipient = objMessage.Recipients.Item(1)
    Set objAddrEntry = objRecipient.AddressEntry
```

continues

Listing 8.40. continued

```
'
' now show the details of the address entry
objAddrEntry.Details
'
End Sub
```

After accessing the first message in the inbox and getting the `AddressEntry` of the first `Recipient` object of the message, this routine invokes the `Details` method to show a dialog box

FIGURE 8.14.

Viewing the `Details` *dialog box for the* `AddressEntry` *object.*

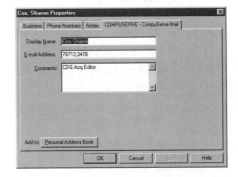

that allows users to modify the fields of the address book entry (see Figure 8.14).

You can modify `AddressEntry` properties without invoking the `Details` method. For example, you can change the `Name` property of an existing `AddressEntry` object. The following code fragment shows how this is done:

```
objAddrEntry.Name = "New Name"
objAddrEntry.Update(True, True) ' update object and reload data
```

You can also delete an entry from the MAPI address book by using the `Delete` method. The following code example shows how this can be done:

```
objAddrEntry.Delete ' mark for delete
objAddrEntry.Update(True, True) ' update the changes
```

> **WARNING**
>
> Once a `Delete`/`Update` method pair is invoked on an `AddressEntry` object, it is permanently removed from the address book and cannot be recovered. Use this method sparingly. And when you do provide delete services in your programs, be sure to add a confirmation option dialog box before permanently deleting the object.

The Attachment Objects and Collections

The Attachment objects contain non-text data that is to be sent along with a standard message. Often this is a binary graphic or formatted document file that is shipped from one user to another. The Attachment object methods and properties allow you to read and write attachments to your messages.

There can be multiple attachments for each message. For this reason, the message object has an Attachments collection object associated with it. All attachment objects are part of the Attachments collection.

The Attachments Collection Object

The Attachments collection object is a child of the Message object and holds all the associated attachments for that message. The Attachments collection is a small collection, so it supports the Count and Item properties and the Attachment object supports the Index property.

Table 8.18 shows the Attachments collection object methods, and Table 8.19 shows the Attachments collection object properties.

Table 8.19. The Attachments collection object methods.

Method name	Parameters	Description
Add	(optional) name as String, (optional) position as Long, (optional) type as Long, (optional) source as String	Adds a new attachment to the attachments collection.
Delete	(none)	Removes all attachments from the collection.

Table 8.20. The Attachments collection object properties.

Property name	Type	Description
Application	String	Name of the library. Always set to OLE/Messaging.
Class	Long	Internal identifying code for all MAPI objects. Always set to 21 for Attachments objects.
Count	Long	The total number of attachments in this collection.
Item	Object	Used to gain access to one of the attachments in the collection based on the Index property of the Attachment object.

To test the Attachments collection object, add a new command button to the control array and set its caption to AttachColl. Then modify the Command1_Click event to match the code in Listing 8.41.

Listing 8.41. Modifying the Command1_Click event.

```
Private Sub Command1_Click(Index As Integer)
    '
    ' handle user selections
    '
    Select Case Index
        Case 0 ' mapi start
            MAPIStart
        Case 1 ' mapi end
            MAPIEnd
        Case 2 ' call address book
            MAPIAddrBook
        Case 3 ' session properties
            SessionProps
        Case 4 ' show infostores collection
            SessionInfoStoreColl
        Case 5 ' show infostore properties
            InfoStoreProps
        Case 6 ' folders collection
            FoldersColl
        Case 7 ' folder object
            FolderProps
        Case 8 ' messsage collection
            MessagesColl
        Case 9 ' message properties
            MessageProps
        Case 10 ' add a message w/ dialogs
            MessageAdd
        Case 11 ' make a message in code
            MessageMake
        Case 12 ' recipients collection
            RecipColl
        Case 13 ' recipient object
            RecipProps
        Case 14 ' add a recipient to a message
            RecipAdd
        Case 15 ' address entry object
            AddrProps
        Case 16 ' address entry details dialog
            AddrDetails
        Case 17 ' attachment collection
            AttachColl
    End Select
    '
End Sub
```

Next you need to add two new variables to the general declaration section of the form. Modify your declarations to match the code in Listing 8.42.

Listing 8.42. Modifying the form-level declarations.

```
Option Explicit
'
Dim objSession As Object ' for mapi session
Dim objInfoStoreColl As Object ' collection of stores
Dim objInfoStore As Object ' single info store
Dim objFolderColl As Object ' collection of folders
Dim objFolder As Object ' single folder
Dim objMessageColl As Object ' messages collection
Dim objMessage As Object ' single message
Dim objRecipColl As Object ' recipient collection
Dim objRecipient As Object ' single recipient
Dim objAddrEntry As Object ' addressentry object
Dim objAttachColl As Object ' attachment collection
Dim objAttachment As Object ' single attachment
```

Now add the `AttachColl` subroutine to the form and enter the code that appears in Listing 8.43.

Listing 8.43. Adding the `AttachColl` routine.

```
Public Sub AttachColl()
    '
    ' inspect the attachment collection
    ' of a message object
    '
    Dim cMsg As String
    Dim x As Integer
    '
    ' first get a message
    Set objMessageColl = objSession.Inbox.Messages
    Set objMessage = objMessageColl.GetFirst
    '
    ' next get attachment collection of message
    Set objAttachColl = objMessage.Attachments
    '
    ' now get properties of the collection
    cMsg = "Application: " & objAttachColl.Application & Chr(13)
    cMsg = cMsg & "Class: " & CStr(objAttachColl.Class) & Chr(13)
    cMsg = cMsg & "Count: " & CStr(objAttachColl.Count) & Chr(13)
    '
    ' now list out attachments
    cMsg = cMsg & Chr(13) & "Attachments:" & Chr(13)
    For x = 1 To objAttachColl.Count
        cMsg = cMsg & CStr(x) & " - " & objAttachColl.Item(x).Name & Chr(13)
    Next x
    '
    MsgBox cMsg, vbInformation, "Attachment Collection Object Properties"
    '
End Sub
```

> **WARNING**
>
> The `AttachColl` routine will crash if there are no attachments on the first message in the inbox. Be sure to add a single message in the inbox with at least one attachment before you run this routine. You can use your MAPI client to create a new message with attachments and send it to yourself.

The `AttachColl` routine accesses the attachments collection of the first message in the inbox and displays its properties. Your output may be different, but it should look something like Figure 8.15.

FIGURE 8.15.

Viewing the `Attachments` *collection object properties.*

You can delete all the attachments in the collection by invoking the `Delete` method on the `Attachments` collection object. The delete is not complete until you invoke the `Update` method on the parent object. And once the delete is complete, you cannot recover the data.

You'll learn about the `Add` method in the next section on `Attachment` objects.

The `Attachment` **Object**

The `Attachment` object contains all the information about the data file attached to a message. In fact, the `Attachment` object includes the actual data file itself. There are several properties and three methods to the `Attachment` object. Table 8.21 shows you the `Attachment` object methods and Table 8.22 shows you the `Attachment` object properties.

Table 8.21. The `Attachment` object methods.

Method name	Parameters	Description
Delete	(none)	Removes the attachment from the attachment collection.
ReadFromFile	fileName as String	Copies the operating system file into the `Attachment` object.
WriteToFile	fileName as String	Copies the data from the `Attachment` object to an operating system file.

Table 8.22. The Attachment object properties.

Property name	Type	Access
Application	String	Name of the library. Always set to OLE/Messaging.
Class	Long	Internal identifying code for all MAPI objects. Always set to 5 for Attachment objects.
Index	Long	A value that indicates the position of the attachment in the attachments collection.
Name	String	The display name of the attachment.
Position	Long	A value indicating the character position in the message body where the attachment should be displayed.
Source	String	For OLE-type data, contains the OLE object name (for example, Word.Document). For File-type data, contains a blank.
Type	Long	The value that indicates the type of attachment. MAPI supports two attachment types: File(0) and OLE(2).

To review the attachment properties, add a new button to the control array and set its caption to AttachProps. Then modify the Command1_Click event to match the code in Listing 8.44.

Listing 8.44. The modified Command1_Click event.

```
Private Sub Command1_Click(Index As Integer)
    '
    ' handle user selections
    '
    Select Case Index
        Case 0 ' mapi start
            MAPIStart
        Case 1 ' mapi end
            MAPIEnd
        Case 2 ' call address book
            MAPIAddrBook
        Case 3 ' session properties
            SessionProps
        Case 4 ' show infostores collection
            SessionInfoStoreColl
        Case 5 ' show infostore properties
            InfoStoreProps
        Case 6 ' folders collection
            FoldersColl
        Case 7 ' folder object
            FolderProps
```

continues

Listing 8.44. continued

```
        Case 8 ' messsage collection
            MessagesColl
        Case 9 ' message properties
            MessageProps
        Case 10 ' add a message w/ dialogs
            MessageAdd
        Case 11 ' make a message in code
            MessageMake
        Case 12 ' recipients collection
            RecipColl
        Case 13 ' recipient object
            RecipProps
        Case 14 ' add a recipient to a message
            RecipAdd
        Case 15 ' address entry object
            AddrProps
        Case 16 ' address entry details dialog
            AddrDetails
        Case 17 ' attachment collection
            AttachColl
        Case 18 ' attachment object properties
            AttachProps
    End Select
    '
End Sub
```

Now add the `AttachProps` subroutine and enter the code from Listing 8.45.

Listing 8.45. Adding the `AttachProps` routine.

```
Public Sub AttachProps()
    '
    ' view the attachment object properties
    '
    Dim cMsg As String
    '
    ' select a message with an attachment
    Set objMessageColl = objSession.Inbox.Messages
    Set objMessage = objMessageColl.GetFirst
    Set objAttachColl = objMessage.Attachments
    Set objAttachment = objAttachColl.Item(1)
    '
    ' now get properties
    cMsg = "Application " & objAttachment.Application & Chr(13)
    cMsg = cMsg & "Class: " & CStr(objAttachment.Class) & Chr(13)
    cMsg = cMsg & "Index: " & CStr(objAttachment.Index) & Chr(13)
    cMsg = cMsg & "Name: " & objAttachment.Name & Chr(13)
    cMsg = cMsg & "Position: " & CStr(objAttachment.position) & Chr(13)
    cMsg = cMsg & "Source: " & objAttachment.Source & Chr(13)
    cMsg = cMsg & "Type: " & CStr(objAttachment.Type)
    '
    MsgBox cMsg, vbInformation, "Attachment object Properties"
    '
End Sub
```

Save and run this routine. When you click on the AttachProps button, you will see the properties of the attachment. Refer to Figure 8.16 for an example of the output.

FIGURE 8.16.
Viewing the Attachment
object properties.

Adding an Attachment to a Message

You can use Visual Basic code to add an attachment directly to a message. This involves setting three properties and invoking the ReadFromFile method. First, add another button to the control array and set its caption to AttachAdd. Then modify the Command1_Click event to match the code in Listing 8.46.

Listing 8.46. Updated Command1_Click event.

```
Private Sub Command1_Click(Index As Integer)
    '
    ' handle user selections
    '
    Select Case Index
        Case 0 ' mapi start
            MAPIStart
        Case 1 ' mapi end
            MAPIEnd
        Case 2 ' call address book
            MAPIAddrBook
        Case 3 ' session properties
            SessionProps
        Case 4 ' show infostores collection
            SessionInfoStoreColl
        Case 5 ' show infostore properties
            InfoStoreProps
        Case 6 ' folders collection
            FoldersColl
        Case 7 ' folder object
            FolderProps
        Case 8 ' messsage collection
            MessagesColl
        Case 9 ' message properties
            MessageProps
        Case 10 ' add a message w/ dialogs
            MessageAdd
        Case 11 ' make a message in code
            MessageMake
        Case 12 ' recipients collection
            RecipColl
        Case 13 ' recipient object
            RecipProps
```

continues

Listing 8.46. continued

```
        Case 14 ' add a recipient to a message
            RecipAdd
        Case 15 ' address entry object
            AddrProps
        Case 16 ' address entry details dialog
            AddrDetails
        Case 17 ' attachment collection
            AttachColl
        Case 18 ' attachment object properties
            AttachProps
        Case 19 ' add attachment
            AttachAdd
    End Select
    '
End Sub
```

Next, add a new subroutine called `AttachAdd` and enter the code shown in Listing 8.47.

Listing 8.47. Adding the `AttachAdd` routine.

```
Public Sub AttachAdd()
    '
    ' add an attachment to a message
    '
    ' first create a new message
    Set objMessageColl = objSession.Outbox.Messages
    Set objMessage = objMessageColl.Add
    objMessage.subject = "Here's the WIN.INI File"
    objMessage.Text = " Here's a copy of the Windows INI File you asked for."
    '
    ' now add an attachment
    Set objAttachColl = objMessage.Attachments
    Set objAttachment = objAttachColl.Add
    objAttachment.Name = "WIN.INI"
    objAttachment.position = 0 ' place at start of message
    objAttachment.ReadFromFile "C:\WINDOWS\WIN.INI"
    '
    ' now address the message
    Set objRecipColl = objMessage.Recipients
    Set objRecipient = objRecipColl.Add
    objRecipient.Name = "MCA" ' a valid name
    objRecipient.Resolve ' validate name
    '
    ' now update and send message
    objMessage.Update ' save it all
    objMessage.Send showdialog:=True ' let's see it
    '
End Sub
```

> **WARNING**
>
> Be sure to address the message to a valid person in your MAPI address book. It is a good idea to address this message to yourself since you will be reading and saving an attachment in the next section.

The `AttachAdd` routine creates a new message, adds the `WIN.INI` file as an attachment (at the first position in the file), and then addresses the message and sends it. Your screen should look something like the one in Figure 8.17.

FIGURE 8.17.

Viewing the attachment to the message.

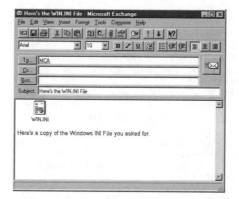

> **TIP**
>
> You could easily send the message without ever seeing the dialog box by just setting the `ShowDialog` parameter to `False`.

Saving a Message Attachment to Disk

Now you can read the message you just sent yourself. Add one more button to the command array and set its caption to `AttachSave`. Then modify the `Command1_Click` event to match the code in Listing 8.48.

Listing 8.48. Updating the `Command1_Click` event.

```
Private Sub Command1_Click(Index As Integer)
    '
    ' handle user selections
    '
    Select Case Index
        Case 0 ' mapi start
            MAPIStart
```

continues

Listing 8.48. continued

```
        Case 1 ' mapi end
            MAPIEnd
        Case 2 ' call address book
            MAPIAddrBook
        Case 3 ' session properties
            SessionProps
        Case 4 ' show infostores collection
            SessionInfoStoreColl
        Case 5 ' show infostore properties
            InfoStoreProps
        Case 6 ' folders collection
            FoldersColl
        Case 7 ' folder object
            FolderProps
        Case 8 ' messsage collection
            MessagesColl
        Case 9 ' message properties
            MessageProps
        Case 10 ' add a message w/ dialogs
            MessageAdd
        Case 11 ' make a message in code
            MessageMake
        Case 12 ' recipients collection
            RecipColl
        Case 13 ' recipient object
            RecipProps
        Case 14 ' add a recipient to a message
            RecipAdd
        Case 15 ' address entry object
            AddrProps
        Case 16 ' address entry details dialog
            AddrDetails
        Case 17 ' attachment collection
            AttachColl
        Case 18 ' attachment object properties
            AttachProps
        Case 19 ' add attachment
            AttachAdd
        Case 20 ' save attachment
            AttachSave
    End Select
    '
End Sub
```

Now add the `AttachSave` subroutine and enter the code from Listing 8.49.

Listing 8.49. Adding the `AttachSave` routine.

```
Public Sub AttachSave()
    '
    ' read a message and save the attachment
    '
    Dim cMsg As String
    '
    ' get the last message in the inbox
```

```
        Set objMessageColl = objSession.Inbox.Messages
        Set objMessage = objMessageColl.GetLast
        '
        ' now save the attachment
        Set objAttachColl = objMessage.Attachments
        Set objAttachment = objAttachColl.Item(1)
        objAttachment.WriteToFile App.Path & "\saved.txt"
        '
        cMsg = "Attachment: " & objAttachment.Name & Chr(13)
        cMsg = cMsg & "Saved as: " & App.Path & "\saved.txt"
        '
        MsgBox cMsg, vbInformation, "Save Attachment"
        '
End Sub
```

The `AttachSave` routine reads the last message added to the inbox collection (the one you sent just a moment ago) and retrieves the attachment from the message's attachment collection. The attachment is then saved in the local disk folder as SAVED.TXT (see Figure 8.18).

FIGURE 8.18.
Saving the attached file.

In production applications, you should add code to the routine to prompt the user for a folder and filename for storing the attachment.

Summary

In this chapter, you learned how to use the OLE Messaging library to access features of MAPI. You learned all the major objects, their methods, and their properties.

- The `Session` object
- The `InfoStore` objects and collections
- The `Folder` objects and collections
- The `Message` objects and collections
- The `Recipient` objects and collections
- The `Address` objects
- The `Attachment` objects and collections

You also wrote several code examples that inspected and modified objects and their properties. You learned to use the OLE Messaging library to

- Read existing messages.
- Create new messages.

- Add recipients to messages.
- Add attachments to messages.
- Modify records in the MAPI address book.

The OLE Messaging library is a rich and powerful set of commands. In the next several chapters, you'll use the OLE Messaging library to build powerful desktop applications that use the advanced features of MAPI 1.0.

9

Creating a MAPI Mailing List Manager with the OLE Messaging Library

Introduction

After reviewing the OLE Messaging Library objects in Chapter 8, "The OLE Messaging Library," you're now ready to build a MAPI application for Win95 and Visual Basic 4.0 that uses these objects.

The Mailing List Manager application lets users define and manage automated mailing lists from the client desktop. Messages can be distributed within a single server or across the Internet (depending on the available transports at the desktop). All access to MAPI services will be performed through the OLE Message objects.

The key features of the Mailing List Manager (MLM) are:

- Automatically scans incoming mail for MLM messages.
- Automatically adds and drops subscribers from the group.
- Automatically distributes messages based on current date.
- Allows subscribers to request copies of archived messages.
- Allows subscribers to request a default FAQ file.
- Most features are modifiable using control files.

The MLM application allows individuals to create a set of text files to be distributed to a controlled list of users at specified times. This project has only one simple form and several support routines. All application rules are stored in a set of ASCII control files similar to INI/registry settings. These control files can be changed by the list manager to determine how the mailing list operates and what features are available to subscribers.

Once you complete this application, you'll be able to establish and manage one or more one-way mailing lists from your own desktop. These mailing lists can be limited to your current attached server or cross over any transport out onto the Internet (depending on the transports installed on your desktop).

Laying Out the MLM Form

The MLM application has only one form. Since the primary purpose of the application is to manage automated lists, there is very little needed in the way of a GUI interface. MLM has a set of command buttons to initiate specific tasks and a single scrollable text box to show progress as the application processes incoming and outgoing mail.

Start a new Visual Basic project and lay out the MLM form. Refer to Table 9.1 and Figure 9.1 for details on the size and position of the controls on the form.

FIGURE 9.1.
Laying out the MLM form.

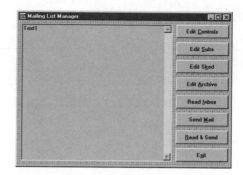

Table 9.1. MLM form controls.

Control	Property	Setting
Form	Name	frmMLM
	Height	5325
	Left	1140
	Top	1230
	Width	7380
Text Box	Name	Text1
	Font	8pt MS Sans Serif, Bold
	Height	4635
	Left	120
	MultiLine	-1 ' True
	Scrollbars	2 ' Vertical
	Top	120
	Width	5115
Command Button	Name	Command1
	Caption	Edit &Controls
	Font	8pt MS Sans Serif, Bold
	Height	450
	Index	0
	Left	5400
	Top	120
	Width	1800

continues

Table 9.1. continued

Control	Property	Setting
Command Button	Name	Command1
	Caption	Edit &Subs
	Font	8pt MS Sans Serif, Bold
	Height	450
	Index	1
	Left	5400
	Top	720
	Width	1800
Command Button	Name	Command1
	Caption	Edit &Sked
	Font	8pt MS Sans Serif, Bold
	Height	450
	Index	2
	Left	5400
	Top	1320
	Width	1800
Command Button	Name	Command1
	Caption	Edit &Archive
	Font	8pt MS Sans Serif, Bold
	Height	450
	Index	3
	Left	5400
	Top	1920
	Width	1800
Command Button	Name	Command1
	Caption	Read &Inbox
	Font	8pt MS Sans Serif, Bold
	Height	450
	Index	4
	Left	5400
	Top	2520
	Width	1800

Control	Property	Setting
Command Button	Name	Command1
	Caption	Send &Mail
	Font	8pt MS Sans Serif, Bold
	Height	450
	Index	5
	Left	5400
	Top	3120
	Width	1800
Command Button	Name	Command1
	Caption	&Read && Send
	Font	8pt MS Sans Serif, Bold
	Height	450
	Index	6
	Left	5400
	Top	3720
	Width	1800
Command Button	Name	Command1
	Caption	E&xit
	Font	8pt MS Sans Serif, Bold
	Height	450
	Index	7
	Left	5400
	Top	4320
	Width	1800

Note that the layout table calls for a control array of command buttons. Add a single button to the form, set its properties (including the Index property), and then use the Edit | Copy, Edit | Paste menu options to make the additional copies of the button. You can then edit the Caption properties as needed.

After you lay out the form, you need to add a handful of variables to the general declaration area, a few routines to handle the standard form events, and one routine to respond to the command-button actions. Listing 9.1 shows the code that declares the form-level variables for this project. Add this code to the general declaration area of the form.

Listing 9.1. Adding the form-level variables.

```
Option Explicit

Dim objMAPISession As Object    ' session object
Dim cMLMFile As String          ' control file
Dim cCtlName() As String        ' control names
Dim cCtlValue() As String       ' control values
Dim bErr As Boolean             ' error flag
Dim nWidth As Integer           ' form width
Dim nHeight As Integer          ' form height
Dim EOL As String               ' end of line
```

Next, add the code in Listing 9.2 to the `Form_Load` event. This code centers the form and then stores its current width and height. This information will be used to prevent users from resizing the form at run-time.

Listing 9.2. Adding code to the `Form_Load` event.

```
Private Sub Form_Load()
    '
    Me.Top = (Screen.Height - Me.Height) / 2
    Me.Left = (Screen.Width - Me.Width) / 2
    '
    nWidth = Me.Width
    nHeight = Me.Height
    EOL = (Chr(13) & Chr(10))
    Text1 = ""
    Me.Caption = "Mailing List Manager [" & cMLMFile & "]"
    '
    ' check for passed parm
    '
    If Len(Command$) <> 0 Then
        cMLMFile = Command$
    Else
        cMLMFile = "mlm.txt"
    End If
    '
End Sub
```

You'll also notice that the `Form_Load` event checks for a parameter passed on the command line at startup. This will be used to determine what set of control files will be used for each run of the MLM application (you'll see more about this later).

Next, add the code in Listing 9.3 to the `Form_Resize` event. This code uses the values established in the `Form_Load` event to keep forcing the form back to its original size whenever a user tries to adjust the form size. Note, however, that this routine *will* allow users to minimize the form.

Listing 9.3. Adding code to the `Form_Resize` event.

```
Private Sub Form_Resize()
    '
    If Me.WindowState <> vbMinimized Then
        Me.Width = nWidth
        Me.Height = nHeight
    End If
    '
End Sub
```

You also need to add code behind the command-button control array. Listing 9.4 contains the code that should be placed in the `Command1_Click` event. This routine just calls a set of custom subroutines that you'll add a bit later in the chapter.

Listing 9.4. Adding the code in the `Command1_Click` event.

```
Private Sub Command1_Click(Index As Integer)
    '
    ' handle user clicks
    '
    Select Case Index
        Case 0 ' edit controls
            ControlsEdit
        Case 1 ' edit subs
            SubEdit
        Case 2 ' edit schedule
            SkedEdit
        Case 3 ' edit archive
            ArchEdit
        Case 4 ' read inbox
            ReadInbox
        Case 5 ' send mail
            SendMail
        Case 6 ' read & send
            ReadInbox
            SendMail
        Case 7 ' exit
            Unload Me
    End Select
    '
End Sub
```

One more line of code is needed to complete this section. The text box control should be a read-only form object. By adding the following line of code to the `Text1_KeyPress` event, you can trick Visual Basic into ignoring any keyboard input performed within the text box control.

```
Private Sub Text1_KeyPress(KeyAscii As Integer)
    KeyAscii = 0
End Sub
```

That's the code needed to support form events and controls. Save this form as MLM.FRM and save the project as MLM.VBP. In the next section you'll add a series of simple support routines to the project.

Coding the Support Routines

Now you'll add a few support routines that are called frequently from other, high-level routines in the project. You'll add all these routines to the general declaration section of the form.

First, add a new subroutine called Status, and add the code shown in Listing 9.5.

Listing 9.5. Adding the Status routine to the project.

```
Public Sub Status(cInfo As String)
    '
    ' send info to status line
    '
    If cInfo = "" Then
        Text1 = ""
    Else
        Text1 = Text1 & cInfo & Chr(13) & Chr(10)
    End If
    '
End Sub
```

The code in the Status routine places a new line in the text box. This will be used to pass progress information to the text box control as the MLM is processing subscriber lists and the Microsoft Exchange inbox.

The MLM project gets its primary instructions from a set of ASCII text control files. The next routine you'll build in this section is the one that reads the master control file. Add a new subroutine called ControlsLoad to the project, and enter the code shown in Listing 9.6.

Listing 9.6. Adding the ControlsLoad routine.

```
Public Sub ControlsLoad()
    '
    ' load control values into variables
    '
    On Error GoTo ControlsLoadErr
    '
    Status ""
    Status "Loading Control Values..."

    Dim nFile As Integer
    Dim nCount As Integer
    Dim cLine As String
    Dim nPos As Integer
    '
    bErr = False
    nCount = 0
    nFile = FreeFile
```

```
    '
    Open cMLMFile For Input As nFile
    While Not EOF(nFile)
        Line Input #nFile, cLine
        If Left(cLine, 1) <> ";" Then
            nPos = InStr(cLine, "=")
            If nPos <> 0 Then
                nCount = nCount + 1
                ReDim Preserve cCtlName(nCount)
                ReDim Preserve cCtlValue(nCount)
                cCtlName(nCount) = Left(cLine, nPos - 1)
                cCtlValue(nCount) = Mid(cLine, nPos + 1, 255)
            End If
        End If
    Wend
    Close #nFile
    Exit Sub
    '
ControlsLoadErr:
    MsgBox Error$, vbCritical, "ControlsLoad Error [" & CStr(Err) & "]"
    bErr = True
    '
End Sub
```

Notice that the `ControlsLoad` routine reads each line of the ASCII text file, and if it is not a comment line (that is, it starts with a ";"), it parses the line into a control name array and a control value array. You'll use these values throughout your project.

Now that the control values are stored in a local array, you need a routine to retrieve a particular control value. Add a new function (not a subroutine) to the project called `ControlSetting`, and add the code shown in Listing 9.7.

Listing 9.7. Adding the `ControlSetting` function.

```
Public Function ControlSetting(cName As String) As String
    '
    ' look up control setting
    '
    Dim cReturn As String
    Dim nCount As Integer
    Dim x As Integer
    '
    nCount = UBound(cCtlName)
    cName = UCase(cName)
    '
    For x = 1 To nCount
        If cName = UCase(cCtlName(x)) Then
            cReturn = cCtlValue(x)
            Exit For
        End If
    Next x
    '
    ControlSetting = cReturn
    '
End Function
```

The ControlSetting function accepts a single parameter (the name of the control value you are requesting) and returns a single value (the value of the control setting you named). This routine accomplishes its task by simply reading through the array of control names until the name is found.

That's all for the general support routines. Save this form and project again before continuing.

Coding the Edit Routines

This next set of routines allows users to edit the various control files required to manage the project. You'll use a call to the NOTEPAD.EXE applet to edit the control files. This is much easier than spending the time to write your own text file editor. Also, the first time you call these routines you'll be prompted to create the new files.

Add a new subroutine called ControlsEdit to the form, and enter the code shown in Listing 9.8.

Listing 9.8. Adding the ControlsEdit routine.

```
Public Sub ControlsEdit()
    '
    Dim rtn As Long
    Dim cEditor
    '
    ControlsLoad
    If bErr <> True Then
        cEditor = ControlSetting("Editor")
        '
        Status "Opening Control File [" & cMLMFile & "]..."
        rtn = Shell(cEditor & " " & cMLMFile, 1)
        Status "Closing Control File..."
    End If
    '
End Sub
```

This routine first attempts to load the master control values, then launches the default editor to allow users to modify those values. You can also see the use of the Status routine to update the form's text box. Go back to the Command1_Click routine (see Listing 9.4) and remove the comment from in front of the ControlsLoad command. Then save this project.

Before you can run this routine, you need to create the default control file. Start NOTEPAD.EXE and enter the information shown in Listing 9.9. Once you complete the entry, save the file in the same folder as the MLM project and call it MLM.TXT.

> **TIP**
>
> If you get errors attempting to launch the editor from these routines, you can include the drive and path qualifiers in the `Editor` control value.

Listing 9.9. Creating the default MLM.TXT control file.

```
; =====================================================
; Mailing List Control values for MLM
; =====================================================
;
; read by MLM.EXE
;
; =====================================================
;
MAPIUserName=MCA
MAPIPassword=
SearchKey=MLM
ListName=MLM Mailing List
NewSub=SUB
NewSubMsg=MLMHello.txt
UnSubMsg=MLMBye.txt
UnSub=UNSUB
GetArchive=GET
ListArchive=LIST
ArchiveFile=MLMArch.txt
ListSchedule=MLMSked.txt
ListSubs=MLMSubs.txt
Editor=notepad.exe
```

> **TIP**
>
> If you don't want to spend time entering this control file information, you can find it in the MLM folder that was created when you installed the source code from the CD-ROM.

There are several entries in this control file. For now, make sure that the control names and values are entered correctly. You'll learn more about how each one works as you go along. Once you get the hang of the control file, you can modify it to suit your own mailing-list needs.

Now add a new subroutine, called SubEdit, to allow the editing of the subscriber list. Enter the code in Listing 9.10 into the routine.

Listing 9.10. Adding the SubEdit routine.

```
Public Sub SubEdit()
    '
    Dim lReturn As Long
    Dim cEditor As String
    Dim cFile As String
    '
    ControlsLoad
    If bErr <> True Then
        cFile = ControlSetting("ListSubs")
        cEditor = ControlSetting("Editor")
        Status "Loading Subscriber List [" & cFile & "]..."
        lReturn = Shell(cEditor & " " & cFile, 1)
        Status "Closing Subscriber List..."
    End If
    '
End Sub
```

Normally you will not need to pre-build the subscriber file. It will be created as you add new subscribers to your mailing list via e-mail requests. However, for testing purposes, open up Notepad and enter the values shown in Listing 9.11. When you are done, save the file as MLMSUBS.TXT in the same folder as the Visual Basic project.

Listing 9.11. Creating the test MLMSUBS.TXT file.

```
; =====================================================
; Mailing List Subscriber File
; =====================================================
;
; Read by MLM.EXE
;
; format:name^address^transport
;
; where:name      = display name
;    address   = e-mail address
;    transport = MAPI transport
;
;    example:Mike Amundsen^mamund@iac.net^SMTP
;
; =====================================================
;
Michael C. Amundsen^mamund@iac.net^SMTP
Mike Amundsen^102461,1267^COMPUSERVE
```

The addresses in the file may not be valid e-mail addresses on your system, but they illustrate the format of the file. Each address entry has three parts:

- ■ *Name*—This is the display name that appears in address books.
- ■ *Address*—This is the full e-mail address of the recipient.
- ■ *Type*—This is the transport type code.

As users request to be on your mailing list, their mailing information is added to this file. Later in the chapter, you'll add yourself to this list by sending yourself an e-mail request.

The next control file needed for the MLM application is the schedule file. This control file contains information on the display name, complete filename, and scheduled delivery date of messages to be sent by MLM. Create a new routine called SkedEdit, and add the code in Listing 9.12.

Listing 9.12. Adding the SkedEdit routine.

```
Public Sub SkedEdit()
    '
    Dim rtn As Long
    Dim cFile As String
    Dim cEditor As String
    '
    ControlsLoad
    If bErr <> True Then
        cFile = ControlSetting("ListSchedule")
        cEditor = ControlSetting("Editor")
        Status "Opening Schedule [" & cFile & "]..."
        rtn = Shell(cEditor & " " & cFile, 1)
        Status "Closing Schdule..."
    End If
    '
End Sub
```

You'll need to create a default schedule file for this project. Listing 9.13 shows the schedule file format. Use NOTEPAD.EXE to build this file and save it in the project directory as MLMSKED.TXT.

Listing 9.13. Building the MLMSKED.TXT file.

```
; ==================================================
; Mailing List Schedule file
; ==================================================
;
; read by MLM.EXE
;
; format:    YYMMDD,uafn,title
;
; where:     YYMMDD = Year, Month, Day
;       uafn   = unambiguous file name
;       title  = descriptive title
;
; example:    960225,MLMFAQ.txt,MLM FAQ Document
;
; ==================================================

960225,mlmhello.txt,Hello and Welcome to MLM!
960226,mlmbye.txt,Goodbye - We'll Miss You!
```

You can see from the sample file that there are three control values for each entry:

- ■ *YYMMDD*—The year, month, and day that the message should be sent.
- ■ *UAFN*—An unambiguous filename. The contents of this text file will be placed in the body of the message to be sent.
- ■ *Title*—This is the title of the message. This value will be placed on the subject line of the message that is sent.

As you build your mailing list message base, you can add lines to this control file.

The last edit routine to add to the project is the one used to edit the archive list. Add a new subroutine called ArchEdit to the project, and enter the code shown in Listing 9.14.

Listing 9.14. Adding the ArchEdit routine.

```
Public Sub ArchEdit()
    '
    Dim rtn As Long
    Dim cEditor As String
    Dim cArchFile As String
    '
    ControlsLoad
    If bErr <> True Then
        cEditor = ControlSetting("Editor")
        cArchFile = ControlSetting("ArchiveFile")
        '
        Status "Opening Archive File [" & cArchFile & "]..."
        rtn = Shell(cEditor & " " & cArchFile, 1)
        Status "Closing Archive File..."
    End If
    '
End Sub
```

Again, you'll need to create an initial archive listing file before you first run your project. Use NOTEPAD.EXE to build a file called MLMARCH.TXT and enter the data shown in Listing 9.15. Save this file in the project directory.

Listing 9.15. Creating the MLMARCH.TXT file.

```
; ====================================================
; Mailing List Archive File
; ====================================================
;
;
; read by MLM.EXE
;
; format:    YYMMDD,uafn,title
;
; where:     YYMMDD = Year, Month, Day
;            uafn   = unambiguous file name
;            title  = descriptive name
;
```

```
; example:    960225,MLMFAQ.txt,MLM FAQ Document
;
; ====================================================

960225,mlmhello.txt,Hello and Welcome to MLM!
960226,mlmbye.txt,Goodbye - We'll Miss You!
```

This file format is identical to the one used in the MLMSKED.TXT file. The contents of this file can be requested by subscribers when they want to retrieve an old message in the database. By passing a GET YYMMDD line in the message subject, subscribers can get a copy of the archive file sent to them automatically.

This is the last of the edit routines for the project. Be sure to save this project before you continue.

Coding the MAPIStart and MAPIEnd routines

Before you can start processing messages, you need to build the routines that will start and end your MAPI sessions. Add a new subroutine called MAPIStart to the project, and enter the code that appears in Listing 9.16.

Listing 9.16. Adding the MAPIStart routine.

```
Public Sub MAPIStart()
    '
    On Error GoTo MAPIStartErr
    '
    Dim cProfile As String
    Dim cPassword As String
    Status "Starting MAPI Session..."
    '
    Set objMAPISession = CreateObject("MAPI.Session")
    cProfile = ControlSetting("MAPIUserName")
    cPassword = ControlSetting("MAPIPassword")
    objMAPISession.Logon profilename:=cProfile, profilePassword:=cPassword
    Exit Sub
    '
MAPIStartErr:
    MsgBox "Unable to Start a MAPI Session", vbCritical, "MAPIStart Error"
    bErr = True
    '
End Sub
```

Note the use of the OLE Messaging Library as the means of access into the MAPI system. Now add the MAPIEnd subroutine to your project and enter the code from Listing 9.17.

Listing 9.17. Adding the MAPIEnd routine.

```
Public Sub MAPIEnd()
    On Error Resume Next
    Status "Closing MAPI Session..."
    objMAPISession.Logoff
End Sub
```

These two routines are the start and end of the ReadMail and SendMail routines you'll add in the next two sections.

Coding the SendMail Routines

The next set of routines will check the schedule control file for the message of the day and automatically format and send messages to all subscribers on the mailing list. This is handled with three routines. The first is the high-level routine that is called from the command button routine. The other two routines handle the details of reading the schedule file, reading the subscriber file, and composing and sending the messages.

Create a new routine called SendMail and add the code shown in Listing 9.18.

Listing 9.18. Adding the SendMail routine.

```
Public Sub SendMail()
    '
    ' read mail
    '
    Status ""
    ControlsLoad
    MAPIStart
    ProcessSubList
    MAPIEnd
    Status "Outbound processing complete."
    MsgBox "Outbound processing complete", vbInformation, "SendMail"
    '
End Sub
```

The SendMail routine first clears the status box and loads the master control file. Then the MAPIStart routine is called. Once the MAPI session is established, the routine calls ProcessSubList to handle all processing of the subscriber list. After the list is processed, the MAPIEnd routine is called and the status box is updated along with message to the user announcing the completion of the processing.

Next add the ProcessSubList subroutine, and enter the code shown in Listing 9.19.

Listing 9.19. Adding the `ProcessSubList` routine.

```
Public Sub ProcessSubList()
    '
    ' read sublist to send messages
    '
    Dim cErr As String
    '
    If bErr <> 0 Then
        Exit Sub
    Else
        bErr = False
    End If
    '
    Dim cSubList As String
    Dim nSubList As Integer
    Dim cListSked As String
    Dim nListSked As Integer
    Dim cSkedFile As String
    Dim cFileDate As String
    Dim cFileName As String
    Dim cFileTitle As String
    Dim cLine As String
    Dim nPos1 As Integer
    Dim nPos2 As Integer
    '
    cSubList = ControlSetting("ListSubs")
    cListSked = ControlSetting("ListSchedule")
    cSkedFile = Format(Now, "YYMMDD")
    '
    Status "Opening Schedule File [" & cListSked & "]..."
    nListSked = FreeFile
    Open cListSked For Input As nListSked
    '
    On Error Resume Next
    Do While Not EOF(nListSked)
        Line Input #nListSked, cLine
        nPos1 = InStr(cLine, ",")
        If nPos1 <> 0 Then
            cFileDate = Left(cLine, nPos1 - 1)
        End If
        nPos2 = InStr(nPos1 + 1, cLine, ",")
        If nPos2 <> 0 Then
            cFileName = Mid(cLine, nPos1 + 1, nPos2 - (nPos1 + 1))
        End If
        If nPos2 + 1 < Len(cLine) Then
            cFileTitle = Mid(cLine, nPos2 + 1, 255)
        Else
            cFileTitle = cFileName
        End If
        If cFileDate = cSkedFile Then
            Exit Do
        End If
    Loop
    Close nListSked
    '
    Status "Opening Subscriber List [" & cSubList & "]..."
    nSubList = FreeFile
```

continues

Listing 9.19. continued

```
    Open cSubList For Input As nSubList
    '
    Do While Not EOF(nSubList)
        Line Input #nSubList, cLine
        If Left(cLine, 1) <> ";" Then
            ProcessSubListMsg cLine, cFileName, cFileTitle
        End If
    Loop
End Sub
```

The main job of the ProcessSubList routine is to open the schedule file, and see if there is a message to send for today's date. If one is found, the routine opens the subscriber control file and calls the ProcessSubListMsg routine to compose and send the message.

Finally, add the ProcessSubListMsg routine and enter the code that appears in Listing 9.20.

Listing 9.20. Adding the ProcessSubListMsg routine.

```
Public Sub ProcessSubListMsg(cListAddr As String, cFile As String, cTitle As
➥String)
    '
    ' send out message
    '
    Dim nFile As Integer
    Dim cLine As String
    Dim cMsgBody As String
    Dim cType As String
    Dim cAddr As String
    Dim cName As String
    Dim objMsg As Object
    Dim objRecip As Object
    Dim nPos1 As Integer
    Dim nPos2 As Integer
    '
    ' parse address line
    nPos1 = InStr(cListAddr, "^")
    If nPos1 <> 0 Then
        cName = Left(cListAddr, nPos1 - 1)
    Else
        Exit Sub
    End If
    '
    nPos2 = InStr(nPos1 + 1, cListAddr, "^")
    If nPos2 <> 0 Then
        cAddr = Mid(cListAddr, nPos1 + 1, nPos2 - (nPos1 + 1))
    Else
        Exit Sub
    End If
    '
    cType = Mid(cListAddr, nPos2 + 1, 255)
    '
    ' now create message
    Status "Sending Msg to " & cName & "..."
    '
```

```
    ' get message text
    nFile = FreeFile
    '
    Open cFile For Input As nFile
    While Not EOF(nFile)
        Line Input #nFile, cLine
        cMsgBody = cMsgBody & EOL & cLine
    Wend
    Close #nFile
    '
    ' now build a new message
    Set objMsg = objMAPISession.Outbox.Messages.Add
    objMsg.subject = ControlSetting("ListName") & " [" & cTitle & "]"
    objMsg.Text = cMsgBody
    ' create the recipient
    Set objRecip = objMsg.Recipients.Add
    If cType = "MS" Then
        objRecip.Name = cName ' handle local users
        objRecip.Type = mapiTo
        objRecip.Resolve
    Else
        objRecip.Name = cType & ":" & cAddr
        objRecip.address = cType & ":" & cAddr
        objRecip.Type = mapiTo
    End If
    ' send the message
    objMsg.Update
    objMsg.Send showDialog:=False
    '
End Sub
```

The most important part of the `ProcessSubListMsg` routine is the last section of code that composes and addresses the message. There are two main processes in this part of the routine. The first process is the creation of a new `Message` object:

```
    ' now build a new message
    Set objMsg = objMAPISession.Outbox.Messages.Add
    objMsg.subject = ControlSetting("ListName") & " [" & cTitle & "]"
    objMsg.Text = cMsgBody
```

The second process is the creation of a new `Recipient` object and the addressing of the message:

```
' create the recipient
    Set objRecip = objMsg.Recipients.Add
    If cType = "MS" Then
        objRecip.Name = cName ' handle local users
        objRecip.Type = mapiTo
        objRecip.Resolve
    Else
        objRecip.Name = cType & ":" & cAddr
        objRecip.address = cType & ":" & cAddr
        objRecip.Type = mapiTo
    End If
```

Notice that addressing is handled a bit differently for MS-type messages. Messages with the address type of MS are addresses within the Microsoft addressing scheme—they're local addresses. To handle these items, you only need to load the Name property, set the recipient type (To:), and then call the MAPI Resolve method to force MAPI to look up the name in the address book(s). When the name is found, MAPI loads the Address property with the complete transport and e-mail address for routing. This is how most MAPI messages are usually sent.

However, for messages of type other than MS, it is likely that they are not in the locally available address books. These messages can still be sent if you load the Address property of the message with both the transport type and the user's e-mail address. This is the way to handle processing for messages that were sent to you from someone who is not in your address book. This is known as *one-off addressing*. One-off addressing ignores the Name property and uses the Address property to route the message.

That is all the code you need to send out daily messages to your subscriber list. The next set of routines will allow your application to scan incoming messages for mailing list-related items and process them as requested.

> **TIP**
>
> It is a good idea to save your project as you go along. The next set of routines are a bit longer and you may want to take a break before continuing.

Coding the Inbox Routines

The next set of routines handles the process of scanning the subject line of incoming messages for mailing-list commands. These commands are then processed and subscribers are added or dropped from the list and archive items are sent to subscribers as requested.

The Inbox processing can recognize four different commands on the subject line. These commands are:

- SUB—When this command appears in the subject line of a message, the sender's name and address are added to the subscriber control file.
- UNSUB—When this command appears in the subject line of a message, the sender's name and address are removed from the subscriber control file.
- LIST—When this command appears in the subject line of a message, MLM will compose and send a message that contains a list of all the archived messages that the subscriber can request.
- GET YYMMDD—When this command appears in the subject line of a message, MLM will retrieve the archived message (indicated by the YYMMDD portion of the command) and send it to the subscriber.

TIP

The exact word used for each of these four commands is determined by settings in the master control file. See Listing 9.9 for an example of the master control file. If you want to change the values for these commands, you can do so in the control file. This is especially useful if you plan to manage more than one list from the same e-mail address. Adding prefixes to the commands will help MLM distinguish which command should be respected and which commands are for some other mailing list.

The first three routines for handling the inbox are rather simple. The first routine clears the progress box, loads the controls, calls the `ProcessInbox` routine, and performs cleanup functions upon return. Add the `ReadInbox` subroutine and add the code shown in Listing 9.21.

Listing 9.21. Adding the `ReadInbox` routine.

```
Public Sub ReadInbox()
    '
    ' read mail
    '
    Status ""
    ControlsLoad
    MAPIStart
    ProcessInbox
    MAPIEnd
    Status "Inbox processing complete."
    MsgBox "Inbox processing complete", vbInformation, "ReadInbox"
    '
End Sub
```

Next, add a new subroutine called `ProcessInbox`, and add the code that appears in Listing 9.22.

Listing 9.22. Adding the `ProcessInbox` routine.

```
Public Sub ProcessInbox()
    '
    ' read inbox for MLM messages
    '
    Dim cErr As String
    '
    If bErr <> 0 Then
        Exit Sub
    Else
        bErr = False
    End If
    '
    Dim objFolder As Object
    Dim objMsgColl As Object
    Dim objMessage As Object
    Dim cSubject As String
    '
```

continues

Listing 9.22. continued

```
    Status "Opening Inbox..."
    Set objFolder = objMAPISession.Inbox
    If objFolder Is Nothing Then
        MsgBox "Unable to Open Inbox", vbCritical, "ProcessInbox Error"
        bErr = True
        Exit Sub
    End If
    '
    Status "Collecting Messages..."
    Set objMsgColl = objFolder.Messages
    If objMsgColl Is Nothing Then
        MsgBox "Unable to access Folder's Messages", vbCritical, "ProcessInbox
➥Error"
        bErr = True
        Exit Sub
    End If
    '
    Status "Scanning Messages for [" & ControlSetting("SearchKey") & "]..."
    Set objMessage = objMsgColl.GetFirst
    Do Until objMessage Is Nothing
        cSubject = objMessage.subject
        If InStr(cSubject, ControlSetting("SearchKey")) Then
            ProcessInboxMsg objMessage
        End If
        Set objMessage = objMsgColl.GetNext
    Loop
    '
End Sub
```

This routine performs three main tasks. The first is to open the messages stored in the Inbox folder. Every message store has an Inbox folder. All new messages are sent to the Inbox folder upon receipt.

```
Status "Opening Inbox..."
    Set objFolder = objMAPISession.Inbox
    If objFolder Is Nothing Then
        MsgBox "Unable to Open Inbox", vbCritical, "ProcessInbox Error"
        bErr = True
        Exit Sub
    End If
```

The second step is to create a collection of all the messages in the Inbox folder. You access messages as a collection of objects in the folder.

```
Status "Collecting Messages..."
    Set objMsgColl = objFolder.Messages
    If objMsgColl Is Nothing Then
        MsgBox "Unable to access Folder's Messages", vbCritical, "ProcessInbox
➥Error"
        bErr = True
        Exit Sub
    End If
```

The third process in this routine is to inspect each message in the collection to see if its subject line contains the search key word from the master control file. If found, the message is passed to the `ProcessInboxMsg` routine for further handling.

```
Status "Scanning Messages for [" & ControlSetting("SearchKey") & "]..."
    Set objMessage = objMsgColl.GetFirst
    Do Until objMessage Is Nothing
        cSubject = objMessage.subject
        If InStr(cSubject, ControlSetting("SearchKey")) Then
            ProcessInboxMsg objMessage
        End If
        Set objMessage = objMsgColl.GetNext
    Loop
```

Now add the `ProcessInboxMsg` subroutine. This routine checks the content of the message for the occurrence of MLM command words (SUB, UNSUB, LIST, GET). If one is found, the appropriate routine is called to handle the request. Enter the code shown in Listing 9.23.

Listing 9.23. Adding the `ProcessInboxMsg` routine.

```
Public Sub ProcessInboxMsg(objMsg As Object)
    '
    ' check out message subject
    '
    Dim cSubject As String
    '
    cSubject = UCase(objMsg.subject)
    '
    If InStr(cSubject, ControlSetting("NewSub")) Then
        ProcessInboxMsgNewSub objMsg
    End If
    '
    If InStr(cSubject, ControlSetting("UnSub")) Then
        ProcessInboxMsgUnSub objMsg
    End If
    '
    If InStr(cSubject, ControlSetting("GetArchive")) Then
        ProcessInboxMsgArcGet objMsg
    End If
    '
    If InStr(cSubject, ControlSetting("ListArchive")) Then
        ProcessInboxMsgArcList objMsg
    End If
    '
End Sub
```

In the next few sections you'll add supporting code to handle all the MLM subject-line commands. It's a good idea to save the project at this point before you continue.

Adding New Subscribers

When a person sends you an e-mail message with the words MLM SUB in the subject line, the MLM application adds that person's e-mail address to the subscriber list. The next set of routines handles all the processing needed to complete that task. This version of the program will also automatically send the new subscriber a greeting message (one that you designate in the control file).

First, add a new subroutine called `ProcessInboxMsgNewSub` to the project, and enter the code shown in Listing 9.24.

Listing 9.24. Adding the `ProcessInboxMsgNewSub` routine.

```
Public Sub ProcessInboxMsgNewSub(objMsg As Object)
    '
    ' add a new sub
    '
    Dim objAddrEntry As Object
    Dim cName As String
    Dim cAddress As String
    Dim cType As String
    '
    On Error Resume Next
    Set objAddrEntry = objMsg.Sender
    If SubFind(objAddrEntry) = False Then
        SubWrite objAddrEntry
        SubGreet objAddrEntry
    End If
    '
End Sub
```

This routine first checks to see if the name already exists in the subscriber control file. If not, it is added and the new subscriber is sent a friendly greeting message.

Create a new function called `SubFind`, and enter the code from Listing 9.25.

Listing 9.25. Adding the `SubFind` function.

```
Public Function SubFind(objAddr As Object) As Boolean
    '
    ' see if sub is in list
    '
    Dim cSubList As String
    Dim bReturn As Boolean
    Dim nFile As Integer
    Dim cRdLine As String
    Dim cSrchLine As String
    '
    cSubList = ControlSetting("ListSubs")
    cSrchLine = objAddr.Name & "^" & objAddr.address & "^" & objAddr.Type
    nFile = FreeFile
    bReturn = False
    '
    Open cSubList For Input As nFile
    While Not EOF(nFile)
        Line Input #nFile, cRdLine
```

```
            If cRdLine = cSrchLine Then
                bReturn = True
            End If
        Wend
        Close #nFile
        SubFind = bReturn
    '
End Function
```

The SubFind routine accepts one parameter (the name to look up), and returns True if the name is found and False if the name is not in the subscriber list.

Next, add the SubWrite subroutine to the project. The code for this routine is in Listing 9.26.

Listing 9.26. Adding the SubWrite routine.

```
Public Sub SubWrite(objAddr As Object)
    '
    ' write new address to subscriber list
    '
    Dim cSubList As String
    Dim nFile As Integer
    '
    cSubList = ControlSetting("ListSubs")
    Status "Adding New Sub..." & objAddr.Name
    '
    nFile = FreeFile
    Open cSubList For Append As nFile
    Print #nFile, objAddr.Name; "^"; objAddr.address; "^"; objAddr.Type
    Close nFile
    '
End Sub
```

Notice that the SubWrite routine copies the Name, Address, and Type properties from the AddressEntry object into the subscriber control file. Each value is separated by a caret (^). This separator character was chosen somewhat arbitrarily. You can change it if you wish.

> **WARNING**
>
> If you change the separator value, be sure you don't use a character that could be part of a valid e-mail address. E-mail addresses today can have a comma (,), colon (:), semicolon (;), slashes (/ or \), and other characters. You'll need to be careful when you choose your separator character!

Next add the SubGreet routine. This composes and sends a friendly greeting message to all new subscribers. Add the code from Listing 9.27 to your project.

Listing 9.27. Adding the SubGreet routine.

```
Public Sub SubGreet(objAddr As Object)
    '
    ' send new sub a welcome greeting
    '
    Dim cSubGreet As String
    Dim nFile As Integer
    Dim cLine As String
    Dim cMsgBody As String
    Dim objMsg As Object
    Dim objRecip As Object
    '
    Status "Sending Greet Msg to " & objAddr.Name & "..."
    '
    ' get greeting message text
    cSubGreet = ControlSetting("NewSubMsg")
    nFile = FreeFile
    '
    Open cSubGreet For Input As nFile
    While Not EOF(nFile)
        Line Input #nFile, cLine
        cMsgBody = cMsgBody & EOL & cLine
    Wend
    Close #nFile
    '
    ' now build a new message
    Set objMsg = objMAPISession.Outbox.Messages.Add
    objMsg.subject = "Welcome to the " & ControlSetting("ListName")
    objMsg.Text = cMsgBody
    ' create the recipient
    Set objRecip = objMsg.Recipients.Add
    If objAddr.Type = "MS" Then
        objRecip.Name = objAddr.Name ' handle local users
        objRecip.Type = mapiTo
        objRecip.Resolve
    Else
        objRecip.Name = objAddr.Type & ":" & objAddr.Address
        objRecip.address = objAddr.Type & ":" & objAddr.Address
        objRecip.Type = mapiTo
    End If
    ' send the message and log off
    objMsg.Update
    objMsg.Send showDialog:=False
    '
End Sub
```

The SubGreet routine looks similar to the routine used to send daily messages to subscribers. The message sent as the greeting pointed to the NewSubMsg parameter in the master control file.

Save your work before adding the code to drop subscribers from the list.

Dropping Subscribers

The routines needed to drop subscribers from the mailing list are very similar to the code needed to add them. You'll create a routine to respond to the request and two supporting routines—one to delete the name from the list, and one to send a goodbye message to the requester.

First add the ProcessInboxMsgUnSub subroutine to the project and enter the code from Listing 9.28.

Listing 9.28. Adding the ProcessInboxMsgUnSub routine.

```
Public Sub ProcessInboxMsgUnSub(objMsg As Object)
    '
    ' drop an existing sub
    '
    Dim objAddrEntry As Object
    Dim cName As String
    Dim cAddress As String
    Dim cType As String
    '
    On Error Resume Next
    Set objAddrEntry = objMsg.Sender
    If SubFind(objAddrEntry) = True Then
        SubDelete objAddrEntry
        SubBye objAddrEntry
    End If
    '
End Sub
```

This routine checks to make sure the name is in the subscriber list. If it is, then the name is dropped and a goodbye message is sent. Add the SubDelete routine to the project by copying the code from Listing 9.29.

Listing 9.29. Adding the SubDelete routine.

```
Public Sub SubDelete(objAddr As Object)
    '
    ' delete an address from the subscriber list
    '
    Dim cSubList As String
    Dim cSubTemp As String
    Dim nList As Integer
    Dim nTemp As Integer
    Dim cRdLine As String
    Dim cSrchLine As String
    '
    cSubList = ControlSetting("ListSubs")
    Status "Dropping a Sub..." & objAddr.Name
    cSrchLine = objAddr.Name & "^" & objAddr.address & "^" & objAddr.Type
    cSubTemp = "tmp001.txt"
    '
```

continues

Listing 9.29. continued

```
    nList = FreeFile
    Open cSubList For Input As nList
    nTemp = FreeFile
    Open cSubTemp For Output As nTemp
    '
    While Not EOF(nList)
        Line Input #nList, cRdLine
        If cRdLine <> cSrchLine Then
        Print #nTemp, cRdLine
        End If
    Wend
    '
    Close #nList
    Close #nTemp
    Kill cSubList
    Name cSubTemp As cSubList
    '
End Sub
```

This routine accomplishes the delete process by copying all the valid names to a temporary file, and then erasing the old file and renaming the temporary file as the new master subscriber list. While this may seem a bit convoluted, it is the quickest and simplest way to handle deletes in a sequential ASCII text file.

> **NOTE**
>
> In a more sophisticated project, you could build the subscriber list in a database and use database INSERT and DELETE operations to manage the list.

Next add the SubBye routine. This sends a goodbye message to the subscriber that was just dropped from the list. The greeting message is kept in the text file pointed to by the value of the UnSubMsg control parameter in the master control file.

Add the code shown in Listing 9.30.

Listing 9.30. Adding the SubBye routine.

```
Public Sub SubBye(objAddr As Object)
    '
    ' send old sub a goodbye msg
    '
    Dim cSubBye As String
    Dim nFile As Integer
    Dim cLine As String
    Dim cMsgBody As String
    Dim objMsg As Object
    Dim objRecip As Object
    '
    Status "Sending Bye Msg to " & objAddr.Name & "..."
    '
```

```
    ' get bye message text
    cSubBye = ControlSetting("UnSubMsg")
    nFile = FreeFile
    '
    Open cSubBye For Input As nFile
    While Not EOF(nFile)
        Line Input #nFile, cLine
        cMsgBody = cMsgBody & EOL & cLine
    Wend
    Close #nFile
    '
    ' now build a new message
    Set objMsg = objMAPISession.Outbox.Messages.Add
    objMsg.subject = "So long from the " & ControlSetting("ListName")
    objMsg.Text = cMsgBody
    ' create the recipient
    Set objRecip = objMsg.Recipients.Add
    If objAddr.Type = "MS" Then
        objRecip.Name = objAddr.Name ' handle local users
        objRecip.Type = mapiTo
        objRecip.Resolve
    Else
        objRecip.Name = objAddr.Type & ":" & objAddr.Address
        objRecip.address = objAddr.Type & ":" & objAddr.Address
        objRecip.Type = mapiTo
    End If
    ' send the message and log off
    objMsg.Update
    objMsg.Send showDialog:=False
    '
End Sub
```

The next code routines will handle subscriber requests for the list of retrievable archive messages.

Listing Archives

One of the added features of MLM is to allow subscribers to send requests for copies of old, archived messages. Users can also request a list of messages that are in the archive. You need two routines to handle the LIST command—the main caller, and the one to actually assemble and send the list.

Add the new subroutine ProcessInboxMsgArcList to the project and enter the code shown in Listing 9.31.

Listing 9.31. Adding the ProcessInboxMsgArcList routine.

```
Public Sub ProcessInboxMsgArcList(objMsg As Object)
    '
    ' get list of archives and
    ' send to requestor
    '
```

continues

Listing 9.31. continued

```
On Error Resume Next
'
Dim objAddrEntry As Object
'
Set objAddrEntry = objMsg.Sender
If SubFind(objAddrEntry) = True Then
    WriteArcList objAddrEntry
End If
'
End Sub
```

Now create the `WriteArcList` subroutine and add the code shown in Listing 9.32.

Listing 9.32. Adding the `WriteArcList` routine.

```
Public Sub WriteArcList(objAddr As Object)
    '
    ' make list of archives
    ' build message and send
    '
    Dim objMsg As Object
    Dim objRecip As Object
    Dim cArcFile As String
    Dim nArcFile As Integer
    Dim cLine As String
    Dim cFileDate As String
    Dim cFileName As String
    Dim cFileTitle As String
    Dim cMsgBody As String
    Dim nPos1 As Integer
    Dim nPos2 As Integer
    '
    Status "Sending Archive List to " & objAddr.Name & "..."
    '
    cMsgBody = "Archive List for " & ControlSetting("ListName") & EOL & EOL
    cMsgBody = cMsgBody & "All records are in the following format:" & EOL
    cMsgBody = cMsgBody & "Date(YYMMDD),FileName,Title" & EOL & EOL
    '
    cArcFile = ControlSetting("ArchiveFile")
    nArcFile = FreeFile
    Open cArcFile For Input As nArcFile
    Do While Not EOF(nArcFile)
        Line Input #1, cLine
        If Left(cLine, 1) <> ";" Then
            cMsgBody = cMsgBody & cLine & EOL
        End If
    Loop
    Close #nArcFile
    '
    ' now add message to outbox
    Set objMsg = objMAPISession.Outbox.Messages.Add
    objMsg.subject = "Archive List from " & ControlSetting("ListName")
    objMsg.Text = cMsgBody
    ' create the recipient
    Set objRecip = objMsg.Recipients.Add
```

```
    If objAddr.Type = "MS" Then
        objRecip.Name = objAddr.Name ' handle local users
        objRecip.Type = mapiTo
        objRecip.Resolve
    Else
        objRecip.Name = objAddr.Type & ":" & objAddr.Address
        objRecip.address = objAddr.Type & ":" & objAddr.Address
        objRecip.Type = mapiTo
    End If
    ' send the message
    objMsg.Update
    objMsg.Send showDialog:=False
    '
End Sub
```

The `WriteArcList` routine reads the `MLMARCH.TXT` control file and creates a message body that has a brief set of instructions and lists all available archived messages. Once this is done, the message is addressed and sent.

Save the project before you go on to the last coding section.

Sending Requested Archives

Once subscribers have received a list of available archives, they can send a MLM GET YYMMDD command on the subject line of a message to ask for a specific message to be sent to them. You need three routines to handle this processing:

■ `ProcessInboxMsgArcGet` to make the initial call for getting the archive;

■ `FindArc` for locating the requested archive message;

■ `WriteArcGet` for retrieving and sending the archive message.

First add the `ProcessInboxMsgArcGet` subroutine to your project and enter the code in Listing 9.33.

Listing 9.33. Adding the `ProcessInboxMsgArcGet` routine.

```
Public Sub ProcessInboxMsgArcGet(objMsg As Object)
    '
    ' get single archive and
    ' send to requestor
    '
    On Error Resume Next
    '
    Dim objAddrEntry As Object
    '
    Set objAddrEntry = objMsg.Sender
    If SubFind(objAddrEntry) = True Then
        WriteArcGet objMsg.subject, objAddrEntry
    End If
    '
End Sub
```

Next, add the FindArc function to the project and enter the code shown in Listing 9.34.

Listing 9.34. Adding the FindArc function.

```
Public Function FindArc(cFile As String) As String
    '
    ' search for requested file in archive list
    '
    Dim cFileDate As String
    Dim cFileName As String
    Dim cFileTitle As String
    Dim cArchFile As String
    Dim nArchFile As Integer
    Dim cLine As String
    Dim nPos1 As Integer
    Dim nPos2 As Integer
    Dim cReturn As String
    '
    cReturn = ""
    cArchFile = ControlSetting("ArchiveFile")
    nArchFile = FreeFile
    Open cArchFile For Input As nArchFile
    Do Until EOF(nArchFile)
        Line Input #nArchFile, cLine
        If Left(cLine, 1) <> ";" Then
            nPos1 = InStr(cLine, ",")
            If nPos1 <> 0 Then
                cFileDate = Left(cLine, nPos1 - 1)
            End If
            nPos2 = InStr(nPos1 + 1, cLine, ",")
            If nPos2 <> 0 Then
                cFileName = Mid(cLine, nPos1 + 1, nPos2 - (nPos1 + 1))
            End If
            If nPos2 < Len(cLine) Then
                cFileTitle = Mid(cLine, nPos2 + 1, 255)
            Else
                cFileTitle = cFileName
            End If
        End If
        '
        ' now compare!
        If UCase(cFileDate) = UCase(cFile) Then
            cReturn = cFileName
            Exit Do
        End If
    Loop
    Close #nArchFile
    '
    FindArc = cReturn
    '
End Function
```

FindArc accepts one parameter (the archive file search number—YYMMDD) and returns the actual operating system filename of the archived message. If no message is found, the return value is a zero-length string.

Finally, add the WriteArcGet routine to the project and enter the code shown in Listing 9.35.

Listing 9.35. Adding the WriteArcGet routine.

```
Public Sub WriteArcGet(cSubject As String, objAddr As Object)
    '
    ' get single archive
    ' build message and send
    '
    Dim objMsg As Object
    Dim objRecip As Object
    Dim cArcFile As String
    Dim nArcFile As Integer
    Dim cLine As String
    Dim cFileDate As String
    Dim cFileName As String
    Dim cFileTitle As String
    Dim cMsgBody As String
    Dim nPos1 As Integer
    Dim nPos2 As Integer
    Dim cArchive As String
    '
    'get archive name
    nPos1 = InStr(UCase(cSubject), "GET")
    If nPos1 <> 0 Then
        nPos2 = InStr(nPos1 + 1, cSubject, " ") ' look for next space
        If nPos2 <> 0 Then
            cArchive = Mid(cSubject, nPos2 + 1, 255)
        Else
            cArchive = ""
        End If
    End If
    '
    cArcFile = FindArc(cArchive)
    If Len(cArcFile) <> 0 Then
        cMsgBody = "Archive File [" & cArchive & "]" & EOL & EOL
        ' read archive file
        nArcFile = FreeFile
        Open cArcFile For Input As nArcFile
        Do While Not EOF(nArcFile)
            Line Input #1, cLine
            If Left(cLine, 1) <> ";" Then
                cMsgBody = cMsgBody & cLine & EOL
            End If
        Loop
        Close #nArcFile
    Else
        cMsgBody = "MLM Archive Error" & EOL & EOL
        cMsgBody = cMsgBody & "*** Unable to locate Archive [" & cArchive & "]." &
➥EOL
    End If
    '
    ' now add message to outbox
    Status "Sending Archive " & cArchive & "to " & objAddr.Name & "..."
    Set objMsg = objMAPISession.Outbox.Messages.Add
    objMsg.subject = "Archive " & cArchive & "from " & ControlSetting("ListName")
```

continues

Listing 9.35. continued

```
    objMsg.Text = cMsgBody
    ' create the recipient
    Set objRecip = objMsg.Recipients.Add
    If objAddr.Type = "MS" Then
        objRecip.Name = objAddr.Name ' handle local users
        objRecip.Type = mapiTo
        objRecip.Resolve
    Else
        objRecip.Name = objAddr.Type & ":" & objAddr.Address
        objRecip.address = objAddr.Type & ":" & objAddr.Address
        objRecip.Type = mapiTo
    End If
    ' send the message
    objMsg.Update
    objMsg.Send showDialog:=False
    '
End Sub
```

The `WriteArcGet` routine picks the archive name out of the subject line and, if it is found, reads the archived message, composes a new message, and sends it to the requestor.

That is all the code for this project. The next step is to test the various MLM functions. Be sure to save the project before you begin testing. Once testing is complete, you can make an executable version of the project for installation on any workstation that has the MAPI OLE Messaging Library installed.

Running the MLM Application

In a production setting, you can set up an e-mail account that is dedicated to processing MLM requests. All e-mail messages regarding that list can be addressed to this dedicated account. You (or someone else) can run the MLM once a day and it can automatically log onto the dedicated account and perform the list processing. Also, since MLM accepts a command-line parameter, you can build control files for several different mailing lists and run them all from the same workstation. You just need to keep in mind that in order to process the messages, you need to start the MLM application and run it at least once a day.

> **TIP**
>
> If you have the Microsoft Plus! pack installed, you can use the System Agent to schedule MLM to run at off-peak times. If you decide to use the System Agent, you need to add additional code to the project to allow you to select the `Read & Send` button automatically. Just add an additional parameter to the command line that will execute the `Command1_Click` event for `Read & Send`.

For testing purposes, set the MLM control file to log onto your own e-mail account. You can then send messages to yourself and test the features of MLM to make sure they are working properly.

Before you start testing you need to make sure you have valid ASCII files for the new subscribe greeting (MLMHELLO.TXT) and the unsubscribe departing message (MLMBYE.TXT). Refer to Listings 9.36 and 9.37 for examples of each of these files.

> **TIP**
>
> You can also find examples in the source code directory Chap08\MLM created when you installed the CD-ROM.

Listing 9.36. Default MLMHELLO.TXT message.

```
You are now added to the MLM Mailing List!

Welcome!

MCA
```

Listing 9.37. Default MLMBYE.TXT message.

```
Sorry you're leaving us!

BYE - MCA
```

Use NOTEPAD.EXE to create these two files and save them in the project directory.

You may also need to modify the MLMSKED.TXT file to match today's date. Change the first entry from 960225 to make sure that any registered subscriber gets a message when you run the SendMail routine.

Testing the MLM Application

Now you're ready to test MLM!

First, add your name to the mailing list. To do this, start up your MAPI client (you could use the one you built in Chapter 7, "Creating a Simple MAPI Client with the MAPI Controls") and send a message with the words MLM SUB in the subject line. It does not matter what you put in the message body; it will be ignored by MLM (see Figure 9.2).

FIGURE 9.2.

*Sending a request to join
the MLM mailing list.*

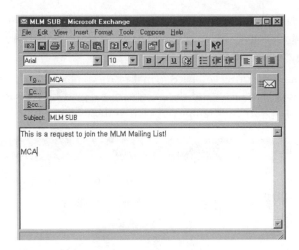

Once the request is sent, load MLM and select the ReadMail button. This will scan all the messages in your inbox, and (if all goes right!) find and process your request to be added to the list. Figure 9.3 shows how the MLM screen looks as it is processing.

FIGURE 9.3.

Running the MLM
ReadMail *process.*

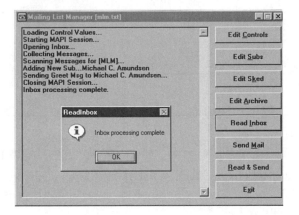

After MLM is done, start up your MAPI client again. You should see a greeting message in your inbox confirming that you have been added to the MLM mailing list (see Figure 9.4).

Next, try sending a message that requests a list of available archives. Use your MAPI client to compose a message with MLM LIST in the subject line. After sending the message, run the MLM ReadMail option again, and then check your inbox with the MAPI client. You should see a message similar to the one in Figure 9.5.

FIGURE 9.4.

Confirmation greeting message from MLM.

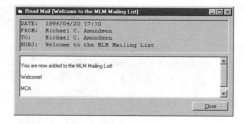

FIGURE 9.5.

Receiving a list of available archives from MLM.

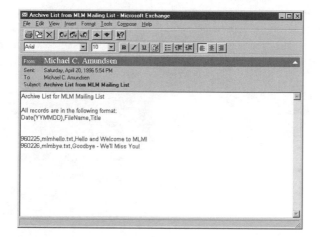

Once you get the list, you can send MLM a command to retrieve a specific message in the archive. Use your MAPI client to send a message that asks for one of the messages. After sending the message, run MLM `ReadMail`, and then recheck your MAPI client for the results. You should get a message like the one in Figure 9.6.

FIGURE 9.6.

Receiving a requested archive message from MLM.

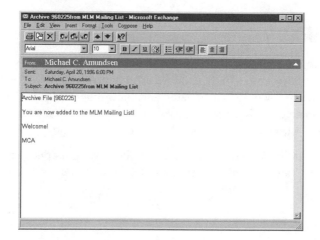

You can test the SendMail option by simply starting MLM and pressing the SendMail button. This will search for a message file tagged with today's date and send it to all subscribers in the list. To test this, modify one of the entries in the MLMSKED.TXT file so that it has the current date as its key number. Figure 9.7 shows what the MLM progress screen looks like as it is working.

FIGURE 9.7.

Running the SendMail
option of MLM.

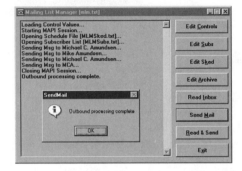

Finally, you can test the unsubscribe feature of MLM by sending a message with MLM UNSUB in the subject. When MLM receives this message, it will drop your name from the subscriber list and send you a departing message.

Summary

In this chapter you built a mailing list manager using Microsoft's OLE Messaging Library. This application lets you define a mailing list, allow others to become list subscribers, publish messages automatically (based on date), and allow others to query and retrieve old messages from the list archives. This program can accept members from within a single network, or from around the world through Internet (or other) transports.

In the next chapter you'll use OLE to build a MAPI application that allows distant users to query databases and other collections of information by way of e-mail.

10

Building a MAPI-Enabled Forum Tool

In this chapter you'll learn how to use MAPI services to create a threaded discussion client. Threaded discussions clients are used quite frequently in groupware settings and on the Internet. The biggest difference between a discussion tool and an e-mail client is that the e-mail client is designed primarily for conducting one-to-one conversations. The discussion tool, however, is designed to support multiple parties, all participating in the same discussion. Even though MAPI services were originally deployed as only an e-mail solution, Microsoft has added several features to MAPI that now make it an excellent platform for building discussion applications.

Before getting into the details of building the tool, you'll learn a bit more about the differences between e-mail and discussion communications. You'll also learn how to take advantage of little-known MAPI properties and new features of the OLE Messaging library that make it easy to put together a standalone discussion tool that can be deployed from within a Local Area Network, over a Wide Area Network, or even across the Internet. You'll learn

- The difference between the MAPI Send and Update methods.
- How to use the ConversationTopic and ConversationIndex properties to create threaded discussions in MAPI messages.
- How to create messages that are posted to a MAPI folder instead of sent to a single individual.

As an added bonus, after you've completed the programming example in this chapter, you'll have a set of library functions that allow you to easily add threaded discussion capabilities to new or existing Visual Basic applications.

Discussion Groups versus E-Mail

By now, most of us have used electronic discussion forums at least once in our lives. And there are many who use them every single day. The advantage of a discussion forum over direct person-to-person e-mail is that you can communicate with a large number of people without generating a large number of messages. In fact, reduced traffic is one of the biggest reasons to consider employing discussion groups as part of your electronic message system.

There are a number of other advantages to using discussion groups instead of e-mail. Often, it is easier to find answers to technical problems if you can go to a place where all the "techies" hang out. Discussion forums can work the same way. Instead of trying to e-mail several people in attempts to solve your problem, you can often find a discussion forum where you can send a single request that will reach hundreds (possibly thousands) of people who may be able to help you. So discussion forums can increase your ability to get your problems solved sooner.

Another good way to highlight the differences between e-mail and discussion groups is by comparing several face-to-face meetings (e-mail messages) with a single staff meeting where everyone shows up at the same place at the same time (the discussion forum). Using forum communications can reduce the amount of time you need to spend communicating. You can say it once and reach lots of people instead of having to repeat your message in lots of single e-mail messages.

Companies use forums as a way to communicate information of general interest as well as a way to take advantage of specialized expertise within an organization. Where corporate e-mail can lead to isolated individuals communicating in a vacuum, discussion groups can foster increased interaction with others and a sense of belonging to a special group—even if one or more of the team members is half-way around the world.

Now that you have a general idea of what discussion groups are and how you can use them in your organization, you're ready to review the three key concepts that make discussion systems different from e-mail systems.

Folders as Destinations

First, and most important, users participating in an online discussion forum do not send messages to individuals. Instead they send their messaging to a single location where all messages are stored. In the MAPI model, the storage location is called a folder. When you create MAPI-based forum tools, you'll select a folder (or folders) to hold all the correspondence from others participating in the forum.

> **NOTE**
>
> There are times when forum participants will initiate private e-mail correspondence in order to cover a topic in more depth or to delve deeper into an aspect of the discussion that would not be interesting to most of the other members.

Then, after each message has been composed, you just *post* the message to the discussion folder for others to see. They, if appropriate, respond to your message with their own comments. The key point to remember is that messages are addressed to locations, not people.

Using the ConversationTopic and ConversationIndex Properties

Another key aspect of discussion groups is the ability to track topics in a *thread* that leads from the beginning of the discussion to the end. As each participant replies to an existing message, a relationship is established between the source message and the reply. Of course, it is perfectly correct (and quite common) to generate a "reply to a reply." This can continue on indefinitely. And in the process an intricate web of ideas and comments all collect in the storage folder that houses the discussion group.

Some discussion tools simply list the messages in the chronological order in which they were received. These are referred to as *non-threaded* or *flat-table* discussion tools (see Figure 10.1).

FIGURE 10.1.

Viewing messages in flat format, chronological order.

Non-threaded tools (often called *readers*) can be handy, but most people prefer the discussion tools that provide threaded discussion tracking. With threaded tools, each conversation that is initiated is a *branch*. Each branch can have its own subsequent conversation thread. And those threads can be combined with others, too. Viewing discussion messages as related threads is really handy (see Figure 10.2).

FIGURE 10.2.

Viewing messages in threaded order.

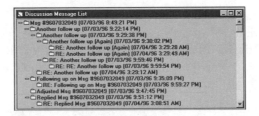

MAPI uses two special properties of the `Message` object to keep track of each branch and sub-branch of a threaded discussion. These two properties are the `ConversationTopic` and the `ConversationIndex` properties. The `ConversationTopic` is usually a readable string. This is much like the subject line of a mail message. Conversation topics for a discussion forum for a typical computer firm might be

- General questions
- Sales
- Technical support
- Press releases

NOTE

Some forums have fixed topics and only allow users to select from a predetermined list when posting messages. Other forums allow users to enter free-form text into the topic field.

MAPI uses the `ConversationIndex` property to keep track of conversation threads within the topic group. This is usually done using some type of numbering scheme. Microsoft recommends that programmers use the same method that is employed by Microsoft Exchange when populating the ConversationIndex field. Microsoft Exchange uses the CoCreateGuid API call to generate a unique number to place in the ConversationIndex field. New messages that respond to an existing message should inherit the ConversationIndex of the previous message and append their own index value to the right. This way, each new branch of the conversation has a longer ConversationIndex. You'll get a better look at this technique when you build the sample Visual Basic project later in this chapter.

> **NOTE**
>
> The CoCreateGuid API generates a unique value based on the system date (among other things). You can use any method you wish to keep track of conversation threads, but it is highly recommended that you use the method described here. It is quick, effective, and requires very few computing resources.

Update **versus** Send

The last major concept to deal with when building discussion tools is the use of the MAPI Update method instead of the Send method. In all the examples covered in the book so far, when you complete a new message and want to place it into the MAPI message pool, you use the Send method (or some type of Send API call) to release the message to MAPI for delivery. This works when you have a person to whom you are addressing the message. However, because discussion messages are not addressed to persons but to folders instead, you cannot "send" new messages. Instead you use the Update method to update the contents of a MAPI folder. In fact, attempting to use the Send method to deliver forum messages will result in a MAPI error.

> **TIP**
>
> The key idea here is to think of updating the contents of a MAPI folder as opposed to sending a message to a person.

The actual process of placing a message in a MAPI folder includes adding a blank message to the target folder, setting that message's subject and text body (just like any mail message) and then setting several other message properties, too. Each of the properties shown in Table 10.1 must be set properly before you invoke the Update method to place a message in a MAPI folder.

Table 10.1. Properties that must be set when updating a message to a folder.

Message Property	Setting	Comment
Type	IPM.xxxx	Where xxxx is a string value you define. Usually you'll use the name of the program that generates this forum message. This can be used to filter incoming messages or for some other use. This is optional but highly recommended. If you leave this property blank, MAPI inserts IPM.Note.
ConversationTopic	<Some Readable String>	For new posts into the folder, this is usually a copy of the Subject property. For replies to an existing folder message, this will be the same as the source message.
ConversationIndex	HHHHHHHHHHHHHH...	Some internal value that shows message inheritance and sequence. It is recommended you use the Microsoft CoCreateGuid API to generate a 16-bit hex value based on workstation time (see the programming example later in this chapter). Reply messages will append their own Guid to the Guid of the message to which they are replying.
TimeSent	Now()	This is the time the message is placed in the target folder.
TimeReceived	Now()	This should be set to the same time as the TimeSent property.
Submitted	TRUE	Indicates the message was queued for delivery. This field is set by MAPI when using the Send method. You must set it yourself when using the Update method.
Unread	TRUE	Indicates that this is a new message. This field is set by MAPI when using the Send method. You must set it yourself when using the Update method.
Sent	TRUE	Indicates that this message was successfully delivered. This field is set by MAPI when using the Send method. You must set it yourself when using the Update method.

> **NOTE**
>
> You'll get to see the details of creating a forum message when you build the forum tool later in this chapter. The main thing to keep in mind now is that you do *not* use the Send method to place messages in folders.

So there are the three key points to remember about the differences between e-mail and discussion messages:

- Discussion messages are addressed to folders, not people.
- MAPI uses the ConversationTopic and ConversationIndex properties to keep track of discussion threads.
- You use the MAPI Update method to deliver discussion messages. You use the MAPI Send method to deliver mail messages.

Now it's time to use Visual Basic to build the example forum tool.

The Discuss Project

For the rest of the chapter, you'll build a complete discussion tool that can be used to track ongoing messages in a target folder. You'll be able to use the program to read messages, generate replies to existing messages, and start new discussion threads. You'll also be able to select the target folder for the discussion. This way, you can use the same tool to monitor more than one discussion.

> **NOTE**
>
> The forum tool described in this chapter is a very basic project. Not much time will be spent on the user interface. This is done to keep focus on the general issues of creating a discussion tool for MAPI systems. If you plan to put a version of this project into production, you'll want to add some bells and whistles to make this a more friendly product.

You'll use the OLE Messaging library (OML) to access MAPI services for this project. The OML gives you all the features you need to be able to manipulate message and folder properties within the MAPI file system. Although you can use the MAPI.OCX to read most of the discussion-related properties, you cannot use the OCX to place messages in a target MAPI folder. Also, you cannot use the simple MAPI API declarations to gain access to target folders or to manipulate message properties.

> **TIP**
>
> If you are planning to build any software that manipulates folders, you'll need to use the OLE Messaging library. No other Microsoft programming interface (besides the C MAPI interface) allows you to gain access to the folders collection.

There is one main code module and several forms in the Discuss project you'll build here.

■ *MAPIPost*—This code module holds all the routines for posting new threads, replying to threads, and collecting information on the available information stores, folders, and messages available to the workstation. You can use the code here in other Visual Basic discussion projects.

■ *modDiscuss*—This code module contains a few constants and global variables used for the Discuss project.

■ *mdiDiscuss*—This is the main form. This acts as a wrapper for the note form and the message list form.

■ *frmNote*—This form is used to read, compose, and reply to existing forum messages.

■ *frmMsgs*—This form is used to display a list of discussion messages within the target folder. The messages are shown in the threaded discussion form.

■ *frmOptions*—This form allows users to change the target folder for the discussion, set the default MAPI logon profile, and control whether the message listing is shown in threaded or flat-table format.

■ *frmAbout*—This is the standard About box for the project.

> **NOTE**
>
> Before you start coding the Discuss project, make sure you have added the OLE Messaging type library. Do this by selecting Tools | References from the main menu of Visual Basic. You will need to install the OLE Messaging library from the MSDN CD-ROM before you can locate it using the "Tools | References" menu option.

The MAPIPost Code Library

The MAPIPost Code Library contains several very important routines. These routines will be used throughout the project to gain access to folder collections and message collections within the folders. This also holds routines for posting new messages and generating replies to existing messages. There are also several routines for performing folder and message searches. You'll be able to use the routines in this module in other MAPI-related projects.

First, start a new Visual Basic project and add a BAS module (Insert | Module). Set its Name property to MAPIPost and save the file as MAPIPOST.BAS. Now add the code shown in Listing 10.1 to the declaration section of the form.

Listing 10.1. Adding the declarations for the module.

```
Option Explicit

'
' OLE message objects
Public objSession As Object
Public objMsgColl As Object
Public objMsg As Object
Public objRecipColl As Object
Public objRecip As Object
Public objAttachColl As Object
Public objAttach As Object
Public objAddrEntry As Object
Public objUserEntry As Object
Public objFolderColl As Object
Public objFolder As Object
Public objInfoStoreColl As Object
Public objInfoStore As Object
Public gnIndentlevel as Integer
Public cStoreID As String

'
' UDT for store/folder pairs
Type FolderType
    Name As String
    FolderID As String
    StoreID As String
End Type
'
Public FolderRec() As FolderType        ' members
Public iFldrCnt As Integer              ' pointer

'
' UDT for message/conversation pairs
Type MsgType
    Subject As String
    Topic As String
    ConvIndex As String
    MsgID As String
    Date As Date
End Type
'
Public MsgRec() As MsgType              ' members
Public iMsgCnt As Integer              ' pointer

'
' type for creating Exchange-compliant timestamp
Type GUID
    guid1 As Long
    guid2 As Long
```

continues

Listing 10.1. continued

```
    guid3 As Long
    guid4 As Long
End Type
'
Declare Function CoCreateGuid Lib "OLE32.DLL" (pGuid As GUID) As Long
Public Const S_OK = 0
```

You'll notice the usual OLE Messaging library object declarations along with two user-defined types that will be used to keep track of message and folder collections. This will come in quite handy as you'll see later on. There is also the `CoCreateGuid` API call. You'll use this to generate unique `ConversationIndex` values for your message threads.

Next you need to add code that starts and ends MAPI services. Listing 10.2 shows the `OLEMAPIStart` and `OLEMAPIEnd` routines. Add them to your project.

Listing 10.2. Adding the `OLEMAPIStart` and `OLEMAPIEnd` routines.

```
Public Sub OLEMAPIStart(cUserProfile As String)
    '
    ' start an OLE MAPI session
    '
    On Error Resume Next
    Set objSession = CreateObject("MAPI.Session")
    objSession.Logon profilename:=cUserProfile
    '
    If Err <> 0 Then
        MsgBox "Unable to Start MAPI Services!", vbCritical, "OLEMAPIStart"
        End
    End If
    '
End Sub

Public Sub OLEMAPIEnd()
    '
    On Error Resume Next
    objSession.Logoff ' end mapi session
    '
End Sub
```

The next routines are used to build a collection of all the folders in all the message stores available to the workstation. You'll remember that MAPI 1.0 allows more than one message store for each workstation. Typically, users will have a personal message store, a server-based collection of messages, and possibly a message store related to an outside messaging service (such as Sprint, CompuServe, and so on). Each one of these stores has its own set of folders, too. The routine in Listing 10.3 shows you how you can enumerate all the folders in all the message stores and build a local user-defined type that you can use to locate and manipulate MAPI folders. Add the code shown in Listing 10.3 to your project.

Listing 10.3. Adding the CollectFolders routine.

```
Public Sub CollectFolders(Optional ctrl As Variant)
    '
    ' build folder tree
    '
    Dim objRootFolder As Object
    Dim lobjFolders As Object
    Dim nIter As Integer
    Dim nStoreCount as Integer
Dim bLoadCtrl As Boolean
    '
    ' loading optional display?
    If IsMissing(ctrl) Or IsNull(ctrl) Then
        ctrl = Null
        bLoadCtrl = False
    Else
        bLoadCtrl = True
    End If
    '
    gnIndentlevel = 0
    cStoreID = ""
    '
    ' get collection of information stores
    Set objInfoStoreColl = objSession.InfoStores
    nStoreCount = objInfoStoreColl.Count
    '
    ' walk through all stores to get folders
    For nIter = 1 To nStoreCount
        iFldrCnt = iFldrCnt + 1
        ReDim Preserve FolderRec(iFldrCnt)
        FolderRec(iFldrCnt).StoreID = objInfoStoreColl.Item(nIter).ID
        FolderRec(iFldrCnt).FolderID = "" ' no folder for a store!
        FolderRec(iFldrCnt).Name = objInfoStoreColl.Item(nIter).Name
        cStoreID = FolderRec(iFldrCnt).StoreID ' hold this for the other folders
        '
        ' add to display control
        If bLoadCtrl = True Then
            ctrl.AddItem FolderRec(iFldrCnt).Name ' add to display
        End If
        '
        ' point to top of store and start loading
        Set objRootFolder = objInfoStoreColl.Item(nIter).RootFolder
        Set objFolderColl = objRootFolder.Folders
        Set lobjFolders = objFolderColl
        LoadFolder lobjFolders, ctrl
        gnIndentlevel = 0
    Next nIter
    '
End Sub
```

You'll see that the routine in Listing 10.3 walks through all the attached message stores and calls the LoadFolders routine to actually collect all the folders in a message store. This routine also allows you to pass an option list control (list box, combo box, or outline control). The routine will use this control to build an onscreen pick list of the available folders.

Now add the LoadFolders routine from Listing 10.4 to your project.

Listing 10.4. Adding the LoadFolders routine.

```
Sub LoadFolder(aFolders As Object, Optional ctrl As Variant)
    '
    ' look for folders in the collection
    '
    Dim mobjFolder As Object
    Dim mFolderCol As Object
    Dim bLoadCtrl As Boolean
    '
    gnIndentlevel = gnIndentlevel + 1
    '
    If IsMissing(ctrl) Or IsNull(ctrl) Then
        bLoadCtrl = False
    Else
        bLoadCtrl = True
    End If
    '
    Set mobjFolder = aFolders.GetFirst
    While Not mobjFolder Is Nothing
        iFldrCnt = iFldrCnt + 1
        ReDim Preserve FolderRec(iFldrCnt)
        '
        FolderRec(iFldrCnt).StoreID = cStoreID
        FolderRec(iFldrCnt).FolderID = mobjFolder.ID
        FolderRec(iFldrCnt).Name = mobjFolder.Name
        '
        ' optionally load screen display
        If bLoadCtrl = True Then
            ctrl.AddItem Space(gnIndentlevel * 5) & FolderRec(iFldrCnt).Name
        End If
        '
        ' look for nested folders
        Set mFolderCol = mobjFolder.Folders
        LoadFolder mFolderCol, ctrl
        '
        ' done with nested folders
        gnIndentlevel = gnIndentlevel - 1
        Set mobjFolder = aFolders.GetNext
    Wend
    '
End Sub
```

Notice that this routine is called recursively in order to collect all the folders that might be found *within* a folder. Since MAPI places no restrictions on how many levels of folders may be defined, you need to use a recursive routine to locate all the available folders.

Once you have built the folder collection, you'll need a method for pulling information out of the collection. Listing 10.5 shows a function that will take the friendly name of a folder and return the unique folder ID and store ID. Add this to your project.

Listing 10.5. Adding the `GetFolderRec` function.

```
Public Function GetFolderRec(cFolderName As String) As FolderType
    '
    ' take name, return structure
    '
    Dim x As Integer
    Dim y As Integer
    '
    ' start w/ a blank return
    GetFolderRec.StoreID = ""
    GetFolderRec.FolderID = ""
    GetFolderRec.Name = ""
    '
    y = UBound(FolderRec) ' get total recs in array
    '
    ' walk through array
    For x = 0 To y - 1
        If Trim(UCase(FolderRec(x).Name)) = Trim(UCase(cFolderName)) Then
            GetFolderRec = FolderRec(x)
            Exit Function
        End If
    Next x
    '
End Function
```

> **WARNING**
>
> This routine will return the folder record of the first folder with the name you request. Because MAPI allows users to define two folders with the same name, this routine may not always return the results expected. This works fine for most projects, but you should keep it in mind when developing MAPI search tools.

You also need some tools for collecting and accessing all the discussion messages in a folder. Listing 10.6 shows the routine that you can use to collect all messages into a local user-defined type. Add the routine to your project.

Listing 10.6. Adding the `OLEMAPIGetMsgs` routine.

```
Public Sub OLEMAPIGetMsgs(cFolderName As String, Optional ctrl As Variant)
    '
    ' get all the discussion messages
    '
    Dim uFolder As FolderType
    ReDim MsgRec(0)
    Dim bLoadCtrl As Boolean
    '
    Set objFolder = Nothing
    Set objMsgColl = Nothing
    Set objMsg = Nothing
```

continues

Listing 10.6. continued

```
'
iMsgCnt = 0
uFolder = GetFolderRec(cFolderName)
'
' check for optional control
If IsMissing(ctrl) Or IsNull(ctrl) Then
    ctrl = Null
    bLoadCtrl = False
Else
    bLoadCtrl = True
    ctrl.Clear
End If
'
' now walk through folder to find discussion msgs
If uFolder.Name = "" Then
    MsgBox "Unable to locate folder!", vbExclamation, uFolder.Name
    Exit Sub
End If
'
' open store, folder
Set objFolder = objSession.GetFolder(uFolder.FolderID, uFolder.StoreID)
If objFolder Is Nothing Then
    MsgBox "Unable to open folder!", vbExclamation, uFolder.Name
    Exit Sub
End If
'
' get message collection
Set objMsgColl = objFolder.Messages
If objMsgColl Is Nothing Then
    MsgBox "No messages in folder", vbExclamation, uFolder.Name
    Exit Sub
End If
'
' ok, get first message
On Error Resume Next
Set objMsg = objMsgColl.GetFirst
'
' now walk through folder to get all discussion msgs
Do Until objMsg Is Nothing
    If objMsg.Type = "IPM.Discuss" Then
        iMsgCnt = iMsgCnt + 1
        ReDim Preserve MsgRec(iMsgCnt)
        MsgRec(iMsgCnt).Subject = objMsg.Subject
        MsgRec(iMsgCnt).Topic = objMsg.ConversationTopic
        MsgRec(iMsgCnt).ConvIndex = objMsg.ConversationIndex
        MsgRec(iMsgCnt).MsgID = objMsg.ID
        MsgRec(iMsgCnt).Date = objMsg.TimeReceived
        '
        ' optionally load control
        If bLoadCtrl = True Then
            ctrl.AddItem objMsg.ConversationIndex
        End If
    End If
    Set objMsg = objMsgColl.GetNext
Loop
'
```

```
    Beep ' tell 'em you're done!
    '
End Sub
```

You'll notice that this routine allows you to place the messages in a list control for sorting and display. You may also have noticed that the field placed in the controls is the ConversationIndex property. Sorting the messages on the ConversationIndex property will automatically give you the threaded list you need. You can then take the sorted list from the list control and use that to generate an onscreen display of the subject or other properties of the message—all in threaded order!

You'll need three different routines to access messages from the user-defined array. First, you need a routine that allows you to pass in a pointer to the sorted list and that returns the ConversationIndex of a message. Listing 10.7 shows how this is done.

Listing 10.7. Adding the MsgIndex function.

```
Public Function MsgIndex(ctrl As Control, iPtr As Integer) As String
    '
    ' accept pointer to sorted list control
    ' and the sorted list control
    ' return msg convIndex property
    '
    MsgIndex = ctrl.List(iPtr)
    '
End Function
```

Next you need a routine that takes the conversation index and returns the complete internal message structure. Listing 10.8 shows you how to do this step.

Listing 10.8. Adding the MsgPtr function.

```
Public Function MsgPtr(cIndex As String) As MsgType
    '
    ' accepts conversation index, returns msg type
    '
    Dim x As Integer
    Dim y As Integer
    '
    y = UBound(MsgRec)
    '
    For x = 1 To y
        If MsgRec(x).ConvIndex = cIndex Then
            MsgPtr = MsgRec(x)
            Exit Function
        End If
    Next x
    '
End Function
```

Finally, you can also use a function that returns the Message user-defined type based on the direct pointer. Add the code from listing 10.9 to your project.

Listing 10.9. Adding the `GetMsgRec` function.

```
Public Function GetMsgRec(iPointer As Integer) As MsgType
    '
    ' accept pointer, return strucutre
    '

    '
    ' start w blank records
    GetMsgRec.MsgID = ""
    GetMsgRec.ConvIndex = ""
    GetMsgRec.Subject = ""
    GetMsgRec.Topic = ""

    '
    ' now try to find it
    If iPointer < 0 Or iPointer > UBound(MsgRec) Then
        MsgBox "Invalid Message pointer!", vbExclamation, "GetMsgRec"
        Exit Function
    Else
        GetMsgRec = MsgRec(iPointer + 1)
    End If
    '
End Function
```

While you're coding the message routines, add the `FillOutline` subroutine shown in Listing 10.10. This routine loads an outline control from the sorted list. The outline can then be displayed to the user.

Listing 10.10. Adding the `FillOutline` routine.

```
Public Sub FillOutline(ctrlIn As Control, ctrlOut As Control)
    '
    ' accept a sorted list box as input
    ' copy the recs to an outline w/ indents
    '
    Dim x As Integer
    Dim uMsg As MsgType
    '
    ctrlOut.Clear ' throw all the old stuff out
    '
    ' load the outline in sorted order
    For x = 0 To ctrlIn.ListCount - 1
        uMsg = MsgPtr(ctrlIn.List(x))
        ctrlOut.AddItem uMsg.Subject & " (" & Format(uMsg.Date, "general date") &
        ➥")"
        If bThreaded = True Then
            ctrlOut.Indent(x) = Len(ctrlIn.List(x)) / 16
        End If
```

```
    Next x
    '
    ' expand all nodes for viewing
    For x = 0 To ctrlOut.ListCount - 1
        If ctrlOut.HasSubItems(x) = True Then
            ctrlOut.Expand(x) = True
        End If
    Next x
    '
End Sub
```

The `FillOutline` routine also makes sure threaded messages are indented properly and expands the entire message tree for users to see the various branches.

One more handy routine is the `MakeTimeStamp` function. This will be used to generate the `ConversationIndex` values. Add the code from Listing 10.11 to your project.

Listing 10.11. Adding the `MakeTimeStamp` routine.

```
Public Function MakeTimeStamp() As String
    '
    ' create Exchange-type time stamp
    '
    Dim lResult As Long
    Dim lGuid As GUID
    '
    On Error GoTo LocalErr
    '
    lResult = CoCreateGuid(lGuid)
    If lResult = S_OK Then
        MakeTimeStamp = Hex$(lGuid.guid1) & Hex$(lGuid.guid2)
    Else
        MakeTimeStamp = "00000000"    ' zeroes
    End If
    Exit Function

LocalErr:
    MsgBox "Error " & Str(Err) & ": " & Error$(Err)
    MakeTimeStamp = "00000000"
    Exit Function
    '
End Function
```

Only two routines remain: `OLEMAPIPostMsg` and `OLEMAPIReplyMsg`. The `OLEMAPIPostMsg` routine builds and posts a new message thread to the target folder. Add the code from Listing 10.12 to your project.

Listing 10.12. Adding the `OLEMAPIPostMsg` routine.

```
Public Sub OLEMAPIPostMsg(cFolderName As String, cTopic As String, cSubject As
String, cBody As String)
    '
    ' post a message to the folder (starts a new thread)
    '
    ' _ _ _ _ _ _ _ _ _ _ _ _ _ _
    ' Inputs:
    '    cFolderName     - name of target folder
    '    cTopic          - general discussion topic
    '    cSubject        - user's subject line
    '    cBody           - user's body text
    ' _ _ _ _ _ _ _ _ _ _ _ _ _ _
    '
    Dim uFolder As FolderType
    '
    ' get folder structure
    uFolder = GetFolderRec(cFolderName) ' get the structure
    If uFolder.FolderID = "" Then
        MsgBox "Unable to Locate Folder!", vbExclamation, cFolderName
        Exit Sub
    End If
    '
    ' open folder, store
    Set objFolder = objSession.GetFolder(uFolder.FolderID, uFolder.StoreID)
    If objFolder Is Nothing Then
        MsgBox "Unable to open folder!", vbExclamation, uFolder.Name
        Exit Sub
    End If
    '
    ' create new message
    Set objMsg = objFolder.Messages.Add
    If objMsg Is Nothing Then
        MsgBox "Unable to create new message in folder!", vbExclamation,
        ↪uFolder.Name
        Exit Sub
    End If
    '
    ' fix up subject/topic
    If cTopic = "" And cSubject = "" Then
        cTopic = "Thread #" & Format(Now(), "YYMMDDHHmm")
    End If
    '
    If cTopic = "" And cSubject <> "" Then
        cTopic = cSubject
    End If
    '
    If cSubject = "" And cTopic <> "" Then
        cSubject = cTopic
    End If
    '
    ' now compose the message
    With objMsg
        '
        ' set user-supplied info
        .Subject = cSubject
        .Text = cBody
```

```
            '
            ' set stock properties
            .Type = "IPM.Discuss"
            .ConversationTopic = cTopic
            .ConversationIndex = MakeTimeStamp
            .TimeSent = Now()
            .TimeReceived = .TimeSent
            .Submitted = True
            .Unread = True
            .Sent = True
            '
            .Update ' force msg into the folder
        End With
        '
        objFolder.Update ' update the folder object
        '
End Sub
```

There are quite a few things going on in this routine. First, it locates the folder and message store where the message will be posted. Then a new message object is created, populated with the appropriate values, and posted (using the Update method) to the target folder.

The OLEMAPIReplyMsg is quite similar, but this method carries information forward from the source message to make sure that the conversation thread is maintained. Add the code from Listing 10.13 to your project.

Listing 10.13. Adding the OLEMAPIReplyMsg routine.

```
Public Sub OLEMAPIReply(FolderName As String, iCount As Integer, cSubject As
➡String, cBody As String)
    '
    ' post a message reply (continues existing thread)
    '
    ' _ _ _ _ _ _ _ _ _ _ _ _ _ _ _ _ _
    ' Inputs:
    '   FolderName  - string name of target folder
    '   iCount      - index into msg array (points to source msg)
    '   cSubject    - user's subject line (if null uses "RE:" & source subject)
    '   cBody       - user's msg body
    ' _ _ _ _ _ _ _ _ _ _ _ _ _ _ _ _ _
    '
    Dim cIndex As String
    Dim uMsg As MsgType
    Dim uFolder As FolderType
    Dim objSourceMsg As Object
    '
    ' check msg pointer
    If iCount < 0 Then
        MsgBox "No Message Selected", vbExclamation, "OLEMAPIReply"
        Exit Sub
    End If
    '
    ' get folder for posting
```

continues

Listing 10.13. continued

```
    uFolder = GetFolderRec(FolderName)
    If uFolder.FolderID = "" Then
        MsgBox "Unable to locate folder!", vbExclamation, FolderName
        Exit Sub
    End If
    '
    ' get source message
    cIndex = MsgIndex(frmMsgs.list1, iCount)
    uMsg = MsgPtr(cIndex)
    Set objSourceMsg = objSession.GetMessage(uMsg.MsgID, uFolder.StoreID)
    If objSourceMsg Is Nothing Then
        MsgBox "Unable to Load selected Message!", vbExclamation, uMsg.Subject
        Exit Sub
    End If
    '
    ' open target store, folder
    Set objFolder = objSession.GetFolder(uFolder.FolderID, uFolder.StoreID)
    If objFolder Is Nothing Then
        MsgBox "Unable to open target folder", vbExclamation, uFolder.Name
        Exit Sub
    End If
    '
    ' create a new blank message object
    Set objMsg = objFolder.Messages.Add
    If objMsg Is Nothing Then
        MsgBox "Unable to add message to folder", vbExclamation, objFolder.Name
        Exit Sub
    End If
    '
    ' fix up target subject, if needed
    If cSubject = "" Then
        cSubject = "RE: " & objSourceMsg.Subject
    End If
    '
    ' now compose reply msg
    With objMsg
        '
        ' user properties
        .Subject = cSubject
        .Text = cBody
        '
        ' stock properties
        .Type = "IPM.Discuss"
        .ConversationTopic = objSourceMsg.ConversationTopic
        .ConversationIndex = objSourceMsg.ConversationIndex & MakeTimeStamp
        .TimeSent = Now()
        .TimeReceived = .TimeSent
        .Submitted = True
        .Unread = True
        .Sent = True
        '
        .Update ' force msg into folder
    End With
    '
    objFolder.Update ' update folder object
    '
End Sub
```

That's all there is to this module. Save the module (MAPIPOST.BAS) and the project (DISCUSS.VBP) before moving on to the next section.

The Discuss and Msgs Forms

The two main forms for the Discuss project are the MDI Discuss form and the Msgs form. The MDI form presents a button array and hosts all the other forms. The Msgs form is used to display the threaded discussion list.

You'll also need to add a few values to a short BAS module. These are project-level values that are used throughout the project. Add a BAS module, set its Name property to ModDiscuss and save it as MODDISCUSS.BAS. Now add the code shown in Listing 10.14 to the general declaration section of the form.

Listing 10.14. Adding project-level declarations.

```
Option Explicit

'
' constants
Public Const dscRead = 0
Public Const dscNewPost = 1
Public Const dscReply = 2

'
' variables
Public cGroup As String
Public cProfile As String
Public bThreaded As Boolean
```

That's all you need to add to this form. Save it (MODDISCUSS.BAS) and close it now.

Laying Out the Discuss Form

The Discuss form is the MDI form that controls the entire project. Refer to Figure 10.3 and Table 10.2 when laying out the Discuss form.

FIGURE 10.3.

Laying out the Discuss form.

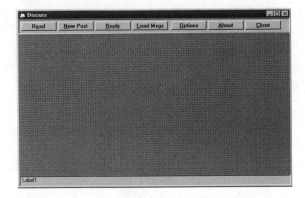

Table 10.2. Controls for the Discuss form.

Control	Property	Setting
VB.MDIForm	Name	mdiDiscuss
	BackColor	&H8000000C&
	Caption	"Discuss"
	ClientHeight	5685
	ClientLeft	735
	ClientTop	1710
	ClientWidth	9210
	Height	6090
	Left	675
	LinkTopic	"MDIForm1"
	Top	1365
	Width	9330
	WindowState	2 'Maximized
VB.PictureBox	Name	Picture2
	Align	2 'Align Bottom
	Height	345
	Left	0
	ScaleHeight	285
	ScaleWidth	9150
	TabIndex	8
	Top	5340
	Width	9210

Control	*Property*	*Setting*
VB.Label	Name	lblStatus
	Caption	"Label1"
	Height	315
	Left	60
	TabIndex	9
	Top	0
	Width	9135
VB.PictureBox	Name	Picture1
	Align	1 'Align Top
	Height	495
	Left	0
	ScaleHeight	435
	ScaleWidth	9150
	TabIndex	0
	Top	0
	Width	9210
VB.CommandButton	Name	cmdMain
	Caption	"&Close"
	Font	
		name="MS Sans Serif"
		charset=0
		weight=700
		size=8.25
		underline=0 'False
		italic=0 'False
		strikethrough=0 'False
	Height	300
	Index	6
	Left	7680
	TabIndex	7
	Top	60
	Width	1200

continues

Table 10.2. continued

Control	Property	Setting
VB.CommandButton	Name	cmdMain
	Caption	"&About"
	Font	
		name= "MS Sans Serif"
		charset=0
		weight=700
		size=8.25
		underline=0 'False
		italic=0 'False
		strikethrough=0 'False
	Height	300
	Index	5
	Left	6420
	TabIndex	6
	Top	60
	Width	1200
VB.CommandButton	Name	cmdMain
	Caption	"&Options"
	Font	
		name="MS Sans Serif"
		charset=0
		weight=700
		size=8.25
		underline=0 'False
		italic=0 'False
		strikethrough=0 'False
	Height	300
	Index	4
	Left	5160
	TabIndex	5
	Top	60
	Width	1200

Control	Property	Setting
VB.CommandButton	Name	cmdMain
	Caption	"&Load Msgs"
	Font	
		name="MS Sans Serif"
		charset=0
		weight=700
		size=8.25
		underline=0 'False
		italic=0 'False
		strikethrough=0 'False
	Height	300
	Index	3
	Left	3840
	TabIndex	4
	Top	60
	Width	1200
VB.CommandButton	Name	cmdMain
	Caption	"&Reply"
	Font	
		name="MS Sans Serif"
		charset=0
		weight=700
		size=8.25
		underline=0 'False
		italic=0 'False
		strikethrough=0 'False
	Height	300
	Index	2
	Left	2580
	TabIndex	3
	Top	60
	Width	1200

continues

Table 10.2. continued

Control	Property	Setting
VB.CommandButton	Name	cmdMain
	Caption	"&New Post"
	Font	
		name="MS Sans Serif"
		charset=0
		weight=700
		size=8.25
		underline=0 'False
		italic=0 'False
		strikethrough=0 'False
	Height	300
	Index	1
	Left	1320
	TabIndex	2
	Top	60
	Width	1200
VB.CommandButton	Name	cmdMain
	Caption	"R&ead"
	Font	
		name="MS Sans Serif"
		charset=0
		weight=700
		size=8.25
		underline=0 'False
		italic=0 'False
		strikethrough=0 'False
	Height	300
	Index	0
	Left	60
	TabIndex	1
	Top	60
	Width	1200

After you complete the form layout, save the form as MDIDISCUSS.FRM before you begin coding.

Coding the Discuss Form

Most of the code in the MDI Discuss form is needed to react to user buttons or basic form events. There are also two custom routines used for reading existing messages and creating new ones.

Listing 10.15 shows the MDIForm_Load event. Add this to your project.

Listing 10.15. Coding the MDIForm_Load event.

```
Private Sub MDIForm_Load()
    '
    ' startup
    '
    cGroup = GetSetting(App.EXEName, "Options", "Group", "CDG")
    cProfile = GetSetting(App.EXEName, "Options", "Profile", "")
    bThreaded = GetSetting(App.EXEName, "Options", "Threaded", True)

    '
    lblStatus = "Logging into Discussion Group [" & cGroup & "]..."
    '
    OLEMAPIStart cProfile
    CollectFolders
    OLEMAPIGetMsgs cGroup, frmMsgs.list1
    FillOutline frmMsgs.list1, frmMsgs.Outline1
    frmMsgs.Show
    lblStatus = ""
    '
End Sub
```

Listing 10.16 shows the code for the Activate and Resize events of the form. Add these two routines to your project.

Listing 10.16. Adding the MDIForm_Activate and MDIForm_Resize events.

```
Private Sub MDIForm_Activate()
    '
    Me.Caption = "Discuss [" & cGroup & "]"
    '
End Sub

Private Sub MDIForm_Resize()
    '
    ' adjust buttons on form
    '
    Dim iFactor As Integer
    Dim iPosition As Integer
    Dim x As Integer
```

continues

Listing 10.16. continued

```
    '
    iFactor = Me.Width / 7 ' # of buttons
    If iFactor < 1200 Then iFactor = 1200
    '
    For x = 0 To 6
        cmdMain(x).Width = iFactor * 0.9
        cmdMain(x).Left = iFactor * x + 60
    Next x
    '
End Sub
```

Finally, add the code from Listing 10.17 to the `MDIForm_Unload` event.

Listing 10.17. Adding the `MDIForm_Unload` event code.

```
Private Sub MDIForm_Unload(Cancel As Integer)
    '
    ' cleanup before leaving
    '


    '
    ' write to registry
    SaveSetting App.EXEName, "Options", "Profile", cProfile
    SaveSetting App.EXEName, "Options", "Group", cGroup
    SaveSetting App.EXEName, "Options", "Threaded", bThreaded


    '
    'drop all loaded forms
    '
    Dim x As Integer
    Dim y As Integer
    '
    x = Forms.Count - 1
    For y = x To 0 Step -1
       Unload Forms(y)
    Next
    End
    '
End Sub
```

Next, you need to add code to the `cmdMain_Click` event to handle user selections from the button array. Listing 10.18 shows the code to handle this.

Listing 10.18. Coding the `cmdMain_Click` event.

```
Private Sub cmdMain_Click(Index As Integer)
    '
    ' handle main user selections
    '
```

```
        Dim uFolder As FolderType
        Dim uMsgRec As MsgType
        Dim objMsg As Object
        '
        Select Case Index
            Case 0 ' read
                LoadMsgRec dscRead
            Case 1 ' new post
                NewMsgRec
            Case 2 ' reply
                LoadMsgRec dscReply
            Case 3 ' load msgs
                OLEMAPIGetMsgs cGroup, frmMsgs.list1
                FillOutline frmMsgs.list1, frmMsgs.Outline1
            Case 4 ' options
                frmOptions.Show
            Case 5 ' about
                frmAbout.Show
            Case 6 ' close
                Unload Me
        End Select
        '
End Sub
```

You can see that the cmdMain routine calls two other routines: LoadMsgRec and NewMsgRec. You need to add these routines to your project. First, add the NewMsgRec subroutine to the form. Add the code from Listing 10.19.

Listing 10.19. Adding the NerwMsgRec routine.

```
Public Sub NewMsgRec()
    '
    ' start a new posting
    '
    Load frmNote
    frmNote.txtSubject = "Msg #" & Format(Now(), "YYMMDDHHmm")
    frmNote.txtTopic = frmNote.txtSubject
    frmNote.txtBody = ""
    frmNote.lblMode = dscNewPost
    frmNote.Show
    '
End Sub
```

The code in Listing 10.19 initializes values on the note form and then calls the form for the user.

The code for the LoadMsgRec routine is a bit more complicated. This routine must first locate the selected message, load it into the form, and then call the note form. Add the code in Listing 10.20 to your form.

Listing 10.20. Adding the `LoadMsgRec` routine.

```
Public Sub LoadMsgRec(iMode As Integer)
    '
    ' read a message record
    '
    Dim uFolder As FolderType
    Dim uMsgRec As MsgType
    Dim cIndex As String
    '
    ' first get folder type
    uFolder = GetFolderRec(cGroup)
    If uFolder.FolderID = "" Then
        MsgBox "Unable to locate Folder", vbExclamation, "ReadMsgRec"
        Exit Sub
    End If
    '
    ' get message type
    cIndex = MsgIndex(frmMsgs.list1, frmMsgs.Outline1.ListIndex)
    uMsgRec = MsgPtr(cIndex)
    If uMsgRec.MsgID = "" Then
        MsgBox "Unable to locate Message", vbExclamation, "ReadMsgRec"
        Exit Sub
    End If
    '
    ' now load real msg from MAPI
    Set objMsg = objSession.GetMessage(uMsgRec.MsgID, uFolder.StoreID)
    If objMsg Is Nothing Then
        MsgBox "Unable to Load Message.", vbExclamation, "ReadMsgRec"
        Exit Sub
    End If
    '
    ' must be good, stuff the form
    Load frmNote
    '
    frmNote.txtTopic = objMsg.ConversationTopic
    If iMode = dscReply Then
        frmNote.txtSubject = "RE: " & objMsg.Subject
    Else
        frmNote.txtSubject = objMsg.Subject
    End If
    frmNote.txtBody = objMsg.Text
    '
    ' mark it for read/reply and show it
    frmNote.lblMode = iMode
    frmNote.lblMsgNbr = frmMsgs.Outline1.ListIndex
    frmNote.Show
    '
End Sub
```

That's all for the MDI Discuss form. Save it as MDIDISCUSS.FRM, and save the project as DISCUSS.VBP before you continue.

FIGURE 10.4.

Laying out the Msgs form.

Laying Out and Coding the Msgs Form

The Msgs form is used to show the threaded discussion list. Refer to Figure 10.4 and Table 10.3 for details on laying out the form.

Table 10.3. Controls for the Msgs form.

Control	Property	Setting
VB.Form	Name	frmMsgs
	Caption	"Form1"
	ClientHeight	2955
	ClientLeft	1140
	ClientTop	1515
	ClientWidth	5175
	Height	3360
	Left	1080
	LinkTopic	"Form1"
	MDIChild	-1 'True
	ScaleHeight	2955
	ScaleWidth	5175
	Top	1170
	Width	5295
VB.ListBox	Name	List1
	Height	840
	Left	3060
	Sorted	-1 'True
	TabIndex	1
	Top	1200
	Visible	0 'False
	Width	1095

continues

Table 10.3. continued

Control	Property	Setting
MSOutl.Outline	Name	Outline1
	Height	2715
	Left	120
	TabIndex	0
	Top	60
	Width	4935
	Font	
		Name="MS Sans Serif"
		Size=8.25
		Charset=0
		Weight=700
		Underline=0 'False
		Italic=0 'False
		Strikethrough=0 'False

> **NOTE**
>
> You'll notice that the form contains both an outline control and a list box control. The list box control is not visible at run time. It is used to automatically sort the messages by conversation index.

There is very little code to the form. Listing 10.21 shows all the code you need to add to the Msgs form.

Listing 10.21. Coding the Msgs form.

```
Private Sub Form_Load()
    '
    Me.Left = 0
    Me.Top = 0
    '
    Me.Caption = "Discussion Message List"
    '
End Sub

Private Sub Form_Resize()
```

```
'
' expand outline control to fill form
'
    If Me.WindowState <> vbMinimized Then
        Outline1.Left = Me.ScaleLeft
        Outline1.Top = Me.ScaleTop
        Outline1.Width = Me.ScaleWidth
        Outline1.Height = Me.ScaleHeight
    End If
End Sub

Private Sub Outline1_DblClick()
'
    mdiDiscuss.LoadMsgRec dscRead
'
End Sub
```

Save this form as DSCMSGS.FRM and update the project before going to the next step.

Building the Other Forms

There are three other forms you need to add to the project. The Note form will be used to read and reply to messages; the Options form allows the user to set and store some program options; and the About dialog box contains typical program information.

The Note Form

Add a new form to the project and set its Name property to frmNote. Refer to Table 10.4 and Figure 10.5 in laying out the note form.

FIGURE 10.5.

Laying out the Note form.

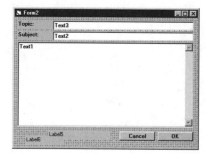

Table 10.4. Controls for the Note form.

Control	Property	Setting
VB.Form	Name	frmNote
	Caption	"Form2"

continues

Table 10.4. continued

Control	Property	Setting
	ClientHeight	4380
	ClientLeft	1080
	ClientTop	1995
	ClientWidth	6255
	Height	4785
	Left	1020
	LinkTopic	"Form2"
	MDIChild	-1 'True
	ScaleHeight	4380
	ScaleWidth	6255
	Top	1650
	Width	6375
VB.CommandButton	Name	cmdBtn
	Caption	"Cancel"
	Font	
		name="MS Sans Serif"
		charset=0
		weight=700
		size=8.25
		underline=0 'False
		italic=0 'False
		strikethrough=0 'False
	Height	300
	Index	1
	Left	3600
	TabIndex	8
	Top	3840
	Width	1200
VB.CommandButton	Name	cmdBtn
	Caption	"OK"
	Font	
		name="MS Sans Serif"

Control	Property	Setting
		charset=0
		weight=700
		size=8.25
		underline=0 'False
		italic=0 'False
		strikethrough=0 'False
	Height	300
	Index	0
	Left	4920
	TabIndex	5
	Top	3840
	Width	1200
VB.TextBox	Name	txtTopic
	Font	
		name="MS Sans Serif"
		charset=0
		weight=700
		size=8.25
		underline=0 'False
		italic=0 'False
		strikethrough=0 'False
	Height	300
	Left	1320
	TabIndex	2
	Text	"Text3"
	Top	120
	Width	4800
VB.TextBox	Name	txtSubject
	Font	
		name="MS Sans Serif"
		charset=0
		weight=700

continues

Table 10.4. continued

Control	Property	Setting
		size=8.25
		underline=0 'False
		italic=0 'False
		strikethrough=0 'False
	Height	300
	Left	1320
	TabIndex	1
	Text	"Text2"
	Top	480
	Width	4800
VB.TextBox	Name	txtBody
	Font	
		name="MS Sans Serif"
		charset=0
		weight=700
		size=8.25
		underline=0 'False
		italic=0 'False
		strikethrough=0 'False
	Height	2835
	Left	120
	MultiLine	-1 'True
	ScrollBars	2 'Vertical
	TabIndex	0
	Text	"dscNote.frx":0000
	Top	840
	Width	6000
VB.Label	Name	lblMsgNbr
	Caption	"Label6"
	Height	255
	Left	420
	TabIndex	7

Control	Property	Setting
	Top	4020
	Visible	0 'False
	Width	1275
VB.Label	Name	lblMode
	Caption	"Label5"
	Height	255
	Left	1200
	TabIndex	6
	Top	3840
	Visible	0 'False
	Width	2055
VB.Label	Name	Label4
	Caption	"Subject:"
	Font	
		name="MS Sans Serif"
		charset=0
		weight=700
		size=8.25
		underline=0 'False
		italic=0 'False
		strikethrough=0 'False
	Height	300
	Left	120
	TabIndex	4
	Top	480
	Width	1200
VB.Label	Name	Label3
	Caption	"Topic:"
	Font	
		name="MS Sans Serif"
		charset=0
		weight=700

continues

Table 10.4. continued

Control	Property	Setting
		size=8.25
		underline=0 'False
		italic=0 'False
VB.Form	Name	frmNote
		strikethrough=0 'False
	Height	300
	Left	120
	TabIndex	3
	Top	120
	Width	1200

After laying out the form, save it (DSCNOTE.FRM) before you add the code.

Along with the typical form-related events, you need to add code to handle user button selections and a custom routine to establish the mode of the form (read, reply, or new message).

First, Listing 10.22 shows all the code for the Form_Load, Form_Activate, and Form_Resize events. Add this to your project.

Listing 10.22. Adding the Form_Load, Form_Activate, and Form_Resize code.

```
Private Sub Form_Load()
    '
    ' init on first entry
    '
    Label1 = "" ' from
    Text1 = "" ' topic
    Text2 = "" ' subject
    Text3 = "" ' body
    '
End Sub

Private Sub Form_Activate()
    '
    StatusUpdate
    '
End Sub


Private Sub Form_Resize()
    '
    ' adjust controls for form
    '
```

```
      If Me.WindowState <> vbMinimized Then
          txtBody.Left = Me.ScaleLeft
          txtBody.Top = 900
          txtBody.Width = Me.ScaleWidth
          txtBody.Height = Me.ScaleHeight - (1320)
          '
          txtTopic.Width = Me.ScaleWidth - 1320
          txtSubject.Width = Me.ScaleWidth - 1320
          '
          cmdBtn(0).Left = Me.ScaleWidth - 1440
          cmdBtn(1).Left = Me.ScaleWidth - 2880
          cmdBtn(1).Top = Me.ScaleHeight - 420
          cmdBtn(0).Top = Me.ScaleHeight - 420
      End If
End Sub
```

Worth mentioning here is the Form_Resize code. This code will adjust controls on the form to fill out as much (or as little) screen area as is allowed.

Another routine that deals with form controls is the StatusUpdate routine (Listing 10.23). This routine toggles the various controls based on the mode of the form (read, reply, or new message). Add the code from Listing 10.23 to your form.

Listing 10.23. Adding the StatusUpdate routine.

```
Public Sub StatusUpdate()
    '
    ' check form status
    '
    Select Case lblMode
        Case Is = dscRead
            txtTopic.Enabled = False
            txtSubject.Enabled = False
            txtBody.Enabled = False
            cmdBtn(0).Caption = "Reply"
            cmdBtn(0).SetFocus
            Me.Caption = "Discussion Read Form [" & txtSubject & "]"
        Case Is = dscReply
            txtTopic.Enabled = False
            txtSubject.Enabled = True
            txtBody.Enabled = True
            cmdBtn(0).Caption = "Post"
            txtSubject.SetFocus
            Me.Caption = "Discussion Reply Form [" & txtSubject & "]"
        Case Is = dscNewPost
            txtTopic.Enabled = True
            txtSubject.Enabled = True
            txtBody.Enabled = True
            cmdBtn(0).Caption = "Post"
            txtTopic.SetFocus
            Me.Caption = "Discussion Post New Topic Form"
    End Select
    '
End Sub
```

The last routine you need to add to the form is the code for the cmdBtn_Click event. This also uses the mode of the form to determine just what the program will do when the user presses the OK button. Add the code from Listing 10.24 to your form.

Listing 10.24. Adding the cmdBtn_Click event code.

```
Private Sub cmdBtn_Click(Index As Integer)
    '
    ' handle use selections
    '
    Select Case Index
        Case 0 ' new post
            Select Case lblMode
                Case Is = dscNewPost
                    OLEMAPIPostMsg cGroup, txtTopic, txtSubject, txtBody
                    MsgBox "Message has been posted!", vbInformation, "Discuss OLE"
                    OLEMAPIGetMsgs cGroup, frmMsgs.list1
                    FillOutline frmMsgs.list1, frmMsgs.Outline1
                    Unload Me
                Case Is = dscReply
                    OLEMAPIReply cGroup, Val(lblMsgNbr), txtSubject, txtBody
                    MsgBox "Reply has been sent!", vbInformation
                    OLEMAPIGetMsgs cGroup, frmMsgs.list1
                    FillOutline frmMsgs.list1, frmMsgs.Outline1
                    Unload Me
                Case Is = dscRead
                    lblMode = dscReply
                    txtSubject = "RE: " & txtSubject
                    txtBody = String(45, 45) & Chr(13) & Chr(10) & txtBody &
Chr(13) & Chr(10) & String(45, 45) & Chr(13) & Chr(10)
                    Form_Activate
            End Select
        Case 1 ' close
            Unload Me
    End Select
    '
End Sub
```

After you complete the code, save the form (DSCNOTE.FRM) and project (DISCUSS.VBP) before you go to the next section.

The Options Form

The Options form allows the user to select the folder for the discussion group, enter a MAPI profile, and turn the message display from flat to threaded. Refer to Figure 10.6 and Table 10.5 for laying out the Options form.

FIGURE 10.6.

Laying out the Options form.

Table 10.5. Controls for the Options form.

Control	Property	Setting
VB.Form	Name	frmOptions
	BorderStyle	3 'Fixed Dialog
	Caption	"Form1"
	ClientHeight	3270
	ClientLeft	2370
	ClientTop	2670
	ClientWidth	5250
	Height	3675
	Left	2310
	LinkTopic	"Form1"
	MaxButton	0 'False
	MDIChild	-1 'True
	MinButton	0 'False
	ScaleHeight	3270
	ScaleWidth	5250
	ShowInTaskbar	0 'False
	Top	2325
	Width	5370
VB.CheckBox	Name	chkThreaded
	Caption	"View Message Threads"
	Font	
		name="MS Sans Serif"
		charset=0
		weight=700
		size=8.25
		underline=0 'False

continues

Table 10.5. continued

Control	Property	Setting
		italic=0 'False
		strikethrough=0 'False
	Height	435
	Left	2700
	TabIndex	7
	Top	900
	Width	2355
VB.CommandButton	Name	cmdBtn
	Caption	"OK"
	Font	
		name="MS Sans Serif"
		charset=0
		weight=700
		size=8.25
		underline=0 'False
		italic=0 'False
		strikethrough=0 'False
	Height	300
	Index	1
	Left	3840
	TabIndex	5
	Top	2340
	Width	1200
VB.CommandButton	Name	cmdBtn
	Caption	"Cancel"
	Font	
		name="MS Sans Serif"
		charset=0
		weight=700
		size=8.25
		underline=0 'False
		italic=0 'False

Control	Property	Setting
		strikethrough=0 'False
	Height	300
	Index	0
	Left	3840
	TabIndex	4
	Top	2700
	Width	1200
VB.TextBox	Name	txtProfile
	Font	
		name="MS Sans Serif"
		charset=0
		weight=700
		size=8.25
		underline=0 'False
		italic=0 'False
		strikethrough=0 'False
	Height	300
	Left	2700
	TabIndex	3
	Top	480
	Width	2400
VB.ListBox	Name	lstGroup
	Font	
		name="MS Sans Serif"
		charset=0
		weight=700
		size=8.25
		underline=0 'False
		italic=0 'False
		strikethrough=0 'False
	Height	2205
	Left	120

continues

Table 10.5. continued

Control	Property	Setting
	TabIndex	1
	Top	840
	Width	2400
VB.Label	Name	lblSelected
	BorderStyle	1 'Fixed Single
	Font	
		name="MS Sans Serif"
		charset=0
		weight=700
		size=8.25
		underline=0 'False
		italic=0 'False
		strikethrough=0 'False
	Height	300
	Left	120
	TabIndex	6
	Top	480
	Width	2400
VB.Label	Name	lblProfile
	BorderStyle	1 'Fixed Single
	Caption	"Enter Login Profile:"
	Font	
		name="MS Sans Serif"
		charset=0
		weight=700
		size=8.25
		underline=0 'False
		italic=0 'False
		strikethrough=0 'False
	Height	300
	Left	2700
	TabIndex	2

Control	Property	Setting
	Top	120
	Width	2400
VB.Label	Name	lblGroup
	BorderStyle	1 'Fixed Single
	Caption	"Select Discussion Group:"
	Font	
		name="MS Sans Serif"
		charset=0
		weight=700
		size=8.25
		underline=0 'False
		italic=0 'False
		strikethrough=0 'False
	Height	300
	Left	120
	TabIndex	0
	Top	120
	Width	2400

It's a good idea to save this form (DSCOPTIONS.FRM) before you start coding.

There is not much code for the Options form. Listing 10.25 shows the code for the Form_Load event.

Listing 10.25. Coding the Form_Load event.

```
Private Sub Form_Load()
    '
    ' set up form
    '
    Me.Caption = "Discuss Options"
    txtProfile = cProfile
    lblSelected = cGroup
    chkThreaded.Value = IIf(bThreaded = 1, 1, 0)

    CollectFolders lstGroup
    '
    Me.Left = (Screen.Width - Me.Width) / 2
    Me.Top = (Screen.Height - Me.Height) / 2
    '
End Sub
```

The next code to add is for the cmdBtn_Click event. This routine will save the user's choices in the system registry for later recall. Add the code from Listing 10.26 to your form.

Listing 10.26. Adding the cmdBtn_Click code.

```
Private Sub cmdBtn_Click(Index As Integer)
    '
    ' handle user selection
    '
    Select Case Index
        Case 0 ' cancel
            ' no action
        Case 1 ' OK
            '
            MousePointer = vbHourglass
            '
            ' save to vars
            cGroup = Trim(lblSelected)
            cProfile = Trim(txtProfile)
            bThreaded = IIf(chkThreaded = 1, True, False)

            '
            ' save to registry
            SaveSetting App.EXEName, "Options", "Profile", Trim(cProfile)
            SaveSetting App.EXEName, "Options", "Group", Trim(cGroup)
            SaveSetting App.EXEName, "Options", "Threaded", IIf(chkThreaded.Value =
            ➥1, 1, 0)
            '
            ' update list & main form
            OLEMAPIGetMsgs cGroup, frmMsgs.list1
            FillOutline frmMsgs.list1, frmMsgs.Outline1
            mdiDiscuss.Caption = "Discuss [" & cGroup & "]"
            '
            MousePointer = vbNormal
            '
    End Select
    '
    Unload Me
    '
End Sub
```

Finally, you need to add one line to the lstGroup_DblClick event:

```
Private Sub lstGroup_DblClick()
    '
    lblSelected = Trim(lstGroup.List(lstGroup.ListIndex))
    '
End Sub
```

Now save the form (DSCOPTIONS.FRM) and update the project. Only one more form to go!

The About Dialog Box

The About dialog box contains basic information about the project. Refer to Figure 10.7 and Table 10.6 for laying out the form.

FIGURE 10.7.

Laying out the About dialog box.

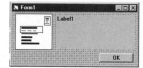

Table 10.6. Controls for the About dialog box.

Control	Property	Setting
VB.Form	Name	frmAbout
	BorderStyle	1 'Fixed Single
	Caption	"Form1"
	ClientHeight	1785
	ClientLeft	2820
	ClientTop	3165
	ClientWidth	4335
	Height	2190
	Left	2760
	LinkTopic	"Form1"
	MaxButton	0 'False
	MDIChild	-1 'True
	MinButton	0 'False
	ScaleHeight	1785
	ScaleWidth	4335
	Top	2820
	Width	4455
VB.CommandButton	Name	cmdOK
	Caption	"OK"
	Font	
		name="MS Sans Serif"
		charset=0
		weight=700
		size=8.25

continues

Table 10.6. continued

Control	Property	Setting
		underline=0 'False
		italic=0 'False
		strikethrough=0 'False
	Height	300
	Left	3000
	TabIndex	0
	Top	1380
	Width	1200
VB.Image	Name	Image1
	Height	1215
	Left	120
	Picture	"dscAbout.frx":0000
	Stretch	-1 'True
	Top	60
	Width	1275
VB.Label	Name	Label1
	Caption	"Label1"
	Font	
		name="MS Sans Serif"
		charset=0
		weight=700
		size=8.25
		underline=0 'False
		italic=0 'False
		strikethrough=0 'False
	Height	1095
	Left	1560
	TabIndex	1
	Top	120
	Width	2655

You only need to add code to the Form_Load event and the cmdOK_click event. Listing 10.27 shows all the code for the About form.

Listing 10.27. Coding the `Form_Load` and `cmdOK_Click` events.

```
Private Sub cmdOK_Click()
    Unload Me
End Sub

Private Sub Form_Load()
    '
    ' set up about box
    '
    Me.Caption = "About " & App.ProductName
    '
    Image1.Stretch = True
    '
    Label1.Caption = App.FileDescription & Chr(13) & Chr(13)
    Label1 = Label1 & App.LegalCopyright & Chr(13) & Chr(13)

    Me.Left = (Screen.Width - Me.Width) / 2
    Me.Top = (Screen.Height - Me.Height) / 2
    '
End Sub
```

That's the last of the code for the Discuss project. Save this form (DSCABOUT.FRM) and update the project before you begin testing.

Testing the Discuss Forum Tool

Once you've coded and compiled the project, you'll be able to load it onto any workstation that has MAPI services installed and available.

> **NOTE**
>
> The discussion tool will not work in a Remote Mail setup. You need to have direct access to at least one message store.

When you first start Discuss, you'll be asked to log into MAPI. One of the first things you should do is open the Options page and select a target folder and set up your default user profile (see Figure 10.8).

You can select any folder as the discussion target. However, since the idea is to carry on discussions with other people, you'll typically select a public folder as the discussion target.

> **NOTE**
>
> If you are working on a standalone machine, you can select any personal folder for this demonstration. Just remember that no one but you can see the results!

FIGURE 10.8.

Setting Discuss options.

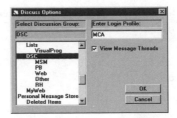

The program will list only messages that have their `Type` property set to `IPM.Discuss`. This means the first time you select a target folder, you won't see any messages. So the next thing you need to do is add a message!

Press `New Post` to add a new thread to the folder (see Figure 10.9).

FIGURE 10.9.

Adding a new thread to the folder.

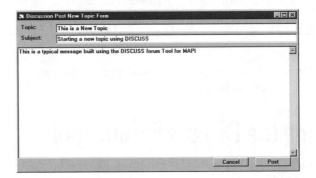

You can also highlight any message in the discussion and double-click it to read it. When you press the `Reply` button at the bottom of a read form, it automatically turns into a reply form. Even the subject and message body are updated to show that this is a reply (see Figure 10.10).

FIGURE 10.10.

Replying to a message.

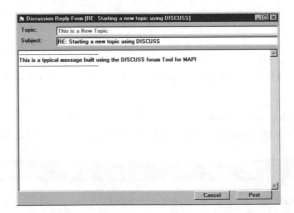

Summary

In this chapter you learned how to use the OLE Messaging library to create online, threaded discussion tools using MAPI services. You learned that there are three ways in which discussion messages differ from mail messages:

- Discussion messages are addressed to folders, not people.
- MAPI uses the `ConversationTopic` and `ConversationIndex` properties to keep track of discussion threads.
- You use the MAPI `Update` method to deliver discussion messages. You use the MAPI `Send` method to deliver mail messages.

You also learned how to build routines that collect all the message stores available to a workstation, all the folders in each of those stores, and all the messages within a folder. You now know how to compose a message for `Update` (rather than `Send`) and how to use the `CoCreateGuid` API to generate unique conversation index values used in threaded discussion tools.

Best of all, most of the heart of this example program can be used to add discussion capabilities to other Visual Basic projects.

11

Creating a MAPI Email Agent

In this chapter you'll learn how to use the OLE Messaging library to create a stand-alone e-mail agent. This agent can scan your incoming mail and, based on rules you establish, automatically handle messages for you. All actions are based on rules you establish in a control file.

Features of the MAPI Email Agent are:

- Timed scanning of your inbox.
- Notification of message arrivals based on level of importance.
- Automatic routing of incoming messages to other e-mail users.
- Automatic replies to messages based on subject or sender.
- Automatic sorting of unread messages into separate folders based on subject, sender, or level of importance.

The first part of the chapter will discuss the concept of e-mail agents and cover the overall design of the program. The next sections will detail the coding of the forms and support routines needed to complete the project. In the final section, you'll install and test the MAPI Email Agent program.

> **NOTE**
>
> The Microsoft Exchange Server clients allow users to establish and code their own mail agent (called the *Inbox Assistant*). If you have the Microsoft Exchange Server client, now is a good time to review the Inbox Assistant to get an idea of its features. The programming project covered in this chapter works independently of the Inbox Assistant and does not require that users have Microsoft Exchange Server installed on their system.

When you complete the programming project in this chapter, you'll have a fully functional MAPI Email Agent that can be installed on any workstation that has access to a MAPI-compliant e-mail system. Also, the techniques used to build this project can be incorporated into other Windows programming projects to add message processing capabilities.

Designing the Email Agent

Before starting to code the project, it's a good idea to discuss the general features and functions of an e-mail agent. Once you have a good idea of what e-mail agents can do, then you can lay out the basic design features of the MAPI Email Agent programming project covered in this chapter.

Basically, an e-mail agent is a program that "acts for you." It is a program that reviews your messages and, based on information you have supplied, processes the messages for you. Typically, e-mail agents process messages in the user's inbox. Users can set up rules that tell the agent how to handle each new message. These rules can tell the e-mail agent to check various parts of the incoming message and then take a specific action.

For example, the agent can be instructed to look for all messages that are received from your boss and then place those messages in a special folder called "Urgent." Or the agent could be told that any message with the word "SALES" in the subject line should be immediately forwarded to another user's inbox and then erased from your inbox without any comment. You might also tell the agent to automatically reply to all senders that you are out on vacation and will return next week.

Features of the MAPI Email Agent

For this chapter, you'll use Visual Basic 4.0 and the OLE Messaging library to build a stand-alone MAPI Email Agent that has the following features:

- *Timed scanning of your inbox*—Users can start the program and allow it to run unattended. It scans the inbox for new messages every *N* minutes. Users can also set configuration values that start the program as an icon on the task bar or as a dialog box.

- *Message notification*—Users can establish a rule that causes a dialog box to pop up each time a specific message is received. This notification can be based on sender ID, subject content, or level of importance.

- *Automatic forwarding*—Users can create rules that automatically forward messages to other addresses. Users can also determine whether the original should be kept or discarded.

- *Automatic replies*—Users can create rules that generate automated replies to senders based on sender ID, subject content, or level of importance.

- *Automatic message copying or moving*—Users can create rules that copy or move incoming messages to other folders in the user's message store. This feature can be used to sort incoming message by sender ID, subject content, or level of importance.

> **NOTE**
>
> The features described here are just the start of what can be accomplished with an e-mail agent. The number of options has been limited to keep this chapter focused on design and coding issues instead of content. As you build your own agent, you can add many other capabilities.

To accomplish this, the MAPI Email Agent will keep track of rules created by the user. These rules will have three parts: *tests*, *comparisons*, and *actions*. The test portion of the rule performs a simple scan of the designated portion of the message, searching for requested content. The MAPI Email Agent described in this chapter is capable of inspecting three message parts:

- *SUBJECT*—Checks the `Subject` property of the message
- *SENDER*—Checks the `Sender.Name` property of the message
- *PRIORITY*—Checks the `Importance` property of the message

For example, the test `SUBJECT MAPI` tells the agent to check the message subject for the word "MAPI." The phrase `SENDER Boss` tells the agent to check for messages sent to the user from the e-mail ID "boss."

All tests must use a logical condition as part of the processing. The MAPI Email Agent uses *comparisons* to do this. The program can check for the following four logical conditions:

- `EQ`—Equals (`SENDER Sharon EQ`)
- `GT`—Greater Than (`PRIORITY 0 GT`)
- `LT`—Less Than (`PRIORITY 1 LT`)
- `CI`—Is Contained In (`SUBJECT VB CI`)

You'll notice that the last value is able to check the selected message part for the occurrence of a word or phrase. Note that all the comparisons are case-insensitive. It is important to note that the LT and GT can be used with character data, too.

The last of the three portions of a rule is the *action*. This is the part of the rule that tells the agent what action to take if the test criteria have been met. The MAPI Email Agent can perform the following actions on a message:

- `MOVE`—Move the message to another folder (`MOVE Urgent`)
- `COPY`—Copy the message to another folder (`COPY Archive`)
- `FORWARD`—Forward the message to another user (`FORWARD mAmund@iac.net`)
- `REPLY`—Send reply text to the user (`REPLY reply.txt`)

The agent allows users to determine whether the forwarded and reply messages are retained or removed once the forward/reply is generated.

Storing the Rules in a Control File

The MAPI Email Agent allows users to build tests and actions, and then use them to create rules. All this information is stored in a text file similar to an INI file. This file also contains general control information, such as the scan interval, whether the agent should create a log file, the default log on profiles, and so on. Listing 11.1 shows a sample rule file.

Listing 11.1. Sample rule file for the MAPI Email Agent.

```
; ************************************************************
; MAPI Email Agent Control File
; ************************************************************
;
```

```
[General]
Editor=notepad.exe
ScanInterval=2
LogFile=mea.log
LogFlag=1
RuleCount=3
ActionCount=4
TestCount=4
Profile=MCA
DeleteForwardFlag=0
NotifyDialog=1
DeleteReplyFlag=0
MinimzeOnStart=0
AutoStart=0
LastUpdated=04/29/96 9:27:30 PM

[Actions]
Action0=MOVE MAPI
Action1=MOVE Urgent
Action2=FORWARD mamund@iac.net
Action3=COPY SavedMail

[Tests]
Test0=SENDER MCA
Test1=SENDER Boss
Test2=SUBJECT SAPI
Test3=SUBJECT MAPI

[Rules]
RuleName0=Boss's Mail
RuleTest0=SENDER Boss
RuleAction0=Move Urgent
RuleCompare0=EQ
RuleName1=Send To ISP
RuleTest1=SENDER MCA
RuleAction1=FORWARD mamund@iac.net
RuleCompare1=EQ
RuleName2=MAPI Mail
RuleTest2=SUBJECT MAPI
RuleAction2=MOVE MAPI
RuleCompare2=CI
```

The next sections show you how to code the MAPI Email Agent forms and support routines that will create and process the rules described here.

Coding the MAPI Email Agent Forms

You'll use Visual Basic 4.0 to create the three forms of the MAPI Email Agent. These forms will allow you to start and stop message processing; add or delete new tests, actions, and rules; and modify default configuration settings for the MAPI Email Agent.

The next three sections of this chapter outline the steps needed to layout and code these three forms. If you haven't done so yet, start Visual Basic 4.0 now and create a new project.

The Main Form

The Main form of the MAPI Email Agent shows the current list of rules, tests, and actions. You can also launch the message scan routine from this screen, access the setup dialog box, and inspect the MAPI Email Agent log file. Figure 11.1 shows an example of the Main form in run-time mode.

FIGURE 11.1.

The MAPI Email Agent Main form.

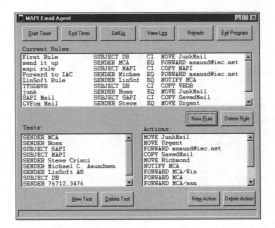

The Main form has a set of command button control arrays to handle the user selections. The first control array covers the top row of buttons. These buttons handle the main processing steps:

- ■ Start Timer starts the timer to count down to the next message scan.
- ■ End Timer disables the timer.
- ■ Setup calls the configuration dialog box.
- ■ View Log displays the contents of the MAPI Email Agent log file.
- ■ Refresh refreshes the list boxes from the control file.
- ■ Exit ends the program.

The second command button control array handles the adding and deleting of tests, actions, and rules. To keep things simple for this project, the system is capable only of adding or deleting rules. Existing rules cannot be edited and saved again. Also, only basic input editing is performed by this program. In a production environment, this program should be enhanced to add an improved user interface with additional input checking and recovery.

Table 11.1 contains a list of all the controls used on the MAPI Email Agent main form along with their property settings. Use this table along with Figure 11.1 to build the MAPI Email Agent Main form.

Table 11.1. Controls for the MAPI Email Agent Main form.

Control	Property	Setting
VB.Form	Name	frmMEA
	Caption	"MAPI Email Agent"
	ClientHeight	6585
	ClientLeft	975
	ClientTop	1575
	ClientWidth	8175
	Height	6990
	Left	915
	LinkTopic	"Form1"
	MaxButton	0 'False
	ScaleHeight	6585
	ScaleWidth	8175
	Top	1230
	Width	8295
VB.CommandButton	Name	Command1
	Caption	"E&xit Program"
	Height	495
	Index	5
	Left	6780
	TabIndex	18
	Top	120
	Width	1200
VB.CommandButton	Name	Command1
	Caption	"Re&fresh"
	Height	495
	Index	4
	Left	5460
	TabIndex	16
	Top	120
	Width	1200
VB.CommandButton	Name	Command2

continues

Table 11.1. continued

Control	Property	Setting
	Caption	"Delete R&ule"
	Height	495
	Index	5
	Left	6900
	TabIndex	15
	Top	3000
	Width	1100
VB.CommandButton	Name	Command2
	Caption	"New &Rule"
	Height	495
	Index	4
	Left	5700
	TabIndex	14
	Top	3000
	Width	1100
VB.CommandButton	Name	Command1
	Caption	"View L&og"
	Height	495
	Index	3
	Left	4140
	TabIndex	13
	Top	120
	Width	1200
VB.CommandButton	Name	Command2
	Caption	"De&lete Action"
	Height	495
	Index	3
	Left	6960
	TabIndex	12
	Top	5700
	Width	1100

Control	Property	Setting
VB.CommandButton	Name	Command2
	Caption	"Ne&w Action"
	Height	495
	Index	2
	Left	5760
	TabIndex	11
	Top	5700
	Width	1100
VB.CommandButton	Name	Command1
	Caption	"SetU&p"
	Height	495
	Index	2
	Left	2820
	TabIndex	10
	Top	120
	Width	1200
VB.CommandButton	Name	Command1
	Caption	"E&nd Timer"
	Height	495
	Index	1
	Left	1500
	TabIndex	9
	Top	120
	Width	1200
VB.CommandButton	Name	Command2
	Caption	"&Delete Test"
	Height	495
	Index	1
	Left	2820
	TabIndex	8
	Top	5700
	Width	1100

continues

Table 11.1. continued

Control	Property	Setting
VB.CommandButton	Name	Command2
	Caption	"&New Test"
	Height	495
	Index	0
	Left	1620
	TabIndex	7
	Top	5700
	Width	1100
VB.ListBox	Name	lstActions
	Font	
		name="Courier"
		charset=0
		weight=400
		size=9.75
		underline=0 'False
		italic=0 'False
		strikethrough=0 'False
	Height	1815
	Left	4200
	TabIndex	3
	Top	3720
	Width	3855
VB.ListBox	Name	lstTests
	Font	
		name="Courier"
		charset=0
		weight=400
		size=9.75
		underline=0 'False
		italic=0 'False
		strikethrough=0 'False
	Height	1815

Control	Property	Setting
	Left	120
	TabIndex	2
	Top	3720
	Width	3795
VB.ListBox	Name	lstRules
	Font	
		name="Courier"
		charset=0
		weight=400
		size=9.75
		underline=0 'False
		italic=0 'False
		strikethrough=0 'False
	Height	1815
	Left	120
	TabIndex	1
	Top	1020
	Width	7875
VB.CommandButton	Name	Command1
	Caption	"&Start Timer"
	Height	495
	Index	0
	Left	180
	TabIndex	0
	Top	120
	Width	1200
VB.Timer	Name	Timer1
	Left	4860
	Top	3000
VB.Label	Name	lblStatus
	BorderStyle	1 'Fixed Single
	Caption	"Label5"

continues

Table 11.1. continued

Control	Property	Setting
	Height	255
	Left	0
	TabIndex	17
	Top	6300
	Width	8115
VB.Label	Name	Label3
	AutoSize	-1 'True
	Caption	"Actions:"
	Font	
		name="Courier"
		charset=0
		weight=400
		size=9.75
		underline=0 'False
		italic=0 'False
		strikethrough=0 'False
	Height	195
	Left	4260
	TabIndex	6
	Top	3480
	Width	960
VB.Label	Name	Label2
	AutoSize	-1 'True
	Caption	"Tests:"
	Font	
		name="Courier"
		charset=0
		weight=400
		size=9.75
		underline=0 'False
		italic=0 'False
		strikethrough=0 'False

Control	Property	Setting
	Height	195
	Left	180
	TabIndex	5
	Top	3420
	Width	720
VB.Label	Name	Label1
	AutoSize	-1 'True
	Caption	"Current Rules:"
	Font	
		name="Courier"
		charset=0
		weight=400
		size=9.75
		underline=0 'False
		italic=0 'False
		strikethrough=0 'False
	Height	195
	Left	180
	TabIndex	4
	Top	780
	Width	1680

Notice that the font size and type used for this form is slightly different. By using a fixed-width font for the text boxes, it is very easy to get consistent alignment. This is a quick way to present a grid-like look to your list boxes. After completing the form layout, save the form as MEA.FRM and save the project as MEA.VBP.

Next you need to add some code to the form. This code covers several key events for the form including the command button selections. The first thing to do is add two form-level variables (see Listing 11.2).

Listing 11.2. Adding the form-level variables to the Main form.

```
Option Explicit

Dim iLocalHeight As Integer
Dim iLocalWidth As Integer
```

These variables are used to retain the original size and shape of the form.

Next add code to the Form_Load event. This code executes some one-time initializations and prepares the form for the user (see Listing 11.3).

Listing 11.3. Adding the Form_Load code.

```
Private Sub Form_Load()
    '
    Left = (Screen.Width - Me.Width) / 2
    Top = (Screen.Height - Me.Height) / 2
    '
    Timer1.Enabled = False ' start as OFF
    Timer1.Interval = 60000 ' tick off the minutes
    lCounter = 0 ' start at zero
    '
    lblstatus = ""
    Me.Icon = LoadPicture(App.Path & "\" & "mail14.ico")
    '
    ' if user set flag, minimize
    If cMinOnStartValue = "1" Then
        Me.WindowState = vbMinimized
    End If
    '
    ' if user set flag, go!
    If cAutoStartValue = "1" Then
        Timer1_Timer ' fire event
        Timer1.Enabled = True
    End If
    '
    ' remember your size
    iLocalHeight = Me.Height
    iLocalWidth = Me.Width
    '
End Sub
```

Note the code that initializes the form-level variables. These variables are used in the next routine: the Form_Resize event, which will prevent users from resizing the form. Add the code shown in Listing 11.4.

Listing 11.4. Adding code to the Form_Resize event.

```
Private Sub Form_Resize()
    '
    ' don't go changin!
    '
    If WindowState = vbNormal Then
        Me.Height = iLocalHeight
        Me.Width = iLocalWidth
    End If
    '
End Sub
```

The next section of code goes in the `Timer1_Timer` event (see Listing 11.5).

Listing 11.5. Adding code to the `Timer1_Timer` event.

```
Private Sub Timer1_Timer()
    '
    ' fire off message scan
    '
    lblstatus = "Minutes to next scan: " & CStr(lCounter)
    lblstatus.Refresh
    Me.Caption = "MAPI Email Agent [" & CStr(lCounter) & " min]"
    DoEvents
    '
    If lCounter = 0 Then
        Timer1.Enabled = False
        StartProcess ' run scan loop
        lCounter = Val(cScanIntervalValue)
        Timer1.Enabled = True
    Else
        lCounter = lCounter - 1
    End If
    '
End Sub
```

This event fires off every minute (see Listing 11.3 where the interval was set to 60000). Each time the event fires, the `lCounter` variable is decremented. When it hits zero, the `StartProcess` routine is called. This is the routine that actually scans the messages. Notice also that the routine is designed to report timer progress on the form title bar. This same information appears as part of the task bar when the form is minimized.

Now it's time to add the code behind the first set of command buttons. This first set of buttons calls all the main operations of the program. Add the code in Listing 11.6 to the `Command1_Click` event.

Listing 11.6. Adding the code for the `Command1_Click` event.

```
Private Sub Command1_Click(Index As Integer)
    '
    ' handle button selection
    '
    Dim x As Long
    '
    Select Case Index
        Case 0 ' start scan countdown
            LogWrite "Message Scan Started"
            lCounter = 0 ' clear counter
            Timer1_Timer ' fire it off right away
            Timer1.Enabled = True ' start counting
        Case 1 ' end scan countdown
            Timer1.Enabled = False
            LogWrite "Message Scan Stopped"
```

continues

Listing 11.6. continued

```
        Case 2 ' view control file
            Timer1.Enabled = False
            frmMEASetUp.Show vbModal
            InitStuff
        Case 3 ' view log file
            x = Shell(cEditorValue & " " & cLogFileValue, 1)
        Case 4 ' refresh lists
            Timer1.Enabled = False
            InitStuff
        Case 5 ' exit program
            Unload Me
    End Select
    '
End Sub
```

WARNING

Most of the code in Listings 11.6 and 11.7 refer to routines and forms that have not been built yet. If you attempt to run the project before all your routines are complete, you'll get error messages from Visual Basic. If you want to test your code by running the project, you'll need to build subroutines to cover the ones that are missing or comment out the lines that call for other routines.

The last code you need to add to the MAPI Email Agent main form is the code for the `Command2_Click` event. This code handles the calls for adding and deleting rules, actions, and tests. Add the code in Listing 11.7 to the `Command2_Click` event.

Listing 11.7. Adding code to the `Command2_Click` event.

```
Private Sub Command2_Click(Index As Integer)
    '
    ' get edit selections
    '
    Dim cInput As String
    Dim cCommand As String
    '
    Select Case Index
        Case 0 ' new test
            cInput = InputBox("Enter Test String [SENDER¦SUBJECT¦PRIORITY Value]:",
"New Test")
            If Trim(cInput) <> "" Then
                cCommand = ParseWord(cInput)
                If InStr(UCase(cTestCommands), UCase(cCommand)) = 0 Then
                    MsgBox "Invalid Test Command - use " & cTestCommands,
vbCritical, "Invalid Command"
                Else
                    MousePointer = vbHourglass
                    AddTest cInput
                    MousePointer = vbNormal
                End If
```

```
                End If
        Case 1 ' delete test
            If lsttests.ListIndex = -1 Then
                MsgBox "Must select a Test item to delete", vbCritical, "Delete
Test"
            Else
                MousePointer = vbHourglass
                DeleteTest lsttests.ListIndex
                MousePointer = vbNormal
            End If
        Case 2 ' new action
            cInput = InputBox("Enter Test String [MsgPart Value]:", "New Test")
            cCommand = ParseWord(cInput)
            If InStr(UCase(cActionCommands), UCase(cCommand)) = 0 Then
                MsgBox "Invalid Action Command - use " & cActionCommands,
vbCritical, "Invalid Command"
            Else
                MousePointer = vbHourglass
                AddAction cInput
                MousePointer = vbNormal
            End If
        Case 3 ' delete action
            If lstactions.ListIndex = -1 Then
                MsgBox "Must select a Action item to delete", vbCritical, "Delete
Test"
            Else
                MousePointer = vbHourglass
                DeleteAction lstactions.ListIndex
                MousePointer = vbNormal
            End If
        Case 4 ' new rule
            AddRule ' call add routine
        Case 5 ' delete rule
            If lstrules.ListIndex = -1 Then
                MsgBox "Must select a Rule to delete", vbCritical, "Delete Test"
            Else
                MousePointer = vbHourglass
                DeleteRule lstrules.ListIndex
                MousePointer = vbNormal
            End If
    End Select
    '
End Sub
```

That's all the coding for the MAPI Email Agent main form. Save this form (MEA.FRM) and this project (MEA.VBP) before continuing.

The Add Rule Form

The rule form is used to compose new rules for the MAPI Email Agent. This form is actually quite simple. It has three list boxes that allow the user to select a test, a compare value, and an action. By combining these three items, the user creates a valid MAPI e-mail agent rule. Once the rule is given a name, it can be saved. All saved rules are acted upon each time MAPI Email Agent scans the incoming messages.

> **NOTE**
>
> This version of MAPI Email Agent does not let you turn rules on or off. If a rule is in the database, it will be processed each time the messages are scanned. The only way to tell the MAPI Email Agent to not process a rule is to permanently remove the rule from the database. Toggling rules on and off would make a nice enhancement for future versions of MAPI Email Agent.

Refer to Figure 11.2 and Table 11.2 when laying out the new MAPI Email Agent Rule form.

FIGURE 11.2.

Laying out the MAPI Email Agent Rule form.

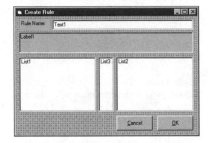

Table 11.2. Controls for the MAPI Email Agent Rule form.

Control	Property	Setting
VB.Form	Name	frmMEARule
	BorderStyle	3 'Fixed Dialog
	Caption	"Create Rule"
	ClientHeight	3990
	ClientLeft	1140
	ClientTop	1515
	ClientWidth	6165
	Height	4395
	Left	1080
	LinkTopic	"Form1"
	MaxButton	0 'False
	MinButton	0 'False
	ScaleHeight	3990
	ScaleWidth	6165
	ShowInTaskbar	0 'False
	Top	1170

Control	Property	Setting
	Width	6285
VB.TextBox	Name	Text1
	Height	315
	Left	1260
	TabIndex	6
	Text	"Text1"
	Top	120
	Width	4755
VB.CommandButton	Name	Command1
	Caption	"&OK"
	Height	495
	Index	1
	Left	4800
	TabIndex	5
	Top	3360
	Width	1215
VB.CommandButton	Name	Command1
	Caption	"&Cancel"
	Height	495
	Index	0
	Left	3420
	TabIndex	4
	Top	3360
	Width	1215
VB.ListBox	Name	List3
	Height	1815
	Left	2820
	TabIndex	2
	Top	1380
	Width	495
VB.ListBox	Name	List2
	Height	1815

continues

Table 11.2. continued

Control	Property	Setting
	Left	3420
	TabIndex	1
	Top	1380
	Width	2595
VB.ListBox	Name	List1
	Height	1815
	Left	120
	TabIndex	0
	Top	1380
	Width	2595
VB.Label	Name	Label2
	Caption	"Rule Name:"
	Height	315
	Left	180
	TabIndex	7
	Top	120
	Width	975
VB.Label	Name	Label1
	BorderStyle	1 'Fixed Single
	Caption	"Label1"
	Height	675
	Left	120
	TabIndex	3
	Top	540
	Width	5895

There are only a few events in the MAPI Email Agent Rule form that need coding. Listing 11.8 shows the code for the Form_Load event.

Listing 11.8. Adding the code for the MAPI Email Agent Rule form `Form_Load` event.

```
Private Sub Form_Load()
    '
    ' fill local lists
    '
    FillList "tests", Me.List1
    FillList "actions", Me.List2
    FillList "compares", Me.List3
    '
    Label1 = "" ' clear rule display
    Text1 = "" ' clear rule name
    '
    Me.Left = (Screen.Width - Me.Width) / 2
    Me.Top = (Screen.Height - Me.Height) / 2
    Me.Icon = LoadPicture(App.Path & "\" & "mail14.ico")
    Me.Caption = "MAPI Email Agent - Create Rule"
    '
End Sub
```

The `Form_Load` event first fills the local list boxes, then initializes the other local controls, centers the form, and sets the form's icon and caption.

The code in Listing 11.9 handles the user selections on the command button control array. Add this code to the `Command1_Click` event.

Listing 11.9. Adding code to the `Command1_Click` event.

```
Private Sub Command1_Click(Index As Integer)
    '
    ' handle button clicks
    '
    Select Case Index
        Case 0 ' cancel
            Unload Me
        Case 1 ' OK
            If Trim(Text1) <> "" Then
                If Trim(Label1) <> "" Then
                    MakeRule Text1.Text, Label1.Caption
                    Text1 = ""
                    Label1 = ""
                Else
                    MsgBox "Must Construct Named Rule", vbCritical, "Rule Error"
                End If
            Else
                MsgBox "Must Name the Rule", vbCritical, "Rule Error"
            End If
    End Select
End Sub
```

Finally, you need to add code to the `DblClick` events of the three list boxes. By double-clicking each box, the user can create a new rule to add to the database. Refer to Listing 11.10 for the code lines to add to each list box.

Listing 11.10. Adding code to the `DblClick_event` of each list box.

```
Private Sub List1_DblClick()
    Label1 = List1.List(List1.ListIndex) & " ¦ "
End Sub

Private Sub List2_DblClick()
    Label1 = Label1 & List2.List(List2.ListIndex)
End Sub

Private Sub List3_DblClick()
    Label1 = Label1 & List3.List(List3.ListIndex) & " ¦ "
End Sub
```

That is all you need to do for the MAPI Email Agent Rule form. Save this form as `MEARULE.FRM` and save the project (`MEA.VBP`) before continuing.

The Setup Form

The last form you need to add to the project is the MAPI Email Agent Setup form. This form allows users to modify the default configuration settings for the MAPI Email Agent. Add a new form to your project called `MEASETUP.FRM`. Refer to Figure 11.3 and Table 11.3 as you lay out the form.

FIGURE 11.3.

*Laying out the MAPI
Email Agent Setup form.*

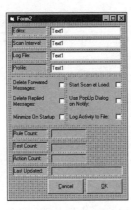

Table 11.3. Controls for the MAPI Email Agent Setup form.

Control	Property	Setting
VB.Form	Name	frmMEASetUp
	BorderStyle	3 'Fixed Dialog
	Caption	"Form2"
	ClientHeight	5940
	ClientLeft	2175

Control	Property	Setting
	ClientTop	1605
	ClientWidth	4005
	Height	6345
	Left	2115
	LinkTopic	"Form2"
	MaxButton	0 'False
	MinButton	0 'False
	ScaleHeight	5940
	ScaleWidth	4005
	ShowInTaskbar	0 'False
	Top	1260
	Width	4125
VB.CommandButton	Name	Command1
	Caption	"&OK"
	Height	495
	Index	1
	Left	2640
	TabIndex	23
	Top	5280
	Width	1215
VB.CommandButton	Name	Command1
	Caption	"&Cancel"
	Height	495
	Index	0
	Left	1320
	TabIndex	22
	Top	5280
	Width	1215
VB.CheckBox	Name	Check6
	Alignment	1 'Right Justify
	Caption	"Log Activity to File:"
	Height	495

continues

Table 11.3. continued

Control	Property	Setting
	Left	2040
	TabIndex	13
	Top	2940
	Width	1800
VB.CheckBox	Name	Check5
	Alignment	1 'Right Justify
	Caption	"Use PopUp Dialog on Notify:"
	Height	495
	Left	2040
	TabIndex	12
	Top	2400
	Width	1800
VB.CheckBox	Name	Check4
	Alignment	1 'Right Justify
	Caption	"Start Scan at Load:"
	Height	495
	Left	2040
	TabIndex	11
	Top	1860
	Width	1800
VB.CheckBox	Name	Check3
	Alignment	1 'Right Justify
	Caption	"Minimize On Startup"
	Height	495
	Left	120
	TabIndex	10
	Top	2940
	Width	1800
VB.CheckBox	Name	Check2
	Alignment	1 'Right Justify
	Caption	"Delete Replied Messages:"

Control	Property	Setting
	Height	495
	Left	120
	TabIndex	9
	Top	2400
	Width	1800
VB.CheckBox	Name	Check1
	Alignment	1 'Right Justify
	Caption	"Delete Forwarded Messages:"
	Height	495
	Left	120
	TabIndex	8
	Top	1860
	Width	1800
VB.TextBox	Name	Text4
	Height	315
	Left	1440
	TabIndex	7
	Text	"Text1"
	Top	1380
	Width	2400
VB.TextBox	Name	Text3
	Height	315
	Left	1440
	TabIndex	6
	Text	"Text1"
	Top	960
	Width	2400
VB.TextBox	Name	Text2
	Height	315
	Left	1440
	TabIndex	5

continues

Table 11.3. continued

Control	Property	Setting
	Text	"Text1"
	Top	540
	Width	2400
VB.TextBox	Name	Text1
	Height	315
	Left	1440
	TabIndex	1
	Text	"Text1"
	Top	120
	Width	2400
VB.Label	Name	Label12
	BorderStyle	1 'Fixed Single
	Height	300
	Left	1440
	TabIndex	21
	Top	3600
	Width	1200
VB.Label	Name	Label11
	BorderStyle	1 'Fixed Single
	Height	300
	Left	1440
	TabIndex	20
	Top	4860
	Width	2415
VB.Label	Name	Label10
	BorderStyle	1 'Fixed Single
	Height	300
	Left	1440
	TabIndex	19
	Top	4440
	Width	1200

Control	Property	Setting
VB.Label	Name	Label9
	BorderStyle	1 'Fixed Single
	Height	300
	Left	1440
	TabIndex	18
	Top	4080
	Width	1200
VB.Label	Name	Label5
	BorderStyle	1 'Fixed Single
	Caption	"Rule Count:"
	Height	300
	Left	120
	TabIndex	17
	Top	3600
	Width	1200
VB.Label	Name	Label8
	BorderStyle	1 'Fixed Single
	Caption	"Last Updated:"
	Height	300
	Left	120
	TabIndex	16
	Top	4860
	Width	1200
VB.Label	Name	Label7
	BorderStyle	1 'Fixed Single
	Caption	"Action Count:"
	Height	300
	Left	120
	TabIndex	15
	Top	4440
	Width	1200

continues

Table 11.3. continued

Control	Property	Setting
VB.Label	Name	Label6
	BorderStyle	1 'Fixed Single
	Caption	"Test Count:"
	Height	300
	Left	120
	TabIndex	14
	Top	4020
	Width	1200
VB.Label	Name	Label4
	BorderStyle	1 'Fixed Single
	Caption	"Profile:"
	Height	300
	Left	120
	TabIndex	4
	Top	1380
	Width	1200
VB.Label	Name	Label3
	BorderStyle	1 'Fixed Single
	Caption	"Log File:"
	Height	300
	Left	120
	TabIndex	3
	Top	960
	Width	1200
VB.Label	Name	Label2
	AutoSize	-1 'True
	BorderStyle	1 'Fixed Single
	Caption	"Scan Interval:"
	Height	300
	Left	120
	TabIndex	2
	Top	540
	Width	1200

Control	Property	Setting
VB.Label	Name	Label1
	AutoSize	-1 'True
	BorderStyle	1 'Fixed Single
	Caption	"Editor:"
	Height	300
	Left	120
	TabIndex	0
	Top	120
	Width	1200

The MAPI Email Agent Setup form needs code for two events and two custom routines. The Custom routines are needed to load the forms controls with the configuration values for editing and then to save them after the values have been modified.

Add a new subroutine called SetupPageLoad to the MAPI Email Agent Setup form and enter the code shown in Listing 11.11.

Listing 11.11. Adding the SetupPageLoad routine.

```
Public Sub SetupPageLoad()
    '
    Text1 = cEditorValue
    Text2 = cScanIntervalValue
    Text3 = cLogFileValue
    Text4 = cProfileValue
    '
    Label9 = cTestCountValue
    Label10 = cActionCountValue
    Label11 = cLastUpdateValue
    Label12 = cRuleCountValue
    '
    Check1.Value = Val(cDelFwdFlagValue)
    Check2.Value = Val(cDelReplyFlagValue)
    Check3.Value = Val(cMinOnStartValue)
    Check4.Value = Val(cAutoStartValue)
    Check5.Value = Val(cNotifyDialogValue)
    Check6.Value = Val(cLogFlagValue)
    '
End Sub
```

Now add another new subroutine called SetupPageSave and enter the code shown in Listing 11.12.

Listing 11.12. Adding the SetupPageSave routine.

```
Public Sub SetupPageSave()
    '
    ' save updated config data
    ' to vars for later
    '
    cEditorValue = Text1
    cScanIntervalValue = Text2
    cLogFileValue = Text3
    cProfileValue = Text4
    '
    cDelFwdFlagValue = CStr(Check1)
    cDelReplyFlagValue = CStr(Check2)
    cMinOnStartValue = CStr(Check3)
    cAutoStartValue = CStr(Check4)
    cNotifyDialogValue = CStr(Check5)
    cLogFlagValue = CStr(Check6)
    '
    ' now save to file
    SaveValues
    '
End Sub
```

Only two events need coding—the Form_Load event and the Command1_Click event. Listing 11.13 shows the code for the Form_Load event.

Listing 11.13. Adding code to the MAPI Email Agent Setup Form_Load event.

```
Private Sub Form_Load()
    '
    ' load controls
    '
    SetupPageLoad
    '
    Me.Left = (Screen.Width - Me.Width) / 2
    Me.Top = (Screen.Height - Me.Height) / 2
    Me.Icon = LoadPicture(App.Path & "\" & "mail14.ico")
    Me.Caption = "MAPI Email Agent - Setup Page"
    '
End Sub
```

WARNING

In the second-to-last line, this code refers to an icon in the local folder. The icon can be found on the CD-ROM that ships with this book, and is copied to your machine when you install the source code from the CD-ROM. If you get an error message on this line, you may need to locate the icon or use another icon for your project.

The last event you need to code for the form is the `Command1_Click` event. This event handles the saving (or canceling) of a new rule. Add the code shown in Listing 11.14 to the `Command1_Click` event.

Listing 11.14. Adding code to the `Command1_Click` event.

```
Private Sub Command1_Click(Index As Integer)
    '
    ' handle key clicks
    '
    Select Case Index
        Case 0 ' cancel
            ' na
        Case 1 ' ok
            SetupPageSave
    End Select
    '
    Unload Me
    '
End Sub
```

That is the end of the coding for the MAPI Email Agent Setup form. Save this form as `MEASETUP.FRM` and save the project (`MEA.VBP`) before you continue to the next section.

In the next section, you'll add the support routines that are needed to make the MAPI Email Agent really work.

Coding the Support Routines

The real heart of the MAPI Email Agent program is the support routines. There are three main sets of routines in the program:

■ Initialization routines
■ List-handling routines
■ Message-processing routines

The next three sections of this chapter walk you through the process of building the support routines for the MAPI Email Agent program.

All the code for the support routines will be added to a BAS module. Before going on to the next sections, add a BAS module called `LIBMEA.BAS` to the MAPI Email Agent project.

The Initialization Routines

The initialization routines declare the global variables and set them to their initial values. There are also routines to handle the reading and writing of configuration values and the storing and retrieving of the test, action, and rule records.

> **NOTE**
>
> All of the control information is kept in a single ASCII text file (MEA.RUL) in the same folder as the program. This format was chosen for simplicity. In a production environment, you will want to consider a more sophisticated storage system including database formats.

Since we will be using an ASCII control file similar to the 16-bit INI files, we need to declare two API calls to handle the reading and writing of those values. Listing 11.15 shows the two API calls needed for this project. Add this code to the general declarations section of the BAS module.

Listing 11.15. Adding the API calls.

```
Option Explicit
'
' APIs for read/write of shared INI settings
Declare Function GetPrivateProfileString Lib "kernel32" Alias
"GetPrivateProfileStringA" (ByVal lpApplicationName As String, ByVal lpKeyName As
Any, ByVal lpDefault As String, ByVal lpReturnedString As String, ByVal nSize As
Long, ByVal lpFileName As String) As Long
Declare Function WritePrivateProfileString Lib "kernel32" Alias
"WritePrivateProfileStringA" (ByVal lpApplicationName As String, ByVal lpKeyName As
Any, ByVal lpString As Any, ByVal lpFileName As String) As Long
```

The next code to add declares the global variables. Listing 11.16 shows all the declarations needed for the project. Add these values to the general declarations section of the module.

Listing 11.16. Declaring the global variables.

```
Global cRuleFile As String
Global cIsEqualTo As String
Global cIsContainedIn As String
Global cIsGreaterThan As String
Global cIsLessThan As String
Global cForwardMsg1 As String
Global cForwardMsg2 As String
Global lCounter As Long
'
' general section
Global cGeneralSection As String
Global cGeneralScanInterval As String
Global cScanIntervalValue As String
Global cGeneralAutoStart As String
Global cAutoStartValue As String
Global cGeneralEditor As String
Global cEditorValue As String
Global cGeneralLogFile As String
Global cLogFileValue As String
Global cGeneralLogFlag As String
```

```
Global cLogFlagValue As String
Global cGeneralRuleCount As String
Global cRuleCountValue As String
Global cGeneralTestCount As String
Global cTestCountValue As String
Global cGeneralActionCount As String
Global cActionCountValue As String
Global cGeneralProfile As String
Global cProfileValue As String
Global cGeneralDelFwdFlag As String
Global cDelFwdFlagValue As String
Global cGeneralDelReplyFlag As String
Global cDelReplyFlagValue As String
Global cGeneralNotifyDialog As String
Global cNotifyDialogValue As String
Global cGeneralMinOnStart As String
Global cMinOnStartValue As String
Global cGeneralLastUpdate As String
Global cLastUpdateValue As String
'
' test section
Global cTestSection As String
Global cTestPriority As String
Global cTestSubject As String
Global cTestSender As String
Global cTestCommands As String
'
' action section
Global cActionSection As String
Global cActionCopy As String ' COPY (folder)
Global cActionMove As String ' MOVE (folder)
Global cActionForward As String ' FORWARD (address)
Global cActionNotify As String ' NOTIFY
Global cActionReply As String ' REPLY (textfile)
Global cActionCommands As String
'
' rules section
Global cRulesSection As String
Global cRuleName() As String
Global cRuleTest() As String
Global cRuleAction() As String
Global cRuleCompare() As String
Global cTest() As String
Global cAction() As String
Global iTestCount As Integer
Global iActionCount As Integer
Global iRuleCount As Integer
'
' standard mapi objects
Global objSession As Object
Global objMsgColl As Object
Global objMessage As Object
Global objOriginator As Object
Global objRecipColl As Object
Global objRecipient As Object
Global objFolderColl As Object
Global objFolder As Object
Global objAddrEntry As Object
```

continues

Listing 11.16. continued

```
Global objInfoStoreColl As Object
Global objInfoStore As Object
Global objAttachColl As Object
Global objAttachments As Object
```

Next add the Main subroutine to the project. This Visual Basic project launches from a Main() subroutine instead of a form. The Main routine first calls a routine that performs the initialization routines, then calls the main form. Once the form is closed by the user, a short cleanup routine is called. Add the code in Listing 11.17 to the project.

Listing 11.17. Adding the Main routine.

```
Public Sub Main()
    '
    ' main start and end
    '
    InitStuff
    frmMEA.Show vbModal
    CloseDown
    '
End Sub
```

Now add the InitStuff subroutine to the project and enter the code in Listing 11.18.

Listing 11.18. Adding the InitStuff routine.

```
Public Sub InitStuff()
    '
    ' it all starts here
    '
    ReDim cAction(0)
    ReDim cTest(0)
    ReDim cRuleName(0)
    ReDim cRuleTest(0)
    ReDim cRuleAction(0)
    ReDim cRuleCompare(0)
    '
    LoadStrings
    LoadValues
    StartMAPI
    LoadLists
    '
End Sub
```

The routine in Listing 11.18 calls four other routines. The first one is LoadStrings. This routine initializes the local variables at startup. Add the LoadStrings subroutine and enter the code in Listing 11.19.

Listing 11.19. Adding the LoadStrings routine.

```
Public Sub LoadStrings()
    '
    ' init all internals
    '
    cRuleFile = App.Path & "\" & App.EXEName & ".RUL"
    cIsEqualTo = "EQ"
    cIsContainedIn = "CI"
    cIsGreaterThan = "GT"
    cIsLessThan = "LT"
    '
    cGeneralSection = "General"
    cGeneralEditor = "Editor"
    cEditorValue = "notepad.exe"
    cGeneralLogFile = "LogFile"
    cLogFileValue = App.Path & "\" & App.EXEName & ".LOG"
    cGeneralLogFlag = "LogFlag"
    cLogFlagValue = "1"
    cGeneralScanInterval = "ScanInterval"
    cScanIntervalValue = "15"
    cGeneralRuleCount = "RuleCount"
    cRuleCountValue = "0"
    cGeneralTestCount = "TestCount"
    cTestCountValue = "0"
    cGeneralActionCount = "ActionCount"
    cActionCountValue = "0"
    cGeneralProfile = "Profile"
    cProfileValue = "MCA"
    cGeneralDelFwdFlag = "DeleteForwardFlag"
    cDelFwdFlagValue = "0"
    cGeneralNotifyDialog = "NotifyDialog"
    cNotifyDialogValue = "0"
    cGeneralDelReplyFlag = "DeleteReplyFlag"
    cDelReplyFlagValue = "0"
    cGeneralMinOnStart = "MinimzeOnStart"
    cMinOnStartValue = "0"
    cGeneralAutoStart = "AutoStart"
    cAutoStartValue = "0"
    cGeneralLastUpdate = "LastUpdated"
    cLastUpdateValue = Now()
    '
    cTestSection = "Tests"
    cTestPriority = "Priority"
    cTestSubject = "Subject"
    cTestSender = "Sender"
    cTestCommands = cTestPriority & " " & cTestSubject & " " & cTestSender
    '
    cActionSection = "Actions"
    cActionCopy = "Copy"
    cActionMove = "Move"
    cActionForward = "Forward"
    cActionReply = "Reply"
    cActionNotify = "Notify"
    cActionCommands = cActionCopy & " " & cActionMove & " " & cActionForward
    cActionCommands = cActionCommands & " " & cActionReply & " " & cActionNotify
    '
    cRulesSection = "Rules"
    '
End Sub
```

> **TIP**
>
> Most of the strings in the LoadString routine are the names of control file keys ("Editor," "ScanInterval," "LogFile," and so on). By storing the *names* of the keys in this way, you can easily localize the project for other languages—because the MAPI Email Agent project checks only variable names, you can change the values in this section to match other languages without having to re-code most of the program.

The next few routines all deal with data transfers to and from the ASCII control file. Listing 11.20 shows two new routines—LoadValues and SaveValues. Add these routines to your module and enter the code shown in Listing 11.20.

Listing 11.20. Adding the LoadValues and SaveValues routines.

```
Public Sub LoadValues()
    '
    ' process rules file
    '
    INIGeneral "LOAD"
    INIRules "LOAD"
    INITests "LOAD"
    INIActions "LOAD"
    '
End Sub

Public Sub SaveValues()
    '
    ' save ini values for next time
    '
    INIGeneral "SAVE"
    INIRules "SAVE"
    INITests "SAVE"
    INIActions "SAVE"
    '
End Sub
```

You can see that both routines call the same subroutines using different parameters for the save and load events. Now add the INIGeneral subroutine to your module and enter the code shown in Listing 11.21.

Listing 11.21. Adding the INIGeneral routine.

```
Public Sub INIGeneral(cAction As String)
    '
    ' load general rule stuff
    '
    cLastUpdateValue = Format(Now(), "general date")
    '
    cEditorValue = INIRegSetting(cAction, cRuleFile, cGeneralSection,
```

```
cGeneralEditor, cEditorValue)
    cScanIntervalValue = INIRegSetting(cAction, cRuleFile, cGeneralSection,
cGeneralScanInterval, cScanIntervalValue)
    cLogFileValue = INIRegSetting(cAction, cRuleFile, cGeneralSection,
cGeneralLogFile, cLogFileValue)
    cLogFlagValue = INIRegSetting(cAction, cRuleFile, cGeneralSection,
cGeneralLogFlag, cLogFlagValue)
    cRuleCountValue = INIRegSetting(cAction, cRuleFile, cGeneralSection,
cGeneralRuleCount, cRuleCountValue)
    cActionCountValue = INIRegSetting(cAction, cRuleFile, cGeneralSection,
cGeneralActionCount, cActionCountValue)
    cTestCountValue = INIRegSetting(cAction, cRuleFile, cGeneralSection,
cGeneralTestCount, cTestCountValue)
    cProfileValue = INIRegSetting(cAction, cRuleFile, cGeneralSection,
cGeneralProfile, cProfileValue)
    cDelFwdFlagValue = INIRegSetting(cAction, cRuleFile, cGeneralSection,
cGeneralDelFwdFlag, cDelFwdFlagValue)
    cNotifyDialogValue = INIRegSetting(cAction, cRuleFile, cGeneralSection,
cGeneralNotifyDialog, cNotifyDialogValue)
    cDelReplyFlagValue = INIRegSetting(cAction, cRuleFile, cGeneralSection,
cGeneralDelReplyFlag, cDelReplyFlagValue)
    cMinOnStartValue = INIRegSetting(cAction, cRuleFile, cGeneralSection,
cGeneralMinOnStart, cMinOnStartValue)
    cAutoStartValue = INIRegSetting(cAction, cRuleFile, cGeneralSection,
cGeneralAutoStart, cAutoStartValue)
    cLastUpdateValue = INIRegSetting(cAction, cRuleFile, cGeneralSection,
cGeneralLastUpdate, cLastUpdateValue)
    '
End Sub
```

You'll notice that the INIRegSetting function called in each line of Listing 11.21 is very similar to the SaveSetting/GetSetting functions built into Visual Basic 4.0. However, unlike the built-in Visual Basic functions, this one routine can be used to both read and write values. Also, this custom version always writes to a disk file. The Visual Basic 4.0 SaveSetting function saves values to the Registry under Windows NT and Windows 95.

Add the INIRegSetting function to your project and enter the code shown in Listing 11.22.

Listing 11.22. Adding the INIRegSetting function.

```
Public Function INIRegSetting(cAction As String, cFile As String, cSection As
String, cKey As String, cValue As String) As String
    '
    ' handle read/write of local ini settings
    ' for public use
    '
    INIRegSetting = ""
    '
    If UCase(cAction) = "LOAD" Then
        INIRegSetting = LocalGetSetting(cFile, cSection, cKey, cValue)
    End If
    '
    If UCase(cAction) = "SAVE" Then
```

continues

Listing 11.22. continued

```
        INIRegSetting = LocalSaveSetting(cFile, cSection, cKey, cValue)
    End If
'
End Function
```

The `INIRegSetting` routine makes one last call down to a pair of custom routines. These custom routines (`LocalGetSetting` and `LocalSaveSetting`) are the wrapper functions for the API declarations you added at the start of this module. Add the two new functions (`LocalGetSetting` and `LocalSaveSetting`) and enter the code shown in Listing 11.23.

Listing 11.23. Adding the `LocalGetSetting` and `LocalSaveSetting` functions.

```
Public Function LocalGetSetting(cFile As String, cSection As String, cKey As
String, cDefault As String) As String
    '
    ' mimic GetSetting/SaveSetting for 32-bit text files
    '
    Dim lRtn As Long
    Dim lSize As Long
    Dim cTemp As String * 1024

    lSize = Len(cTemp)
    lRtn = GetPrivateProfileString(cSection, cKey, cDefault, cTemp, lSize, cFile)
    If Trim(cTemp) = "" Then
        cTemp = Trim(cDefault)
        lRtn = WritePrivateProfileString(cSection, cKey, cTemp, cFile)
    End If
    '
    LocalGetSetting = Left(cTemp, lRtn)
    '
End Function

Public Function LocalSaveSetting(cFile As String, cSection As String, cKey As
String, cValue As String)
    '
    ' mimic INI/Registry stuff for public use
    '
    Dim lRtn As Long
    '
    lRtn = WritePrivateProfileString(cSection, cKey, cValue, cFile)
    LocalSaveSetting = cValue ' return what was saved
    '
End Function
```

Next you need to add the routines to load the rules, actions, and tests from the control file into memory variables. Listing 11.24 contains the code for the `INIRules` routine.

Listing 11.24. Adding the `INIRules` routine.

```
Public Sub INIRules(cAction As String)
    '
    ' load all rules
    '
    Dim x As Integer
    '
    iRuleCount = Val(cRuleCountValue)
    ReDim Preserve cRuleName(iRuleCount)
    ReDim Preserve cRuleTest(iRuleCount)
    ReDim Preserve cRuleAction(iRuleCount)
    ReDim Preserve cRuleCompare(iRuleCount)
    '
    If iRuleCount > 0 Then
        For x = 0 To iRuleCount - 1
            cRuleName(x) = INIRegSetting(cAction, cRuleFile, cRulesSection,
"RuleName" & CStr(x), cRuleName(x))
            cRuleTest(x) = INIRegSetting(cAction, cRuleFile, cRulesSection,
"RuleTest" & CStr(x), cRuleTest(x))
            cRuleAction(x) = INIRegSetting(cAction, cRuleFile, cRulesSection,
"RuleAction" & CStr(x), cRuleAction(x))
            cRuleCompare(x) = INIRegSetting(cAction, cRuleFile, cRulesSection,
"RuleCompare" & CStr(x), cRuleCompare(x))
        Next x
    End If
    '
End Sub
```

Listing 11.25 shows the code for the `INITests` and `INIActions` routines. Add these to your project.

Listing 11.25. Adding the `INITests` and `INIActions` routines.

```
Public Sub INITests(cAction As String)
    '
    ' load all tests
    '
    Dim x As Integer
    '
    iTestCount = Val(cTestCountValue)
    ReDim Preserve cTest(iTestCount)
    '
    If iTestCount > 0 Then
        For x = 0 To iTestCount - 1
            cTest(x) = INIRegSetting(cAction, cRuleFile, cTestSection, "Test" &
CStr(x), cTest(x))
        Next x
    End If
    '
End Sub

Public Sub INIActions(cEvent As String)
    '
    ' load all actions
    '
    Dim x As Integer
```

continues

Listing 11.25. continued

```
    '
    iActionCount = Val(cActionCountValue)
    ReDim Preserve cAction(iActionCount)
    '
    If iActionCount > 0 Then
        For x = 0 To iActionCount - 1
            cAction(x) = INIRegSetting(cEvent, cRuleFile, cActionSection, "Action"
& CStr(x), cAction(x))
        Next x
    End If
    '
End Sub
```

The last routines needed for the initialization section are the ones that start and end your MAPI sessions (you remember MAPI, right?), and the routine that handles program exit cleanup.

First add the `CloseDown` cleanup routine to your project and enter the code shown in Listing 11.26.

Listing 11.26. Adding the `CloseDown` routine.

```
Public Sub CloseDown()
    '
    ' close down system
    '
    SaveValues
    MAPIEnd
    '
End Sub
```

Now add the `StartMAPI` and `MAPIEnd` routines and enter the code from Listing 11.27.

Listing 11.27. Adding the `StartMAPI` and `MAPIEnd` routines.

```
Public Sub StartMAPI()
    '
    ' log into mapi system
    '
    Set objSession = CreateObject("MAPI.Session")
    objSession.Logon profilename:=cProfileValue, profilepassword:="",
newsession:=True
    '
End Sub

Public Sub MAPIEnd()
    '
    ' log off mapi system
    objSession.Logoff
    Set objSession = Nothing
    '
End Sub
```

That is the end of the support routines for initialization. Save this module (MEA.BAS) and project (MEA.VBP) before continuing to the next section.

The List-Handling Routines

The next set of routines handle the addition and deletion of records from the rules, tests, and actions lists. There are also two routines that handle the populating of the list controls on the MAPI Email Agent forms.

First, add a new subroutine called LoadLists to the module and enter the code shown in Listing 11.28. This routine simply calls the low-level function that actually fills the list box control.

Listing 11.28. Adding the LoadLists routine.

```
Public Sub LoadLists()
    '
    ' load the main form lists
    '
    FillList "rules", frmMEA.lstrules
    FillList "tests", frmMEA.lsttests
    FillList "actions", frmMEA.lstactions
    '
End Sub
```

Next, add the low-level routine that is called by LoadLists. Add the subroutine FillList to the project and enter the code shown in Listing 11.29.

Listing 11.29. Adding the FillList routine.

```
Public Sub FillList(cListName As String, lstControl As Control)
    '
    ' fill form lists with data
    '
    Dim x As Integer
    Dim ln As Integer
    Dim cLine As String
    '
    Select Case UCase(cListName)
        Case "RULES"
            lstControl.Clear
            For x = 0 To iRuleCount - 1
                If Len(cRuleName(x)) > 18 Then
                    ln = 18
                Else
                    ln = Len(cRuleName(x))
                End If
                cLine = Left(cRuleName(x), 18) & Space(20 - ln)
                '
```

continues

Listing 11.29. continued

```
                     If Len(cRuleTest(x)) > 13 Then
                         ln = 13
                     Else
                         ln = Len(cRuleTest(x))
                     End If
                     '
                     cLine = cLine & Left(cRuleTest(x), 13) & Space(15 - ln)
                     cLine = cLine & cRuleCompare(x)
                     cLine = cLine & Space(2)
                     cLine = cLine & cRuleAction(x)
                     lstControl.AddItem cLine
             Next x
         Case "TESTS"
             lstControl.Clear
             For x = 0 To iTestCount - 1
                 lstControl.AddItem cTest(x)
             Next x
         Case "ACTIONS"
             lstControl.Clear
             For x = 0 To iActionCount - 1
                 lstControl.AddItem cAction(x)
             Next x
         Case "COMPARES"
             lstControl.Clear
             lstControl.AddItem cIsEqualTo
             lstControl.AddItem cIsGreaterThan
             lstControl.AddItem cIsLessThan
             lstControl.AddItem cIsContainedIn
     End Select
     '
End Sub
```

Notice the use of column-like spacing for the rules list. By computing length and setting spacing evenly, you can give the effect of a grid format while still using a list box control.

TIP

This technique works well only if you set your list box control font type to a fixed-width font such as Courier or System.

The next two routines deal with the addition and deletion of tests. First, add the new routine AddTest to the project and enter the code shown in Listing 11.30.

Listing 11.30. Adding the AddTest routine.

```
Public Sub AddTest(cTestLine As String)
    '
    ' add a new test to system
    '
    Dim x As Integer
    Dim p As Integer
```

```
'
' look for empty spot
p = -1
For x = 0 To iTestCount - 1
    If cTest(x) = "" Then
        p = x
        Exit For
    End If
Next x
'
' no empty spot, make a new one
If p = -1 Then
    iTestCount = iTestCount + 1
    cTestCountValue = CStr(iTestCount)
    ReDim Preserve cTest(iTestCount)
    p = iTestCount - 1
End If
'
cTest(p) = cTestLine ' save item
'
' refresh lists
SaveValues
LoadValues
LoadLists
'
End Sub
```

This routine works by adding an item to the Test() array. First, the routine attempts to find an open slot in the existing list. If none is found, the routine will expand the list and add the new item at the bottom of the list. As a final step, AddTest saves the new data to the control file and then reloads the control data to refresh the local variables.

The DeleteTest function is quite simple. It just removes the selected item from the array by blanking it out. This is simple, but not the most desirable. When you run the program you'll see that each deletion leaves a hole in the list. As new items are added, these holes are filled. The holes do not adversely affect processing, but they are a bit unsightly in the list controls. In a production application, more time can be spent on the user interface. For now, just keep in mind you have a routine that works—you can add the bells and whistles later.

Add the DeleteTest subroutine to your project and enter the code in Listing 11.31.

Listing 11.31. Adding the DeleteTest routine.

```
Public Sub DeleteTest(itest As Integer)
    '
    ' remove test from list
    '
    cTest(itest) = ""
    '
    SaveValues
    LoadValues
    LoadLists
    '
End Sub
```

The AddAction and DeleteAction routines are almost identical to the AddTest and DeleteTest routines. Add these two new subroutines to your project and enter the code from Listings 11.32 and 11.33.

Listing 11.32. Adding the AddAction routine.

```
Public Sub AddAction(cInput As String)
    '
    ' add a new test to system
    '
    Dim x As Integer
    Dim p As Integer
    '
    ' look for empty spot
    p = -1
    For x = 0 To iActionCount - 1
        If cAction(x) = "" Then
            p = x
            Exit For
        End If
    Next x
    '
    ' no empty spot, make a new one
    If p = -1 Then
        iActionCount = iActionCount + 1
        cActionCountValue = CStr(iActionCount)
        ReDim Preserve cAction(iActionCount)
        p = iActionCount - 1
    End If
    '
    cAction(p) = cInput ' save item
    '
    ' refresh lists
    SaveValues
    LoadValues
    LoadLists
    '
End Sub
```

Listing 11.33. Adding the DeleteAction routine.

```
Public Sub DeleteAction(iAction As Integer)
    '
    ' remove action from list
    '
    cAction(iAction) = ""
    '
    SaveValues
    LoadValues
    LoadLists
    '
End Sub
```

The `AddRule` routine is a bit different. The `AddRule` routine calls the MAPI Email Agent Rule form to add new rules. This form then calls a function to actually add the new rule to the control file. So there are really three routines:

- AddRule
- MakeRule
- DeleteRule

First, add the new `AddRule` subroutine and enter the code shown in Listing 11.34.

Listing 11.34. Adding the `AddRule` routine.

```
Public Sub AddRule()
    '
    ' handle adding new rule
    '
    frmMEARule.Show vbModal
    '
    frmMEA.MousePointer = vbHourglass
    '
    SaveValues
    LoadValues
    LoadLists
    '
    frmMEA.MousePointer = vbNormal
    '
End Sub
```

Now add the `MakeRule` subroutine to your project. This is the routine that actually saves the results of data entry on the MAPI Email Agent Rule form. Enter the code from Listing 11.35.

Listing 11.35. Adding the `MakeRule` routine.

```
Public Sub MakeRule(cName As String, cRule As String)
    '
    ' store new rule
    '
    Dim x As Integer
    Dim p As Integer
    Dim cTestPart As String
    Dim cComparePart As String
    Dim cActionPart As String
    Dim nPos1 As Integer
    Dim nPos2 As Integer
    '
    ' first get parts
    '
    nPos1 = 1
    nPos2 = InStr(nPos1, cRule, " ¦ ")
    If nPos2 <> 0 Then
        cTestPart = Trim(Mid(cRule, nPos1, nPos2 - nPos1))
```

continues

Listing 11.35. continued

```
    End If
    '
    nPos1 = nPos2 + 3
    nPos2 = InStr(nPos1, cRule, " ¦ ")
    If nPos2 <> 0 Then
        cComparePart = Trim(Mid(cRule, nPos1, nPos2 - nPos1))
    End If
    '
    nPos1 = nPos2 + 3
    cActionPart = Trim(Mid(cRule, nPos1, 255))
    '
    '
    ' look for empty spot
    p = -1
    For x = 0 To iRuleCount - 1
        If Trim(cRuleName(x)) = "" Then
            p = x
            Exit For
        End If
    Next x
    '
    ' no empty spot, make a new one
    If p = -1 Then
        iRuleCount = iRuleCount + 1
        cRuleCountValue = CStr(iRuleCount)
        ReDim Preserve cRuleName(iRuleCount)
        ReDim Preserve cRuleTest(iRuleCount)
        ReDim Preserve cRuleCompare(iRuleCount)
        ReDim Preserve cRuleAction(iRuleCount)
        p = iRuleCount - 1
    End If
    '
    ' save it
    cRuleName(p) = cName
    cRuleTest(p) = cTestPart
    cRuleCompare(p) = cComparePart
    cRuleAction(p) = cActionPart
    '
    ' refresh storage
    SaveValues
    LoadValues
    '
End Sub
```

The last list-handling routine you need to add is the DeleteRule subroutine. After adding the routine, enter the code you see in Listing 11.36.

Listing 11.36. Adding the DeleteRule routine.

```
Public Sub DeleteRule(iAction As Integer)
    '
    ' remove rule from list
    '
    cRuleName(iAction) = ""
```

```
        cRuleTest(iAction) = ""
        cRuleCompare(iAction) = ""
        cRuleAction(iAction) = ""
        '
        SaveValues
        LoadValues
        LoadLists
        '
End Sub
```

There is one more support routine needed before you are done with this section. You need a routine to write out log messages when requested. Add a new subroutine called LogWrite to your project and enter the code shown in Listing 11.37. This routine writes lines to a text file along with the date and time the line was written. This routine also sends the same message to the status line of the MAPI Email Agent main form.

Listing 11.37. Adding the LogWrite routine.

```
Public Sub LogWrite(cLine As String)
    '
    ' write an entry in the log
    '
    Dim nFile As Integer
    Dim cWriteLine As String
    '
    If cLogFlagValue <> "1" Then
        Exit Sub ' write is OFF
    End If
    '
    cWriteLine = Format(Now, "general date")
    cWriteLine = cWriteLine & Space(3)
    cWriteLine = cWriteLine & cLine
    '
    nFile = FreeFile
    Open cLogFileValue For Append As nFile
    Print #nFile, cWriteLine
    Close #nFile
    '
    frmMEA.lblstatus = cWriteLine
    '
End Sub
```

You now have all the routines needed to add and delete items from the lists. Actually you have everything built except the message processing routines. This is a good time to test the forms and list-handling routines. First, you need to add a "stub" routine to your project. This routine does nothing on its own, but it allows you to test your forms without getting errors. Just create a new subroutine called StartProcess.

```
Public Sub StartProcess()
    '
End Sub
```

Now save the module (MEA.BAS) and the project (MEA.VBP) before doing any test runs. After you are satisfied the routines are working properly, you can go on to the next section for the last bit of coding—the message processing routines.

The Message Processing Routines

This last set of routines is where the MAPI services are finally used. The goal of the message processing routines is to inspect each message in the user's inbox and check the messages against the rules that have been established for the MAPI Email Agent.

The top-level routines are StartProcess and ScanMsgs. The StartProcess routine is called by the Timer1_Timer event or by pressing the Start button on the main form. StartProcess checks to see if there are any messages in the user's inbox. If there are, then the ScanMsg routine is called to process each message.

If you already added the StartProcess routine, locate it now. Otherwise, add the new routine and enter the code shown in Listing 11.38.

Listing 11.38. Adding the StartProcess code.

```
Public Sub StartProcess()
    '
    ' start main process loop
    '
    Set objMsgColl = objSession.Inbox.Messages
    If objMsgColl Is Nothing Then
        MsgBox "No Messages to scan"
    Else
        ScanMsgs
        Set objMsgColl = Nothing
    End If
    '
End Sub
```

The StartProcess routine attempts to create a message collection object based on the Session inbox. If that is successful, the ScanMsgs routine can be called. Now add the ScanMsgs subroutine and enter the code in Listing 11.39.

Listing 11.39. Adding the ScanMsgs routine.

```
Public Sub ScanMsgs()
    '
    ' check each message for hits
    '
    Dim x As Long
    '
    Set objMessage = objMsgColl.GetFirst
    If objMessage Is Nothing Then
        Exit Sub ' no messages!
```

```
        End If
        Do Until objMessage Is Nothing
            CheckRule
            Set objMessage = objMsgColl.GetNext
        Loop
        '
        LogWrite "Msg Scan Completed"
        '
End Sub
```

The ScanMsgs routine selects each message in the collection and submits it to the CheckRule routine for processing.

Now add the CheckRule subroutine and type in the code shown in Listing 11.40.

Listing 11.40. Adding the CheckRule routine.

```
Public Sub CheckRule()
    '
    ' check for rule hit
    '
    Dim x As Integer
    Dim cCmd As String
    Dim bRtn As Boolean
    Dim objAddrEntry As Object
    '
    On Error GoTo CheckRuleErr
    '
    For x = 0 To iRuleCount - 1
        cCmd = ParseWord(cRuleTest(x))
        '
        Select Case UCase(cCmd)
            Case UCase(cTestSender)
                Set objAddrEntry = objMessage.Sender
                If objAddrEntry Is Nothing Then
                    ' na
                Else
                    If CheckSender(x, objMessage.Sender.Name) = True Then
                        DoAction x
                    End If
                End If
            Case UCase(cTestSubject)
                If CheckSubject(x, objMessage.subject) = True Then
                    DoAction x
                End If
            Case UCase(cTestPriority)
                If CheckPriority(x, objMessage.importance) = True Then
                    DoAction x
                End If
        End Select
        '
    Next x
    '
    Exit Sub
    '
```

continues

Listing 11.40. continued

```
CheckRuleErr:
    MsgBox Error$, vbCritical, "CheckRuleErr [" & CStr(Err) & "]"
    '
End Sub
```

Several things are going on in this routine. First, the first "word" on the line is removed using the ParseWord() function. This word is then used to determine the type of test to perform on the message. The appropriate check subroutine is called (CheckSender, CheckSubject, CheckPriority) and, if the return is positive, the DoAction routine is called to handle the action portion of the rule.

Now add the ParseWord function and enter the code shown in Listing 11.41.

Listing 11.41. Adding the ParseWord function.

```
Public Function ParseWord(cLine As String) As String
    '
    ' pick a word off line
    '
    Dim nPos As Integer
    '
    nPos = InStr(cLine, " ")
    If nPos <> 0 Then
        ParseWord = Left(cLine, nPos - 1)
    Else
        ParseWord = ""
    End If
    '
End Function
```

The ParseWord() function accepts a string and returns the first full word found in the string. For example ParseWord("SENDER Smith") would return SENDER. This is used to pull the command portion of a test or action record.

The CheckRule routine you entered earlier (in Listing 11.40) uses ParseWord() to get the message portion command of a rule (SENDER, SUBJECT, PRIORITY). This value is then used to call the three message-part-specific check routines (CheckSender, CheckSubject, and CheckPriority). You need to add these routines next.

First add the CheckSender function, and enter the code shown in Listing 11.42.

Listing 11.42. Adding the CheckSender function.

```
Public Function CheckSender(nRule As Integer, cName As String)
    '
    ' check name against sender test
    '
    Dim nPos As Integer
```

```
    Dim cSender As String
    '
    nPos = InStr(cRuleTest(nRule), " ")
    If nPos <> 0 Then
        cSender = Trim(Mid(cRuleTest(nRule), nPos + 1, 255))
    End If
    '
    cSender = Trim(UCase(cSender))
    cName = Trim(UCase(cName))
    '
    Select Case UCase(cRuleCompare(nRule))
        Case UCase(cIsEqualTo)
            If cSender = cName Then
                CheckSender = True
            Else
                CheckSender = False
            End If
        Case UCase(cIsGreaterThan)
            If cSender > cName Then
                CheckSender = True
            Else
                CheckSender = False
            End If
        Case UCase(cIsLessThan)
            If cSender < cName Then
                CheckSender = True
            Else
                CheckSender = False
            End If
        Case UCase(cIsContainedIn)
             If InStr(cSender, cName) <> 0 Then
                CheckSender = True
            Else
                CheckSender = False
            End If
     End Select
     '
End Function
```

Note that this routine uses a SELECT CASE structure to handle the compare portion of the rule. After locating the correct compare operation, CheckSender tests the Sender portion against the Name in the rule and returns the result (TRUE or FALSE).

The CheckSubject and CheckPriority functions work the same way. The only difference is that the CheckPriority function does not test for CI ("is contained in"). Add the CheckSubject function and enter the code from Listing 11.43.

Listing 11.43. Adding the CheckSubject routine.

```
Public Function CheckSubject(nRule As Integer, cSubjMsg As String) As Boolean
    '
    ' check subject against message test
    '
```

continues

Listing 11.43. continued

```
    Dim nPos As Integer
    Dim cSubjRule As String
    '
    nPos = InStr(cRuleTest(nRule), " ")
    If nPos <> 0 Then
        cSubjRule = Trim(Mid(cRuleTest(nRule), nPos + 1, 255))
    End If
    '
    cSubjRule = UCase(Trim(cSubjRule))
    cSubjMsg = UCase(Trim(cSubjMsg))
    '
    Select Case UCase(cRuleCompare(nRule))
        Case UCase(cIsEqualTo)
            If cSubjRule = cSubjMsg Then
                CheckSubject = True
            Else
                CheckSubject = False
            End If
        Case UCase(cIsLessThan)
            If cSubjRule < cSubjMsg Then
                CheckSubject = True
            Else
                CheckSubject = False
            End If
        Case UCase(cIsGreaterThan)
            If cSubjRule > cSubjMsg Then
                CheckSubject = True
            Else
                CheckSubject = False
            End If
        Case UCase(cIsContainedIn)
            If InStr(cSubjRule, cSubjMsg) <> 0 Then
                CheckSubject = True
            Else
                CheckSubject = False
            End If
    End Select
    '
End Function
```

Finally, add the CheckPriority function and enter the code from Listing 11.44.

Listing 11.44. Adding the CheckPriority routine.

```
Public Function CheckPriority(nRule As Integer, nImpMsg) As Boolean
    '
    ' check subject against message test
    '
    Dim nPos As Integer
    Dim cImpRule As String
    Dim nImpRule As Integer
    '
    nPos = InStr(cRuleTest(nRule), " ")
    If nPos <> 0 Then
```

```
            cImpRule = Trim(Mid(cRuleTest(nRule), nPos + 1, 255))
    End If
    '
    nImpRule = Val(cImpRule)
    '
    Select Case UCase(cRuleCompare(nRule))
        Case UCase(cIsEqualTo)
            If nImpRule = nImpMsg Then
                CheckPriority = True
            Else
                CheckPriority = False
            End If
        Case UCase(cIsLessThan)
            If nImpRule < nImpMsg Then
                CheckPriority = True
            Else
                CheckPriority = False
            End If
        Case UCase(cIsGreaterThan)
            If nImpRule > nImpMsg Then
                CheckPriority = True
            Else
                CheckPriority = False
            End If
    End Select
    '
End Function
```

If the Check*nnn* routine returns TRUE, an action must take place. The DoAction routine is used to execute the appropriate e-mail action. DoAction accepts the index to the rule as its only parameter. Like the CheckRule routine, DoAction uses a SELECT CASE structure to act on each command word (NOTIFY, COPY, MOVE, FORWARD, and REPLY).

Add the DoAction subroutine to the project and enter the code shown in Listing 11.45.

Listing 11.45. Adding the DoAction routine.

```
Public Sub DoAction(nRule As Integer)
    '
    ' handle valid action
    ' nRule points to rule in array
    ' use current objMessage
    '
    Dim cCmd As String ' action command
    Dim cTarget As String ' action target
    Dim nPos As Integer
    '
    ' get command and target
    cCmd = ParseWord(cRuleAction(nRule))
    nPos = InStr(cRuleAction(nRule), " ")
    If nPos <> 0 Then
        cTarget = Trim(Mid(cRuleAction(nRule), nPos + 1, 255))
    End If
    '
```

continues

Listing 11.45. continued

```
    ' now execute command
    Select Case UCase(cCmd)
        Case UCase(cActionMove)
            MsgMoveCopy "MOVE", cTarget, objMessage
        Case UCase(cActionCopy)
            MsgMoveCopy "COPY", cTarget, objMessage
        Case UCase(cActionForward)
            MsgFwdReply "FORWARD", cTarget, objMessage
        Case UCase(cActionReply)
            MsgFwdReply "REPLY", cTarget, objMessage
        Case UCase(cActionNotify)
            MsgNotify cTarget, objMessage
    End Select
    '
End Sub
```

There are only three routines used to act on all five commands. This is because the FORWARD and REPLY commands act on messages, and the COPY and MOVE commands act on folders. Only one routine is needed for each (with slight behavior changes within each routine).

The NOTIFY option is the easiest to handle. All that is needed is a pop-up dialog box when the message arrives. Add the MsgNotify routine and type in the code from Listing 11.46.

Listing 11.46. Adding the MsgNotify routine.

```
Public Sub MsgNotify(cNotify As String, objMsg As Object)
    '
    Dim cMsg As String
    '
    cMsg = "Message Notification for ["
    cMsg = cMsg & objMsg.subject
    cMsg = cMsg & "] from ["
    cMsg = cMsg & objMsg.Sender.Name & "]"
    '
    ' send out pop-up?
    If cNotifyDialogValue = "1" Then
        MsgBox cMsg, vbExclamation, "MAPI Email Agent Notification"
    End If
    LogWrite (cMsg)
    '
End Sub
```

The routine needed for forwarding and replying to messages involves making a new message (with the contents of the original) and sending it to a new address. Since this is actually a messaging operation, you'll use the .Send function to force the message into the transport for delivery. Add the MsgFwdReply subroutine and enter the code in Listing 11.47.

Listing 11.47. Adding the `MsgFwdReply` routine.

```
Public Sub MsgFwdReply(cEvent As String, cDestAddr As String, objMsg As Object)
    '
    Dim cMsg As String
    '
    Dim objLocalMsgColl As Object
    Dim objCopyMsg As Object
    Dim cHeader As String
    Dim cSubjPrefix As String
    '
    cTarget = UCase(cEvent)
    '
    cHeader = "<------ Message " & cEvent
    cHeader = cHeader & " from ["
    cHeader = cHeader & objSession.Name
    cHeader = cHeader & "] by MAPI Email Agent ------>"
    cHeader = cHeader & Chr(13) & Chr(10) & Chr(13) & Chr(10)
    '
    If cEvent = "REPLY" Then
        cSubjPrefix = "RE: "
    Else
        cSubjPrefix = "FW: "
    End If
    '
    Set objLocalMsgColl = objSession.Outbox.Messages
    Set objCopyMsg = objLocalMsgColl.Add
    With objCopyMsg
        .subject = cSubjPrefix & objMsg.subject
        .Text = cHeader & objMsg.Text
    End With
    '
    ' add recipient
    Set objRecipient = objCopyMsg.Recipients.Add
    objRecipient.Name = cDestAddr
    objRecipient.Type = mapiTo
    objCopyMsg.Recipients.Resolve showdialog:=False
    objCopyMsg.Update
    objCopyMsg.Send showdialog:=False
    '
    ' delete old message?
    If cDelFwdFlagValue = "1" And cEvent = "FORWARD" Then
        objMessage.Delete
    End If
    If cDelReplyFlagValue = "1" And cEvent = "REPLY" Then
        objMessage.Delete
    End If
    objSession.Outbox.Update
    '
    ' send out status
    cMsg = cEvent & " Message ["
    cMsg = cMsg & objMsg.subject
    cMsg = cMsg & "] to [" & cDestAddr & "]"
    '
    LogWrite (cMsg)
    '
End Sub
```

There are a few things to keep in mind about this routine. First, a good REPLY routine should allow users to attach, or append, a text message to the original. Here, that code is left out for brevity. You'll also notice that only one recipient is added to the note. In some cases, it is possible that more than one person should receive the forwarded message. This can be handled by using distribution lists. Finally, there is no code here to handle any attachments to the original note. This should be added in a production environment.

The other action to be handled by the MAPI Email Agent is copying or moving messages to other folders. This is accomplished using the .Update method. Moving messages is similar to posting them. For this reason you do not want to attempt to "send" the message. Add the MsgMoveCopy subroutine and enter the code shown in Listing 11.48.

Listing 11.48. Adding the MsgMoveCopy routine.

```
Public Sub MsgMoveCopy(cEvent As String, cFolder As String, objMsg As Object)
    '
    Dim objLocalFolder As Object
    Dim objLocalMsg As Object
    Dim objLocalRecipient As Object
    '
    Dim cMsg As String
    Dim cFldrID As String
    Dim cRecipName As String
    Dim cHeader As String
    Dim i As Integer
    '
    ' carry sender info with you
    cHeader = "<------ " & UCase(cEvent) & " from ["
    cHeader = cHeader & objMsg.Sender.Name
    cHeader = cHeader & "] by MAPI Email Agent ------>"
    cHeader = cHeader & Chr(13) & Chr(10) & Chr(13) & Chr(10)
    '
    ' look for folder
    cFldrID = FindFolder(cFolder)
    If cFldrID = "" Then
        Exit Sub
    End If
    '
    ' move to folder
    Set objLocalFolder = objSession.GetFolder(cFldrID)
    Set objLocalMsg = objLocalFolder.Messages.Add
    '
    ' copy from objmsg to objlocalmsg
    With objLocalMsg
        .DeliveryReceipt = objMsg.DeliveryReceipt
        .Encrypted = objMsg.Encrypted
        .importance = objMsg.importance
        .ReadReceipt = objMsg.ReadReceipt
        .Sent = objMsg.Sent
        .Signed = objMsg.Signed
        .subject = objMsg.subject
        .Submitted = objMsg.Submitted
        .Text = cHeader & objMsg.Text
        .TimeReceived = objMsg.TimeReceived
```

```
        .TimeSent = objMsg.TimeSent
        .Type = objMsg.Type
        .Unread = objMsg.Unread
    End With
    '
    ' add recipients
    For i = 1 To objMsg.Recipients.Count Step 1
        cRecipName = objMsg.Recipients.Item(i).Name
        If cRecipName <> "" Then
            Set objLocalRecipient = objLocalMsg.Recipients.Add
            objLocalRecipient.Name = cRecipName
        End If
    Next i
    '
    ' now save the update
    objLocalMsg.Update
    '
    ' if a move, dump the original message
    If UCase(cEvent) = "MOVE" Then
        objMsg.Delete
    End If
    '
    ' send out notices
    cMsg = UCase(cEvent) & " Message ["
    cMsg = cMsg & objMsg.subject
    cMsg = cMsg & "] to [" & cFolder & "]"
    LogWrite (cMsg)
    '
End Sub
```

Again, a few things worth pointing out here. First, moving or copying messages to other folders requires that you actually *find* the target folder first. This is not as simple as looking up a name in a list. MAPI message stores are recursively hierarchical. That means that folders can exist within folders. And MAPI does not publish a list of the folder tree—you must traverse it each time yourself. This means you need your own `FindFolder` routine (you'll add that in a minute).

> **WARNING**
>
> Since traversing the folder tree can be time-consuming, you might be tempted to build a tree at startup and use that throughout your program. Be careful! Since the Microsoft Exchange message stores can be shared among users, the tree can change rather rapidly. Not only could you encounter new folders or discover that old folders have been deleted, it is also possible that your target folder has been moved. It is a good idea to traverse the folder tree each time you attempt to find a folder.

Notice that the process of moving a message really involves creating a copy in the new folder. The code here copies the most commonly used items, but does not copy any attachments. Keep in mind that some properties may not exist for some messages. You'll need error trapping to prevent program crashes.

The last routine you need for the MAPI Email Agent application is the FindFolder function. This routine accepts a folder name and returns its unique MAPI ID value. Add the FindFolder function and enter the code shown in Listing 11.49.

Listing 11.49. Adding the FindFolder function.

```
Public Function FindFolder(cFldrName As String) As String
    '
    ' see if you can locate the requested folder
    ' if  found, return the unqiue Folder ID
    '
    Dim cRtnID As String
    Dim cTempID As String
    Dim objInfoStore As Object
    Dim objTempFldr As Object
    Dim objTempColl As Object
    Dim x As Integer
    '
    cRtnID = "" ' assume not found
    '
    ' scan the folder collection
    Set objTempColl = objSession.Inbox.Folders
    Set objTempFldr = objTempColl.GetFirst
    Do
        cTempID = objTempFldr.ID
        If UCase(objTempFldr.Name) = UCase(cFldrName) Then
            cRtnID = objTempFldr.ID
            Exit Do
        End If
        Set objTempFldr = objTempColl.GetNext
    Loop While objTempFldr.Name <> ""
    '
    FindFolder = cRtnID ' return the result
    '
End Function
```

You'll notice that the MAPI Email Agent inspects only the top-level folder collection of the Session.InBox. This is done to keep the code brief. If you wanted to search all the folders, you'd need to start at the Session.RootFolder and, after collecting the folders, inspect each of them for the existence of folders, and so on and so forth. For now, the MAPI Email Agent program only works with folders in the inbox. You can add code to expand the search capabilities of the Findfolder routine in future MAPI projects.

Save this module (MEA.BAS) and the project (MEA.VBP) before you start testing the MAPI Email Agent.

Installing and Testing the MAPI Email Agent

After you have completed the MAPI Email Agent project, you can install it on any workstation that has access to MAPI services. You do not have to have Microsoft Exchange or Microsoft Mail clients running in order to use the MAPI Email Agent.

In order to set up MAPI Email Agent to process your incoming mail you need to build test, action, and rule records. You also need to use your Microsoft Exchange or Microsoft Mail client to build any new target folders you want to include as parts of COPY or MOVE actions.

Once your folders are built and your rules are entered, you can launch the MAPI Email Agent at startup each day and let the program do its thing!

The next few sections talk you through a simple example of running the MAPI Email Agent on your workstation.

Setting Up Your Email Folders

First, start up your MAPI e-mail client and make sure you have the following folders within your inbox:

- Urgent
- MAPI
- Sales

After adding these folders to your inbox, it should look something like the one in Figure 11.4.

FIGURE 11.4.

Adding folders to your inbox.

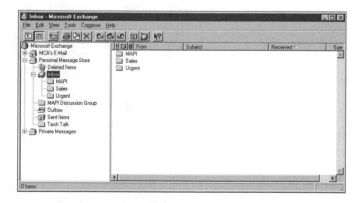

You'll use these folders as destinations when you add rules to your MAPI Email Agent database.

Building MAPI Email Agent Actions, Tests, and Rules

Next you need to add test, action, and rule records to the MAPI Email Agent database. Start the MAPI Email Agent program and enter the tests and actions shown in Table 11.4.

Table 11.4. MAPI Email Agent tests and actions.

Record Type	Contents
Test	SENDER Boss
	SUBJECT MAPI
	SUBJECT SALES
	PRIORITY 0
	SENDER Assistant
Action	FORWARD Boss
	MOVE Urgent
	COPY MAPI
	REPLY Sales
	NOTIFY Me

Figure 11.5 shows how the MAPI Email Agent looks after the tests and actions have been entered.

FIGURE 11.5.

Adding the test and action records.

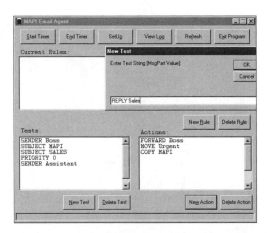

Now you're ready to create some rules for the MAPI Email Agent. Enter the rules shown in Table 11.5.

Table 11.5. Adding rules to the MAPI Email Agent.

Rule Name	Test	Compare	Action
Bosses Mail	SENDER Boss	EQ	COPY Urgent
Save MAPI	SUBJECT MAPI	CI	COPY MAPI
Assistant Routing	SENDER Assistant	EQ	FORWARD Boss
Wake Me Up	PRIORITY 0	EQ	NOTIFY Me
Sales Handler	SUBJECT SALES	CI	REPLY Sales

Figure 11.6 shows what your screen should look like as you build your MAPI Email Agent rules.

FIGURE 11.6.
Building MAPI Email Agent rules.

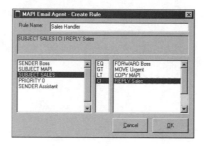

You're now ready to test your MAPI Email Agent!

Running the MAPI Email Agent

You can easily test the MAPI Email Agent by sending yourself some messages that meet the entered criteria. Send yourself a note that has MAPI in the subject or send a note that is marked high priority. Once the messages are sent, click the Start Timer button on the MAPI Email Agent to scan your inbox. You'll see messages along the status bar as the program scans; when the program finishes, check the log file by clicking the View Log button.

Summary

In this chapter you learned how to use the OLE Messaging library to create a stand-alone e-mail agent. This agent can scan your incoming mail and, based on rules you establish, automatically handle messages for you. All actions are based on rules you establish in a control file.

Features of the MAPI Email Agent include:

- Timed scanning of your inbox.
- Notification of message arrivals based on level of importance.

- Automatic routing of incoming messages to other e-mail users.
- Automatic replies to messages based on subject or sender.
- Automatic sorting of unread messages into separate folders based on subject, sender, or level of importance.

You also learned that the process of sending messages is handled differently than posting messages (`.Send` versus `.Update`), and you learned how to traverse the folder tree to locate a desired MAPI storage folder.

12

Creating Windows Messaging Client Extensions

Up to this point, you've learned how to create standalone MAPI applications and how to use the Exchange Forms Designer to create MAPI-enabled forms that run under the Windows Messaging client interface. In this chapter, you'll learn how to use C++ to create direct extensions to the Microsoft Exchange interface. You'll see how easy it is to add new property pages to the Microsoft Exchange menus. You'll also see how you can build programs that execute at selected times throughout the life of a Microsoft Exchange session.

In the first part of the chapter, you'll get a review of the Microsoft Exchange extension interface. You'll learn about the various extension types and how you can use context mapping to determine when your client extension is called by Microsoft Exchange.

In the second part of the chapter, you'll use C++ to create a program that adds a property sheet and several message event extensions to the Windows Messaging client. This program will act as a message checksum verifier. You'll be able to turn this new message extension on and off by selecting Tools ¦ Options from the main Microsoft Exchange menu to find your extension property page.

When you're finished with this chapter, you'll understand the theory behind Windows Messaging client extensions and have experience creating your own working extension.

> **NOTE**
>
> The project in this chapter was built using Microsoft Visual C++ 4.1. You may need to make slight changes to the code if you plan to compile it using another version of C++. If you do not have a C++ compiler, you can still get a lot out of this chapter. The complete source code and a compiled version of the project can be found on the CD-ROM. You can review the source code as you read the chapter and install the compiled extension as instructed.

What Are Exchange Client Extensions?

Before we jump into the task of creating a Windows Messaging client extension, it's worthwhile spending some time reviewing the theory behind Windows Messaging client extensions and how they can be used to create programs that work within the Windows Messaging client environment.

This section of the chapter covers

- How Windows Messaging client extensions work
- Advantages of Windows Messaging client extensions
- The Windows Messaging client contexts
- Mapping Microsoft Exchange contexts to Microsoft Exchange COM interfaces

- Event extensions
- Property extensions
- Registering extensions

In the next section, you'll build a working Windows Messaging client extension using VC++.

How Microsoft Exchange Client Extensions Work

The heart of the Windows Messaging client extension model is to expose all major process events of the Windows Messaging client to make them available for other programs to monitor and, when appropriate, modify or replace standard Windows Messaging client actions. For example, you can write an extension that scans the incoming message for selected words and then immediately moves that message to another folder or even forwards the message directly to another user. You can write extensions that automatically add additional text at the bottom of the message body when the user saves the message or submits it for delivery. You can even write extension code that executes when a user attempts to resolve recipient names to the installed address books. You can also write an extension that will be executed when a user accesses an attachment (for example, to check for viruses).

There are additional extension sets that allow you to add property pages to the Microsoft Exchange main menu (*Property extensions*); extension sets to add entirely new menu commands to Microsoft Exchange (*Command extensions*); new features for message searching (*Advanced Criteria extensions*) and others.

To accomplish all this, Microsoft has created a large set of API calls and callback functions that can be used to create Dynamic Link Libraries (DLLs) that intercept Windows Messaging client messages and then, when appropriate, jump in and perform any desired task before returning control to the Windows Messaging client. In effect, your extension program becomes part of the Windows Messaging client (see Figure 12.1).

FIGURE 12.1.
Windows Messaging client extensions become part of the Windows Messaging client.

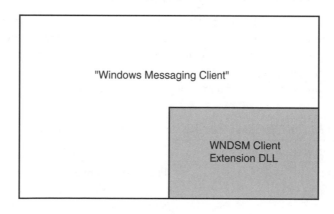

"Windows Messaging Client"

WNDSM Client
Extension DLL

Microsoft Exchange is designed to allow several extension DLLs to be loaded at one time. In fact, many of the Windows Messaging client features that appear on the menu are simple extension DLLs designed and shipped by Microsoft. For example, if you have installed the Internet Mail features of Microsoft Exchange, you have really installed an extension DLL. There are several Microsoft Exchange extension DLLs currently available, and many more will be available in the future.

Advantages of Microsoft Exchange Client Extensions

There are some real advantages to creating Windows Messaging client extensions instead of creating standalone MAPI applications. First, if you want to add just one or two features to the client interface, it's a lot easier to code those few additional features instead of doing the work to code a complete MAPI client to replace the Windows Messaging client. Second, by using client extensions, you can customize the Microsoft Exchange interface to meet your needs without losing the power of Microsoft Exchange.

An added benefit is that not only can you install your own special Microsoft Exchange features, you can also take advantage of other extension DLLs by other vendors. And, because the interface is well defined and open to all programmers, it is not too likely that you'll design an extension that is incompatible with other DLLs you'll install later.

Finally, by using the DLL extension to add features to Microsoft Exchange, users can use a familiar interface while taking advantage of the unique add-ins you've developed. Also, Microsoft has pledged to make sure that any extensions built for Microsoft Exchange will run under all versions of the Windows Messaging client. This means you can write routines that can potentially be installed on NT, Windows 95, Windows for Workgroups, and Windows 3.1 Windows Messaging client software.

The Microsoft Exchange Client Contexts

In order to allow DLLs to monitor Windows Messaging client processes, a set of context messages has been developed to inform any DLLs of the current Windows Messaging client process in progress. These context messages make up what is called the *Context Map*. This map lists all the general process events that can be monitored by an installed extension DLL. Table 12.1 shows the list of contexts along with a short description.

Table 12.1. The Windows Messaging client extension context map.

Context Map Name	Description
TASK	This context covers the entire Microsoft Exchange program session, from program start to program exit. Note that this may cover more than one logon, since users can log off a session without exiting the Windows Messaging client.

Context Map Name	Description
SESSION	This context spans a single MAPI session, from the logon to logoff. As noted above, multiple logons can occur during a single execution of Microsoft Exchange. These sessions may or may not overlap (that is, the user could log into MAPI services from another instance of Microsoft Exchange).
VIEWER	This context covers the time when the main viewer window has focus. You can use this to add features to the process of selecting messages or folders.
REMOTEVIEWER	This context covers the time when the Remote Mail window is displayed when the user chooses the `Remote Mail` command.
SEARCHVIEWER	This context covers the Find window that is displayed when the user chooses the `Find` command.
ADDRBOOK	The context for the Address Book window that is displayed when the user chooses the `Address Book` command.
SENDNOTEMESSAGE	The context for the standard Compose Note window in which messages of class `IPM.Note` are composed.
READNOTEMESSAGE	The context for the standard read note window in which messages of class `IPM.Note` are read after they are received.
READREPORTMESSAGE	The context for the read report message window in which report messages (Read, Delivery, Non-Read, Non-Delivery) are read after they are received.
SENDRESENDMESSAGE	The context for the resend message window that is displayed when the user chooses the `Send Again` command on the non-delivery report.
SENDPOSTMESSAGE	The context for the standard posting window in which existing posting messages are composed.
READPOSTMESSAGE	The context for the standard posting window in which existing posting messages are read.
PROPERTYSHEETS	A property sheet window.
ADVANCEDCRITERIA	The context for the dialog box in which the user specifies advanced search criteria.

As you can see from Table 12.1, there are quite a few different context messages that you can use to monitor Windows Messaging client processing. Also, more than one of these contexts can be active at the same time. For example, the TASK context is always active when the Windows Messaging client is loaded. At the same time, as soon as the user logs onto a MAPI session, the SESSION context is active, too. As users perform finds, read messages, post notes, and so on, each of the contexts becomes active. And as each process ends, the context becomes inactive. This can be a bit confusing at first glance. However, you needn't worry about knowing what contexts are active at any given moment. You'll write your extension to become active when a certain context becomes active. When that happens, your code executes.

The Microsoft Exchange COM Interface

Along with the Microsoft Exchange contexts, Microsoft has developed a set of *Component Object Model* (COM) interfaces to react to the various events associated with a Windows Messaging client process. Most of the Microsoft Exchange COM interfaces relate directly to a Microsoft Exchange context. Table 12.2 shows a list of the Microsoft Exchange COM interfaces and gives short descriptions of them.

Table 12.2 The Windows Messaging client COM interfaces.

Microsoft Exchange COM Interface	Description
IExchExt:Iunknown	Can be used to load extension objects in all contexts. Most extension objects are designed to operate only within a particular context or set of contexts, but some can operate in all contexts. Use this primarily in conjunction with the IExchExtCallBack interface.
IExchExtAdvancedCriteria	Used to enable extension objects to replace or enhance the functionality of the Advanced dialog box that appears when the user selects the Advanced button from the Find dialog box.
IExchExtAttachedFileEvents	Used to enable extension objects to replace or enhance the default attachment-handling behavior of Microsoft Exchange.
IExchExtCallBack	Enables extension objects to retrieve information about the current context. IExchExtCallBack uses the methods of the IUnknown interface for reference management.
IExchExtCommands	Used by extension objects to add and execute custom menu or toolbar command buttons. Extension

Microsoft Exchange COM Interface	Description
	objects can also replace existing Microsoft Exchange commands or enhance their behavior before Microsoft Exchange carries them out.
IExchExtMessageEvents	Used by extension objects to give them the ability to replace or enhance the default message-handling behavior of Microsoft Exchange.
IExchExtPropertySheets	Used to enable extension objects to append pages to Microsoft Exchange property sheets.
IExchExtSessionEvent	Used to enable an extension object to respond to the arrival of new messages. Use this interface to build custom inbox processing routines.
IExchExtUserEvents	Used to enable an extension object to handle changes to the currently selected list box item, text, or object.

Most of the COM interfaces are self-explanatory. However, a few deserve some extra attention. The IExchExt:IUnknown interface is used mostly by the IExchExtCallBack interface. Although it is possible to build complete context interfaces using IExchExt:IUnknown, it's not very practical—especially when you have all the other COM objects to work with.

Also, the IExchExtUserEvents interface returns general information about user actions in the Windows Messaging client. Whenever the focus changes from one Microsoft Exchange object to another (that is, the selected folder or message), you can have your application execute some code.

Finally, there are two other interfaces not listed in Table 12.2. The IExchExtModeless:IUnknown and IExchExtModelessCallBack interfaces can be used to develop non-modal processes that run alongside the Windows Messaging client and intercept messages normally addressed to the client.

NOTE

Creating modeless add-ins is beyond the scope of this book. If you're interested in creating a modeless extension for Microsoft Exchange, you can find additional information in the Microsoft MAPI SDK documentation.

Mapping Contexts to COM Interfaces

In order to write your program to become active for the various contexts, you need to use one (or more) of the Component Object Model interfaces that match up to the Microsoft Exchange contexts. In other words, you "map" your program code to contexts using the COM interfaces. When you register your program with one or more of the COM interfaces, your program receives alerts from Microsoft Exchange that fire off methods within the COM interface. You can place code within these methods to make sure that your program performs the desired actions at the right time.

For example, if you want your program to execute whenever the SESSION context occurs, you'll need to use the IExchExtSession COM interface object in your program. Some of the contexts can be accessed using more than one COM interface. For example, The IExchExtMessage COM interface is called from several of the Microsoft Exchange contexts (SENDNOTEMESSAGE, READNOTEMESSAGE, SENDPOSTMESSAGE, READPOSTMESSAGE, READREPORTMESSAGE, and SENDRESENDMESSAGE). To make it a bit more complex, a single context can alert more than one COM interface. For example, the ADDRBOOK context notifies the IExchExtCommands, IExchExtUserEvents, and IExchExtPropertySheets interfaces.

Table 12.3 shows the Microsoft Exchange contexts along with the COM interfaces that can be used to monitor those contexts.

Table 12.3. Mapping Microsoft Exchange contexts to Microsoft Exchange COM interfaces.

Context Name	Interfaces Called
TASK	None. Only IexchExt::Install and IUnknown::Release are called from this context.
SESSION	IExchExtSessionEvents
VIEWER, REMOTEVIEWER, SEARCHVIEWER	IExchExtCommands, IExchExtUserEvents, IExchExtPropertySheets
ADDRBOOK	IExchExtCommands, IExchExtUserEvents, IExchExtPropertySheets
SENDNOTEMESSAGE, READNOTEMESSAGE, READREPORTMESSAGE, SENDRESENDMESSAGE, READPOSTMESSAGE, SENDPOSTMESSAGE	IExchExtCommands, IExchExtUserEvents, IExchExtMessageEvents, IExchExtAttachedFileEvents, IExchExtPropertySheets
PROPERTYSHEETS	IExchExtPropertySheets
ADVANCEDCRITERIA	IExchExtAdvancedCriteria

Now that you have a good idea of how the Windows Messaging client extensions and the Windows Messaging client contexts work together, it's time to focus on two of the COM interfaces that you'll use in the Message Signing project for this chapter:

■ The Message Events interface

■ The Property Sheets interface

Message Event Extensions

These message event extensions can be used to monitor the Windows Messaging client actions on incoming and outgoing messages. When your application registers the IExchExtMessageEvents interface, you can receive notifications whenever the user attempts to read, write, address, or submit a MAPI message. Table 12.4 shows the methods associated with the IExchExtMessageEvents interface along with a short description.

Table 12.4. The methods of the IExchExtMessageEvents interface.

Interface Method	Description
OnCheckNames	Used to replace or enhance the behavior of Microsoft Exchange when recipient names typed by the user are being resolved to their address book entries.
OnCheckNamesComplete	Used to roll back the implementation of the OnCheckNames method in case of an error, or to release resources allocated by OnCheckNames.
OnRead	Used to replace or enhance the behavior of Microsoft Exchange when reading information from a message.
OnReadComplete	Used to roll back implementation of the OnRead method in case of an error or to release resources allocated by OnRead.
OnSubmit	Used to replace or enhance the behavior of Microsoft Exchange when a message is being submitted.
OnSubmitComplete	Used to roll back implementation of the OnSubmit method in case of an error, or to release resources allocated by OnSubmit.
OnWrite	Used to replace or enhance the behavior of Microsoft Exchange when writing information to a message.
OnWriteComplete	Used to roll back implementation of the OnWrite method in case of an error, or to release resources allocated by OnWrite.

You should notice that all eight of the message event methods can be sorted into four groups of two:

■ OnCheckNames/OnCheckNamesComplete

■ OnRead/OnReadComplete

- ■ OnSubmit/OnSubmitComplete
- ■ OnWrite/OnWriteComplete

The first method of the pair (for example, OnWrite) is called when the user attempts the suggested operation within the Windows Messaging client. The second method of the pair (for example, OnWriteComplete) is executed immediately after the first method. This second event can be used to check results from code execution under the first method, and to perform any error recovery or cleanup that might be needed.

For example, if you decide to add an extension that encrypts messages upon submission for delivery, you could write code in the OnSubmit method of the Message Event interface that would copy the message body to a temporary file and convert it into its encrypted form. You might then write code in the OnSubmitComplete method that would check the results of the encryption to make sure all went well. If not, you could then inform the user of the problem and restore the original text. If all went well, the OnSubmitComplete method could copy the encrypted message over the original and then erase the temporary file.

In the example you'll build later in this chapter, you'll use the OnWrite and OnRead method pairs to create and check message checksums before saving and reading MAPI messages.

Property Extensions

The Windows Messaging client also has an extension for managing the creation of custom property pages. You can create a simple dialog box and then register it as one of the tabbed property pages of a Windows Messaging client object. The Windows Messaging client displays property pages for four different objects. Table 12.5 shows the four objects along with short descriptions of them.

Table 12.5. The Microsoft Exchange objects that display property pages.

Property Page Object	*Description*
Information Store Properties	This shows the properties of the selected MAPI Information Store object.
Folder Properties	This shows the properties of the selected MAPI Folder object.
Message Properties	This shows the properties of the selected MAPI Message object.
Tools Options Menu	This shows the properties page from the Tools ¦ Options menu selection of the Windows Messaging client.

There are three methods to the IExchExtPropertySheets COM interface. These methods allow you to determine the number of pages that are currently registered for display, allow you to define and add a new property page, and allow you to release the property page you added to the object. Table 12.6 describes the three methods.

Table 12.6. The methods of the IExchExtPropertySheets COM interface.

Interface Method	Description
GetMaxPageCount	Returns the maximum number of pages an extension will add to the property sheet.
GetPages	Adds property sheet page to the current list of pages.
FreePages	Frees any resources allocated by the GetPages method.

In the project shown later in this chapter, you'll use these three methods to add a property page to the Tools ¦ Options menu of the Windows Messaging client.

NOTE

The other COM interfaces mentioned here also have associated methods. These methods are not covered in this chapter. This was done to focus on the creation of a complete Windows Messaging client extension application. You can learn more about all the Microsoft Exchange COM interfaces and their methods by reviewing the MAPI SDK documentation.

Registering Extensions

Once you have successfully created a Windows Messaging client extension, you must inform the Windows Messaging client that the extension exists before it will be able to use it. This is done by making entries in the system registry database. All Windows Messaging client extensions must be registered. On 32-bit Windows systems, the client extension entries are placed in the HKEY_LOCAL_MACHINE\Software\Microsoft\Exchange\Client\Extensions section of the registry. On 16-bit systems, the registration is stored in the [Extensions] section of the EXCHNG.INI file. Figure 12.2 shows the system registry editor open to the [Extensions] section.

NOTE

In network environments, Windows Messaging client extensions can be shared among several clients. Shared Microsoft Exchange DLLs are registered in the SHARED32.INI file on 32-bit systems and in the SHARED.INI file on 16-bit systems.

FIGURE 12.2.

Viewing the Exchange\
Client\Extensions
*section of the System
Registry.*

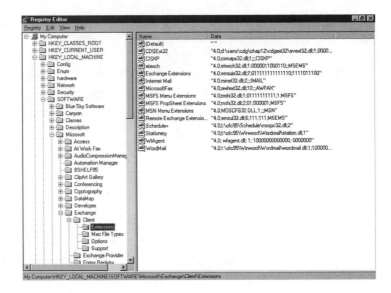

The registry entry tells the Windows Messaging client several important things about the extension DLL. The syntax of an extension entry is as follows:

```
Tag=Version;<ExtsDir>DllName;[Ordinal];[ContextMap];[InterfaceMap];[Provider]
```

Table 12.7 shows each of the parts of the registration entry and explains its meaning and use.

Table 12.7. The Windows Messaging client extension registration entry.

Entry Parameter	Description
Tag	An extension identifier that uniquely distinguishes the registry entry from other entries.
Version	The version number of the syntax. Use 4.0 for the current release of Microsoft Exchange.
DllName	The complete path and filename of the DLL containing the extension.
Ordinal	An optional field that specifies the entry point into the VTable of the DLL to retrieve the extension object. If this field is empty, the default value is 1.
ContextMap	An optional string made up of "0" and "1" characters that indicate the contexts in which the extension should be loaded. Any unspecified values after the end of the string are assumed to be zero. If no context map is provided, the extension is loaded in all contexts.

Entry Parameter	Description
InterfaceMap	An optional string made up of "0" and "1" characters that indicates the interfaces the extension supports.
Provider	An optional string containing the PR_SERVICE_NAME of the service provider that your extension is designed to work with. For example, if your extension is designed to work with a custom address book provider, this entry would contain the PR_SERVICE_NAME of the address book provider. You should only use this parameter if your extension is provider-specific.

The ContextMap and InterfaceMap entries need some clarification. By placing "1" or "0" values in these strings, you are telling Microsoft Exchange which context events and COM interfaces you want your client to participate in. Table 12.8 shows the meaning of each position in the ContextMap parameter.

Table 12.8. The ContextMap parameter positions.

Parameter Position	Context
1	SESSION
2	VIEWER
3	REMOTEVIEWER
4	SEARCHVIEWER
5	ADDRBOOK
6	SENDNOTEMESSAGE
7	READNOTEMESSAGE
8	SENDPOSTMESSAGE
9	READPOSTMESSAGE
10	READREPORTMESSAGE
11	SENDRESENDMESSAGE
12	PROPERTYSHEETS
13	ADVANCEDCRITERIA
14	TASK

For example, if your DLL extension should execute each time one of the message events occurred, you would create the following ContextMap parameter:

```
"00000111111000"
```

In addition to the `ContextMap` parameter, there is a parameter to inform Microsoft Exchange which COM interfaces your extension will use. Table 12.9 shows the list of COM interfaces and their positions in the `InterfaceMap` parameter.

Table 12.9. The COM `InterfaceMap` parameter positions.

Parameter Position	Interface
1	IExchExtCommands
2	IExchExtUserEvents
3	IExchExtSessionEvents
4	IExchExtMessageEvents
5	IExchExtAttachedFileEvents
6	IExchExtPropertySheets
7	IExchExtAdvancedCriteria

For example, if your DLL extension used the property sheet and message interfaces, you'd create an `InterfaceMap` parameter that looks like the following:

`"0001010"`

Later in this chapter, you'll make a registry entry to match the Message Signing Extension example described in this chapter.

> **WARNING**
>
> It is acceptable to leave out trailing bits in the interface and context map parameters and allow Microsoft Exchange to assume these missing entries are zero ("0"). However, it is not recommended. It is much better to construct a complete string, even if most of them are set to zero.

Now that you know the theory behind creating Windows Messaging client extensions and how to register them for use, you're ready to build the sample project.

Creating the Message Signing Extension

The sample Windows Messaging client extension described in this chapter creates a checksum of each message body and stores that value before it is sent to the recipient. The same extension also checks the stored value against the computed checksum each time the user attempts to read a message. If, upon reading the message, the stored checksum is not equal to the computed checksum, it is likely that the message has been altered in some way since it was submitted for delivery by the original author. In this way, you can implement a rather simple message signature process that will give a high degree of confidence that the messages users receive have not been tampered with before they arrive at their destination.

There are four main steps to creating the Message Signing extension DLL:

- *Building the initial header file*—This file will contain global declarations along with prototypes for the Microsoft Exchange class objects and their associated methods.

- *Coding the main DLL routines*—These are the actual routines that register the DLL for callbacks to the COM interfaces and establish code behavior for the necessary COM interface methods.

- *Laying out the Property Sheet dialog box*—This dialog box will be registered and accessed from the Tools ¦ Options menu of the Windows Messaging client.

- *Coding the Property Sheet dialog box events*—This is the code to handle user interaction with the registered property page.

> **NOTE**
>
> If you own a copy of Microsoft Visual C++, you can load the CDGEXT32 project found on the CD-ROM that ships with this book. If you do not have a copy of C++, you can still load the source code files and review them as you read along in this chapter.

Building the Initial Header File

The initial header file (CDGEXT32.H) contains basic defines, includes, and global declarations. It also contains the prototypes for the Microsoft Exchange class objects and their associated methods. Listing 12.1 shows the first part of the CDGEXT32.H file.

Listing 12.1. The first half of the CDGEXT32.H header file.

```
// =======================================================================
//   CDGEXT32.H
// =======================================================================
#ifndef __CDGEXT32_H__
#define __CDGEXT32_H__

//
// include files
//
#include <WINDOWS.H>
#include <COMMCTRL.H>
#include <MAPIX.H>
#include <MAPIUTIL.H>
#include <MAPIFORM.H>
#include <EXCHEXT.H>
```

continues

Listing 12.1. continued

```
#include "RESOURCE.H"

//
// function prototypes
//
extern "C"
{
 LPEXCHEXT CALLBACK ExchEntryPoint(void);
}

void ErrMsgBox(HWND hWnd,  HRESULT hr,  PSTR szFunction, LPSTR szMessage);
HRESULT CheckMsgSignature(LPMESSAGE pMsg, ULONG *pulCheckSum);
BOOL CALLBACK MsgSigningDlgProc(HWND hDlg, UINT uMsg, WPARAM wParam, LPARAM
➡lParam);

// global declarations
extern BOOL bSignatureOn;

//
// class declarations
//
class CDGExt;
class CDGExtPropSheets;
class CDGExtMsgEvents;
```

The code in Listing 12.1 first lists all the include files needed for the project (these are part of the MAPI SDK that can be found on MSDN Professional Level CD-ROMs and above). Next is the declaration of the initial entry point for the Microsoft Exchange DLL extension, along with three custom functions used in the project, along with a single variable declaration. Finally, the three COM objects that will be used in the project are declared.

Listing 12.2 shows the CDGEXT32.H code that defines the methods and properties of the high-level IExchExt interface object. This object will be used to install the extension and register the DLL for property sheet and message events.

Listing 12.2. Defining the IExchExt interface object.

```
//
// overall exchange extension class
//
class CDGExt : public IExchExt
{
 public:
    CDGExt();
    STDMETHODIMP QueryInterface(REFIID riid, LPVOID * ppvObj);
    inline STDMETHODIMP_(ULONG) AddRef() { ++m_cRef; return m_cRef; };
    STDMETHODIMP_(ULONG) Release();
    STDMETHODIMP Install (LPEXCHEXTCALLBACK pmecb, ULONG mecontext, ULONG ulFlags);

 private:
    ULONG m_cRef;
```

```
    UINT  m_context;
    CDGExtPropSheets * m_pExchExtPropertySheets;
    CDGExtMsgEvents * m_pExchExtMessageEvents;

};
```

Next, Listing 12.3 shows the definition of the Property Sheets object.

Listing 12.3. Defining the IExchExtPropertySheets COM interface.

```
//
// property sheet extension class
//
class CDGExtPropSheets : public IExchExtPropertySheets
{
 public:
    CDGExtPropSheets (LPUNKNOWN pParentInterface) {
    m_pExchExt = pParentInterface;
    m_cRef = 0;
    };

    STDMETHODIMP QueryInterface(REFIID   riid, LPVOID * ppvObj);
    inline STDMETHODIMP_(ULONG) AddRef() { ++m_cRef; return m_cRef; };
    inline STDMETHODIMP_(ULONG) Release()
         { ULONG ulCount = —m_cRef;
           if (!ulCount) { delete this; }
          return ulCount;};

       STDMETHODIMP_ (ULONG) GetMaxPageCount(ULONG ulFlags);
       STDMETHODIMP  GetPages(LPEXCHEXTCALLBACK peecb, ULONG ulFlags,
➥LPPROPSHEETPAGE ppsp, ULONG FAR * pcpsp);
    STDMETHODIMP_ (VOID) FreePages(LPPROPSHEETPAGE ppsp, ULONG ulFlags, ULONG
➥cpsp);

 private:
    ULONG m_cRef;
    LPUNKNOWN m_pExchExt;
};
```

Finally, Listing 12.4 shows the code that defines the Message Event COM interface.

Listing 12.4. Defining the IExchExtMessageEvents COM interface.

```
//
// message event extension class
//
class CDGExtMsgEvents : public IExchExtMessageEvents
{
 public:
    CDGExtMsgEvents (LPUNKNOWN pParentInterface) {
    m_pExchExt = pParentInterface;
```

continues

Listing 12.4. continued

```
    m_cRef = 0;
    m_bInSubmitState = FALSE;
    };

    STDMETHODIMP QueryInterface(REFIID riid, LPVOID * ppvObj);
    inline STDMETHODIMP_(ULONG) AddRef() { ++m_cRef; return m_cRef; };
    inline STDMETHODIMP_(ULONG) Release()
                { ULONG ulCount = —m_cRef;
                    if (!ulCount) { delete this; }
                return ulCount;}};

    STDMETHODIMP OnRead(LPEXCHEXTCALLBACK lpeecb);
    STDMETHODIMP OnReadComplete(LPEXCHEXTCALLBACK lpeecb, ULONG ulFlags);
    STDMETHODIMP OnWrite(LPEXCHEXTCALLBACK lpeecb);
    STDMETHODIMP OnWriteComplete(LPEXCHEXTCALLBACK lpeecb, ULONG ulFlags);
    STDMETHODIMP OnSubmit(LPEXCHEXTCALLBACK lpeecb);
    STDMETHODIMP_ (VOID)OnSubmitComplete(LPEXCHEXTCALLBACK lpeecb, ULONG ulFlags);
    STDMETHODIMP OnCheckNames(LPEXCHEXTCALLBACK lpeecb);
    STDMETHODIMP OnCheckNamesComplete(LPEXCHEXTCALLBACK lpeecb, ULONG ulFlags);


private:
    ULONG    m_cRef;
    HRESULT m_hrOnReadComplete;
    BOOL     m_bInSubmitState;
    LPUNKNOWN m_pExchExt;

};
```

This is all there is to the CDGEXT32.H header file. Next, you'll review the code for the main extension DLL.

Coding the Main DLL Routines

The CDGEXT32.CPP file contains the main body of code for the extension. The code file can be divided into five parts:

■ Initialization and main entry code

■ Code for the high-level IExchExt object

■ Code for the IExchExtPropertySheets object

■ Code for the IExchExtMessageEvents object

■ Helper code for local routines

Listing 12.5 shows the initialization and main entry code for CDGEXT32.CPP. This code handles some basic housekeeping and then establishes the DLL entry point (DLLMain) and the callback address for the IExchExt object (ExchEntryPoint).

Listing 12.5. The initialization and main entry code for CDGEXT32.CPP.

```
// ================================================================
// CDGEXT32.CPP
// ================================================================

//
// module-level defines
//
#define INITGUID
#define USES_IID_IExchExt
#define USES_IID_IExchExtAdvancedCriteria
#define USES_IID_IExchExtAttachedFileEvents
#define USES_IID_IExchExtCommands
#define USES_IID_IExchExtMessageEvents
#define USES_IID_IExchExtPropertySheets
#define USES_IID_IExchExtSessionEvents
#define USES_IID_IExchExtUserEvents
#define USES_IID_IMessage
#define USES_PS_MAPI

//
// include files
//
#include "CDGEXT32.H"
#include <INITGUID.H>
#include <MAPIGUID.H>

//
// local declarations
//
MAPINAMEID NamedID[1]; // for new property
BOOL bSignatureOn = TRUE; // assume it's on
static HINSTANCE ghInstDLL = NULL;  // DLL handle


// ----------------------------------------------------------------
// Main Body of routines
//
// These two routines are the initial entry point for the DLL and
// the code that registers the extension DLL.
// ----------------------------------------------------------------

//
// to start things off as a DLL
//
BOOL WINAPI DllMain(
    HINSTANCE  hinstDLL,
    DWORD  fdwReason,
    LPVOID  lpvReserved)
{
 if (DLL_PROCESS_ATTACH == fdwReason)
 {
    ghInstDLL = hinstDLL;

 }
 return TRUE;
}
```

continues

Listing 12.5. continued

```
//
// register the extension
//
LPEXCHEXT CALLBACK ExchEntryPoint(void)
{
     return new CDGExt;
}
```

Next is the code for the methods and properties of the IExchExt object. Along with the initial object constructor code, three methods must be coded:

- The QueryInterface method
- The Install method
- The Release method

Listing 12.6 shows the code for the IExchExt object.

Listing 12.6. Code for the IExchExt interface.

```
// ----------------------------------------
// Handle the creation of the CDGExt object
// ----------------------------------------
//
// These routines establish the initial
// extension interface.
//
// CDGExt::CDGExt() - constructor
// CDGExt::Release() - frees up resources
// CDGExt::QueryInterface() - main entry
// CDGExt::Install() - installs extensions
// ----------------------------------------

//
// constructor for the propertysheet and message event extension
//
CDGExt::CDGExt()
{
  m_cRef = 1;
  m_pExchExtPropertySheets = new CDGExtPropSheets(this);
  m_pExchExtMessageEvents = new CDGExtMsgEvents(this);

};


//
// frees up resources when done
//
STDMETHODIMP_(ULONG) CDGExt::Release()
{
 ULONG ulCount = —m_cRef;

  if (!ulCount)
```

```
 {
  delete this;
 }

return ulCount;

}

//
// initial interface query
// for both propertysheets and message events
//
STDMETHODIMP CDGExt::QueryInterface(REFIID riid, LPVOID FAR * ppvObj)
{
    HRESULT hResult = S_OK;

    *ppvObj = NULL;

    if (( IID_IUnknown == riid) ¦¦ ( IID_IExchExt == riid) )
    {
        *ppvObj = (LPUNKNOWN)this;
    }
    else if (IID_IExchExtPropertySheets == riid) // for property sheets?
    {
     // ignore send/read contexts (for property sheet)
        if ( (m_context == EECONTEXT_SENDNOTEMESSAGE)    ¦¦
             (m_context == EECONTEXT_SENDPOSTMESSAGE)    ¦¦
             (m_context == EECONTEXT_SENDRESENDMESSAGE)  ¦¦
             (m_context == EECONTEXT_READNOTEMESSAGE)    ¦¦
             (m_context == EECONTEXT_READPOSTMESSAGE)    ¦¦
             (m_context == EECONTEXT_READREPORTMESSAGE) )
            return E_NOINTERFACE;

      // otherwise return the interface
        *ppvObj = (LPUNKNOWN) m_pExchExtPropertySheets;
    }
    else if (IID_IExchExtMessageEvents == riid) // for message events?
    {
        *ppvObj = (LPUNKNOWN) m_pExchExtMessageEvents;
    }
    else
        hResult = E_NOINTERFACE;

    if (NULL != *ppvObj)
        ((LPUNKNOWN)*ppvObj)->AddRef();

    return hResult;
}


//
// actually installs the extension
//
STDMETHODIMP CDGExt::Install(LPEXCHEXTCALLBACK peecb, ULONG eecontext, ULONG
➥ulFlags)
{
    ULONG ulBuildVersion;
```

continues

Listing 12.6. continued

```
    HRESULT hr;

    m_context = eecontext;

    // compare versions
    peecb->GetVersion(&ulBuildVersion, EECBGV_GETBUILDVERSION);
    if (EECBGV_BUILDVERSION_MAJOR != (ulBuildVersion &
                                      EECBGV_BUILDVERSION_MAJOR_MASK))
        return S_FALSE;  // oops!

    switch (eecontext)
    {
     case EECONTEXT_PROPERTYSHEETS:
     case EECONTEXT_SENDNOTEMESSAGE:
     case EECONTEXT_SENDPOSTMESSAGE:
     case EECONTEXT_SENDRESENDMESSAGE:
     case EECONTEXT_READNOTEMESSAGE:
     case EECONTEXT_READPOSTMESSAGE:
     case EECONTEXT_READREPORTMESSAGE:
        hr = S_OK;
        break;

     default:
        hr = S_FALSE;
        break;
    }


    return hr;

}
//
// end of CDGExt Object
// ----------------------------------------------------------------
```

The next section of code in the CDGEXT32.CPP file is the code that implements the methods of the IExchExtMessageEvents interface. Listing 12.7 shows the initial QueryInterface function for the object.

Listing 12.7. The initial QueryInterface function for the MessageEvents object.

```
// ----------------------------------------------------------------
// Handle creation of Messge Event object
// ----------------------------------------------------------------
//
// Routines for the Message Event extension
//
// CDGExtMsgEvents::QueryInterface() - [not used]
// CDGExtMsgEvents::OnRead() - at start of read msg
// CDGExtMsgEvents::OnReadComplete() - at end of read
// CDGExtMsgEvents::OnWrite() - ad start of write msg
// CDGExtMsgEvents::OnWriteComplete() - at end of write
// CDGExtMsgEvents::OnSubmit() - at start of msg submit
```

```
//  CDGExtMsgEvents::OnSubmitComplete() - end of submit
//  CDGExtMsgEvents::OnCheckNames() - start of resolve
//  CDGExtMsgEvents::OnCheckNamesComplete() - resolve end
//  ------------------------------------------------------------

//
// sample queryinterface for message events
// not used now
//
STDMETHODIMP CDGExtMsgEvents::QueryInterface(REFIID riid, LPVOID FAR * ppvObj)
{

    *ppvObj = NULL;
    if (riid == IID_IExchExtMessageEvents)
    {
        *ppvObj = (LPVOID)this;
        AddRef(); // using one more!
        return S_OK;
    }
    if (riid == IID_IUnknown)
    {
        *ppvObj = (LPVOID)m_pExchExt;  // return parent interface
        m_pExchExt->AddRef();
        return S_OK;
    }
    return E_NOINTERFACE;
);
```

> **TIP**
>
> The Windows Messaging client does not call the `QueryInterface()` methods directly. The code is added here in anticipation of changes to the client that might result in calls to this method. It is also a good rule to code the `QueryInterface` method for all COM objects.

Listing 12.8 shows the code for the `OnRead` and `OnReadComplete` methods. These methods check for the existence of the `CheckSum` property and, if found, compare the stored value to a freshly computed value. If the results do not match, the user is warned that the message may have been altered.

Listing 12.8. Code for the `OnRead` and `OnReadComplete` methods.

```
//
// fires when user attempts to Read a message
//
HRESULT CDGExtMsgEvents::OnRead(LPEXCHEXTCALLBACK lpeecb)
{
  HRESULT hr;
  LPMESSAGE pMsg;
```

continues

Listing 12.8. continued

```
LPMDB pMDB;
ULONG ulCheckSum;
LPSPropTagArray pNamedPropTags;
LPSPropValue pPropValues;
ULONG ulcValues;
HWND hWnd;
HCURSOR hOldCursor;

m_hrOnReadComplete = S_FALSE; // assume all will go fine

pMsg = NULL;
pMDB = NULL;
pPropValues = NULL;
pNamedPropTags = NULL;

// turned OFF?
if (!bSignatureOn)
{
    goto error_return;
}

// get the message
hr = lpeecb->GetObject(&pMDB, (LPMAPIPROP *)&pMsg);
if (FAILED(hr))
{
  goto error_return;
}

// save current state of window and cursor
lpeecb->GetWindow(&hWnd);
hOldCursor = SetCursor(LoadCursor(NULL, IDC_WAIT));

// check to see if MsgChecksum exists
NamedID[0].lpguid = (LPGUID)&IID_IMessage;
NamedID[0].ulKind = MNID_STRING;
NamedID[0].Kind.lpwstrName = L"MsgChecksum";

hr = pMsg->GetIDsFromNames(1, (LPMAPINAMEID *)&NamedID, 0, &pNamedPropTags);
if (FAILED(hr)) // maybe not there first time
{
    goto error_return;
}

hr = pMsg->GetProps(pNamedPropTags, 0, &ulcValues, &pPropValues);
if (FAILED(hr))     // must be some other error
{
  goto error_return;
}

if (hr == MAPI_W_ERRORS_RETURNED) // not signed
{
  goto error_return;
}

// must be signed, check the signature
hr = CheckMsgSignature(pMsg, &ulCheckSum);
if (FAILED(hr))
```

```
    {
      ErrMsgBox(hWnd, hr, "OnRead",
          "An error occured while calculating\n"
          "the message signature.");
       goto error_return;
    }

  //
  // got a value back
  //
  if (pPropValues[0].Value.ul == ulCheckSum)
  {
      MessageBox(hWnd,
          "Signed Message Verified.",
          "CDG Message Signing Extension",
          MB_OK);
  }
  else
  {
   int nRet = MessageBox(hWnd,
       "Signed Message was altered.\n"
       "Do you wish to view the message anyway?",
       "CDG MEssage Signing Extension",
       MB_YESNO);

   if (nRet == IDNO)
   // tell OnReadComplete to not display the message
      m_hrOnReadComplete = MAPI_E_CALL_FAILED;
  }

  error_return:

  hr = S_FALSE;

  //
  // free up resources
  //
  if (pMDB != NULL)
      pMDB->Release();

  if (pMsg != NULL)
      pMsg->Release();

  if (pNamedPropTags != NULL)
      MAPIFreeBuffer(pNamedPropTags);

  if (pPropValues != NULL)
      MAPIFreeBuffer(pPropValues);

  SetCursor(hOldCursor);

  return hr;
}

//
// fires after the read is complete
//
```

continues

Listing 12.8. continued

```
HRESULT CDGExtMsgEvents::OnReadComplete(LPEXCHEXTCALLBACK lpeecb, ULONG ulFlags)
{

  return m_hrOnReadComplete;

}
```

Listing 12.9 shows the code for the OnWrite and OnWriteComplete methods. These methods are called when the user attempts to write a message back to the message store. This is the routine that computes a checksum signature and places it in a new message field before sending it to the recipient(s).

Listing 12.9. Coding the OnWrite and OnWrite complete methods.

```
//
// fires when user starts to write message
//
HRESULT CDGExtMsgEvents::OnWrite(LPEXCHEXTCALLBACK lpeecb)
{
  HRESULT hr;

  hr = S_FALSE;

  return hr;
}

//
// fires after message has been written
//
HRESULT CDGExtMsgEvents::OnWriteComplete(LPEXCHEXTCALLBACK lpeecb, ULONG ulFlags)
{
  HRESULT hr;
  LPMESSAGE pMsg;
  LPMDB pMDB;
  ULONG ulCheckSum;
  SPropValue pChksumProp[1];
  LPSPropTagArray pNamedPropTags;
  LPSPropProblemArray pPropProblems;
  HWND hWnd;
  HCURSOR hOldCursor;

  // turned OFF?
  if (!bSignatureOn)
  {
      return S_FALSE;
  }

  // just saving or really sending?
  if (!m_bInSubmitState)
  {
      return S_FALSE;
  }
```

```
pMsg = NULL;
pMDB = NULL;
pPropProblems   = NULL;
pNamedPropTags = NULL;

hOldCursor = SetCursor(LoadCursor(NULL, IDC_WAIT));


hr = lpeecb->GetObject(&pMDB, (LPMAPIPROP *)&pMsg);
if (FAILED(hr))
{
  goto error_return;
}

hr = CheckMsgSignature(pMsg, &ulCheckSum);
if (FAILED(hr))
{
  lpeecb->GetWindow(&hWnd);

  ErrMsgBox(hWnd, hr, "OnWriteComplete",
      "An error occured while calculating\n"
      "the message signature.");
  goto error_return;
}

// use a named property for the message body checksum
NamedID[0].lpguid = (LPGUID)&IID_IMessage;
NamedID[0].ulKind = MNID_STRING;
NamedID[0].Kind.lpwstrName = L"MsgChecksum";

hr = pMsg->GetIDsFromNames(1, (LPMAPINAMEID *)&NamedID, MAPI_CREATE,
➥&pNamedPropTags);
if (FAILED(hr))
{
 goto error_return;
}

pChksumProp[0].ulPropTag = PROP_TAG(PT_LONG, HIWORD(pNamedPropTags-
➥>aulPropTag[0]));
pChksumProp[0].dwAlignPad = 0L;
pChksumProp[0].Value.ul = ulCheckSum;

hr = pMsg->SetProps(1, pChksumProp, &pPropProblems);
if (FAILED(hr))
{
 goto error_return;
}


// all fine, keep going
hr = S_FALSE;

error_return:


//
// free up resources
```

continues

Listing 12.9. continued

```
//
if (pMDB != NULL)
  pMDB->Release();

if (pMsg != NULL)
    pMsg->Release();

if (pNamedPropTags != NULL)
    MAPIFreeBuffer(pNamedPropTags);

if (pPropProblems != NULL)
    MAPIFreeBuffer(pPropProblems);

SetCursor(hOldCursor);

return hr;
}
```

The last bit of code for the Message Events interface is found in Listing 12.10. Not much is happening here. This code is included for completeness.

Listing 12.10. The remaining Message Event object code.

```
//
// fires when user attempts to submit a msg to the outbox
//
HRESULT CDGExtMsgEvents::OnSubmit(LPEXCHEXTCALLBACK lpeecb)
{
  HRESULT hr;

  hr = S_FALSE;
  m_bInSubmitState = TRUE;  // submit is called

  return hr;
}

//
// fires after message was submitted
//
VOID CDGExtMsgEvents::OnSubmitComplete(LPEXCHEXTCALLBACK lpeecb, ULONG ulFlags)
{

  m_bInSubmitState = FALSE;  // out of submit state

}

//
// fires when user attempts to resolve addresses
//
HRESULT CDGExtMsgEvents::OnCheckNames(LPEXCHEXTCALLBACK lpeecb)
{
  return S_FALSE; // not used
}
```

```
//
// fires after resolve is done
//
HRESULT CDGExtMsgEvents::OnCheckNamesComplete(LPEXCHEXTCALLBACK lpeecb, ULONG
➥ulFlags)
{
  return S_FALSE; // not used
}
```

The last section of code that deals with objects is the code for the IExchExtPropertySheets interface. Listing 12.11 shows the code for implementing custom property sheets for the Windows Messaging client.

Listing 12.11. Code for the custom property sheet objects.

```
// -------------------------------------------------------------
// Handle creation CDGExtPropSheets object
// -------------------------------------------------------------
//
// Routines for the propertysheet extension
//
// CDGExtPropSheets::QueryInterface() - [not used]
// CDGExtPropSheets::GetMaxPageCount() - count pages
// CDGExtPropSheets::GetPages() - add a new page
// CDGExtPropSheets::FreePages() - free up resources
// -------------------------------------------------------------


//
// sample queryinterface for propertysheets
// not used right now
//
STDMETHODIMP CDGExtPropSheets::QueryInterface(REFIID riid, LPVOID FAR * ppvObj)
{

    *ppvObj = NULL;
    if (riid == IID_IExchExtPropertySheets)
    {
        *ppvObj = (LPVOID)this;
        // Increase usage count of this object
        AddRef();
        return S_OK;
    }
    if (riid == IID_IUnknown)
    {
        *ppvObj = (LPVOID)m_pExchExt;  // return parent interface
        m_pExchExt->AddRef();
        return S_OK;
    }

    return E_NOINTERFACE;

}
```

continues

Listing 12.11. continued

```
//
// get property page count
//
ULONG CDGExtPropSheets::GetMaxPageCount(ULONG ulFlags)
{
 ULONG ulNumExtSheets;

    switch (ulFlags)
    {
     // ignore these objects.
     case EEPS_FOLDER:
     case EEPS_STORE:
     case EEPS_MESSAGE:
         ulNumExtSheets = 0;
         break;

     // add a tab to the Tools¦Options page
     case EEPS_TOOLSOPTIONS:
         ulNumExtSheets = 1;
         break;

     default:
          ulNumExtSheets = 0;
         break;
    }

    return ulNumExtSheets;
}


//
// to add a new page
//
STDMETHODIMP CDGExtPropSheets::GetPages(LPEXCHEXTCALLBACK peecb,
                      ULONG ulFlags, LPPROPSHEETPAGE ppsp, ULONG FAR * pcpsp)
{
 LPMDB pMDB = NULL;
 LPMESSAGE pItem = NULL;

    *pcpsp = 0;


    // members for the new property page
    ppsp[0].dwSize = sizeof (PROPSHEETPAGE);
    ppsp[0].dwFlags = PSP_DEFAULT ¦ PSP_HASHELP;
    ppsp[0].hInstance = ghInstDLL;
    ppsp[0].pszTemplate = MAKEINTRESOURCE(IDD_SIGNATURE);
    ppsp[0].hIcon = NULL;      // not used
    ppsp[0].pszTitle = NULL;   // not used
    ppsp[0].pfnDlgProc = (DLGPROC)MsgSigningDlgProc;
    ppsp[0].lParam = 0;
    ppsp[0].pfnCallback = NULL;
    ppsp[0].pcRefParent = NULL; // not used

    *pcpsp = 1;

    return S_OK;
```

```
}


//
// free up any resources
//
VOID CDGExtPropSheets::FreePages(LPPROPSHEETPAGE ppsp, ULONG ulFlags, ULONG cpsp)
{
    // not used
}
//
// end of CDGExtPropSheets object
// ----------------------------------------------------------------
```

Only the code for the local helper functions remains. This code section contains two routines:
an error message handler and the code that actually computes the signature checksum. Listing
12.12 shows both these routines.

Listing 12.12. The `ErrMsgBox` and `CheckMsgSignature` routines.

```
// ----------------------------------------------------------------
// Local Helper routines
// ----------------------------------------------------------------
//
// ErrMsgBox() - used to handle error msgs
// CheckMsgSignature() - calculates checksum
// ----------------------------------------------------------------

//
// ErrMsgBox()
//
//      Params:
//        hWnd         - parent window
//        hr           - HRESULT value (0 to suppress)
//        szFunction   - function name in which the error occurred (NULL to suppress)
//        szMessage    - error message (required)
//
void ErrMsgBox(HWND hWnd, HRESULT hr, LPSTR szFunction, LPSTR szMessage)
{
 static char szError[256];

 if (szMessage == NULL)
 {
    MessageBox(hWnd,
        "An unknown error occured in\nextension",
        "CDG Message Signing Extension", MB_ICONEXCLAMATION | MB_OK);
    return;
 }

 if ((hr == 0) && (szFunction == NULL))
 {
    MessageBox(hWnd, szMessage, "CDG Message Signing Extension Error",
➥MB_ICONEXCLAMATION | MB_OK);
```

continues

Listing 12.12. continued

```
    return;
 }


 if (szFunction != NULL)
 {
  wsprintf(szError, "Error %08X in %s\n%s", hr, szFunction, szMessage);
  MessageBox(hWnd, szError, "CDG Message Signing Extension Error",
➥MB_ICONEXCLAMATION ¦ MB_OK);
 }

}



//
// CheckMsgSignature(pMsg, &ulCheckSum)()
//
//    Params:
//      pMsg         - points to message object
//        *pulCheckSum - points to checksum
//
HRESULT CheckMsgSignature(LPMESSAGE pMsg, ULONG *pulCheckSum)
{
 HRESULT hr;
 LPSTREAM pStreamBody;
 ULONG ulValue;
 ULONG ulRead;
 LARGE_INTEGER LgInt;
 ULARGE_INTEGER uLgInt;

 //
 // make sure you have a valid msg body
 //
 if ( (pMsg == NULL) ¦¦(pulCheckSum == NULL) )
 {
     hr = MAPI_E_INVALID_PARAMETER;
     goto error_return;
 }

 //
 // access the message body
 //
 pStreamBody = NULL;
 hr = pMsg->OpenProperty(PR_BODY, &IID_IStream, STGM_DIRECT ¦ STGM_READ, 0,
➥(LPUNKNOWN *) &pStreamBody);
 if (FAILED(hr))
 {
     goto error_return;
 }

 //
 // point to starting position
 //
 LgInt.LowPart = 0;
 LgInt.HighPart = 0;
 pStreamBody->Seek(LgInt, STREAM_SEEK_SET, &uLgInt);
```

```
//
// add up ascii values
//
(*pulCheckSum) = 0;
ulValue = 0;
while ( (S_OK == (hr = pStreamBody->Read((LPVOID)&ulValue, 4, &ulRead)))  &&
        (ulRead > 0) )
{
   (*pulCheckSum) += ulValue;
   ulValue = 0;
}


//
// clean up
//
error_return:

if (pStreamBody != NULL)
    pStreamBody->Release();

return hr;

}
//
// End of Helper routines
// ---------------------------------------------------------------
```

That is the end of the code for the CDGEXT32.CPP file. In the next section, you'll create the dialog box that will be added to the collection of property pages for the Windows Messaging client.

Laying Out and Coding the Property Sheet Dialog Box

The next step is to design the dialog page that will appear on the Tools ¦ Options tabbed dialog box of the Windows Messaging client. Although you'll build this as if it were a standalone dialog box, Microsoft Exchange will use the information to create an additional tab in the property pages displayed by the Windows Messaging client.

The dialog box consists of a frame control (IDC_STATIC), a check box (IDC_ENABLESGN), and a label control (IDC_STATIC). Figure 12.3 shows the layout of the dialog box.

FIGURE 12.3.

Laying out the Property Sheet dialog box.

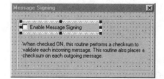

Once the dialog box is designed and saved into the CDGEXT32.RC, you need to create a code module to handle the user events on the property sheet. Listing 12.13 shows the code for the CDGPRP32.CPP file that handles all the dialog messages.

Listing 12.13. Code for the CDGPRP32.CPP file.

```
// ================================================================
//   CDGPRP32.CPP
// ================================================================
//

#include "CDGEXT32.H"

// ----------------------------------------------------------------
// MsgSigningDlgProc
//
//     Params:
//        hDlg   - handle to modeless dialog, the property page
//        uMsg   - message
//        wParam - wParam of wndproc
//        lParam - lParam of wndproc, points to NMHDR for notifications
//
// Handles events for the custom property page
// ----------------------------------------------------------------

BOOL CALLBACK MsgSigningDlgProc(HWND hDlg, UINT uMsg,
        WPARAM wParam, LPARAM lParam)
{
 BOOL bMsgResult;
 static HBRUSH hBrush;
 static COLORREF GrayColor;
 static LPNMHDR pnmhdr;
 static HWND hWndPage;

 switch (uMsg)
 {

  case WM_INITDIALOG:
  {
   LOGBRUSH lb;

    GrayColor = (COLORREF)GetSysColor(COLOR_BTNFACE);

    memset(&lb, 0, sizeof(LOGBRUSH));
    lb.lbStyle = BS_SOLID;
    lb.lbColor = GrayColor;
    hBrush = CreateBrushIndirect(&lb);

    return TRUE;
  }
  break;

  case WM_CTLCOLORDLG:
  case WM_CTLCOLORBTN:
  case WM_CTLCOLORSTATIC:
```

```
     if (hBrush != NULL)
   {
     SetBkColor((HDC)wParam, GrayColor);

     return (BOOL)hBrush;
   }

break;

case WM_DESTROY:
{
 if (hBrush != NULL)
         DeleteObject(hBrush);


 return TRUE;
}

case WM_COMMAND:
{
 if (LOWORD(wParam) == IDC_ENABLESGN)
 {
     SendMessage(GetParent(hDlg), PSM_CHANGED, (WPARAM)hDlg, 0L);
     bSignatureOn = SendDlgItemMessage(hDlg, IDC_ENABLESGN, BM_GETCHECK, 0, 0L);
 }
}
break;

case WM_NOTIFY:
{
 pnmhdr = ((LPNMHDR) lParam);

 switch ( pnmhdr->code)
 {
  case PSN_KILLACTIVE:
      bMsgResult = FALSE;   // allow this page to receive PSN_APPLY
      break;

  case PSN_SETACTIVE:

      // initialize controls
      if (bSignatureOn)
         SendDlgItemMessage(hDlg, IDC_ENABLESGN, BM_SETCHECK, 1, 0L);
      else
         SendDlgItemMessage(hDlg, IDC_ENABLESGN, BM_SETCHECK, 0, 0L);

      hWndPage = pnmhdr->hwndFrom;    // to be used in WM_COMMAND

      bMsgResult = FALSE;
      break;

  case PSN_APPLY:

      // get user input
      bSignatureOn = SendDlgItemMessage(hDlg, IDC_ENABLESGN, BM_GETCHECK, 0, 0L);

      bMsgResult = PSNRET_NOERROR;
```

continues

Listing 12.13. continued

```
      break;

  case PSN_HELP:
      MessageBox( pnmhdr->hwndFrom,
                  "CDG Message Signing Extension\n"
                  "(c)1996 MCA/SAMS Publishing",
                  "About",
                  MB_OK);
      bMsgResult = TRUE;
      break;

  default:
      bMsgResult = FALSE;
      break;
 }  // switch

    SetWindowLong( hDlg, DWL_MSGRESULT, bMsgResult);
    break;

 }       // case WM_NOTIFY

 default:
    bMsgResult = FALSE;
   break;

 }  // switch


 return bMsgResult;
}
```

This is the end of the code for the project. If you have Microsoft Visual C++ (or some other compatible C compiler), you can compile this code to create the DLL extension that will be installed into the Windows Messaging client.

Those who cannot (or choose not to) compile the source code shown here can copy the CDGEXT32.DLL from the CD-ROM that ships with the book to your local hard drive instead. You can then install this version of the extension.

Installing and Testing the Message Signing Extension

There are two main steps to installing the compiled version of the Message Signing Extension. First, you should compile the project or produce the CDGEXT32.DLL and copy that to a folder on your local hard drive.

> **NOTE**
>
> If you are not compiling your own version of the source code, copy the `CDGEXT32.DLL` from the CD-ROM to a local directory on your machine.

Next, you need to add an entry to your system registry database to inform Microsoft Exchange that a new extension is available. Listing 12.14 shows the exact registry entry you need to add to the `HKEY_LOCAL_MACHINE\Software\Microsoft\Exchange\Client\Extensions` section of your registry database.

Listing 12.14. The registry entry for the `CDGEXT32.DLL`.

```
CDGEXT32 = 4.0;d:\sams\cdg\chap12\cdgext32\CDGEXT32.dll;1;00000111111100
```

> **NOTE**
>
> The exact drive and directory should reflect the correct location of the `CDGEXT32.DLL` on your system.

Once you've added the entry, close the registry to update it and then start the Windows Messaging client to force it to install the new extension. Now you're ready to try the new Windows Messaging client feature!

Running the Message Signing Extension

When you start up the Windows Messaging client and select `Tools | Options` from the main menu, you should see a new property page for the message signing feature (see Figure 12.4).

FIGURE 12.4.

Viewing the new Message Signing *property page.*

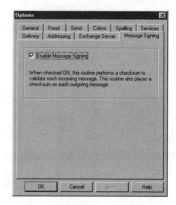

While you have the property page up, make sure that Message Signing is enabled (that is, the check mark is *on*).

Next, send yourself a new message. When the new message is written, the CDGEXT32.DLL kicks in and creates a checksum signature for the message. When you receive this message and open it, you should see a dialog box telling you the message was verified (see Figure 12.5).

FIGURE 12.5.

The CDGEXT32.DLL *in action.*

And that's all there is to it! You now have a working Windows Messaging client extension that can perform simple security checks on incoming messages. And you can turn the verification feature on and off using the new property page you created.

Summary

In this chapter, you learned the theory behind the Windows Messaging client extension model and the advantages of using Microsoft Exchange extensions instead of building your own standalone MAPI client. You also learned the following key concepts:

- The Microsoft Exchange Client has fourteen separate contexts that can be monitored by an extension DLL.
- The Microsoft Exchange Client has seven COM interfaces that can be used by C++ programmers to create programs that respond to Windows Messaging client events.
- Programmers need to map Microsoft Exchange contexts to Microsoft Exchange COM interfaces.

You also learned how to register Microsoft Exchange extension DLLs in the system registry (for 32-bit systems) or the EXCHNG.INI files for 16-bit systems. You also learned that you can install an extension as a shared resource on the network by making the correct entry in the SHARED32.INI file (32-bit systems) or the SHARED.INI file (16-bit systems).

Finally, you learned the details about the methods and properties of the Message Events and Property Sheets COM interfaces, and used that knowledge to build a working Message Signing extension.

13

Part II Summary—The Messaging API

In this section of the book you learned the details of the Messaging API (MAPI) services interface and how to use the various programming tools to access MAPI services. Throughout the section you used the programming techniques and tools to build several useful desktop applications including:

- A simple e-mail client
- A mailing list server
- A forum tool
- A custom form for the Microsoft Exchange client
- An e-mail inbox agent

You learned that there are two versions of MAPI currently active—Simple MAPI (or MAPI 0) and MAPI 1.0. Simple MAPI is available through the MAPI controls that ship with Visual Basic and through a library of Simple MAPI API calls. Most of the MAPI 1.0 features are available via the OLE Messaging Library that is shipped with the MSDN Professional Level CDs. The only MAPI services you cannot perform with the OLE Messaging Library are adding new entries to the address book, and creating and deleting folders from the message store. For this you need the power of C++ and access to the full MAPI 1.0 API set.

Here's a short summary of each of the chapters in Part II:

Chapter 3, "What Is MAPI?"

This chapter explained that the Messaging Application Programming Interface (MAPI) is a part of the Windows Open Systems Architecture (WOSA) model. MAPI is designed to offer three key benefits over other messaging services:

- *Flexibility*—Since MAPI is implemented within the WOSA model, there are three distinct layers:
    - The client layer (the end-user software)
    - The MAPI DLL layer (the MAPI service broker)
    - The service layer (the actual message service provider)

    Because the MAPI DLL layer acts as the service request broker between the MAPI client and the MAPI server, you can interchange servers and clients without having to modify your MAPI software modules.

- *Consistency*—MAPI services and the methods for accessing them are the same no matter what vendor you use to provide the message services.

- *Portability*—MAPI services are available on all supported versions of Windows (Win3.11, WFW, WinNT, and Win95). As Microsoft moves WOSA services to non-Windows platforms, MAPI services will be available within those operating systems, too.

There are three general types of MAPI messages:

■ *Text messages*—These are the standard plain ASCII text messages commonly known as e-mail. Some MAPI service providers support the use of rich-text formatted messages (for example, the Microsoft Exchange Mail client).

■ *Formatted documents and binary files*—These are word processing documents, graphics files, databases, and so on. MAPI allows you to send these binary files as attachments to the body of text messages.

■ *Control messages*—These messages are used by operating systems and specialized batch programs to relay information about the operating system, or to send commands that tell remote machines how to process attached data or run special jobs.

Finally, you learned about the various types of MAPI applications:

■ *Electronic mail clients*—The sole purpose of these programs is to give users direct access to the available MAPI services (for example, the Microsoft Mail Exchange client that ships with Windows 95).

■ *Message-aware applications*—These are programs that offer MAPI services as an added feature. Usually these programs offer users a send button or menu option. The standard output of the program can then be routed to another location through MAPI. The Send... menu option of Microsoft Word95 is an example of a message-aware application.

■ *Message-enabled applications*—These programs offer MAPI services as a basic part of their functionality. Message-enabled applications usually will not operate properly unless MAPI services are available to the workstation. Examples of message-enabled applications are data entry forms that collect data and automatically route it to the appropriate e-mail address, sometimes without asking the user for MAPI logons or addresses.

Two more application types are:

■ *Electronic forms applications*—These programs are fully functional data entry forms that are MAPI-enabled. Users can treat the form like any Windows program. Once data entry is completed and the message is sent, the addressee can open the message and see the same data form.

■ *Message-driven applications*—These are programs that can inspect portions of a message (body, header, attachments) and perform requested actions based on the contents of the message parts. Examples of message-driven applications include e-mail filtering agents, file transfer and update routines, and long-distance data search and retrieval programs.

Chapter 4, "MAPI Architecture"

In this chapter you learned about the general architecture of the MAPI system. You learned that there are two main components to the system:

- The MAPI Client
- The MAPI Server

The MAPI Client resides on the user's desktop and handles three main MAPI objects:

- Messages and attachments
- Storage folders
- MAPI addresses

Chapter 4 also reviewed the basic properties and features of MAPI messages, including message headers, folders, and address objects.

You learned that the MAPI Server usually resides on a stand-alone workstation connected to the network (although not always). Like the MAPI Client, the MAPI Server handles three main objects:

- Message transports
- Message stores
- Address books

The MAPI model allows users to use multiple versions of message transports (such as Microsoft Exchange Server messages and SMTP Internet messages), message storage, and address books. You also learned about the MAPI Spooler, which moves items from the message store to the appropriate provider.

Chapter 5, "Using the Microsoft Exchange Forms Designer"

In this chapter you learned how to use the Microsoft Exchange Forms Designer kit that ships with Microsoft Exchange Server. You learned how to design, code, test, and install custom message forms for use at individual workstations or over a large network.

Topics in this chapter included:

- Using the Microsoft Exchange Forms Designer
- Creating custom forms

■ Testing and compiling custom forms

■ Installing custom forms

You also learned how to set up Microsoft Exchange folders for use with custom forms. Related topics included:

■ Creating shared folders

■ Setting folder views, including sorting, filtering, and grouping messages

■ Installing custom forms in folders

Chapter 6, "Creating MAPI-Aware Applications"

In Chapter 6 you learned how to use low-level MAPI function calls to add e-mail capabilities to existing Windows applications.

You learned that MAPI-aware applications are programs that provide electronic send and/or receive services as a part of their basic feature set. Mail-aware software is able to use the available mail services in much the same way that programs use available printers, modems, or storage media (disk drives, CD-ROMs, and so on). For example, most office suite applications (word processors, spreadsheets, for example) provide a send feature on the main menu of all their programs. Basically, whatever documents you can create with the program can be sent to other locations using the mail services available on the network.

You learned to add MAPI-aware features to an Excel spreadsheet by adding a few API calls and some code to package up sections of the spreadsheet to be forwarded to another e-mail user.

You also modified a text editor project built with Visual Basic 4.0 by adding a Send... option to the main menu. In this way you added MAPI features to the application with a minimum of additional coding.

Part of this chapter described the details of the MAPI 0 API call set. This API set gives you the same abilities as the Visual Basic 4.0 MAPI controls with a few advantages:

■ *Crash protection*—Using the Visual Basic 4.0 MAPI controls will cause your program to crash if MAPI services are not available at the workstation. Using the API set means you can trap for missing MAPI services and modify your program accordingly.

■ *Portability*—You can use the API call set with any VBA-compliant system, including Access, Excel, and Word. You cannot use the Visual Basic MAPI controls with these applications.

Chapter 7, "Creating a Simple MAPI Client with the MAPI Controls"

This chapter covered two main topics:

■ The Visual Basic MAPI controls
■ Building a Simple MAPI client application

You learned the properties and methods of the two Visual Basic MAPI controls. The MAPISession control is used to gain access to MAPI service providers through the SignOn and SignOff methods. The MAPIMessages control is used to read, create, delete, address, and send MAPI messages.

The Simple MAPI client described in this chapter showed you how to build a complete MAPI-enabled application with a minimum of coding. This example application showed how you can use the Visual Basic MAPI controls to create a fully-functional e-mail client that can read and delete incoming messages, compose new messages, address them, and send them to their recipients.

You also learned that Simple MAPI services allow only limited access to the MAPI address book. You can search and edit the address book only through the pre-defined MAPI.Show method. You cannot directly search for existing addresses or add, edit, or delete addresses without using the address dialog box supplied by the MAPI service provider.

Simple MAPI does not allow you access to any of the existing mail folders. You can only see the inbox folder and its contents.

Chapter 8, "The OLE Messaging Library"

In Chapter 8 you learned how to use the OLE Messaging Library (OML) to access features of MAPI. You learned all the major objects, their methods, and their properties.

■ The Session object
■ The Folder objects and collections
■ The Message objects and collections
■ The Attachment objects and collections
■ The Recipient objects and collections
■ The Address objects
■ The InfoStore objects and collections

You also wrote several code examples that inspected and modified objects and their properties. You learned to use the OLE Messaging Library to:

■ Read existing messages
■ Create new messages
■ Add recipients to messages
■ Add attachments to messages
■ Modify records in the MAPI address book

Chapter 9, "Creating a MAPI Mailing List Manager with the OLE Messaging Library"

In Chapter 9 you built a Mailing List Manager (MLM) using Microsoft's OLE Messaging Library. This application let users define a mailing list, allowed others to become list subscribers, published messages automatically (based on date), and allowed other users to query and retrieve old messages from the list archives. The program accepted members from within a single network, or from around the world via Internet (or other) transports.

Here are the key features of the Mailing List Manager:

■ Automatically scans incoming mail for MLM messages
■ Automatically adds and drops subscribers from the group
■ Automatically distributes messages based on the current date
■ Allows subscribers to request copies of archived messages
■ Allows subscribers to request a default FAQ file
■ Allows most features to be modified through the use of control files

The MLM application allowed individuals to create a set of text files to be distributed to a controlled list of users at specified times. This project had only one simple form and several support routines. All application rules were stored in a set of ASCII control files similar to INI/registry settings. These control values can be changed by the list manager to determine how the mailing list operates, and what features are available to subscribers.

Chapter 10, "Building a MAPI-Enabled Forum Tool"

In Chapter 10 you learned how to use the OLE Messaging Library to build a Visual Basic 4.0 application that can track discussion threads in the shared Microsoft Exchange folder. You learned how to use the ConversationIndex and ConversationTopic properties of message objects in order to track and link messages in a series of related threads.

You also used the Visual Basic 4.0 Windows 95 controls to create a Forum Client reader that graphically represents the progress of a discussion and allows users to read threads and add new items to a thread. You added discussion manager features that control the expiration, deletion, and archiving of threads and allow users to set memberships and security levels for discussion groups.

In addition to building your own Forum Tool with Visual Basic 4.0, you learned how to use the Folder Views options of Microsoft Exchange Client to create both personal and public views of message folders. This gives you the ability to create discussion forums within Microsoft Exchange without having to install additional MAPI software.

Chapter 11, "Creating a MAPI E-Mail Agent"

In this chapter you learned how to use the OLE Messaging Library and some API calls to create a stand-alone e-mail agent. This agent scanned your incoming mail and, based on rules you established, automatically handled messages for you. It also archived and purged old messages. All actions were based on rules you established in a control file.

Features of the e-mail agent included:

- Timed scanning of your inbox
- Notification of message arrivals based on level of importance
- Automatic routing of incoming messages to other e-mail users
- Automatic replies to messages based on subject or sender
- Automatic sorting of unread messages into separate folders based on subject, sender, or level of importance.
- Automatic archiving and purging of messages based on subject, date received, or date last read.

Chapter 12, "Creating Microsoft Exchange Client Extensions"

In Chapter 12 you learned how to add custom routines to your existing MAPI clients. You learned how to do this using the MAPI 0 extension interface and by using the Microsoft Exchange client extension.

You learned that there are four types of Microsoft Exchange client extensions:

- Command extensions
- Event extensions
- Property sheet extensions
- Advanced criteria extensions

You also learned that there are several possible Microsoft Exchange extension message events that you can use to build special processing routines into the Microsoft Exchange client (see Table 13.1).

Table 13.1. Microsoft Exchange client message events.

Message Event	*Description*
OnRead	Replaces or enhances the behavior of Microsoft Exchange when reading information from a message.
OnReadComplete	Enables extension objects to roll back their implementation of the OnRead method in case of an error, or to release resources allocated by OnRead.
OnWrite	Replaces or enhances the behavior of Microsoft Exchange when writing information to a message.
OnWriteComplete	Enables extension objects to roll back their implementation of the OnWrite method in case of an error, or to release resources allocated by OnWrite.
OnCheckNames	Replaces or enhances the behavior of Microsoft Exchange when recipient names typed by the user are being resolved to their address book entries.
OnCheckNamesComplete	Enables extension objects to roll back their implementation of the OnCheckNames method in case of an error, or to release resources allocated by OnCheckNames.
OnSubmit	Replaces or enhances the behavior of Microsoft Exchange when a message has been submitted.
OnSubmitComplete	Enables extension objects to roll back their implementation of the OnSubmit method in case of an error, or to release resources allocated by OnSubmit.

You designed a simple extension that computes and reports the size of the message at the OnRead event. You also added a simple property page to the Microsoft Exchange client to turn the size checker on and off.

You learned how to register MAPI clients by modifying the [Register] section of the local INI file. Also, you learned that there are several places where extension registration can be found, depending on the Windows platform:

■ MSMAIL.INI—Local extensions on 16-bit MSMAIL clients.

■ EXCHNG.INI—Local extensions on 16-bit Exchange clients.

- `SHARED.INI`—Shared extensions on 16-bit clients.
- `SHARED32.INI`—Shared extensions on 32-bit clients.
- `HKEY_LOCAL_MACHINE\Software\Microsoft\Exchange\Client\Options`—Local extensions on 32-bit Exchange clients.

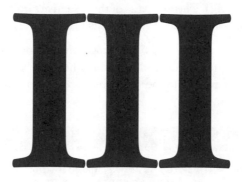

The Speech API (SAPI)

The newest member of the Windows Open Services Architecture (WOSA) team is the Microsoft Windows *Speech Application Program Interface* (SAPI). Close on the heels of the release of Windows 95, Microsoft has introduced a set of speech services that brings the power and possibilities of speech recognition and text-to-speech technology to the desktop.

As usual, Microsoft has designed SAPI to act as a full member of WOSA. All speech services are delivered using a back-end service provider interface (SPI) and a client-side application programming interface (API). The two parts of the system are linked by a dynamic link library (DLL) that passes information and service requests between the API and SPI.

This section of the book introduces the SAPI programming model, covers the basic concepts behind Microsoft's speech technology, and illustrates how to use the SAPI programming tools to build your own speech-aware and speech-enabled applications for the Windows 95 operating system.

NOTE

As of this writing, the SAPI system is only available for the Win95 operating system. Microsoft plans to release a version of SAPI for the NT operating system in the near future.

Let's take a quick tour of the chapters in this section.

In the first three chapters, you'll learn all about the SAPI object interface (Chapter 14, "What Is SAPI?") and its underlying architecture (Chapter 15, "SAPI Architecture"), and review the basics of accessing the SAPI services for Win95 (Chapter 16, "SAPI Basics"). When you finish these chapters you'll understand the SAPI model and know how to design programs that access speech services.

The next three chapters in this section deal with programming tools and technical issues regarding speech engines. Chapter 17, "SAPI Tools—Using SAPI Objects with Visual Basic 4.0," reviews SAPI programming techniques, and Chapter 18, "SAPI Behind the Scenes," covers the concepts behind the current grammar technologies and the use of phonetic alphabets. You'll design and implement speech applications using techniques covered in Chapter 19, "Creating SAPI Applications with C++," and Chapter 20, "Building the Voice-Activated Text Reader."

Finally Chapter 21, "Part III Summary—The Speech API," reviews all the material covered in this section and helps you put it all together.

When you complete the chapters in this section you will understand and know how to use the SAPI service model, you'll know the details behind the underlying grammar engine used in the SAPI service providers, and you'll know how to design and code speech applications in the Windows 95 environment.

14

What Is SAPI?

One of the newest extensions for the Windows 95 operating system is the *Speech Application Programming Interface* (SAPI). This Windows extension gives workstations the ability to recognize human speech as input, and create human-like audio output from printed text. This ability adds a new dimension to human/PC interaction. Speech recognition services can be used to extend the use of PCs to those who find typing too difficult or too time-consuming. Text-to-speech services can be used to provide aural representations of text documents to those who cannot see typical display screens because of physical limitations or due to the nature of their work.

Like the other Windows services described in this book, SAPI is part of the Windows Open Services Architecture (WOSA) model. Speech recognition (SR) and text-to-speech (TTS) services are actually provided by separate modules called *engines*. Users can select the speech engine they prefer to use as long as it conforms to the SAPI interface.

In this chapter you'll learn the basic concepts behind designing and implementing a speech recognition and text-to-speech engine using the SAPI design model. You'll also learn about creating grammar definitions for speech recognition.

Speech Recognition

Any speech system has, at its heart, a process for recognizing human speech and turning it into something the computer understands. In effect, the computer needs a translator. Research into effective speech recognition algorithms and processing models has been going on almost ever since the computer was invented. And a great deal of mathematics and linguistics go into the design and implementation of a speech recognition system. A detailed discussion of speech recognition algorithms is beyond the scope of this book, but it is important to have a good idea of the commonly used techniques for turning human speech into something a computer understands.

Every speech recognition system uses four key operations to listen to and understand human speech. They are:

- ■ *Word separation*—This is the process of creating discreet portions of human speech. Each portion can be as large as a phrase or as small as a single syllable or word part.
- ■ *Vocabulary*—This is the list of speech items that the speech engine can identify.
- ■ *Word matching*—This is the method that the speech system uses to look up a speech part in the system's vocabulary—the *search engine* portion of the system.
- ■ *Speaker dependence*—This is the degree to which the speech engine is dependent on the vocal tones and speaking patterns of individuals.

These four aspects of the speech system are closely interrelated. If you want to develop a speech system with a rich vocabulary, you'll need a sophisticated word matching system to quickly search the vocabulary. Also, as the vocabulary gets larger, more items in the list could sound similar (for example, *yes* and *yet*). In order to successfully identify these speech parts, the word separation portion of the system must be able to determine smaller and smaller differences between speech items.

Finally, the speech engine must balance all of these factors against the aspect of speaker dependence. As the speech system learns smaller and smaller differences between words, the system becomes more and more dependent on the speaking habits of a single user. Individual accents and speech patterns can confuse speech engines. In other words, as the system becomes more responsive to a single user, that same system becomes less able to translate the speech of other users.

The next few sections describe each of the four aspects of a speech engine in a bit more detail.

Word Separation

The first task of the speech engine is to accept words as input. Speech engines use a process called *word separation* to gather human speech. Just as the keyboard is used as an input device to accept physical keystrokes for translation into readable characters, the process of word separation accepts the sound of human speech for translation by the computer.

There are three basic methods of word separation. In ascending order of complexity they are:

- Discrete speech
- Word spotting
- Continuous speech

Systems that use the *discrete speech* method of word separation require the user to place a short pause between each spoken word. This slight bit of silence allows the speech system to recognize the beginning and ending of each word. The silences separate the words much like the space bar does when you type. The advantage of the discrete speech method is that it requires the least amount of computational resources. The disadvantage of this method is that it is not very user-friendly. Discrete speech systems can easily become confused if a person does not pause between words.

Systems that use *word spotting* avoid the need for users to pause in between each word by listening only for key words or phrases. Word spotting systems, in effect, ignore the items they do not know or care about and act only on the words they can match in their vocabulary. For example, suppose the speech system can recognize the word *help*, and knows to load the Windows Help engine whenever it hears the word. Under word spotting, the following phrases will all result in the speech engine invoking Windows Help:

Please load Help.

Can you help me, please?

These definitions are no help at all!

As you can see, one of the disadvantages of word spotting is that the system can easily misinterpret the user's meaning. However, word spotting also has several key advantages. Word spotting allows users to speak normally, without employing pauses. Also, since word spotting systems simply ignore words they don't know and act only on key words, these systems can give the appearance of being more sophisticated than they really are. Word spotting requires more computing resources than discreet speech, but not as much as the last method of word separation—continuous speech.

Continuous speech systems recognize and process every word spoken. This gives the greatest degree of accuracy when attempting to understand a speaker's request. However, it also requires the greatest amount of computing power. First, the speech system must determine the start and end of each word without the use of silence. This is much like readingtextthathasnospacesinit (see!). Once the words have been separated, the system must look them up in the vocabulary and identify them. This, too, can take precious computing time. The primary advantage of continuous speech systems is that they offer the greatest level of sophistication in recognizing human speech. The primary disadvantage is the amount of computing resources they require.

Speaker Dependence

Speaker dependence is a key factor in the design and implementation of a speech recognition system. In theory, you would like a system that has very little speaker dependence. This would mean that the same workstation could be spoken to by several people with the same positive results. People often speak quite differently from one another, however, and this can cause problems.

First, there is the case of accents. Just using the United States as an example, you can identify several regional sounds. Add to these the possibility that speakers may also have accents that come from outside the U.S. due to the influence of other languages (Spanish, German, Japanese), and you have a wide range of pronunciation for even the simplest of sentences. Speaker speed and pitch inflection can also vary widely, which can pose problems for speech systems that need to determine whether a spoken phrase is a statement or a question.

Speech systems fall into three categories in terms of their speaker dependence. They can be:

- Speaker independent
- Speaker dependent
- Speaker adaptive

Speaker-independent systems require the most resources. They must be able to accurately translate human speech across as many dialects and accents as possible. *Speaker-dependent* systems require the least amount of computing resources. These systems require that the user "train" the system before it is able to accurately convert human speech. A compromise between the two approaches is the speaker-adaptive method. *Speaker-adaptive* systems are prepared to work without training, but increase their accuracy after working with the same speaker for a period of time.

The additional training required by speaker-dependent systems can be frustrating to users. Usually training can take several hours, but some systems can reach 90 percent accuracy or better after just five minutes of training. Users with physical disabilities, or those who find typing highly inefficient, will be most likely to accept using speaker-dependent systems.

Systems that will be used by many different people need the power of speaker independence. This is especially true for systems that will have short encounters with many different people, such as greeting kiosks at an airport. In such situations, training is unlikely to occur, and a high degree of accuracy is expected right away.

For systems where multiple people will access the same workstation over a longer period of time, the speaker-adaptive system will work fine. A good example would be a workstation used by several employees to query information from a database. The initial investment spent training the speech system will pay off over time as the same staff uses the system.

Word Matching

Word matching is the process of performing look-ups into the speech database. As each word is gathered (using the word separation techniques described earlier), it must be matched against some item in the speech engine's database. It is the process of word matching that connects the audio input signal to a meaningful item in the speech engine database.

There are two primary methods of word matching:

- Whole-word matching
- Phoneme matching

Under *whole-word matching*, the speech engine searches the database for a word that matches the audio input. Whole-word matching requires less search capability than phoneme matching. But, whole-word matching requires a greater amount of storage capacity. Under the whole-word matching model, the system must store a word template that represents each possible word that the engine can recognize. While quick retrieval makes whole-word matching attractive, the fact that all words must be known ahead of time limits the application of whole-word matching systems.

Phoneme matching systems keep a dictionary of language phonemes. *Phonemes* are the smallest unique sound part of a language, and can be numerous. For example, while the English language has 26 individual letters, these letters do not represent the total list of possible phonemes. Also, phonemes are not restricted by spelling conventions.

Consider the words *Philip* and *fill up*. These words have the same phonemes: *f, eh, ul, ah*, and *pah*. However, they have entirely different meanings. Under the whole-word matching model, these words could represent multiple entries in the database. Under the phoneme matching model, the same five phonemes can be used to represent both words.

As you may expect, phoneme matching systems require more computational resources, but less storage space.

Vocabulary

The final element of a speech recognition system is the vocabulary. There are two competing issues regarding vocabulary: size and accuracy. As the vocabulary size increases, recognition improves. With large vocabularies, it is easy for speech systems to locate a word that matches the one identified in the word separation phase. However, one of the reasons it is easy to find a match is that more than one entry in the vocabulary may match the given input. For example, the words *no* and *go* are very similar to most speech engines. Therefore, as vocabulary size grows, the accuracy of speech recognition can decrease.

Contrary to what you might assume, a speech engine's vocabulary does not represent the total number of words it understands. Instead, the vocabulary of a speech engine represents the number of words that it can recognize in a current state or moment in time. In effect, this is the total number of "unidentified" words that the system can resolve at any moment.

For example, let's assume you have registered the following word phrases with your speech engine: "Start running Exchange" and "Start running Word." Before you say anything, the current state of the speech engine has four words: *start, running, Exchange*, and *Word*. Once you say "Start running" there are only two words in the current state: *Exchange* and *Word*. The system's ability to keep track of the possible next word is determined by the size of its vocabulary.

Small vocabulary systems (100 words or less) work well in situations where most of the speech recognition is devoted to processing commands. However, you need a large vocabulary to handle dictation systems. Dictation vocabularies can reach into tens of thousands of words. This is one of the reasons that dictation systems are so difficult to implement. Not only does the vocabulary need to be large, the resolutions must be made quite quickly.

Text-to-Speech

A second type of speech service provides the ability to convert written text into spoken words. This is called *text-to-speech* (or *TTS*) technology. Just as there are a number of factors to consider when developing speech recognition engines (SR), there are a few issues that must be addressed when creating and implementing rules for TTS engines.

The four common issues that must be addressed when creating a TTS engine are as follows:

- Phonemes
- Voice quality
- TTS synthesis
- TTS diphone concatenation

The first two factors deal with the creation of audio tones that are recognizable as human speech. The last two items are competing methods for interpreting text that is to be converted into audio.

Voice Quality

The quality of a computerized voice is directly related to the sophistication of the rules that identify and convert text into an audio signal. It is not too difficult to build a TTS engine that can create recognizable speech. However, it is extremely difficult to create a TTS engine that does not sound like a computer. Three factors in human speech are very difficult to produce with computers:

- Prosody
- Emotion
- Pronunciation anomalies

Human speech has a special rhythm or *prosody*—a pattern of pauses, inflections, and emphasis that is an integral part of the language. While computers can do a good job of pronouncing individual words, it is difficult to get them to accurately mimic the tonal and rhythmic inflections of human speech. For this reason, it is always quite easy to differentiate computer-generated speech from a computer playing back a recording of a human voice.

Another factor of human speech that computers have difficulty rendering is emotion. While TTS engines are capable of distinguishing declarative statements from questions or exclamations, computers are still not able to convey believable emotive qualities when rendering text into speech.

Lastly, every language has its own pronunciation anomalies. These are words that do not "play by the rules" when it comes to converting text into speech. Some common examples in English are *dough* and *tough* or *comb* and *home*. More troublesome are words such as *read* which must be understood in context in order to figure out their exact pronunciation. For example, the pronunciations are different in "He *read* the paper" or "She will now *read* to the class." Even more likely to cause problems is the interjection of technobabble such as "SQL," "MAPI," and "SAPI." All these factors make the development of a truly human-sounding computer-generated voice extremely difficult.

Speech systems usually offer some way to correct for these types of problems. One typical solution is to include the ability to enter the phonetic spelling of a word and relate that spelling to the text version. Another common adjustment is to allow users to enter control tags in the text to instruct the speech engine to add emphasis or inflection, or alter the speed or pitch of the audio output. Much of this type of adjustment information is based on phonemes, as described in the next section.

Phonemes

As we've discussed, phonemes are the sound parts that make up words. Linguists use phonemes to accurately record the vocal sounds uttered by humans when speaking. These same phonemes also can be used to generate computerized speech. TTS engines use their knowledge of grammar rules and phonemes to scan printed text and generate audio output.

> **NOTE**
>
> If you are interested in learning more about phonemes and how they are used to analyze speech, refer to the *Phonetic Symbol Guide* by Pullum and Ladusaw (Chicago University Press, 1996).

The SAPI design model recognizes and allows for the incorporation of phonemes as a method for creating speech output. Microsoft has developed an expression of the International Phonetic Alphabet (IPA) in the form of Unicode strings. Programmers can use these strings to improve the pronunciation skills of the TTS engine, or to add entirely new words to the vocabulary.

> **NOTE**
>
> If you wish to use direct Unicode to alter the behavior of your TTS engine, you'll have to program using Unicode. SAPI does not support the direct use of phonemes in ANSI format.

As mentioned in the previous section on voice quality, most TTS engines provide several methods for improving the pronunciation of words. Unless you are involved in the development of a text-to-speech engine, you probably will not use phonemes very often.

TTS Synthesis

Once the TTS knows what phonemes to use to reproduce a word, there are two possible methods for creating the audio output: *synthesis* or *diphone concatenation*.

The synthesis method uses calculations of a person's lip and tongue position, the force of breath, and other factors to synthesize human speech. This method is usually not as accurate as the diphone method. However, if the TTS uses the synthesis method for generating output, it is very easy to modify a few parameters and then create a new "voice."

Synthesis-based TTS engines require less overall computational resources, and less storage capacity. Synthesis-based systems are a bit more difficult to understand at first, but usually offer users the ability to adjust the tone, speed, and inflection of the voice rather easily.

TTS Diphone Concatenation

The diphone concatenation method of generating speech uses pairs of phonemes (*di* meaning two) to produce each sound. These diphones represent the start and end of each individual speech part. For example, the word *pig* contains the diphones *silence-p, p-i, i-g,* and *g-silence.* Diphone TTS systems scan the word and then piece together the correct phoneme pairs to pronounce the word.

These phoneme pairs are produced not by computer synthesis, but from actual recordings of human voices that have been broken down to their smallest elements and categorized into the various diphone pairs. Since TTS systems that use diphones are using elements of actual human speech, they can produce much more human-like output. However, since diphone pairs are very language-specific, diphone TTS systems are usually dedicated to producing a single language. Because of this, diphone systems do not do well in environments where numerous foreign words may be present, or where the TTS might be required to produce output in more than one language.

Grammar Rules

The final elements of a speech engine are the grammar rules. Grammar rules are used by speech recognition (SR) software to analyze human speech input and, in the process, attempt to understand what a person is saying. Most of us suffered through a series of lessons in grade school where our teachers attempted to show us just how grammar rules affect our everyday speech patterns. And most of us probably don't remember a great deal from those lessons, but we all use grammar rules every day without thinking about them, to express ourselves and make sense of what others say to us. Without an understanding of and appreciation for the importance of grammars, computer speech recognition systems would not be possible.

There can be any number of grammars, each composed of a set of rules of speech. Just as humans must learn to share a common grammar in order to be understood, computers must also share a common grammar with the speaker in order to convert audio information into text.

Grammars can be divided in to three types, each with its own strengths and weaknesses. The types are:

- Context-free grammars
- Dictation grammars
- Limited domain grammars

Context-free grammars offer the greatest degree of flexibility when interpreting human speech. Dictation grammars offer the greatest degree of accuracy when converting spoken words into printed text. Limited domain grammars offer a compromise between the highly flexible context-free grammar and the restrictive dictation grammar.

The following sections discuss each grammar type in more detail.

Context-Free Grammars

Context-free grammars work on the principle of following established rules to determine the most likely candidates for the next word in a sentence. Context-free grammars *do not* work on the idea that each word should be understood within a context. Rather, they evaluate the relationship of each word and word phrase to a known set of rules about what words are possible at any given moment.

The main elements of a context-free grammar are:

- *Words*—A list of valid words to be spoken
- *Rules*—A set of speech structures in which words are used
- *Lists*—One or more word sets to be used within rules

Context-free grammars are good for systems that have to deal with a wide variety of input. Context-free systems are also able to handle variable vocabularies. This is because most of the rule-building done for context-free grammars revolves around declaring lists and groups of words that fit into common patterns or rules. Once the SR engine understands the rules, it is very easy to expand the vocabulary by expanding the lists of possible members of a group.

For example, rules in a context-free grammar might look something like this:

```
<NameRule>=ALT("Mike","Curt","Sharon","Angelique")

<SendMailRule>=("Send Email to", <NameRule>)
```

In the example above, two rules have been established. The first rule, `<NameRule>`, creates a list of possible names. The second rule, `<SendMailRule>`, creates a rule that depends on `<NameRule>`. In this way, context-free grammars allow you to build your own grammatical rules as a predictor of how humans will interact with the system.

Even more importantly, context-free grammars allow for easy expansion at run-time. Since much of the way context-free grammars operate focuses on lists, it is easy to allow users to add list members and, therefore, to improve the value of the SR system quickly. This makes it easy to install a system with only basic components. The basic system can be expanded to meet the needs of various users. In this way, context-free grammars offer a high degree of flexibility with very little development cost or complication.

The construction of quality context-free grammars can be a challenge, however. Systems that only need to do a few things (such as load and run programs, execute simple directives, and so on) are easily expressed using context-free grammars. However, in order to perform more complex tasks or a wider range of chores, additional rules are needed. As the number of rules and the length of lists increases, the computational load rises dramatically. Also, since context-free grammars base their predictions on predefined rules, they are not good for tasks like dictation, where a large vocabulary is most important.

Dictation Grammars

Unlike context-free grammars that operate using rules, dictation grammars base their evaluations on vocabulary. The primary function of a dictation grammar is to convert human speech into text as accurately as possible. In order to do this, dictation grammars need not only a rich vocabulary to work from, but also a sample output to use as a model when analyzing speech input. Rules of speech are not important to a system that must simply convert human input into printed text.

The elements of a dictation grammar are:

- *Topic*—Identifies the dictation topic (for example, medical or legal).
- *Common*—A set of words commonly used in the dictation. Usually the common group contains technical or specialized words that are expected to appear during dictation, but are not usually found in regular conversation.
- *Group*—A related set of words that can be expected, but that are not directly related to the dictation topic. The group usually has a set of words that are expected to occur frequently during dictation. The grammar model can contain more than one group.
- *Sample*—A sample of text that shows the writing style of the speaker or general format of the dictation. This text is used to aid the SR engine in analyzing speech input.

The success of a dictation grammar depends on the quality of the vocabulary. The more items on the list, the greater the chance of the SR engine mistaking one item for another. However, the more limited the vocabulary, the greater the number of "unknown" words that will occur during the course of the dictation. The most successful dictation systems balance vocabulary depth and the uniqueness of the words in the database. For this reason, dictation systems are usually tuned for one topic, such as legal or medical dictation. By limiting the vocabulary to the words most likely to occur in the course of dictation, translation accuracy is increased.

Limited Domain Grammars

Limited domain grammars offer a compromise between the flexibility of context-free grammars and the accuracy of dictation grammars. Limited domain grammars have the following elements:

- *Words*—This is the list of specialized words that are likely to occur during a session.
- *Group*—This is a set of related words that could occur during the session. The grammar can contain multiple word groups. A single phrase would be expected to include one of the words in the group.
- *Sample*—A sample of text that shows the writing style of the speaker or general format of the dictation. This text is used to aid the SR engine in analyzing the speech input.

Limited domain grammars are useful in situations where the vocabulary of the system need not be very large. Examples include systems that use natural language to accept command statement, such as "How can I set the margins?" or "Replace all instances of 'New York' with 'Los Angeles.'" Limited domain grammars also work well for filling in forms or for simple text entry.

Summary

In this chapter you learned about the key factors behind creating and implementing a complete speech system for PCs. You learned the three major parts to speech systems:

- *Speech recognition*—Converts audio input into printed text or directly into computer commands.
- *Text-to-speech*—Converts printed text into audible speech.
- *Grammar rules*—Used by speech recognition systems to analyze audio input and convert it into commands or text.

In the next chapter, you'll learn the specifics behind the Microsoft speech recognition engine.

15

SAPI Architecture

Introduction

The Speech API is implemented as a series of Component Object Model (COM) interfaces. This chapter identifies the top-level objects, their child objects, and their methods.

The SAPI model is divided into two distinct levels:

■ *High-level SAPI*—This level provides basic speech services in the form of command-and-control speech recognition and simple text-to-speech output.

■ *Low-level SAPI*—This level provides detailed access to all speech services, including direct interfaces to control dialogs and manipulation of both speech recognition (SR) and text-to-speech (TTS) behavior attributes.

Each of the two levels of SAPI services has its own set of objects and methods.

Along with the two sets of COM interfaces, Microsoft has also published an OLE Automation type library for the high-level SAPI objects. This set of OLE objects is discussed at the end of the chapter.

When you complete this chapter you'll understand the basic architecture of the SAPI model, including all the SAPI objects and their uses. Detailed information about the object's methods and parameters will be covered in the next chapter—"SAPI Basics."

> **NOTE**
>
> Most of the Microsoft Speech API is accessible only through C++ code. For this reason, many of the examples shown in this chapter are expressed in Microsoft Visual C++ code. You do not need to be able to code in C++ in order to understand the information discussed here. At the end of this chapter, the OLE Automation objects available through Visual Basic are also discussed.

High-Level SAPI

The high-level SAPI services provide access to basic forms of speech recognition and text-to-speech services. This is ideal for providing voice-activated menus, command buttons, and so on. It is also sufficient for basic rendering of text into speech.

The high-level SAPI interface has two top-level objects—one for voice command services (speech recognition), and one for voice text services (text-to-speech). The following two sections describe each of these top-level objects, their child objects, and the interfaces available through each object.

Voice Command

The Voice Command object is used to provide speech recognition services. It is useful for providing simple command-and-control speech services such as implementing menu options, activating command buttons, and issuing other simple operating system commands.

The Voice Command object has one child object and one collection object. The child object is the Voice Menu object and the collection object is a collection of enumerated menu objects (see Figure 15.1).

FIGURE 15.1.
The Voice Command *object.*

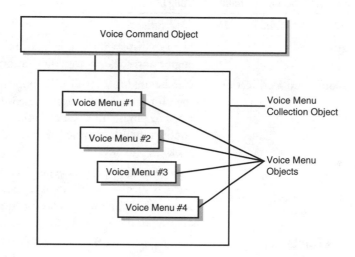

Voice Command **Object**

The Voice Command object supports three interfaces:

- The Voice Command interface
- The Attributes interface
- The Dialogs interface

The Voice Command interface is used to enumerate, create, and delete voice menu objects. This interface is also used to register an application to use the SR engine. An application must successfully complete the registration before the SR engine can be used. An additional method defined for the Voice Command interface is the Mimic method. This is used to play back a voice command to the engine; it can be used to "speak" voice commands directly to the SR engine. This is similar to playing keystroke or mouse-action macros back to the operating system.

The Attributes interface is used to set and retrieve a number of basic parameters that control the behavior of the voice command system. You can enable or disable voice commands, adjust input gain, establish the SR mode, and control the input device (microphone or telephone).

The Dialogs interface gives you access to a series of dialog boxes that can be used as a standard set of input screens for setting and displaying SR engine information. The SAPI model identifies five different dialog boxes that should be available through the Dialogs interface. The exact layout and content of these dialog boxes is not dictated by Microsoft, but is determined by the developer of the speech recognition engine. However, Microsoft has established general guidelines for the contents of the SR engine dialog boxes. Table 15.1 lists each of the five defined dialog boxes along with short descriptions of their suggested contents.

Table 15.1. The Voice Command dialog boxes.

Dialog Box Name	Description
About Box	Used to display the dialog box that identifies the SR engine and show its copyright information.
Command Verification	Can be used as a verification pop-up window during a speech recognition session. When the engine identifies a word or phrase, this box can appear requesting the user to confirm that the engine has correctly understood the spoken command.
General Dialog	Can be used to provide general access to the SR engine settings such as identifying the speaker, controlling recognition parameters, and the amount of disk space allotted to the SR engine.
Lexicon Dialog	Can be used to offer the speaker the opportunity to alter the pronunciation lexicon, including altering the phonetic spelling of troublesome words, or adding or deleting personal vocabulary files.

The Voice Menu Object and the Menu Object Collection

The Voice Menu object is the only child object of the Voice Command object. It is used to allow applications to define, add, and delete voice commands in a menu. You can also use the Voice Menu object to activate and deactivate menus and, optionally, to provide a training dialog box for the menu.

The voice menu collection object contains a set of all menu objects defined in the voice command database. Microsoft SAPI defines functions to select and copy menu collections for use by the voice command speech engine.

The Voice Command Notification Callback

In the process of registering the application to use a voice command object, a notification *callback* (or *sink*) is established. This callback receives messages regarding the SR engine activity.

Typical messages sent out by the SR engine can include notifications that the engine has detected commands being spoken, that some attribute of the engine has been changed, or that spoken commands have been heard but not recognized.

> **NOTE**
>
> Notification callbacks require a pointer to the function that will receive all related messages. Callbacks cannot be registered using Visual Basic; you need C or C++. However, the voice command OLE Automation type library that ships with the Speech SDK has a notification callback built into it.

Voice Text

The SAPI model defines a basic text-to-speech service called *voice text*. This service has only one object—the Voice Text object. The Voice Text object supports three interfaces:

- The Voice Text interface
- The Attributes interface
- The Dialogs interface

The Voice Text interface is the primary interface of the TTS portion of the high-level SAPI model. The Voice Text interface provides a set method to start, pause, resume, fast forward, rewind, and stop the TTS engine while it is speaking text. This mirrors the VCR-type controls commonly employed for PC video and audio playback.

The Voice Text interface is also used to register the application that will request TTS services. An application must successfully complete the registration before the TTS engine can be used. This registration function can optionally pass a pointer to a callback function to be used to capture voice text messages. This establishes a notification callback with several methods, which are triggered by messages sent from the underlying TTS engine.

> **NOTE**
>
> Notification callbacks require a pointer to the function that will receive all related messages. Callbacks cannot be registered using Visual Basic; you need C or C++. However, the voice text OLE Automation type library that ships with the Speech SDK has a notification callback built into it.

The Attribute interface provides access to settings that control the basic behavior of the TTS engine. For example, you can use the Attributes interface to set the audio device to be used, set the playback speed (in words per minute), and turn the speech services on and off. If the

TTS engine supports it, you can also use the `Attributes` interface to select the TTS speaking mode. The TTS speaking mode usually refers to a predefined set of voices, each having its own character or style (for example, male, female, child, adult, and so on).

The `Dialogs` interface can be used to allow users the ability to set and retrieve information regarding the TTS engine. The exact contents and layout of the dialog boxes are not determined by Microsoft but by the TTS engine developer. Microsoft does, however, suggest the possible contents of each dialog box. Table 15.2 shows the four voice text dialogs defined by the SAPI model, along with short descriptions of their suggested contents.

Table 15.2. The Voice Text dialog boxes.

Dialog Name	Description
About Box	Used to display the dialog box that identifies the TTS engine and shows its copyright information.
Lexicon Dialog	Can be used to offer the speaker the opportunity to alter the pronunciation lexicon, including altering the phonetic spelling of troublesome words, or adding or deleting personal vocabulary files.
General Dialog	Can be used to display general information about the TTS engine. Examples might be controlling the speed at which the text will be read, the character of the voice that will be used for playback, and other user preferences as supported by the TTS engine.
Translate Dialog	Can be used to offer the user the ability to alter the pronunciation of key words in the lexicon. For example, the TTS engine that ships with Microsoft Voice has a special entry that forces the speech engine to express all occurrences of "TTS" as "text to speech," instead of just reciting the letters "T-T-S."

Low-Level SAPI

The low-level SAPI services provide access to a much greater level of control of Windows speech recognition and text-to-speech services. This level is best for implementing advanced SR and TTS services, including the creation of dictation systems.

Just as there are two basic service types for high-level SAPI, there are two primary COM interfaces defined for low-level SAPI—one for speech recognition and one for text-to-speech services. The rest of this chapter outlines each of the objects and their interfaces.

> **NOTE**
>
> This section of the chapter covers the low-level SAPI services. These services are available only from C or C++ programs—not Visual Basic. However, even if you do not program in C, you can still learn a lot from this section of the chapter. The material in this section can give you a good understanding of the details behind the SAPI OLE automation objects, and may also give you some ideas on how you can use the VB-level SAPI services in your programs.

Speech Recognition

The Speech Recognition object has several child objects and collections. There are two top-level objects in the SR system: the SR Engine Enumerator object and the SR Sharing object. These two objects are created using their unique CLSID (class ID) values. The purpose of both objects is to give an application information about the available speech recognition engines and allow the application to register with the appropriate engine. Once the engine is selected, one or more grammar objects can be created, and as each phrase is heard, an SR Results object is created for each phrase. This object is a temporary object that contains details about the phrase that was captured by the speech recognition engine. Figure 15.2 shows how the different objects relate to each other, and how they are created.

FIGURE 15.2.
Mapping the low-level SAPI objects.

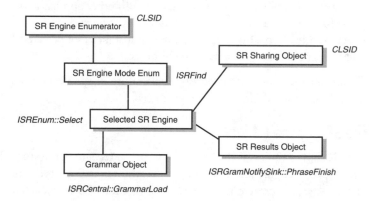

When an SR engine is created, a link to a valid audio input device is also created. While it is possible to create a custom audio input device, it is not required. The default audio input device is an attached microphone, but can also be set to point to a telephone device.

The rest of this section details the low-level SAPI SR objects and their interfaces.

The SR Enumerator **and** Engine Enumerator **Objects**

The role of the SR Enumerator and Engine Enumerator objects is to locate and select an appropriate SR engine for the requesting application. The Enumerator object lists all available speech recognition modes and their associated installed engines. This information is supplied by the child object of the Enumerator object: the Engine Enumerator object. The result of this search is a pointer to the SR engine interface that best meets the service request.

The Enumerator and Engine Enumerator objects support only two interfaces:

- The ISREnum interface is used to get a list of all available engines.
- The ISRFind interface is used to select the desired engine.

> **NOTE**
>
> The SR Enumerator and Engine Enumerator objects are used only to locate and select an engine object. Once that is done, these two objects can be discarded.

The SR Sharing **Object**

The SR Sharing object is a possible replacement for the SR Enumerator and Engine Enumerator objects. The SR Sharing object uses only one interface, the ISRSharing interface, to locate and select an engine object that will be shared with other applications on the PC. In essence, this allows for the registration of a requesting application with an out-of-process memory SR server object. While often slower than creating an instance of a private SR object, using the Sharing object can reduce strain on memory resources.

The SR Sharing interface is an optional feature of speech engines and may not be available depending on the design of the engine itself.

The SR Engine **Object**

The SR Engine Object is the heart of the speech recognition system. This object represents the actual speech engine and it supports several interfaces for the monitoring of speech activity. The SR Engine is created using the Select method of the ISREnum interface of the SR Enumerator object described earlier. Table 15.3 lists the interfaces supported by the SR Engine object along with a short description of their uses.

Table 15.3. The interfaces of the SR Engine **object.**

Interface Name	Description
ISRCentral	The main interface for the SR Engine object. Allows the loading and unloading of grammars, checks information status of the engine, starts and stops the engine, and registers and releases the engine notification callback.
ISRDialogs	Used to display a series of dialog boxes that allow users to set parameters of the engine and engage in training to improve the SR performance.
ISRAttributes	Used to set and get basic attributes of the engine, including input device name and type, volume controls, and other information.
ISRSpeaker	Allows users to manage a list of speakers that use the engine. This is especially valuable when more than one person uses the same device. This is an optional interface.
ISRLexPronounce	This interface is used to provide users access to modify the pronunciation or playback of certain words in the lexicon. This is an optional interface.

The SR Engine object also provides a notification callback interface (ISRNotifySink) to capture messages sent by the engine. These messages can be used to check on the performance status of the engine, and can provide feedback to the application (or speaker) that can be used to improve performance.

The Grammar **Object**

The Grammar object is a child object of the SR Engine object. It is used to load parsing grammars for use by the speech engine in analyzing audio input. The Grammar object contains all the rules, words, lists, and other parameters that control how the SR engine interprets human speech. Each phrase detected by the SR engine is processed using the loaded grammars.

The Grammar object supports three interfaces:

■ ISRGramCFG—This interface is used to handle grammar functions specific to context-free grammars, including the management of lists and rules.

■ ISRGramDictation—This interface is used to handle grammar functions specific to dictation grammars, including words, word groups, and sample text.

■ IRSGramCommon—This interface is use to handle tasks common to both dictation and context-free grammars. This includes loading and unloading grammars, activating or deactivating a loaded grammar, training the engine, and possibly storing SR results objects.

The Grammar object also supports a notification callback to handle messages regarding grammar events. Optionally, the grammar object can create an SR Results object. This object is discussed fully in the next section.

The SR Results Object

The SR Results object contains detailed information about the most recent speech recognition event. This could include a recorded representation of the speech, the interpreted phrase constructed by the engine, the name of the speaker, performance statistics, and so on.

> **NOTE**
>
> The SR Results object is optional and is not supported by all engines.

Table 15.4 shows the interfaces defined for the SR Results object, along with descriptions of their use. Only the first interface in the table is required (the ISRResBasic interface).

Table 15.4. The defined interfaces for the SR Results object.

Interface Name	Description
ISRResBasic	Used to provide basic information about the results object, including an audio representation of the phrase, the selected interpretation of the audio, the grammar used to analyze the input, and the start and stop time of the recognition event.
ISRResAudio	Used to retrieve an audio representation of the recognized phrase. This audio file can be played back to the speaker or saved as a WAV format file for later review.
ISRResGraph	Used to produce a graphic representation of the recognition event. This graph could show the phonemes used to construct the phrase, show the engine's "score" for accurately detecting the phrase, and so on.
ISRResCorrection	Used to provide an opportunity to confirm that the interpretation was accurate, possibly allowing for a correction in the analysis.
ISRResEval	Used to re-evaluate the results of the previous recognition. This could be used by the engine to request the speaker to repeat training phrases and use the new information to re-evaluate previous interpretations.
ISRResSpeaker	Used to identify the speaker performing the dictation. Could be used to improve engine performance by comparing stored information from previous sessions with the same speaker.

Interface Name	Description
ISRResModifyGUI	Used to provide a pop-up window asking the user to confirm the engine's interpretation. Could also provide a list of alternate results to choose from.
ISRResMerge	Used to merge data from two different recognition events into a single unit for evaluation purposes. This can be done to improve the system's knowledge about a speaker or phrase.
ISRResMemory	Used to allocate and release memory used by results objects. This is strictly a housekeeping function.

Text-to-Speech

The low-level text-to-speech services are provided by one primary object—the TTS Engine object. Like the SR object set, the TTS object set has an Enumerator object and an Engine Enumerator object. These objects are used to locate and select a valid TTS Engine object and are then discarded (see Figure 15.3).

FIGURE 15.3.
Mapping the low-level SAPI objects.

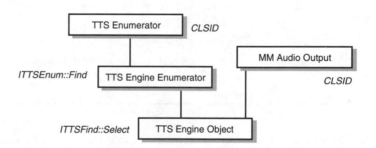

The TTS services also use an audio output object. The default object for output is the PC speakers, but this can be set to the telephone device. Applications can also create their own output devices, including the creation of a WAV format recording device as the output for TTS engine activity.

The rest of this section discusses the details of the low-level SAPI TTS objects.

The TTS Enumerator and Engine Enumerator Objects

The TTS Enumerator and Engine Enumerator objects are used to obtain a list of the available TTS engines and their speaking modes. They both support two interfaces:

■ ITTSEnum—Used to obtain a list of the available TTS engines.

■ ITTSFind—Used to obtain a pointer to the requested TTS engine.

Once the objects have provided a valid address to a TTS engine object, the TTS Enumerator and Engine Enumerator objects can be discarded.

The TTS Engine Object

The TTS Engine object is the primary object of low-level SAPI TTS services. The Engine object supports several interfaces. Table 15.5 lists the interfaces used for the translations of text into audible speech.

Table 15.5. The TTS Engine object interfaces.

Interface Name	Description
ITTSCentral	The main interface for the TTS engine object. It is used to register an application with the TTS system, starting, pausing, and stopping the TTS playback, and so on.
ITTSDialogs	Used to provide a connection to several dialog boxes. The exact contents of each dialog box is determined by the engine provider, not by Microsoft. Dialog boxes defined for the interface are: About Box General Dialog Lexicon Dialog Training Dialog
ITTSAttributes	Used to set and retrieve control parameters of the TTS engine, including playback speed and volume, playback device, and so on.

In addition to the interfaces described in Table 15.5, the TTS Engine object supports two notification callbacks:

- ITTSNotifySink—Used to send the application messages regarding the playback of text as audio output, including start and stop of playback and other events.
- ITTSBufNotifysink—Used to send messages regarding the status of text in the playback buffer. If the content of the buffer changes, messages are sent to the application using the TTS engine.

Speech Objects and OLE Automation

Microsoft supplies an OLE Automation type library with the Speech SDK. This type library can be used with any VBA-compliant software, including Visual Basic, Access, Excel, and others. The OLE Automation set provides high-level SAPI services only. The objects, properties, and methods are quite similar to the objects and interfaces provided by the high-level SAPI services described at the beginning of this chapter.

There are two type library files in the Microsoft Speech SDK:

- VCAUTO.TLB supplies the speech recognition services.
- VTXTAUTO.TLB supplies the text-to-speech services.

You can load these libraries into a Visual Basic project by way of the Tools ¦ References menu item (see Figure 15.4).

FIGURE 15.4.

Loading the Voice Command and Voice Text type libraries.

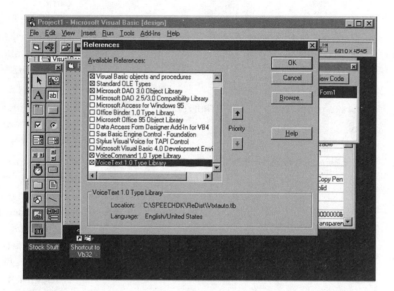

OLE Automation Speech Recognition Services

The OLE Automation speech recognition services are implemented using two objects:

- The OLE Voice Command object
- The OLE Voice Menu object

The OLE Voice Command object has three properties and two methods. Table 15.6 shows the Voice Command object's properties and methods, along with their parameters and short descriptions.

Table 15.6. The properties and methods of the OLE Voice Command **object.**

Property/Method Name	Parameters	Description
Register method		This method is used to register the application with the SR engine. It must be called before any speech recognition will occur.
CallBack property	Project.Class as string	Visual Basic 4.0 programs can use this property to identify an existing class module that has two special methods defined. (See the following section, "Using the Voice Command Callback.")
Awake property	TRUE/FALSE	Use this property to turn on or off speech recognition for the application.
CommandSpoken property	cmdNum as integer	Use this property to determine which command was heard by the SR engine. VB4 applications do not need to use this property if they have installed the callback routines described earlier. All other programming environments must poll this value (using a timer) to determine the command that has been spoken.
MenuCreate method	appName as String, state as String, langID as Integer, dialect as String, flags as Long	Use this method to create a new menu object. Menu objects are used to add new items to the list of valid commands to be recognized by the SR engine.

Using the Voice Command Callback

The Voice Command type library provides a unique and very efficient method for registering callbacks using a Visual Basic 4.0 class module. In order to establish an automatic notification from the SR engine, all you need to do is add a VB4 class module to your application. This class module must have two functions created:

■ CommandRecognize—This event is fired each time the SR engine recognizes a command that belongs to your application's list.

■ CommandOther—This event is fired each time the SR engine receives spoken input it cannot understand.

Listing 15.1 shows how these two routines look in a class module.

Listing 15.1. Creating the notification routines for the Voice Command **object.**

```
'Sent when a spoken phrase was either recognized as being from another
➥application's
'command set or was not recognized.
Function CommandOther(pszCommand As String, pszApp As String, pszState As String)
    If Len(pszCommand) = 0 Then
        VcintrForm.StatusMsg.Text = "Command unrecognized" & Chr(13) & Chr(10) &
➥VcintrForm.StatusMsg.Text
    Else
        VcintrForm.StatusMsg.Text = pszCommand & " was recognized from " & pszApp &
➥"'s " & pszState & " menu" & Chr(13) & Chr(10) & VcintrForm.StatusMsg.Text
    End If

End Function


'Sent when a spoken phrase is recognized as being from the application's
➥commandset.
Function CommandRecognize(pszCommand As String, dwID As Long)
    VcintrForm.StatusMsg.Text = pszCommand & Chr(13) & Chr(10) &
➥VcintrForm.StatusMsg.Text
End Function
```

NOTE

You'll learn more about how to use the Voice Command object in Chapter 19, "Creating SAPI Applications with C++."

The Voice Menu **Object**

The OLE Voice Menu object is used to add new commands to the list of valid items that can be recognized by the SR engine. The Voice Menu object has two properties and three methods. Table 15.7 shows the Voice Menu object's methods and properties, along with parameters and short descriptions.

Table 15.7. The properties and methods of the OLE Voice Menu **object.**

Property/Method	Parameters	Description
hWndMenu property	hWnd as long	Sets the window handle for a voice menu. Whenever this window is the foreground window, the voice menu is automatically activated; otherwise, it is deactivated. If this property is set to NULL, the menu is global.
Active property	TRUE/FALSE	Use this to turn the menu on or off. If this is set to TRUE, the menu is active. The menu must be active before its commands will be recognized by the SR engine.
Add method	id as Long, command as String, category as String, description as String	Adds a new menu to the list of recognizable menus. The command parameter contains the actual menu item the SR engine will listen for. The id parameter will be returned when the SR engine recognizes that the command has been spoken. The other parameters are optional.
Remove method	id as Long	Removes an item from the menu list. The id parameter is the same value used to create the menu in the Add method.
ListSet method	Name as String, Elements as Long, Data as String	Add a list of possible entries for use with a command (see "Using Command Lists with the Voice Menu Object" later in this chapter). Name is the name of the list referred to in a command. Elements is the total number of elements in this list. Data is the set of elements, separated by a chr(0).

Using Command Lists with the Voice Menu Object

The Voice Menu object allows you to define a command that refers to a list. You can then load this list into the grammar using the ListSet method. For example, you can use the Add method to create a command to send e-mail messages. Then you can use the `ListSet` method to create a list of people to receive e-mail (see Listing 15.2).

Listing 15.2. Using the `Add` and `ListSet` methods of the `Voice Menu` object.

```
Dim Names
Dim szNULL as String
szNULL = Chr(0)
.
.
Call vMenu.Add(109, "Send email to <Names>")
Names = "Larry" & szNULL & "Mike" & szNULL & "Gib" & szNULL & "Doug" & szNULL &
➥"George" & szNull
Call Vmenu.ListSet("Names", 5, Names)
```

OLE Automation Text-to-Speech Services

You can gain access to the OLE Automation TTS services using only one object—the `Voice Text` object. The `Voice Text` object has four properties and seven methods. Table 15.8 shows the properties and methods, along with their parameters and short descriptions.

Table 15.8. The properties and methods of the `Voice Text` object.

Property/Method	Parameters	Description
Register method	AppName as string	Used to register the application with the TTS engine. This must be called before any other methods are called.
Callback property	Project.Class as string	This property is used to establish a callback interface between the `Voice Text` object and your program. See the "Using the Voice Text Callback" section later in this chapter.
Enabled property	TRUE/FALSE	Use this property to turn the TTS service on or off. This must be set to TRUE for the `Voice Text` object to speak text.
Speed property	lSpeed as Long	Setting this value controls the speed (in words per minute) at which text is spoken. Setting the value to 0 sets the slowest speed. Setting the value to -1 sets the fastest speed.

continues

Table 15.8. continued

Property/Method	Parameters	Description
IsSpeaking	TRUE/FALSE	Indicates whether the TTS engine is currently speaking text. You can poll this read-only property to determine when the TTS engine is busy or idle. Note that VB4 programmers should use the Callback property instead of this property.
Speak method	cText as string, lFlags as Long	Use this method to get the TTS engine to speak text. The lFlags parameter can contain a value to indicate this is a statement, question, and so on.
StopSpeaking method	(none)	Use this method to force the TTS engine to stop speaking the current text.
AudioPause	(none)	Use this method to pause all TTS activity. This affects all applications using TTS services at this site (PC).
AudioResume	(none)	Use this method to resume TTS activity after calling AudioPause. This affects all applications using TTS services at this site (PC).
AudioRewind	(none)	Use this method to back up the TTS playback approximately one phrase or sentence.
AudioFastForward	(none)	Use this method to advance the TTS engine approximately one phrase or sentence.

Using the Voice Text Callback

The Voice Text type library provides a unique and very efficient method for registering callbacks using a Visual Basic 4.0 class module. In order to establish an automatic notification from the TTS engine, all you need to do is add a VB4 class module to your application. This class module must have two functions created:

- SpeakingStarted—This event is fired each time the TTS engine begins speaking text.
- SpeakingDone—This event is fired each time the TTS engine stops speaking text.

Listing 15.3. Creating the notification routines for a Voice Text **object.**

```
Function SpeakingDone()
    VtintrForm.StatusMsg.Text = "Speaking Done notification" & Chr(13) & Chr(10) &
➥VtintrForm.StatusMsg.Text
End Function

Function SpeakingStarted()
    VtintrForm.StatusMsg.Text = "Speaking Started notification" & Chr(13) & Chr(10)
➥& VtintrForm.StatusMsg.Text
End Function
```

Only VB4 applications can use this method of establishing callbacks through class modules. If you are using the TTS objects with other VBA-compatible languages, you need to set up a routine, using a timer, that will regularly poll the IsSpeaking property. The IsSpeaking property is set to TRUE while the TTS engine is speaking text.

Summary

In this chapter you learned the details of the SR and TTS interfaces defined by the Microsoft SAPI model. You learned that the SAPI model is based on the Component Object Model (COM) interface and that Microsoft has defined two distinct levels of SAPI services:

- *High-level SAPI*—This provides a command-and-control level of service. This is good for detecting menu and system-level commands and for speaking simple text.
- *Low-level SAPI*—This provides a much more flexible interface and allows programmers access to extended SR and TTS services.

You learned that the two levels of SAPI service each contain several COM interfaces that allow C programmers access to speech services. These interfaces include the ability to set and get engine attributes, turn the services on or off, display dialog boxes for user interaction, and perform direct TTS and SR functions.

Since the SAPI model is based on the COM interface, high-level languages such as Visual Basic cannot directly call functions using the standard API calls. Instead, Microsoft has developed OLE Automation type libraries for use with Visual Basic and other VBA-compliant systems. The two type libraries are:

- *Voice Command Objects*—This provides access to speech recognition services.
- *Voice Text Objects*—This provides access to text-to-speech services.

You now have a good understanding of the types of speech recognition and text-to-speech services that are available with the Microsoft SAPI model. In the next chapter, you'll learn about details surrounding the design and implementation of SAPI applications, including typical hardware required, technology limits, and design considerations when building SAPI applications.

16

SAPI Basics

This chapter covers a handful of issues that must be addressed when designing and installing SR/TTS applications, including hardware requirements, and the state of current SR/TTS technology and its limits. The chapter also includes some tips for designing your SR/TTS applications.

SR/TTS applications can be resource hogs. The section on hardware shows you the minimal, recommended, and preferred processor and RAM requirements for the most common SR/TTS applications. Of course, speech applications also need special hardware, including audio cards, microphones, and speakers. In this chapter, you'll find a general list of compatible devices, along with tips on what other options you have and how to use them.

You'll also learn about the general state of SR/TTS technology and its limits. This will help you design applications that do not place unrealistic demands on the software or raise users' expectations beyond the capabilities of your application.

Finally, this chapter contains a set of tips and suggestions for designing and implementing SR/TTS services. You'll learn how to design SR and TTS interfaces that reduce the chance of engine errors, and increase the usability of your programs.

When you complete this chapter, you'll know just what hardware is needed for speech systems and how to design programs that can successfully implement SR/TTS services that really work.

SAPI Hardware

Speech systems can be resource intensive. It is especially important that SR engines have enough RAM and disk space to respond quickly to user requests. Failure to respond quickly results in additional commands spoken into the system. This has the effect of creating a spiraling degradation in performance. The worse things get, the worse things get. It doesn't take too much of this before users decide your software is more trouble than it's worth!

Text-to-speech engines can also tax the system. While TTS engines do not always require a great deal of memory to operate, insufficient processor speed can result in halting or unintelligible playback of text.

For these reasons, it is important to establish clear hardware and software requirements when designing and implementing your speech-aware and speech-enabled applications. Not all PCs will have the memory, disk space, and hardware needed to properly implement SR and TTS services. There are three general categories of workstation resources that should be reviewed:

- *General hardware*, including processor speed and RAM memory
- *Software*, including operating system and SR/TTS engines
- *Special hardware*, including sound cards, microphones, speakers, and headphones

The following three sections provide some general guidelines to follow when establishing minimal resource requirements for your applications.

General Hardware Requirements

Speech systems can tax processor and RAM resources. SR services require varying levels of resources depending on the type of SR engine installed and the level of services implemented. TTS engine requirements are rather stable, but also depend on the TTS engine installed.

The SR and TTS engines currently available for SAPI systems usually can be successfully implemented using as little as a 486/33 processor chip and an additional 1MB of RAM. However, overall PC performance with this configuration is pretty poor and is not recommended. A good suggested processor is a Pentium processor (P60 or better) with at least 16MB of total RAM. Systems that will be supporting dictation SR services require the most computational power. It is not unreasonable to expect the workstation to use 32MB of RAM and a P100 or higher processor. Obviously, the more resources, the better the performance.

SR Processor and Memory Requirements

In general, SR systems that implement command and control services will only need an additional 1MB of RAM (not counting the application's RAM requirement). Dictation services should get at least another 8MB of RAM—preferably more. The type of speech sampling, analysis, and size of recognition vocabulary all affect the minimal resource requirements. Table 16.1 shows published minimal processor and RAM requirements of speech recognition services.

Table 16.1. Published minimal processor and RAM requirements of SR services.

Levels of Speech-Recognition Services	Minimal Processor	Minimal Additional RAM
Discrete, speaker-dependent, whole word, small vocabulary	386/16	64K
Discrete, speaker-independent, whole word, small vocabulary	386/33	256K
Continuous, speaker-independent, sub-word, small vocabulary	486/33	1MB
Discrete, speaker-dependent, whole word, large vocabulary	Pentium	8MB
Continuous, speaker-independent, sub-word, large vocabulary	RISC processor	8MB

These memory requirements are in addition to the requirements of the operating system and any loaded applications. The minimal Windows 95 memory model should be 12MB. Recommended RAM is 16MB and 24MB is preferred. The minimal NT memory should be 16MB with 24MB recommended and 32MB preferred.

TTS Processor and Memory Requirements

TTS engines do not place as much of a demand on workstation resources as SR engines. Usually TTS services only require a 486/33 processor and only 1MB of additional RAM. TTS programs themselves are rather small—about 150K. However, the grammar and prosody rules can demand as much as another 1MB depending on the complexity of the language being spoken. It is interesting to note that probably the most complex and demanding language for TTS processing is English. This is primarily due to the irregular spelling patterns of the language.

Most TTS engines use speech synthesis to produce the audio output. However, advanced systems can use diphone concatenation. Since diphone-based systems rely on a set of actual voice samples for reproducing written text, these systems can require an additional 1MB of RAM. To be safe, it is a good idea to suggest a requirement of 2MB of additional RAM, with a recommendation of 4MB for advanced TTS systems.

Software Requirements—Operating Systems and Speech Engines

The general software requirements are rather simple. The Microsoft Speech API can only be implemented on Windows 32-bit operating systems. This means you'll need Windows 95 or Windows NT 3.5 or greater on the workstation.

> **NOTE**
>
> All the testing and programming examples covered in this book have been performed using Windows 95. It is assumed that Windows NT systems will not require any additional modifications.

The most important software requirements for implementing speech services are the SR and TTS engines. An SR/TTS engine is the back-end processing module in the SAPI model. Your application is the front end, and the SPEECH.DLL acts as the broker between the two processes.

The new wave of multimedia PCs usually has SR/TTS engines as part of their initial software package. For existing PCs, most sound cards now ship with SR/TTS engines.

Microsoft's Speech SDK does not include a set of SR/TTS engines. However, Microsoft does have an engine on the market. Their Microsoft Phone software system (available as part of modem/sound card packages) includes the Microsoft Voice SR/TTS engine. You can also purchase engines directly from third-party vendors.

> **NOTE**
>
> Refer to Appendix B, "SAPI Resources," for a list of vendors that support the Speech API. You can also check the CD-ROM that ships with this book for the most recent list of SAPI vendors. Finally, the Microsoft Speech SDK contains a list of SAPI engine providers in the ENGINE.DOC file.

Special Hardware Requirements—Sound Cards, Microphones, and Speakers

Complete speech-capable workstations need three additional pieces of hardware:

- A *sound card* for audio reproduction
- *Speakers* for audio playback
- A *microphone* for audio input

Just about any sound card can support SR/TTS engines. Any of the major vendors' cards are acceptable, including Sound Blaster and its compatibles, Media Vision, ESS technology, and others. Any card that is compatible with Microsoft's Windows Sound System is also acceptable.

Many vendors are now offering multifunction cards that provide speech, data, FAX, and telephony services all in one card. You can usually purchase one of these cards for about $250-$500. By installing one of these new cards, you can upgrade a workstation and reduce the number of hardware slots in use at the same time.

A few speech-recognition engines still need a *DSP* (*digital signal processor*) card. While it may be preferable to work with newer cards that do not require DSP handling, there are advantages to using DSP technology. DSP cards handle some of the computational work of interpreting speech input. This can actually reduce the resource requirements for providing SR services. In systems where speech is a vital source of process input, DSP cards can noticeably boost performance.

SR engines require the use of a microphone for audio input. This is usually handled by a directional microphone mounted on the PC base. Other options include the use of a *lavaliere microphone* draped around the neck, or a headset microphone that includes headphones. Depending on the audio card installed, you may also be able to use a telephone handset for input.

Most multimedia systems ship with a suitable microphone built into the PC or as an external device that plugs into the sound card. It is also possible to purchase high-grade unidirectional microphones from audio retailers. Depending on the microphone and the sound card used, you may need an amplifier to boost the input to levels usable by the SR engine.

The quality of the audio input is one of the most important factors in successful implementation of speech services on a PC. If the system will be used in a noisy environment, close-talk microphones should be used. This will reduce extraneous noise and improve the recognition capabilities of the SR engine.

Speakers or headphones are needed to play back TTS output. In private office spaces, free-standing speakers provide the best sound reproduction and fewest dangers of ear damage through high-levels of playback. However, in larger offices, or in areas where the playback can disturb others, headphones are preferred.

> **TIP**
>
> As mentioned earlier in this chapter, some systems can also provide audio playback through a telephone handset. Conversely, the use of free-standing speakers and a microphone can be used successfully as a speaker-phone system.

Technology Issues

As advanced as SR/TTS technology is, it still has its limits. This section covers the general technology issues for SR and TTS engines along with a quick summary of some of the limits of the process and how this can affect perceived performance and system design.

SR Techniques

Speech recognition technology can be measured by three factors:

- Word selection
- Speaker dependence
- Word analysis

Word selection deals with the process of actually perceiving "word items" as input. Any speech engine must have some method for listening to the input stream and deciding when a word item has been uttered. There are three different methods for selecting words from the input stream. They are:

- Discrete speech
- Word spotting
- Continuous speech

Discrete speech is the simplest form of word selection. Under discrete speech, the engine requires a slight pause between each word. This pause marks the beginning and end of each word item. Discrete speech requires the least amount of computational resources. However, discrete speech is not very natural for users. With a discrete speech system, users must speak in a halting voice. This may be adequate for short interactions with the speech system, but rather annoying for extended periods.

A much more preferred method of handling speech input is word spotting. Under *word spotting*, the speech engine listens for a list of key words along the input stream. This method allows users to use continuous speech. Since the system is "listening" for key words, users do not need to use unnatural pauses while they speak. The advantage of word spotting is that it gives users the perception that the system is actually listening to every word while limiting the amount of resources required by the engine itself. The disadvantage of word spotting is that the system can easily misinterpret input. For example, if the engine recognizes the word *run*, it will interpret the phrases "Run Excel" and "Run Access" as the same phrase. For this reason, it is important to design vocabularies for word-spotting systems that limit the possibility of confusion.

The most advanced form of word selection is the continuous speech method. Under *continuous speech*, the SR engine attempts to recognize each word that is uttered in real time. This is the most resource-intensive of the word selection methods. For this reason, continuous speech is best reserved for dictation systems that require complete and accurate perception of every word.

The process of word selection can be affected by the speaker. *Speaker dependence* refers to the engine's ability to deal with different speakers. Systems can be speaker dependent, speaker independent, or speaker adaptive. The disadvantage of speaker-dependent systems is that they require extensive training by a single user before they become very accurate. This training can last as much as one hour before the system has an accuracy rate of over 90 percent. Another drawback to speaker-dependent systems is that each new user must re-train the system to reduce confusion and improve performance. However, speaker-dependent systems provide the greatest degree of accuracy while using the least amount of computing resources.

Speaker-adaptive systems are designed to perform adequately without training, but they improve with use. The advantage of speaker-adaptive systems is that users experience success without tedious training. Disadvantages include additional computing resource requirements and possible reduced performance on systems that must serve different people.

Speaker-independent systems provide the greatest degree of accuracy without performance. Speaker-independent systems are a must for installations where multiple speakers need to use the same station. The drawback of speaker-independent systems is that they require the greatest degree of computing resources.

Once a word item has been selected, it must be analyzed. *Word analysis* techniques involve matching the word item to a list of known words in the engine's vocabulary. There are two methods for handling word analysis: *whole-word matching* or *sub-word matching*. Under whole-word matching, the SR engine matches the word item against a vocabulary of complete word templates. The advantage of this method is that the engine is able to make an accurate match very quickly, without the need for a great deal of computing power. The disadvantage of whole-word matching is that it requires extremely large vocabularies—into the tens of thousands of entries. Also, these words must be stored as spoken templates. Each word can require as much as 512 bytes of storage.

An alternate word-matching method involves the use of sub-words called *phonemes*. Each language has a fixed set of phonemes that are used to build all words. By informing the SR engine of the phonemes and their representations it is much easier to recognize a wider range of words. Under sub-word matching, the engine does not require an extensive vocabulary. An additional advantage of sub-word systems is that the pronunciation of a word can be determined from printed text. Phoneme storage requires only 5 to 20 bytes per phoneme. The disadvantage of sub-word matching is that is requires more processing resources to analyze input.

SR Limits

It is important to understand the limits of current SR technology and how these limits affect system performance. Three of the most vital limitations of current SR technology are:

- Speaker identification
- Input recognition
- Recognition accuracy

The first hurdle for SR engines is determining when the speaker is addressing the engine and when the words are directed to someone else in the room. This skill is beyond the SR systems currently on the market. Your program must allow users to inform the computer that you are addressing the engine. Also, SR engines cannot distinguish between multiple speakers. With speaker-independent systems, this is not a big problem. However, speaker-dependent systems cannot deal well in situations where multiple users may be addressing the same system.

Even speaker-independent systems can have a hard time when multiple speakers are involved. For example, a dictation system designed to transcribe a meeting will not be able to differentiate between speakers. Also, SR systems fail when two people are speaking at the same time.

SR engines also have limits regarding the processing of identified words. First, SR engines have no ability to process natural language. They can only recognize words in the existing vocabulary and process them based on known grammar rules. Thus, despite any perceived "friendliness" of speech-enabled systems, they do not really understand the speaker at all.

SR engines also are unable to hear a new word and derive its meaning from previously spoken words. The system is incapable of spelling or rendering words that are not already in its vocabulary.

Finally, SR engines are not able to deal with wide variations in pronunciation of the same word. For example, words such as either (*ee-ther* or *I-ther*) and potato (*po-tay-toe* or *po-tah-toe*) can easily confuse the system. Wide variations in pronunciation can greatly reduce the accuracy of SR systems.

Recognition accuracy can be affected by regional dialects, quality of the microphone, and the ambient noise level during a speech session. Much like the problem with pronunciation, dialect variations can hamper SR engine performance. If your software is implemented in a location where the common speech contains local slang or other region-specific words, these words may be misinterpreted or not recognized at all.

Poor microphones or noisy office spaces also affect accuracy. A system that works fine in a quiet, well-equipped office may be unusable in a noisy facility. In a noisy environment, the SR engine is more likely to confuse similar-sounding words such as *out* and *pout*, or *in* and *when*. For this reason it is important to emphasize the value of a good microphone and a quiet environment when performing SR activities.

TTS Techniques

TTS engines use two different techniques for turning text input into audio output—synthesis or diphone concatenation. *Synthesis* involves the creation of human speech through the use of stored phonemes. This method results in audio output that is understandable, but not very human-like. The advantage of synthesis systems is that they do not require a great deal of storage space to implement and that they allow for the modification of voice quality through the adjustment of only a few parameters.

Diphone-based systems produce output that is much closer to human speech. This is because the system stores actual human speech phoneme sets and plays them back. The disadvantage of this method is that it requires more computing and storage capacity. However, if your application is used to provide long sessions of audio output, diphone systems produce a speech quality much easier to understand.

TTS Limits

TTS engines are limited in their ability to re-create the details of spoken language, including the rhythm, accent, and pitch inflection. This combination of properties is call the *prosody* of speech. TTS engines are not very good at adding prosody. For this reason, listening to TTS output can be difficult, especially for long periods of time. Most TTS engines allow users to edit text files with embedded control information that adds prosody to the ASCII text. This is useful for systems that are used to "read" text that is edited and stored for later retrieval.

TTS systems have their limits when it comes to producing individualized voices. Synthesis-based engines are relatively easy to modify to create new voice types. This modification involves the adjustment of general pitch and speed to produce new vocal personalities such as "old man,". "child," "female," "male," and so on. However, these voices still use the same prosody and grammar rules.

Creating new voices for diphone-based systems is much more costly than for synthesis-based systems. Since each new vocal personality must be assembled from pre-recorded human speech, it can take quite a bit of time and effort to alter an existing voice set or to produce a new one. Diphone concatenation is costly for systems that must support multiple languages or need to provide flexibility in voice personalities.

General SR Design Issues

There are a number of general issues to keep in mind when designing SR interfaces to your applications.

First, if you provide speech services within your application, you'll need to make sure you let the user know the services are available. This can be done by adding a graphic image to the display, telling the user that the computer is "listening," or you can add caption or status items that indicate the current state of the SR engine.

It is also a good idea to make speech services an optional feature whenever possible. Some installations may not have the hardware or RAM required to implement speech services. Even if the workstation has adequate resources, the user may experience performance degradation with the speech services active. It is a good idea to have a menu option or some other method that allows users to turn off speech services entirely.

When you add speech services to your programs, it is important to make sure you give users realistic expectations regarding the capabilities of the installation. This is best done through user documentation. You needn't go into great length, but you should give users general information about the state of SR technology, and make sure users do not expect to carry on extensive conversations with their new "talking electronic pal."

Along with indications that speech services are active, it is a good idea to provide users with a single speech command that displays a list of recognized speech inputs, and some general online help regarding the use and capabilities of the SR services of your program. Since the total number of commands might be quite large, you may want to provide a type of voice-activated help system that allows users to query the current command set and then ask additional questions to learn more about the various speech commands they can use.

It is also a good idea to add confirmations to especially dangerous or ambiguous speech commands. For example, if you have a voice command for "Delete," you should ask the user to confirm this option before continuing. This is especially important if you have other commands that may sound similar—if you have both "Delete" and "Repeat" in the command list you will want to make sure the system is quite sure which command was requested.

In general, it is a good idea to display the status of all speech processing. If the system does not understand a command, it is important to tell users rather than making them sit idle while your program waits for understandable input. If the system cannot identify a command, display a message telling the user to repeat the command, or bring up a dialog box that lists likely possibilities from which the user can select the requested command.

In some situations, background noise can hamper the performance of the SR engine. It is advisable to allow users to turn off speech services and only turn them back on when they are needed. This can be handled through a single button press or menu selection. In this way, stray noise will not be misinterpreted as speech input.

There are a few things to avoid when adding voice commands to an application. SR systems are not very successful when processing long series of numbers or single letters. "M" and "N" sound quite alike, and long lists of digits can confuse most SR systems. Also, although SR systems are capable of handling requests such as "move mouse left," "move mouse right," and so on, this is not a good use of voice technology. Using voice commands to handle a pointer device is a bit like using the keyboard to play musical notes. It is possible, but not desirable.

Voice Command Menu Design

The key to designing good command menus is to make sure they are complete, consistent, and that they contain unique commands within the set. Good command menus also contain more than just the list of items displayed on the physical menu. It is a good idea to think of voice commands as you would keyboard shortcuts.

Useful voice command menus will provide access to all the common operations that might be performed by the user. For example, the standard menu might offer a top-level menu option of Help. Under the Help menu might be an About item to display the basic information about the loaded application. It makes sense to add a voice command that provides direct access to the About box with a Help About command.

These shortcut commands may span several menu levels or even stand independent of any existing menu. For example, in an application that is used to monitor the status of manufacturing operations within a plant, you might add a command such as Display Statistics that would gather data from several locations and present a graph onscreen.

When designing menus, be sure to include commands for all dialog boxes. It is not a good idea to provide voice commands for only some dialog boxes and not for others.

> **TIP**
>
> You do not have to create menu commands for Windows-supplied dialog boxes (the Common Dialogs, the Message Box, and so on). Windows automatically supplies voice commands for these dialogs.

Be sure to include voice commands for the list and combo boxes within a dialog box, as well as the command buttons, check boxes, and option buttons.

In addition to creating menus for all the dialog boxes of your applications, you should consider creating a "global" menu that is active as long as the application is running. This would allow users to execute common operations such as *Get New Mail* or *Display Status Log* without having to first bring the application into the foreground.

> **TIP**
>
> It is advisable to limit this use of speech services to only a few vital and unique commands since any other applications that have speech services may also activate global commands.

It is also important to include common alternate wordings for commonly used operations, such as *Get New Mail* and *Check for New Mail*, and so on. Although you may not be able to include all possible alternatives, adding a few will greatly improve the accessibility of your speech interface.

Use consistent word order in your menu design. For example, for action commands you should use the verb-noun construct, as in *Save File* or *Check E-Mail*. For questions, use a consistent preface such as *How do I...* or *Help Me...*, as in *How do I check e-mail?* or *Help me change font*. It is also important to be consistent with the use of singular and plural. In the above example, you must be sure to use *Font* or *Fonts* throughout the application.

Since the effectiveness of the SR engine is determined by its ability to identify your voice input against a list of valid words, you can increase the accuracy of the SR engine by keeping the command lists relatively short. When a command is spoken, the engine will scan the list of valid inputs in this state and select the most likely candidate. The more words on the list, the greater the chance the engine will select the wrong command. By limiting the list, you can increase the odds of a correct "hit."

Finally, you can greatly increase the accuracy of the SR engine by avoiding similar-sounding words in commands. For example, *repeat* and *delete* are dangerously similar. Other words that are easily confused are *go* and *no*, and even *on* and *off*. You can still use these words in your application if you use them in separate states. In other words, do not use *repeat* in the same set of menu options as *delete*.

TTS Design Issues

There are a few things to keep in mind when adding text-to-speech services to your applications. First, make sure you design your application to offer TTS as an option, not as a required service. Your application may be installed on a workstation that does not have the required resources, or the user may decided to turn off TTS services to improve overall performance.

For this reason, it is also important to provide visual as well as aural feedback for all major operations. For example, when processing is complete, it is a good idea to inform the user with a dialog box as well as a spoken message.

Because TTS engines typically produce a voice that is less than human-like, extended sessions of listening to TTS output can be tiring to users. It is a good idea to limit TTS output to short phrases. For example, if your application gathers status data on several production operations on the shop floor, it is better to have the program announce the completion of the process (for example, *Status report complete*) instead of announcing the details of the findings. Alternatively, your TTS application could announce a short summary of the data (for example, *All operations on time and within specifications*).

If your application must provide extended TTS sessions you should consider using pre-recorded WAV files for output. For example, if your application should allow users aural access to company regulations or documentation, it is better to record a person reading the documents, and then play back these recordings to users upon request. Also, if your application provides a limited set of vocal responses to the user, it is advisable to use WAV recordings instead of TTS output. A good example of this would be telephony applications that ask users questions and respond with fixed answers.

Finally, it is not advisable to mix WAV output and TTS output in the same session. This highlights the differences between the quality of recorded voice and computer-generated speech. Switching between WAV and TTS can also make it harder for users to understand the TTS voice since they may be expecting a familiar recorded voice and hear computer-generated TTS instead.

Summary

This chapter covered three main topics:

■ Hardware and software requirements for SAPI applications
■ The state of the art and limits of SR/TTS technology
■ Design tips for adding speech services to Windows applications

The Microsoft Speech SDK only works on 32-bit operating systems. This means you will need Windows 95 or Windows NT version 3.5 or greater in order to run SAPI applications.

The minimum, recommended, and preferred processor and RAM requirements for SAPI applications vary depending on the level of services your application provides. The minimum SAPI-enabled system may need as little as 1MB of additional RAM and be able to run on a 486/33 processor. However, it is a good idea to require at least Pentium 60 processor and an additional 8MB RAM. This will give your applications the additional computational power needed for the most typical SAPI implementations.

SAPI systems can use just about any of the current sound cards on the market today. Any card that is compatible with the Windows Sound System or with Sound Blaster systems will work fine. You should use a close-talk, unidirectional microphone, and use either external speakers or headphones for monitoring audio output.

You learned that SR technology uses three basic processes for interpreting audio input:

- Word selection
- Word analysis
- Speaker dependence

You also learned that SR systems have their limits. SR engines cannot automatically distinguish between multiple speakers, cannot learn new words, guess at spelling, or handle wide variations in word pronunciation (for example, *to-may-toe* or *to-mah-toe*).

TTS engine technology is based on two different types of implementation. Synthesis systems create audio output by generating audio tones using algorithms. This results in unmistakably computer-like speech. Diphone concatenation is an alternate method for generating speech. Diphones are a set of phoneme pairs collected from actual human speech samples. The TTS engine is able to convert text into phoneme pairs and match them to diphones in the TTS engine database. TTS engines are not able to mimic human speech patterns and rhythms (called *prosody*) and are not very good at communicating emotions. Also, most TTS engines experience difficulty with unusual words. This can result in odd-sounding phrases.

Finally, you learned some tips on designing and implementing speech services. Some of the tips covered here were:

- Make SR and TTS services optional whenever possible.
- Design voice command menus to provide easy access to all major operations.
- Avoid similar-sounding words and inconsistent word order and keep command lists short.
- Limit TTS use to short playback, use WAV recordings for long playback sessions.
- Don't mix TTS and WAV playback in the same session.

In the next chapter, you'll use the information you learned here to start creating SAPI-enabled applications.

17

SAPI Tools—Using SAPI Objects with Visual Basic 4.0

The Microsoft Speech SDK contains a set of OLE library files for implementing SAPI services using Visual Basic and other VBA-compatible languages. In this chapter, you'll learn how to use the objects, methods, and properties in the OLE library to add speech recognition (SR) and text-to-speech (TTS) services to your Windows applications.

There are two OLE libraries:

- The OLE Voice Text library (VTXTAUTO.TLB)
- The OLE Voice Command library (VCMDAUTO.TLB)

> **NOTE**
>
> The Microsoft SDK supplies these files in the REDIST folder that is created when you install the SDK. You should copy these files from the REDIST folder into the WINDOWS\SYSTEM folder before you begin the examples in this book.

You will first learn to use the Voice Text object to add TTS services to Visual Basic applications. Once you know how to use the Voice Text object, you'll learn how to use the Voice Command and Voice Menu objects to add SR services to Visual Basic applications.

If you have not yet done so, start Visual Basic 4.0 and begin a new project. You'll use Visual Basic to complete all the examples in this section.

OLE Voice Text Object

The Voice Text object is used to provide access to the text-to-speech services of the installed TTS engine. Using the Voice Text object involves only a few simple steps. First, you must register your application with the SAPI services on the workstation. Then you can send text to the Voice Text object for playback. You can use several other methods to rewind, fast-forward, pause, and restart audio playback of the text message.

Using the Visual Basic Object Browser

When using Visual Basic, you can use the Tools ¦ References menu option to load the object library into the Visual Basic design-time environment (see Figure 17.1).

The advantage of this method is that you can use the Visual Basic Object browser to view all the objects, methods, and properties of the library at design time (see Figure 17.2).

FIGURE 17.1.

Loading the OLE Voice Text library into Visual Basic at design time.

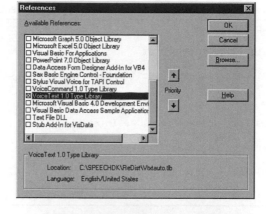

FIGURE 17.2.

Using the Visual Basic Object Browser to inspect the Voice Text library.

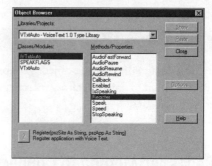

NOTE

Other VBA-compliant languages (Excel, Word, Access, and so on) cannot pre-load the object library. You can still use the SAPI OLE objects as described here, but you will not be able to use the object browser to view the object details at run-time.

Start a new Visual Basic project and add the following code to the general declarations section:

```
Dim objVText as Object ' declare TTS object variable
```

You'll use this variable throughout the project. This is the top-level object for all TTS services. Next you need to add code to the Form_Load event to initialize the TTS object. Also, you need to add code to the Form_Unload event to destroy the TTS object upon exit. Add the code shown in Listing 17.1 to your project.

Listing 17.1. Adding code to the `Form_Load` and `Form_Unload` events.

```
Private Sub Form_Load()
    '
    ' create voice text object
    '
    Set objVText = CreateObject("Speech.VoiceText")
    '
End Sub

Private Sub Form_Unload(Cancel As Integer)
    '
    ' destroy voice object
    '
    Set objVText = Nothing
    '
End Sub
```

> **TIP**
>
> It's always a good idea to destroy the object variable once you no longer need it.
> Setting the object equal to `Nothing` clears memory of any remaining references to the
> unused objects.

Using the `Register` Method to Connect to the TTS Engine

Once you create a valid TTS object, you must use the `Register` method to register your application with the TTS engine. There are two parameters that you can use with the `Register` method. The first parameter allows you to select the output device that the TTS engine will use for playback. You can leave this parameter empty in order to use the default device. You can also enter the name of any other valid line device such as an attached telephone handset. The second parameter is the name of the application that is requesting TTS services. This second parameter cannot be left blank.

To test the `Register` method, add a new command button to the project, and set its `Name` property to `cmdReg` and its caption to `&Register`. Then add the code shown in Listing 17.2 to the `CmdReg_Click` event.

Listing 17.2. Adding code to the `cmdReg_Click` event.

```
Private Sub cmdReg_Click()
    '
    ' register the app w/ TTS engine
    '
    Dim cDevice As String
    Dim cAppName As String
    '
```

```
        cDevice = "" ' use default value
        cAppName = "Voice Text Demo"
        '
        objVText.register cDevice, cAppName
        '
End Sub
```

Now save the form as VTEXT.FRM and the project as VTEXT.VBP, and run the project. When you press the Register button, you will register your application as ready for TTS services.

Using the Enable Property to Start and Stop the TTS Engine

Once you have registered your application with the TTS engine, you must set the Enabled property to TRUE before you can actually send text to the engine for output.

Add two new buttons to the form. Set the Name property and Caption property of one button to cmdEnable and &Enable, respectively. Set the Name and Caption properties of the next button to cmdDisable and &Disable. Then add the code shown in Listing 17.3.

Listing 17.3. Adding code to the cmdEnable and cmdDisable buttons.

```
Private Sub cmdDisable_Click()
    '
    ' disabling the engine for this site
    '
    objVText.Enabled = False
    '
End Sub

Private Sub cmdEnable_Click()
    '
    ' enable the engine for this site
    '
    objVText.Enabled = True
    '
End Sub
```

NOTE

The Enabled property affects all applications using TTS services at your workstation. *Use this setting with caution.* Changing the Enabled property to FALSE will disable all TTS services registered on your PC. For this reason, it is a good idea to check the Enabled property each time you attempt to speak text.

Using the Speak Method to Play Text

Once you have registered your application with the TTS engine and set the Enabled property to TRUE, you can send text to the engine for playback. The Speak method takes two parameters. The first parameter is the text to play back, and the second parameter is a flag parameter that can be used to establish the statement type and queue priority of the text being sent to the TTS engine.

Every text message sent to the TTS engine must be declared as one of seven types. The OLE Voice Text library has a set of pre-defined constants that can be used to set the statement type of the Speak method option flag. These types are shown in Table 17.1.

Table 17.1. Statement types used by the SAPI TTS engine.

Pre-Defined Constant	Value	Description
Vtxtst_STATEMENT	1	A neutral informative statement, such as *You have new messages.* This is the default type of speech.
Vtxtst_QUESTION	2	A question, such as *Do you want to save the file?*
Vtxtst_COMMAND	4	An instruction to the user, such as *Insert the disk.*
Vtxtst_WARNING	8	A warning, such as *Your printer is out of paper.*
Vtxtst_READING	16	Text that is being read from a document, such as an e-mail message.
Vtxtst_NUMBERS	32	Text that is numeric and that should be read in numeric style.
Vtxtst_SPREADSHEET	64	Text that is being read from a spreadsheet, such as columns of numbers.

WARNING

The flag parameter of the Speak method is *not* optional, but how the value is used depends on the installed TTS engine. It is possible that setting this flag to various values will *not* result in different inflections of voice during playback.

The TTS engine is responsible for playing back messages sent in from all speech-enabled applications on your PC. Each message sent to the TTS engine is played back in the order in which it was received. You can use the flag parameter to control the priority level of the text message you send to the TTS engine. There are three priority levels for a message. The OLE library has a set of pre-defined constants to match the priority values. Table 17.2 shows each of the priority levels, their values, and a short description.

Table 17.2. Priority values used by the SAPI TTS engine.

Pre-Defined Constant	Value	Description
Vtxtsp_VERYHIGH	128	Play the text immediately, interrupting text that is currently being spoken, if any. The interrupted text resumes playing as soon as the very high-priority text is finished, although the interrupted text may not be correctly synchronized.
Vtxtsp_HIGH	256	Play the text as soon as possible, after text that is currently being spoken but before any other text in the queue.
Vtxtsp_NORMAL	512	Add the text to the end of the queue. This is the default priority.

To test the Speak method, you need to add a command button to the form along with a text box and several option buttons with two frame controls. Refer to Figure 17.3 and Table 17.3 as you arrange the controls on the form.

FIGURE 17.3.

Laying out the controls for adding the Speak method to the project.

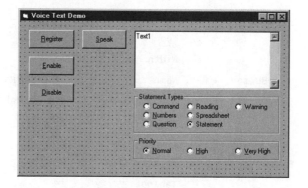

Table 17.3. Control table for the Voice Text Demo form.

Control	Property	Setting
VB.Frame	Name	fraPriority
	Caption	"Priority"
	Height	615
	Left	3120
	TabIndex	13
	Top	3120
	Width	3975
VB.OptionButton	Name	OptPriority
	Caption	"&Very High"
	Height	255
	Index	2
	Left	2760
	TabIndex	16
	Top	240
	Width	1095
VB.OptionButton	Name	OptPriority
	Caption	"&High"
	Height	255
	Index	1
	Left	1440
	TabIndex	15
	Top	240
	Width	1215
VB.OptionButton	Name	OptPriority
	Caption	"&Normal"
	Height	255
	Index	0
	Left	240
	TabIndex	14
	Top	240
	Value	−1 'True
	Width	1215

Control	Property	Setting
VB.Frame	Name	fraType
	Caption	"Statement Types"
	Height	1095
	Left	3120
	TabIndex	5
	Top	1920
	Width	3975
VB.OptionButton	Name	optType
	Caption	"Warning"
	Height	255
	Index	6
	Left	2760
	TabIndex	12
	Top	240
	Width	975
VB.OptionButton	Name	optType
	Caption	"Statement"
	Height	255
	Index	5
	Left	1440
	TabIndex	11
	Top	720
	Value	−1 'True
	Width	1095
VB.OptionButton	Name	optType
	Caption	"Spreadsheet"
	Height	255
	Index	4
	Left	1440
	TabIndex	10
	Top	480
	Width	1215

continues

Table 17.3. continued

Control	Property	Setting
VB.OptionButton	Name	optType
	Caption	"Reading"
	Height	255
	Index	3
	Left	1440
	TabIndex	9
	Top	240
	Width	975
VB.OptionButton	Name	optType
	Caption	"Question"
	Height	255
	Index	2
	Left	240
	TabIndex	8
	Top	720
	Width	1095
VB.OptionButton	Name	optType
	Caption	"&Numbers"
	Height	255
	Index	1
	Left	240
	TabIndex	7
	Top	480
	Width	1095
VB.OptionButton	Name	optType
	Caption	"Command"
	Height	255
	Index	0
	Left	240
	TabIndex	6
	Top	240
	Width	1095

Control	Property	Setting
VB.TextBox	Name	txtSpeak
	Height	1575
	Left	3120
	MultiLine	−1 'True
	ScrollBars	2 'Vertical
	TabIndex	4
	Top	240
	Width	3975
VB.CommandButton	Name	cmdSpeak
	Caption	"&Speak"
	Height	495
	Left	1680
	TabIndex	3
	Top	240
	Width	1215

Note that the option buttons are built as members of control arrays. You'll use this array when you add the code behind the Speak command button. Now add the code from Listing 17.4 to the cmdSpeak_Click event.

Listing 17.4. Adding code to the cmdSpeak_Click event.

```
Private Sub cmdSpeak_Click()
    '
    ' get text and play it back
    '
    Dim iType As Integer ' statement type
    Dim iPriority As Integer ' queue priority
    Dim cText As String ' text to speak
    '
    ' read statement type selection
    iType = IIf(optType(0), vtxtst_COMMAND, iType)
    iType = IIf(optType(1), vtxtst_NUMBERS, iType)
    iType = IIf(optType(2), vtxtst_QUESTION, iType)
    iType = IIf(optType(3), vtxtst_READING, iType)
    iType = IIf(optType(4), vtxtst_SPREADSHEET, iType)
    iType = IIf(optType(5), vtxtst_STATEMENT, iType)
    iType = IIf(optType(6), vtxtst_WARNING, iType)
    '
    ' get priority value
    iPriority = IIf(OptPriority(0), vtxtsp_NORMAL, iPriority)
```

continues

Listing 17.4. continued

```
    iPriority = IIf(OptPriority(1), vtxtsp_HIGH, iPriority)
    iPriority = IIf(OptPriority(2), vtxtsp_VERYHIGH, iPriority)
    '
    ' get text to speak
    cText = txtSpeak.Text
    '
    objVText.Speak cText, iType + iPriority
    '
End Sub
```

This is the minimal set of commands needed to implement speech services. You can provide speech services by simply registering your application, enabling the engine, and executing the Speak method. However, there are additional properties and methods that you can use to control the behavior of the TTS engine.

Adjusting the Speed of Voice Playback

You can adjust the speed of audio playback using the Speed property. The speed of audio playback is measured in *words per minute* (*wpm*). The default speed of playback is 150wpm. Setting the Speed property to 0 causes the engine to speak at the lowest possible speed. Setting it to −1 results in the highest possible speaking speed.

You can use the Speed property to both read and write the playback value. Add a single command button to the form. Set its Name property to cmdSpeed and its Caption property to S&peed. Then add the code shown in Listing 17.5 to the cmdSpeed_Click event.

Listing 17.5. Adding code to the cmdSpeed_Click event.

```
Private Sub cmdSpeed_Click()
    '
    ' determine min and max speed
    ' for this TTS engine
    '
    Dim iMin As Integer
    Dim iMax As Integer
    Static iDefault As Integer
    Dim cMsg As String
    '
    ' get default first time
    If iDefault = 0 Then
        iDefault = objVText.Speed ' get default speed
    End If
    '
    ' get slowest speed
    objVText.Speed = 0 ' set to slowest speed
    iMin = objVText.Speed ' get slowest speed
    '
    ' set fastest speed
    objVText.Speed = -1 ' set to fastest speed
```

```
    iMax = objVText.Speed ' get fastest speed
    '
    ' set back to default value
    objVText.Speed = iDefault
    '
    ' show results
    cMsg = "Slowest Speed: " & CStr(iMin) & Chr(13)
    cMsg = cMsg & "Fastest Speed: " & CStr(iMax) & Chr(13)
    cMsg = cMsg & "Default Speed: " & CStr(iDefault)
    '
    MsgBox cMsg, vbInformation, "Voice Command Speed Settings"
    '
End Sub
```

When you save and run the project, press the Speed button (be sure to press Register and Enabled first). You'll see a message box showing the speed limits of your TTS engine. Your message box should look like the one in Figure 17.4.

FIGURE 17.4.

Displaying the TTS engine speeds.

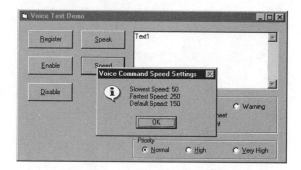

To test the effects of changing playback speed, add two buttons, one label control, and one text box control to the form. Use Table 17.4 and Figure 17.5 as guides when adding these controls.

Table 17.4. Controls for adjusting playback speed.

Control	Property	Setting
VB.CommandButton	Name	cmdSpGet
	Caption	"&Get Speed"
	Height	300
	Left	4560
	TabIndex	20
	Top	3840
	Width	1215

continues

Table 17.4. continued

Control	Property	Setting
VB.CommandButton	Name	cmdSpSet
	Caption	"Se&t Speed"
	Height	300
	Left	5880
	TabIndex	19
	Top	3840
	Width	1215
VB.TextBox	Name	txtSpeed
	Height	300
	Left	3960
	TabIndex	17
	Top	3840
	Width	495
VB.Label	Name	lblSpeed
	Alignment	1 'Right Justify
	Caption	"Speed:"
	Height	300
	Left	3120
	TabIndex	18
	Top	3840
	Width	615

FIGURE 17.5.

Adding the speed controls to the form.

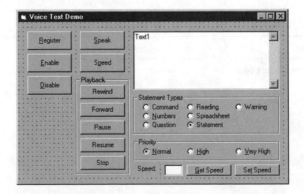

Adding Playback Controls for TTS Services

You can also add the ability to pause, rewind, fast-forward, and restart TTS playback. The TTS fast-forward and rewind methods cause the engine to move the playback pointer approximately one sentence. Refer to Table 17.5 and Figure 17.5 to add the playback button controls to the form.

Table 17.5. Adding the playback buttons to the form.

Control	Property	Setting
VB.Frame	Name	fraAudio
	Caption	"Playback"
	Height	2655
	Left	1560
	TabIndex	26
	Top	1440
	Width	1455
VB.CommandButton	Name	cmdAudio
	Caption	"Stop"
	Height	375
	Index	4
	Left	1680
	TabIndex	27
	Top	3600
	Width	1215
VB.CommandButton	Name	cmdAudio
	Caption	"Resume"
	Height	375
	Index	3
	Left	1680
	TabIndex	25
	Top	3120
	Width	1215
VB.CommandButton	Name	cmdAudio
	Caption	"Pause"

continues

Table 17.5. continued

Control	Property	Setting
	Height	375
	Index	2
	Left	1680
	TabIndex	24
	Top	2640
	Width	1215
VB.CommandButton	Name	cmdAudio
	Caption	"Forward"
	Height	375
	Index	1
	Left	1680
	TabIndex	23
	Top	2160
	Width	1215
VB.CommandButton	Name	cmdAudio
	Caption	"Rewind"
	Height	375
	Index	0
	Left	1680
	TabIndex	22
	Top	1680
	Width	1215

After adding the command button array and the frame control to the form, add the code shown in Listing 17.6 behind the cmdAudio_Click event.

Listing 17.6. Adding code behind the cmdAudio_Click event.

```
Private Sub cmdAudio_Click(Index As Integer)
    '
    ' handle audio playback buttons
    '
    On Error GoTo cmdAudioErr
    '
    Select Case Index
        Case 0 ' rewind
```

```
            objVText.AudioRewind
        Case 1 ' forward
            objVText.AudioFastForward
        Case 2 ' pause
            objVText.AudioPause
        Case 3 ' resume
            objVText.AudioResume
        Case 4 ' stop
             objVText.StopSpeaking
    End Select
    '
    Exit Sub
    '
cmdAudioErr:
    MsgBox Error$, vbCritical, "Audio Playback Error [" & CStr(Err) & "]"
    '
End Sub
```

Getting TTS Status Reports with the `IsSpeaking` Property

You can use the `IsSpeaking` property to check the status of the TTS engine. The `IsSpeaking` property returns `TRUE` if the engine is currently speaking a message, `FALSE` when the engine is idle. You must check the property on a regular basis in order to get up-to-date status reports. The best way to do this is in a timed loop. In Visual Basic, this can be done using the timer control.

Add three new controls to the form: a new frame control (`Name=fraIsSp, Caption=Is Speaking`), a new label control (`Name=lblIsSpeaking, Caption=False`), and a timer control. Refer to Figure 17.6 for the position and size of the controls.

FIGURE 17.6.

Placing the Is Speaking *controls on the form.*

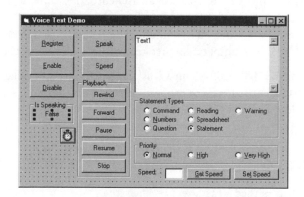

After you place the controls on the form, add the code shown in Listing 17.7 to the `Timer1_Timer` event and the `cmdEnabled_Click` event.

Listing 17.7. Adding code to check the `IsSpeaking` property.

```
Private Sub Timer1_Timer()
    '
    ' update label display
    lblIsSpeaking = CStr(objVText.IsSpeaking)
    '
End Sub

Private Sub cmdEnable_Click()
    '
    ' enable the engine for this site
    '
    objVText.Enabled = True
    '
    ' add code to get voice speed
    cmdSpGet_Click
    '
    ' start timer to check IsSpeaking
    Timer1.Interval = 500
    Timer1.Enabled = True
    '
End Sub
```

After saving and running the program, you can register and enable the TTS services and enter text to be spoken. When you press the Speak button, you can watch the Is Speaking label change from False to True and back again to False.

Establishing a TTS Callback in Visual Basic 4.0

If you are using Visual Basic 4.0 as the platform for the OLE Voice Text library, you can use the Callback property to establish an asynchronous callback from the TTS engine to your Visual Basic program. This link is established by adding a class module to your Visual Basic program. This class module must contain two methods: SpeakingStarted and SpeakingDone. These methods will be automatically invoked by the TTS engine at the appropriate time.

To establish a TTS callback in Visual Basic 4.0, first add a class module. Set its Name property to clsCallBack, its Instance property to MultiUse, Creatable, and its Public property to TRUE. Then add the code in Listing 17.8.

Listing 17.8. Adding methods to the `clsCallBack` class module.

```
Public Function SpeakingDone()
    '
    ' this method will execute when the
    ' TTS engine stops speaking text
    '
    frmVText.lblCallBack = "TTS Engine Idle"
    '
End Function
```

```
Public Function SpeakingStarted()
    '
    ' this method will execute when the
    ' TTS engine starts speaking text
    '
    frmVText.lblCallBack = "TTS Engine Active"
    '
End Function
```

The code in Listing 17.8 creates the class and methods required to link the TTS engine with your Visual Basic application. The next step is to initialize the Callback property. In this step, you are telling the TTS engine the name of the project and the name of the class module that has the two required methods.

To do this, add another command button, frame control, and label control to the form. Use Figure 17.7 and Table 17.6 to place and size the controls.

FIGURE 17.7.

Placement of the
Callback *controls on the*
form.

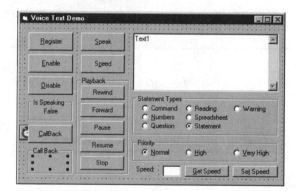

Table 17.6. The Callback controls.

Control	Property	Setting
VB.CommandButton	Name	cmdCallBack
	Caption	"&CallBack"
	Height	495
	Left	240
	TabIndex	32
	Top	2760
	Width	1215
VB.Frame	Name	fraCallBack
	Caption	"Call Back"

continues

Table 17.6. continued

Control	Property	Setting
	Height	735
	Left	240
	TabIndex	30
	Top	3360
	Width	1215
VB.Label	Name	lblCallBack
	Alignment	2 'Center
	Height	375
	Left	120
	TabIndex	31
	Top	240
	Width	975

After adding the controls, place the code shown in Listing 17.9 behind the `CallBack_Click` event.

Listing 17.9. Adding the code to the `CallBack_Click` event.

```
Private Sub cmdCallBack_Click()
    '
    ' register call back for VB4
    '
    objVText.Callback = "VText.clsCallBack"
    '
End Sub
```

This code sets the `Callback` property and informs the TTS engine of the application and class module to use for sending notification messages.

> **WARNING**
>
> Be sure to include the proper application name (found by inspecting the `ProjectName` value on the `Tools ¦ Project` command dialog box) and the proper class name (check the `Name` property of the class module). Failure to do this will result in OLE Automation error 440.

After adding the callback controls, you can save the form (VTEXT.FRM) and the project (VTEXT.VBP) and run the application. After registering and enabling the application, establish the callback by pressing the CallBack button. Then, when you have the TTS engine speak text in the text box, you'll see the TTS engine status messages appear in the Callback frame.

You now know how to use all the methods and properties of the Voice Text object. Next, you'll learn how to use the Voice Command objects to make Visual Basic applications listen to a human voice and translate the audio input into computer commands from a menu.

OLE Voice Command Objects

The Microsoft SR engine is implemented in an OLE object library called VCAUTO.TLB. This file can be added to the Visual Basic 4.0 design-time library through the Tools ¦ References menu, and then you can view the library's objects, methods, and properties using the View ¦ Object Browser option on the main menu.

The OLE Voice Command library contains two objects:

■ The Voice Command object—This is the top-level object used to initialize and control the SR engine.

■ The Voice Menu object—This is the only child object of the Voice Command object. It is used to add and delete voice menu items. Each menu item represents a command recognized by the SR engine.

> **NOTE**
>
> In order to use these examples, you need to have the Microsoft Speech SDK installed on your machine and have the files from the REDIST folder (created when you install the Speech SDK) copied to your WINDOWS\SYSTEM folder. You also need to have an SR engine installed and running. All the examples here were created using the Microsoft Voice SR/TTS engine that ships with Microsoft Phone.

Creating the Voice Command Menu Object

The first step in the process is the creation and initialization of a programming object variable. This variable will act as the top-level object for accessing the SR engine.

Load Visual Basic and start a new project. You need to create two form-level variables that will be used throughout the program. You also need to add code to the Form_Load and Form_Unload events. Listing 17.10 shows the code for these events and the declaration section.

Listing 17.10. Adding code to the `Form_Load` and `Form_Unload` events.

```
Option Explicit

Dim objVCmd As Object
Dim objVMenu As Object

.........

Private Sub Form_Load()
    '
    ' create new voice command object
    '
    Set objVCmd = CreateObject("Speech.VoiceCommand")
    '
End Sub

Private Sub Form_Unload(Cancel As Integer)
    '
    ' destroy the voice command objects
    '
    Set objVCmd = Nothing
    Set objVMenu = Nothing
    '
End Sub
```

Using the `Register` Method to Connect to the SR Engine

After creating the `Voice Command` object, you can use the `Register` method to connect the object to the installed SR engine. Add a command button to the form. Set its `Name` property to `cmdReg` and its `Caption` property to `&Register`. Then add the code shown in Listing 17.11.

Listing 17.11. Adding code to the `cmdReg_Click` event.

```
Private Sub cmdReg_Click()
    '
    ' register w/ SR engine
    '
    objVCmd.Register "" ' use default location
    '
End Sub
```

The `Register` method of the `Voice Command` object takes only one parameter: the device identifier. Passing an empty string results in registering the default input device (usually an attached microphone).

Using the Awake Property to Start and Stop SR Processing

Before the SR engine will attempt to interpret audio input, you must "wake it up" by setting the Awake property to TRUE. You can tell the SR engine to stop listening for commands by setting the Awake property to FALSE.

Add two buttons to the form, named CmdAwake and CmdSleep. Set their Caption properties to &Awake and &Sleep, respectively. Finally, add a label control named lblAwake. This label will contain a status message telling you when the SR engine is listening to you. Then add the code shown in Listing 17.12.

Listing 17.12. Adding code to the cmdAwake and cmdSleep buttons.

```
Private Sub cmdAwake_Click()
    '
    ' wake up the SR engine
    '
    objVCmd.Awake = True
    lblAwake.Caption = "SR Engine is Awake"
    '
End Sub


Private Sub cmdSleep_Click()
    '
    ' tell SR engine to stop listening
    '
    objVCmd.Awake = False
    lblAwake.Caption = "SR Engine is Sleeping"
    '
End Sub
```

Each time you press the Awake button or the Sleep button, the contents of the lblAwake control are updated.

Creating the Menu Object

After establishing the TTS connection and enabling it, you must create a menu object and fill it with menu commands. Then you can activate the menu, and it will respond to your voice.

First, add two new buttons to the form. Set their Name properties to cmdCreate and cmdAdd. Set their Caption properties to &Create Menu and &Add Menu. Next, add the code shown in Listing 17.13 behind the cmdCreate_Click event.

Listing 17.13. Adding code to the `cmdCreate` and `cdmAdd` buttons.

```
Private Sub cmdCrMenu_Click()
    '
    ' create a new menu
    '
    Dim iType As Integer
    Dim cMenuCmd As String
    Dim cMenuState As String
    Dim lMenuLangID As Long
    Dim cDialect As String
    Dim cAppName As String
    '
    ' set default stuff
    cAppName = App.EXEName ' this app
    cMenuState = frmVCmd.Caption ' this window
    cDialect = "" ' use default
    lMenuLangID = 1033 ' US lang nbr
    '
    ' get menu creation type
    iType = IIf(optMenuCmd(0), vcmdmc_CREATE_NEW, iType)
    iType = IIf(optMenuCmd(1), vcmdmc_CREATE_ALWAYS, iType)
    iType = IIf(optMenuCmd(2), vcmdmc_CREATE_TEMP, iType)
    iType = IIf(optMenuCmd(3), vcmdmc_OPEN_ALWAYS, iType)
    iType = IIf(optMenuCmd(4), vcmdmc_OPEN_EXISTING, iType)
    '
    ' now create an empty menu
    Set objVMenu = objVCmd.MenuCreate(cAppName, cMenuState, lMenuLangID, cDialect,
➡iType)
    '
End Sub
```

Creating a menu involves setting several parameters. First, you need to tell the SR engine the name of the application that is requesting services. This must be a unique name, since all responses will be directed by the SR engine, based on this published application name. Next, you need to initialize the MenuState parameter. The menu state is much like the level of a menu. It groups menu items together. All the menus in the same group are considered at the same time when the SR engine is analyzing audio input.

The lMenuLangID helps the engine interpret user input. Most SR engines support only one language. Setting this parameter tells the SR engine what language you plan to speak. You can set the values using the pre-defined Visual Basic 4.0 constants, or by looking up the values in the Visual Basic help files under "Collating Order." Table 17.7 shows the possible language constants in Visual Basic.

Table 17.7. Visual Basic language constants.

Language ID	Description
dbLangGeneral	English, German, French, Portuguese, Italian, and Modern Spanish

Language ID	Description
dbLangArabic	Arabic
dbLangCzech	Czech
dbLangCyrillic	Russian
dbLangDutch	Dutch
dbLangGreek	Greek
dbLangHebrew	Hebrew
dbLangHungarian	Hungarian
dbLangIcelandic	Icelandic
dbLangNordic	Nordic languages (Microsoft Jet database engine version 1.0 only)
dbLangNorwdan	Norwegian and Danish
dbLangPolish	Polish
dbLangSwedfin	Swedish and Finnish
dbLangSpanish	Traditional Spanish
dbLangTurkish	Turkish

NOTE

If you are using Visual Basic 4.0, you can find these constants using the Object Browser. Once you find them, make sure you use only the language portion of the constant. SAPI needs only the language number, not the country code and other items stored in the collating-order constants.

The next value is the `Dialect` parameter. This value can control the character of the spoken word. It is also possible that the SR engine does not use this parameter. A NULL string will use the default dialect built into the speech engine.

Lastly, you need to indicate the type of menu you wish to work with. The SAPI model defines three ways to create new menus and ways to open existing menus. Table 17.8 shows the various versions of the `MenuType` parameter.

Table 17.8. The MenuType parameters.

Pre-Defined VB4 Constant	Value	Description
Vcmdmc_CREATE_NEW	2	Creates an empty menu with the given name. If a menu by that name already exists in the voice command database, the method fails. The new menu is stored in the database when the Voice Menu object is released.
Vcmdmc_CREATE_ALWAYS	4	Creates an empty menu with the given name. If a menu by that name already exists in the voice command database, it is erased. The new menu is stored in the database when the Voice Menu object is released.
Vcmdmc_CREATE_TEMP	1	Creates an empty menu with the given name. If a menu by that name already exists in the voice command database, the method fails. The new menu is temporary and is discarded when the Voice Menu object is released.
Vcmdmc_OPEN_ALWAYS	8	Opens an existing menu with the given name. If the menu does not exist, the method creates a new, empty menu. The new menu is stored in the database when the Voice Menu object is released.
Vcmdmc_OPEN_EXISTING	16	Opens an existing menu. If the menu does not exist, the method fails.

Creating the empty menu is only half of the process. Creating the menu object does not populate that menu with commands. You must add voice command items to the new menu using the Add method of the Voice Menu object.

Adding Commands to the Voice Menu Object

Once you have created the Voice Menu object, you can start adding actual commands to the menu. This is done with the Add method of the Voice Menu object. The Add method takes the four parameters shown in Table 17.9.

Table 17.9. The Add method parameters.

Parameter	Description
identifier	Unique number for the command. The CommandSpoken property is set to this number when the command is recognized.
command	Voice command string—for example, *Open the file.* This is the command that users will speak.
category	String that indicates the category to which the command belongs.
description	String that describes the action performed by the command. This is for comment purposes only.

The identifier parameter must be a unique number. This value is returned when the SR engine recognizes the spoken command in the command parameter. The category parameter is used to organize lists of commands. This is similar to using "File," "Edit," or "Help"-type menu categories. The description parameter is used only for comment purposes and does not affect the performance of the SR engine at all.

To add some commands to the menu you created earlier, add a new button to the project. Set its Name property to cmdAdd and its Caption property to Add Items. Then add the code shown in Listing 17.14.

Listing 17.14. Adding code to the cmdAdd_Click event.

```
Private Sub cmdAdd_Click()
    '
    ' add a new item to the menu
    '
    Dim x As Integer
    '
    For x = 1 To 4
        lMenuIndex = x
        objVMenu.Add lMenuIndex, "Line " & CStr(x), "Item List", "Make an Item
        ➡List"
        '
        objVMenu.hWndMenu = Me.hWnd ' for this window
        objVMenu.Active = True ' turn it on
        '
    Next x
    '
    MsgBox "Menu Complete"
    '
End Sub
```

Your form should look something like the one in Figure 17.8.

FIGURE 17.8.

The VCMD *screen layout.*

There are two other steps to completing the process of adding commands to a menu. First, all commands added to a menu are global unless they are assigned a window handle. Global menus can be called at any time during a Windows session, regardless of what window is active or what programs are loaded. If a menu command is assigned to a particular window, it will only be available when the window is loaded and has focus.

> **TIP**
>
> It is a good idea to limit the use of global menu commands. The more global commands you have registered, the more analysis will be required before the SR engine can identify your command. Additional commands also increase the error rate of the SR engine.

After entering the code from Listing 17.14, save and run the project. Press `Register` and `Awake`; then press `Create Menu` and `Add Items`. This will add the four items to the list of available voice commands. Figure 17.9 shows a list of the available voice commands. You can see the new commands added by the VCMD application at the end of the command list.

FIGURE 17.9.

Viewing the active voice commands.

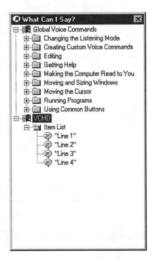

> **NOTE**
>
> Figure 17.9 shows the output of the "What Can I Say?" voice command for Microsoft Voice. If you are using another SR/TTS engine, you may have a different method for viewing the active voice commands.

At this point, you have created a new voice command menu and added new commands that can be recognized by the engine. However, you still need to add additional code to get the application to respond to the menu commands themselves.

Using the CommandSpoken Property to Respond to Menu Commands

Once you have registered commands with the SAPI system, you need to have a way to detect when commands have been spoken and to react to them accordingly. To do this, you need to check the CommandSpoken property of the Voice Command object.

The CommandSpoken property will contain the identifier number of the menu command the SR engine has recognized. You can then use this number to execute program code.

You need to regularly check the CommandSpoken property using a timer loop. To do this, you need to add one timer control and three label controls to the form. After placing the timer control on the form, add the three label controls. Name the first one lblResults and set its BorderStyle property to Fixed Single and its Alignment property to Centered. Set the name of the second label control to lblStatus and give it the same properties as the lblResults control. Finally, set the name of the third label control to lblPolling with the Caption set to Polling Results. Refer to Figure 17.10 for sizing and placement of these three controls.

FIGURE 17.10.

Adding the controls for polling the CommandSpoken *property.*

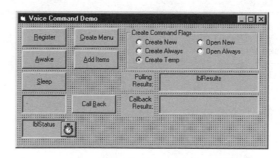

Now add two new lines of code to the Form_Load event. This code will start the timer cycle (see Listing 17.15).

Listing 17.15. Adding timer code to the Form_Load event.

```
Private Sub Form_Load()
    '
    ' create new voice command object
    '
    Set objVCmd = CreateObject("Speech.VoiceCommand")
    '
    Timer1.Interval = 500
    Timer1.Enabled = True
    '
End Sub
```

Finally, you need to add code to the Timer1_Timer event. This code will fire each time the timer interval loop reaches zero. Here you can test the value of CommandSpoken and respond according to the number returned. Add the code shown in Listing 17.16.

Listing 17.16. Adding code to respond to the CommandSpoken property.

```
Private Sub Timer1_Timer()
    '
    ' look for menu hit
    '
    Dim lHeard As Long
    '
    lHeard = objVCmd.CommandSpoken
    lblstatus = "Menu ID: [" & CStr(lHeard) & "]"
    '
    Select Case lHeard
        Case 0 ' no command
            ' na
        Case 1 ' beep command
            lblResults = "Line 1"
        Case 2
            lblResults = "Line 2"
        Case 3
            lblResults = "Line 3"
        Case 4
            lblResults = "Line 4"
    End Select
    '
    lHeard = 0
    objVCmd.CommandSpoken = 0
    '
End Sub
```

As soon as you get a non-zero value, you can check this value against a list of known identifier numbers and then fire off your own code based on the returned value. In this case, you will update the lblStatus box to show the command value returned, and the lblResults box will be updated to show the action to be taken.

You can test this by saving and running the project. After pressing `Register`, `Awake`, `Create Menu`, and `Add Items`, you will be able to speak any of the four registered commands (Line 1 through Line 4), and you'll see the `lblResults` label reflect the spoken command. In a real program, this code could fire off new forms, load files, save data to disk, and so on.

Establishing an SR Callback in Visual Basic 4.0

In Visual Basic 4.0, you establish a callback notification using a *class module*. This is a better method for receiving information about the spoken commands than polling the `CommandSpoken` property. To create a callback link between SAPI and your Visual Basic program, you must first add a class module to the project and then add two subroutines:

- `CommandRecognize`—Used to capture spoken commands understood by the SR engine.
- `CommandOther`—Used to capture spoken commands not recognized by the SR engine.

To add these elements, add a new class module to your project (`Insert ¦ Class Module`) and set its `Name` property to `clsCallBack`. Also set its `Instancing` property to `Creatable`, `Multiuse` and its `Public` property to `TRUE`. Then add the code shown in Listing 17.17.

Listing 17.17. Adding the `Callback` routines to the `clsCallBack` module.

```
Function CommandRecognize(szCommand As String, dwID As Long)
    '
    ' trap recognized command
    '
    frmVCmd.lblcallback = szCommand & " [" & CStr(dwID) & "]"
    '
End Function

Function CommandOther(szCommand As String, szApp As String, szState As String)

End Function
```

Notice that the `CommandRecognize` function returns two parameters. The first one is the actual command string spoken by the user. The second is the identifier number of the command. The single line of code added to the routine will update a label control with the results of the spoken command.

The `CommandOther` function allows you to trap commands that were meant for other applications. In this way, you can monitor all voice commands from a single location. For now, you do not need to add any code to this routine.

Next, you need to add two more label controls and one button control to the project. Add a label control and set its `Name` property to `lblCallBack`, its `Alignment` property to `Centered`, and its `BorderStyle` property to `Fixed Single`. Set the name of the second label control to `lblCBResults` and its `Caption` to `CallBack Results`. Now add a command button to the project with its `Name` property set to `cmdCallBack` and its `Caption` set to `CallBack`.

Finally, you need to add code behind the `cmdCallBack_Click` event to actually register the call-back notification. Listing 17.18 shows you how to do this.

Listing 17.18. Adding code to the `cmdCallBack_Click` event.

```
Private Sub cmdCBack_Click()
    '
    ' register callback
    '
    objVCmd.Callback = "Vcmd.clsCallBack"
    '
End Sub
```

Now save and run the project. You'll see the `lblCallBack` label show the exact command spoken along with the identifier number. This will match the information shown in the `lblResults` box.

Creating List Commands for the Voice Menu Object

The `Voice Menu` object allows you to create a list of items to be applied to a single command. For example, you could create a command that displays a customer address (such as *Show Smith and Sons*). But what if you wanted to show every customer address? Instead of creating a menu command for each address, you can create a list of customers and then apply that list to a special command string that has the list name as a part of the command (for example, *Show <CustomerName>*).

You can create lists using the `ListSet` method of the `Voice Menu` object. The `ListSet` method accepts two parameters. The first is the name of the list. The second parameter is the list of items, each separated by `Chr(0)`.

To test this, add a new command button to the form. Set its `Name` property to `cmdList` and its `Caption` to `Make List`. Then add the code shown in Listing 17.19.

Listing 17.19. Adding code behind the `cmdList_Click` event.

```
Private Sub cmdList_Click()
    '
    ' add a list command
    ' build a list
    ' activate the menu
    '
    lMenuIndex = lMenuIndex + 1
    objVMenu.Active = False
    objVMenu.Add lMenuIndex, "Show <CustomerName>", "Name List", "Display Names"
    objVMenu.ListSet "CustomerName", 3, "Smith" & Chr(0) & "Lee" & Chr(0) &
➡"Shannon" & Chr(0)
    objVMenu.Active = True
    '
End Sub
```

Notice that you must first create a valid menu command that refers to the list. Also, it is a good idea to set the Active property to FALSE while you edit a menu and set it back to TRUE when you are done.

Since you have added a new command to the menu, you also need to update the Timer1_Timer event to look for the new command. Modify the code in Timer1_Timer to match the code in Listing 17.20.

Listing 17.20. Modifying the Timer1_Timer event.

```
Private Sub Timer1_Timer()
'
    ' look for menu hit
    '
    Dim lHeard As Long
    '
    lHeard = objVCmd.CommandSpoken
    lblstatus = "Menu ID: [" & CStr(lHeard) & "]"
    '
    Select Case lHeard
        Case 0 ' no command
            ' na
        Case 1 ' beep command
            lblResults = "Line 1"
        Case 2
            lblResults = "Line 2"
        Case 3
            lblResults = "Line 3"
        Case 4
            lblResults = "Line 4"
        Case 5
            lblResults = "Show"
    End Select
    '
    lHeard = 0
    objVCmd.CommandSpoken = 0
    '
End Sub
```

Now save and run the project. After starting the SR engine (press Register, Awake, Create Menu, Add Items, and CallBack), press the Make List button to add the new commands to the list. At this point, you should be able to view the command list from Microsoft Voice by invoking the "What Can I Say?" command. Your screen should look something like the one in Figure 17.11.

Now when you speak the command *Show Lee,* you'll see the command appear in the lblCallBack window (see Figure 17.12).

Notice that the callback window shows the complete spoken command (that is, both the command and the list item), but the CommandSpoken window just displays the word *Show.* The CommandSpoken property can return only the identifier of the command recognized by the SR engine, not the actual command itself. This means that if you plan to use lists as part of your voice commands, you will have to use the `Callback` property and class module to return the complete spoken command.

FIGURE 17.11.

Viewing the new command list.

FIGURE 17.12.

The results of speaking a list command.

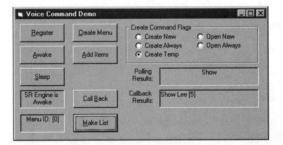

Removing Commands from the `Voice Menu` Object

You can remove commands from the `Voice Menu` object using the `Remove` method. It is a good idea to remove any commands that are no longer needed. The fewer commands the SR engine has to deal with, the faster and more accurate the engine will be.

Add one more button to the form. Set its Name property to cmdRemove and its Caption property to Remove. Now add the code shown in Listing 17.21 to the cmdRemove_Click event.

Listing 17.21. Adding code to the cmdRemove_Click event.

```
Private Sub Command1_Click()
    '
    ' remove menus from the list
    '
    Dim lLoop As Long
    '
    For lLoop = lMenuIndex To 1 Step -1
        objVMenu.Remove (lLoop)
    Next lLoop
    '
    lMenuIndex = 0
    '
    MsgBox "Menus Removed"
    '
End Sub
```

TIP

In this code example, you are creating a temporary menu. This menu will be removed automatically when the program exits. It is still a good practice to remove old menu items, because these items take up storage space and can cause slower recognition.

Summary

In this chapter, you learned how to use the SAPI OLE objects to create real, working TTS and SR Windows programs using Visual Basic 4.0. You learned that there are two OLE libraries for use with Visual Basic 4.0 and all other VBA-compatible languages:

■ The OLE Voice Text library (VTXTAUTO.TLB)
■ The OLE Voice Command library (VCMDAUTO.TLB)

The Voice Text library provides TTS services and the Voice Command library provides SR services.

You learned how to use the Voice Text object to register and enable the TTS engine and how to send text to the engine for playback. You also learned how to adjust the speed of playback and how to add rewind, pause, fast-forward, and resume options to TTS playback. Finally, you learned how to use the IsSpeaking property in a timer loop and the Callback property to get notification on the status of the TTS engine.

You learned how to use the Voice Command object and the Voice Menu object to register and awaken the SR engine. You also learned how to create and populate command menus and how to use the CommandSpoken and Callback properties to return the identifier of the command spoken and to respond by executing code associated with the command. You also learned how to create command lists to allow users to speak a single command with replaceable parameters.

In the next chapter, you'll learn more about command lists and parameters used by the grammar engine that underlies the Speech system. You'll also learn how to use control tags to improve TTS engine playback and about the International Phonetic Alphabet and how it is used to improve both SR and TTS services.

18

SAPI Behind the Scenes

In this chapter, you'll learn about three aspects of the SAPI system that are not often used in the course of normal speech services operations:

- *Control tags* are used to modify the audio output of TTS engines.
- *Grammar rules* are used to tell SR engines how to analyze audio input.
- The *International Phonetic Alphabet* is used by Unicode systems to gain additional control over both TTS output and SR input.

You'll learn how to add control tags to your TTS text input in order to change the speed, pitch, volume, mood, gender, and other characteristics of TTS audio output. You'll learn how to use the 15 control tags to improve the sound of your TTS engine.

You'll also learn how grammar rules are used by the SR engine to analyze spoken input. You'll learn how to design your own grammars for specialized uses. You'll also learn how to code and compile your own grammars using tools from the Microsoft Speech SDK. Finally, you'll load your custom grammar into a test program and test the results of your newly designed grammar rules.

The last topic in this chapter is the International Phonetic Alphabet (*IPA*). The IPA is a standard system for documenting the various sounds of human speech. The IPA is an implementation option for SAPI speech services under Unicode. For this reason, the IPA can be implemented only on WinNT systems. In this chapter, you'll learn how the IPA can be used to improve both TTS playback and SR recognition performance.

Control Tags

One of the most difficult tasks for a TTS system is the rendering of complete sentences. Most TTS systems do quite well when converting a single word into speech. However, when TTS systems begin to string words together into sentences, they do not perform as well because human speech has a set of inflections, pitches, and rhythms. These characteristics of human speech are called *prosody*.

There are several reasons that TTS engines are unsuccessful in matching the prosody of human speech. First, very little of it is written down in the text. Punctuation marks can be used to estimate some prosody information, but not all. Much of the inflection of a sentence is tied to subtle differences in the speech of individuals when they speak to each other—interjections, racing to complete a thought, putting in a little added *emphasis to make a point*. These are all aspects of human prosody that are rarely found in written text.

When you consider the complexity involved in rendering a complete thought or sentence, the current level of technology in TTS engines is quite remarkable. Although the average output of TTS engines still sounds like a poor imitation of Darth Vader, it is amazingly close to human speech.

One of the ways that the SAPI model attempts to provide added control to TTS engines is the inclusion of what are called *control tags* in text that is to be spoken. These tags can be used to adjust the speed, pitch, and character of the voice used to render the text. By using control tags, you can greatly improve the perceived performance of the TTS engine.

The SAPI model defines 15 different control tags that can be used to modify the output of TTS engines. Microsoft defined these tags but does not determine how the TTS engine will respond to them. It is acceptable for TTS engines that comply with the TAPI model to ignore any and all control tags it does not understand. It is possible that the TTS engine you install on your system will not respond to some or all of these tags. It is also possible that the TTS engine will attempt to interpret them as part of the text instead of ignoring them. You will need to experiment with your TTS engine to determine its level of compliance with the SAPI model.

> **NOTE**
>
> All of the examples in this section were created using the Microsoft Voice TTS engine that ships with Microsoft Phone.

The SAPI control tags fall into three general categories:

- *Voice character* control tags
- *Phrase modification* control tags
- *Low-level TTS* control tags

The *voice character* tags can be used to set high-level general characteristics of the voice. The SAPI model allows users to select gender, dialect, accent, message context types, speaker's age, even the general mood of the speaker.

The *phrase modification* tags can be used to adjust the pronunciation at a word-by-word or phrase-by-phrase level. Users can control the word emphasis, pauses, pitch, speed, and volume of the playback.

The *low-level TTS* tags deal with attributes of the TTS engine itself. Users can add comments to the text, control the pronunciation of a word, turn prosody rules on and off, reset the engine to default settings, or even call a control tag based on its own GUID (guaranteed unique identifier).

You add control tags to the text sent to the TTS engine by surrounding them with the backslash (\) character. For example, to adjust the speed of the text playback from 150 to 200 words per minute, you would enter the \Spd=\ control tag. The text below shows how this looks:

```
\Spd=150\This sentence is normal. \Spd=200\This sentence is faster.
```

Control tags are not case sensitive. For example, \spd=200\ is the same as \Spd=200\ or \SPD=200\. However, control tags are white-space sensitive. \Spd=200\ is *not* the same as \ Spd=200 \. As mentioned above, if the TTS engine encounters an unknown control tag, it ignores it. The next three sections of this chapter go into the details of each control tag and show you how to use them.

Before continuing, load the TTSTEST.EXE program from the SPEECHSDK\BIN\ANSI.API directory (Win95) or the SPEECHSDK\BIN\UNICODE.API directory (WinNT). This program will be used to illustrate examples throughout the chapter. After loading your program, press the Register button to start the TTS engine on your workstation. Then press the Add Mode button to select a voice for playback. Finally, make sure TTSDATAFLAG_TAGGED is checked. This informs the application that you will be sending control tags with your text. Your screen should now look something like the one in Figure 18.1.

FIGURE 18.1.

Starting the TTSTEST.EXE *application.*

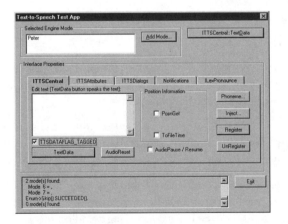

The Voice Character Control Tags

There are three control tags that allow you to alter the general character of the speaking voice. Microsoft has identified several characteristics of playback voices that can be altered using control tags. However, your TTS engine may not recognize all of them. The three control tags in this group are

- `Chr`—Used to set the character of the voice.
- `Ctx`—Used to set the context of the spoken text.
- `Vce`—Used to set additional characteristics of the voice, including language, accent, dialect, gender, name, and age.

Using the `Chr` Tag to Set the Voice Character

The `Chr` tag allows you to set the general character of the voice. The syntax for the `Chr` tag is

```
\Chr=string[[,string...]]\
```

More than one characteristic can be applied at the same time. The default value is `Normal`. Others that are recognized by the Microsoft Voice TTS engine are `Monotone` and `Whisper`. Additional characteristics suggested by Microsoft are

Angry	Business	Calm	Depressed	Excited
Falsetto	Happy	Loud	Perky	Quiet
Sarcastic	Scared	Shout	Tense	

To test the `Chr` tag, enter the text shown in Listing 18.1 into the input box of `TTSTEST.EXE`.

Listing 18.1. Testing the `Chr` control tag.

```
\chr="monotone"\
How are you today?
\chr="whisper"\
I am fine.
\chr="normal"\
Good to hear.
```

Each sentence will be spoken using a different characteristic. After entering the text, press the `TextData` button to hear the results.

Using the `Ctx` Tag to Set the Message Context

Another valuable control tag is `Ctx`, the context tag. You can use this tag to tell the TTS engine the context of the message you are asking it to render. Like the `Chr` tag, the `Ctx` tag takes `string` as a parameter. Microsoft has defined the strings in Table 18.1 for the context tag.

Table 18.1. The context tag parameters.

Context Tag Parameter	Description
Address	Addresses and/or phone numbers.
C	Code in the C or C++ programming language.
Document	Text document.
E-Mail	Electronic mail.
Numbers	Numbers, dates, times, and so on.
Spreadsheet	Spreadsheet document.
Unknown	Context is unknown (default).

Setting the context helps the TTS engine better interpret the text. To test this, enter the text shown in Listing 18.2 into the text box.

Listing 18.2. Testing the `Ctx` control tag.

```
\ctx="Address"\
1204 W. 7th Street
Oak Ridge, TN
\ctx="E-Mail"\
BillGates@msn.com
\ctx="Unknown"\
129 W. First Avenue
```

When you press the `TextData` button to hear the results, you'll notice that the TTS engine automatically converts the "W." to "West" when given the `\Ctx="Address"\` tag but fails to do so when the `\Ctx="Unknown"\` tag is used. You'll also notice that the e-mail address is spoken using the phrase "Bill Gates at msn dot com" when the `\Ctx="E-Mail"\` tag is used.

Using the `Vce` Tag to Control Additional Voice Characteristics

The last voice character control tag is the `Vce` tag. This tag can be used to set several aspects of a voice in a single control tag. The exact syntax of the `Vce` tag is

```
\Vce=chartype=string[[,chartype=string...]]\
```

Several character types can be set in a single call. Microsoft has defined six different character type classes. These classes, along with their possible settings and brief descriptions, are shown in Table 18.2.

Table 18.2. The Vce character types and their parameters.

Character Type	*Description*
Language=*language*	Tells the TTS engine to speak in the specified language.
Accent=*accent*	Tells the TTS engine to use the specified accent. For example, if Language="English" and Accent="French", the engine will speak English with a French accent.
Dialect=*dialect*	Tells the TTS engine to speak in the specified dialect.
Gender=*gender*	Used to set the gender of the voice as "Male," "Female," or "Neutral."
Speaker=*speakername*	Specifies the name of the voice, or NULL if the name is unimportant. The Microsoft Voice engine can respond using the following names: Peter Sidney Eager Eddie Deep Douglas Biff Grandpa Amos Melvin Alex Wanda Julia
Age=*age*	Sets the age of the voice, which can be one of the following values: Baby (about 1 year old) Toddler (about 3 years old) Child (about 6 years old) Adolescent (about 14 years old) Adult (between 20 and 60 years old) Elderly (over 60 years old)

Style=*style*	Sets the personality of the voice. For example:
	`Business`
	`Casual`
	`Computer`
	`Excited`
	`Singsong`

To test the Vce control tag, enter the text shown in Listing 18.3 and press TextData to hear the results.

Listing 18.3. Testing the Vce control tag.

```
\Vce=Speaker="Sidney"\
Hello there Peter.
\Vce=Speaker="Peter"\
Hi Sid. How are you?
\Vce=Speaker="Sidney"\
Not good really. Bad head cold.
```

You can use the Vce control tag to program the TTS engine to carry on a multiperson dialog.

The Phrase Modification Control Tags

The second set of control tags—the phrase modification tags—can be used to modify words or phrases within the message stream. Phrase modification tags give you added control over TTS output. There are five phrase modification control tags:

- ■ Emp—Used to add emphasis to a single word.
- ■ Pau—Used to place a silent pause into the output stream.
- ■ Pit—Used to alter the base pitch of the output.
- ■ Spd—Used to set the base speed of the output.
- ■ Vol—Used to set the base volume of the output.

Using the Emp Tag to Add Emphasis to a Word

You can insert the \Emp\ tag before a word to force the TTS engine to give it added emphasis. Enter the text shown in Listing 18.4 and press TextData to hear the results.

Listing 18.4. Testing the Emp control tag.

```
I \Emp\told you never to go running in the street.

Didn't you \Emp\hear me?

You must listen to me when I tell you something \Emp\important.
```

You can quickly compare this phrase to one without emphasis by simply adding a space to each \Emp\ tag so that is looks like \ Emp\. Since this will appear to be a new tag, the TTS engine will ignore it and speak the text with standard prosody.

Using the Pau Control Tag to Add Pauses to the Text

You can use the Pau tag to add pauses to the playback. The pause is measured in milliseconds. Here's an example of the Pau tag syntax:

```
\Pau=1000\
```

To test the `Pau` tag, add two tags to the speech you entered from the previous example. Your text should now look like the text in Listing 18.5.

Listing 18.5. Testing the `Pau` control tag.

```
I \Emp\told you never to go running in the street.
\pau=1000\
Didn't you \Emp\hear me?
\pau=2000\
You must listen to me when I tell you something \Emp\important.
```

Using the `Pit` Control Tag to Modify the Pitch of the Voice

The `Pit` control tag can be used to modify the base pitch of the voice. This base pitch is used to set the normal speaking pitch level. The actual pitch hovers above and below this value as the TTS engine mimics human speech prosody. The pitch is measured in hertz. There is a minimum and maximum pitch: the minimum pitch is 50 hertz and the maximum is 400 hertz.

Listing 18.6 shows modifications to the previous text adding `\Pit\` control tags to the text.

Listing 18.6. Testing the `Pit` control tag.

```
\Pit=100\
I \Emp\told you never to go running in the street.
\pau=1000\ \Pit=200\
Didn't you \Emp\hear me?
\pau=2000\ \Pit=400\
You must listen to me when I tell you something \Emp\important.
\Pit=50\
```

> **TIP**
>
> Notice that the last line of Listing 18.6 shows a pitch tag setting the pitch back to normal (`\Pit=50\`). This is done because the pitch setting does not automatically revert to the default level after a message has been spoken. If you want to return the pitch to its original level, you must do so using the `Pit` control tag.

Using the `Spd` Control Tag to Modify the Playback Speed

You can modify the playback speed of the TTS engine using the `\Spd\` control tag. The speed is measured in words per minute (wpm). The minimum value is 50wpm and the maximum is 250wpm. Setting `Spd` to 0 sets the slowest possible speed. Setting `Spd` to –1 sets the fastest possible speed. Listing 18.7 shows additional modifications to the previous text. Enter this text and press the `TextData` button to hear the results.

Listing 18.7. Testing the Spd control tag.

```
\Spd=150\
I \Emp\told you never to go running in the street.
\pau=1000\ \Spd=75\
Didn't you \Emp\hear me?
\pau=2000\ \Spd=200\
You must listen to me when I tell you something \Emp\important.
\Spd=150\
```

Using the Vol Control Tag to Adjust Playback Volume

The Vol control tag can be used to adjust the base line volume of the TTS playback. The value can range from 0 (the quietest) to 65535 (the loudest). The actual pitch hovers above and below the value set by Vol. Make the changes to the text shown in Listing 18.8 and press TextData to hear the results.

Listing 18.8. Testing the Vol control tag.

```
\Spd=150\ \Vol=30000\
I \Emp\told you never to go running in the street.

\pau=1000\ \Spd=75\ \Vol=65000\
Didn't you \Emp\hear me?

\Vol=15000\ \pau=2000\ \Spd=200\
You must listen to me when I tell you something \Emp\important.
\Spd=150\ \Vol\=65000
```

The Low-Level TTS Control Tags

There are seven low-level TTS control tags, which are used to handle TTS adjustments not normally seen by TTS users. Most of these control tags are meant to be used by people who are designing and training complex TTS engines and grammars.

Of the event low-level TTS control tags, only one is used frequently—the \Rst\ tag. This tag resets the control values to those that existed at the start of the current session.

The remaining control tags are summarized in Table 18.3.

Table 18.3. The low-level TTS control tags.

Control Tag	Syntax	Description
Com	\Com=*string*\	Use this tag to add comments to the text passed to the TTS engine. These comments will be ignored by the TTS engine.

Control Tag	Syntax	Description
Eng	\Eng;*[GUID]:command*\	Use this tag to call an engine-specific command. This can be used to call special hardware-specific commands supported by third-party TTS engines.
Mrk	\Mrk=*number*\	Use this tag to fire the BookMark event of the ITTSBufNotifySink. You can use this to signal such things as page turns or slide changes once the place in the text is reached.
Prn	\Prn=*text=IPA*\	Use this tag to embed custom pronunciations of words using the International Phonetic Alphabet. This may not be supported by your engine.
Pro	\Pro=*number*\	Use this tag to turn on and off the TTS prosody rules. Setting the Pro value to 1 turns the rules on; setting it to 0 turns the rules off.
Prt	\Prt=*string*\	Use this tag to tell the engine what part of speech the current word is. Microsoft has defined these general categories: Abbr (abbreviation) N (noun) Adj (adjective) Ord (ordinal number) Adv (adverb) Prep (preposition) Card (cardinal number) Pron (pronoun) Conj (conjunction) Prop (proper noun) Cont (contraction) Punct (punctuation) Det (determiner) Quant (quantifier) Interj (interjection) V (verb)

> **NOTE**
>
> With the exception of the \Rst\ tag, none of the other tags produced noticeable results using the TTS engine that ships with Microsoft Voice. For this reason, there are no examples for these control tags.

Now that you know how to modify the way the TTS engine processes input, you are ready to learn how to use grammar rules to control the way SR engines behave.

Grammar Rules

The grammar of the SR engine controls how the SR engine interprets audio input. The grammar defines the objects for which the engine will listen and the rules used to analyze the objects. SR engines require that one or more grammars be loaded and activated before an engine can successfully interpret the audio stream.

As mentioned in earlier chapters, the SAPI model defines three types of SR grammars:

- *Context-free* grammars—Words are analyzed based on syntax rules instead of content rules. Interpretation is based on the placement and order of the objects, not their meaning or context.
- *Dictation* grammars—Words are compared against a large vocabulary, a predefined topic (or context), and an expected speaking style.
- *Limited-domain* grammars—This grammar is a cross between rule-based context-free and word-based dictation grammars.

The context-free grammar format is the most commonly used format. It is especially good at interpreting command and control statements from the user. Context-free grammars also allow a great deal of flexibility since the creation of a set of rules is much easier than building and analyzing large vocabularies, as is done in dictation grammars. By defining a small set of general rules, the SR engine can successfully respond to hundreds (or even thousands) of valid commands—without having to actually build each command into the SR lexicon. The rest of this section deals with the design, compilation, and testing of context-free grammars for the SAPI SR engine model.

General Rules for the SAPI Context-Free Grammar

The SAPI Context-Free Grammar (CFG) operates on a limited set of rules. These rules are used to analyze all audio input. In addition to rules, CFGs also allow for the definition of individual words. These words become part of the grammar and can be recognized by themselves or as part of a defined rule.

Defining Words in a CFG

In SAPI CFGs, each defined word is assigned a unique ID number. This is done by listing each word, followed by a number. Listing 18.9 shows an example.

Listing 18.9. Defining words for a CFG file.

```
//
// defining names
//
Lee = 101 ;
Shannon = 102 ;
Jesse = 103 ;
Scott = 104 ;
Michelle = 105 ;
Sue = 106 ;
```

Notice that there are spaces between each item on the line. The Microsoft GRAMCOMP.EXE program requires that each item be separated by white space. Also note that a semicolon (;) must appear at the end of each definition.

TIP

If you are using the GRAMCOMP.EXE compiler, you are not required to define each word and give it a number. The GRAMCOMP.EXE program automatically assigns a number to each new word for you. However, it is a good idea to predefine words to prevent any potential conflicts at compile time.

The list of words can be as short or as long as you require. Keep in mind that the SR engine can only recognize words that appear in the vocabulary. If you fail to define the word "Stop," you can holler *Stop!* to the engine as long as you like, but it will have no idea what you are saying! Also, the longer the list, the more likely it is that the engine will confuse one word for another. As the list increases in size, the accuracy of the engine decreases. Try to keep your lists as short as possible.

Defining Rules in a CFG

Along with words, CFGs require rules to interpret the audio stream. Each rule consists of two parts—the rule name and the series of operations that define the rule:

```
<RuleName> = [series of operations]
```

There are several possible operations within a rule. You can call another rule, list a set of recognizable words, or refer to an external list of words. There are also several special functions defined for CFGs. These functions define interpretation options for the input stream. There are four CFG functions recognized by the GRAMCOMP.EXE compiler:

- alt()—Use this function to list a set of alternative inputs.
- seq()—Use this function to indicate to the SR engine the sequence in which input will occur.
- opt()—Use this function to inform the SR engine that the word or rule is optional and may not appear as part of the input stream.
- rep()—Use this function to tell the SR engine that this word or rule could be repeated several times.

Using the alt() Rule Function

When building a rule definition, you can tell the SR engine that only one of the items in the list is expected. Listing 18.10 shows how this is done.

Listing 18.10. An example of the alt() rule function.

```
<Names> = alt(
        Scott
        Wayne
        Curt
)alt ;
```

The <Names> rule in Listing 18.10 defines three alternative names for the rule. This tells the SR engine that only one of the names will be spoken at a single occurrence.

Using the seq() Rule Function

You can also define a rule that indicates the sequence in which words will be spoken. Listing 18.11 shows how you can modify the <Names> rule to also include last names as part of the rule.

Listing 18.11. An example of the seq() rule function.

```
<Names> = alt(
    Scott
    seq( Scott Ivey )seq
    Wayne
```

```
seq( Wayne Ivey )seq
Curt
seq( Curt Smith )seq
)alt ;
```

The `<Names>` rule now lists six alternatives. Three of them include two-word phrases that must be spoken in the proper order to be recognized. For example, users could say *Scott* or *Scott Ivey*, and the SR engine would recognize the input. However, if the user said *Ivey Scott*, the system would not understand the input.

Using the `opt()` Rule Function

You can define rules that show that some of the input is optional—that it may or may not occur in the input stream. The `opt()` function can simplify rules while still giving them a great deal of flexibility. Listing 18.12 shows how to apply the `opt()` function to the `<Names>` rule.

Listing 18.12. An example of the `opt()` rule function.

```
<Names> = alt(
    seq( Scott opt( Ivey )opt )seq
    seq( Wayne opt( Ivey )opt )seq
    seq( Curt opt( Smith )opt )seq
    )alt ;
```

The `<Names>` rule now has only three alternative inputs again. This time, each input has an optional last name to match the first name.

Using the `rep()` Rule Function

The `rep()` rule function can be used to tell the SR engine to expect more than one of the objects within the context of the rule. A good example would be the creation of a phone-dialing rule. First, you can define a rule that dials each phone number (see Listing 18.13).

Listing 18.13. A phone-dialing rule.

```
<Dial> = alt(
    3215002
    4975501
    3336363
    )alt ;
```

Listing 18.13 meets all the requirements of a well-formed rule, but it has some problems. First, SR engines are not very good at recognizing objects such as "3336363" as individual words.

Second, this list can easily grow to tens, even hundreds, of entries. As the list grows, accuracy will decrease, especially since it is likely that several phone numbers will sound alike.

Instead of defining a rule that contains all the phone numbers, you can define a rule using the rep() function that tells the engine to listen for a set of numbers. Listing 18.14 is an improved version of the <Dial> rule.

Listing 18.14. An improved Dial rule.

```
<Dial> = alt(
    seq( Dial rep( <Numbers> )rep )seq
    )alt ;

<Numbers> = alt(
    zero
    one
    two
    three
    four
    five
    six
    seven
    eight
    nine
    )alt ;
```

Now the <Dial> rule knows to wait for a series of numbers. This allows it to be used for any possible combination of digits that can be used to dial a telephone number.

> **TIP**
>
> The <Dial> rule described here is still not very good. The SR engine has a hard time interpreting long sets of numbers. It is better to define words that will aid in the dialing of phone numbers. For example, *Dial New York Office* is more likely to be understood than *Dial 1-800-555-1212.*

Using Run-Time Lists with CFG Rules

You can define a rule that uses the contents of a list built at run-time. This allows the SR engine to collect information about the workstation (loadable applications, available Word documents, and so on) while the system is up and running rather than having to build everything into the grammar itself. The list name is added to the rule surrounded by braces ({}). At run-time, programmers can use the SetList method of the Voice Menu object in the OLE library to create and populate the list. Listing 18.15 shows how to build a rule that refers to a run-time list.

Listing 18.15. An example of referring to a run-time list.

```
<RunProgram> = alt( seq( Run {ProgList} )seq )alt ;
```

`<RunProgram>` allows the user to say "Run *name*" where *name* is one of the program names that was loaded into the list at run-time.

Creating and Compiling a SAPI Context-Free Grammar

Now that you know the basic building blocks used to create CFGs, it is time to build and compile actual grammar rules using NOTEPAD.EXE and the GRAMCOMP.EXE grammar compiler that ships with the Microsoft Speech SDK. The first step in the process is to define the general scope and function of the grammar. For example, you might want a grammar that can handle typical customer requests for directions in a shopping center.

Once you define the scope and function of a grammar, you need to identify the words and rules needed to populate the CFG. Since an SR engine can only recognize words it already knows, you must be sure to include all the words needed to complete operations.

TIP

You do not, however, need to include all the possible words users may utter to the SR engine. The software package that is using the SR engine should have some type of error response in cases where the audio input cannot be interpreted.

To use the shopping center example, you'd need a list of all the locations that users might request. This would include all the stores, restaurants, major landmarks within the building, public services such as restrooms, exits, drinking fountains, security office, and so on. Then you need to collect a set of typical phrases that you expect users to utter. Examples might be "Where is the ....?" or "Show me ... on the map," or "How can I locate the ....?" After you have collected all this material, you are ready to create the grammar.

Coding the MALL.TXT Context-Free Grammar

Let's assume you have the job of building a workstation that will allow shoppers to ask directions in order to locate their favorite shops within the mall. Listing 18.16 shows a list of the store names and some other major landmarks in the mall. Load NOTEPAD.EXE and enter this information into a file called MALL.TXT.

Listing 18.16. Adding words to the MALL grammar.

```
// ********************************************************
// MALL GRAMMAR RULES
// ********************************************************
//
// Title:    MALL.TXT
// Version:   1.0 - 05/16/96 (MCA)
//
// Site:    Win95 SAPI
// Compiler:  GRAMCOMP.EXE
//
// Desc:   Used to direct customers to their favorite
//        shops in the mall.
//
// ********************************************************


//
// define words
//
J = 9900 ;
C = 9901 ;
Penneys = 9902 ;
Sears = 9903 ;
Bobs = 9904 ;
Bagels = 9905 ;
Michelles = 9906 ;
Supplies = 9906 ;
The = 9907 ;
Sports = 9908 ;
Barn = 9909 ;

Security = 9910 ;
Office = 9911 ;
Main = 9912 ;
Food = 9913 ;
Court = 9914 ;
Shops = 9915 ;
Specialty = 9916 ;

Exits = 9917 ;
Restroom = 9918 ;
Fountain = 9919 ;
```

Next, you need to define a top-level rule that calls all other rules. This one rule should be relatively simple and provide for branches to other more complicated rules. By creating branches, you can limit SR errors since the possible words or phrases are limited to those defined in a branch. In other words, by creating branches to other rules, you limit the scope of words and rules that must be analyzed by the SR engine at any one moment. This improves accuracy.

Listing 18.17 shows a top-level rule that calls several other possible rules. Add this to your MALL.TXT grammar file.

Listing 18.17. Adding the top-level rule to the MALL grammar file.

```
// **************************************
// Define starting rule
//
// This rule calls any one of the other
// internal rules.
//
<Start> = alt(
    <_Locations>
    <_TellMeWhere>
    <_HowCanIFind>
    <_ShowMe>
    <_WhereIs>
    )alt ;
```

Notice that each of the rules called by <Start> begins with an underscore (_). This underscore tells the compiler that this is an internal rule and should not be exported to the user. The more exported rules the SR engine has to review, the greater the chance of failure. It is a good idea to limit the number of exported rules to a bare minimum.

The first internal rule on the list is called <_Locations>. This rule contains a list of all the locations that customers may ask about. Notice the use of seq() and opt() in the rule. This allows customers to ask for the same locations in several different ways without having to add many items to the vocabulary. Enter the data shown in Listing 18.18 into the MALL.TXT grammar file.

Listing 18.18. Adding the Locations rule.

```
// **************************************
// Define Locations rule
//
// This rule lists all possible locations
//
<_Locations> = alt(
    // JC Penneys, Penneys
    seq( opt( seq( J C )seq )opt Penneys )seq

    // sears
    Sears

    // Bobs, Bobs Bagels
    seq( Bobs opt( Bagels )opt )seq

    // Michelles, Michelles Supplies
    seq( Michelles opt( Supplies )opt )seq

    // The Sports Barn, Sports Barn
    seq( opt( The )opt Sports Barn )seq

    // Security, Security Office
    seq( Security opt( Office )opt )seq
```

continues

Listing 18.18. continued

```
// Main Office
seq( Main Office )seq

// Food, Food Court, Food Shops
seq( Food opt( alt( Court Shops )alt )opt )seq

// Specialty Shops
seq( Specialty Shops )seq

// Exits
Exits

// Restroom
Restroom

// Fountain
Fountain

)alt ;
```

The last step is to build a set of query rules. These are rules that contain the questions customers will commonly ask of the workstation. Each of these questions is really a short phrase followed by a store or location name. Listing 18.19 shows how you can implement the query rules defined in the <Start> rule.

Listing 18.19. Adding the query rules to the MALL.TXT grammar file.

```
// **************************************
// Define simple queries
//
// These rules respond to customer
// queries
//
<_TellMeWhere> = seq( Tell me where <_Locations> is )seq ;
<_HowCanIFind> = seq( How can I find opt( the )opt <_Locations> )seq ;
<_ShowMe> = seq( Show me opt( where )opt <_Locations> opt( is )opt )seq ;
<_WhereIs> = seq( Where is <_Locations> )seq ;

//
// eof
//
```

Notice the use of the opt() functions to widen the scope of the rules. These add flexibility to the grammar without adding extra rules.

> **NOTE**
>
> Be sure to save the file as MALL.TXT before you continue on to the next step.

Compiling the MALL.TXT Grammar File

After you have constructed the grammar file, you are ready to compile it into a binary form understood by the SAPI SR engine.

> **NOTE**
>
> To do this, you need to use the GRAMCOMP.EXE program that ships with the Speech SDK. You can find this program in the SPEECHSDK\BIN folder that was created when you installed the Speech SDK.

The GRAMCOMP.EXE program is a command-line application with no defined window. To run the program, open an MS-DOS window and move to the directory that contains the GRAMCOMP.EXE file. Then type the following on the command line:

```
gramcomp /ansi mall.txt mall.grm<return>
```

> **WARNING**
>
> If you are using WinNT, do not include the /ansi portion of the command. This is needed only for Win95 workstations that do not support the default Unicode compilation mode.

You may need to include the directory path to locate the MALL.TXT file. Once the compiler is running, it will read in the MALL.TXT file and compile it into binary format and save it as MALL.GRM. Your screen should look something like the one in Figure 18.2.

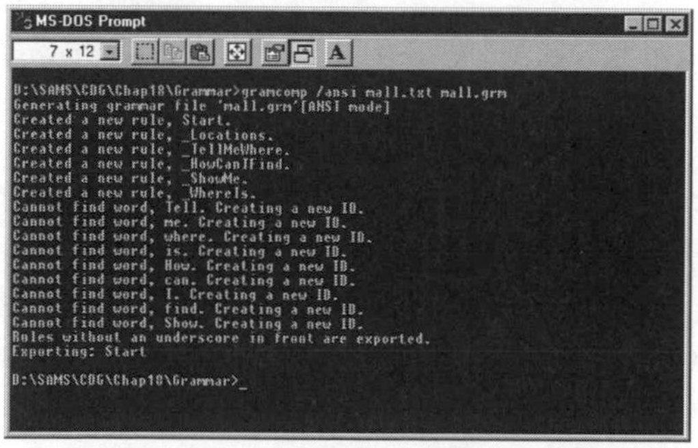

FIGURE 18.2.

Compiling the MALL grammar.

You should get a message telling you that one rule has been exported (Start). If you receive error messages, return to the MALL.TXT file to fix them and recompile. Once you complete compilation successfully, you are ready to test your grammar using SRTEST.EXE.

Loading and Testing SAPI Context-Free Grammars

You can test your new grammar by loading it into the SRTEST.EXE application that ships with the Speech SDK. The ANSI version of the program can be found in the SPEECHSDK\BIN\ANSI.API. You can find the Unicode version in \SPEECHSDK\BIN\UNICODE.API.

Once you load the grammar, you can use the same software to test the SR engine's response to your spoken queries.

Loading and Activating the MALL grammar

When you first start the program, press the Add Mode button to select an engine mode. You should then see one or more modes available. It does not matter which one you pick as long as it supports the same language you used to build the grammar (see Figure 18.3).

FIGURE 18.3.
Selecting an SR mode.

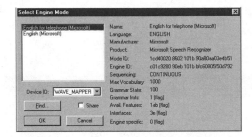

After selecting the SR mode, you need to load the new MALL.GRM file. To do this, press the Rescan Files button and enter the directory path that contains the MALL.GRM grammar file (see Figure 18.4).

FIGURE 18.4.
Loading the MALL.GRM
grammar file.

You will see the MALL.GRM file appear in the list of available grammars. Double-click the name to load it into the SR engine.

Next, you need to activate the MALL grammar. To do this, select the Grammar option button on the left side of the screen and bring up the ISRGramCom tab of the form. Set the Rule combo box to Start and the Window combo box to MainWnd and press Activate. The MALL.GRM grammar should activate, and your screen should look like the one in Figure 18.5.

FIGURE 18.5.

Activating the MALL *grammar.*

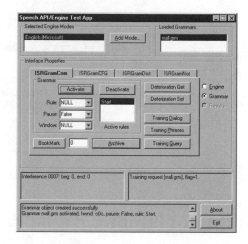

The status box at the bottom of the form should contain messages like the ones in Listing 18.20.

Listing 18.20. Messages showing successful grammar activation.

```
Grammar object created successfully.
Grammar mall.grm activated, hwnd: c0c, pause: False, rule: Start,
```

Testing the MALL Grammar

You are now ready to test the grammar by speaking to your system. The responses will appear in the status box at the lower left of the form.

For example, ask your system the following question: *How can I find Sears?* You should see the application flash a few status messages across the bottom of the screen and then return with the selected response. The message in the lower portion of the screen should look like the one in Figure 18.6.

You can experiment with the grammar by speaking phrases and watching the response. You can also make changes to your MALL.TXT file and recompile it to add new features or refine the grammar to meet your needs.

FIGURE 18.6.

Testing the MALL *grammar.*

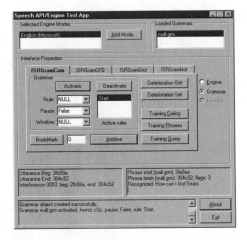

International Phonetic Alphabet

The Unicode versions of the SAPI model can support the use of the International Phonetic Alphabet (IPA) to aid in the analysis and pronunciation of words. The IPA is a standardized set of symbols for documenting phonemes.

On IPA-supported TTS systems, the IPA values can be used to adjust the pronunciation of troublesome words. This is done by associating the Unicode strings with the word in the dictionary. Some TTS engines will store this set of IPA codes as a permanent part of the dictionary. In this way, the TTS system can be refined over time to handle difficult words.

> **NOTE**
>
> Since the IPA system is only supported through Unicode, Win95 systems do not support the IPA. You can check for IPA support on WinNT-based speech systems by inspecting the TTSMODEINFO structure of TTS engines and the ILexPronounce interface of the SR engine.

SR systems that support IPA will allow users to enter IPA codes into the SR lexicon as a way of teaching the system how some words will sound. These IPA values are then used to match audio input to words in the SR engine's vocabulary, thereby improving recognition performance.

The IPA defines a common set of English consonants and vowels along with a more complex set of phoneme sets that are used to further describe English language sounds. Table 18.4 shows the list of IPA consonants and vowels with their associated Unicode values.

Table 18.4. IPA consonants and vowels.

Consonant	Examples	Unicode values
b	big, able, tab	U+0062
ch	chin, archer, march	U+0074 U+0283
d	dig, idea, wad	U+0064
f	fork, after, if	U+0066
g	gut, angle, tag	U+0261
h	help, ahead, hotel	U+0068
j	joy, agile, edge	U+0064 U+0292
k	cut, oaken, take	U+006B
l	lid	U+006C
	elbow, sail	U+026B
m	met, amid, aim	U+006D
n	no, end, pan	U+006E
ng	sing, anger, drink	U+014B
p	put, open, tap	U+0070
r	red, part, far	U+0072
s	sit, cast, toss	U+0073
sh	she, cushion, wash	U+0283
t	talk, sat	U+0074
	meter	U+027E
th	thin, nothing, truth	U+03B8
dh	then, father, scythe	U+00F0
v	vat, over, have	U+0076
w	with, away, wit	U+0077
z	zap, lazy, haze	U+007A
zh	azure, measure	U+0292
Neutral (schwa)	ago, comply	U+0259
a	at, carry, gas	U+00E6
	ate, day, tape	U+0065
	ah, car, father	U+0251
e	end, berry, ten	U+025B
	eve, be, me	U+0069

continues

Table 18.4. continued

Consonant	Examples	Unicode values
i	is, hit, lid	U+026A
	ice, bite, high	U+0061 U+026A
o	own, tone, go	U+006F
	look, pull, good	U+028A
	tool, crew, moo	U+0075
	oil, coin, toy	U+0254
	out, how, our	U+0061 U+028A
u	up, bud, cut	U+028C
	urn, fur, meter,	U+025A
y	yet, onion, yard	U+006A

The IPA system also defines a set of phonemes that describe the various complex sounds of a language. There are several general categories of sounds. Each has its own set of Unicode characters associated with it. The basic sound categories are

- *Pulmonic obstruents*—These are "stop" sounds in which the breath is obstructed in some way. Examples are words like *pig, fork,* and *chip.*
- *Pulmonic resonants*—These are "stop" sounds in which the breath is not obstructed. Examples are words such as *mouse, look, rock,* and *with.*
- *Rounded vowels*—These are sounds that are produced when the lips are rounded. Examples are *boot* and *coat.*
- *Unrounded vowels*—These are sounds that are produced without rounding the lips. Examples of unrounded vowels are *beef, father,* and *how.*

Additional information on the IPA and its use can be found in the Appendix section of the Microsoft Speech SDK documentation.

Summary

In this chapter, you learned about three aspects of the SAPI interface that are usually not seen by the average user. You learned the following:

- Control tags are used to adjust TTS engine output.
- Grammar rules are used by SR engines to interpret input.
- The International Phonetic Alphabet can be used on Unicode systems to adjust both TTS and SR performance.

You learned that Microsoft has defined 15 control tags and that they fall into three general categories:

- *Voice character control tags*—These are used to control the general character of the voice including gender, mood, age, and so on.
- *Phrase modification control tags*—These are used to control the playback speed, volume, pitch, and word emphasis.
- *Low-level TTS control tags*—These are used to inform the TTS engine of the correct pronunciation of words, identify the part of speech, call special commands, and so on.

You learned that the SAPI model supports three types of grammar: *context-free*, *dictation*, and *limited-domain*. You learned how to create your own context-free grammar with defined words and rules. You compiled and tested that grammar, too.

You learned that the context-free grammar compiler supplied by Microsoft supports the definition of words, rules, and external lists that can be filled at run-time. You also learned that there are four compiler functions:

- alt()—Used to list a set of alternative inputs.
- seq()—Used to indicate to the SR engine the sequence in which input will occur.
- opt()—Used to inform the SR engine that the word or rule is optional and may not appear as part of the input stream.
- rep()—Used to tell the SR engine that this word or rule could be repeated several times.

You designed, coded, compiled, and tested a grammar that could be used to support a voice-activated help kiosk at a shopping center.

Finally, you learned about the International Phonetic Alphabet (IPA) and how Unicode-based speech systems can use IPA to improve TTS and SR engine performance.

19

Creating SAPI Applications with C++

Most of the things you'll want to add to Windows applications can be handled using the OLE automation libraries for speech recognition (VCMDAUTO.TLB) and text-to-speech (VTXTAUTO.TLB). These libraries can be called from Visual Basic or any VBA-compliant application such as Excel, Access, Word, and so on. However, there are some things that you can only do using C or C++ languages. This includes building permanently stored grammars, calling SAPI dialog boxes, and other low-level functions. For this reason, it is a good idea to know how to perform some basic SAPI functions in C. Even if you do not regularly program in C or C++, you can still learn a lot by reading through the code in these examples.

In this chapter, you'll get a quick tour of a TTS demonstration application and an SR demonstration application. The applications reviewed here are part of the Microsoft Speech SDK. If you have the Speech SDK installed on your workstation, you can follow along with the code and compile and test the resulting application. If you do not have the SDK installed or do not have a copy of C++ with which to compile the application, you can still follow along with the review of the various functions used in the C++ programs.

When you are finished with this chapter, you will know how to build simple TTS and SR programs using C++ and the Microsoft Speech SDK.

> **NOTE**
>
> All the examples in this chapter are shipped with the Microsoft Speech SDK. The compiler used in this chapter is Microsoft Visual C++ 4.1 (VC++). If you are using another compiler, you may need to modify some of the code in order for it to work for you.

The TTS Demo Project

Creating a TTS application with C++ involves just a few basic steps. To see how this is done, you can look at the TTSDEMO.CPP source code that ships with the Microsoft Speech SDK. You can find this file in the \SPEECHSDK\SAMPLES\TTSDEMO folder that was created when you installed the Microsoft Speech SDK.

> **NOTE**
>
> If you do not have the Microsoft Speech SDK installed or do not have Visual C++, you can still follow along with the code examples shown in this chapter.

The rest of this section reviews the contents of the TTSDEMO.MAK project. There are two components to review: the DEMO.CPP source code file and the DEMO.RC file. The DEMO.CPP source code file contains all the code needed to implement TTS services for Windows using C++. The `DEMO.RC` file contains a simple dialog box that you can use to accept text input from the user and then send that text to the TTS engine for playback.

The Initial Header and Declarations for DEMO.CPP

Before you code the various routines for the TTS demo, there are a handful of include statements and a couple of global declarations that must be added. Listing 19.1 shows the include statements needed to implement TTS services in VC++.

Listing 19.1. The include statements and global declarations for DEMO.CPP.

```
/*************************************************************************
Demo.Cpp - Code to demo tts.

Copyright c. 1995 by Microsoft Corporation

*/


#include <windows.h>
#include <string.h>
#include <stdio.h>
#include <mmsystem.h>
#include <initguid.h>
#include <objbase.h>
#include <objerror.h>
#include <ole2ver.h>

#include <speech.h>
#include "resource.h"


/*************************************************************************
Globals */

HINSTANCE          ghInstance;                    // instance handle
PITTSCENTRALW      gpITTSCentral = NULL;
```

Most of the include files are part of VC++. The `speech.h` header file is shipped as part of the Microsoft Speech SDK. And the `resource.h` header file is created when you build the dialog box for the project.

The WinMain Procedure of DEMO.CPP

Since the SAPI model is implemented using the Component Object Model (COM) interface, you need to begin and end an OLE session as part of normal processing. After starting the OLE session, you need to use the `TTSCentral` interface to locate and initialize an available TTS engine. Once you have a session started with a valid TTS engine, you can use a simple dialog box to accept text input and send that text to the TTS engine using the TextData method of the TTSCentral interface. After exiting the dialog box, you need to release the connection to TTSCentral and then end the OLE session.

The code in Listing 19.2 shows the WinMain procedure for the TTSDEMO.CPP file.

Listing 19.2. The WinMain procedure of the TTSDEMO project.

```
/***************************************************************************
winmain - Windows main code.
*/

int PASCAL WinMain(HINSTANCE hInstance, HINSTANCE hPrevInstance,
                   LPSTR lpszCmdLine, int nCmdShow)
{
TTSMODEINFOW    ModeInfo;

// try to begin ole

    if (!BeginOLE())
       {
       MessageBox (NULL, "Can't create OLE.", NULL, MB_OK);
       return 1;
       }

// find the right object
    memset (&ModeInfo, 0, sizeof(ModeInfo));
    gpITTSCentral = FindAndSelect (&ModeInfo);
    if (!gpITTSCentral) {
       MessageBox (NULL, "Can't create a TTS engine.", NULL, MB_OK);
       return 1;
       };

// Bring up the dialog box
    DialogBox (hInstance, MAKEINTRESOURCE(IDD_TTS),
       NULL, (FARPROC) DialogProc);

// try to close ole
    gpITTSCentral->Release();

    if (!EndOLE())
       MessageBox (NULL, "Can't shut down OLE.", NULL, MB_OK);

    return 0;
}
```

You can see the basic steps mentioned earlier: start the OLE session, get a TTS object, and start the dialog box. Once the dialog is completed, you need to release the TTS object and end the OLE session. The rest of the code all supports the code in WinMain.

Starting and Ending the OLE Session

The code needed to start and end the OLE session is pretty basic. The code in Listing 19.3 shows both the `BeginOLE` and `EndOLE` procedures.

Listing 19.3. The `BeginOLE` and `EndOLE` procedures.

```
/****************************************************************************
BeginOLE - This begins the OLE.

inputs
    none
returns
    BOOL - TRUE if is succedes
*/

BOOL BeginOLE (void)
{
    DWORD     dwVer;

// Initialize OLE

    SetMessageQueue(96);
    dwVer = CoBuildVersion();

    if (rmm != HIWORD(dwVer)) return FALSE;          // error

    if (FAILED(CoInitialize(NULL))) return FALSE;

    return TRUE;
}


/****************************************************************************
EndOLE - This closes up the OLE.

inputs
    none
returns
    BOOL - TRUE if succede
*/

BOOL EndOLE (void)
{
// Free up all of OLE

    CoUninitialize ();

    return TRUE;
}
```

The code in Listing 19.3 shows three steps in the BeginOLE routine. The first line creates a message queue that can hold up to 96 messages. The next two lines check the OLE version, and the last line actually initializes the OLE session. The EndOLE session simply releases the OLE session you created in BeginOLE.

Selecting the TTS Engine Object

After creating the OLE session, you need to locate and select a valid TTS engine object. There are just a few steps to the process. First, you need a few local variables to keep track of your progress. Listing 19.4 shows the initial declarations for the FindAndSelect procedure.

Listing 19.4. Declarations for the FindAndSelect procedure.

```
/****************************************************************************
FindAndSelect - This finds and selects according to the specific TTSMODEINFOW.

inputs
   PTTSMODEINFOW        pTTSInfo - desired mode
returns
   PITTSCENTRAL - ISRCentral interface to TTS engine
sets:

*/

PITTSCENTRALW FindAndSelect (PTTSMODEINFOW pTTSInfo)
{
   HRESULT          hRes;
   TTSMODEINFOW          ttsResult;        // final result
   WCHAR          Zero = 0;
   PITTSFINDW       pITTSFind;        // find interface
   PIAUDIOMULTIMEDIADEVICE       pIAMM;  // multimedia device interface for audio-dest
   PITTSCENTRALW  pITTSCentral;         // central interface
```

Next, you need to create an instance of the TTSFind object. This will be used to select an available TTS engine. Listing 19.5 shows how this is done.

Listing 19.5. Creating the TTSFind object.

```
hRes = CoCreateInstance(CLSID_TTSEnumerator, NULL, CLSCTX_ALL, IID_ITTSFindW,
                                               (void**)&pITTSFind);
   if (FAILED(hRes)) return NULL;

   hRes = pITTSFind->Find(pTTSInfo, NULL, &ttsResult);

   if (hRes)
      {
      pITTSFind->Release();
      return NULL;     // error
      }
```

The next step is to locate and select an audio output object. This will be used by the TTS engine for playback of the text. Listing 19.6 shows the code needed to select an available audio device.

Listing 19.6. Selecting an available audio device.

```
// Get the audio dest
   hRes = CoCreateInstance(CLSID_MMAudioDest, NULL, CLSCTX_ALL,
➡IID_IAudioMultiMediaDevice,(void**)&pIAMM);
   if (hRes)
      {
      pITTSFind->Release;
      return NULL;      // error
      }
   pIAMM->DeviceNumSet (WAVE_MAPPER);
```

The code in Listing 19.6 uses the `DeviceNumSet` method of the `MMAudioDest` interface to find the available WAVE output device for the PC.

Once you have successfully created the `TSFind` object and the `MMAudioDest` object, you're ready to use the `Select` method of `TTSFind` to return a handle to a valid TTS engine object. After getting the handle, you can release the `TTSFind` object because it was needed only to locate a valid TTS engine object. Listing 19.7 shows how this is done.

Listing 19.7. Selecting the TTS engine and releasing `TTSFind`.

```
// Pass off the multi-media-device interface as an IUnknown (since it is one)

// Should do select now

   hRes = pITTSFind->Select(ttsResult.gModeID, &pITTSCentral, (LPUNKNOWN) pIAMM);

   if (hRes) {
      pITTSFind->Release();
      return NULL;
      };

// free random stuff up

   pITTSFind->Release();

   return pITTSCentral;
}
```

After getting a valid TTS engine and a valid audio output, you can start sending text to the TTS engine using the `TextData` method of the `TTSCentral` interface.

Sending Text to the TTS Engine

The TTSDEMO project uses a simple dialog box to accept text from the user and send it to the TTS engine. Figure 19.1 shows the dialog box in design mode.

FIGURE 19.1.

The dialog box from the TTSDEMO *project.*

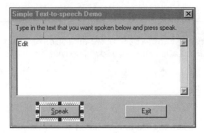

This dialog box has a single text window and two command buttons—Speak and Exit. When the user presses the OK button, the text typed into the window is sent to the TTS engine for playback. The code in Listing 19.8 shows the CallBack routine that handles the dialog box events.

Listing 19.8. Handling the dialog box callback.

```
/***********************************************************************
DialogProc
*/
BOOL CALLBACK DialogProc(HWND hWnd, UINT uMsg, WPARAM wParam, LPARAM lParam)
{
switch (uMsg) {
   case WM_COMMAND:
        switch (LOWORD(wParam))
           {
           case IDOK:
              {
              char   szSpeak[1024];
              WCHAR wszSpeak[1024];
              SDATA data;

              // Speak
              GetDlgItemText (hWnd, IDC_EDIT, szSpeak, sizeof(szSpeak));
              data.dwSize = (DWORD)
                 MultiByteToWideChar(CP_ACP, 0, szSpeak, -1, wszSpeak,
                 sizeof(wszSpeak) / sizeof(WCHAR)) * sizeof(WCHAR);
              data.pData = wszSpeak;
              gpITTSCentral->TextData (CHARSET_TEXT, 0,
                 data, NULL,
                 IID_ITTSBufNotifySinkW);
              }
              return TRUE;
           case IDCANCEL:
              EndDialog (hWnd, IDCANCEL);
              return TRUE;
```

```
        }
    break;
    };

return FALSE;  // didn't handle
}
```

Note that there are a couple of extra steps involved in sending the text to the TTS engine. The whole process involves filling an SDATA structure to pass to the TTS engine. First, the GetDlgItemText copies the text in the window into a memory location. The size of the string is inserted into the SDATA structure. Next, the MultiByteToWideChar function is used to convert the data to wide character format, and the results are loaded into the SDATA structure. Finally, the structure is passed to the TTS engine using the TextData method of the TTSCentral interface.

That's all there is to it. You can test the application by compiling it yourself or by loading the TTSDEMO.EXE application from the CD-ROM that ships with this book.

The VCMD Demo Project

Building SR applications in C++ is not much different. The biggest change is that you need to create a menu object and load it with commands that will be spoken to the SR engine. In fact, the process of loading the commands and then checking the spoken phrase against the command list is the largest part of the code.

The C++ example reviewed here is part of the Microsoft Speech SDK. The project VCMDDEMO.MAK is installed when you install the SDK. If you have the SDK installed and own a copy of C++, you can load the project and review the source code while you read this chapter.

> **NOTE**
>
> If you do not have a copy of the SDK or C++, you can still learn a lot by reviewing the code shown here.

There are two main parts to the project. The first is the DEMO.CPP source code. This file contains the main C++ code for the project. The second part of the project is the VCMDDEMO.RC resource file. This file contains the definitions of two dialog boxes used in the project.

The Initial Header and Declarations for the VCMDDEMO Project

The first thing that must be done is to add the include and declaration statements to the source code. These will be used throughout the project. Most of the include files are a part of the VC++ system. However, the last two items (speech.h and resource.h) are unique. The speech.h file ships with the SDK. The resource.h file contains information about the two dialog boxes used in the project. The define statements establish some constant values that will be used to track timer events later in the project. Listing 19.9 shows the header and include code for the project.

Listing 19.9. The include and header code for the VCMDDEMO project.

```
/*************************************************************************
Demo.Cpp - Code to quickly demo voice commands.

Copyright c. 1995 by Microsoft Corporation

*/


#include <windows.h>
#include <string.h>
#include <stdio.h>
#include <mmsystem.h>
#include <initguid.h>
#include <objbase.h>
#include <objerror.h>
#include <ole2ver.h>

#include <speech.h>
#include "resource.h"

#define   TIMER_CHANGECOMMAND      (52)
#define   TIMER_CLEARRESULT        (53)
```

The VCMDDEMO project uses notification callbacks to receive messages from the SR engine. Since the SAPI system is based on the Component Object Model (COM), you'll need to include some code that creates the needed class object and associated methods. Listing 19.10 shows the code needed to declare the class and methods of the event notification routine.

Listing 19.10. Declaring the event notification class and methods.

```
// Voice Command notifications
class CIVCmdNotifySink : public IVCmdNotifySink {
    private:
    DWORD    m_dwMsgCnt;
    HWND     m_hwnd;

    public:
    CIVCmdNotifySink(void);
    ~CIVCmdNotifySink(void);


    // IUnknown members that delegate to m_punkOuter
    // Non-delegating object IUnknown
    STDMETHODIMP          QueryInterface (REFIID, LPVOID FAR *);
    STDMETHODIMP_(ULONG) AddRef(void);
    STDMETHODIMP_(ULONG) Release(void);
```

```
        // IVCmdNotifySink members
        STDMETHODIMP CommandRecognize (DWORD, PVCMDNAME, DWORD, DWORD, PVOID,
                                       DWORD,PSTR, PSTR);
        STDMETHODIMP CommandOther     (PVCMDNAME, PSTR);
        STDMETHODIMP MenuActivate     (PVCMDNAME, BOOL);
        STDMETHODIMP UtteranceBegin   (void);
        STDMETHODIMP UtteranceEnd     (void);
        STDMETHODIMP CommandStart     (void);
        STDMETHODIMP VUMeter          (WORD);
        STDMETHODIMP AttribChanged    (DWORD);
        STDMETHODIMP Interference     (DWORD);
};
typedef CIVCmdNotifySink * PCIVCmdNotifySink;
```

There is one more step needed as part of the initial declarations. The VCMDDEMO project must declare a list of commands to be loaded into the menu. These are the commands that the SR engine will be able to recognize when a user speaks. The project also uses a handful of other global-level declarations in the project. Listing 19.11 shows the final set of declarations for the project.

Listing 19.11. Declaring the menu commands for the project.

```
/***********************************************************************
Globals */

HINSTANCE          ghInstance;                    // instance handle
CIVCmdNotifySink   gVCmdNotifySink;
HWND               ghwndResultsDisplay = NULL;
HWND               ghwndDialog = NULL;
PIVOICECMD         gpIVoiceCommand = NULL;
PIVCMDDIALOGS      gpIVCmdDialogs = NULL;
PIVCMDMENU         gpIVCmdMenu = NULL;
char               *gpszCommands = NULL; // Commands
char               *gpszCurCommand = NULL;  // current command that looking at

char  gszDefaultSet[] = // default command set
    "Help\r\n"
    "Minimize window.\r\n"
    "Maximize window.\r\n"
    "What time is it?\r\n"
    "What day is it?\r\n"
    "Create a new file.\r\n"
    "Delete the current file\r\n"
    "Open a file\r\n"
    "Switch to Word.\r\n"
    "Switch to Excel.\r\n"
    "Switch to calculator.\r\n"
    "Change the background color.\r\n"
    "Go to sleep.\r\n"
    "Wake up.\r\n"
    "Print the document.\r\n"
    "Speak the text.\r\n"
    "Paste\r\n"
```

continues

Listing 19.11. continued

```
  "Copy\r\n";

BOOL       bNonFatalShutDown = FALSE;
int CheckNavigator(void);
DWORD VCMDState(PIVCMDATTRIBUTES);
```

The `WinMain` **Procedure of the** `VCMDDEMO` **Project**

The main routine of the project is quite simple. First, the project performs basic initialization by starting the OLE session, initializing the SR engine, and making sure it is up and running. After the OLE routines are done, the default list of commands is loaded, and the first dialog box is presented. This first dialog box simply displays a list of possible commands and listens to see if the user utters any of them (see Figure 19.2).

FIGURE 19.2.

Main dialog box of the
VCMDDEMO project.

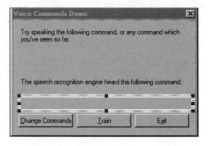

This same dialog box has a button that the user can press to bring up a secondary dialog box. This second dialog box allows the user to create a custom list of commands to recognize. Once the commands are entered, they are used to replace the default set, and the listening dialog box returns (see Figure 19.3).

FIGURE 19.3.

Secondary dialog box of the
VCMDDEMO project.

Once the user exits the top dialog box, string resources are freed and the OLE objects are released. Listing 19.12 shows the complete WinMain procedure.

Listing 19.12. The VCMDDEMO project WinMain procedure.

```
/**************************************************************************
winmain - Windows main code.
*/

int PASCAL WinMain(HINSTANCE hInstance, HINSTANCE hPrevInstance,
                  LPSTR lpszCmdLine, int nCmdShow)
{
ghInstance = hInstance;

// try to begin ole

   if (!BeginOLE())
   {
      if(!bNonFatalShutDown)
         MessageBox (NULL, "Can't open. OLE or a VoiceCommands call failed", NULL,
➥MB_OK);
      return 1;
   }


// Create a menu out of the default
gpszCommands = (char*) malloc (strlen(gszDefaultSet)+1);
if (!gpszCommands)
   return 1;
strcpy (gpszCommands, gszDefaultSet);
gpszCurCommand = gpszCommands;

// Bring up the dialog box
   DialogBox (hInstance, MAKEINTRESOURCE(IDD_VCMD),
      NULL, (FARPROC) DialogProc);

if (gpszCommands)
   free (gpszCommands);

// try to close ole
   if (!EndOLE())
      MessageBox (NULL, "Can't shut down OLE.", NULL, MB_OK);

   return 0;
}
```

Starting and Ending the OLE Session

All C++ programs need to use the OLE services of Windows to access SAPI services. The BeginOLE routine of the VCMDDEMO project covers a lot of ground. This one routine handles OLE initialization, the registration of SAPI services, creation of several SR objects, checking the registry for SAPI-related entries, and checking the status of the SR engine on the workstation.

The first step is to establish the start of OLE services. Listing 19.13 shows this part of the BeginOLE routine.

Listing 19.13. Starting the OLE services.

```
/*************************************************************************
BeginOLE - This begins the OLE and creates the voice commands object,
   registers with it, and creates a temporary menu.

inputs
   none
returns
   BOOL - TRUE if is succedes
*/

BOOL BeginOLE (void)
{
   DWORD    dwVer; // OLE version
   HRESULT  hRes;
   VCMDNAME VcmdName; // Command Name
   LANGUAGE Language; // language to use
   PIVCMDATTRIBUTES  pIVCmdAttributes;


   gpIVoiceCommand = NULL;
   gpIVCmdDialogs = NULL;
   gpIVCmdMenu = NULL;

// Initialize OLE

   SetMessageQueue(96);
   dwVer = CoBuildVersion();

   if (rmm != HIWORD(dwVer)) return FALSE;          // error

   if (FAILED(CoInitialize(NULL))) return FALSE;
```

The next step is to create a Voice Command object, get a pointer to one of the training dialog boxes provided by SAPI, and register the VCMDDEMO application to receive notifications when the SR engine recognizes a command. Listing 19.14 shows this part of the BeginOLE routine.

Listing 19.14. Creating the Voice Command object and registering the application.

```
// Create the voice commands object
if (CoCreateInstance(CLSID_VCmd,
   NULL,
   CLSCTX_LOCAL_SERVER,
   IID_IVoiceCmd,
   (LPVOID *)&gpIVoiceCommand) != S_OK)
      goto fail;

// Get the dialogs object
hRes = gpIVoiceCommand->QueryInterface(
```

```
        IID_IVCmdDialogs, (LPVOID FAR *)&gpIVCmdDialogs);
if (hRes)
   goto fail;

// Register
hRes = gpIVoiceCommand->Register("", &gVCmdNotifySink,
      IID_IVCmdNotifySink, VCMDRF_ALLMESSAGES, NULL);
if (hRes)
   goto fail;
```

If all that goes well, the next section of code creates a link to a command object attribute interface and checks the status of SAPI services on the workstation. The CheckNavigator routine checks the registry to see if speech services are present. If they are, the VCMDState routine is used to return a value indicating the status of SAPI services. Based on the return value, several different messages are displayed in dialog boxes for the user to review. These two routines are reviewed later in this chapter. Listing 19.15 shows the next part of the BeginOLE routine.

Listing 19.15. Checking the attributes of the SR engine.

```
//The following code checks for a navigator app and
//checks the state of voice commands

hRes = gpIVoiceCommand->QueryInterface(
   IID_IVCmdAttributes, (LPVOID FAR *)&pIVCmdAttributes);
if (pIVCmdAttributes)
{
      int      iRes;
   DWORD     dwRes;

   iRes = CheckNavigator();

   if (iRes == -1)//navigator not installed or has never been run(entries not in
►registry)
   {
         MessageBox(NULL, "A navigator application is not installed on your system
►or it has \
been installed but has not been run. \r\nVCMD Demo can not continue", "Error",
►MB_OK ¦ MB_ICONSTOP);
         pIVCmdAttributes->Release();
         bNonFatalShutDown = TRUE;
         goto fail;
   }

   else if(iRes == 0)// navigator installed but not running
   {
         int iMBRes;

         iMBRes = MessageBox(NULL, "A navigator application is installed but not
►running. \
You can press \"Cancel\" and enable speech recognition by starting the navigator
►application or \
press \"OK\" and VCMD Demo will enable Speech Recognition without starting the
```

continues

Listing 19.15. continued

```
navigator application", "Speech Recognition Status", MB_OKCANCEL |
➥MB_ICONQUESTION);

        if(iMBRes == IDCANCEL)
        {
            pIVCmdAttributes->Release();
            bNonFatalShutDown = TRUE;
            goto fail;
        }
        else if(iMBRes == IDOK)
        {
            pIVCmdAttributes->EnabledSet( TRUE );
            pIVCmdAttributes->AwakeStateSet( TRUE );
        }
    }

    else if (iRes == 1)// navigator installed and running
    {
        dwRes = VCMDState(pIVCmdAttributes);
        if(dwRes == 0)
            MessageBox(NULL, "Speech recognition is currently turned off. Please
➥turn it on using the Navigator application.", "Speech Recognition Status",
➥MB_ICONINFORMATION);
        else if(dwRes == 1)
            MessageBox(NULL, "Speech recognition is currently in standby mode.
➥Please turn it on using the Navigator application.", "Speech Recognition Status",
➥MB_ICONINFORMATION);
        else if(dwRes == 3)
        {
            MessageBox(NULL, "Voice Commands Call failed. This application will
➥terminate.", "Error", MB_ICONSTOP | MB_OK);
            pIVCmdAttributes->Release();
            goto fail;
        }
    }

    pIVCmdAttributes->Release();
};
```

Finally, the routine creates a menu object to hold the command list. The final part of the routine contains code that is invoked in case of errors. This code releases any collected resources. Listing 19.16 shows the final portion of the BeginOLE routine.

Listing 19.16. Creating the Voice Command menu object.

```
// Create a menu object
lstrcpy (VcmdName.szApplication, "Voice Commands Demo");
lstrcpy (VcmdName.szState, "Main");
Language.LanguageID = LANG_ENGLISH;
lstrcpy (Language.szDialect, "US English");
hRes = gpIVoiceCommand->MenuCreate( &VcmdName,
    &Language,
    VCMDMC_CREATE_TEMP,
```

```
      &gpIVCmdMenu
      );
if (hRes)
   goto fail;

return TRUE;


   // else failed

fail:
   if (gpIVoiceCommand)
      gpIVoiceCommand->Release();
   if (gpIVCmdDialogs)
      gpIVCmdDialogs->Release();
   if (gpIVCmdMenu)
      gpIVCmdMenu->Release();
   gpIVoiceCommand = NULL;
   gpIVCmdDialogs = NULL;
   gpIVCmdMenu = NULL;

   return FALSE;
}
```

After the user exits the main dialog box, the WinMain routine calls the EndOLE procedure. This procedure releases SAPI resources and closes out the OLE session. Listing 19.17 shows the code for the EndOLE procedure.

Listing 19.17. The EndOLE procedure.

```
/***************************************************************************
EndOLE - This closes up the OLE and frees everything else.

inputs
   none
returns
   BOOL - TRUE if succeed
*/

BOOL EndOLE (void)
{
// Free the interfaces
   if (gpIVoiceCommand)
      gpIVoiceCommand->Release();
   if (gpIVCmdDialogs)
      gpIVCmdDialogs->Release();
   if (gpIVCmdMenu)
      gpIVCmdMenu->Release();
   gpIVoiceCommand = NULL;
   gpIVCmdDialogs = NULL;
   gpIVCmdMenu = NULL;

// Free up all of OLE
```

continues

Listing 19.17. continued

```
    CoUninitialize ();

    return TRUE;
}
```

Checking the Status of Speech Services

The VCMDDEMO project contains two routines that check the status of speech services on the workstation. The first routine (CheckNavigator) checks the Windows registry to see if speech services have been installed on the machine. Listing 19.18 shows the CheckNavigator procedure.

Listing 19.18. The CheckNavigator procedure.

```
/***************************************************************************
*    CheckNavigator:
*
*    Checks the registry entries to see if a navigator application
*    has been installed on the machine. If the Navigator is installed
*    CheckNavigator returns its state(0 [not running], 1 [running]) else if no
*    navigator is found it returns -1.
***************************************************************************/
int CheckNavigator(void)
{
    HKEY   hKey;
    DWORD dwType=REG_DWORD, dwSize=sizeof(DWORD), dwVal;

    if( RegOpenKeyEx(HKEY_CURRENT_USER, "Software\\Voice", 0, KEY_READ, &hKey) !=
➥ERROR_SUCCESS )
        return -1;

    if( RegQueryValueEx (hKey, "UseSpeech", 0, &dwType, (LPBYTE)&dwVal, &dwSize) !=
➥ERROR_SUCCESS )
        return -1;

    RegCloseKey (hKey);

    return (int)dwVal;
}
```

The second routine in VCMDDEMO that checks the status of speech services is the VCMDState procedure. This routine uses the EnabledGet method of the Attributes interface to see whether the SR engine is already listening for audio input. Listing 19.19 shows the code for the VCMDState routine.

Listing 19.19. The VCMDState procedure.

```
/****************************************************************************
*     VCMDState:
*
*     Determines what listening state Voice Commands is in. Returns an int
*     specifying a state( 0 [not listening state], 1 [sleep state], 2 [listening
*     state]) or in case of error returns 3.
****************************************************************************/

DWORD VCMDState(PIVCMDATTRIBUTES pIVCmdAttributes)
{
    DWORD dwAwake, dwEnabled;

    dwAwake = dwEnabled = 0;
    if((FAILED(pIVCmdAttributes->EnabledGet(&dwEnabled))) ||
➡(FAILED(pIVCmdAttributes->AwakeStateGet(&dwAwake))))
        return 3;// function failed
    else
    {
        if(dwEnabled == 0)
            return 0; //not listening state
        else if(dwEnabled == 1 && dwAwake == 0)
            return 1; //sleep state
        else
            return 2; //listening state
    }
}
```

Handling the Main Dialog Box Events

Once the main dialog box starts, there are four possible events to handle. First, upon initiation of the dialog box, the commands are loaded into the menu object, and the timer is activated. The next possible event is the user pressing one of the three command buttons on the form. Here, if Cancel is selected, the program is ended. If the Train button is selected, a general dialog box (supplied by the engine) is called. Finally, if the Change button is pressed, the secondary dialog box is presented.

While waiting for the user to press a button, the timer event fires every two seconds. Each time the timer event occurs, the program displays a new command on the main form and waits for the user to speak the phrase. Finally, upon exiting the dialog box, the timer is canceled and the routine is exited. Listing 19.20 shows the code for this procedure.

Listing 19.20. Handling the main dialog box events.

```
/****************************************************************************
DialogProc
*/
BOOL CALLBACK DialogProc(HWND hWnd, UINT uMsg, WPARAM wParam, LPARAM lParam)
{
```

continues

Listing 19.20. continued

```
switch (uMsg) {
    case WM_INITDIALOG:
        ghwndResultsDisplay = GetDlgItem (hWnd, IDC_HEARD);
        ghwndDialog = hWnd;

        if (UseCommands (gpszCommands, gpIVCmdMenu))
            return 1;   // error

        SetTimer (hWnd, TIMER_CHANGECOMMAND, 2000, NULL);
        PostMessage (hWnd, WM_TIMER, TIMER_CHANGECOMMAND, 0);
        return FALSE;
    case WM_COMMAND:
        switch (LOWORD(wParam))
            {
            case IDC_CHANGE:
                // Change commands dialog box
                DialogBox (ghInstance, MAKEINTRESOURCE(IDD_CHANGE),
                    hWnd, (FARPROC) ChangeProc);
                return TRUE;
            case IDC_TRAIN:
                gpIVCmdDialogs->GeneralDlg (hWnd, "Demo Training & General
➥Control");
                return TRUE;
            case IDCANCEL:
                EndDialog (hWnd, IDCANCEL);
                return TRUE;
            }
        break;
    case WM_TIMER:
        if (wParam == TIMER_CHANGECOMMAND) {
            char     *pszToDisplay;
            DWORD    dwSize;
            char     cTemp;

            // go to the next command
            if (!gpszCurCommand)
                gpszCurCommand = gpszCommands;
            gpszCurCommand = NextCommand (gpszCurCommand,
                &pszToDisplay, &dwSize);
            if (gpszCurCommand) {
                cTemp = pszToDisplay[dwSize];
                pszToDisplay[dwSize] = '\0';
                SetDlgItemText (hWnd, IDC_COMMAND, pszToDisplay);
                pszToDisplay[dwSize] = cTemp;
                };
            }
        else {
            // clear the static
            KillTimer (hWnd, TIMER_CLEARRESULT);
            SetDlgItemText (hWnd, IDC_HEARD, "");
            };
        return TRUE;
    case WM_DESTROY:
        KillTimer (hWnd, TIMER_CHANGECOMMAND);
        break;   // continue on
```

```
    };

return FALSE;   // didn't handle
}
```

Handling the Change Dialog Box Events

The secondary dialog box allows the user to create a new, customized menu. When the OK button is pressed, the new command list is copied to the menu object using the UseCommands routine. Listing 19.21 contains the code for the ChangeProc procedure.

Listing 19.21. Handling the change dialog events.

```
/**********************************************************************
ChangeProc
*/
BOOL CALLBACK ChangeProc(HWND hWnd, UINT uMsg, WPARAM wParam, LPARAM lParam)
{
switch (uMsg) {
    case WM_INITDIALOG:
        SetDlgItemText (hWnd, IDC_EDIT, gpszCommands);
        return FALSE;
    case WM_COMMAND:
        switch (LOWORD(wParam))
            {
            case IDOK:
                {
                char      *pszNew;
                DWORD     dwSize;
                // Throw out the old buffer & copy the
                // new one in. Then set us to use it
                pszNew = (char*) malloc (dwSize =
                    GetWindowTextLength(GetDlgItem(hWnd, IDC_EDIT)) + 1);
                if (pszNew) {
                    GetDlgItemText (hWnd, IDC_EDIT, pszNew, dwSize);
                    free (gpszCommands);
                    gpszCommands = pszNew;
                    gpszCurCommand = pszNew;
                    if (UseCommands (gpszCommands, gpIVCmdMenu))
                        return 1;    // error

                    };
                EndDialog (hWnd, IDOK);
                }
                return TRUE;
            case IDCANCEL:
                EndDialog (hWnd, IDCANCEL);
                return TRUE;
            }
        break;
    };

return FALSE;   // didn't handle
}
```

Handling the Menu Commands

The VCMDDEMO project uses three routines to handle the process of loading commands into the voice menu object and responding to recognized spoken commands. The UseCommands procedure is the high-level routine that loads the voice menu object. There are five steps to complete for loading the menu. First, the current menu is deactivated. Then the number of commands in the menu is updated (pMenu->Num). Next, all the commands in the existing menu are removed using the pMenu->Remove method.

Once all commands are removed, the GetCommands procedure is called to collect all the new commands into a single data block. This block is then used as the source for adding the new menus (pMenu->Add). Notice that the C++ Add method allows you to add all menus at once by telling the SR engine to total the number of commands in the data block. After the data is loaded, the memory is freed and the menu is reactivated using the pMenu->Activate method. Listing 19.22 shows how this looks in the VCMDDEMO code.

Listing 19.22. The UseCommands procedure.

```
/****************************************************************************
UseCommands - This accepts a NULL-terminated string with commands
    separated by new-lines and loads them into the voice-menu object,
    replacing any old commands.

inputs
    char      *pszCommands - String.
    PIVCMDMENU  pMenu - Menu
returns
    HRESULT - error
*/
HRESULT UseCommands (char *pszCommands, PIVCMDMENU pMenu)
{
HRESULT  hRes;
SDATA    data;
DWORD    dwNum, dwStart;

hRes = pMenu->Deactivate ();
if (hRes) return hRes;

hRes = pMenu->Num (&dwNum);
if (hRes) return hRes;

if (dwNum)
    hRes = pMenu->Remove (1, dwNum, VCMD_BY_POSITION);
if (hRes) return hRes;

if (!GetCommands(pszCommands, &data, &dwNum))
    return ResultFromScode (E_OUTOFMEMORY);

hRes = pMenu->Add (dwNum, data, &dwStart);
if (hRes) return hRes;
```

```
// free memory
free (data.pData);

hRes = pMenu->Activate(ghwndDialog, 0);
return hRes;
}
```

The GetCommands procedure converts the text strings stored in the memory block into the menu commands structure understood by the SAPI system. The first step is a call to NextCommand to get a command line to load. Then, after computing the total length of the command, a series of steps is executed to build a valid menu structure. This continues in a loop until the NextCommand procedure reports that all command strings have been converted. Listing 19.23 shows the source code for the GetCommands procedure.

Listing 19.23. The GetCommands procedure.

```
/******************************************************************
GetCommands - Takes a block of memory containing command strings and
    converts it into a list of VCMDCOMMAND structures.

inputs
    char     *pszMemory - NULL terminated string. Commands are
                 separated by \n or \r.
    PSDATA   pData - This is filled in with a pointer to memory and
                 size for the vcmdcommand structure. The memory
                 must be freed by the caller with free().
    DWORD    *pdwNumCommands - Filled with the number of commands
*/
BOOL GetCommands(char *pszMemory, PSDATA pData, DWORD *pdwNumCommands)
{
    PSTR pTemp;
    DWORD dwTotal, dwSize, dwSizeDesc, dwSizeCat;
    DWORD dwSizeCmd;
    PVCMDCOMMAND pCmd, pCmdNew;
    CHAR    *pszBegin;
    DWORD   dwCmdSize;
    DWORD   dwCmds = 0;   // Current count
    DWORD   dwCount = 1;  // Command number
    char    szCat[] = "Main";

    dwTotal = dwSize = 0;

    pTemp = (PSTR)malloc(0);
    if (!pTemp)
        return FALSE;

    pCmd = (PVCMDCOMMAND)pTemp;
    for( ;; ) {
        pszMemory = NextCommand (pszMemory, &pszBegin, &dwCmdSize);
        if (!pszMemory)
            break;   // no more
```

continues

Listing 19.23. continued

```
        // size of header
        dwSize = sizeof(VCMDCOMMAND);

        // get command length
        dwSizeCmd = (dwCmdSize + 1);

        // doubleword align
        dwSizeCmd += 3;
        dwSizeCmd &= (~3);
        dwSize += dwSizeCmd;

        // get description length
        dwSizeDesc = (dwCmdSize + 1);

        // doubleword align
        dwSizeDesc += 3;
        dwSizeDesc &= (~3);
        dwSize += dwSizeDesc;

        // get category length
        dwSizeCat = lstrlen(szCat) + 1;

        // doubleword align
        dwSizeCat += 3;
        dwSizeCat &= (~3);
        dwSize += dwSizeCat;

        // action indicator
        dwSize += sizeof(DWORD);

        // accumulate total size
        dwTotal += dwSize;

        // reallocate enough memory to hold this command
        pTemp = (PSTR)realloc((PVOID)pCmd, dwTotal);

        // fill in the new command
        pCmd = (PVCMDCOMMAND)pTemp;
        pTemp += (dwTotal-dwSize);
        pCmdNew = (PVCMDCOMMAND)pTemp;
        memset (pCmdNew, 0, dwSize);

        pCmdNew->dwSize = dwSize;
        pCmdNew->dwFlags = 0;
        pCmdNew->dwAction = (DWORD)(pCmdNew->abData-(PBYTE)pTemp);
        pCmdNew->dwActionSize = sizeof(DWORD);
        pCmdNew->dwCommandText = NULL;

        // point past header to begin of data
        pTemp += (pCmdNew->abData-(PBYTE)pTemp);

        // action index
        *(DWORD *)pTemp = dwCount++;
        pTemp += sizeof(DWORD);
```

```
        // command
        pCmdNew->dwCommand = (DWORD)((PBYTE)pTemp - (PBYTE)pCmdNew);
        strncpy(pTemp, pszBegin, dwCmdSize);
        pTemp += dwSizeCmd;

        // description
        pCmdNew->dwDescription = (DWORD)((PBYTE)pTemp - (PBYTE)pCmdNew);
        strncpy(pTemp, pszBegin, dwCmdSize);
        pTemp += dwSizeDesc;

        // category
        pCmdNew->dwCategory = (DWORD)((PBYTE)pTemp - (PBYTE)pCmdNew);
        strcpy(pTemp, szCat);

        // we just added another command
        dwCmds++;
    }

    pData->pData = (PVOID)pCmd;
    pData->dwSize = dwTotal;
    *pdwNumCommands = dwCmds;
    return TRUE;
}
```

The final routine that handles the processing of menu commands is the `NextCommand` procedure. This routine searches the command list data block for characters until a newline character is found. The resulting string is assumed to be a valid command. This command is returned, and the starting position is updated for the next call to this routine. Listing 19.24 shows the code for the `NextCommand` routine.

Listing 19.24. The `NextCommand` procedure.

```
/******************************************************************
NextCommand - This looks in the memory and finds the next command.

inputs
    CHAR    *pszMemory - Memory to start looking at
    PCHAR   *pBegin - Filled in with a pointer to the
        beginning of the command string.
    DWORD   *pdwSize - Filled in with the number of bytes in
        the string (excluding any NULL termination)
returns
    CHAR * - The next place that NextCommand should be called from,
        or NULL if no command string was found.
*/
CHAR * NextCommand (CHAR *pszMemory, PCHAR *pBegin,
    DWORD *pdwSize)
{
DWORD i;

for( ;; ) {
    // try to find a non-newline
    while ((*pszMemory == '\n') || (*pszMemory == '\r')) {
```

continues

Listing 19.24. continued

```
    if (*pszMemory == '\0')
        return NULL;
    pszMemory++;
    };

// Try to find a new-line
for (i = 0;
    (pszMemory[i] != '\n') && (pszMemory[i] != '\r') && (pszMemory[i] != '\0');
    i++);
if (!i) {
    if (!pszMemory[i])
        return NULL;    // end
    pszMemory++;
    continue;    // try again
    };

// Else, we've found a string
*pBegin = pszMemory;
*pdwSize = i;
return pszMemory + i;
    };
}
```

The Notification Events

The final code section to review is the code that handles the various notification events of the voice command menu object. In this program, most of the events are ignored. However, the two most important events—CommandRecognized and CommandOther—contain code that will display the command spoken. The standard COM methods (QueryInterface, AddRef, and Release) are also coded. Listing 19.25 contains the code for the notification events.

Listing 19.25. Handling the notification events.

```
/***************************************************************************
 *  Voice Command notification objects
 ***************************************************************************/

CIVCmdNotifySink::CIVCmdNotifySink (void)
{
    m_dwMsgCnt = 0;
}

CIVCmdNotifySink::~CIVCmdNotifySink (void)
{
// this space intentionally left blank
}

STDMETHODIMP CIVCmdNotifySink::QueryInterface (REFIID riid, LPVOID *ppv)
{
    *ppv = NULL;
```

```
    /* always return our IUnknown for IID_IUnknown */
    if (IsEqualIID (riid, IID_IUnknown) || IsEqualIID(riid,IID_IVCmdNotifySink)) {
        *ppv = (LPVOID) this;
        return NOERROR;
    }

    // otherwise, can't find
    return ResultFromScode (E_NOINTERFACE);
}

STDMETHODIMP_ (ULONG) CIVCmdNotifySink::AddRef (void)
{
    // normally this increases a reference count, but this object
    // is going to be freed as soon as the app is freed, so it doesn't
    // matter
    return 1;
}

STDMETHODIMP_(ULONG) CIVCmdNotifySink::Release (void)
{
    // normally this releases a reference count, but this object
    // is going to be freed when the application is freed so it doesn't
    // matter
    return 1;
};


STDMETHODIMP CIVCmdNotifySink::CommandRecognize(DWORD dwID, PVCMDNAME pName,
    DWORD dwFlags, DWORD dwActionSize, PVOID pAction, DWORD dwNumLists,
    PSTR pszListValues, PSTR pszCommand)
{
// This is called when a recognition occurs for the current application

if (!ghwndResultsDisplay)
    return NOERROR;

SetWindowText (ghwndResultsDisplay,
    pszCommand ? pszCommand : "[Unrecognized]");

// Kill the timer & restart it
if (ghwndDialog) {
    KillTimer (ghwndDialog, TIMER_CLEARRESULT);
    SetTimer (ghwndDialog, TIMER_CLEARRESULT, 2000, NULL);
    };

return NOERROR;
}


STDMETHODIMP CIVCmdNotifySink::CommandOther(PVCMDNAME pName, PSTR pszCommand)
{
// This is called when a recognition occurs for another application,
// or an unknown recognition occurs

if (!ghwndResultsDisplay)
    return NOERROR;
```

continues

Listing 19.25. continued

```
SetWindowText (ghwndResultsDisplay,
   pszCommand ? pszCommand : "[Unrecognized]");

// Kill the timer & restart it
if (ghwndDialog) {
   KillTimer (ghwndDialog, TIMER_CLEARRESULT);
   SetTimer (ghwndDialog, TIMER_CLEARRESULT, 2000, NULL);
   };


return NOERROR;
}

STDMETHODIMP CIVCmdNotifySink::MenuActivate(PVCMDNAME pName, BOOL bActive)
{
// Called when a menu is activated or deactivated. We don't care.

   return NOERROR;
}

STDMETHODIMP CIVCmdNotifySink::AttribChanged(DWORD dwAttribute)
{
// Called when an attribute changes. We don't care.
   return NOERROR;
}

STDMETHODIMP CIVCmdNotifySink::Interference(DWORD dwType)
{
// Called when audio interference is happening. We don't care.
   return NOERROR;
}

STDMETHODIMP CIVCmdNotifySink::CommandStart(void)
{
// Called when SR starts processing a command. We don't care.
   return NOERROR;
}

STDMETHODIMP CIVCmdNotifySink::UtteranceBegin(void)
{
// Called when an utterance begins. We don't care.
   return NOERROR;
}

STDMETHODIMP CIVCmdNotifySink::UtteranceEnd()
{
// Called when an utterance finishes. We don't care.
   return NOERROR;
}

STDMETHODIMP CIVCmdNotifySink::VUMeter(WORD wLevel)
{
// Called for VU meter notifications. We don't care.
   return NOERROR;
}
```

That completes the review of the VCMDDEMO project. You can test this project by compiling the project or just by running the VCMDDEMO.EXE program. You'll find this in the SPEECH\BIN directory that was created when you installed the Microsoft Speech SDK. You can also find this program on the CD-ROM that ships with this book.

Summary

In this chapter, you learned how to write simple TTS and SR applications using C++. You reviewed (and hopefully were able to build) a simple TTS program that you can use to cut and paste any text for playback. You also reviewed (built and tested) a simple SR interface to illustrate the techniques required to add SR services to existing applications.

In the next chapter, you'll build a complete program in Visual Basic 4.0 that uses both SR and TTS services to implement a voice-activated text reader.

20

Building the Voice-Activated Text Reader

In this chapter, you'll build a complete Visual Basic 4.0 application that uses both speech recognition and text-to-speech services. You'll use the MDINOTE project that ships with Visual Basic 4.0 as a starting framework for creating a voice-activated text reader. This application will allow users to use voice commands to load text documents and then tell the workstation to play back the loaded documents using TTS services.

You'll learn how to declare your own custom voice commands and how to use the voice commands automatically built by Windows each time you load an application. You'll also learn how to add menu options and toolbar buttons that provide TTS services for your application. When you are done with the example project in this chapter, you'll know how to build SAPI-enabled applications using Visual Basic 4.0 or any other VBA-compliant language.

Designing the Application

The first stage in the process of building a SAPI-enabled Windows application is designing the SAPI interface. Adding SAPI services to an application is much like adding other Windows extensions (such as messaging, telephony, and so on). Usually, you can start from an existing application framework and add SAPI services where appropriate.

In order for you to focus on the process of incorporating SAPI services into an application, the project in this chapter starts from a working Visual Basic 4.0 application—the MDINOTE.VBP project. This application allows users to create, edit, and save text files.

> **NOTE**
>
> This project ships with Visual Basic 4.0 and can be found in the SAMPLES\MDI folder of the Visual Basic home directory. You can also find it on the CD-ROM that ships with this book.

For the example in this chapter, you'll add both speech recognition and text-to-speech services to this application. When you complete the project outlined here, you'll have a fully functional text editor that provides both SR and TTS services to users.

Adding TTS Services

Adding TTS services to the MDINOTE.VBP project is really quite simple. You will need to provide an option that allows users to tell the TTS engine to read the selected text. You should also allow users to fast-forward the reader, rewind it, and stop it as needed. The easiest way to do this is to provide a set of menu options that correspond to the SAPI TTS Speak, FastForward, Rewind, and StopSpeaking services. In addition to adding menu options, you'll also add command buttons to appear on the toolbar.

Adding TTS services also requires some initialization code to declare and initialize the Voice Text object.

Adding SR Services

Adding speech recognition services to Windows 95 applications is very easy. First, as soon as the SAPI services are installed and activated, all the menu options of a Windows application are valid voice commands. In other words, even if you have done no coding at all, your Windows 95 applications are ready to receive and respond to voice commands.

> **TIP**
>
> As soon as you load a Windows application, the menu options are activated as valid voice commands. You can view the valid voice commands at any moment by saying *What Can I Say?* or by selecting the alternate mouse button while pointing to the Microsoft Voice balloon icon in the system tray.

In addition to the default menu option commands, you'll also add a set of custom commands for the MDINOTE.VBP project. These are one-word commands that the user can speak. They correspond to the set of toolbar buttons that appear on the form while the project is running.

Along with the code that declares the menu commands and their objects, you'll also write code to check the CommandSpoken property and respond to the voice commands as needed.

Coding the MDISpeech Module

The first job in adding speech services to a project is declaring global variables and adding the initialization routines for starting and ending the application. If you are adding TTS services, you need to add code that will respond to the various TTS engine requests (Speak, FastForward, Rewind, and Stop). If you are enabling custom SR voice commands, you'll need to add code that registers the new commands.

> **NOTE**
>
> You'll also need code that checks the CommandSpoken property of the Voice Command object to see if one of your custom commands was uttered by the user. You'll add that code to the main form later in this chapter.

Declaring the Global Variables

For the project described in this chapter, you'll need to add both SR and TTS services. First, load the MDINOTE project and add a new BAS module. Set its Name property to modSpeech and save it as MDISP.BAS. Next add the code shown in Listing 20.1 to the general declaration section of the module.

Listing 20.1. Adding code to the declaration section.

```
Option Explicit
'
' **********************************************
' This module adds SAPI support to the program.
' **********************************************

'
' VCmd speech stuff
Global objVCmd As Object ' SR Command object
Global objVMenu As Object ' SR Menu object
Global cVCmdMenu() As String ' SR command strings
Global lSRCmd As Long ' SR command ID
'
' VTxt Speech stuff
Global objVText As Object ' TTS object
Global bVText As Boolean ' TTS flag
Global Const vTxtSpeak = 0
Global Const vTxtForward = 1
Global Const vTxtRewind = 2
Global Const vTxtStop = 3
```

The first several code lines declare the variables and objects needed to provide SR services. The SAPI voice command object library requires two different objects: the Voice Command object and the Voice Menu object. You'll also need an array to hold the commands to be added to the menu and a variable to hold the menu ID returned in the CommandSpoken property.

The TTS service requires only one object. You'll use a Boolean flag to hold the activity status of the TTS engine returned by the IsSpeaking property. The last four constants are used by Visual Basic to keep track of menu and button options selected by the user.

Save the code module as MDISP.BAS and the project as MDINOTE.VBP before continuing on to the next section.

Coding the InitSAPI and UnInitSAPI Routines

The next code section you need to add is the code that will initialize and uninitialize SAPI services for the application. The first routine (InitSAPI) will be called when the program first starts. The last routine (UnInitSAPI) will be called when the project ends. Add a new subroutine called InitSAPI to the modSpeech module. Enter the code shown in Listing 20.2.

Listing 20.2. Adding the `InitSAPI` routine.

```
Public Sub InitSAPI()
    '
    ' voice command objects
    Set objVCmd = CreateObject("Speech.VoiceCommand")
    objVCmd.Register "" ' use default location
    objVCmd.Awake = True ' awaken speech services
    Set objVMenu = objVCmd.MenuCreate(App.EXEName, "MDI", 1033, "",
vcmdmc_CREATE_TEMP)
    InitVoice ' go build command list
    '
    ' voice text objects
    Set objVText = CreateObject("Speech.VoiceText")
    objVText.Register "", App.EXEName
    objVText.Enabled = True
    InitVText ' go build menu/buttons
    '
End Sub
```

This routine first initializes the Voice Command objects, registers the application, and starts the SR engine. The call to the InitVoice routine adds the custom voice commands to the declared menu. You'll see that code in the next section.

After handling the registration of SR services, the routine adds TTS services to the project. After initializing the Voice Text object, registering the application, and enabling TTS, the InitVText routine is called to build the menu and button options on the forms. You'll see this code later.

The next set of code to add is the UnInitSAPI routine. This routine will be called at the end of the program. The UnInitSAPI routine deactivates all SAPI objects and releases all links to SAPI services. Add a new subroutine to the modSpeech module and enter the code shown in Listing 20.3.

Listing 20.3. Adding the `UnInitSAPI` code.

```
Public Sub UnInitSAPI()
    '
    ' remove sapi services
    '
    objVMenu.Active = False ' stop menu
    Set objVMenu = Nothing  ' remove link
    objVCmd.Awake = False    ' close down SR
    Set objVCmd = Nothing    ' remove link
    '
    objVText.Enabled = False ' stop TTS
    Set objVText = Nothing   ' remove link
    '
End Sub
```

Coding the `InitVoice` Routine

The `InitVoice` routine adds all the new custom commands to the menu object declared in the `InitSAPI` routine. After it adds the new commands, a timer object is initialized and enabled. The timer will be used to check for a valid voice command. Add a new subroutine called `InitVoice` and enter the code shown in Listing 20.4.

Listing 20.4. Adding the `InitVoice` routine.

```
Public Sub InitVoice()
    '
    ' build added voice menu commands
    '
    Dim x As Integer
    ReDim Preserve cVCmdMenu(11) As String
    '
    cVCmdMenu(1) = "New"
    cVCmdMenu(2) = "Open"
    cVCmdMenu(3) = "Exit"
    cVCmdMenu(4) = "Toggle Toolbar"
    cVCmdMenu(5) = "Read"
    cVCmdMenu(6) = "Forward"
    cVCmdMenu(7) = "Rewind"
    cVCmdMenu(8) = "Stop"
    cVCmdMenu(9) = "Cut"
    cVCmdMenu(10) = "Copy"
    cVCmdMenu(11) = "Paste"
    '
    For x = 1 To 11
        objVMenu.Add 100 + x, cVCmdMenu(x), "MDI Menu", cVCmdMenu(x)
    Next x
    objVMenu.Active = True
    '
    ' start timer loop
    frmMDI!SRTimer.Interval = 500 ' every 1/2 second
    frmMDI!SRTimer.Enabled = True ' turn it on
    '
End Sub
```

As you can see, adding custom menu options involves adding the command strings to the menu object and then activating the menu object. The code that sets the timer is needed to poll the `SpokenCommand` property every half second.

> **TIP**
>
> You do not have to add custom commands to SAPI-enabled applications that have a declared menu. All menu items are automatically registered as voice commands by the operating system. The commands added here are really shortcuts to existing menu options.

Coding the `InitVText` Routine

When you add TTS services to the application, you need only to initialize the TTS object and then "turn on" the menu and/or command buttons that allow users to gain access to the TTS engine. In this application a set of buttons for the toolbar needs initialization. The code in Listing 20.5 shows how this is done.

Listing 20.5. Adding the `InitVText` routine.

```
Public Sub InitVText()
    '
    ' set up vText buttons and menu
    '
    Dim cDir As String
    Dim cPic(4) As String
    Dim x As Integer
    '
    cDir = "d:\sams\cdg\chap20\mdi\"
    cPic(0) = "arw01rt.ico" ' read
    cPic(1) = "arw01up.ico" ' forward
    cPic(2) = "arw01lt.ico" ' rewind
    cPic(3) = "arw01dn.ico" ' stop
    '
    For x = 0 To 3
        frmMDI.ImgVText(x).Picture = LoadPicture(cDir & cPic(x))
    Next x
    '
    VTextAction vTxtStop ' force "stop"
    '
    ' start timer loop
    frmMDI.TTSTimer.Interval = 500 ' every 1/2 second
    frmMDI.TTSTimer.Enabled = True ' turn it on
    '
End Sub
```

You'll notice a call to the `VTextAction` routine. This routine handles the TTS service requests (`Speak`, `FastForward`, `Rewind`, and `StopSpeaking`). A timer is also enabled in order to track the active status of the TTS engine.

Coding the `VTextAction` Routine

The `VTextAction` routine is the code that handles the various TTS service requests made by the user. This one set of code can handle all of the playback options for the program. It also handles the enabling of the toolbar buttons and the menu options. Listing 20.6 shows the code needed for the `VTextAction` subroutine.

Listing 20.6. Adding the VTextAction routine.

```
Public Sub VTextAction(Index As Integer)
    '
    ' handle request to start/stop reading
    '
    Static bVPause As Boolean
    '
    Screen.ActiveForm.MousePointer = vbHourglass
    '
    ' handle service request
    Select Case Index
        Case vTxtSpeak ' speak=0
            If Not bVText Then
                If Len(Trim(Screen.ActiveForm.Text1.Text)) <> 0 Then
                    objVText.Speak Screen.ActiveForm.Text1.Text, vtxtsp_NORMAL
                    bVText = True
                End If
            End If
        Case vTxtForward ' fast forward=1
            If bVText Then
                objVText.AudioFastForward
            End If
        Case vTxtRewind ' rewind=2
            If bVText Then
                objVText.AudioRewind
            End If
        Case vTxtStop ' stop speaking=3
            If bVText Then
                objVText.StopSpeaking
                bVText = False
                bVPause = False
            End If
    End Select
    '
    ' update menu
    If bVText Then
        With Screen.ActiveForm
            .mnuVText(0).Enabled = False
            .mnuVText(1).Visible = True
            .mnuVText(2).Visible = True
            .mnuVText(3).Visible = True
        End With
    Else
        If Screen.ActiveForm.Caption <> "MDI NotePad" Then
            With Screen.ActiveForm
                .mnuVText(0).Enabled = True
                .mnuVText(1).Visible = False
                .mnuVText(2).Visible = False
                .mnuVText(3).Visible = False
            End With
        End If
    End If
    '
    ' update buttons
    If bVText Then
        frmMDI.ImgVText(0).Visible = True
        frmMDI.ImgVText(1).Visible = True
```

```
        frmMDI.ImgVText(2).Visible = True
        frmMDI.ImgVText(3).Visible = True
    Else
        frmMDI.ImgVText(0).Visible = True
        frmMDI.ImgVText(1).Visible = False
        frmMDI.ImgVText(2).Visible = False
        frmMDI.ImgVText(3).Visible = False
    End If
    '
    ' no open text pages
    If Not AnyPadsLeft() Then
        frmMDI.ImgVText(0).Visible = False
    End If
    '
    Screen.ActiveForm.MousePointer = vbNormal
    '
End Sub
```

There are three parts to this one routine. The first part of the code handles the actual TTS request. Only the first option (vTxtSpeak) involves any coding. Since the MDINOTE project uses a single text box for user input, this text box is automatically used as the source for all TTS playback.

> **NOTE**
>
> You'll notice that an index value is used to power this routine. This index value comes from an array of command buttons or from a menu array. You'll build these later. Control and menu arrays are excellent ways to build compact code in Visual Basic.

The second part of the code handles the enabling and disabling of the menu items on the edit form. When the edit form is opened, a single menu item is activated (Read). Once the TTS engine starts reading, the other options (Rewind, Forward, and Stop) are made visible. The third and last part of this routine makes sure the proper buttons appear on the toolbar. This works the same as the menu array. You'll build the menu and control array in the next section.

This is the end of the code module for the project. Save the module as MDISP.BAS and the project as MDINOTE.VBP before continuing.

Modifying the MDINote Forms

There are two forms in the MDINOTE project that must be modified: the frmMDI form and the frmNotePad form. The frmMDI form holds the button array and calls the InitSAPI and UnInitSAPI routines. It also has code to handle the timer controls. The frmNotePad form holds the menu array and has code to control the starting and stopping of the TTS engine.

Modifying the MDI Form

The first task in modifying the frmMDI form is adding the button array to the toolbar. You'll use image controls to hold the buttons views. You'll also need to add code to the Form_Load and Form_Unload events. Finally, you'll add code for the two timer events.

Adding the Timer and Button Objects

First, you need to open the frmMDI form and add an array of four image controls and then add two timers. Table 20.1 shows the controls that need to be added to the form. Refer to Figure 20.1 and Table 20.1 for the placement of the image controls on the form.

Table 20.1. Adding the controls to the frmMDI form.

Control	Property	Setting
VB.Timer	Name	SRTimer
	Left	6180
	Top	0
VB.Timer	Name	TTSTimer
	Left	6480
	Top	60
VB.Image	Name	ImgVText
	Height	330
	Index	3
	Left	3120
	Stretch	-1 'True
	Top	0
	Visible	0 'False
	Width	375
VB.Image	Name	ImgVText
	Height	330
	Index	2
	Left	2760
	Stretch	-1 'True
	Top	0
	Visible	0 'False
	Width	375

Control	Property	Setting
VB.Image	Name	ImgVText
	Height	330
	Index	1
	Left	2400
	Stretch	-1 'True
	Top	0
	Visible	0 'False
	Width	375
VB.Image	Name	ImgVText
	Height	330
	Index	0
	Left	2040
	Stretch	-1 'True
	Top	0
	Visible	0 'False
	Width	375

FIGURE 20.1.

Placing the controls on the frmMDI *form.*

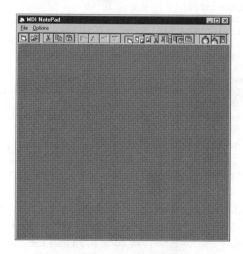

Be sure to *paint* the image controls and the timers onto the toolbar. Also note that the imgVText control is a control array of four controls. You'll use the index value returned by this array to tell the VTextAction routine what service was requested by the user.

> **NOTE**
>
> You don't need to set the picture property of the image controls at design time. This is handled by the InitText routine you wrote earlier.

After adding these controls, save the form (MDI.FRM) and the project (MDINOTE.VBP) before continuing.

Adding Code to the Form_Load and Form_Unload Events

After adding the controls, you need to add some code to the Form_Load and Form_UnLoad events. This code will be executed only once at the start or end of the program. Listing 20.7 shows the complete Form_Load code with the single line that calls the InitSAPI routine added at the end. Modify the Form_Load event code to look like the code in Listing 20.7.

Listing 20.7. Modifying the Form_Load event code.

```
Private Sub MDIForm_Load()
    '
    ' Application starts here (Load event of Startup form).
    Show
    ' Always set the working directory to the directory containing the application.
    ChDir App.Path
    ' Initialize the document form array, and show the first document.
    ReDim Document(1)
    ReDim FState(1)
    Document(1).Tag = 1
    FState(1).Dirty = False
    ' Read System registry and set the recent menu file list control array
➥appropriately.
    GetRecentFiles
    ' Set global variable gFindDirection which determines which direction
    ' the FindIt function will search in.
    gFindDirection = 1
    '
    InitSAPI ' <<< added for SAPI >>>
    '
End Sub
```

You also need to make a similar modification to the Form_Unload event code. Listing 20.8 shows the entire code listing for the Form_Unload event with the call to UnInitSAPI at the start of the routine. Modify the Form_Unload code to match the code in Listing 20.8.

Listing 20.8. Modifying the Form_Unload event code.

```
Private Sub MDIForm_Unload(Cancel As Integer)
    '
    UnInitSAPI ' <<< added for SAPI >>>
```

```
    '
    ' If the Unload event was not cancelled (in the QueryUnload events for the
➡Notepad forms),
    ' there will be no document window left, so go ahead and end the application.
    If Not AnyPadsLeft() Then
        End
    End If
    '
End Sub
```

Coding the Timer and Button Events

The final code you need to add to the frmMDI form is the code to handle the button array and the code to handle the timer events. First, add the code in Listing 20.9 to the ImgVText_Click event. This will pass the array index to the VTextAction routine to handle the TTS service request.

Listing 20.9. Adding code to the ImgVText_Click event.

```
Private Sub ImgVText_Click(Index As Integer)
    '
    VTextAction Index ' handle vText SAPI request
    '
End Sub
```

The code for the TTSTimer event is also quite simple. The timer event simply checks to see if the TTS engine is actually speaking any text. The results of this check are loaded into the global variable bVText to inform the VTextAction routine how to display the menu and button array objects. Add the code in Listing 20.10 to the TTSTimer_Timer event.

Listing 20.10. Adding code to the TTSTimer_Timer event

```
Private Sub TTSTimer_Timer()
    '
    bVText = objVText.IsSpeaking ' load results
    '
End Sub
```

The code for the SRTimer_Timer event is more involved. The SRTimer must check the value returned by the CommandSpoken property to see if it is a valid custom command. If the value is part of the Select Case structure, the corresponding program routine is called. Add the code shown in Listing 20.11 to the SRTimer_Timer event.

Listing 20.11. Adding code to the SRTimer_Timer event.

```
Private Sub SRTimer_Timer()
    '
    ' check status of SR Engine
    '
    lSRCmd = objVCmd.CommandSpoken
    objVCmd.CommandSpoken = 0 ' clear command
    '
    Select Case lSRCmd
        Case 101 ' new
            FileNew
        Case 102 ' open
            FOpenProc
        Case 103 ' exit
            Unload frmMDI
        Case 104 ' toggle toolbar
            OptionsToolbarProc frmMDI
        Case 105 ' read
            VTextAction vTxtSpeak
        Case 106 ' forward
            VTextAction vTxtForward
        Case 107 ' rewind
            VTextAction vTxtRewind
        Case 108 ' stop
            VTextAction vTxtStop
        Case 109 ' cut
            EditCutProc
        Case 110 ' copy
            EditCopyProc
        Case 111 'paste
            EditPasteProc
    End Select
    '
    lSRCmd = 0
End Sub
```

> **WARNING**
>
> You'll notice that the CommandSpoken property is loaded into a local variable and then set to zero. This is an important step. Failure to clear the CommandSpoken property can result in locking your program into a loop that keeps executing the last requested command. To prevent getting caught in a loop, be sure to clear the CommandSpoken property as soon as you read it.

Those are all the modifications needed to the frmMDI form. Save the form and the project before continuing.

Modifying the NotePad Form

There are only two main modifications to the `frmNotePad` form. First, you need to add the TTS menu options to the form. Next, you need to add a few lines of code to the `Form_Load` and `Form_Unload` events. Once these are done, you are ready to test your finished application.

Adding the Menu Options

You need to add four menu options to the `File` menu. These four options correspond to the TTS engine service options: `Speak`, `FastForward`, `Rewind`, and `StopSpeaking`. Refer to Table 20.2 and Figure 20.2 to see how to add these menu options to the `frmNotePad` form.

Table 20.2. Adding the TTS engine options to the menu.

Control	*Property*	*Setting*
VB.Menu	Name	mnuVText
	Caption	"&Read"
	Index	0
VB.Menu	Name	mnuVText
	Caption	"&Forward"
	Index	1
	Visible	0 'False
VB.Menu	Name	mnuVText
	Caption	"R&ewind"
	Index	2
	Visible	0 'False
VB.Menu	Name	mnuVText
	Caption	"S&top"
	Index	3
	Visible	0 'False
VB.Menu	Name	mnuFileSp02
	Caption	"-"

Note that all but the first menu option (`Read`) have their `Visible` property set to `FALSE`. You'll only show the other options after the TTS engine starts speaking some text.

FIGURE 20.2.
Using the Menu Editor to add the TTS engine options.

After adding the menu object, you need to add some code to the mnuVText_Click event to handle menu selections. Since this is a menu array, you'll only need one line of code to pass the selected service request to the VTextAction routine. Listing 20.12 shows the code you should add to the mnuVText_Click event.

Listing 20.12. Adding code to the mnuVText_Click event.

```
Private Sub mnuVText_Click(Index As Integer)
    '
    VTextAction Index ' handle vtext service request
    '
End Sub
```

Adding Code to the Form_Load and Form_Unload Events

You need to add only one line to the Form_Load and Form_Unload events. This line forces the TTS engine to stop speaking any code already in progress. That prevents the engine from attempting to speak two sets of text at once.

Listing 20.13 shows the complete Form_Load event with the SAPI-related line at the end. Modify the code in Form_Load to match the code in Listing 20.13.

Listing 20.13. Modifying the Form_Load event.

```
Private Sub Form_Load()
    Dim i As Integer

    mnuFontName(0).Caption = Screen.Fonts(0)
    For i = 1 To Screen.FontCount - 1
        Load mnuFontName(i)
        mnuFontName(0).Caption = Screen.Fonts(i)
    Next
    '
    VTextAction vTxtStop ' <<< force stop all speaking >>>
    '
End Sub
```

The code modification to the Form_Unload event is also quite easy. Listing 20.14 shows the whole Form_Unload event code with the SAPI-related line at the end. Modify the Form_Unload event code to match that shown in Listing 20.14.

Listing 20.14. Modifying the Form_Unload event code.

```
Private Sub Form_Unload(Cancel As Integer)
    FState(Me.Tag).Deleted = True

    ' Hide the toolbar edit buttons if no notepad windows exist.
    If Not AnyPadsLeft() Then
        frmMDI!imgcutbutton.Visible = False
        frmMDI!imgcopybutton.Visible = False
        frmMDI!imgPasteButton.Visible = False
        gToolsHidden = True
        GetRecentFiles
    End If
    '
    VTextAction vTxtStop ' force stop all speaking
    '
End Sub
```

That is the end of the code modification for the MDINOTE.VBP project. Save this form (MDINOTE.FRM) and the project (MDINOTE.VBP) before beginning to test your new SAPI-enabled version of the MDINOTE project.

Testing the SAPI-Enabled MDI NotePad

You now have a SAPI-enabled MDI NotePad project ready to test.

Once you compile the MDINOTE project, you can view the new voice commands that were added and also test the TTS playback of text documents.

> **WARNING**
>
> Be sure your workstation has speech services installed and activated before you start this project. If not, you may encounter an error and may have to reboot your system.

First, start the MDINOTE application and ask your workstation to tell you what commands are available (ask *What can I say?*). You should see two additional sections in the voice menu. The first one ("MDI NotePad voice commands") was added by the operating system when you first loaded the program. The Windows operating system will automatically create a set of voice commands that matches the menus of the program. Figure 20.3 shows the list of commands automatically built by Windows under the "MDI NotePad…" heading.

FIGURE 20.3.

Viewing the automatic voice commands.

You'll also see the custom commands added to the command list under the "MDINOTE" heading. These were added by the InitVoice routine in the project.

You can test the SR options of the program by speaking any of the menu commands or custom voice commands. When you say *New*, you should see a new blank page appear, ready for text input. You can test the TTS services by loading a text document and selecting Read from the menu or speaking the *Read* voice command. You'll see a set of buttons appear on the toolbar and an expanded list on the File menu (see Figure 20.4).

FIGURE 20.4.

Viewing the expanded file menu during a Read *command.*

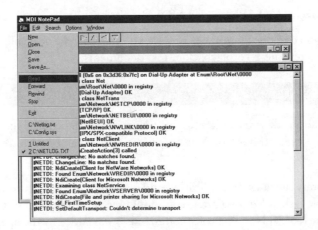

Summary

In this chapter, you learned how to add SR and TTS services to Visual Basic 4.0 applications using the OLE `Voice Command` and `Voice Text` libraries. You modified the `MDINOTE` project that ships with Visual Basic 4.0 to add options to speak command words and have the TTS engine read loaded text documents back to you.

You also learned that you do not need to add any code to Windows programs in order to make them SR-capable. Every menu option that is declared in a Windows program is automatically loaded as a valid SAPI voice command by the Windows operating system (as long as SAPI services are active). You also learned how to add custom voice commands to speed access to key menu items.

The next chapter is a summary of the SAPI section. The next section of the book describes the Windows telephony application programming interface and how you can use it to control incoming and outgoing voice and data telephone calls.

21

Part III Summary—
The Speech API

Chapter 14, "What Is SAPI?"

Chapter 14 covered the key factors in creating and implementing a complete speech system for PCs. You learned the three major parts of speech systems:

- *Speech recognition* converts audio input into printed text or directly into computer commands.
- *Text-to-speech* converts printed text into audible speech.
- *Grammar rules* are used by speech recognition systems to analyze audio input and convert it into commands or text.

Chapter 15, "SAPI Architecture"

In Chapter 15 you learned the details of the SR and TTS interfaces defined by the Microsoft SAPI model. You also learned that the SAPI model is based on the Component Object Model (COM) interface and that Microsoft has defined two distinct levels of SAPI services:

- *High-level SAPI* provides a "command-and-control" level of service. This is good for detecting menu and system-level commands and for speaking simple text.
- *Low-level SAPI* provides a much more flexible interface and allows programmers access to extended SR and TTS services.

You learned that the two levels of SAPI service each contain several COM interfaces that allow C programmers access to speech services. These interfaces include the ability to set and get engine attributes, turn the services on or off, display dialog boxes for user interaction, and perform direct TTS and SR functions.

Since the SAPI model is based on the COM interface, high-level languages such as Visual Basic cannot call functions directly using the standard API calls. Instead, Microsoft has developed OLE automation type libraries for use with Visual Basic and other VBA-compliant systems. The two type libraries are:

- *Voice Command Objects*—This library provides access to speech recognition services.
- *Voice Text Objects*—This library provides access to text-to-speech services.

Chapter 16, "SAPI Basics"

Chapter 16 focused on the hardware and software requirements of SAPI systems, the general technology and limits of SAPI services, and some design tips for creating successful SAPI implementations.

The Microsoft Speech SDK only works on 32-bit operating systems. This means you need Windows 95 or Windows NT Version 3.5 or greater in order to run SAPI applications.

The minimum, recommended, and preferred processor and RAM requirements for SAPI applications vary depending on the level of services your application provides. The minimum SAPI-enabled system may need as little as 1MB of additional RAM and be able to run on a 486/33 processor. However, it is a good idea to require at least a Pentium 60 processor and an additional 8MB RAM. This will give your applications the additional computational power needed for the most typical SAPI implementations.

SAPI systems can use just about any of the current sound cards on the market today. Any card that is compatible with the Windows Sound System or with Sound Blaster systems will work fine. You should use a close-talk, unidirectional microphone, and you can use either external speakers or headphones for monitoring audio output.

You learned that SR technology uses three basic processes for interpreting audio input:

■ Word selection
■ Word analysis
■ Speaker dependence

You also learned that SR systems have their limits. SR engines cannot automatically distinguish between multiple speakers, cannot learn new words, guess at spelling, or handle wide variations in word pronunciation (for example, "toe- may- toe" versus "toe- mah- toe").

TTS engine technology is based on two different types of implementations. *Synthesis systems* create audio output by generating audio-tones using algorithms. This results in unmistakably computer-like speech. *Diphone concatenation* is an alternate method for generating speech. *Diphones* are sets of phoneme pairs collected from actual human speech samples. The TTS engine is able to convert text into phoneme pairs and match them to diphones in the TTS engine database. TTS engines are not able to mimic human speech patterns and rhythms (called *prosody*), and are not very good at communicating emotions. Also, most TTS engines experience difficulty with unusual words. This can result in odd-sounding phrases.

Finally, you learned some tips for designing and implementing speech services, including:

■ Make SR and TTS services optional whenever possible.
■ Design voice command menus to provide easy access to all major operations.
■ Avoid similar-sounding words and inconsistent word order, and keep command lists short.
■ Limit TTS use to short playback; use WAV recordings for long playback sessions.
■ Don't mix TTS and WAV playback in the same session.

Chapter 17, "SAPI Tools—Using SAPI Objects with Visual Basic 4.0"

In Chapter 17 you learned that the Microsoft Speech SDK contains a set of OLE library files for implementing SAPI services using Visual Basic and other VBA-compatible languages. There is an OLE Automation Library for TTS services (VTXTAUTO.TLB), and one for SR services (VMCDAUTO.TLB). Chapter 17 showed you how to use the objects, methods, and properties in the OLE library to add SR and TTS services to your Windows applications.

You learned how to register and enable TTS services using the Voice Text object. You also learned how to adjust the speed and how to control the playback, rewind, fast forward, and pause methods of TTS output. Finally, you learned how to use a special Callback method to register a notification sink using a Visual Basic Class module.

You also learned how to register and enable SRT services using the Voice Command and Voice Menu objects. You learned how to build temporary and permanent menu commands and how to link them to program operations. You also learned how to build commands that accept a list of possible choices and how to use that list in a program. Finally, you learned how to use the Callback property to register a notification sink using the Visual Basic Class module.

Chapter 18, "SAPI Behind the Scenes"

In Chapter 18 you learned how the speech system uses grammar rules, control tags, and the International Phonetic Alphabet to perform its key operations.

You built simple grammars and tested them using the tools that ship with the Speech SDK. You also learned how to load and enable those grammars for use in your SAPI applications.

You added control tag information to your TTS input to improve the prosody and overall performance of TTS interfaces. You used Speech SDK tools to create and play back text with control tags, and you learned how to edit the stored lexicon to maintain improved TTS performance over time.

Finally, you learned how the International Phonetic Alphabet is used to store and reproduce common speech patterns. The IPA can be used by SR and TTS engines as a source for analysis and playback.

Chapter 19, "Creating SAPI Applications with C++"

In Chapter 19 you learned how to write simple TTS and SR applications using C++. Since many of the SAPI features are available only through C++ coding, this chapter gave you a quick review of how to use C++ to implement SAPI services.

You built a simple TTS program that you can use to cut and paste any text for playback. You also built and tested a simple SR interface to illustrate the techniques required to add SRT services to existing applications.

Chapter 20, "Building the Voice-Activated Text Reader"

In Chapter 20 you used all the information gathered from previous chapters to build a complete application that implements both TTS and SR services. The Voice-Activated Text Reader allows users to select text files to load, loads them into the editor page, and then reads them back to the user on command. All major operations can be performed using speech commands.

You also learned how to add SR services to other existing applications using a set of library modules that you can add to any Visual Basic project.

The Future of SAPI

The future of SAPI is wide open. This section of the book gave you only a first glimpse of the possibilities ahead. At present, SAPI systems are most successful as command-and-control interfaces. Such interfaces allow users to use voice commands to start and stop basic operations that usually require keyboard or mouse intervention. Current technology offers limited voice playback services. Users can get quick replies or short readings of text without much trouble. However, long stretches of text playback are still difficult to understand.

With the creation of the generalized interfaces defined by Microsoft in the SAPI model, it will not be long before new versions of the TTS and SR engine appear on the market ready to take advantage of the larger base of Windows operating systems already installed. With each new release of Windows, and new versions of the SAPI interface, speech services are bound to become more powerful and more user-friendly.

Although we have not yet arrived at the level of voice interaction depicted in *Star Trek* and other futuristic tales, the release of SAPI for Windows puts us more than one step closer to that reality!

IV

The Telephony API (TAPI)

The Telephony API (TAPI) is a very powerful services model. First introduced for Windows 3.1, TAPI provides easy access to telephony services at the Windows desktop. The TAPI model is a fully WOSA-compliant system that works with just about any modem or telephony card. With TAPI, you can develop voice and data applications that use the telephone as their file transfer medium.

> **NOTE**
>
> The most recent version of TAPI (1.4) is designed specifically for the Windows 95 operating system. Microsoft is planning to release TAPI 2.0 late in 1996 for the Windows NT operating system. It will be released after WinNT 4.0 is on the market.

Here's a quick tour of the telephony section of the book:

In Chapter 22, "What Is TAPI?," you'll get a general overview of the TAPI model and its capabilities. Chapter 23, "TAPI Architecture," goes into details on the API model, including the major objects exposed and the methods and properties available to the programmer. In Chapter 24, "TAPI Basics," you'll learn TAPI programming techniques to handle the basic operations of a TAPI-compliant application.

The next four chapters cover specific programming techniques and some of the technical details behind the model. Chapter 25, "TAPI Hardware Considerations," reviews typical hardware configurations and outlines the capabilities and limitations of the various setups. In Chapter 26, "TAPI Tools—Using the TAPILine Control," you'll learn how to use the Microsoft TAPI development tools to build TAPI applications. This includes Microsoft tools and third-party TAPI development kits. Chapter 27, "TAPI Behind the Scenes—The TELEPHON.INI File," covers technical aspects of the API that most programmers don't often use, but that could come in handy. You'll also learn some of the ins and outs of program installation and configuration when dealing with telephony applications. Finally, Chapter 28, "Using TAPI to Handle Incoming Calls," reviews the various aspects of selecting and using TAPI server-side software for your desktop applications.

In Chapter 29, "Writing TAPI-Assisted Applications," you'll learn how to build basic TAPI programs using the Assisted TAPI level of service. In Chapter 30, "Creating TAPI-Enabled Applications," you'll learn how to use the more powerful Basic TAPI services to build interactive voice and data programs. Then, in Chapter 31, "Third-Party TAPI Tools," you'll get a tour of some of the most popular third-party TAPI development tools. You'll even get a chance to use demo versions of the development tools on the CD-ROM that comes with this book.

Chapter 32, "Part IV Summary—The Telephony API," pulls it all together with a quick review of the entire TAPI section of the book.

After you complete this section of the book, you'll understand the TAPI service model and you'll know how to use TAPI services to create voice and data applications for the Windows 95 operating system that access telephony services. You'll also have a chance to test and evaluate some third-party TAPI development tools in the process.

22

What Is TAPI?

The *Telephony Application Programming Interface* (TAPI) is one of the most significant API sets to be released by Microsoft. The telephony API is a single set of function calls that allows programmers to manage and manipulate any type of communications link between the PC and the telephone line(s). While telephony models for the PC have been around for several years, the telephony API establishes a uniform set of calls that can be applied to any type of hardware that supplies a TAPI-compliant service provider interface (SPI).

This chapter provides a general overview of the Telephony API and how it fits into the WOSA (Windows Open Services Architecture) model. You'll learn about the two main devices defined within the TAPI model:

■ Line devices

■ Phone devices

You'll also learn about the typical physical configurations used in a TAPI model, which can be:

■ Phone-based

■ PC-based

■ Shared or unified line

■ Multiline

You'll also learn about the different types of telephone service lines used to provide media transport services for TAPI applications, including:

■ POTS

■ Digital T1

■ ISDN service

■ PBX service

When you complete this chapter you should have a good understanding of the TAPI model, including the meaning and use of line and phone devices. You'll also know the most common TAPI hardware configurations, their advantages, and their drawbacks. Finally, you'll understand the various physical telephone services available for use in TAPI applications.

The Telephony API Model

The telephony API model is designed to provide an abstracted layer for access to telephone services on all Windows platforms. In other words, the telephony API is a single set of functions that can be used to access all aspects of telephony services within the Windows operating system.

This is a huge undertaking. The aim of TAPI is to allow programmers to write applications that work regardless of the physical telephone medium available to the PC. Applications written using TAPI to gain direct access to telephone-line services work the same on analog or digital phone lines. Applications that use TAPI can generate a full set of dialing tones and flash-hook functions (like that of the simple analog handset found in most homes), and can also communicate with sophisticated multiline digital desktop terminals used in high-tech offices.

The TAPI design model is divided into two areas, each with its own set of API calls. Each API set focuses on what TAPI refers to as a *device*. The two TAPI devices are:

■ *Line devices* to model the physical telephony lines used to send and receive voice and data between locations.

■ *Phone devices* to model the desktop handset used to place and receive calls.

Lines

The line device is used to model the physical telephone line. It is important to understand that, in TAPI, the line device is not really a physical line; it's just a model or object representing a physical line. In TAPI applications, a program could keep track of several line devices, each of which is connected to a physical line. That same TAPI application could also keep track of multiple line devices that number more than the total physical lines available to the PC.

For example, a single TAPI application could be designed to provide voice, fax, and data links for a user. The TAPI application would identify three line devices. One for voice calls, one for fax transmission, and one for sending and receiving data via an attached modem. If the PC has only one physical phone line attached, the TAPI application would share the one line between the three defined line devices. This is called *dynamic line mapping* (see Figure 22.1).

FIGURE 22.1.
TAPI dynamically maps line devices to physical lines.

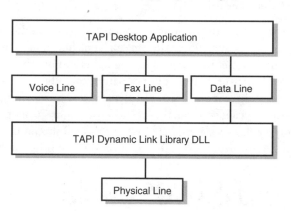

Each time the TAPI application starts a line device, it requests the first available physical line that has the capabilities needed (voice, fax, data, and so on). If a line is not available, a message to that effect is returned to the calling program. In some cases, such as fax transmissions, the TAPI application may "queue up" the line request for processing at a later time.

If two lines are available, the TAPI application uses them as they are needed. If a third line device becomes active, the TAPI application knows that there are no other available open lines and notifies the user (or possibly queues up the outbound call for later).

TAPI is also able to keep track of the types of lines available. For example, one of the two lines connected to the PC may be a dedicated, high-speed data transmission line (such as a Switched 56Kbps line), and the other a basic voice-grade line (such as a 3.1KHz line). If the TAPI application requested a high-speed data line, the SPI would return the *handle* of the Switch 56Kbps line. If the application requested a voice-grade line, the SPI would return the handle of the voice line. If, however, the second request was for another data line, the SPI would know that the voice-grade line was not acceptable and would return a message telling the TAPI application that all data lines were busy.

Phones

The second type of device modeled by TAPI is the phone device. This model allows TAPI programmers to easily create "virtual phones" within the PC workspace. For example, a standard PC with a sound card, speakers, and microphone can emulate all the functions of a desktop phone. These virtual phones, like their line device counterparts, need not exist in a one-to-one relationship to physical phones. A single PC could model several phone devices, each with their own unique characteristics. When an actual call must be made, the user could select one of the phone devices, enter the desired number and then the TAPI application would attach the phone device to an available line device. Note that the phone devices link to line devices (which eventually link to physical telephone lines).

One of the primary uses of multiple phone devices would be the modeling of an office switchboard. The typical switchboard has several trunk lines that terminate at a single multiline handset. Usually this handset has several flashing lights and pushbuttons. The buttons are used to connect trunk lines to extension phones within the office. The extension phones could be modeled as phone devices on a receptionist's screen. The incoming trunk lines could be modeled as line devices. As calls come in, the receptionist would "pick up" a line, "drop" it onto the switchboard phone device, determine to whom the call should be routed, and then pick up the call off the switchboard phone and drop it onto the appropriate extension (see Figure 22.2).

TAPI and the WOSA Model

TAPI is able to accomplish its task by dividing the job into two distinct layers: the client API and the SPI. Each interface is a set of functions designed to complete generic telephony tasks such as opening a line, checking for a dial tone, dialing a number, checking for a ring or a busy signal, and so on. The client API sends requests from the application to the SPI for each task. It is the job of the SPI to complete the task and pass the results back to the calling program through the client API. Does any of this sound familiar? It should. TAPI is a full member of the WOSA (Windows Open Services Architecture) model.

FIGURE 22.2.
A virtual switchboard using TAPI phone and line devices.

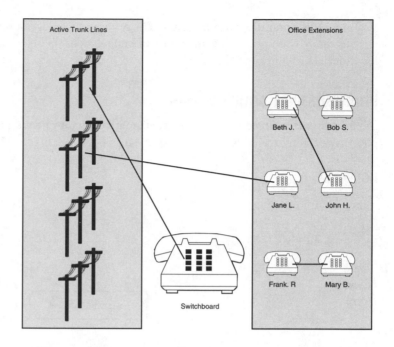

By acting as part of the WOSA model, TAPI provides a complete telephony implementation for Windows operating systems without forcing the programmer to learn vendor-specific APIs. Application developers can focus on delivering the features needed most by users and leave the details of vendor-specific implementation to the hardware driver (SPI) programmers. At the same time, hardware vendors can spend time implementing a single set of SPI calls that they can be assured will work on all Windows platforms.

Typical Configurations

The TAPI model is designed to function in several different physical configurations, which each have advantages and drawbacks. There are four general physical configurations:

- *Phone-based*—This configuration is best for voice-oriented call processing where the standard handset (or some variation) is used most frequently.

- *PC-based*—This configuration is best for data-oriented call processing where the PC is used most frequently for either voice or data processing.

- *Shared* or *unified line*—This is a compromise between phone-based and PC-based systems. It allows all devices to operate as equals along the service line.

- *Multiline*—There are several variations of the multiline configuration. The primary difference between this configuration and the others is that the PC acts as either a voice-server or a call switching center that connects the outside phone lines to one or more PCs and telephone handsets. The primary advantage of multiline configurations is that you do not need a direct one-to-one relationship between phone lines and end devices (phones or PCs).

Phone-Based Configurations

In phone-based TAPI configurations, the standard telephone handset is connected to the telephone switch and the PC is connected to the telephone (see Figure 22.3).

FIGURE 22.3.
A typical phone-based TAPI configuration.

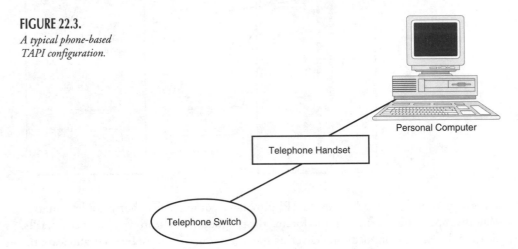

This configuration is most useful when the telephone handset is the primary device for accessing the telephone line. Since the telephone rests between the PC and the switch, the PC may not be able to share in all the activity on the line. In the example shown in Figure 22.3, the PC could not be included in a conference call if the handset originated the call since no line can be "conferenced" with itself and the call originates "upstream" from the PC.

A phone-based configuration does not preclude the use of the PC to originate calls. As long as the PC is equipped with a phone card that allows dialing, the PC can originate a call and then allow the handset to pick up on that call at any time. In other words, even in a phone-based configuration, the PC can be used as a dialing tool, and then hand the voice calls off to the upstream handset device.

PC-Based Configurations

PC-based TAPI configurations place the PC between the telephone switch and the standard handset (see Figure 22.4).

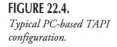

FIGURE 22.4.
Typical PC-based TAPI configuration.

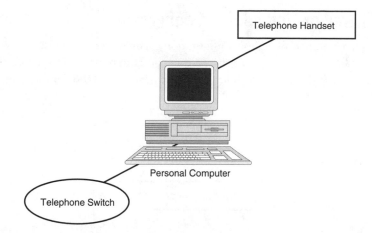

This configuration is most useful when the PC is the primary device for accessing the telephone line. In this configuration, the PC most often originates phone calls. Typically, this is done via a phone card and software on the PC that manages a list of phone numbers and handles the dialing of the phone. Depending on the exact media mode of the call, the PC can be used to display digital data on screen while handling voice information, too.

The PC-based configuration illustrated in Figure 22.4 also allows for originating calls from the handset. In this case, calls can be shared by the PC since the data stream is passing through the PC to the switch. Users could originate a voice call through the handset and then switch to the PC to capture and display digital data sent over the same line.

Another major advantage of the PC-based configuration is that the PC can act as a call manager for the handset. This is especially valuable in a mixed-mode environment where voice, data, and fax are all coming in to the same phone address. For example, as a call comes in to the attached phone line, the PC can answer the call and determine the media mode of the call. If it is a fax call, the PC can route the call directly to an attached fax machine (or to the fax driver on the PC). Data calls can be handled directly by the PC and voice calls can be forwarded to the attached handset.

In a PC-based configuration, the PC can also be used for call screening and message handling. TAPI-compliant software could record incoming messages for the user and place them in a queue for later review, or forward calls to another address. With the addition of caller ID services from the local telephone company, the PC could also act as a call filter agent, screening the calls as they arrive and allowing only designated callers access to the PC or the handset.

Shared or Unified Line Configurations

The shared or unified line configuration is a bit of a compromise between PC-based and phone-based configurations. The shared line configuration involves a split along the line leading to the switch. Both the PC and the phone have equal (and simultaneous) access to the line (see Figure 22.5).

FIGURE 22.5.

Typical shared line TAPI configuration.

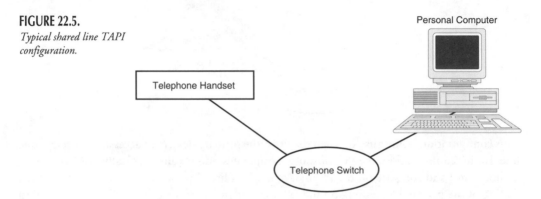

The advantage of the shared-line configuration is that either device can act as the originator of a call. The primary disadvantage is that both devices have equal access to incoming calls. In other words, as a call comes in, both devices will ring. Depending on the software operating on the PC, it is possible that both devices would attempt to answer the same incoming call. This situation is much like having two extension phones along the same access line.

The unified line configuration offers the combined benefits of the PC-based configuration and the shared-line configuration. In the unified line configuration, the access line goes directly from the switch into a telephone card in the PC. The PC also has handset equipment either attached to the phone card or integrated into the PC itself. All that is really needed is a microphone for input and speakers for output, but some systems offer headphones or a keypad to simulate the familiar telephone handset (see Figure 22.6).

With the unified line arrangement the PC can act as either a handset device or a PC data device. In fact, the unified line arrangement is virtually the same as the PC-based configuration except that the phone is internal to the PC instead of attached directly to the PC. As new calls come in to the device, software on the PC can determine the media mode of the call (data, fax, voice, and so on) and route the call to the proper hardware on the PC. Also, with the unified arrangement, users do not need to worry about two devices ringing at the same time when a call comes in.

FIGURE 22.6.
Typical unified line TAPI configuration.

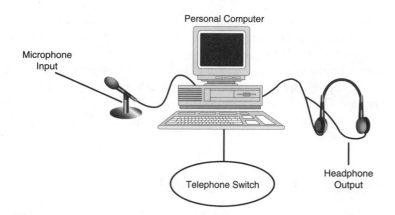

Personal Computer

Microphone
Input

Headphone
Output

Telephone Switch

Multiline Configurations

So far, all the configurations reviewed here have been single-line models. This is commonly referred to as *first-party call control.* TAPI is also designed to support multiline configurations. In this arrangement, TAPI is used to provide *third-party call control.*

Single lines act as the first (and only) party in a telephone call. In a multiline environment, a device can act as a third party in a telephone call. The most common form of third-party call control is a central switchboard in an office. When a call comes in, the switchboard (the third party) accepts the call, determines the final destination of the call, routes the call to the correct extension, and then drops out of the call stream.

These are the two basic multiline TAPI configurations:

- *Voice server*—Used to provide voice mail and other services from a central location.
- *PBX server*—Used to provide call control for inbound and outbound trunk lines.

In a voice server configuration, the TAPI-enabled PC acts as a message storage device accessible from any other telephone handset. Handsets can be configured to forward all "ring/no answer" calls to the voice server where inbound callers are instructed to leave recorded messages. Later, users can dial into the voice server to retrieve their messages. Alternatively, users could consult a *universal in-box* that contains voice-mail, faxes, and e-mail. Upon selecting the voice-mail items, the PC would play the message over the PC speakers and allow the user to speak a reply using either the phone handset or an attached microphone.

In a PBX server configuration, the TAPI-enabled PC acts as a sort of first line of defense for all incoming calls to a multiline location, usually an office building. In this mode, TAPI functions are used to accept calls, present them to an operator for review, and then forward them to the final destination. This is using the TAPI PC as a true third-party control system.

While a Voice Server does its work behind a standard desktop phone, the PBX Server does its work in front of any desktop phone. In other words, the Voice Server is designed to handle calls when the desktop phone is busy or in some other way unable to accept calls. The PBX Server, on the other hand, is used to accept all calls coming into the office and route those calls to the appropriate desktop phone. Many offices employ both PBX Server and Voice Server systems. The PBX Server answers the incoming line and routes it to the desktop phone. If the desktop phone is unable to accept the call, the Voice Server takes a message and stores it for later retrieval.

Telephone Line Services

One of the primary aims of the TAPI model is to allow programmers to design systems that will work the same way regardless of the physical characteristics of the telephone line. TAPI functions behave the same on analog, digital, and cellular phone lines. TAPI is able to operate in single-line or multiline configurations. In fact, the real value of the TAPI model for the programmer is that users can usually install TAPI-compliant software on systems with different physical line types and still operate properly.

It is important to know that some physical line types offer options not available on other line types. For example, ISDN lines offer simultaneous data and voice channels not available on POTS or T1 lines. TAPI cannot make a POTS line offer the same services an ISDN line offers. TAPI does, however, provide a consistent interface to all services options shared by line types (such as line open, dial, send data, close line, and so on).

Line types can be divided into three main groups:

- Analog lines
- Digital lines
- Private protocol lines

Analog lines are the kind of lines available in most homes. Digital lines are usually used by large organizations, including local telephone service providers, to transfer large amounts of voice and data channels. T1 and ISDN lines are typical types of digital lines. Private protocol lines are a special kind of digital line. These lines are used within private branch exchanges (PBXs). PBX-type lines are used to transport voice, data, and special control information used by the switching hardware to provide advanced telephony features such as call transfer, conferencing, and so on.

The Telephone Switching Network

Regardless of the type of telephone line service used (POTS, T1, ISDN, PBX), signal transmission (voice or data) must move from the source location (the *call originator*) to the desired destination. Along the way, a typical call can be converted from analog to digital, move from physical wires, through fiber optical cables, and possibly even by way of microwave satellite transmission before it finally arrives at the designated destination address. Figure 22.7 shows how an overseas call might travel through the telephone network.

FIGURE 22.7.

Transmission modes for a typical overseas telephone call.

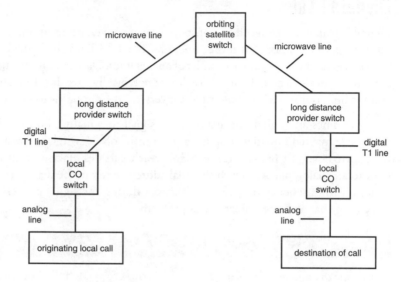

The rest of this section describes each of the telephone line service types in greater detail.

Plain Old Telephone Service (POTS)

Plain Old Telephone Service (POTS) is the line service type provided to most homes in the United States. POTS is an analog service that provides basic connection to the telephone company's central office by way of a single-line link. Standard POTS users cannot perform advanced telephone operations such as call transfers, forwarding, or conferencing.

The analog POTS is designed to send voice signals, not data. For this reason, POTS users must employ a data modulator-demodulator (or *modem*) to send digital information over POTS lines. The analog aspects of POTS lines limits the amount of digital data that can be fed through the line. While 28.8Kbps service over analog dial-up lines is quite reliable, data rates beyond that limit require special line conditioning. Available in some locations in the U.S. is a special dial-up service known as Switched 56 service. Switched 56 service provides for data rates of up to 56Kbps over dial-up lines.

Recently, local telephone companies have begun offering additional services for POTS users. Caller ID, call forwarding, and voice message services can be purchased from local switch operators for an additional charge. Also, a specialized set of services, called Centrex, can be purchased from almost all local telephone companies. Centrex services allow POTS lines to behave much like a line tied to a private branch exchange (PBX). Centrex services offer call waiting, call forwarding, call transfers, and other services that provide the appearance of a multiline phone system while still using POTS lines.

Digital T1 Lines

Digital T1 lines are designed to transport several conversations at once. T1 lines can send 24 multiple phone connections at the same time. Since T1 lines are digital instead of analog, data rates can extend well beyond the limits of analog lines. Data rates in the megabytes-per-minute are typical for dedicated T1 lines. T1 lines are typically used for dedicated data transmission and for bulk transmission of multiple conversations from point to point.

Since T1 lines are digital, the analog voice signals originating on POTS lines at a residence must be converted into digital signals at the central office switch before a voice conversation is transported over T1 lines. Once the signal reaches its destination, it must often be converted back to an analog signal to reach the final address. Early in the deployment of T1 lines, it was common to experience time delays or echoes during the signal conversion. The advance of technology has all but eliminated this problem.

> **NOTE**
>
> European telephone lines have a similar format to the US T1 line digital format, called *E1*. E1 lines can handle up to 30 simultaneous conversations at one time. Although the digital format of E1 lines is different than the T1 format, central office switching handles all translations needed and TAPI users need to do nothing special to handle calls over E1 lines.

Integrated Services Digital Network (ISDN)

The *Integrated Services Digital Network* (ISDN) was developed to handle voice, data, and video services over the same line. Although developed more than 20 years ago, ISDN lines have only recently become available in major service markets in the United States. In some major metropolitan areas, ISDN service is available at price levels approaching that of analog dial-up lines. The increased expansion of data services (such as the Internet), along with the upcoming deregulation of the U.S. telecommunications industry, will contribute to lowering the price and increasing the availability of ISDN in the U.S.

The most common form of ISDN service, called *Basic Rate Interface* or *BRI-ISDN*, provides two 64Kbps channels and one 16Kbps *control* or *signal information* channel. The advantage of ISDN is that the two 64Kbps B channels can be configured to provide a single 128Kbps pipe for voice, video, or data, or the line can be configured to provide one 64Kbps data channel and a simultaneous 64Kbps digital voice channel. Thus ISDN service provides for transporting more than one media mode at the same time. In addition to the two B channels,

BRI-ISDN provides a 16Kbps control channel, called the *D* channel, that can be used to send signaling information and additional control data. This control data can contain information about the calling party (name, location, and so on) or other supplemental information needed to complete the media transmission.

An advanced ISDN format, called *Primary Rate Interface* or *PRI-ISDN*, can provide up to 32 separate channels. The PRI-ISDN format used in the US, Canada, and Japan provides 23 64Kbps B channels and one 64Kbps D channel. The PRI-ISDN format used in Europe allows for 30 64Kbps B channels and two 64Kbps D channels.

BRI-ISDN offers high-speed data services at very competitive costs when compared to T1 or even Switched 56 services. In fact, ISDN is arriving "at the curb" in some major metropolitan areas, and residential users are now able to purchase BRI-ISDN services for Internet use at relatively low cost. PRI-ISDN, however, is a much more expensive service and is used by businesses that need to quickly move large amounts of data.

Private Branch Exchange (PBX)

The *Private Branch Exchange* (PBX) format is used in commercial switching equipment to handle multiline phone systems in offices. Typically, the local telephone provider brings multiline service up to the PBX switch and then the PBX handles all call control and line switching within the PBX network. PBX phones operate on proprietary formats and are usually digital-only lines.

PBX format most often includes more than just the voice/data signal. Impulses to control flashing lights on desktop phones, data strings that appear on display panels, and additional information to handle call conferencing, forward, and call screening are all usually sent along the same line.

The exact data format of PBX lines varies between vendors. However, TAPI applications work on all PBX lines for which the vendor has supplied a TAPI-compliant service provider.

Summary

In this chapter you were presented with a general outline of the TAPI model, including the definition and purpose of two devices defined within the TAPI model:

- *Line devices* are used to model physical telephone lines.
- *Phone devices* are used to model physical telephone handsets.

You should also know the relative advantages and disadvantages of the four main types of TAPI hardware configurations:

- *Phone-based configurations* are for use in mostly voice-oriented calling.
- *PC-based configurations* are for use in mostly PC-oriented calling.

- *Shared* or *unified line configurations* are for use when both voice and data share the phone use equally.
- *Multiline configurations* are for use as a voice server (for voice-mail) or as a PBX server (for computerized switchboards).

Finally, you should be able to identify the four main types of telephone service used to transmit the voice and data signal:

- Analog *POTS* (*Plain Old Telephone Service*) for general voice-grade transmissions and for data transmission up to 28.8Kbps speed.
- Digital *T1* for dedicated high-speed voice or data services (56Kbps and above).
- *ISDN* (*Integrated Services Digital Network*) for high-speed multichannel simultaneous voice and data services.
- *PBX* (*Private Branch Exchange*) for use within proprietary switchboard hardware in an office setting.

Now that you have a general idea of the TAPI model, it's time to learn the specifics of the TAPI architecture. That is the topic of the next chapter.

23

TAPI Architecture

In this chapter, you'll learn how the Telephony API is organized and how its various function calls are used to provide TAPI services to Windows applications. You'll learn about the four different levels of TAPI services:

- *Assisted Telephony*—This is the simplest form of TAPI service.
- *Basic Telephony*—This provides basic in- and outbound telephony services for a single-line phone.
- *Supplemental Telephony*—This provides advanced telephone services such as hold, park, conference, and so on, to single and multiline phones.
- *Extended Telephony*—This provides a direct interface between Windows programs and vendor-specific TAPI services.

You'll also learn how these levels of service are implemented using API calls and how they work together to provide complete TAPI services, from a simple Dial button, through handling inbound and outbound calls, to acting as a switchboard in a multiline setting, and finally to providing access to vendor-specific features of telephony cards.

When you complete this chapter you'll understand how the Telephony API is organized and how you can use it to add telephony services to your Windows applications.

Assisted Telephony Services

The simplest form of TAPI service is *Assisted Telephony*. Under the Assisted Telephony interface, programmers can place outbound calls and check the current dialing location of the workstation. This type of telephony service can be used to provide a simple Dial button to existing applications or add dialing capabilities to new applications that will use telephony as an added service.

In fact, the Assisted Telephony model only provides access for programs to request the *placement* of an outbound call. The actual dialing of the call is handled by another Windows/TAPI application. The default application is DIALER.EXE. This application ships with the Windows TAPI SDK and is part of the Windows 95 operating system.

There are two API calls used to provide Assisted TAPI services. Table 23.1 shows the two calls, their parameters, and descriptions of what they do and how they can be used.

Table 23.1. The Assisted Telephony API.

API Call	Parameters	Comments
TapiRequestMakeCall	DestAddress, AppName, CalledParty, Comment	Use this function to request an outbound call placement. Only the DestAddress is required.

API Call	Parameters	Comments
TapiGetLocationInfo	CountryCode, CityCode	Use this function to return the current country code and city code of the workstation. These values are stored in the TELEPHON.INI file.

The TapiRequestMakeCall has four parameters. Only the DestAddess is required. The DestAddress is a string of numbers that represents the telephone number to dial. For example, "999-555-1212" is a valid DestAddress in the United States format. The AppName parameter is the name of the application that requested the TAPI service. This would be the name of your application. The CalledParty is a string that represents the name of the person you are calling. This information could be used by the DIALER.EXE application to log the person called. The Comment parameter could contain a string of text describing the reason for the call.

The TapiGetLocation function returns two parameters: the CountryCode and CityCode of the current location set by the Windows control panel TAPI applet. These two parameters are stored in the TELEPHON.INI file in the Windows folder of the workstation. The country code is a value used to place out-of-country calls. The country code for the United States is "1." The CityCode is known as the *area code* in the United States. The combination of the country code and the city code is used to determine how the TAPI dialer will place the requested call.

For example, if the requested call contained "1-312-555-1212" and the current workstation location indicated a country code of "1" and a city code of "312," then the TAPI DIALER.EXE program would attempt to place the call without including the country or city codes: "555-1212." If, however, the requested call contained "43-80-12 33 45" then the DIALER program would assume that the user was attempting to place an out-of-country call and would use the appropriate dialing prefixes.

NOTE

You'll learn more about the dialing prefixes and how they are used in Chapter 27, "TAPI Behind the Scenes—The TELEPHON.INI File." For now it is only important to know that TAPI uses the location information stored in TELEPHON.INI to determine how to place a requested call.

Basic Telephony Services

Basic Telephony is the next level up in the TAPI service model. Basic Telephony function calls allow programmers to create applications that can provide basic in- and outbound voice and data calls over a single-line analog telephone. The analog phone line most often used for this level of service is often referred to as a *POTS* or *Plain Old Telephone Service* line. The Basic Telephony API set can also be used with more sophisticated lines such as T1, ISDN, or digital lines. However, the added features of these advanced line devices (such as call forwarding, park, hold, conference, and so on) are not available when using the Basic Telephony API set.

The Basic Telephony level of service focuses on the use of a *line device* as a means of transporting information from one place to the next. A line device to TAPI can be a handset, a fax board, a data modem, a telephony card, or any other physical device that can be attached to a telephone line, But it is treated as a virtual device, not a physical one.

Line devices are not associated directly with any physical telephone line. This way, TAPI can "see" multiple TAPI devices on the same machine (data modem, handset, and fax board) while there is only one physical telephone line attached to the workstation (see Figure 23.1).

FIGURE 23.1.

The relationship between TAPI line devices and physical phone lines.

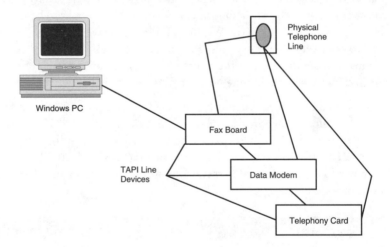

One of the primary functions of the TAPI interface is to handle multiple TAPI service requests from the workstation. It is possible that several applications running on the workstation may request TAPI services at some time. The call control application (DIALER.EXE) accepts each request and places them in a queue for processing in the requested order.

The Basic Telephony Line Device API Set

The Basic Telephony service model has several API calls for handling and fulfilling service requests. These calls can be collected into logical groups:

■ *Basic line-handling calls* handle the initialization and opening and closing of TAPI lines.

■ *Line settings and status* calls handle the reading and writing of various parameter values that control the behavior of the line device.

■ *Outbound and inbound functions* handle the details of placing an outbound voice or data call and answering an inbound voice or data call.

■ *Addressing functions* handle the details of recognizing, translating, and/or building telephone "addresses" or dialing strings.

■ *Miscellaneous features* handle other TAPI-related functions, such as managing call-monitoring privileges and manipulating call handles.

Table 23.2 shows the Basic Telephony API calls, sorted by functional group, along with a short description of their use. You'll learn more about how these API calls can be used in a program in Chapter 30, "Creating TAPI-Enabled Applications."

Table 23.2. The Basic Telephony line device API set.

Function Group	API Call	Description
Basic line-handling	lineInitialize	Initializes the Telephony API line abstraction for use by the invoking application.
	lineShutdown	Shuts down the application's use of the Telephony API line.
	lineNegotiateAPIVersion	Allows an application to negotiate an API version to use.
	lineOpen	Opens a specified line device for providing subsequent monitoring and/or control of the line.
	lineClose	Closes a specified opened line device.
	lineDrop	Disconnects a call, or abandons a call attempt in progress.
	lineDeallocateCall	De-allocates the specified call handle.

continues

Table 23.2. continued

Function Group	API Call	Description
Line settings and status	lineGetDevCaps	Returns the capabilities of a given line device.
	lineGetDevConfig	Returns the configuration of a media stream device.
	lineGetlineDevStatus	Returns the current status of the specified open line device.
	lineSetDevConfig	Sets the configuration of the specified media stream device.
	lineSetStatusMessages	Specifies the status changes for which the application wants to be notified.
	lineGetStatusMessages	Returns the application's current line and address status message settings.
	lineGetID	Retrieves a device ID associated with the specified open line, address, or call.
	lineSetNumRings	Indicates the number of rings after which inbound calls are to be answered.
	lineGetNumRings	This function returns the minimum number of rings requested with lineSetNumRings.
	lineGetIcon	Allows an application to retrieve an icon for display to the user.
	lineConfigDialog	Causes the provider of the specified line device to display a dialog that allows the user to configure parameters related to the line device.
Inbound and outbound calls	lineMakeCall	Makes an outbound call and returns a call handle for it.
	lineDial	Dials (parts of one or more) dialable addresses.
	lineAnswer	Answers an inbound call.
Addresses	lineGetAddressCaps	Returns the telephony capabilities of an address.

Function Group	API Call	Description
	lineGetAddressStatus	Returns the current status of a specified address.
	lineGetAddressID	Retrieves the address ID of an address specified using an alternate format.
	lineTranslateAddress	Translates between an address in canonical format and an address in dialable format.
	lineSetCurrentLocation	Sets the location used as the context for address translation.
	lineSetTollList	Manipulates the toll list.
	lineGetTranslateCaps	Returns address translation capabilities.
Miscellaneous features	lineGetCallInfo	Returns mostly constant information about a call.
	lineGetCallStatus	Returns complete call status information for the specified call.
	lineSetAppSpecific	Sets the application-specific field of a call's information structure.
	LineRegisterRequest ➥Recipient	Registers or de-registers the application as a request recipient for the specified request mode.
	lineGetRequest	Gets the next request from the Telephony DLL.
	lineSetCallPrivilege	Sets the application's privilege to the privilege specified.
	lineHandoff	Hands off call ownership and/or changes an application's privileges to a call.
	lineGetNewCalls	Returns call handles to calls on a specified line or address for which the application does not yet have handles.
	lineGetConfRelatedCalls	Returns a list of call handles that are part of the same conference call as the call specified as a parameter.

The Basic Telephony Line Device Structures

Along with the extensive API set for Basic Telephony, the TAPI model defines several data structures that are used to pass information between TAPI and the requesting application. The layout of the structures contains variable as well as fixed data. This allows the API set to contain information of indeterminate length without prior knowledge of the contents of the structure.

In order to handle variable-length structures, the defined data structures contain fields that indicate the total size needed to fill in all variable data (dwNeededSize) along with the total size used by TAPI when filling in the structure (dwUsedSize). Listing 23.1 shows how this looks in the LINECALLLIST structure.

Listing 23.1. Viewing the LINECALLLIST structure.

```
typedef struct linecalllist_tag {
  DWORD   dwTotalSize;
  DWORD   dwNeededSize;
  DWORD   dwUsedSize;

  DWORD   dwCallsNumEntries;
  DWORD   dwCallsSize;
  DWORD   dwCallsOffset;
} LINECALLLIST, FAR *LPLINECALLLIST;
```

The dwTotalSize field is first set by the calling application to tell TAPI how much memory has been allocated for the structure. If TAPI cannot fill in all values without running out of allocated space, an error is returned and it is the job of the requesting application to re-allocate space and make the call again.

Along with the total size and total needed fields, each variable-length structure has a fixed portion and a variable portion. The fixed portion contains values that indicate the size of the variable-length field and the offset (from the start of the structure) at which the field is located. Note the fields dwCallsSize and dwCallsOffset in the LINECALLLIST structure shown in Listing 23.1.

Table 23.2 shows the list of data structures used by the Basic Telephony API set along with short descriptions of their use.

Table 23.2. The Basic Telephony API line device structures.

Structure	Description
LINEADDRESSCAPS	Describes the capabilities of a specified address.
LINEADDRESSSTATUS	Describes the current status of an address.
LINECALLINFO	Contains information about a call.

Structure	Description
LINECALLLIST	Describes a list of call handles.
LINECALLPARAMS	Describes parameters supplied when making calls using `lineMakeCall`.
LINECALLSTATUS	Describes the current status of a call.
LINECARDENTRY	Describes a calling card.
LINECOUNTRYENTRY	Provides the information for a single country entry.
LINECOUNTRYLIST	Describes a list of countries.
LINEDEVCAPS	Describes the capabilities of a line device.
LINEDEVSTATUS	Describes the current status of a line device.
LINEDIALPARAMS	Specifies a collection of dialing-related fields.
LINEEXTENSIONID	Describes an extension ID. Extension IDs are used to identify service provider-specific extensions for line devices.
LINEFORWARD	Describes an entry of the forwarding instructions.
LINEFORWARDLIST	Describes a list of forwarding instructions.
LINEGENERATETONE	Contains information about a tone to be generated.
LINELOCATIONENTRY	Describes a location used to provide an address translation context.
LINEMEDIACONTROLCALLSTATE	Describes a media action to be executed when detecting transitions into one or more call states.
LINEMEDIACONTROLDIGIT	Describes a media action to be executed when detecting a digit.
LINEMEDIACONTROLMEDIA	Describes a media action to be executed when detecting a media-mode change.
LINEMEDIACONTROLTONE	Describes a media action to be executed when a tone has been detected.
LINEMONITORTONE	Describes a tone to be monitored.
LINEPROVIDERENTRY	Provides the information for a single-service provider entry.
LINEPROVIDERLIST	Describes a list of service providers.
LINEREQMAKECALL	Describes a `tapiRequestMakeCall` request.
LINETERMCAPS	Describes the capabilities of a line's terminal device.
LINETRANSLATECAPS	Describes the address translation capabilities.
LINETRANSLATEOUTPUT	Describes the result of an address translation.

> **NOTE**
>
> A detailed listing of all TAPI structures is included in the Microsoft Visual C++ Win32 documentation. You can also find complete TAPI documentation on the MSDN Professional Level CD-ROMs.

Basic Telephony Line Device Messages

The Telephony API uses Windows messages to communicate with the requesting application. When the requesting application first performs a `LineInitialize` function, a callback function address must be supplied. All messages are then sent to this callback function.

> **NOTE**
>
> The fact that TAPI uses callbacks for messages means that any high-level language such as Visual Basic must use either a DLL or OCX or establish the callback link or use some other tool that can capture Windows messages. A sample OCX is included on the CD-ROM that ships with this book. This OCX is used throughout the book to show how you can link Visual Basic and other VBA-compliant languages to TAPI services.

Each message returns the same set of parameters. The first is the relevant handle. Usually this is the call handle, but it may also be a line handle. The second parameter is the callback instance value. This value will always be the instance handle of the current running application. The next three values vary depending on the message. One or more of these return values will contain non-zero data. Table 23.3 contains a list of the Basic Telephony messages, their parameters, and short descriptions.

Table 23.3. Basic Telephony line device messages.

Message	*Parameters*	*Description*

LINE_ADDRESSSTATE	dwDevice = hLine;
	dwCallbackInstance = Callback;
	dwParam1 = idAddress;
	dwParam2 = AddressState;
	dwParam3 = (DWORD) 0;
		Sent when the status of an address changes on a line that is currently open by the application. The application can invoke lineGetAddressStatus to determine the current status of the address.

Message	Parameters	Description

LINE_CALLINFO	dwDevice = hCall;
	dwCallbackInstance =
	hCallback;
	dwParam1 = CallInfoState;
	dwParam2 = (DWORD) 0;
	dwParam3 = (DWORD) 0;
		Sent when the call information about the specified call has changed. The application can invoke lineGetCallInfo to determine the current call information.

LINE_CALLSTATE	dwDevice = hCall;
	dwCallbackInstance =
	hCallback;
	dwParam1 = CallState;
	dwParam2 =
	CallStateDetail;
	dwParam3 = CallPrivilege;
		Sent when the status of the specified call has changed. Several such messages will typically be received during the lifetime of a call.

LINE_CLOSE	dwDevice = hLine;
	dwCallbackInstance =
	hCallback;
	dwParam1 = (DWORD) 0;
	dwParam2 = (DWORD) 0;
	dwParam3 = (DWORD) 0;
		Sent when the specified line device has been forcibly closed. The line device handle or any call handles for calls on the line are no longer valid once this message has been sent.

LINE_CREATE	dwDevice = 0;
	dwCallbackInstance = 0;
	dwParam1 = idDevice;
	dwParam2 = 0;
	dwParam3 = 0;
		Sent to inform the application of the creation of a new line device.

LINE_DEVSPECIFIC	dwDevice = hLineOrCall; dwCallbackInstance = hCallback; dwParam1 = DeviceSpecific1; dwParam2 = DeviceSpecific2; dwParam3 = DeviceSpecific3;	Sent to notify the application about device-specific events occurring on a line, address, or call. The meaning of the message and the interpretation of the parameters is device specific.

continues

Table 23.3. continued

Message	Parameters	Description
LINE_DEVSPECIFICFEATURE	dwDevice = hLineOrCall; dwCallbackInstance = hCallback; dwParam1 = DeviceSpecific1; dwParam2 = DeviceSpecific2; dwParam3 = DeviceSpecific3;	Sent to notify the application about device-specific events occurring on a line, address, or call. The meaning of the message and the interpretation of the parameters is device specific.

LINE_GATHERDIGITS	dwDevice = hCall;
	dwCallbackInstance =
	hCallback;
	dwParam1 =
	GatherTermination;
	dwParam2 = 0;
	dwParam3 = 0;
		Sent when the current buffered digit-gathering request has terminated or is canceled. The digit buffer may be examined after this message has been received by the application.

LINE_GENERATE	dwDevice = hCall;
	dwCallbackInstance =
	hCallback;
	dwParam1 =
	GenerateTermination;
	dwParam2 = 0;
	dwParam3 = 0;
		Sent to notify the application that the current digit or tone generation has terminated. Note that only one such generation request can be in progress on a given call at any time. This message is also sent when digit or tone generation is canceled.

LINE_LINEDEVSTATE	dwDevice = hLine;
	dwCallbackInstance =
	hCallback;
	dwParam1 = DeviceState;
	dwParam2 =
	DeviceStateDetail1;
	dwParam3 =
	DeviceStateDetail2
		Sent when the state of a line device has changed. The application can invoke lineGetLineDevStatus to determine the new status of the line.

Message	Parameters	Description

LINE_MONITORDIGITS	dwDevice = hCall;
	dwCallbackInstance =
	hCallback;
	dwParam1 = Digit;
	dwParam2 = DigitMode;
	dwParam3 = 0;
		Sent when a digit is detected. The sending of this message is controlled with the lineMonitorDigits function.

LINE_MONITORMEDIA	dwDevice = hCall;
	dwCallbackInstance =
	hCallback;
	dwParam1 = MediaMode;
	dwParam2 = 0;
	dwParam3 = 0;
		Sent when a change in the call's media mode is detected. The sending of this message is controlled with the lineMonitorMedia function.

LINE_MONITORTONE	dwDevice = hCall;
	dwCallbackInstance =
	hCallback;
	dwParam1 = dwAppSpecific;
	dwParam2 = 0;
	dwParam3 = 0;
		Sent when a tone is detected. The sending of this message is controlled with the lineMonitorTones function.

LINE_REPLY	dwDevice = 0;
	dwCallbackInstance =
	hCallback;
	dwParam1 = idRequest;
	dwParam2 = Status;
	dwParam3 = 0;
		Sent to report the results of function calls that completed asynchronously.

LINE_REQUEST	dwDevice = 0;
	dwCallbackInstance =
	hRegistration;
	dwParam1 = RequestMode;
	dwParam2 =
	RequestModeDetail1;
	dwParam3 =
	RequestModeDetail2;
		Sent to report the arrival of a new request from another application.

NOTE

Additional information about the TAPI line messages can be found in the Win32 documentation that ships with Microsoft Visual C++ and in the TAPI documentation that ships with the MSDN Professional Level CD-ROM pack.

Supplemental Telephony Services

The Supplemental Telephony functions provide advanced line device handling (conference, park, hold, forward, and so on). Access to these advanced services is dependent on the type of telephone line to which the workstation is connected. In other words, even if you implement call forwarding functions within your TAPI application, these functions will only work if call forwarding services are available on the telephone line provided by the local telephone company.

The Supplemental Telephony functions also allow programmers to handle service requests for multiple-line phones. You can use Supplemental Telephony to mange a physical handset that has access to multiple physical lines (see Figure 23.2).

FIGURE 23.2.

Using Supplemental TAPI to manage a single handset linked to multiple physical lines.

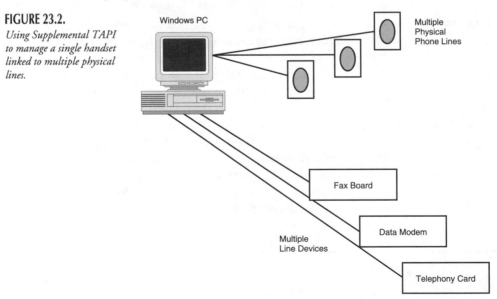

You can also use the Supplemental Telephony functions to manage multiple handsets using one or more physical lines. Because TAPI "virtualizes" both line and phone devices, there need not be a direct one-to-one correspondence between a defined phone device and a defined line device. In this way you can use TAPI to create a switchboard application to manage telephony services (see Figure 23.3).

FIGURE 23.3.
Using Supplemental TAPI to provide switchboard services.

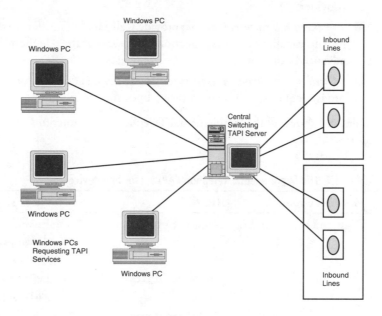

Supplemental Telephony also provides access to defining and manipulating phone devices. To TAPI a phone device is any device that can accept or place calls. In effect, you can register your workstation as a phone device. Then you can use resources on your workstation to place or accept calls without the need of a handset or desktop phone. Of course, in order to act successfully as a phone device, your workstation must have audio input and output hardware.

NOTE

You'll learn more about telephony hardware under the TAPI model in Chapter 25, "TAPI Hardware Considerations."

Supplemental Telephony API for Line Devices

The Supplemental API set for line devices adds advanced call control and other features to the API library. The set can be divided into the following related groups of functions:

■ *Digit and tone handling functions* allow programmers to detect and generate digits or tones along the phone line. This capability is needed to allow some systems to perform advanced line operations such as forwarding, call holds, and so on.

■ *Advanced line-handling functions* provide call acceptance, rejection, redirection, and other operations. These are most useful in an environment where the phone line is connected to a central switch instead of directly to the external telephone service provider.

■ *Advanced call features functions* provide Call Hold, Transfer, Park, Forward, and Pickup capabilities. These functions only work if the telephone line supports the advanced call features.

■ *Miscellaneous advanced features functions* provide added features specific to TAPI service requests, such as monitoring lines and setting call parameters.

Table 23.4 shows all the Supplemental Telephony API functions for the advanced line device features.

Table 23.4. The Supplemental Telephony API set for line devices.

Function Group	API Call	Description
Digit and tone handling	lineMonitorDigits	Enables or disables digit detection notification on a specified call.
	lineGatherDigits	Performs the buffered gathering of digits on a call.
	lineMonitorTones	Specifies which tones to detect on a specified call.
	lineGenerateDigits	Generates inband digits on a call.
	lineGenerateTone	Generates a given set of tones inband on a call.
Advanced call handling	lineAccept	Accepts an offered call and starts alerting both caller (ring-back) and called party (ring).
	lineRedirect	Redirects an offering call to another address.
	lineSecureCall	Secures an existing call from interference by other events such as call-waiting beeps on data connections.
	lineCompleteCall	Places a call completion request.

Function Group	API Call	Description
	lineUncompleteCall	Cancels a call completion request.
Call hold	lineHold	Places the specified call on hard hold.
	lineUnhold	Retrieves a held call.
Call transfer	lineSetupTransfer	Prepares a specified call for transfer to another address.
	lineCompleteTransfer	Transfers a call that was set up for transfer to another call, or enters a three-way conference.
	lineBlindTransfer	Transfers a call to another party.
	lineSwapHold	Swaps the active call with the call currently on consultation hold.
Call conference	lineSetupConference	Prepares a given call for the addition of another party.
	linePrepareAddToConference	Prepares to add a party to an existing conference call by allocating a consultation call that can later be added to the conference call that is placed on conference hold.
	lineAddToConference	Adds a consultation call to an existing conference call.
	lineRemoveFromConference	Removes a party from a conference call.
Call park	linePark	Parks a given call at another address.
	lineUnpark	Retrieves a parked call.
Call forwarding	lineForward	Sets or cancels call forwarding requests.
Call pickup	linePickup	Picks up a call that is alerting at another number. Picks up a call alerting at another destination address

continues

Table 23.4. continued

Function Group	API Call	Description
		and returns a call handle for the picked up call (linePickup can also be used for call waiting).
Miscellaneous advanced features	lineSendUserUserInfo	Sends user-to-user information to the remote party on the specified call (ISDN only).
	lineSetTerminal	Specifies the terminal device to which the specified line, address events, or call media stream events are routed.
	lineSetCallParams	Requests a change in the call parameters of an existing call.
	lineMonitorMedia	Enables or disables media mode notification on a specified call.
	lineSetMediaControl	Sets up a call's media stream for media control.
	lineSetMediaMode	Sets the media mode(s) of the specified call in its LINECALLINFO structure.

Supplemental Telephony API for Phone Devices

The Supplemental Telephony API also provides function calls for the handling of phone devices. To TAPI, any device that can place or accept calls can be a phone device. The phone device API set allows programmers to invent their own phone devices in code. In effect, you can create a virtual handset using the TAPI phone device. This allows properly equipped workstations to act as single- or multiple-line phones in an office environment. If your PC has appropriate audio input and output hardware (speakers, sound card, microphone, and so on) and is connected to the telephone service, you can create a "handset" using the phone device API set.

The Supplemental Telephony API set for phone devices can be divided into the following function groups:

- *Basic phone-handling functions* provide basic initialization and shutdown, opening and closing a phone device, and ringing the open device.
- *Phone settings and status functions* allow programmers to read and write various settings of the phone device such as volume, gain, hookswitch behavior, and so on.
- *Physical display, data, button, and lamp functions* can be used to read and write display information to desktop units. Since TAPI can be used to support more than just PC workstations, these functions allow a central TAPI program to monitor and update LCD displays, to flash lamps, to change buttons labels, and to store and retrieve data from desktop terminals.

Table 23.5 shows all the Supplemental Telephony phone device API calls along with short descriptions of their use.

Table 23.5. The Supplemental Telephony API for phone devices.

Function Group	API Call	Description
Basic phone handling	phoneInitialize	Initializes the Telephony API phone device for use by the invoking application.
	phoneShutdown	Shuts down the application's use of the phone Telephony API.
	phoneNegotiateAPIVersion	Allows an application to negotiate an API version to use.
	phoneOpen	Opens the specified phone device, giving the application either owner or monitor privileges.
	phoneClose	Closes a specified open phone device.
	phoneSetRing	Rings an open phone device according to a given ring mode.
	phoneGetRing	Returns the current ring mode of an opened phone device.

continues

Table 23.5. continued

Function Group	API Call	Description
Phone settings and status	phoneGetDevCaps	Returns the capabilities of a given phone device.
	phoneGetID	Returns a device ID for the given device class associated with the specified phone device.
	phoneGetIcon	Allows an application to retrieve an icon for display to the user.
	phoneConfigDialog	Causes the provider of the specified phone device to display a dialog that allows the user to configure parameters related to the phone device.
	phoneSetStatusMessages	Specifies the status changes for which the application wants to be notified.
	phoneGetStatusMessages	Returns the status changes for which the application wants to be notified.
	phoneGetStatus	Returns the complete status of an open phone device.
	phoneSetHookSwitch	Sets the hookswitch mode of one or more of the hookswitch devices of an open phone device.
	phoneGetHookSwitch	Queries the hookswitch mode of a hookswitch device of an open phone device.
	phoneSetVolume	Sets the volume of a hookswitch device's speaker of an open phone device.
	phoneGetVolume	Returns the volume setting of a hookswitch device's speaker of an open phone device.

Function Group	API Call	Description
	phoneSetGain	Sets the gain of a hookswitch device's mic of an open phone device.
	phoneGetGain	Returns the gain setting of a hookswitch device's mic of an open phone device.
Physical display, data, buttons, and lamps	phoneSetDisplay	Writes information to the display of an open phone device.
	phoneGetDisplay	Returns the current contents of a phone's display.
	phoneSetButtonInfo	Sets the information associated with a button on a phone device.
	phoneGetButtonInfo	Returns information associated with a button on a phone device.
	phoneSetLamp	Lights a lamp on a specified open phone device in a given lamp-lighting mode.
	phoneGetLamp	Returns the current lamp mode of the specified lamp.
	phoneSetData	Downloads a buffer of data to a given data area in the phone device.
	phoneGetData	Uploads the contents of a given data area in the phone device to a buffer.

The Supplemental Telephony Phone Device Structures

Just as the line device API set has a series of data structures, the phone device set also has related data structures. These structures are used to pass information between the desktop program and the TAPI service provider.

The phone device structures most often used are the PHONECAPS and PHONESTATUS structures. Table 23.6 shows all the phone device structures along with brief descriptions of their use.

Table 23.6. The Supplemental Telephony phone device structures.

Structure	Description
PHONEBUTTONINFO	Contains information about a button on a phone device.
PHONECAPS	Describes the capabilities of a phone device.
PHONEEXTENSIONID	Describes an extension ID. Extension IDs are used to identify service provider-specific extensions for phone device classes. Used mostly for Extended Telephony.
PHONESTATUS	Describes the current status of a phone device.
VARSTRING	Used for returning variably sized strings. It is used both by the line device class and the phone device class.

The Supplemental Telephony Phone Device Messages

The Supplemental Telephony phone device also uses a callback function to register a function address to receive Windows messages. This callback address is established during the phoneInitialize API call.

> **NOTE**
>
> The fact that TAPI uses callbacks for messages means that any high-level languages such as Visual Basic must use either a DLL or OCX or establish the callback link or use some other tool that can capture windows messages. A sample OCX is included on the CD-ROM that ships with this book. This OCX is used throughout the book to show how you can link Visual Basic and other VBA-compliant languages to TAPI services.

Each message returns the same set of parameters. The first is the handle of the phone device. The second parameter is the callback instance value. This value will always be the instance handle of the current running application. The next three values vary depending on the message. One or more of these return values will contain non-zero data. Table 23.7 contains a list of the Basic Telephony messages, their parameters, and short descriptions.

Table 23.7. The Supplemental Telephony phone device messages.

Message	*Parameters*	*Description*

PHONE_BUTTON	hPhone = hPhoneDevice;
	dwCallbackInstance = hCallback;
	dwParam1 = idButtonOrLamp;
	dwParam2 = ButtonMode;
	dwParam3 = ButtonState;
		Sent to notify the application that button press monitoring is enabled if it has detected a button press on the local phone.

PHONE_CLOSE	hPhone = hPhoneDevice;
	dwCallbackInstance = hCallback;
	dwParam1 = 0;
	dwParam2 = 0;
	dwParam3 = 0;
		Sent when an open phone device has been forcibly closed as part of resource reclamation. The device handle is no longer valid once this message has been sent.

PHONE_CREATE	hPhone = hPhoneDev;
	dwCallbackInstance = 0;
	dwParam1 = idDevice;
	dwParam2 = 0;
	dwParam3 = 0;
		This message is sent to inform applications of the creation of a new phone device.

PHONE_DEVSPECIFIC	hPhone = hPhoneDevice;
	dwCallbackInstance = hCallback;
	dwParam1 = DevSpecific1;
	dwParam2 = DevSpecific2;
	dwParam3 = DevSpecific3;
		This message is sent to notify the application about device-specific events occurring at the phone. The meaning of the message and the interpretation of the parameters is defined by the hardware vendor.

PHONE_REPLY	hPhone = 0;
	dwCallbackInstance = hCallback;
	dwParam1 = idRequest;
	dwParam2 = Status;
	dwParam3 = 0;
		This message is sent to report the results of a function call that completed asynchronously.

PHONE_STATE	hPhone = hPhoneDevice;
	dwCallbackInstance = hCallback;
	dwParam1 = PhoneState;
	dwParam2 = PhoneStateDetails;
	dwParam3 = 0;
		The service provider sends this message to an application's callback function whenever the status of a phone device changes.

Extended Telephony Services

The last level of Telephony services is Extended Telephony. Extended Telephony service allows hardware vendors to define their own device-specific functions and services and still operate under the TAPI service model. By adding a small set of extended service API functions, Microsoft allows hardware vendors to continue to provide unique services not previously defined by TAPI. The TAPI model defines both line and phone device API calls for Extended Telephony.

Table 23.8 shows the Extended Telephony API set along with short descriptions of their use.

Table 23. 8. The Extended Telephony API set.

Function Group	API Call	Description
Extended Line service	lineNegotiateExtVersion	Allows an application to negotiate an extension version to use with the specified line device.
	lineDevSpecific	Device-specific escape function.
	lineDevSpecificFeature	Device-specific escape function to allow sending switch features to the switch.
Extended Phone service	phoneNegotiateExtVersion	Allows an application to negotiate an extension version to use with the specified phone device.
	phoneDevSpecific	Device-specific escape function to allow vendor dependent extensions.

The actual meaning and use of extended TAPI calls is defined by the service provider or hardware vendor. Extended Telephony providers define the parameters of the calls and their meaning, and publish this information to the programmer. The programmer can then check the version information with the service provider before attempting to make an extended service call.

Summary

In this chapter you learned how the TAPI service model is implemented as a set of API calls. You learned there are four levels of TAPI services:

- ■ *Assisted Telephony*—The simplest form of TAPI service.
- ■ *Basic Telephony*—Provides basic in- and outbound telephony services for a single-line phone.
- ■ *Supplemental Telephony*—Provides advanced telephone services such as hold, park, conference, and so on, to single and multiline phones.
- ■ *Extended Telephony*—Provides a direct interface between Windows programs and vendor-specific TAPI services.

You also learned that the TAPI function set defines two different devices to handle telephony services:

- ■ A *line device* is used to control the connection between a data source and the physical telephone line.
- ■ A *phone device* is used to control the connection between a desktop handset and a line device.

Finally, you reviewed the API calls, data structures, and Windows messages defined for each level of TAPI service.

In the next chapter, you'll learn the basic programming steps needed to create a TAPI application.

24

TAPI Basics

In this chapter, you'll learn how to build a simple TAPI dialer application in C using the Basic Telephony level of service. This application will be used to highlight the basic operations required to build TAPI applications (in any language).

You'll learn how to perform line initialization, locate a usable outbound line, and open it in preparation for dialing. You'll also learn how to place an outbound call and use the TAPI line callback function to monitor call progress. Finally, you'll learn how to safely close down a line after the call has been completed.

When you are done with the example in this chapter, you'll understand the basics of writing TAPI applications and know how to use Basic Telephony services in your own applications.

> **NOTE**
>
> The project in this chapter was written using the Microsoft Visual C++ 4.1 compiler. However, the code is compatible with the Microsoft VC 2.0 compiler. If you do not have a C compiler, you can still get a lot out of the chapter. The same techniques covered here will be used when you build TAPI applications in Microsoft Visual Basic 4.0 later in this section of the book.

Using TAPI to Place Outbound Calls

Before starting the review of the TAPIOUT project, it is a good idea to cover the minimal steps needed to place an outbound call using TAPI services. There are really only a few steps:

- Call `lineInitialize` to start the TAPI session.
- Call `lineNegotiateAPIVersion` to make sure you can use the installed TAPI services.
- Call `lineOpen` to get a line that is appropriate for your needs (data, fax, voice, and so on).
- Use the `LINECALLPARAMS` structure to set up calling parameters before you place your call.
- Call `lineMakeCall` to actually attempt to place a TAPI call.

After you complete these steps, you can use the messages received by the registered callback function to track call progress and respond accordingly. The next few sections cover the outbound calling steps in greater detail.

Calling `lineInitialize` to Start the TAPI Session

The first thing you need to do to start a TAPI session is to call the `lineInitialize` routine to initialize the link between your application and the TAPI service provider. The `lineInitialize` routine includes a pointer to the callback function in your code that will handle all messages.

After successful initialization, the routine returns a value in the lineHandle parameter. You'll use this value throughout your TAPI session. You will also get a count of the total number of TAPI lines defined for this workstation. You'll use that information to check the API version and line parameters of each line before you attempt to place a call.

If an error occurs, a non-zero value is returned. You can check the errors using a case switch and present a message to the user.

Calling lineNegotiateAPIVersion to Check TAPI Services

After you successfully open the TAPI session, you need to call the lineNegotiateAPIVersion function for each line in the collection. The total number of lines was returned as part of the lineInitialize routine. You need to check this value because it is possible that you will be requesting a version of TAPI this is not available for this machine.

You pass your API version request to the function and get a value back that is the version of TAPI that the workstation can provide to your application. You can also get a pointer to a structure that holds information about vendor-specific extension services available on this workstation. This is a method for allowing non-TAPI services to be recognized using the TAPI interface.

Using lineOpen to Locate an Appropriate TAPI Line Device

Once you have successfully negotiated an API version, you must use the lineOpen function to pass through each line and request the appropriate level of service. For example, if you wanted to place an interactive voice call, you'd use the lineOpen function to locate a line that supports interactive voice.

This is an important point. It is quite possible that the workstation will have several TAPI devices defined, but only one may provide the type of service you need (voice, fax, data, and so on). If there is no device available (none exists or the current one is busy), you'll get an error message. However, if an appropriate line is available, you'll receive a zero as a return code and a value indicating the handle of the open line. You'll use this value in subsequent TAPI calls.

Setting Call Parameters with the LINECALLPARAMS Structure

Once you locate an appropriate line, you can set calling parameters using the LINECALLPARAMS structure. You use this structure to tell TAPI the speed and media type (data, voice, and so on) of your call and other values.

Setting the LINECALLPARAMS structure is optional. If you do not set any value for the LINECALLPARAMS, Microsoft TAPI will use default values. For most calls, the default values will work just fine.

Using `lineMakeCall` to Place the Call

The last step in the process is actually placing the call using the `lineMakeCall` function. This function passes the string that contains the phone number to call, a handle for the open line (you got that from `lineOpen`) and, optionally, a pointer to the `LINECALLPARAMS` structure.

If the call is placed successfully, a call handle is returned. You'll use this call handle in subsequent TAPI functions. If there is trouble making the call, the return code is non-zero and can be checked for appropriate action.

It is important to note that at this point the call has been *placed* but not completed. All TAPI knows for sure is that digits have been dialed and the phone line is active. TAPI will continue to receive status information and route that to your application through the callback function registered when you called `lineInitialize`. The quality of the status information (dialing, ringing, busy, idle, and so on) is all determined by the hardware vendor and TAPI service provider application. The more sophisticated the hardware, the more accurate the progress information.

For example, standard data/fax modems do not report call progress information. When you place your TAPI call, you'll be notified by the hardware that the call is in progress and will see nothing else until the call is completed or a time-out occurs. Other hardware (advanced voice/data modems) may provide additional call-progress data. High-end telephony cards provide the most accurate information.

Now that you know the basics of placing an outbound call using TAPI, it's time to review the `TAPIOUT` project on the CD-ROM that accompanies this book.

The `TAPIOut` Project

The `TAPIOUT` project that ships on the CD-ROM is a C program that allows users to enter a phone number and use TAPI to place an outbound call. This project is very rudimentary. There are no extra bells and whistles. However, the code in this project gives a good review of what it takes to provide basic TAPI services. The next several sections of this chapter review the `TAPIOUT` project step-by-step. You'll see how you can use the TAPI functions described earlier in the chapter to create a functional TAPI dialer.

If you have a copy of Microsoft VC++ 2.0 or later, start it now and load the `TAPIOUT.MAK` (or `TAPIOUT.MDP`) project from the CD-ROM. You can follow along with the examples in the chapter.

> **TIP**
>
> You'll need to have the TAPI SDK installed on your machine before you can compile this project. Once you load the project, be sure to select `Tools ¦ Update All Dependencies` to resolve references to the `TAPI.H` and `TAPI32.LIB` files in the project. You may need to reload these files into the project using `Insert ¦ Files into Project...`

The Initial Declarations

This first step in the process is declaring all the needed includes, defines, function prototypes, and global variables. Listing 24.1 shows how this looks in the TAPIOUT project.

Listing 24.1. The initial declarations of the TAPIOUT project.

```
// ********************************************************************
// SIMPLE OUTBOUND TAPI DIALER APPLICATION
// ********************************************************************
//
// Title:    TAPIOut
// Version:  1.0 - 05/24/96 (MCA)
//
// Equip:    VC++ 4.0 / Win95 / TAPI SDK
//
// Client:   MAPI, SAPI, TAPI Developer's Guide (SAMS 1996)
//
// Desc:     Simple dialog to show how to use TAPI to place outbound
//           calls. Takes dialing string and shows progress as the
//           program attempts to complete the call.
//
// Files:    TAPIOUT.C
//           TAPIOUT.RC
//           TAPIOUT.DEF
//           RESOURCE.H
//           TAPI.H
//           TAPI32.LIB
//
// ********************************************************************

// ****************************************
// Includes and defines
//
#include "windows.h"
#include "tapi.h"
#include "resource.h"

#define tapiVersionCur  (MAKELONG(4,1)) // ver 1.4
#define    TAPI_LINE_REPLY          5000
#define TAPI_LINECALLSTATE_CONNECTED      5001
#define TAPI_LINECALLSTATE_IDLE        5002
#define TAPI_LINECALLSTATE_DISCONNECTED   5003
#define TAPI_LINECALLSTATE_BUSY        5004
#define TAPI_LINECALLSTATE_ACCEPTED       5005
#define TAPI_LINECALLSTATE_PROCEEDING      5006
#define TAPI_LINECALLSTATE_OFFERING       5007
#define TAPI_LINECALLSTATE_DIALTONE       5008
#define TAPI_LINECALLSTATE_DIALING       5009

// ****************************************
// global declares
//
LONG PlaceCall( HWND, LPTSTR );
void CALLBACK LineCallBackProc(DWORD hDevice,DWORD dwMessage,DWORD dwInstance,DWORD
➥dwParam1,DWORD dwParam2,DWORD dwParam3);
```

continues

Listing 24.1. continued

```
BOOL WINAPI MainDialog(HWND hDlg, WORD msg, WORD wParam, LONG lParam);
void ShowProgress( HWND hWnd, LPSTR OutputString );
void SetVarProps( HWND hWnd, DWORD hDevice );

LINECALLPARAMS LineParams;    // need this structure
DWORD lines;                  // count of available lines
HINSTANCE hInst;              // this instance of the app
HWND MainWin, ButtonWnd;      // window handles
HLINEAPP LineHandle = NULL;    // tapi line handle
```

Notice the inclusion of the `TAPI.H` and `WINDOWS.H` files. You'll need these on your system if you want to compile this project. You'll also need the `TAPI32.LIB` file.

The defines added here make it easy to provide a local message handler that responds to pre-defined TAPI messages. You'll see how these are used in the `MainDialog` and `lineCallBack` routines later in this chapter.

Notice also the declaration of global handles and a `lineParams` structure. You'll use these throughout the project.

The User Dialog Box and the `WinMain` Procedure

The `WinMain` code for this project is quite simple. Declare a message queue, get the current instance of this program, and then call the main dialog box. All other activity is generated by the dialog box. Listing 24.2 shows the code for the `WinMain` routine.

Listing 24.2. The `WinMain` routine for the `TAPIOUT` project.

```
// *********************************************
// Initial Entry
//
// establish a message queue
// get the instance handle
// start the user dialog
//
int PASCAL WinMain( HANDLE hInstance, HANDLE hPrev, LPSTR lpCmd, int nShow )
{
      SetMessageQueue( 100 );
      hInst = hInstance;
    DialogBox( hInstance, MAKEINTRESOURCE( ID_MAIN_SCREEN ), NULL, MainDialog );
      return( FALSE );
}
```

The main dialog box contains only a few controls. An input box for the phone number, a list box to show the status messages supplied by TAPI, and three command buttons (`PlaceCall`, `Disconnect`, and `Exit`). Figure 24.1 shows the layout of the main dialog box.

FIGURE 24.1.

The main dialog box of the
TAPIOUT *project.*

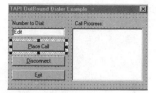

The code for the main dialog box is a bit lengthy; however, it is rather simple, too. The code
can be broken down into three main sections:

■ Responding to user commands (button presses).

■ Displaying posted messages from the callback routine.

■ Performing code operations based on posted messages from the callback function.

The first part of the MainDialog code responds to the initial loading of the dialog box and to
user actions on the command buttons. Listing 24.3 shows how this code looks.

Listing 24.3. The first part of the MainDialog code.

```
// *********************************************
// Main Dialog to handle user interface
//
BOOL WINAPI MainDialog(HWND hDlg, WORD msg, WORD wParam, LONG lParam)
{
    switch (msg)
    {
        case WM_INITDIALOG:     // when dialgo first starts up
        {
            // Set the necessary properties to null
            SetProp( hDlg, "HCALL", NULL );
            SetProp( hDlg, "HLINE", NULL );
            SetProp( hDlg, "HCOMM", NULL );
            break;
        }
        case WM_COMMAND:     // user pressed a button
        {
            switch( wParam )
            {
                case ID_CALL:     // user press PLACE CALL
                {
                    char PhoneNumber[ 100 ];    // save some space
                    HCALL hCall;               // declare a local handle
                    //
                    // Gotta call going? - Uh, oh!
                    hCall = (HCALL)GetProp( hDlg, "HCALL" );
                    if( hCall != NULL  )
                    {
```

continues

Listing 24.3. continued

```
                        MessageBox( hDlg,"Please Disconnect before making another
                                        ➥call!",
                                        " Tapi Error",
                                        MB_ICONSTOP );
                    break;
                }
                //
                // Get digits from input box
                GetDlgItemText( hDlg, ID_PHONE, PhoneNumber, sizeof(
➥PhoneNumber ) );
                //
                // place the call (check return value)
                if( PlaceCall( hDlg, PhoneNumber ) < 0 )
                    ShowProgress( hDlg, "Unable to start a TAPI Function" );
                break;
            }
            case ID_DISCONNECT:     // user press DISCONNECT
            {
                LONG retcode;    // some local stuff
                HCALL hCall;
                HANDLE hComm;
                //
                // try to get the handles
                hCall = (HCALL)GetProp( hDlg, "HCALL" );
                hComm = (HANDLE)GetProp( hDlg, "HCOMM" );
                //
                // if we have a comm handle, drop it
                if( hComm != NULL )
                {
                    CloseHandle( hComm );
                    SetProp( hDlg, "HCALL", NULL );
                }
                //
                // if we have a call handle, drop it
                if( hCall != NULL )
                {
                    retcode = lineDrop( hCall, NULL, 0 );
                    ShowProgress( hDlg, "Call is Dropped" );
                    SetProp( hDlg, "HCALL", NULL );
                }
                break;
            }
            case IDOK:    // user pressed the EXIT button
            {
                HCALL hCall; // declare some local vars
                HLINE hLine;
                HANDLE hComm;
                //
                // load the values
                hCall = (HCALL)GetProp( hDlg, "HCALL" );
                hLine = (HLINE)GetProp( hDlg, "HLINE" );
                hComm = (HANDLE)GetProp( hDlg, "HCOMM" );
                //
```

```
                    // if we have a comm handle, close it
                    if( hComm != NULL )
                    {
                        CloseHandle( hComm );
                        SetProp( hDlg, "HCOMM", NULL );
                    }
                    //
                    // if we have a call handle, close it
                    if( hCall != NULL )
                    {
                        lineDrop( hCall, NULL, 0 );
                        SetProp( hDlg, "HCALL", NULL );
                    }
                    //
                    // if we have a line handle, close it
                    if( hLine != NULL )
                    {
                        lineClose( hLine );
                        SetProp( hDlg, "HLINE", NULL );
                    }
                    //
                    // close down open line
                    if( LineHandle != NULL )
                    {
                        lineShutdown( LineHandle );
                        LineHandle = NULL;
                    }
                    //
                    // drop the save properties
                    RemoveProp( hDlg, "HCALL" );
                    RemoveProp( hDlg, "HLINE" );
                    RemoveProp( hDlg, "HCOMM" );
                    //
                    // close down the dialog
                    EndDialog( hDlg, FALSE );
                    break;
                                                              }
```

The code here deserves some review. First, when the dialog box first starts, three properties are created. These will hold values used throughout the dialog. The next event is the pressing of the ID_CALL button. This tells the dialog box to attempt to place a call. The first step is to check to see if a call is already in progress. If so, a message is displayed to the user. If no call is currently in progress, the phone number is gathered from the input box and then passed to the PlaceCall function for final dispatch (you'll see the PlaceCall function in the next section of this chapter).

If the user presses the ID_DISCONNECT button, the program checks the comm and call handles and, if they are set, clears them using the ClearHandle and lineDrop functions.

Finally, when the user presses the Exit button (IDOK), the same types of routines executed in ID_DISCONNECT must also occur here. In addition to the ClearHandle and lineDrop functions, the lineClose and lineShutdown routines are called. This performs final closure on all TAPI services for this session.

The second section of the MainDialog is used to respond to TAPI messages received via the lineCallBack function and passed onto the MainDialog. The only message that needs attention is when a call goes idle. If a call goes idle, the MainDialog needs to close down the line resources just as if the user had pressed the Disconnect button. Listing 24.4 shows how this code looks in the TAPIOUT project.

Listing 24.4. Responding to the TAPI Messages in the MainDialog.

```
//
// **************************************
// respond to TAPI Messages
// **************************************
//
case TAPI_LINE_REPLY:
{
    ShowProgress( hDlg, "Line Reply" );
     break;
}
//
case TAPI_LINECALLSTATE_CONNECTED:
{
    ShowProgress( hDlg, "Line Call State is Connected" );
    break;
}
//
case TAPI_LINECALLSTATE_IDLE:
{
    LONG retcode;     // local stuff
    HLINE hLine;
    //
    // call went idle, do cleanup
    hLine = (HLINE)GetProp( hDlg, "HLINE" );
    //
    // if we have a live line, close it
    if( hLine != NULL )
    {
        retcode = lineClose( hLine );
        SetProp( hDlg, "HLINE", (HANDLE)NULL );
    }
    ShowProgress( hDlg, "Line Call State is idle" );
    break;
}
```

Notice that, unlike the disconnect which performs both a lineDrop and a lineClose, the idle line handler only calls lineClose. This is because idle lines have already experienced the lineDrop. This is why they are idle!

The last section of the MainDialog is used to simply post status messages to the list box on the dialog box. The code is added here to show you progress during the call. You may not need to code these messages at all in production applications. Listing 24.5 shows how this code looks.

Listing 24.5. Posting TAPI messages from the MainDialog.

```
//
// *********************************************
// respond to forwarded TAPI messages
// *********************************************
//
case TAPI_LINECALLSTATE_DISCONNECTED:
{
    ShowProgress( hDlg, "Line Call State is Disconnected" );
    break;
}
//
case TAPI_LINECALLSTATE_BUSY:
{
    ShowProgress( hDlg, "Line Call State is Busy" );
    break;
}
//
case TAPI_LINECALLSTATE_ACCEPTED:
{
    ShowProgress( hDlg, "Line Call State is Accepted" );
    break;
}
//
case TAPI_LINECALLSTATE_PROCEEDING:
{
    ShowProgress( hDlg, "Line Call State is Proceeding" );
    break;
}
//
case TAPI_LINECALLSTATE_OFFERING:
{
    ShowProgress( hDlg, "Line Call State is Offering" );
    break;
}
//
case TAPI_LINECALLSTATE_DIALTONE:
{
    ShowProgress( hDlg, "Line Call State is DialTone" );
    break;
}
//
case TAPI_LINECALLSTATE_DIALING:
{
    ShowProgress( hDlg, "Line Call State is Dialing" );
    break;
```

continues

Listing 24.5. continued

```
            }
            default:
                break;
        } // switch (wParam)
        break;
    } // case WM_COMMAND
    default:
        break;
    } // switch (msg)
    return (FALSE);
} // main dialog
```

The `PlaceCall` Function

The real heart of the project is the `PlaceCall` function. This routine is the one that actually places the requested call. The code here follows the outline in the first part of this chapter. The steps of initialize, check API, look for open line, set call parameters, and place call are all here in this one routine. You can use this code as a shell routine to place in your other TAPI applications. Listing 24.6 shows the code for the `PlaceCall` function.

Listing 24.6. The code for the `PlaceCall` function.

```
// ***************************************************
// This routine places the actual call
//
LONG PlaceCall( HWND hWnd, LPTSTR PhoneNumber )
{
    LONG    retcode;                // local returns
    DWORD   i;                      // counter for lines
    DWORD   ApiVersion;             // expected API version
    DWORD   RetApiVersion;          // return version
    LINEEXTENSIONID    ExtensionID; // struc for API call
    HLINE   hLine;                  // local line handle
    HCALL   hCall;                  // local call handle
    //
    // make sure you have a phone number
    if( lstrlen( PhoneNumber ) < 1 )
        return( -1 );
    //
    // Initialize the line, register the callback
    if( LineHandle == NULL )
        retcode = lineInitialize( &LineHandle, hInst,
➥(LINECALLBACK)LineCallBackProc, "TAPI Out", &lines );
    if( retcode < 0 )
        return( retcode );
    //
    // go through all lines to get API and properties
    // if you find one that has the right properties,
    // jump out and continue to next section of code
```

```
    //
    hLine = (HLINE)GetProp( hWnd, "HLINE" );
    if( hLine == NULL )
    {
        for( i=0; i < lines; i++ )
        {
            // Negotiate the API Version for each line
            ApiVersion = tapiVersionCur;
            retcode = lineNegotiateAPIVersion( LineHandle, i, ApiVersion,
➥ApiVersion, &RetApiVersion,
                &ExtensionID );
            retcode = lineOpen( LineHandle, i, &hLine, RetApiVersion, 0,
➥(DWORD)hWnd,
                LINECALLPRIVILEGE_OWNER | LINECALLPRIVILEGE_MONITOR,
                LINEMEDIAMODE_DATAMODEM, NULL );
            if( retcode == 0 )
                break;
        }
        if( retcode != 0 )
            return( -1 );
    }
    //
    // found a good line
    SetProp( hWnd, "HLINE",(HANDLE)(HLINE)hLine );
    //
    // now set of properties of the line for outbound dialing
    memset( &LineParams, 0, sizeof( LINECALLPARAMS ) );
    LineParams.dwTotalSize = sizeof( LINECALLPARAMS );
    LineParams.dwMinRate = 9600;    // setting data rates
    LineParams.dwMaxRate = 9600;    //
    LineParams.dwMediaMode = LINEMEDIAMODE_DATAMODEM;    // doing a data call
    //
    // finally place the call!
    retcode = lineMakeCall( hLine, &hCall, PhoneNumber, 0, &LineParams );
    return( retcode );    // tell'em how it turned out!
}
```

This code hardly needs review—you've seen this explained before. The key points to remember are:

- Use `lineInitialize` to register your callback function.
- Use `lineNegotiateAPIVersion` to check for valid TAPI services.
- Use `lineOpen` to ask for a line that can suit your needs (data, fax, voice, and so on).
- Use `LINECALLPARAMS` to optionally set calling parameters.
- Use `lineMakeCall` to actually place the call.

It is also important to remember that once TAPI performs the `lineMakeCall` successfully you still are not connected to your called party. You need to check callback messages to check the status of your call.

The ShowProgress and SetVarProps Procedures

There are two helper routines in the TAPIOUT project. The first, ShowProgress, is used to post messages to the list box on the main dialog form. Listing 24.7 shows how this code looks.

Listing 24.7. Posting messages to the main dialog box.

```
// **************************************************
// update list box to show TAPI progress
//
void ShowProgress( HWND hDlg, LPTSTR OutputString )
{
    DWORD dwIndex;
    int i;
    dwIndex = SendDlgItemMessage( hDlg, ID_STATUS_LIST, LB_ADDSTRING, 0,
➥(LPARAM)(LPSTR)OutputString );
    if( dwIndex == LB_ERR )           // clear some space for full box
    {
        for( i = 0; i < 10; i++ )
            SendDlgItemMessage( hDlg, ID_STATUS_LIST, LB_DELETESTRING, 0, 0 );
        // now send the message
        dwIndex = SendDlgItemMessage( hDlg, ID_STATUS_LIST, LB_ADDSTRING, 0,
➥(LPARAM)(LPSTR)OutputString );
    }
    SendDlgItemMessage( hDlg, ID_STATUS_LIST, LB_SETCURSEL, (WPARAM)dwIndex, 0 );
    return;
}
```

The second routine is used to pick the line ID out of the LINECALLINFO structure and store it in the dialog properties set. Listing 24.8 shows the SetVarProps routine.

Listing 24.8. The code for the SetVarProps routine.

```
// **************************************************
// get line handle from LINECALLINFO structure
//
void SetVarProps( HWND hWnd, DWORD hDevice )
{
    LINECALLINFO LineCallInfo;
    memset( &LineCallInfo, 0, sizeof( LINECALLINFO ) );
    SetProp( hWnd, "HCALL", (HANDLE)(HCALL)hDevice );
    LineCallInfo.dwTotalSize = sizeof( LINECALLINFO );
    lineGetCallInfo( (HCALL)hDevice, &LineCallInfo );
     SetProp( hWnd, "HLINE", (HANDLE)(HLINE)LineCallInfo.hLine );
    return;
}
```

The `lineCallBackProc` Procedure

The `lineCallBackProc` is the routine registered (using `lineInitialize`) to receive all TAPI messages for this application. Since this routine must handle all messages from TAPI, it can get a bit long. In this chapter, the code is broken into three segments:

■ Handling `LINE_CALLSTATE` messages

■ Passing status information to the `MainDialog`

■ Other messages currently ignored by `TAPIOUT`

The first section of the `lineCallBackProc` contains code to respond to changes in the `LINE_CALLSTATE` message. Only two messages get our attention here: `LINE_CALLSTATE_IDLE` and `LINE_CALLSTATE_CONNECTED`. Listing 24.9 shows the code that responds to these two messages.

Listing 24.9. Responding to the `LINE_CALLSTATE_IDLE` and `LINE_CALLSTATE_CONNECTED` messages.

```
// ********************************************
// The callback to handle TAPI messages
//
// This routine handles all messages generated by TAPI services.
// Most of these messages are ignored here or just passsed on to
// the main dialog for posting to the progress window.
//
void CALLBACK LineCallBackProc(DWORD hDevice,DWORD dwMessage,DWORD dwInstance,DWORD
➥dwParam1,DWORD dwParam2,DWORD dwParam3)
{

    switch (dwMessage)
        {
        case LINE_CALLSTATE:     // review the call state messages
            {
                switch( dwParam1 )
                {
                    case LINECALLSTATE_IDLE:     // went idle
                    {
                        LONG retcode;
                        LINECALLINFO LineCallInfo;
                        //
                        // load call info into structure
                        memset( &LineCallInfo, 0, sizeof( LINECALLINFO ) );
                        LineCallInfo.dwTotalSize = sizeof( LINECALLINFO );
                        lineGetCallInfo( (HCALL)hDevice, &LineCallInfo );
                        //
                        // deallocate the call
                        retcode = lineDeallocateCall( (HCALL)hDevice );
                        //
                        // post message to main dialog
                        PostMessage((HWND)dwInstance, WM_COMMAND,
➥TAPI_LINECALLSTATE_IDLE, (LPARAM)(HLINE)LineCallInfo.hLine );
                        break;
                    }
```

continues

Listing 24.9. continued

```
                        case LINECALLSTATE_CONNECTED:    // hey, we got through!
                        {
                            //
                            // local vars for processing
                            LPVARSTRING lpVarStringStruct = NULL;
                            size_t sizeofVarStringStruct = sizeof( VARSTRING ) + 1024;
                            HANDLE CommFile = NULL;
                            long lreturn;
                            // get the comm handle.  Be sure to drop this handle when
                            // the call is done or you'll get device unavailable errors
                            // and have to REBOOT!
                            lpVarStringStruct = LocalAlloc( 0, sizeofVarStringStruct );
                            do
                            {
                                memset( lpVarStringStruct, 0, sizeofVarStringStruct );
                                lpVarStringStruct->dwTotalSize =
➥(DWORD)sizeofVarStringStruct;
                                lreturn = lineGetID( 0, 0, (HCALL)hDevice,
➥LINECALLSELECT_CALL, lpVarStringStruct, "comm/datamodem" );
                            } while( lreturn != 0 );
                            //
                            // get comm device handle and save it to properties area
                            CommFile = *( (LPHANDLE )( ( LPBYTE )lpVarStringStruct +
➥lpVarStringStruct->dwStringOffset ) );
                            SetProp( (HWND)dwInstance, "HCOMM", CommFile );
                            SetVarProps( (HWND)dwInstance, hDevice );
                            //
                            // tell main dialog we got through
                            PostMessage( (HWND)dwInstance, WM_COMMAND,
➥TAPI_LINECALLSTATE_CONNECTED, (LPARAM)(HANDLE)CommFile );
                            LocalFree( lpVarStringStruct ); // drop mem space
                            break;
                                                                                    }
```

Notice that the LINE_CALLSTATE_CONNECTED routine contains code that retrieves the comm handle and gets the lineID. You'll need these values in subsequent calls to TAPI services. The LINE_CALLSTATE_IDLE routine simply de-allocates the device handle to free up resources for the next call.

The second segment of the callback routine passes messages to the main dialog box for display. These are added here to show you how the messages work and how call progress can be reported. You may not need to add these messages to your production applications. Listing 24.10 shows the portion of lineCallBackProc that posts messages to the MainDialog routine.

Listing 24.10. Passing messages from lineCallBack to MainDialog.

```
                    case LINECALLSTATE_ACCEPTED:    // just pass message on...
                    {
                        SetVarProps( (HWND)dwInstance, hDevice );
                        PostMessage( (HWND)dwInstance, WM_COMMAND,
➥TAPI_LINECALLSTATE_ACCEPTED,(LPARAM)(HCALL)hDevice );
                        break;
```

```
                }

                case LINECALLSTATE_PROCEEDING:      // post progress message
                {
                     SetVarProps( (HWND)dwInstance, hDevice );
                     PostMessage( (HWND)dwInstance, WM_COMMAND,
➥TAPI_LINECALLSTATE_PROCEEDING,(LPARAM)(HCALL)hDevice );
                     break;
                }

                case LINECALLSTATE_OFFERING:      // pass it on
                {
                     SetVarProps( (HWND)dwInstance, hDevice );
                     PostMessage( (HWND)dwInstance, WM_COMMAND,
➥TAPI_LINECALLSTATE_OFFERING, (LPARAM)(HCALL)hDevice );
                     break;
                }

                case LINECALLSTATE_DIALTONE:      // pass it on
                {
                     SetVarProps( (HWND)dwInstance, hDevice );
                     PostMessage( (HWND)dwInstance, WM_COMMAND,
➥TAPI_LINECALLSTATE_DIALTONE, (LPARAM)(HCALL)hDevice );
                     break;
                }

                case LINECALLSTATE_DIALING:          // pas it on...
                {
                     SetVarProps( (HWND)dwInstance, hDevice );
                     PostMessage( (HWND)dwInstance, WM_COMMAND,
➥TAPI_LINECALLSTATE_DIALING, (LPARAM)(HCALL)hDevice );
                     break;
                }

                case LINECALLSTATE_BUSY:          // pass it on...
                {
                     SetVarProps( (HWND)dwInstance, hDevice );
                     PostMessage( (HWND)dwInstance, WM_COMMAND,
➥TAPI_LINECALLSTATE_BUSY, 0 );
                     break;
                }

                case LINECALLSTATE_DISCONNECTED:      // pass it on...
                {
                     SetVarProps( (HWND)dwInstance, hDevice );
                     PostMessage( (HWND)dwInstance, WM_COMMAND,
➥TAPI_LINECALLSTATE_DISCONNECTED, (LPARAM)(HCALL)hDevice );
                     break;
                }
            }
          break;
        }
```

In the final section of the lineCallBack routine, several other potential messages are listed, but no code is added. This is just to give you an idea of the other messages that can be received by lineCallBackProc. Listing 24.11 shows the final section of the lineCallBackProc routine.

Listing 24.11. The last section of `lineCallBackProc`.

```
        case LINE_LINEDEVSTATE:      // we'll ignore these for now...
            switch (dwParam1)
            {
                case LINEDEVSTATE_REINIT:
                    break;

                case LINEDEVSTATE_RINGING:
                    break;
            }
            break;

        case LINE_CLOSE: // the line has been closed!
            {
            break;
            }
        case LINE_REPLY:      // pass on TAPI_REPLY messages
        {
            PostMessage( (HWND)dwInstance, WM_COMMAND, TAPI_LINE_REPLY, 0 );
            break;
        }

        //
        // other messages that we'll ignore here
        //
        case LINE_REQUEST:
        case LINE_ADDRESSSTATE:
            break;
        case LINE_CALLINFO:
            break;
        case LINE_DEVSPECIFIC:
            break;
        case LINE_DEVSPECIFICFEATURE:
            break;
        case LINE_GATHERDIGITS:
            break;
        case LINE_GENERATE:
            break;
        case LINE_MONITORDIGITS:
            break;
        case LINE_MONITORMEDIA:
            break;
        case LINE_MONITORTONE:
            break;
    } /* switch */

} /* LineCallBackProc */
```

That concludes the code review for the TAPIOUT project. In the next section, you'll get to test the TAPIOUT project.

Testing the `TAPIOut` Project

If you have a C compiler that can handle the `TAPIOUT` code, compile it now. If you do not have a compiler, you can load the `TAPIOUT.EXE` from the CD-ROM that ships with the book.

When you first load `TAPIOUT` you'll see a simple dialog box. Enter a valid phone number in the input box and press `PlaceCall`. You'll see several messages appear in the status box as TAPI attempts to complete your call (see Figure 24.2).

FIGURE 24.2.
Running the `TAPIOUT`
project.

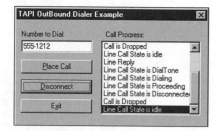

In a production application you would add code that responded to the `LINE_CALLSTATE_CONNECTED` message by notifying the user to pick up a connected handset (for voice calls), beginning a data send (for fax or data calls), or possibly starting a recorded message (for automated voice calls).

Summary

In this chapter you learned how to use the Basic Telephony API functions to write a short dialer program in C. The techniques you learned here will be used throughout all the TAPI projects in this book. Even the projects written in Visual Basic 4.0 will use the same API calls in the same order.

In the next chapter, you'll learn about the details of hardware configurations including the limitations and advantages of standard modem cards, voice-modem cards, and telephony hardware.

25

TAPI Hardware Considerations

In this chapter, you'll learn the differences between the three primary types of telephony hardware for PCs:

- Basic data modems
- Voice-data modems
- Telephony cards

These three types of interface cards provide a wide range of telephony service for desktop workstations. You'll learn the advantages and limits of each of the interface card types and how you can use them in your telephony applications.

Basic data modems can support Assisted Telephony services (outbound dialing) and usually are able to support only limited inbound call handling.

Voice-data modems are a new breed of low-cost modems that provide additional features that come close to that of the higher-priced telephony cards. These modems usually are capable of supporting the Basic Telephony services and many of the Supplemental services. The key to success with voice-data modems is getting a good service provider interface for your card.

Finally, telephony cards offer the greatest level of service compatibility. Telephony cards usually support all of the Basic Telephony and all of the Supplemental Telephony services, including phone device control. Most telephony cards also offer multiple lines on a single card. This makes them ideal for supporting commercial-grade telephony applications.

You'll also get a quick review of how modems work and how Win95 and WinNT use modem drivers to communicate with hardware devices.

Modems and the UniModem Drivers for Win95 and WinNT

All TAPI services are routed through some type of modem. These modems also depend on the Windows operating system to supply device drivers to communicate between programs and the device itself. While a detailed discussion of device drivers is beyond the scope of this book, it is a good idea to have a general understanding of how Windows uses device drivers and how modems work. In this section you'll get a quick review of modem theory and a short discussion of the Universal Modem Driver that ships with Win95 and WinNT.

A Quick Review of How Modems Work

Before getting into the details of how the three types of telephony hardware differ, it is important to do a quick review of how modems work. If you've seen all this before, you can skip to the next section.

Sending computer data over voice-grade phone lines is a bit of a trick. All data stored on a PC (documents, programs, graphics, sound and video files, and so on) is stored as 1s and 0s—binary data. However, standard telephone lines are not capable of sending binary data—only sounds. That means that any information sent over the telephone line has to be in the form of sound waves. In order to accomplish this feat, hardware was invented to convert digital information into sound (that is, to *modulate* it), then back again from sound into digital information (*demodulate* it). This process of modulating and demodulating is how the device got its name: mo-dem (*mo*dulate-*dem*odulate).

Sending data over phones lines involves three main steps. First, a connection must be established between two modem devices over a telephone line. This is typically done by having one modem place a telephone call to the other modem. If the second modem answers the telephone call, the two modems go through a process of determining if they understand each other called *handshaking*. If that is successful, then information can be passed.

In the second step, the digital information is modulated into sound and then sent over the voice-grade telephone line to the second modem. In the last step, the modem at the other end of the call converts (demodulates) the sound back into digital information and presents it to the computer for processing (view the graphic, save the file, play the video or audio, and so on).

The Universal Modem Drivers and TAPI Service Providers

TAPI requires each workstation to have not just a TAPI-compliant application, but also a *Telephony Service Provider Interface* (*TSPI*). This interface talks directly to the hardware to convert your TAPI service requests into commands understood by the hardware. The TSPI is usually supplied by the hardware vendor, but Microsoft Win95 ships with a simple TSPI called the *UniModem Driver* (Universal Modem Driver). The UniModem driver is designed to support Assisted Telephony and some Basic Telephony. You can build simple applications that allow users to place and receive voice and data calls using basic data modems and the UniModem driver that ships with Win95 and WinNT.

> **NOTE**
>
> You'll learn more about TSPI and modem drivers in Chapter 27, "TAPI Behind the Scenes—The `TELEPHON.INI` File."

Microsoft has released a modem driver that supports additional voice features including playing and recording audio files. This driver is called the *UniModemV Driver* (Universal Modem for Voice). This driver supports the use of voice commands along with recording and playing back voice files. It can also handle caller ID and some other added service features. Exactly what the UniModemV driver can do is also dependent on the hardware. The telephony hardware must recognize any advanced features and be able to communicate them to the driver.

> **TIP**
>
> You can find a copy of the UniModemV driver on the CD-ROM that ships with this book.

Basic Data Modems

The most basic type of hardware that supports TAPI is the basic data modem. This type of modem is designed to use analog phone lines to send digital data. Any computer that can access online services (BBS, Internet, commercial information services, and so on) has at least this level of modem hardware. You can get basic data modems with speeds of 9600 to 14,400bps (bits per second) for $100 U.S. or less. You can get data modems that can handle 28,800bps for a bit more.

It is not easy to find data modems for PCs that are rated beyond 28.8Kbps. The primary reason for this is that voice-grade telephone lines cannot handle error-free throughput at speeds much faster than 28.8Kbps. Although there are now some 33.3 modems on the market, your local lines may not be able to handle those speeds. You can contact your local telephone service provider to get an idea of the line quality in your area. Usually, if you want to use speeds faster than 28.8, you'll need to purchase special lines from your local telephone service provider.

Almost all basic data modems recognize a common set of control codes. This set of control codes is called the *Hayes* or *AT* command set. This set of controls was developed by the makers of the Hayes modem. The first command in the set (AT) is the "attention" command. This tells the device you are about to send control codes directly to the hardware. The command set is known by the original author's name ("Hayes") or by the first command in the set ("AT").

Basic data modems support Assisted Telephony services without any problem (that is, placing outbound calls). Most basic modems are capable of supporting some of the Basic Telephony services, including accepting inbound calls. However, if you want to perform any of the more advanced TAPI services, such as playing or recording audio files, you'll need more advanced hardware. Also, if you want to access advanced features available for voice telephones such as caller ID, call hold, park, forward, and so on, you'll need more than a basic data modem. Figure 25.1 shows the TAPI service levels and telephony hardware classes. The highlighted areas give you an idea of how basic data modems do in supporting TAPI services.

If you are designing applications that allow users to select names or phone numbers and then place outbound voice or data calls, basic modems will work just fine. In fact, unless you are planning to add voice recording, playback, or other advanced telephony features to your application, the basic modem will provide all your TAPI needs.

FIGURE 25.1.

Basic modem support for TAPI services.

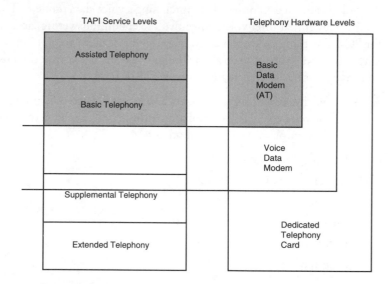

Data Modems with Voice

There is a new type of modem available that offers all the services of a data modem, but also has added support for voice services. These modems are often called voice-data modems (or data-voice modems). This hardware has additional programming built into the chips that will support advanced telephone features such as caller ID, call hold, park, forward, and so on. Just as basic data modems use the AT command set, the voice-data modems use an extension of that set called the *AT+V* command set (*AT plus Voice*).

AT+V modems cost a bit more than basic data modems. You can find them in the U.S. packaged with sound cards and other multimedia hardware. Generally the cost is about $250 U.S. If the modem is part of a bundled multimedia kit, you could end up paying twice that amount.

Voice-data modems also require a TAPI-compliant modem driver in order to work with TAPI services. This driver is usually supplied by the hardware vendor. Microsoft also supplies a modem driver that supports voice services—the UniModemV driver. If your modem does not ship with a TAPI-compliant driver, you might be able to install the UniModemV driver to enable your voice features.

> **TIP**
>
> A copy of the UniModemV driver ships with the latest version of Windows 95 and the new Windows NT 4.0. If you have an older version of Windows 95 or Windows NT, you can use the copy of UniModemV on the CD-ROM that ships with this book.

A word of caution is in order when purchasing a voice-data modem. There are several modems on the market that offer voice, voice-mail, telephone answering, and other TAPI-like services for PCs. The thing to keep in mind is that many of them are not TAPI-compliant. While you may get a modem that can do all the things you want, it may not do it using the TAPI calls and you many not be able to program it using TAPI services.

As of the writing of this book, there are a handful of voice-data modem vendors that have announced the release of TAPI-compliant hardware. Here is a list of some vendors currently offering TAPI-compliant voice-data modems:

- Compaq Presario Systems
- Creative Labs Phone Blaster
- Logicode 14.4 PCMCIA
- Diamond Telecommander 2500
- Cirrus Logic
- Aztech Systems

> **TIP**
>
> This list is growing all the time. For the most recent updates on this list you can check the CD-ROM that ships with this book. You can also check out the Communications Developer's Guide Web site for updates on MAPI, SAPI, and TAPI development. Point your browser to `www.iac.net/~mamund/mstdg`.

Voice-data modems with supporting TAPI drivers offer a wide range of access to TAPI services. You can use voice-data modems to perform both outbound and inbound call handling, play and record voice files, and (if the feature is available on the telephone line) support caller

ID and other advanced services for single-line phones. Figure 25.2 shows how voice-data modems shape up in their support of TAPI services.

FIGURE 25.2.

Voice-data modem support for TAPI services.

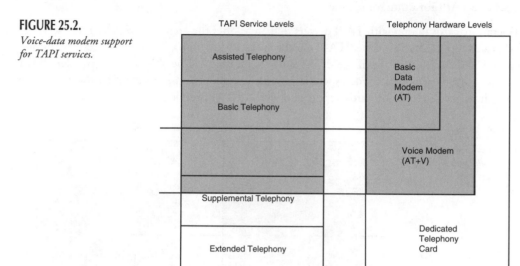

Telephony Cards

The most advanced level of hardware you can get for TAPI services on a desktop PC is a dedicated telephony card. This is a piece of hardware dedicated to handling telephone services. Most telephony cards are designed to handle more than one line at a time, too. If you are planning an application that must answer several phone lines or perform any line transfers, and so on, you'll need a telephony card.

Most telephony cards are sold as part of a kit. You can get software development tools, cards for the PC, cables, and documentation all for one price. This price usually starts at around $1000 U.S. and can easily climb depending on the number of lines you wish to support. Even though the price is a bit high, if you are doing any serious TAPI work, you'll need this kind of equipment.

As with other telephony hardware, telephony cards need an accompanying TAPI driver in order to recognize TAPI calls from your program. While most telephony card vendors are working on TAPI drivers, not all of them supply one as of this writing. It is important to check the specifications of the hardware and supporting materials before you buy.

It is also important to point out that there are lots of very sophisticated hardware and software tools for handling telephony services that are not TAPI-based. It is possible that you will be able to find the right hardware and software to meet your needs without using TAPI services at all. The only drawback is that you'll be using a proprietary system that may (or may not) become obsolete in the future. If it is possible, it is a good idea to use TAPI-compliant products since the power of Microsoft and the Windows operating system is likely to support interfaces like TAPI for quite some time.

Telephony cards (along with TAPI drivers to match) offer the greatest access to TAPI services. You can support all the Assisted TAPI and Basic TAPI functions along with access to Supplemental TAPI services. Also, if the driver supports it, you will be able to use Extended TAPI services to gain access to vendor-specific functions unique to the installed hardware. Figure 25.3 shows how telephony cards support all levels of TAPI services.

FIGURE 25.3.
Telephony cards can support all levels of TAPI services.

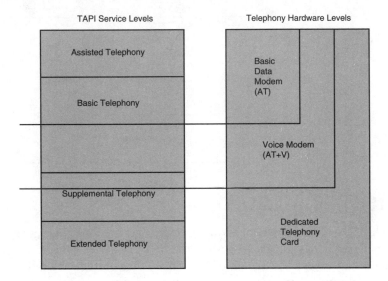

Summary

In this chapter you learned the differences between the three types of hardware options and how they rate in offering support for TAPI services on PC workstations:

- *Basic data modems* support Assisted Telephony services (outbound dialing) and can support only limited inbound call handling. Use this type of hardware if you are building simple outbound dialing applications.

- *Voice-data modems* are capable of supporting the Assisted Telephony and Basic Telephony services and many of the Supplemental services. Use this type of hardware if you want to provide both inbound and outbound services on a single-line phone.

- *Telephony cards* support all of the Basic Telephony and all of the Supplemental Telephony services, including phone device control. Most telephony cards also offer multiple lines on a single card. This make them ideal for supporting commercial-grade telephony applications.

You also got a quick review of modems and modem drivers. You learned that Win95 and WinNT rely on the UniModem or UniModemV modem drivers to communicate between the telephony hardware and your program. You also learned that, no matter what hardware you purchase, you will need a TAPI-compliant *TSPI* (*Telephony Service Provider Interface*) that matches the hardware you purchased. Hardware vendors may recognize the UniModem or UniModemV drivers, or ship their own TSPI drivers with their hardware.

In the next chapter, you'll learn how to use Visual Basic and a special custom OCX control to gain direct access TAPI services for your Visual Basic programs.

26

TAPI Tools—Using the TAPILINE Control

In this chapter, you'll learn how to use a special custom control, the TAPILine control, to gain access to TAPI services from within your Visual Basic 4.0 programs. You'll also learn about the TAPILine control's properties and methods, and how to use a series of accompanying DLL calls that allow you to pass data structures between your Visual Basic program and the TAPI32.DLL.

After a review of the control itself, you'll build a demonstration project in Visual Basic 4.0 that will use the methods, properties, and DLL calls you learned about in the first part of the chapter. In the process you'll learn how to access all the major operations of Basic Telephony from within your Visual Basic programs.

When you complete this chapter, you'll know how to use the new control and how to add Basic Telephony services to your Visual Basic applications.

The TAPILINE Control

Accessing all but the simplest TAPI services requires the use of a notification callback (also known as a *sink*). Because Visual Basic is not capable of passing a callback address to TAPI, there is a special TAPI control included with this book, called TAPILINE.OCX, which allows the TAPI.DLL to notify your Visual Basic program whenever a critical event happens during a TAPI operation. This is done through an OCX event called TAPICallBack.

There is also a handful of properties that can be set or read. These allow you to get information from the TAPI services about the application ID, the line devices, and the identifying number of the call that is currently in progress at your workstation.

TAPILINE.OCX has a wealth of methods. In fact, TAPILINE.OCX includes every single method for TAPI line devices. You can use these methods to invoke dialog boxes, call TAPI functions, and get and read critical TAPI settings and return values.

The TAPILINE development kit also includes a DLL file that is used to pass data structures between your Visual Basic program and the TAPI system. This DLL file is needed because Visual Basic cannot use API calls to pass structured data directly. Rather than create routines that handle long byte arrays, you'll use DLL helper functions to read and write data structures used by the TAPI system.

Installing the TAPILINE Control

Before you can use the TAPILINE control in your projects, you must add several files to your WINDOWS\SYSTEM folder. Table 26.1 shows the files you must add:

Table 26.1. Required files for using TAPILINE.OCX with Visual Basic.

File Name	*Description*
TAPILINE.OCX	This is the actual OLE control that appears in your Visual Basic tool box.
TAPILINE.LIC	A short license file to verify you have a legal copy of TAPILINE.
TAPILINE.OCA	An additional control file used by Visual Basic.
TAPILINE.TLB	A type library file. You can use this to access TAPILINE services without loading the control on the form.
PSTAPIDLL32.DLL	The DLL that holds supporting routines for passing structured data between Visual Basic and TAPI.
MCF40.DLL	The DLL that provides support for Microsoft Foundation Class services.
MSVCRT40.DLL	The DLL that supports Microsoft Visual C++.

You can find these files in the TAPISYS and RUNTIMEC folders on the CD-ROM that ships with this book.

> **WARNING**
>
> It is possible that you have the last two files already in your WINDOWS\SYSTEM directory. If you already have them, do *not* copy them from the CD-ROM to your system.

After you copy the files to the WINDOWS\SYSTEM directory, you can start up Visual Basic 4.0 and add the TAPILINE control to your tool box. To do this, select Tools ¦ Custom Controls... from the main menu. A dialog box will appear showing all the controls that Visual Basic knows about. You should see one called "TAPILINE OLE Custom Control Module" (see Figure 26.1).

FIGURE 26.1.

Loading the TAPILINE *custom control.*

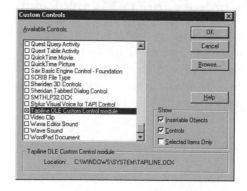

Once you locate the control, click it to turn the check mark on and then press OK to close the dialog box.

After loading the `TAPILINE` control into your toolbox, you'll be able to double-click the control to load it onto a Visual Basic form. You'll notice that you cannot resize the control once it is on your form. You will also notice that it disappears when you run your Visual Basic program. This is normal behavior for the `TAPILINE` control (see Figure 26.2).

FIGURE 26.2.

Placing the `TAPILINE` *control on a Visual Basic form.*

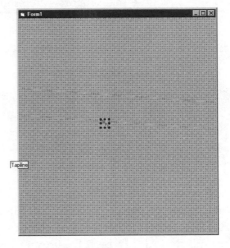

The TAPI Control's `TapiCallBack` Event

The one event recognized by the `TAPILINE.OCX` control is the `TapiCallBack` event. This event fires each time the TAPI system sends out a message. The `TapiCallBack` event receives a device ID, the message ID and program instance, and three additional parameters. It is up to the Visual Basic program to respond to the messages appropriately. Listing 26.1 shows how the event declaration appears within Visual Basic.

Listing 26.1. The TapiCallBack event declaration.

```
Private Sub Tapiline1_TapiCallBack(ByVal hDevice As Long, ByVal dwMessage As Long,
➥ByVal dwInstance As Long, ByVal dwParam1 As Long, ByVal dwParam2 As Long, ByVal
➥dwParam3 As Long)

End Sub
```

The TAPI system can generate 14 different messages that will be passed to the TapiCallBack event. Listing 26.2 shows the message names along with their unique values. These are the values that Visual Basic must check for in the TapiCallBack event.

Listing 26.2. The TAPI event messages.

```
'
' Line callback messages
'
Global Const LINE_ADDRESSSTATE = 0&
Global Const LINE_CALLINFO = 1&
Global Const LINE_CALLSTATE = 2&
Global Const LINE_CLOSE = 3&
Global Const LINE_DEVSPECIFIC = 4&
Global Const LINE_DEVSPECIFICFEATURE = 5&
Global Const LINE_GATHERDIGITS = 6&
Global Const LINE_GENERATE = 7&
Global Const LINE_LINEDEVSTATE = 8&
Global Const LINE_MONITORDIGITS = 9&
Global Const LINE_MONITORMEDIA = 10&
Global Const LINE_MONITORTONE = 11&
Global Const LINE_REPLY = 12&
Global Const LINE_REQUEST = 13&
```

> **NOTE**
>
> Chapter 23, "TAPI Architecture," describes the TAPILINE messages, their parameters, and their use.

The TAPILINE.OCX Properties

The TAPILINE.OCX has 12 unique, TAPI-related properties. TAPILINE uses these properties to keep track of important handles, ID values, and other settings. You can read or write these values using standard Visual Basic code or manipulate them at design time through the Properties window of Visual Basic. Table 26.2 shows the 12 TAPI-related properties along with short descriptions.

Table 26.2. The `TAPILINE.OCX` properties.

Property	Description
AddressID	This is a value from 0 to the maximum number of addresses available on a line device. Use this value to identify multiple addresses for the same line (multiple-line phones only).
APIVersion	This is the value of the TAPI API version currently in use. This is set by TAPI.
CompletionID	This is a unique value set by TAPI to identify a call that is in progress. Used in multiline systems that allow call camp and other advanced features.
GatheredDigits	This is a string of digits pressed by the user. This is the results of the `lineGatherDigits` function.
HandleToCall	This is the unique handle of the current call.
HandleToConfCall	This is the unique handle of a conference call in progress.
HandleToConsultCall	This is the unique handle of a call transfer that is in progress. This is used by several Supplemental TAPI functions.
LineApp	This is the unique ID of this session between Visual Basic and TAPI.
LineHandle	This is the unique ID of the line that has been opened for use.
NumberOfRings	This is the maximum number of rings to allow for an outbound call.
NumDevices	This is the total number of devices TAPI recognizes on the workstation.
PermanentProviderID	This is the unique ID of the TAPI service provider that is being used to complete the TAPI service request.
Priority	This is the priority value used to complete the last TAPI service request.

Most of these values are set at run-time by TAPI. You can read them to get status information about the state of a TAPI service request. As you will see in the example project built later in this chapter, there are a few properties here which you can manipulate safely during run-time. However, most should be treated as read-only properties.

The `TAPILINE.OCX` Methods

The `TAPILINE.OCX` has numerous methods that can be used to make TAPI service requests. In fact, all of the TAPI line functions have been recreated as methods for the `TAPILINE.OCX` control. Instead of listing all the methods here, you can use the TAPILINE.HLP file that ships with the TAPILINE.OCX control. This file contains detailed information on each of the methods. To use the help file as a reference, click the TAPILINE.HLP file and then press the Help Topics button to bring up the search dialog box. You can browse the search list or type in search strings to locate the desired function. Figure 26.3 shows you how the help file looks when it is first loaded.

FIGURE 26.3.

Loading the TAPILINE
help file.

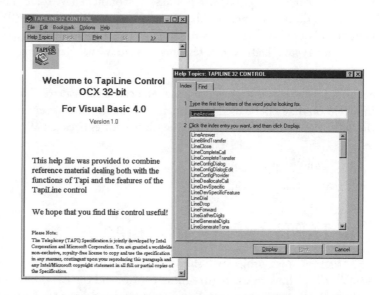

<table>
<tr><td>

TIP

You can also refer to Chapter 23, "TAPI Architecture," to get a complete list of all TAPILINE functions, including short descriptions.

</td></tr>
</table>

The TAPILINE DLL Functions

The TAPI system makes extensive use of data structures. In fact, several of the structures are variable in length. These are difficult to pass between Visual Basic and Windows DLLs or OCX controls. In order to simplify the process, the TAPILINE control comes with a helper DLL called PSTAPIDLL32. This DLL contains 17 functions that are used to pass data structures. Listing 26.3 shows a sample of the API declarations used to link these helper functions to your Visual Basic programs.

Listing 26.3. Declaring the DLL helper functions for TAPILINE.

```
Declare Sub LineMonitorToneFunc Lib "pstapidll32" (ByVal nMode As Long, structdata
➥As LINEMONITORTONE)
Declare Sub LineTranslateOutputFunc Lib "pstapidll32" (ByVal nMode As Long,
➥structdata As LINETRANSLATEOUTPUT, ByVal ExtraData As String)
```

Each call has at least two parameters and several of them have three. The first parameter (nMode) is used to indicate whether you are attempting to read (1) or write (0) TAPI data. The second parameter is a pre-defined data structure that contains the TAPI-related information. You will have other Type...End Type statements in your Visual Basic program that match these data structures.

Some of the DLL calls have a third parameter called sExtraData. This parameter contains string information that will be used to augment the structured data sent in the same call. This is how the TAPILINE control passes variable-length structures between Visual Basic and the TAPI system.

You'll see all 17 of the helper DLL calls in the next section of the chapter when you build the TAPILine Test application.

The TAPILINE Test Project

The TAPILINE Test project will show you how to build TAPI applications using Visual Basic 4.0. You'll see how to use the TAPILINE control and the PSTAPIDLL32 dynamic link library to perform TAPI service requests. You'll see how these two added resources (along with a bit of Visual Basic code) can give you extensive access to the TAPI services built into every Win95 and WinNT machine.

Before you can begin running TAPI applications from Visual Basic, you need a few support modules that contain DLL declarations, structured data types, global constants, and several internal help routines to decipher the messages returned by TAPI.

Once you have the DLL declarations, the line constants and structures, and the helper functions, you are ready to lay out the TAPILINE Test form and place code behind several buttons to see how TAPI services work from within Visual Basic programs.

Creating the support code of declarations, data structures, and constants is a big (and tedious) job. Instead of asking you to type all the code yourself, a set of support modules is included on the CD-ROM that accompanies this book. You can find the code support routines in the TAPILINE\VBTAPI folder on the CD-ROM. Table 26.3 lists the Visual Basic support modules along with short descriptions of their uses.

Table 26.3. The TAPILINE support modules for Visual Basic.

Module Name	Description
TAPILINE.BAS	All the DLL declarations, line constants, and line data structures needed for creating TAPI applications that use line devices.
TAPIPHON.BAS	All the constants and data structures needed to handle phone devices.
TAPICALL.BAS	A set of helper functions that handle TAPI callback messages and other routines.

NOTE

The TAPILINE.OCX can only handle line devices. The TAPIPHON.BAS module is included to help you if you wish to develop additional OCX or DLL code to support phone device programming from Visual Basic. It is possible that TAPILINE will support phone device programming in the future.

Copy the modules listed in Table 26.3 onto your own hard disk and use them whenever you use the TAPILINE.OCX file. The next section of the chapter reviews the modules listed to help you understand what is in them and to give you a good idea of how they work.

The DLL Declarations and General TAPI Constants

The first code in the TAPILINE.BAS module is the set of DLL declarations needed to call the TAPILINE helper functions for passing structured data. Listing 26.4 shows the code that handles the DLL declarations.

Listing 26.4. PSTAPIDLL32 DLL declarations.

```
'
' DLL declares for TAPILine control
'
Declare Sub LineCallParamsFunc Lib "pstapidll32" (ByVal nMode As Long, structdata
➥As LINECALLPARAMS, ByVal ExtraData As String)
Declare Sub LineForwardListFunc Lib "pstapidll32" (ByVal nMode As Long, structdata
➥As LINEFORWARDLIST, ByVal ExtraData As String)
Declare Sub LineGenerateToneFunc Lib "pstapidll32" (ByVal nMode As Long, structdata
➥As LINEGENERATETONE_TYPE, ByVal ExtraData As String)
Declare Sub LineAddressCapsFunc Lib "pstapidll32" (ByVal nMode As Long, structdata
➥As LINEADDRESSCAPS, ByVal ExtraData As String)
```

continues

Listing 26.4. continued

```
Declare Sub LineCallInfoFunc Lib "pstapidll32" (ByVal nMode As Long, structdata As
➥LINECALLINFO, ByVal ExtraData As String)
Declare Sub LineCallStatusFunc Lib "pstapidll32" (ByVal nMode As Long, structdata
➥As LINECALLSTATUS, ByVal ExtraData As String)
Declare Sub LineCallListFunc Lib "pstapidll32" (ByVal nMode As Long, structdata As
➥LINECALLLIST, ByVal ExtraData As String)
Declare Sub LineDevCapsFunc Lib "pstapidll32" (ByVal nMode As Long, structdata As
➥LINEDEVCAPS, ByVal ExtraData As String)
Declare Sub VarStringFunc Lib "pstapidll32" (ByVal nMode As Long, structdata As
➥VARSTRING, ByVal ExtraData As String)
Declare Sub LineDevStatusFunc Lib "pstapidll32" (ByVal nMode As Long, structdata As
➥LINEDEVSTATUS, ByVal ExtraData As String)
Declare Sub LineTranslateCapsFunc Lib "pstapidll32" (ByVal nMode As Long,
➥structdata As LINETRANSLATECAPS, ByVal ExtraData As String)
Declare Sub LineMonitorToneFunc Lib "pstapidll32" (ByVal nMode As Long, structdata
➥As LINEMONITORTONE)
Declare Sub LineExtensionIDFunc Lib "pstapidll32" (ByVal nMode As Long, structdata
➥As LINEEXTENSIONID)
Declare Sub LineDialParmsFunc Lib "pstapidll32" (ByVal nMode As Long, structdata As
➥LINEDIALPARAMS)
Declare Sub LineMediaControlDigitFunc Lib "pstapidll32" (ByVal nMode As Long,
➥structdata As LINEMEDIACONTROLDIGIT)
Declare Sub LineTranslateOutputFunc Lib "pstapidll32" (ByVal nMode As Long,
➥structdata As LINETRANSLATEOUTPUT, ByVal ExtraData As String)
Declare Sub LineAddressStatusFunc Lib "pstapidll32" (ByVal nMode As Long,
➥structdata As LINEADDRESSSTATUS, ByVal ExtraData As String)

'
' constants for read/write of params
'
Global Const TAPI_WRITE = 0
Global Const TAPI_READ = 1
```

You'll notice that the global constants for TAPI_WRITE and TAPI_READ appear at the end of the DLL declarations. These are used for the nMode parameter of the DLL calls.

After the DLL declares, you'll see a list of TAPI error message values that could be returned. Listing 26.5 shows the error values that appear in the TAPILINE.BAS module.

Listing 26.5. The TAPI error message values.

```
'
' **************************************************
' general TAPI constants
' **************************************************
'
Global Const TAPI_REPLY = &H400& + 99&

Global Const TAPIERR_CONNECTED = 0&
Global Const TAPIERR_DROPPED = -1&
Global Const TAPIERR_NOREQUESTRECIPIENT = -2&
Global Const TAPIERR_REQUESTQUEUEFULL = -3&
Global Const TAPIERR_INVALDESTADDRESS = -4&
```

```
Global Const TAPIERR_INVALWINDOWHANDLE = -5&
Global Const TAPIERR_INVALDEVICECLASS = -6&
Global Const TAPIERR_INVALDEVICEID = -7&
Global Const TAPIERR_DEVICECLASSUNAVAIL = -8&
Global Const TAPIERR_DEVICEIDUNAVAIL = -9&
Global Const TAPIERR_DEVICEINUSE = -10&
Global Const TAPIERR_DESTBUSY = -11&
Global Const TAPIERR_DESTNOANSWER = -12&
Global Const TAPIERR_DESTUNAVAIL = -13&
Global Const TAPIERR_UNKNOWNWINHANDLE = -14&
Global Const TAPIERR_UNKNOWNREQUESTID = -15&
Global Const TAPIERR_REQUESTFAILED = -16&
Global Const TAPIERR_REQUESTCANCELLED = -17&
Global Const TAPIERR_INVALPOINTER = -18&
Global Const TAPIMAXDESTADDRESSSIZE = 80&
Global Const TAPIMAXAPPNAMESIZE = 40&
Global Const TAPIMAXCALLEDPARTYSIZE = 40&
Global Const TAPIMAXCOMMENTSIZE = 80&
Global Const TAPIMAXDEVICECLASSSIZE = 40&
Global Const TAPIMAXDEVICEIDSIZE = 40&
```

Next, there is the list of callback message values. These will be used to check the `MessageID` values returned in the `TapiCallBack` event of the TAPILINE control. Listing 26.6 shows the list of 14 possible messages.

Listing 26.6. The `TAPICallBack` message IDs.

```
'
' Line callback messages
'
Global Const LINE_ADDRESSSTATE = 0&
Global Const LINE_CALLINFO = 1&
Global Const LINE_CALLSTATE = 2&
Global Const LINE_CLOSE = 3&
Global Const LINE_DEVSPECIFIC = 4&
Global Const LINE_DEVSPECIFICFEATURE = 5&
Global Const LINE_GATHERDIGITS = 6&
Global Const LINE_GENERATE = 7&
Global Const LINE_LINEDEVSTATE = 8&
Global Const LINE_MONITORDIGITS = 9&
Global Const LINE_MONITORMEDIA = 10&
Global Const LINE_MONITORTONE = 11&
Global Const LINE_REPLY = 12&
Global Const LINE_REQUEST = 13&
```

The Line Structures and Constants

There are numerous constants and declarations needed to support all the TAPI line device functions. There are too many to include here, but one is shown in Listing 26.7 to give you an example.

Listing 26.7. An example line constant and type declaration.

```
Global Const LINEADDRCAPFLAGS_FWDNUMRINGS = &H1&
Global Const LINEADDRCAPFLAGS_PICKUPGROUPID = &H2&
Global Const LINEADDRCAPFLAGS_SECURE = &H4&
Global Const LINEADDRCAPFLAGS_BLOCKIDDEFAULT = &H8&
Global Const LINEADDRCAPFLAGS_BLOCKIDOVERRIDE = &H10&
Global Const LINEADDRCAPFLAGS_DIALED = &H20&
Global Const LINEADDRCAPFLAGS_ORIGOFFHOOK = &H40&
Global Const LINEADDRCAPFLAGS_DESTOFFHOOK = &H80&
Global Const LINEADDRCAPFLAGS_FWDCONSULT = &H100&
Global Const LINEADDRCAPFLAGS_SETUPCONFNULL = &H200&
Global Const LINEADDRCAPFLAGS_AUTORECONNECT = &H400&
Global Const LINEADDRCAPFLAGS_COMPLETIONID = &H800&
Global Const LINEADDRCAPFLAGS_TRANSFERHELD = &H1000&
Global Const LINEADDRCAPFLAGS_TRANSFERMAKE = &H2000&
Global Const LINEADDRCAPFLAGS_CONFERENCEHELD = &H4000&
Global Const LINEADDRCAPFLAGS_CONFERENCEMAKE = &H8000&
Global Const LINEADDRCAPFLAGS_PARTIALDIAL = &H10000
Global Const LINEADDRCAPFLAGS_FWDSTATUSVALID = &H20000
Global Const LINEADDRCAPFLAGS_FWDINTEXTADDR = &H40000
Global Const LINEADDRCAPFLAGS_FWDBUSYNAADDR = &H80000
Global Const LINEADDRCAPFLAGS_ACCEPTTOALERT = &H100000
Global Const LINEADDRCAPFLAGS_CONFDROP = &H200000
Global Const LINEADDRCAPFLAGS_PICKUPCALLWAIT = &H400000

Type LINEADDRESSCAPS
    dwTotalSize As Long
    dwNeededSize As Long
    dwUsedSize As Long

    dwLineDeviceID As Long

    dwAddressSize As Long
    dwAddressOffset As Long

    dwDevSpecificSize As Long
    dwDevSpecificOffset As Long

    dwAddressSharing As Long
    dwAddressStates As Long
    dwCallInfoStates As Long
    dwCallerIDFlags As Long
    dwCalledIDFlags As Long
    dwConnectedIDFlags As Long
    dwRedirectionIDFlags As Long
    dwRedirectingIDFlags As Long
    dwCallStates As Long
    dwDialToneModes As Long
    dwBusyModes As Long
    dwSpecialInfo As Long
    dwDisconnectModes As Long

    dwMaxNumActiveCalls As Long
    dwMaxNumOnHoldCalls As Long
    dwMaxNumOnHoldPendingCalls As Long
```

```
        dwMaxNumConference As Long
        dwMaxNumTransConf As Long

        dwAddrCapFlags As Long
        dwCallFeatures As Long
        dwRemoveFromConfCaps As Long
        dwRemoveFromConfState As Long
        dwTransferModes As Long
        dwParkModes As Long

        dwForwardModes As Long
        dwMaxForwardEntries As Long
        dwMaxSpecificEntries As Long
        dwMinFwdNumRings As Long
        dwMaxFwdNumRings As Long

        dwMaxCallCompletions As Long
        dwCallCompletionConds As Long
        dwCallCompletionModes As Long
        dwNumCompletionMessages As Long
        dwCompletionMsgTextEntrySize As Long
        dwCompletionMsgTextSize As Long
        dwCompletionMsgTextOffset As Long
End Type
Global Const LINEADDRESSCAPS_FIXEDSIZE = 176

Type LINEADDRESSCAPS_STR
    Mem As String * LINEADDRESSCAPS_FIXEDSIZE
End Type
```

You'll notice a set of constants that appear before the type declaration. These can be used to set various TAPI parameters within the data structure. Some declarations are return values that can be read once TAPI has set or modified the data within the structure. The TAPILINE.BAS module contains many of these sets of constants and data structure declarations. The VBTAPI folder also contains a similar module for phone device declarations. Although the TAPILINE control currently only supports line devices, a future version may provide support for phone devices.

For now, you can load the TAPILINE.BAS module into your Visual Basic programs that use the TAPILINE.OCX control.

The TAPILine Function Module

The TAPICALL.BAS module contains several routines needed to support TAPI calls using TAPILINE.OCX and the PSTAPIDLL file. Again, typing them all in is boring. Instead, this section reviews several of the more important example routines. You can load the TAPICALL.BAS module into your Visual Basic projects and use these routines without having to re-enter all the code.

The TAPICallBackHandler Function

The most important routine in the TAPICALL.BAS module is the TAPICallBackHandler function. This routine takes the parameters returned in the TAPICallBack event of the TAPILINE.OCX and dispatches messages based on the return values. Listing 26.8 shows the code for the TAPICallBackHandler.

Listing 26.8. Code for the TAPICallBackHandler function.

```
Public Function TapiCallBackHandler(hDevice As Long, dwMessage As Long, dwInstance
As Long, dwParam1 As Long, dwParam2 As Long, dwParam3 As Long) As String
    '
    ' handle messages from TAPI control
    '
    Dim cMsg As String
    '
    Select Case dwMessage
        Case LINE_ADDRESSSTATE  '(= 0&)
            cMsg = "MSG: Line_AddressState"
            cMsg = cMsg & "..."
            cMsg = cMsg & "AddressID=" & CStr(dwParam1)
            cMsg = cMsg & ", State=" & LineAddressStateMsg(dwParam2)
        Case LINE_CALLINFO  '(= 1&)
            cMsg = "MSG: Line_CallInfo"
        Case LINE_CALLSTATE   '(= 2&)
            cMsg = "MSG: Line_CallState"
            cMsg = cMsg & "..."
            cMsg = cMsg & "CallState=" & LineCallStateMsg(dwParam1)
            '
            Select Case dwParam1
                Case LINECALLSTATE_BUSY
                    cMsg = cMsg & ", StateDependent=" & _
➥LineCallStateBusyMsg(dwParam2)
                Case LINECALLSTATE_DIALTONE
                    cMsg = cMsg & ", StateDependent=" & _
➥LineCallStateDialtoneMsg(dwParam2)
                Case LINECALLSTATE_DISCONNECTED
                    cMsg = cMsg & ", StateDependent=" & _
➥LineCallStateDisconnectedMsg(dwParam2)
                Case Else
                    cMsg = cMsg & ", StateDependent=" & CStr(dwParam2)
            End Select
            '
            cMsg = cMsg & ", Privilege=" & CStr(dwParam3)
        Case LINE_CLOSE '(= 3&)
            cMsg = "MSG: Line_Close"
        Case LINE_DEVSPECIFIC  '(= 4&)
            cMsg = "MSG: Line_DevSpecific"
        Case LINE_DEVSPECIFICFEATURE  '(= 5&)
            cMsg = "MSG: Line_DevSpecificFeature"
        Case LINE_GATHERDIGITS  '(= 6&)
            cMsg = "MSG: Line_GatherDigits"
        Case LINE_GENERATE  '(= 7&)
            cMsg = "MSG: Line_Generate"
```

```
            Case LINE_LINEDEVSTATE  '(= 8&)
                cMsg = "MSG: Line_LineDevState"
            Case LINE_MONITORDIGITS  '(= 9&)
                cMsg = "MSG: Line_MonitorDigits"
            Case LINE_MONITORMEDIA  '(= 10&)
                cMsg = "MSG: Line_MonitorMedia"
            Case LINE_MONITORTONE  '(= 11&)
                cMsg = "MSG: Line_MonitorTone"
            Case LINE_REPLY  '(= 12&)
                cMsg = "MSG: Line_Reply...idRequest=" & CStr(dwParam1) & " - Status = "
➥& LineErr(dwParam2)
            Case LINE_REQUEST  '(= 13&)
                cMsg = "MSG: Line_Request"
            Case Else
                cMsg = "MSG: Unknown Message..." + CStr(dwMessage)
        End Select
        '
        TapiCallBackHandler = cMsg
        '
End Function
```

This routine is designed to turn the callback MessageID value and other parameters into a meaningful message to display in a status box on a form. In production applications, you could use this same SELECT CASE structure to enclose calls to subroutines and functions that fire appropriate Visual Basic code based on the messages received.

You'll also notice that there are several calls to other support routines that translate parameters into meaningful strings for extended messages. These routines could be replaced by Visual Basic code that performs other tasks based on the parameters passed by TAPI into the TAPICallBack event.

A Sample CallState Message Function

There are several functions that convert call-state parameters into messages. These routines could be used to fire off Visual Basic code based on the state of the current call. Listing 26.9 shows one of these routines.

Listing 26.9. A sample CallState message function.

```
Public Function LineCallStateDisconnectedMsg(dwParam As Long) As String
    '
    ' handle message values
    '
    Dim cReturn As String
    '
    Select Case dwParam
        Case LINEDISCONNECTMODE_NORMAL  ' &H1&
            cReturn = "Normal"
        Case LINEDISCONNECTMODE_UNKNOWN  ' &H2&
```

continues

Listing 26.9. continued

```
            cReturn = "Unknown"
    Case LINEDISCONNECTMODE_REJECT ' &H4&
            cReturn = "Rejected"
    Case LINEDISCONNECTMODE_PICKUP ' &H8&
            cReturn = "Picked Up"
    Case LINEDISCONNECTMODE_FORWARDED ' &H10&
            cReturn = "Forwarded"
    Case LINEDISCONNECTMODE_BUSY ' &H20&
            cReturn = "Busy"
    Case LINEDISCONNECTMODE_NOANSWER ' &H40&
            cReturn = "No Answer"
    Case LINEDISCONNECTMODE_BADADDRESS ' &H80&
            cReturn = "Invalid Address"
    Case LINEDISCONNECTMODE_UNREACHABLE ' &H100&
            cReturn = "Unreachable"
    Case LINEDISCONNECTMODE_CONGESTION ' &H200&
            cReturn = "Congested Network"
    Case LINEDISCONNECTMODE_INCOMPATIBLE ' &H400&
            cReturn = "Incompatible Equipment"
    Case LINEDISCONNECTMODE_UNAVAIL ' &H800&
            cReturn = "Reason Unavailable"
    Case Else
            cReturn = "Unknown LineCallStateDisconnected Msg [" & CStr(dwParam) &
➥"]"
    End Select
    '
    LineCallStateDisconnectedMsg = cReturn
    '
End Function
```

This routine handles one of the parameters returned from a line disconnect event.

The `Clean` and `Offset` Functions

Some of the TAPI functions return data in variable-length strings. These data strings usually contain several items, separated by zeros. You need two routines to help read the data in these strings. First, you need a routine to clean out the zero character (0) values in a returned string. Second, you need a routine that can pick a block of characters out of the data string based on an offset and a string size. This offset and size are returned as part of the fixed-size data structure.

The `Clean` function removes all character string 0 values from the returned data. Listing 26.10 shows how this is done.

Listing 26.10. The `Clean` function.

```
Function Clean(c As String) As String
    '
    ' strip 0s from string
```

```
'
    Dim l As Integer
    Dim x As Integer
    Dim s As String
    Dim n As Integer
    '
    l = Len
    s = ""
    For x = 1 To Len
        If Mid(c, x, 1) <> Chr(0) Then
            s = s + Mid(c, x, 1)
        Else
            s = s + " "
        End If
    Next
    '
    Clean = s
End Function
```

You'll notice that the routine replaces all character zeros with character 32 (space). This maintains the original size of the string, but prevents Visual Basic from encountering errors when it tries to read a string that contains character 0 values.

The second routine needed to handle the variable strings is one that picks out a substring based on the offset and size values found in the fixed data structure. Listing 26.11 shows how the GetOffset function works.

Listing 26.11. The GetOffset function.

```
Public Function GetOffset(lLenStru As Long, lOffset As Long, lSize As Long,
➥cExtraData As String) As String
    '
    ' return the data at the offset
    '
    GetOffset = Mid(cExtraData, (lOffset - lLenStru) + 1, lSize)
    '
End Function
```

TAPI returns an offset value computed from the start of the original data structure. For this reason, the length of the data structure is passed as a first parameter into the function. This length is the size of the fixed portion of the data structure. The GetOffset routine subtracts the fixed-length amount to get the starting position in the cExtraData string space. This position is used to pick out a data string that is the length of lSize. The resulting string is then returned to the calling program.

That gives you a good idea of how the support routines work and how they are used throughout the program. In the next section, you'll build a demonstration program that uses the tools you have reviewed so far.

Laying Out the `TAPILine` Form

For our example program, you'll build a form that has a series of buttons you can press to invoke various TAPI service requests. The status of your requests will be displayed in a scrollable text box on the form. In a real application, you'd capture the status information and use it to control program flow. But for now, you'll see each message sent back from TAPI and you'll see how you can write code to capture those messages.

First, start Visual Basic and open a new project. Then add the `TAPILINE.OCX` control to the form.

> **TIP**
>
> If you do not see the `TAPILINE.OCX` in your Visual Basic toolbox window, add it by using the `Tools | Custom Controls` menu option. For more information on adding the `TAPILINE.OCX` to your project see the `TAPILINE.OCX` section of this chapter.

Next, add the `TAPILINE.BAS` and `TAPICALL.BAS` modules to your project (`File | Add File...`). You can find these in the `VBTAPI` folder on the CD-ROM.

Now you're ready to place the controls on the form. Refer to Figure 26.4 and Table 26.4 when laying out the form.

FIGURE 26.4.

Laying out the `TAPITest` *form.*

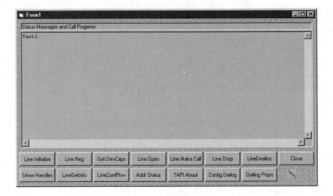

Table 26.4. The `TAPITest` form controls.

Control	Property	Setting
VB.Form	Name	frmTapiLine
	Caption	"Form1"
	Height	6000

Control	Property	Setting
	Left	1035
	Top	1305
	Width	10260
VB.CommandButton	Name	cmdLineConfProv
	Caption	"LineConfProv"
	Height	450
	Left	2580
	TabIndex	15
	Top	5040
	Width	1200
VB.CommandButton	Name	cmdLineDeallocate
	Caption	"LineDealloc"
	Height	450
	Left	7620
	TabIndex	14
	Top	4500
	Width	1200
VB.CommandButton	Name	cmdLineGetInfo
	Caption	"LineGetInfo"
	Height	450
	Left	1320
	TabIndex	13
	Top	5040
	Width	1200
VB.CommandButton	Name	cmdLineShowHandles
	Caption	"Show Handles"
	Height	450
	Left	60
	TabIndex	12
	Top	5040
	Width	1200

continues

Table 26.4. continued

Control	Property	Setting
VB.TextBox	Name	Text1
	BackColor	&H00C0C0C0&
	Font	name="MS LineDraw"
		charset=2
		weight=400
		size=8.25
		underline=0 'False
		italic=0 'False
		strikethrough=0 'False
	Height	3915
	Left	120
	MultiLine	-1 'True
	ScrollBars	3 'Both
	TabIndex	11
	Top	420
	Width	9915
VB.CommandButton	Name	cmdLineAbout
	Caption	"TAPI About"
	Height	450
	Left	5100
	TabIndex	10
	Top	5040
	Width	1200
VB.CommandButton	Name	cmdLineDrop
	Caption	"Line Drop"
	Height	450
	Left	6360
	TabIndex	9
	Top	4500
	Width	1200
VB.CommandButton	Name	cmdLineDialProps

Control	Property	Setting
	Caption	"Dialing Props"
	Height	450
	Left	7620
	TabIndex	8
	Top	5040
	Width	1200
VB.CommandButton	Name	cmdLineAddrStatus
	Caption	"Addr Status"
	Height	450
	Left	3840
	TabIndex	7
	Top	5040
	Width	1200
VB.CommandButton	Name	cmdLineConfDialog
	Caption	"Config Dialog"
	Height	450
	Left	6360
	TabIndex	6
	Top	5040
	Width	1200
VB.CommandButton	Name	cmdLineDevCaps
	Caption	"Get DevCaps"
	Height	450
	Left	2580
	TabIndex	5
	Top	4500
	Width	1200
VB.CommandButton	Name	cmdLineClose
	Caption	"Close"
	Height	450
	Left	8880
	TabIndex	4

continues

Table 26.4. continued

Control	Property	Setting
	Top	4500
	Width	1200
VB.CommandButton	Name	cmdLineMakeCall
	Caption	"Line Make Call"
	Height	450
	Left	5100
	TabIndex	3
	Top	4500
	Width	1200
VB.CommandButton	Name	cmdLineOpen
	Caption	"Line Open"
	Height	450
	Left	3840
	TabIndex	2
	Top	4500
	Width	1200
VB.CommandButton	Name	cmdLineNegApi
	Caption	"Line Neg"
	Height	450
	Left	1320
	TabIndex	1
	Top	4500
	Width	1200
VB.CommandButton	Name	cmdLineInit
	Caption	"Line Initialize"
	Height	450
	Left	60
	TabIndex	0
	Top	4500
	Width	1200
VB.Label	Name	Label1
	BorderStyle	1 'Fixed Single

Control	Property	Setting
	Caption	"Status Messages and Call Progress:"
	Height	255
	Left	120
	TabIndex	16
	Top	120
	Width	9915
TapilineLib.Tapiline	Name	Tapiline1
	Left	9180
	Top	5100

After completing the form, save the form as TAPITEST.FRM and the project as TAPITEST.VBP. Now you're ready to place code into the form.

Coding the TAPILine Form

There are two sets of code for the TAPILine form. The first set is for the support routines. These are called by several other routines on the form. Next you get to add the code behind all the buttons. This code is the actual TAPI service requests.

Adding the Support Routines

Before adding code behind the buttons on the form, you need to add a few support routines to the project. First, three form-level declarations are needed. Add the code in Listing 26.12 to the general declaration area of the form.

Listing 26.12. Form-level variables.

```
Option Explicit

Dim nline As Integer ' line to select
Dim lNumDev As Long ' number of devices
Dim cLine As String
```

Next, you need to add code to clear the values in four key properties used in this project. Create a subroutine called ClearHandles and add the code shown in Listing 26.13.

Listing 26.13. The ClearHandles routine.

```
Public Sub ClearHandles()
    '
    ' set all control handles to zero
    '
    Me.Tapiline1.LineApp = 0
    Me.Tapiline1.LineHandle = 0
    Me.Tapiline1.HandleToCall = 0
    Me.Tapiline1.AddressID = 0
    '
End Sub
```

You'll also need a routine to display the contents of these same four properties. Add a subroutine called ShowHandles and add the code in Listing 26.14.

Listing 26.14. The ShowHandles routine.

```
Public Sub ShowHandles()
    '
    AddText Me.Text1, "LineApp (Session)......" & Hex(Tapiline1.LineApp)
    AddText Me.Text1, "LineHandle (Line)......" & Hex(Tapiline1.LineHandle)
    AddText Me.Text1, "HandleToCall (Call)...." & Hex(Tapiline1.HandleToCall)
    AddText Me.Text1, "AddressID (internal)..." & Hex(Tapiline1.AddressID)
    '
    AddText Me.Text1, cLine ' msg separator
    '
End Sub
```

Next, add a new function called GetVarInfo. This will be used to parse some of the return values from the GetDevCaps TAPI function. Place the code shown in Listing 26.15 into the GetVarInfo function.

Listing 26.15. The GetVarInfo function.

```
Function GetVarInfo(nSize As Long, nOffset As Long, cString As String, nLen As
➥Long) As String
    Dim cValue As String
    '
    If nSize <> 0 Then
       cValue = Mid(cString, ((nOffset - nLen - 3)), nSize)
    Else
        cValue = ""
    End If
    '
    GetVarInfo = cValue
    '
End Function
```

Next comes a routine to fill the LINECALLPARAMS data structure before placing a call. This takes a bit of coding, so it's better to place it in its own routine. You can modify this routine to contain parameters that meet your modem's specifications. Add a subroutine called FillCallParams and enter the code from Listing 26.16.

Listing 26.16. The FillCallParams routine.

```
Function GetVarInfo(nSize As Long, nOffset As Long, cString As String, nLen As
➥Long) As String
    Dim cValue As String
    '
    If nSize <> 0 Then
       cValue = Mid(cString, ((nOffset - nLen - 3)), nSize)
    Else
        cValue = ""
    End If
    '
    GetVarInfo = cValue
    '
End Function
```

The last support routine you need to code for this project is the one used to read the LINECALLINFO data structure. This structure is quite long and contains a great deal of data. This routine (LocalGetLineInfo) reads the data, cleans up the returned strings, and then calls a routine in the TAPICALL.BAS file to actually show the results. Add the code from Listing 26.17 to your form.

Listing 26.17. The LocalGetLineInfo routine.

```
Function GetVarInfo(nSize As Long, nOffset As Long, cString As String, nLen As
➥Long) As String
    Dim cValue As String
    '
    If nSize <> 0 Then
       cValue = Mid(cString, ((nOffset - nLen - 3)), nSize)
    Else
        cValue = ""
    End If
    '
    GetVarInfo = cValue
    '
End Function
```

Adding the Form Event Code

So you've added the pre-built BAS modules and you've entered the support routines—now you're ready to build the real TAPI code! First, you need to add some code to the Form_Load and Form_Unload events. Listing 26.18 shows the code for the Form_Load event.

Listing 26.18. The Form_Load event code.

```
Private Sub Form_Load()
    Text1 = ""
    Me.Caption = "TAPILine Test Form"
    '
    Me.Left = (Screen.Width - Me.Width) / 2
    Me.Top = (Screen.Height - Me.Height) / 2
    '
    cLine = String(80, 45) ' for message box
    '
    ClearHandles ' clear out control handles
    '
End Sub
```

This code sets the form caption, centers the form on the screen, initializes a display line, and clears the handle values.

Next, add the Form_Unload event code shown in Listing 26.19.

Listing 26.19. The Form_Unload event code.

```
Private Sub Form_Unload(Cancel As Integer)
    '
    ' be sure to close the line before leaving
    '
    Dim a As Long
    a = Tapiline1.LineClose
    '
End Sub
```

This code just makes sure the TAPI session is closed out before exiting the program.

The next code you need to add is the code for the TAPICallBack event of the TAPILINE1 control. All you need to do is pass the parameter list to the TAPICallBackHandler function and then display the results. Listing 26.20 shows the code you need to add to the TAPICallBack event.

Listing 26.20. Code for the TapiLine1_TapiCallBack event.

```
Private Sub Tapiline1_TapiCallBack(ByVal hDevice As Long, ByVal dwMessage As Long,
➡ByVal dwInstance As Long, ByVal dwParam1 As Long, ByVal dwParam2 As Long, ByVal
➡dwParam3 As Long)
    '
```

```
    ' send all messages to generic handler
    '
    Dim cMsg As String
    '
    cMsg = TapiCallBackHandler(hDevice, dwMessage, dwInstance, dwParam1, dwParam2,
➥dwParam3)
    AddText Me.Text1, cMsg
    '
    AddText Me.Text1, cLine ' msg separator
    '
End Sub
```

Adding the Button Event Code

Now you're ready to start programming TAPI from Visual Basic! First add the code shown in Listing 26.21 to the cmdLineInit_Click event.

Listing 26.21. The cmdLineInit_Click code.

```
Private Sub cmdLineInit_Click()
    '
    ' initialize TAPI interface'
    '
    Dim a As Long
    '
    a = Me.Tapiline1.LineInitialize("TAPITEST")
    If a < 0 Then
      AddText Me.Text1, "<<<ERROR>>> LineInit..." & LineErr(a)
    End If
    '
    lNumDev = Tapiline1.NumDevices
    AddText Me.Text1, "LineInit (NumDev: " & CStr(lNumDev) & ")"
    '
    AddText Me.Text1, cLine ' msg separator
    '
End Sub
```

This code initializes TAPI services for your program and displays the number of TAPI devices by reading the property value set by the LineInitialize method.

Next add the code for the cmdLineNegAPI_Click event. This code walks through all the devices found by TAPI and makes sure they all support the current TAPI version. Add the code shown in Listing 26.22.

Listing 26.22. The cmdLineNegAPI_Click code.

```
Private Sub cmdLineNegApi_Click()
    '
```

continues

Listing 26.22. continued

```
' get api info for all devices
'
Dim a As Long
Dim x As Integer
' 65536= 10000, 65540 = 10004 (version 1.0, version 1.4)
For x = 0 To lNumDev - 1
    a = Me.Tapiline1.LineNegotiateAPIVersion(x, 65536, 65540)
    If a < 0 Then
        AddText Me.Text1, "<<<ERROR>>> LineNegAPI..." & LineErr(a)
    Else
        AddText Me.Text1, "LineNegAPI... Dev #" & CStr(x) & " OK"
    End If
Next x
'
AddText Me.Text1, cLine ' msg separator
'
End Sub
```

Now save and run the project. After clicking the first two buttons, you should see a number of lines on your screen along with messages saying the API negotiation routine was successful (see Figure 26.5).

FIGURE 26.5.

Results from line initialize and NegAPI *calls.*

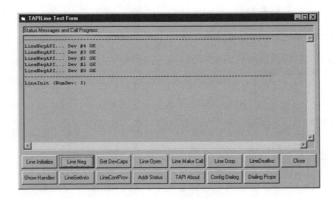

The next set of code collects the device capabilities of all the line devices recognized by TAPI. Add the code from Listing 26.23 to the cmdLineGetDevCaps_Click event of the form.

Listing 26.23. The cmdLineGetDevCaps_Click code.

```
Private Sub cmdLineDevCaps_Click()
    '
    ' display capabilites of each line
    '
    Dim a As Long
    Dim b As LINEDEVCAPS
    Dim c As String * 2048
    Dim x As Integer
```

```
    '
    Dim nSize As Long
    Dim nOffset As Long
    Dim cValue As String
    '
    For x = 0 To lNumDev - 1
        ' make the call to get dev caps
        a = Tapiline1.LineGetDevCaps(x)
        If a < 0 Then
            AddText Me.Text1, "<<<ERROR>>> DevCaps..." & LineErr(a)
        End If
        ' read the results
        LineDevCapsFunc TAPI_READ, b, c
        '
        ' strip out non-printables
        c = Clean
        '
        ' show user device capabilities
        AddText Me.Text1, "Line Device #" & CStr(x)
        AddText Me.Text1, "TerminalCaps..." & GetVarInfo(b.dwTerminalCapsSize,
b.dwTerminalCapsOffset, c, Len(b))
        AddText Me.Text1, "ProviderInfo..." & GetVarInfo(b.dwProviderInfoSize,
b.dwProviderInfoOffset, c, Len(b))
        AddText Me.Text1, "TerminalText..." & GetVarInfo(b.dwTerminalTextSize,
b.dwTerminalTextOffset, c, Len(b))
        AddText Me.Text1, "DevSpecific..." & GetVarInfo(b.dwDevSpecificSize,
b.dwDevSpecificOffset, c, Len(b))
        AddText Me.Text1, "LineName..." & GetVarInfo(b.dwLineNameSize,
b.dwLineNameOffset, c, Len(b))
        AddText Me.Text1, "TotalSize..." & CStr(b.dwTotalSize)
        AddText Me.Text1, "NeededSize..." & CStr(b.dwNeededSize)
        AddText Me.Text1, "UsedSize..." & CStr(b.dwUsedSize)
        AddText Me.Text1, "MaxNumActiveCalls..." & CStr(b.dwMaxNumActiveCalls)
        AddText Me.Text1, cLine ' msg separator
    Next x
    '
End Sub
```

Not only does this routine get the capabilities of each device, the routine also displays the results in the text box on screen. You can scroll through this screen to inspect the various devices recognized by TAPI.

After initializing, negotiating the API, and getting the device capabilities, you are now ready to open a line for outbound calls. The code behind the cmdLineOpen_Click event will handle this task. Add the code from Listing 26.24 to the project.

Listing 26.24. The cmdLineOpen_Click event code.

```
Private Sub cmdLineOpen_Click()
    '
    ' open a selected line
    ' and show results
    '
```

continues

Listing 26.24. continued

```
    Dim a As Long
    Dim b As LINECALLPARAMS
    Dim c As String * 2048
    Dim s As String
    Dim cValue As String
    '
    ' get line number from user
    nline = InputBox("Enter Line to Open:")
    '
    ' perform the open
    a = Me.Tapiline1.LineOpen(nline, 0, LINECALLPRIVILEGE_NONE,
➡LINEMEDIAMODE_INTERACTIVEVOICE)
    If a < 0 Then
      AddText Me.Text1, "<<<ERROR>>> LineOpen..." & LineErr(a)
    End If
    '
    ' get parameters
    FillCallParams ' prep area first
    LineCallParamsFunc TAPI_READ, b, c ' then read it
    '
    ' show them to user
    AddText Me.Text1, "TotalSize..." & CStr(b.dwTotalSize)
    AddText Me.Text1, "BearerMode..." & CStr(b.dwBearerMode)
    AddText Me.Text1, "MinRate..." & CStr(b.dwMinRate)
    AddText Me.Text1, "MaxRate..." & CStr(b.dwMaxRate)
    AddText Me.Text1, "MediaMode..." & CStr(b.dwMediaMode)
    AddText Me.Text1, "CallParamFlags..." & CStr(b.dwCallParamFlags)
    AddText Me.Text1, "AddressMode..." & CStr(b.dwAddressMode)
    AddText Me.Text1, "AddressID..." & CStr(b.dwAddressID)
    AddText Me.Text1, "OrigAddressSize..." & CStr(b.dwOrigAddressSize)
    AddText Me.Text1, "OrigAddressOffset..." & CStr(b.dwOrigAddressOffset)
    AddText Me.Text1, "Originating Address..." & GetOffset(Len(b),
➡b.dwOrigAddressOffset, b.dwOrigAddressSize, c)
    '
    AddText Me.Text1, cLine ' msg separator
    '
End Sub
```

You'll notice that the routine first prompts the user for a line number. For now, select a line that is capable of handling outbound voice calls. In a production application, you could inspect the values returned by the GetDevCaps method to locate a line device with the needed capabilities.

Next, the routine performs a line-open and then sets the LINECALLPARAMS structure and displays the results. Setting the LINECALLPARAMS structure will affect how the call is finally placed. This is optional. If no LINECALLPARAMS are set, TAPI will use the default values for the selected line device. Figure 26.6 shows how the status box looks after selecting a line and displaying the call parameters.

FIGURE 26.6.
*Displaying call parameters
on an open line.*

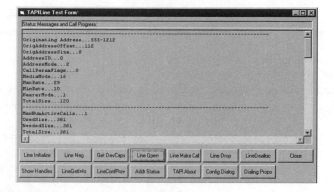

After a line is opened successfully, you are ready to place an outbound call. Add the code shown
in Listing 26.25 in the cmdLineMakeCall_Click event.

Listing 26.25. The cmdLineMakeCall_Click event code.

```
Private Sub cmdLineMakeCall_Click()
    '
    ' make a real call
    '
    Dim a As Long
    Dim b As LINECALLPARAMS
    Dim c As String * 2048
    Dim cAddress As String
    '
    ' read current parameters
    LineCallParamsFunc TAPI_READ, b, c
    '
    ' show them to the user
    AddText Me.Text1, "TotalSize..." & CStr(b.dwTotalSize)
    AddText Me.Text1, "BearerMode..." & CStr(b.dwBearerMode)
    AddText Me.Text1, "MinRate..." & CStr(b.dwMinRate)
    AddText Me.Text1, "MaxRate..." & CStr(b.dwMaxRate)
    AddText Me.Text1, "MediaMode..." & CStr(b.dwMediaMode)
    AddText Me.Text1, "CallParamFlags..." & CStr(b.dwCallParamFlags)
    AddText Me.Text1, "AddressMode..." & CStr(b.dwAddressMode)
    AddText Me.Text1, "AddressID..." & CStr(b.dwAddressID)
    '
    ' get phone number to dial
    cAddress = InputBox("Enter Address to Dial:", "Dialing String")
    '
    ' make the call
    a = Me.Tapiline1.LineMakeCall(cAddress, 1)
    If a < 0 Then
        AddText Me.Text1, "<<<ERROR>>> LineMakeCall..." & LineErr(a)
    End If
    '
    AddText Me.Text1, cLine ' message separator
    '
End Sub
```

This code reads the LINECALLPARAMS structure, displays the results, and then prompts the user for a phone number. After the number is entered, the LineMakeCall method is invoked to place the call.

Once the call is placed, several TAPI messages cross through the TAPICallBack event. When you run the program and place a call, you'll see the progress messages appear in the status box. Figure 26.7 shows an example of what you should see when you run the program.

FIGURE 26.7.

Monitoring call progress.

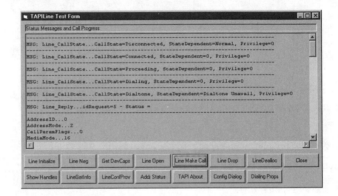

The next three buttons handle code that drops the current call, de-allocates the line handle, and closes the line device. All these steps should occur at the end of a call. Listing 26.26 shows the code for the three button routines (cmdLineDrop, cmdLineDealloc, and cmdLineClose). Add this code to your project.

Listing 26.26. The cmdLineDrop, cmdLineDealloc, and cmdLineClose code.

```
Private Sub cmdLineDrop_Click()
    '
    ' drop idle line
    '
    Dim lRtn As Long
    '
    lRtn = Tapiline1.LineDrop("", 0)
    If lRtn < 0 Then
        AddText Me.Text1, "<<<ERROR>>> LineDrop..." & LineErr(lRtn)
    Else
        AddText Me.Text1, "LineDrop Successful"
    End If
    '
    AddText Me.Text1, cLine ' msg separator
    '
End Sub

Private Sub cmdLineDeallocate_Click()
    '
    ' de-allocate memory from unused line
    '
```

```
    Dim lRtn As Long
    '
    lRtn = Tapiline1.LineDeallocateCall
    If lRtn < 0 Then
        AddText Me.Text1, "<<<ERROR>>> LineDeallocateCall..." & LineErr(lRtn)
    Else
        AddText Me.Text1, "LineDeallocateCall Successful"
    End If
    '
    Me.Tapiline1.HandleToCall = 0 ' clear call handle
    '
    AddText Me.Text1, cLine ' msg separator
    '
End Sub

Private Sub cmdLineClose_Click()
    '
    ' close open line
    '
    Dim a As Long
    '
    a = Tapiline1.LineClose
    If a < 0 Then
        AddText Me.Text1, "<<<ERROR>>> LineClose..." & LineErr(a)
    Else
        AddText Me.Text1, "Line Close Successful"
    End If
    '
    Me.Tapiline1.LineHandle = 0 ' clear line handle
    '
    AddText Me.Text1, cLine ' msg separator
    '
End Sub
```

Notice that the cmdLineDealloc_Click event contains code that clears the HandletoCall property of the TAPILine control. Also, the cmdLineClose_Click event contains code that clears the LineHandle property. It is a good idea to clear these handles when you are done with a call. Figure 26.8 shows how the status messages look as you drop, de-allocate, and close a line.

FIGURE 26.8.

Dropping, de-allocating, and closing the line.

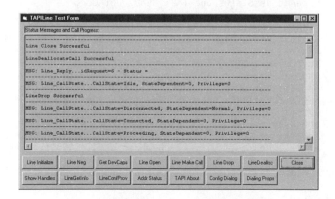

Those are the steps to completing an outbound call using the TAPILine control. The other routines in this project all illustrate additional line device functions you can access from the TAPILINE.OCX.

Displaying Call Information and Address Status

Once a line is open and a call is active, you can get call information about the line through the LineGetCallInfo method. You can also get information about the address originating the call (that's you!) using the LineGetAddressStatus method. Listing 26.27 shows the code for these two buttons. Add this code to your project.

Listing 26.27. The cmdLineGetCallInfo and cmdLineGetAddrStatus code.

```
Private Sub cmdLineGetInfo_Click()
    '
    ' get lots of info on this line
    '
    LocalGetLineInfo
    '
End Sub

Private Sub cmdLineAddrStatus_Click()
    '
    ' get address status of the line
    '
    Dim udtAddr As LINEADDRESSSTATUS
    Dim c As String * 2048
    Dim lRtn As Long
    '
    ' make the call to GetAddressStatus
    lRtn = Tapiline1.LineGetAddressStatus
    If lRtn < 0 Then
        AddText Me.Text1, "<<<ERROR>>> LineGetAddressStatus..." & LineErr(lRtn)
        Exit Sub
    End If
    '
    ' get the results
    LineAddressStatusFunc TAPI_READ, udtAddr, c
    '
    ' show them to user
    AddText Me.Text1, "TotalSize..." & CStr(udtAddr.dwTotalSize)
    AddText Me.Text1, "NeededSize..." & CStr(udtAddr.dwNeededSize)
    AddText Me.Text1, "UsedSize..." & CStr(udtAddr.dwUsedSize)
    AddText Me.Text1, "NumInUse..." & CStr(udtAddr.dwNumInUse)
    AddText Me.Text1, "NumActiveCalls..." & CStr(udtAddr.dwNumActiveCalls)
    AddText Me.Text1, "NumOnHoldCalls..." & CStr(udtAddr.dwNumOnHoldCalls)
    AddText Me.Text1, "NumOnHoldPendCalls..." & CStr(udtAddr.dwNumOnHoldPendCalls)
    AddText Me.Text1, "AddressFeatures..." & CStr(udtAddr.dwAddressFeatures)
    AddText Me.Text1, "NumRingsNoAnswer..." & CStr(udtAddr.dwNumRingsNoAnswer)
    AddText Me.Text1, "ForwardNumEntries..." & CStr(udtAddr.dwForwardNumEntries)
    '
    AddText Me.Text1, cLine ' msg separator
    '
End Sub
```

The companion CD-ROM contains all the sample projects from the book.

Windows 95 Installation Instructions

1. Insert the CD-ROM disc into your CD-ROM drive.
2. From the Windows 95 desktop, double-click the My Computer icon.
3. Double-click the icon representing your CD-ROM drive.
4. Double-click the icon titled Install.EXE to run the installation program.

Installation creates a program group named "MAPI SAPI TAPI Dev Guide." This group contains icons to browse the CD-ROM.

> **NOTE**
>
> If Windows 95 is installed on your computer, and you have the AutoPlay feature enabled, the INSTALL program starts automatically whenever you insert the disc into your CD-ROM drive.

Windows NT Installation Instructions

1. Insert the CD-ROM disc into your CD-ROM drive.
2. From File Manager or Program Manager, choose Run from the File menu.
3. Type `<drive>\Install` and press Enter, where `<drive>` corresponds to the drive letter of your CD-ROM. For example, if your CD-ROM is drive D:, type `D:\Install` and press Enter.

Installation creates a program group named "MAPI SAPI TAPI Dev Guide." This group contains icons to browse the CD-ROM.

What's on the CD-ROM

The cmdLineGetCallInfo_Click code simply calls a routine you build earlier. This displays information about the active call on the specified line device. The cmdLineGetAddrStatus_Click code gets information about the originating address (or extension). When you run your project and place a call, you can monitor the call information and address status by pressing these two buttons during the call (see Figure 26.9).

FIGURE 26.9.
Checking call information and address status.

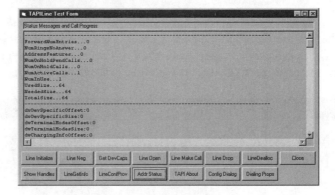

You can also watch the values of call handles change as you progress through completing a call. Add the code shown in Listing 26.28 to the cmdShowHandles_Click event.

Listing 26.28. The cmdShowHandles_Click event code.

```
Private Sub cmdLineShowHandles_Click()
    '
    '  show handle properties
    '
    ShowHandles
    '
End Sub
```

Save the project and then run it. Now you can press the cmdShowHandles button at various times—while you open a line, place a call and then drop, de-allocate, and close the line—to monitor the creation and clearing of handles throughout the call process.

Displaying TAPI Dialog Boxes

The TAPILINE control supports four dialog boxes that you can call from within Visual Basic. They are:

- The control's About box
- The Provider Configuration dialog box
- The Line Configuration dialog box
- The Dialing Properties dialog box

The About box is supplied by the TAPILINE control itself. All you need to do is call the AboutBox method (see Figure 26.10).

FIGURE 26.10.
The TAPILINE *control About box.*

The Provider Configuration dialog box is called by using the LineConfigProvider method. This brings up a dialog box supplied by the TAPI Service Provider. The list of TAPI Service Providers is kept in the TELEPHON.INI file in the WINDOWS\SYSTEM directory.

> **NOTE**
>
> You'll learn more about the TELEPHON.INI file in Chapter 27, "TAPI Behind the Scenes—The TELEPHON.INI File."

Figure 26.11 shows the dialog box that appears on workstations where the UniModemV device driver is installed.

FIGURE 26.11.
The TAPI Service Provider dialog box.

The Line Configuration dialog box is called using the LineConfigDialog method. This brings up a dialog box supplied by the operating system. Figure 26.12 shows an example line configuration dialog box.

FIGURE 26.12.
The TAPI line configuration dialog box.

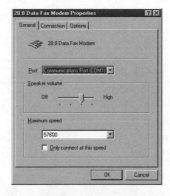

> **TIP**
>
> Don't be confused by the similarity of the dialog boxes from the LineConfigDialog and the LineConfigProvider methods. The first method (LineConfigDialog) calls the dialog box for configuring the device associated with the selected line. The second method (LineConfigProvider) calls the dialog box for configuring the device access for the selected TAPI service provider. A TSP may have access to more than one device. That is why you can use the LineConfigProvider dialog box to access all the devices on the workstation, but you can only access one device from LineConfigDialog.

The last dialog box supported by the TAPILINE control is the Dialing Properties dialog box. This is called using the LineTranslateDialog method. You must invoke the LineInitialize method before you call this dialog box. This is the only dialog box that requires that TAPI be up and running. Figure 26.13 shows the Dialing Properties dialog box.

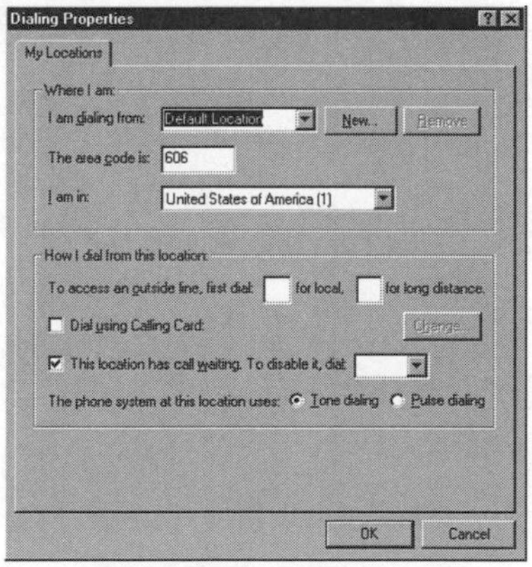

FIGURE 26.13.
The Dialing Properties dialog box.

Listing 26.29 shows the code for the four buttons mentioned above. Add this code to your project.

Listing 26.29. The code for the dialog boxes.

```
Private Sub cmdLineAbout_Click()
    '
    ' show TAPILine about box
    '
    Tapiline1.AboutBox
    '
End Sub

Private Sub cmdLineConfProv_Click()
    '
    ' call provider's config
    '
    Dim lRtn As Long
    '
    Tapiline1.PermanentProviderID = InputBox("Enter PermProviderID:")
    AddText Me.Text1, "PermProvider..." & CStr(Tapiline1.PermanentProviderID)
    lRtn = Tapiline1.LineConfigProvider(Me.hWnd)
    If lRtn < 0 Then
        AddText Me.Text1, "<<<ERROR>>> LineConfigProvider..." & LineErr(lRtn)
    Else
        AddText Me.Text1, "LineConfigProvider successfull"
    End If
    '
    AddText Me.Text1, cLine ' msg separator
    '
End Sub

Private Sub cmdLineConfDialog_Click()
    '
    ' show config dialog(s)
    '
    Dim a As Long
    Dim n As Integer
    Dim x As Integer
    Dim y As Integer
    Dim z As Integer
    '
    ' get a device from user
    n = InputBox("Enter Device # (-1 for all):")
    '
    ' set loop params
    If n = -1 Then
        ' user wants them all!
        y = 0
        z = lNumDev - 1
    Else
        ' user just wants one
        y = n
        z = n
    End If
```

```
        '
        ' call up dialog(s)
        For x = y To z
            a = Tapiline1.LineConfigDialog(x, Me.hWnd, "comm")
            If a <> 0 Then
                MsgBox LineErr(a), vbCritical, "lineConfigDialog Error!"
            End If
        Next x
        '
End Sub

Private Sub cmdLineDialProps_Click()
    '
    ' show the dialing properties dialog
    '
    Dim lReturn As Long
    Dim nDevice As Integer
    Dim x As Integer
    '
    ' get device from user
    nDevice = InputBox("Enter Device # (-1 for all):")
    If nDevice <> -1 Then
        ' user wants just one
        lReturn = Tapiline1.LineTranslateDialog(nDevice, Me.hWnd, "")
        If lReturn <> 0 Then
            MsgBox LineErr(lReturn), vbCritical, "LineTranslateDialog Error!"
        End If
    Else
        ' show them all to user
        For x = 0 To lNumDev - 1
            lReturn = Tapiline1.LineTranslateDialog(x, Me.hWnd, "")
            If lReturn <> 0 Then
                MsgBox LineErr(lReturn), vbCritical, "LineTranslateDialog Error!"
            End If
        Next x
    End If
    '
End Sub
```

That is all the code for the TAPITEST.VBP project. You can use the code here to place simple voice outbound calls and watch your progress using the status window. Later in this section, you use the code shown here to build a complete telephony application in Visual Basic.

Summary

In this chapter you learned the properties, methods, and events of the TAPILINE control found on the CD-ROM that accompanies this book. You also learned how to use this control to gain access to TAPI services from within Visual Basic programs.

You learned how to perform the following TAPI service requests:

- Initialize a TAPI session.
- Confirm the TAPI version you are using.
- Get a list of device capabilities.
- Open a line for outbound calling.
- Place an outbound call.
- Drop an active call.
- De-allocate the idle call.
- Close an open line device.

You also learned how to monitor call progress using TAPI messages and the `LineGetCallInfo` and `LineGetAddress` methods. Finally, you learned how to call the four TAPI dialog boxes to gain access to configuration dialogs to customize your TAPI interface.

In the next chapter you'll learn about the `TELEPHON.INI` file. This file contains control information affected by the dialog boxes you learned about in this chapter.

27

TAPI Behind the Scenes— The TELEPHON.INI File

In this chapter you'll learn how the TAPI system uses entries in the TELEPHON.INI file to determine what TAPI service providers are installed, how to handle outbound dialing rules, the current dialing location, and which providers are to be used for TAPI service requests.

Almost all of this information is updated from the various configuration dialog boxes available through calls to TAPI functions. As part of this chapter, you'll build a short program that calls the TAPI Line dialog boxes and allows you to inspect the resulting changes to the TELEPHON.INI file.

Building the TAPI Dialog Utility Program

Before getting into the details of how the TELEPHON.INI file is used for TAPI services, let's build a short Visual Basic program that gives you easy access to the TAPI dialog boxes that affect the file, and a quick TELEPHON.INI viewer.

> **NOTE**
>
> If you do not have Visual Basic on your machine or you want to skip over this section, you can find the completed program (TAPIDLG.EXE) on the CD-ROM that comes with this book. You can use this compiled version of the program to follow along with the rest of the chapter.

Creating the TAPI Dialog Utility project takes only a few controls and a small amount of code. The following two sections of the chapter will walk you through the details of building this handy utility.

Laying Out the TAPI Dialog Utility Form

Start by loading Visual Basic 4.0 and creating a new project. Next, you need to lay out the form. Refer to Table 27.1 and Figure 27.1 as guides. Be sure to load the TAPILINE.OCX into your toolbox before you start coding. Also, make sure you add the frame control *before* you add the option buttons, and paint the option buttons within the frame control. That way they will be registered as child controls of the frame.

> **TIP**
>
> If you plan to do a lot of coding with the TAPILINE control, add it to your startup project. Open AUTO32LD.VBP (or AUTO16LD.VBP) and add the TAPILINE control. Then save the project. Now every new project you create will have the TAPILINE control in the toolbox.

Table 27.1. Controls for the TAPI Dialog Utility project.

Control	Property	Setting
VB.Form	Name	Form1
	Caption	"Form1"
	Height	2670
	Left	1530
	Top	1770
	Width	5685
VB.CommandButton	Name	cmdButton
	Caption	"&Telepho.ini"
	Height	495
	Index	2
	Left	60
	TabIndex	8
	Top	1620
	Width	1215
VB.ListBox	Name	List1
	Height	1035
	Left	60
	TabIndex	6
	Top	420
	Width	2595
VB.CommandButton	Name	cmdButton
	Caption	"&Apply"
	Height	495
	Index	1
	Left	4200
	TabIndex	5
	Top	1680
	Width	1215

continues

Table 27.1. continued

Control	Property	Setting
VB.CommandButton	Name	cmdButton
	Caption	"E&xit"
	Height	495
	Index	0
	Left	2820
	TabIndex	4
	Top	1680
	Width	1215
VB.Frame	Name	Frame1
	Caption	"Dialog Selection"
	Height	1395
	Left	2820
	TabIndex	0
	Top	120
	Width	2595
VB.OptionButton	Name	optDialog
	Caption	"Line Configure Provider"
	Height	195
	Index	2
	Left	120
	TabIndex	3
	Top	960
	Width	2295
VB.OptionButton	Name	optDialog
	Caption	"Line Configure Dialog"
	Height	195
	Index	1
	Left	120
	TabIndex	2
	Top	660
	Width	2295

Control	Property	Setting
`VB.OptionButton`	`Name`	optDialog
	`Caption`	"Line Translate Dialog"
	`Height`	195
	`Index`	0
	`Left`	120
	`TabIndex`	1
	`Top`	360
	`Width`	2295
`VB.Label`	`Name`	Label1
	`BorderStyle`	1 'Fixed Single
	`Caption`	"TAPI Line Devices:"
	`Height`	255
	`Left`	60
	`TabIndex`	7
	`Top`	120
	`Width`	2595
`TapilineLib.Tapiline`	`Name`	Tapiline1
	`Left`	1980
	`Top`	1680

FIGURE 27.1.

Laying out the TAPI Dialog Utility project.

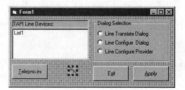

Once you complete the layout of the dialog box, save the form as `TAPIDLG.FRM` and the project as `TAPIDLG.VBP`. Now you're ready to add code to the form.

Coding the TAPI Dialog Utility Project

There isn't much code to add here, just a few lines to initialize TAPI and then some code to respond to user selections on the option buttons, command buttons, and the list control.

First, add a new subroutine called StartTAPI to the form. This will hold the code that initializes the TAPI session and confirms the available devices. Listing 27.1 shows the code for the StartTAPI routine. Add this to your project.

Listing 27.1. Adding the StartTAPI routine.

```
Public Sub StartTAPI()
    '
    ' start up tapi
    '
    Dim lRtn As Long
    Dim x As Integer
    '
    ' init tapi
    lRtn = Tapiline1.LineInitialize(App.EXEName)
    If lRtn <> 0 Then
        MsgBox "Unable to Start TAPI!", vbCritical
        Unload Me
    End If
    '
    ' get devices
    For x = 0 To Tapiline1.NumDevices - 1
        Tapiline1.LineNegotiateAPIVersion x, 65536, 65540
        List1.AddItem "TAPI Line #" & CStr(x)
    Next x
    '
End Sub
```

As you can see, this routine just calls the lineInitialize method, gets the total number of devices, and then performs the lineNegotiateAPIVersion method for all the available TAPI line devices. In the process, the line devices are loaded into the list box for the user.

Next you need to add some code to the Form_Load event. This code is executed when the program first starts. Listing 27.2 shows the code you need to add to your project.

Listing 27.2. Adding the Form_Load event code.

```
Private Sub Form_Load()
    '
    Me.Caption = "TAPI Dialog Utility"
    Me.Left = (Screen.Width - Me.Width) / 2
    Me.Top = (Screen.Height - Me.Height) / 2
    '
    StartTAPI
    '
End Sub
```

The code in the Form_Load event sets the form caption, centers the form, and then calls the StartTAPI routine to initialize TAPI services.

The really important code is in the cmdButton_Click event. This is the code that handles the user's dialog box selections. Listing 27.3 shows the code needed for the cmdButton_Click event. Add it to your project.

Listing 27.3. Adding the cmdButton_Click event code.

```
Private Sub cmdButton_Click(Index As Integer)
    '
    ' handle button selections
    '
    Dim lRtn As Long
    Dim nLine As Integer
    '
    ' get line to work with
    nLine = List1.ListIndex
    If nLine = -1 Then
        nLine = 0
    End If
    '
    ' get button selection
    Select Case Index
        Case 0 ' exit
            Tapiline1.LineClose
            Unload Me
        Case 1 ' start dialog
            '
            ' call line translate
            If optDialog(0) = True Then
                Tapiline1.LineTranslateDialog nLine, Me.hWnd, "+1 (606)555-1212"
            End If
            '
            ' call line config
            If optDialog(1) = True Then
                Tapiline1.LineConfigDialog nLine, Me.hWnd, "tapi/line"
            End If
            '
            ' call provider config
            If optDialog(2) = True Then
                Tapiline1.PermanentProviderID = 1
                Tapiline1.LineConfigProvider Me.hWnd
            End If
        Case 2 ' load telephon.ini w/ notepad
            lRtn = Shell("notepad.exe c:\windows\telephon.ini", 1)
    End Select
    '
End Sub
```

TIP

If you do not have a copy of NOTEPAD.EXE, or it is in some directory other than your Windows directory, change the Shell call in Listing 27.3 to point to your favorite ASCII editor.

The first few lines of code make sure one of the line devices in the list box has been selected. If not, it automatically selects the first one in the list. Next, the SELECT CASE statements determine which button has been pressed.

If the Exit button was pressed, the program executes the lineClose method before unloading the form. This is not strictly needed, since this project does not open any available line devices. However, it is a good practice to release any remaining TAPI resources before exiting.

If the user selects the Apply button, the program checks to see which option button was selected and then calls the requested dialog box. Notice that the call to the Translate dialog box contains an optional dialing address. This will be displayed in the lower left of the dialog box to show the user how the dialing rules will be applied to the selected phone number.

If the user selects the Telephon.ini button, the program launches a shell operation which calls NOTEPAD.EXE and loads the TELEPHON.INI file for viewing. You can use this option to view the results of editing the various settings in the dialog boxes.

The last bit of code to add to the project is a single line behind the List1_DblClick event. This will automatically launch the selected dialog box each time the user double-clicks the item in the list. Add the code shown in Listing 27.4 to your project.

Listing 27.4. Adding the List1_DblClick event code.

```
Private Sub List1_DblClick()
    '
    cmdButton_Click 1 ' call apply button
    '
End Sub
```

That's all the code you need. Save this form (TAPIDLG.FRM) and project (TAPIDLG.VBP) and then test it out. When running the project, you should see a list of available line devices in the list box and be able to call up each of the TAPI dialogs for the various devices (see Figure 27.2).

FIGURE 27.2.
Testing the TAPI dialog utility.

Once you are sure the program is working correctly, compile it (TAPIDLG.EXE) to disk. You'll use the TAPIDLG.EXE program in the next several sections of the chapter.

The TELEPHON.INI File

The TAPI system uses the TELEPHON.INI file to hold important control parameters. Even though the TAPI system is implemented on Win95 and WinNT, the control values are *not* stored in the system registry. This is because TAPI was originally deployed as part of the Windows 3.1 operating system. Also, as of this writing, all TAPI service providers (TSPs) are 16-bit applications. For these reasons, the old 16-bit INI file is still used by TAPI.

Most of the TELEPHON.INI file is updated through TAPI dialog boxes. In fact, it is not a good idea to modify the INI file directly, since this may result in invalidating your TAPI installation. Still, you can call up the TELEPHON.INI file using NOTEPAD.EXE (or some other ASCII editor) and view the contents. This is a good way to learn a lot about how TAPI services are managed by the Windows operating system.

> **WARNING**
>
> If you are working with the old TAPI 1.3 system on Windows 3.1 machines, your TELEPHON.INI file will look quite different. In fact, you cannot use the TELEPHON.INI file from TAPI 1.3 for TAPI 1.4 installations. Any attempt to do so will cause an error when you try to start any TAPI service. All the material covered here is based on TAPI 1.4 TELEPHON.INI file layouts.

The TELEPHON.INI file is divided into four main sections:

- The *Service Provider* section holds information on all the Telephony Service Providers (TSPs) installed on the workstation.

- The *HandOff Priorities* section holds information about which line devices can support which media modes and the order in which the line devices should be called.

- The *Location* section holds information on the dialing location of the workstation. TAPI allows multiple locations to be defined for a single workstation. That way a user with a laptop can set up several location definitions and easily switch from one to the other when traveling.

- The *Credit Card* section holds dialing instructions for using telephone service credit cards to control billing. TAPI ships with a number of standard credit card instructions, but you can also add your own, if needed.

The rest of this chapter reviews each of the four main sections and shows you examples of how to modify the information using the TAPI dialog utility you built earlier in the chapter.

> **TIP**
>
> Now is a good time to load the TAPIDLG.EXE file you created earlier. If you did not enter and compile the program described above, you can find a completed version of it on the CD-ROM, which you can load instead.

TAPI Service Provider Information

The TAPI service provider information is actually stored in two separate sections of the TELEPHON.INI file. The [Providers] section lists all the TSPs installed on the machine. This section gives each of them a unique ID value. Each TSP then has its own section in the TELEPHON.INI file. That section is named based on the provider ID that appears in the [Providers] section. The provider-specific section contains data about the services supported by the TSP and any other TSP-related data for that provider.

TAPI uses this information to initialize all available service providers when the lineInitialize method is first invoked on the workstation.

The Providers Section

The [Providers] section of the TELEPHON.INI file has three main parts:

■ The total number of installed providers
■ The next provider ID
■ The ProviderID and ProviderFileName pair

Listing 27.5 shows how a typical [Providers] section of a TELEPHON.INI file looks.

Listing 27.5. A typical [Providers] section of TELEPHON.INI.

```
[Providers]
NumProviders=2
NextProviderID=5
ProviderID0=1
ProviderFilename0=unimdm.tsp
ProviderID1=4
ProviderFileName1=esp.tsp
```

In the example shown in Listing 27.4, there are two TSPs active on the workstation, the UNIMDM.TSP and the ESP.TSP. They are given the provider IDs "0" and "4" respectively. You can see that the next TSP added to the workstation will be given the ID "5." The values in this section are altered by the TSPs themselves.

There is no dialog box from TAPI that makes changes to these settings. Changing these settings manually can cause your system to lock up when you start TAPI services.

The Provider-Specific Section

For each ProviderFileName, ProviderID pair in the [Providers] section, there is a separate section header that bears the ProviderID value. This section contains entries used to describe the properties of the lines and phones supported by the service provider. Listing 27.6 shows the set of provider sections that match the [Providers] section that appears in Listing 27.5.

Listing 27.6. Example provider-specific sections.

```
[Provider1]
NumLines=1
NumPhones=0

[Provider4]
NumLines=8
NumPhones=4
```

In Listing 27.6, Provider1 supports only one line device and no phone devices. Provider4 supports up to eight lines and four phones.

The entries shown in Listing 27.6 are the required minimum entries for each provider-specific section. TSPs can also add other values to their sections if they wish. These values could identify individual lines and phones, provide additional configuration settings used by the TSP, and so on. Microsoft suggests TSPs establish a system for identifying line or phone parameters similar to the one used for identifying providers. For example, each line could have an ID and name value along with any special settings. Listing 27.7 shows how this might look in the TELEPHON.INI file.

Listing 27.7. Extended provider-specific entries.

```
[Provider1]
NumLines=2
NumPhones=1
NextLineID=2
NextPhoneID=1
LineID0=1
LineName1=MCA's Data Line
LinePort1=COM1
LineInitString1=ATH0
LineID1=2
LineName2=Voice Line
LinePort2=COM2
LineInitString2=
```

Notice the use of the `NextLineID` and `NextPhoneID` settings. This will allow the TSP to add future lines or phones with unique values. The additional settings here are related to communications ports and initialization strings, but they could be anything at all that the TSP needs to manage the TAPI service on the line.

The main thing to keep in mind about the provider settings is that they are managed by the Telephony service provider application—not the `TAPI.DLL` or your own desktop applications. All settings that appear here are the result of actions by the TSPs. You run the risk of trashing your TAPI installation if you meddle with these values!

Handoff Priorities Information

When there is more than one TAPI application registered on the workstation, the TAPI system must have some process for deciding which service request is handled by which TAPI application. The `[HandOffProrities]` section of the `TELEPHON.INI` file helps TAPI handle this situation. The `[HandOffPriorities]` section lists all the applications that can handle inbound and outbound calls. Also, the applications are listed in preference order. The first items on the list should be called before the last items on the list.

Each entry in the `[HandOffPriorities]` section lists the type of TAPI service request followed by one or more registered programs capable of handling the request. Listing 27.8 shows a typical `[HandOffPriorities]` section from the `TELEPHON.INI` file.

Listing 27.8. A typical `[HandOffPriorities]` section.

```
[HandoffPriorities]
datamodem=rasapi32.dll,
interactivevoice=AMENGINE.DLL,MSPHONE.EXE,
automatedvoice=AMENGINE.DLL,
RequestMakeCall=C:\PROGRA~1\MICROS~3\MSPHONE.EXE,C:\WINDOWS\DIALER.EXE,
```

Listing 27.8 shows that the workstation can support four TAPI service request types:

- ■ `datamodem`—Used for handling data-oriented calls.
- ■ `interactivevoice`—Used for handling live voice calls.
- ■ `automatedvoice`—Used for handling recorded voice calls.
- ■ `RequestMakeCall`—Used for handling assisted TAPI requests from other programs on the workstation.

You'll notice that the last entry in the section (`RequestMakeCall`) shows that there are two different programs on the workstation that can handle the TAPI service request. In this case, when a program makes a call to the `RequestMakeCall` TAPI function, TAPI will attempt to hand the request to the MSPHONE.EXE application first. If that application does not respond (it is busy with another call or not working properly), then TAPI will attempt to pass the service request to DIALER.EXE.

The [HandOffPriorities] section can contain several different entries, each corresponding to a media mode recognized by TAPI. Listing 27.9 shows a prototype of the [HandOffPriorities] section with all the known media modes and a sample extended media mode listed.

Listing 27.9. A prototype [HandOffPriorities] section.

```
 [HandoffPriorities]
RequestMakeCall=[<appname>[,<appname>]...]
RequestMediaCall=[<appname>[,<appname>]...]
unknown=[<appname>[,<appname>]...]
interactivevoice=[<appname>[,<appname>]...]
automatedvoice=[<appname>[,<appname>]...]
g3fax=[<appname>[,<appname>]...]
g4fax=[<appname>[,<appname>]...]
datamodem=[<appname>[,<appname>]...]
teletex=[<appname>[,<appname>]...]
videotex=[<appname>[,<appname>]...]
telex=[<appname>[,<appname>]...]
mixed=[<appname>[,<appname>]...]
tdd=[<appname>[,<appname>]...]
adsi=[<appname>[,<appname>]...]
digitaldata=[<appname>[,<appname>]...]
```

> **NOTE**
>
> TAPI also allows TSPs to define their own media modes and place them in the [HandOffPriorities] section. These settings are important only to those developing TSPs and are not covered in this book. For more on TSPs and extended media modes, you can refer to the Win32 Extensions documentation that ships with Microsoft Visual C++, or versions of the TAPI documentation that appear on the MSDN Professional Level CD-ROMs.

Like the provider section, the values in this section are manipulated by the TAPI applications that are designed to fulfill TAPI service requests. If you develop an application that is designed to process a particular type of media, you can place its name in this section. Most of the examples covered in this book are designed to make TAPI requests, not respond to them. For this reason, you will not be making any changes to the entries in the [HandOffPriorities] section of the TELEPHON.INI file.

Dialing Location Information

The next important section is the [Locations] section. This section holds information on the current location from which the workstation is placing calls. The values here are used to determine how to actually dial the telephone numbers provided to TAPI. For example, TAPI will attempt to determine if the telephone number can be handled using local dialing rules, long distance rules, or international rules.

The TAPI system allows users to define more than one location entry for the workstation. This way, users can move their computer to different locations and not have to reinstall or reinitialize the TAPI location each time. The best example of this is a laptop user who travels to different locations, but still wants to use TAPI services to place and receive calls. When the user arrives at a new location, the TAPI system need only be informed of the current location (and its dialing rules) and all applications will behave as normal, without any changing of phone numbers or dialing rules.

There are three main entries in the [Locations] section of the TELEPHON.INI:

- Locations—This entry tells TAPI how many locations are defined in the [Locations] section.

- CurrentLocation—This entry tells TAPI which of the location entries is currently selected.

- Location—This entry contains information about the dialing parameters for the defined location. There is one of these entries for each location defined in the [Locations] section.

Listing 27.10 shows a typical [Locations] section of the TELEPHON.INI file.

Listing 27.10. A typical [Locations] section.

```
[Locations]
CurrentLocation=5,3
Locations=4,6
Location0=0,"Default Location","","","606",1,0,0,1,"",0,""
Location1=1,"Office","","","513",1,0,0,0,"",0,""
Location2=3,"Oak Ridge, TN","","","423",1,0,0,0,"",0,""
Location3=5,"Sweden Office","9","8","013",46,1,0,0,"",0,""
```

The first entry in the section (CurrentLocation) tells TAPI that the current location is location index "5". The second parameter tells TAPI apps that they can find location index "5" by looking at the third location item in the list. This speeds selection of the record.

The second entry in the section (Locations) tells TAPI how many locations are defined here (4) and what the index value of the next location will be ("6"). This is used when adding new locations to the list.

The rest of the entries in the [Locations] section contain information about each defined location for this workstation. Listing 27.11 shows the prototype for all location entries in the TELEPHON.INI file.

Listing 27.11. The Location entry prototype.

```
Location<index>=<LocationID>,"<FriendlyName>","<LocalPrefix>","<LDPrefix>","<AreaCode>",<CountryCode>,
➥<PreferredCardID>,<CardHint>,<InsertAreaCode>,"<TollPrefixes>",<TonePulseDialing>,
➥<DisableCallWaiting>
```

Table 27.2 shows the list of parameters in the location line along with a short description of their use and meaning. The parameters are listed in the order in which they appear in the Location entry.

Table 27.2. The Location entry parameters.

Parameter	Description
<LocationID>	This is the unique ID value for this location.
<FriendlyName>	This is the easy-to-read name for this location (such as "Cincinnati, OH" or "My Home Office").
<LocalPrefix>	This is the digit(s) that must be dialed in order to place a local call from the location. This can be used in offices where users must dial "9" to reach an outside line, and so on.
<LdPrefix>	This is the digit(s) that must be dialed in order to place a long distance call from the location. This can be used in offices that must gain direct access to long distance lines before placing a call.
<AreaCode>	This is the area or city code for the location. This is compared against the requested outbound number to see if long distance must be used to complete the call.
<CountryCode>	This is the country code for the current location. This is used to determine whether international dialing rules must be employed to complete the requested outbound call.
<PreferredCardID>	This is the calling card that should be used to complete the long distance call.
<CardHint>	This is the direct index value of the calling card indicated in the <PreferredCardID> entry. This speeds the collection of the calling card entry data.

continues

Table 27.2. continued

Parameter	Description
<InsertAreaCode>	This entry must be set to 1 or 0. If set to 1, the area code will be used when placing calls to phone addresses that have the same area code and have a dialing prefix that appears in the <TollPrefixes> entry for this location (see the following description).
<TollPrefixes>	This is a list of three-digit phone address prefixes that require long distance dialing even though they are in the same area code as the current location. In order for TAPI to treat these as toll calls, the <InsertAreaCode> value for this location must be set to 1.
<TonePulseDialing>	This value must be set to 1 or 0. If it is set to 0, tone dialing will be used to place calls from this location. If it is set to 1, pulse dialing will be used.
<DisableCallWaiting>	This parameter contains the digit(s) that must be dialed to disable call waiting on the line. This can be used to turn off call waiting during data transmission calls in order to prevent loss of data during the call.

Modifying the Location Values with the lineTranslateDialog Method

You can adjust the values for location entries by using the lineTranslateDialog method of the TapiLine control. To test this out, run the TAPIDLG.EXE program and select the Telephon.ini button to view the current settings for the [Location] section. Figure 27.3 shows what your screen might look like at this point.

FIGURE 27.3.

Displaying the TELEPHON.INI *file from* TAPIDLG.EXE.

Now close the instance of NOTEPAD.EXE (be sure not to save any incidental changes you might have made). Now select the Line Translate Dialog option button and press Apply. This will bring up the Dialing Properties dialog box. You are ready to add a new location entry into the TELEPHON.INI file.

Press the New... button and create a new location. Use the information in Table 27.3 and Figure 27.4 to set the location parameters.

Table 27.3. New location parameters.

Setting Name	Setting Value
Name	TAPI Book
Area Code	999
Local Outside Line Access	9
Long Distance Outside Line Access	8
Disable Call Waiting	1170
Dialing Method	Tone Dialing

FIGURE 27.4.

Building a new location.

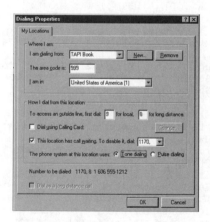

After you enter and save the new location data, press the Telephon.ini button to bring up the TELEPHON.INI file. Find the new entry in the [Location] section to see how the dialog box updated the INI file. Your new entry should look like the one in Listing 27.12.

Listing 27.12. The results of adding a new location to TELEPHON.INI.

```
Location4=6,"TAPI Book","9","8","999",1,2,0,1,"",0,"1170,"
```

You have now used the TAPI dialog boxes to add new locations to your TELEPHON.INI file. Next you'll use the same dialog box to add calling card information for the location.

Credit Card Dialing Instructions

Another very important section in the TELEPHON.INI file is the [Cards] section. This section holds information on the calling cards defined for this workstation. The first entry in the [Cards] section tells TAPI how many calling card definitions are in the section and the next available entry ID. Each additional entry in the [Cards] section represents one set of calling parameters. Listing 27.13 shows what a typical [Cards] section of the TELEPHON.INI file looks like.

Listing 27.13. A typical [Cards] section.

```
[Cards]
Cards=23,23
Card0=0,"None (Direct Dial)","","","","",1
Card1=1,"AT&T Direct Dial via 10ATT1","","G","102881FG","10288011EFG",1
Card2=4,"MCI Direct Dial via 102221","","G","102221FG","10222011EFG",1
Card3=5,"MCI via 102220","","G","102220FG$TH","1022201EFG$TH",1
Card4=6,"MCI via 1-800-888-8000","","G","18008888000,,,,,,TH,,FG","
➥18008888000,,,,,,TH,,011EFG",1
Card5=7,"MCI via 1-800-674-0700","","G","18006740700,,,,,,TH,,FG","
➥18006740700,,,,,,TH,,011EFG",1
Card6=8,"MCI via 1-800-674-7000","","G","18006747000,,,,,,TH,,FG","
➥18006747000,,,,,,TH,,011EFG",1
Card7=9,"US Sprint Direct Dial via 103331","","G","103331FG","10333011EFG",1
Card8=10,"US Sprint via 103330","","G","103330FG$TH","1033301EFG$TH",1
Card9=11,"US Sprint via 1-800-877-8000","","G","18008778000,,,T0FG,,H","
➥18008778000,,,T01EFG#,H",1
Card10=12,"Calling Card via 0","","G","0FG$TH","01EFG$TH",1
Card11=13,"Carte France Telecom","","T3610,H,G#","T3610,H,16,FG#","
➥T3610,H,19,EFG#",1
Card12=14,"Mercury (UK)","","0500800800$TH,0FG","0500800800$TH,0FG","
➥0500800800$TH,0FG",1
Card13=15,"British Telecom (UK)","","144$H,0FG","144$H,0FG","144$H,010EFG",1
Card14=16,"CLEAR Communications (New Zealand)","","0502333$TH,0FG","
➥0502333$TH,0FG","0502333$TH,00EFG",1
Card15=17,"Telecom New Zealand","","012,0FG?H","012,0FG?H","012,00EFG?H",1
Card16=18,"Global Card (Taiwan to USA)","","G","0FG","0080,102880$TFG$H",1
Card17=19,"Telecom Australia via 1818 (voice)","","1818$TH,FG#","1818$TH,FG#","
➥1818$TH,0011EFG#",1
Card18=20,"Telecom Australia via 1818 (fax)","","1818$TH,FG#","1818$TH,FG#","
➥1818$TH,0015EFG#",1
Card19=21,"Optus (Australia) via 1812","","FG","FG","1812@TH,0011EFG",1
Card20=22,"Optus (Australia) via 008551812","","FG","FG","008551812@TH,0011EFG",1
Card21=3,"AT&T via 1-800-321-0288","634567890","G","18003210288$TFG$TH","
➥18003210288$T01EFG$TH",1
Card22=2,"AT&T via 10ATT0","42345678","G","102880FG$TH","1028801EFG$TH",1
```

Every calling card entry has seven parts. Listing 27.14 shows the prototype entry for the [Cards] section. Table 27.4 shows the [Cards] entry parameters and short descriptions of their use.

Listing 27.14. The prototype entry for the `[Cards]` section.

```
Card<index>=<CardID>,"<FriendlyName>","<ScrambledCardNum>","<SameArea>","<LongDistance>",
➥"<International>",<Hidden>
```

Table 27.4. The card entry parameters.

Parameter Name	Description
`<CardID>`	This is the unique card ID for this entry.
`<FriendlyName>`	This is an easy-to-read name for the card entry (such as "ATT Calling Card").
`<ScrambledCardNum>`	This is the calling card number. It is scrambled by the TAPI dialog box in order to increase security.
`<SameArea>`	This is the dialing rule for placing a call within the same area code using the calling card.
`<LongDistance>`	This is the dialing rule for placing a long distance call using the calling card.
`<International>`	This is the dialing rule for placing an international call using the calling card.
`<Hidden>`	This value must be 0, 1, 2, or 3. It controls the user's access to the calling card entry. 1 = User can see and edit the entry 2 = User can see, but not edit the entry 3 = User can edit the entry, but not see it 4 = User can neither see nor edit the entry

Understanding the TAPI Dialing Rules

Several entries in the `[Cards]` section contain dialing rules used by TAPI. These rules are expressed in a series of codes that appear as part of the dialing string. The dialing string can contain the standard values of "0" through "9" along with many other values. These values can be divided into three groups:

- Dialable digits or tones
- Pauses or other control values
- Insertion codes

Dialable digits or tones include 0 through 9, A through D, and # and *. TAPI recognizes several pause or control codes and insertion codes. Table 27.5 shows the valid control and insertion codes for TAPI dialing strings.

Table 27.5. Valid control and insertion codes for dialing strings.

Dialing Code	Description
T	Use tone (DTMF) dialing
P	Use pulse dialing
!	Flash the hookswitch (to make a transfer)
,	Pause (for about one second)
W	Wait for second dial tone (for DID calls)
@	Wait for quiet answer (call pick-up only)
$	Wait for "bong" tone (for billing cards)
E	Insert the country code
F	Insert the area code
G	Insert the phone number
H	Insert the calling card number
I	Optionally insert the area code

You can use the information in Table 27.5 to decipher entries in the [Cards] section of the TELEPHON.INI file. For example, the dialing rules for placing calls using the card entry shown in Listing 27.15 indicate the dialing rules for local, long distance, and international calls.

Listing 27.15. A sample dialing rule set.

```
Card1=1,"AT&T Direct Dial via 10ATT1","","G","102881FG","10288011EFG",1
```

Local calls are placed by simply dialing the phone number ("G"). Long distance calls require dialing "102881" plus the area code ("F") and the phone number ("G"). While the international calls must be placed using "10288011" plus the country code ("E"), the area code ("F"), and the phone number ("G").

Testing the Calling Card Settings of TAPIDLG.EXE

You can check the effects of TAPI dialog boxes on the long distance dialing rules by clicking the Dial Using Calling Card check box and selecting a calling card to use. Fill in the calling card number as eight 9s ("99999999"). Refer to Figure 27.5. Then click OK to save the calling card data and OK to save the location data.

FIGURE 27.5.
Entering calling card data.

After saving the data, press the Telephon.ini button to bring up the TELEPHON.INI file and find the [Cards] entry you modified. It should look something like the one in Listing 27.16.

Listing 27.16. The modified [Cards] entry.

```
Card22=2,"AT&T via 10ATT0","42345678","G","102880FG$TH","1028801EFG$TH",1
```

Notice that the dialog box scrambled the calling card number before saving it to the INI file.

> **WARNING**
>
> Be sure to restore your location settings after you finish with this chapter. If you do not, your TSPs will not know how to place a call from your "experimental" location.

Summary

In this chapter you learned a bit about how TAPI works behind the scenes to place call requests generated by your programs. You learned that the TAPI system keeps track of vital information in the TELEPHON.INI file kept in the WINDOWS folder on the workstation. You learned there are four main sections in the TELEPHON.INI file:

- The *Service Provider* section holds information on all the Telephony Service Providers (TSPs) installed on the workstation.
- The *HandOff Priorities* section holds information about which line devices can support which media modes and the order in which the line devices should be called.
- The *Location* section holds information on the dialing locations of the workstation.
- The *Credit Card* section holds dialing instructions for using telephone service credit cards to control billing.

You learned the different predefined media modes that can be handled by registered TAPI applications in the [HandOffPriorities] section. You also learned the dialing codes that are used in the [Cards] section to tell TAPI how to place requested calls.

Finally, you built a small Visual Basic application that allowed you to gain direct access to the various TAPI line dialog boxes that can affect the TELEPHON.INI file.

In the next chapter, you'll learn how the Telephony Service Providers work and how they fit into the TAPI model.

28

Using TAPI to Handle Incoming Calls

Now that you know how to use TAPI services to handle outbound calling, it's time to create an example of handling inbound calls. In this chapter, you'll learn how to use the TAPILINE control that ships with the book to create a simple Visual Basic program that will wait for an incoming call and notify you with "ring." You can then pick up an attached receiver to accept the call. If you have a speaker phone card in your workstation, you can simply click a button on the screen and begin to talk.

Before you can accept incoming calls, you need to open an available line device with parameters that tell TAPI you plan to use the line for incoming calls. This chapter will show you how to select a valid line device and how to use the lineOpen method to prepare TAPI to respond to inbound calls.

In order to respond to and accept incoming calls, you need to know how to interpret a new set of TAPI messages. These messages are sent to the TapiCallBack event of the TAPILINE control. In this chapter, you'll learn which messages are used to monitor inbound calls and how to write Visual Basic code that responds to each message.

Finally, you'll learn how to end inbound calls properly, including how to respond when the caller on the other line hangs up unexpectedly. When you finish the project in this chapter, you'll know how to write telephone answering routines for all your Visual Basic and VBA-language programs.

Process Flow for Inbound Calls

Before you start to code the example, it's important to go over the basics of how to use TAPI services to handle inbound calls. The process is not very complex, but it can be tricky because you need to write a program that can wait for a telephone event and then respond accordingly. Since the program is designed to wait for a call, it is the telephone that really controls the program flow.

There are a total of six basic steps to using TAPI to process inbound calls (see Figure 28.1). Several of these steps are pretty much the same as those used to handle outbound calls.

The six steps are

■ Initialize TAPI services on the workstation.

■ Select and open valid line devices for incoming calls.

■ Wait for an inbound call to appear on the line.

■ When a call appears, accept the call and begin conversation.

■ When the call ends, close the line and prepare for the next call.

■ When the session is over, shut down TAPI services on the workstation.

FIGURE 28.1.
The process flow for handling inbound calls.

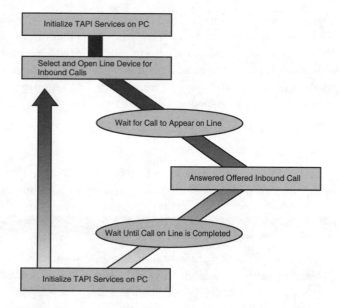

This process can best be illustrated using a typical voice call between two people. Let's assume you need to create a Visual Basic program that will answer incoming calls and route them to a telephone handset or speakerphone. You'll want to allow the user to start TAPI, wait for a call, accept any inbound calls, and, at the end of a conversation, end the call and wait for another one.

Starting TAPI services on the workstation requires initializing the TAPI driver (lineInitialize), verifying the current TAPI API version (lineNegotiateAPIVersion), and collecting information on all the available TAPI devices on the workstation (lineGetDevCaps). Then you must select one of the line devices that is capable of handling inbound calls and open it for inbound handling (lineOpen). By opening the device in this way, you are telling TAPI that you want to be told whenever an inbound call shows up on the line.

At this point, all you need to do is wait for TAPI to tell you when a call appears on the selected line. When it does, your program will receive a message (through the TapiCallBack event) telling you that a call is being "offered" to you. If you decide to accept the call, you can retrieve the handle to the call and answer (using the lineAnswer method). Once this is done, your program can pass the call to the user and wait until the conversation is completed.

There are basically two ways a phone conversation ends: Either you hang up or the person (machine) on the other end hangs up. In the first case, you can use the lineDrop and lineClose methods to end the call. If, however, the other party hangs up (possibly unexpectedly), the line is automatically closed by TAPI. However, you still need to release your program's hold on the call handle (using lineDeallocateCall). In either case, performing lineClose or lineDeallocateCall will prepare the line device for receiving additional inbound calls.

There are two main points to keep in mind when building applications to accept inbound calls. First, after you open the device using parameters that inform TAPI that you want to be notified of any inbound calls, you need to watch for (and respond to) TAPI messages that occur when a call appears. The second main point is that once a call is accepted and in progress, your program needs to watch for (and respond to) TAPI messages that indicate the call has ended. In other words, your inbound call handler has two main jobs:

- Wait for a call to appear.
- Wait for a call to end.

The rest of this chapter shows you how to use the TAPILINE control and Visual Basic to create a program that performs all the tasks necessary for handling inbound voice calls.

> **NOTE**
>
> The example in this chapter assumes your workstation has a modem or telephony card that is capable of handling voice calls. If your modem is able to handle only data calls, you can still build the project described here. However, you will be able to complete only data modem calls, not voice calls.

The TAPIANS Project

The rest of this chapter is devoted to building a Visual Basic application that handles inbound calls. You need to write code that will handle initializing and opening an inbound line device, and code that will respond to TAPI messages regarding calls appearing on the line. Along with the code you write, you'll need to use the TAPILINE control and the Visual Basic TAPI library files that are on the CD-ROM that ships with this book.

> **NOTE**
>
> For more information on the TAPILINE control and the TAPI library files, see Chapter 26, "TAPI Tools—Using the TAPILINE Control."

Finally, you'll need to design an input form that allows users to start the TAPI call monitor, accept offered calls, and hang up completed calls.

When you are done with this example, you'll have a handful of TAPI answering routines that you can use in all your Visual Basic or VBA-compatible programs.

Creating the TAPIANS Form

First, you need to lay out a Visual Basic form with four command buttons, one list box, and one multiline text box. This form will be used to start TAPI services and accept and end calls on the selected line. Refer to Table 28.1 and Figure 28.2 when building the TAPIANS form.

FIGURE 28.2.

Laying out the TAPIANS *form.*

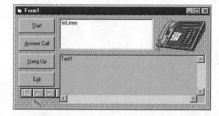

Table 28.1. Controls for the TAPIANS form.

Control	Property	Setting
VB.Form	Name	frmTapiAns
	Caption	"Form1"
	Height	3525
	Left	1245
	Top	1215
	Width	6750
VB.TextBox	Name	txtStatus
	BackColor	&H00C0C0C0&
	Height	1635
	Left	1500
	MultiLine	-1 'True
	ScrollBars	3 'Both
	TabIndex	5
	Top	1320
	Width	4995
VB.ListBox	Name	lstLines
	Height	1035
	Left	1500
	TabIndex	4
	Top	120
	Width	3195

continues

Table 28.1. continued

Control	Property	Setting
VB.CommandButton	Name	cmdButton
	Caption	"E&xit"
	Height	495
	Index	3
	Left	120
	TabIndex	3
	Top	1920
	Width	1215
VB.CommandButton	Name	cmdButton
	Caption	"&Hang Up"
	Height	495
	Index	2
	Left	120
	TabIndex	2
	Top	1320
	Width	1215
VB.CommandButton	Name	cmdButton
	Caption	"&Answer Call"
	Height	495
	Index	1
	Left	120
	TabIndex	1
	Top	720
	Width	1215
VB.CommandButton	Name	cmdButton
	Caption	"&Start"
	Height	495
	Index	0
	Left	120
	TabIndex	0
	Top	120
	Width	1215

Control	Property	Setting
VB.Image	Name	Image1
	Height	1035
	Left	4800
	Stretch	-1 'True
	Top	180
	Width	1695
MCI.MMControl	Name	MMControl1
	Height	330
	Left	180
	TabIndex	6
	Top	2460
	Visible	0 'False
	Width	3540
TapilineLib.Tapiline	Name	Tapiline1
	Left	600
	Top	2820

There are a few things that you need to keep in mind when building this form. First, be sure to add the TAPILINE control to your project (Tools | Custom Controls) before you start building the form. Also notice that you need to add the MCI Multimedia control to the form. You'll use that control to produce the sound of a ringing telephone whenever a call appears on the monitored line. Notice that the MCI control has its Visible property set to FALSE. There is also an Image control on the form. You'll load an image of a multiline telephone into this control at run-time. Be sure to set the Stretch property of the Image control to TRUE. Finally, by now you should recognize the control array used with the command buttons. Be sure to add the first button, set its values (including the Index value), and then use Edit | Copy and Edit | Paste to add all the buttons in the control array.

When you are finished building the form, save it as TAPIANS.FRM and save the project as TAPIANS.VBP before you go on to the next section.

Coding the TAPIANS Form

There are a handful of code routines you need to add to the TAPIANS form. But, before you add code to the form, you need to add two BAS modules to the project (File | Add File). These modules can be found on the CD-ROM that ships with this book. The first is the `TAPILINE.BAS` module. This module contains all the TAPI constants, structures, and helper APIs needed to support the `TAPILINE` control. The second BAS module you need to add to the project is the `TAPICALL.BAS` module. This routine contains several helper functions and subroutines for decoding TAPI messages. There are also several general routines in this module to handle typical TAPI operations for Visual Basic programs.

> **TIP**
>
> The easiest way to add the `TAPICALL` and `TAPILINE` modules to your project is to first copy them into the project directory, and then use the `File | Add File` menu option to place them into your project. You probably have more than one copy of these routines on your hard disk. You used them in Chapter 26, "TAPI Tools—Using the `TAPILINE` Control." If you can't find them on your hard disk, you can find them on the CD-ROM that ships with this book.

Coding the `Form_Load` and `Form_Unload` Events

The first code to add to the project is the code for the `Form_Load` event. This code calls several support routines and handles general initialization controls. Add the code shown in Listing 28.1 to the `Form_Load` event of the form.

Listing 28.1. Coding the `Form_Load` event.

```
Private Sub Form_Load()
    '
    ClearHandles ' start clean
    TapiStart ' init tapi & get version
    TapiGetDevCaps ' get device names
    MCIStart ' init multimedia control
    '
    Me.Left = (Screen.Width - Me.Width) / 2
    Me.Top = (Screen.Height - Me.Height) / 2
    '
    Me.Caption = "TAPI Answer Demo"
    Me.Image1.Picture = LoadPicture(App.Path & "\phone.wmf")
    txtStatus.Text = ""
    '
    cmdButton(1).Enabled = False
    cmdButton(2).Enabled = False
    '
End Sub
```

The code in the `Form_Load` event calls for support routines to set up TAPI and the MCI control. The rest of the code centers the form and sets properties for the form and various controls on the form.

Listing 28.2 shows the code for the `Form_Unload` event. This code makes sure that TAPI services are properly closed down before exiting the program. Add this code to the `TAPIANS` form.

Listing 28.2. Adding code to the `Form_Unload` event.

```
Private Sub Form_Unload(Cancel As Integer)
    '
    ' close up shop
    '
    Tapiline1.LineDrop "", 0 ' drop active call
    Tapiline1.LineClose ' close open line
    Tapiline1.LineShutdown ' uninit TAPI
    '
End Sub
```

Nothing complex here. The only item to note is the inclusion of the two parameters for the `lineDrop` method. These parameters are used only when passing user information on ISDN lines. Since this program assumes you'll be using voice-grade telephone lines, the values are left empty.

Adding the `TAPIANS` Support Routines

There are just a few support routines needed for the `TAPIANS` project. These routines handle the initialization of TAPI and multimedia services for the workstation. You'll also add a routine to clear out TAPI pointers at the start of the project and the end of a call.

First, you need a routine to handle the initial startup of TAPI services for the workstation. This routine should start TAPI, get a count of all the available line devices, and confirm the API version of the devices. The code in Listing 28.3 shows you how to do this. Add a new subroutine called `TAPIStart` on the form (use `Insert | Procedure`), and enter the code shown in Listing 28.3.

Listing 28.3. Adding the `TAPIStart` procedure.

```
Public Sub TapiStart()
    '
    ' start tapi and get lines
    '
    Dim x As Integer
    Dim lRtn As Long
    '
    lRtn = Tapiline1.LineInitialize(App.EXEName)
    If lRtn < 0 Then
        MsgBox "Unable to Start TAPI!", vbCritical
        Unload Me
    End If
    '
    For x = 0 To Tapiline1.NumDevices - 1
        Tapiline1.LineNegotiateAPIVersion x, &H10000, &H10004
```

continues

Listing 28.3. continued

```
    Next x
    '
End Sub
```

You've seen most of this before. Notice that the lRtn value is checked after attempting to start TAPI. You'll see that the test is for a value *less* than zero. Several TAPI functions return positive values instead of zero when they are successful. However, error values are always less than zero. You'll also notice the hexadecimal values &H10000 (decimal 65536) and &H10004 (decimal 65540) as parameters in the lineNegotiateAPIVersion method. These are the minimum (1.0) and maximum (1.4) API versions supported by the TAPILINE control. Notice also that the numDevices property of the TAPILINE control is set to the total number of recognized line devices for the workstation. You'll use this value to collect information on all the registered line devices.

Next, you need to add a routine to get the capabilities of all the line devices you discovered in the TAPIStart routine. You'll use the numDevices property just mentioned above. Listing 28.4 shows the new routine TapiGetDevCaps. This routine fills a list box with the names of all the registered devices. With this list, the user can select the device most appropriate for voice calls. Add the code in Listing 28.4 to your form.

Listing 28.4. Adding the TapiGetDevCaps routine.

```
Public Sub TapiGetDevCaps()
    '
    ' load device names into list box
    '
    Dim a As Long
    Dim b As LINEDEVCAPS
    Dim c As String * 2048
    Dim x As Integer
    '
    For x = 0 To Tapiline1.NumDevices - 1
        ' make the call to get dev caps
        a = Tapiline1.LineGetDevCaps(x)
        If a < 0 Then
            lstLines.AddItem "<<<ERROR>>> DevCaps..." & LineErr(a)
        Else
            LineDevCapsFunc TAPI_READ, b, c
            c = Clean(c)
            lstLines.AddItem GetOffset(Len(b) + 4, b.dwLineNameOffset,
➥b.dwLineNameSize, c)
        End If
    Next x
    '
End Sub
```

You can see that after calling the `lineGetDevCaps` method of the `TAPILINE` control, you need to call the `lineDevCapsFunc` API function to retrieve the data in the `LINEDEVCAPS` structure. This data is filled in by TAPI when you use the `lineGetDevCaps` method. This routine uses the `GetOffset` helper function (from the TAPICALLS library) to pull out the line device name and insert it into the list control on the form.

Since this project will use a WAV file to signal a ringing phone, you'll need to add some code to initialize the `MCI Multimedia` control to handle WAV output. Add a new subroutine called `MCIStart` and enter the code shown in Listing 28.5.

Listing 28.5. Adding the `MCIStart` routine.

```
Public Sub MCIStart()
    '
    ' init MCI control for ringing phone
    '
    MMControl1.Notify = False
    MMControl1.Wait = True
    MMControl1.Shareable = False
    MMControl1.DeviceType = "WaveAudio"
    MMControl1.filename = App.Path & "\ringin.wav"
    MMControl1.Command = "Open"
    '
End Sub
```

Not too much to comment on here, either. Just note that the control accesses the RINGIN.WAV file. This should be placed in your application directory. It is included on the CD-ROM that accompanies this book. If you have it stored in another location, be sure to modify the code in Listing 28.5 to point to the proper folder.

The last support routine you need to add to the project is one that clears `TAPILINE` control properties related to a completed call. You'll use this routine at the very beginning of the program (for initialization) and at the end of each call (for cleanup). Add a new subroutine called `ClearHandles` and enter the code shown in Listing 28.6.

Listing 28.6. Adding the `ClearHandles` routine.

```
Public Sub ClearHandles()
    '
    ' set all control handles to zero
    '
    Tapiline1.LineHandle = 0
    Tapiline1.HandleToCall = 0
    Tapiline1.AddressID = 0
    '
End Sub
```

These properties are all set when a call is accepted on a line device. Once a call is ended, you need to clear these properties in preparation for the next call.

Save the form (TAPIANS.FRM) and project (TAPIANS.VBP) before continuing.

Adding the `TapiCallBack` Event Code

The next code you need to add to the project relates to detecting and responding to TAPI messages (TapiCallBack). The TapiCallBack event of the TAPILINE control receives all messages generated by the TAPI system. As mentioned in earlier chapters, there are several different messages, each with their own set of accompanying parameters.

> **NOTE**
>
> For more information on TAPI messages, their use, and meaning, refer to Chapter 23, "TAPI Architecture."

In this example, you need to keep track of only two messages:

- LINE_CALLSTATE
- LINE_CLOSE

The LINE_CALLSTATE message is sent whenever the state of the selected line has changed. This program will watch for messages that indicate there is a new call on the line (dwParam1 = LINECALLSTATE_OFFERED) or when the party on the other end of the line closed the call unexpectedly (dwParam1 = LINECALLSTATE_IDLE). The LINE_CLOSE message is sent whenever the user ends the call normally.

You can monitor the message activity by adding code to the TapiCallBack event that checks each message sent by TAPI. This is done using a SELECT CASE structure to compare the incoming message to a list of messages for which you are waiting. The code in Listing 28.7 shows how this is done. Add this code to the TapiCallBack event.

Listing 28.7. Adding code to the `TapiCallBack` event.

```
Private Sub Tapiline1_TapiCallBack(ByVal hDevice As Long, ByVal dwMessage As Long,
➥ByVal dwInstance As Long, ByVal dwParam1 As Long, ByVal dwParam2 As Long, ByVal
➥dwParam3 As Long)
    '
    ' handle TAPI messages
    '
    Dim cMsg As String
    '
    ' handle call actions
    Select Case dwMessage
        Case LINE_CALLSTATE ' state of call on line changed
            Select Case dwParam1
```

```
                Case LINECALLSTATE_OFFERING ' get call handle
                    Tapiline1.HandleToCall = hDevice ' update handle to call
                    MMControl1.Command = "play" ' ring me!
                Case LINECALLSTATE_IDLE ' they hung up on me!
                    Tapiline1.LineDeallocateCall ' dump pointer
                    Tapiline1.HandleToCall = 0 ' clear property
                    AddText txtStatus, "LineDeallocate Successful"
            End Select
        Case LINE_CLOSE ' line was closed
            cmdButton_Click 2 ' force hangup
    End Select
    '
    ' report status to user
    cMsg = TapiCallBackHandler(hDevice, dwMessage, dwInstance, dwParam1, dwParam2,
➥dwParam3)
    AddText txtStatus, cMsg
    '
End Sub
```

The code in Listing 28.7 shows the SELECT CASE structure monitoring two messages—
LINE_CALLSTATE and LINE_CLOSE. When the LINE_CALLSTATE message appears, additional checking
is performed to determine the exact state of the call. If a new call is appearing on the line
(LINECALLSTATE_OFFERING), the program updates the HandleToCall property and then rings the
workstation to tell the user a call is coming in.

If the call state has changed to completed (LINECALLSTATE_IDLE), the routine releases memory
allocated to the call and clears the HandleToCall property in preparation for the next incoming
call.

When the LINE_CLOSE message appears, that means the user has completed the call. The code
here makes a call to the cmdButton array that will act as if the user pressed the HangUp button
(you'll code that in just a moment).

You'll also notice that the routine contains calls to the TapiCallBackHandler function. This
function interprets the TAPI message and creates a text string that can be shown to the user to
indicate the progress of the call.

Coding the cmdButton Array

The last code you need to add will handle the user's actions on the command buttons. There
are four possible actions that the user can select:

- Start opens the selected line for incoming calls.
- Answer is used to accept an incoming (ringing) call.
- HangUp is used to end a call connection.
- Exit ends TAPI services and stops the program.

Listing 28.8 shows the complete code for the cmdButton_Click event.

Listing 28.8. The code for the cmdButton_Click event.

```
Private Sub cmdButton_Click(Index As Integer)
    '
    ' open a line for monitoring
    '
    Dim lRtn As Long
    Dim lPrivilege As Long
    Dim lMediaMode As Long
    '
    ' check for start up selection only
    If Index = 0 Then
        If lstLines.ListIndex = -1 Then
            MsgBox "Select a line first!", vbInformation
            Exit Sub
        End If
    End If
    '
    ' set line parameters
    lPrivilege = LINECALLPRIVILEGE_OWNER + LINECALLPRIVILEGE_MONITOR
    lMediaMode = LINEMEDIAMODE_INTERACTIVEVOICE
    '
    ' react to user selection
    Select Case Index
        Case 0 ' start looking
            lRtn = Tapiline1.LineOpen(lstLines.ListIndex, 0, lPrivilege,
➥lMediaMode)
            If lRtn < 0 Then
                AddText txtStatus, "<<LineOpen ERROR>> " & LineErr(lRtn)
            Else
                AddText txtStatus, "LineOpen Successful"
                AddText txtStatus, "Waiting for an incoming call..."
                '
                cmdButton(0).Enabled = False
                cmdButton(1).Enabled = True
                cmdButton(2).Enabled = True
                '
            End If
        Case 1 ' answer call
            lRtn = Tapiline1.LineAnswer("", 0) ' only needed for ISDN
            If (lRtn < 0) Then
                AddText txtStatus, "<<LineAnswer ERROR>> " & LineErr(lRtn)
            Else
                AddText txtStatus, "LineAnswer Successful"
            End If
        Case 2 ' disconnect call
            Tapiline1.LineDrop "", 0 ' no parms unless ISDN!
            Tapiline1.LineClose
            '
            cmdButton(0).Enabled = True
            cmdButton(1).Enabled = False
            cmdButton(2).Enabled = False
            '
            ClearHandles ' clean up control handles
            AddText txtStatus, "Line Dropped and Closed"
```

```
        Case 3 ' exit program
            Unload Me
    End Select
    '
End Sub
```

There's a lot going on in this code section, so it is worth reviewing in greater detail.

First, if the user has pressed the Start button, the code checks to make sure a line device has been selected from the list box. If no line device was selected, the user gets an error message, and the code exits the procedure (see Listing 28.9).

Listing 28.9. Checking for a selected line device.

```
' check for start up selection only
    If Index = 0 Then
        If lstLines.ListIndex = -1 Then
            MsgBox "Select a line first!", vbInformation
            Exit Sub
        End If
    End If
```

If the user has selected a valid device and pressed the Start button, the routine attempts to open the selected line device for interactive voice services with owner and monitor privileges.

> **NOTE**
>
> The privilege values tell TAPI that the program wants to "own" any incoming calls. But, if for some reason this workstation cannot own the calls, at least it wants to be able to "see" (monitor) them. This is the standard privilege profile for incoming calls.

If an error occurs when attempting to open the line, an error message is delivered to the text box. If the line is opened successfully, the appropriate message is sent to the text box, and the Answer and HangUp buttons are enabled while the Start button is disabled (see Listing 28.10).

Listing 28.10. Opening a line for incoming calls.

```
' set line parameters
    lPrivilege = LINECALLPRIVILEGE_OWNER + LINECALLPRIVILEGE_MONITOR
    lMediaMode = LINEMEDIAMODE_INTERACTIVEVOICE
    '
    ' react to user selection
    Select Case Index
        Case 0 ' start looking
            lRtn = Tapiline1.LineOpen(lstLines.ListIndex, 0, lPrivilege,
➥lMediaMode)
```

continues

Listing 28.10. continued

```
        If lRtn < 0 Then
            AddText txtStatus, "<<LineOpen ERROR>> " & LineErr(lRtn)
        Else
            AddText txtStatus, "LineOpen Successful"
            AddText txtStatus, "Waiting for an incoming call..."
            '
            cmdButton(0).Enabled = False
            cmdButton(1).Enabled = True
            cmdButton(2).Enabled = True
            '
        End If
```

Once the line is opened, the user will receive a notice (the sound of a ringing phone) when a call appears on the line. The user can press the Answer button to accept the call. Listing 28.11 shows the code that calls the LineAnswer method to accept a call.

Listing 28.11. Accepting an incoming call.

```
Case 1 ' answer call
        lRtn = Tapiline1.LineAnswer("", 0) ' only needed for ISDN
        If (lRtn < 0) Then
            AddText txtStatus, "<<LineAnswer ERROR>> " & LineErr(lRtn)
        Else
            AddText txtStatus, "LineAnswer Successful"
        End If
```

This code is quite simple, but it hides a very important aspect of accepting an incoming call. The lineAnswer method assumes that you already have the HandleToCall property set to point to the call handle provided by TAPI. However, this property is not automatically set for you. Since you may not want to accept a given call, TAPI supplies you with only the call handle. This is done as part of the LINE_CALLSTATE message. Check out the code in Listing 28.7 to see where the HandleToCall property is set for you.

The last bit of code in the cmdButton_Click event that needs some attention is the code that handles the HangUp button. This button is pressed to close out an active call. When a user decides to end a call, both the lineClose and lineDrop methods should be invoked to clear resources. It is also a good idea to clear any handle properties that relate to the previous call. Listing 28.12 shows the HangUp code in detail.

Listing 28.12. Ending a TAPI call.

```
Case 2 ' disconnect call
        Tapiline1.LineDrop "", 0 ' no parms unless ISDN!
        Tapiline1.LineClose
        '
        cmdButton(0).Enabled = True
```

```
        cmdButton(1).Enabled = False
        cmdButton(2).Enabled = False
        '
        ClearHandles ' clean up control handles
        AddText txtStatus, "Line Dropped and Closed"
```

That completes the coding of the TAPIANS project. Be sure to save the form (TAPIANS.FRM) and the project (TAPIANS.VBP) before you continue. In the next section, you'll test the TAPIANS project to make sure it is working properly.

Testing TAPIANS

Now that you have completed the TAPIANS project, you're ready to test it out. To do this, you'll need a workstation configuration that includes either a built-in TAPI-compliant speakerphone or a standard telephone handset connected to the "out" jack of a voice-capable modem. Figure 28.3 shows an example of how you can arrange a standard voice-data modem and telephone handset to handle inbound TAPI calls.

FIGURE 28.3.

Example hardware arrangement for handling incoming calls.

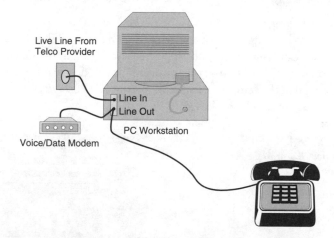

NOTE

If you do not have a voice-capable modem or telephony card, you can still test this project. You'll need to change the MONITORMEDIA_ mode from INTERACTIVEVOICE to DATAMODEM. This will set up your application to accept data modem calls. When the call is answered, TAPI will immediately begin sending data handshaking signals to the party at the other end of the phone.

In order to fully test the project, you'll need to answer an incoming phone call. If you are working from a home or office that has multiple phone lines, you can simply set up the TAPIANS program to monitor a line and call that line from another phone in the same building.

If you are working where you have only one line for both incoming and outgoing calls, you'll need to arrange for assistance from a friend. After running the TAPIANS project and pressing the Start button, call a friend and ask him or her to call you back at the same number that TAPIANS is monitoring.

> **TIP**
>
> You can purchase from office and telephone equipment suppliers devices that will simulate an incoming call on the line. These devices cost very little and are handy if you want to take your TAPI software to demonstrations, shows, or other events where you cannot rely on access to active telephone lines.

Once you have your test call lined up, you can run the TAPIANS project and begin testing.

The first thing you'll see is a list of all the line devices that TAPI recognizes on your workstation. Scroll through the list and select the one that will be able to handle the media mode for your test call (voice-data modem). Once you highlight the line device, you can press the Start button to tell TAPI to begin monitoring the line device for incoming calls. You should receive a message in the status box that tells you that TAPI services were started and that the program is waiting for a call (see Figure 28.4).

FIGURE 28.4.

TAPIANS *is waiting for an incoming call.*

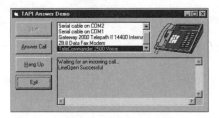

Now you need to get TAPIANS to see an incoming call appear on the line. If you have another phone line available to you, use it to call the phone line that TAPI is monitoring. If you don't have multiple phone lines, now is the time to call one of your friends to ask him or her to call the TAPI-monitored line.

> **NOTE**
>
> If you are using a call simulator, you can just flip the switch that sends a "tip-and-ring" signal along the line. This will tell TAPI a call is coming in.

When a call appears on the line, TAPI sends a LINE_CALLSTATE message with a dwParam1 equal to LINECALLSTATE_OFFERING. This tells your program that a new call is being offered to you for acceptance. At this point, the TAPIANS program will copy the hDevice value passed in the LINE_CALLSTATE message into the HandleToCall property of the TAPILINE control. This prepares the control to answer the offered call.

When the user presses the Answer button, TAPIANS invokes the lineAnswer method. If this function call is successful, TAPI returns three messages in quick succession. First, TAPI sends a LINE_REPLY message back to TAPIANS. This message is sent by TAPI whenever an asynchronous TAPI service request is completed. This message is not important for this application and can be disregarded.

> **NOTE**
>
> LINE_REPLY messages are useful for applications that deal in multiple phone lines. Since there are several possible asynchronous activities that can occur during TAPI services, keeping track of the RequestID is important. Since this application is working with only a single phone line, it is not so important to keep track of the RequestID value.

The next message TAPI returns is a LINE_CALLSTATE message with a dwParam1 equal to LINECALLSTATE_ACCEPTED. This message tells TAPIANS that the lineAnswer method was successful. Finally, TAPI will return a message of LINE_CALLSTATE with a dwParam1 set to LINECALLSTATE_CONNECTED. This message indicates that the telephone call has been successfully connected. You can now pick up the telephone handset and talk to the person at the other end of the line (or to yourself, depending on how you placed the call!).

This set of messages and responses from your Visual Basic program happens quite quickly. Figure 28.5 shows how the messages appear in a typical call appearance.

FIGURE 28.5.

Viewing call progress for an incoming call.

When you are ready to end the telephone call, you press the HangUp button on the TAPIANS dialog box. This will cause the program to drop the call and close the line. You'll get a short message telling you the line was closed successfully.

That's all there is to it. You now have a functional Visual Basic program that can see calls coming in on the line and give users the chance to answer those calls using a Visual Basic program.

Summary

In this chapter, you learned how to use the TAPILINE control to create a Visual Basic application that can monitor a telephone line for incoming calls and allow users to answer those calls. In the process, you learned about the six steps needed to handle inbound calls using TAPI services:

■ Initialize TAPI services on the workstation.

■ Select and open valid line devices for incoming calls.

■ Wait for an inbound call to appear on the line.

■ When a call appears, accept the call and begin conversation.

■ When the call ends, close the line and prepare for the next call.

■ When the session is over, shut down TAPI services on the workstation.

You also learned the importance of the LINE_CALLSTATE message sent by TAPI whenever a new call appears on the line and when an active call becomes idle (the other party hangs up). You learned how to write code in the TapiCallBack event of the TAPILINE control to watch for and respond to LINE_CALLSTATE messages.

Finally, you learned the importance of getting the call handle from the LINECALLSTATE_OFFERING message and placing this value into the HandleToCall property of the TAPILINE control. This must be done before you can invoke the lineAnswer method to accept the incoming call.

In the next chapter, you'll combine the skills you learned here with the techniques you learned in Chapter 26 for placing outbound calls to build a "virtual phone" for your PC. This application will allow users to place outbound calls and accept inbound calls.

29

Writing TAPI-Assisted Applications

Now that you have a good idea of how the TAPI system is designed, it's time to start writing some TAPI programs! This chapter covers the simplest form of TAPI—the outbound voice-phone call. When you complete this chapter you'll know how to add phone-dialing capabilities to Excel spreadsheets (or any other VBA-compatible system) and you'll build a complete Visual Basic 4.0 online phone book that can store names and numbers, place calls, and log your call history into an Access database for tracking and reporting purposes.

The Assisted Telephony API Calls

Before jumping into the coding routines for Assisted TAPI, it is a good idea to review and test out the two API calls that you'll use throughout the chapter. The two functions you need to work with in order to complete Assisted TAPI calls are:

- `tapiGetLocationInfo`—Returns the current country and city (area) codes set in the `TELEPHON.INI` file.

- `tapiRequestMakeCall`—Initiates a voice-phone call by passing the dialing address (phone number) and other optional parameters including the dialing application to use, the name of the person you are calling, and a comment about the nature of the call.

The TAPI system uses the `tapiGetLocationInfo` to determine the current country/area code settings when attempting to dial a phone number passed in the `tapiRequestMakeCall` function. For example, if the code supplied in the call request includes an area code, TAPI will check to see if it matches the current area code. If the two codes match, TAPI will not dial the area code since it is understood that it is not needed to successfully place a call. This means that you can store complete area code information with all your phone numbers in your address book. Just like you, TAPI is smart enough to skip the area code when it's appropriate.

> **TIP**
>
> Although TAPI's ability to strip out area codes is handy, it can cause minor problems. In several areas of the world, phone companies allow local calls across area codes—especially in locations where both parties live close to one another along the "dividing line." In these cases, TAPI will notice the area code difference and attempt to place the call using the area code. This usually results in error tones from the phone exchange. If you are in an area where this occurs, you'll need to leave out area codes from the affected address entries.

`tapiGetLocationInfo` is a read-only function. You cannot use it to set the current country or area code. However, you can use this function to return the country/area code string to be used as a default in building new entries in an online address book. You'll see how this works later in the chapter.

Testing the Assisted TAPI Functions

For now, let's put together a short project that illustrates the two Assisted TAPI functions you'll use throughout the chapter. You'll need a modem connected to your PC and a telephone handset connected to the same line as the modem. Figure 29.1 shows how the equipment should be connected for all Assisted TAPI calls.

FIGURE 29.1.

Modem, PC, and phone connections for Assisted TAPI.

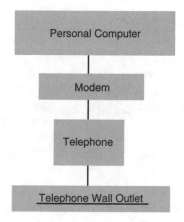

To test the Assisted TAPI functions, start a new Visual Basic 4.0 project and place buttons on the form. Set the caption of Command1 to Get Info and the caption of Command2 to Place Call. Next add a code module to the project (select Insert | Module from the main menu) and add the code shown in Listing 29.1 to the declaration section of the module.

Listing 29.1. Declaring the TAPI functions.

```
Option Explicit

'
' declare assisted tapi functions
'
#If Win32 Then
    Declare Function tapiRequestMakeCall Lib "TAPI32.DLL" (ByVal lpszDestAddress As
➥String, ByVal lpszAppName As String, ByVal lpszCalledParty As String, ByVal
➥lpszComment As String) As Long
    Declare Function tapiGetLocationInfo Lib "TAPI32.DLL" (ByVal lpszCountryCode As
➥String, ByVal lpszCityCode As String) As Long
#Else
    Declare Function tapiRequestMakeCall Lib "TAPI.DLL" (ByVal lpszDestAddress As
➥String, ByVal lpszAppName As String, ByVal lpszCalledParty As String, ByVal
➥lpszComment As String) As Long
    Declare Function tapiGetLocationInfo Lib "TAPI.DLL" (ByVal lpszCountryCode As
➥String, ByVal lpszCityCode As String) As Long
#End If
```

These are the two Assisted TAPI functions in their 16-bit and 32-bit form. If you are only working in one environment, you can remove the extra code. But, if you plan to use this application code in more than one environment, leave the two sets of declares in the file.

Now you need to add code behind the two buttons. Listing 29.2 shows the code for the Command1 (Get Info) button. Add this code to the Command1_Click event.

Listing 29.2. Adding code for the Get Info button.

```
Private Sub Command1_Click()
    '
    Dim lTapi As Long
    Dim cCountry As String * 1
    Dim cCity As String * 3
    '
    lTapi = tapiGetLocationInfo(cCountry, cCity)
    MsgBox Mid(cCountry, 1, 1) + "-(" + Mid(cCity, 1, 3) + ")", 0, "Location Info"
    '
End Sub
```

Pressing this button causes Visual Basic to display a message box showing the current country and city code (area code) stored in the TELEPHON.INI file/registry.Notice the variable declaration sets string sizes for the cCountry and cCity variables. This is needed in order to make sure the tapiGetLocationInfo function returns clean data. You also need to make sure you trim the returned variables. TAPI will return these two variables as zero-terminated strings (the last character is a zero—Chr(0)). Zero characters are unprintable in Visual Basic and can produce unexpected results. It's always a good idea to clean your string upon return from API calls.

The code in Listing 29.3 shows how to place a call using the tapiRequestMakeCall function. Add this code to the Command2_Click event.

Listing 29.3. Adding code for the Place Call button.

```
Private Sub Command2_Click()
    '
    Dim cAddress As String
    Dim lTapi As Long
    '
    cAddress = InputBox("Enter Phone Number to Call:", "Place Call")
    cAddress = Trim(cAddress)
    '
    If Len(cAddress) <> 0 Then
        lTapi = tapiRequestMakeCall(cAddress, "", "", "")
        If lTapi <> 0 Then
            MsgBox "Error placing call!", vbCritical, "TAPI Error Code [" +
➥CStr(lTapi) + "]"
        End If
    End If
    '
End Sub
```

Only the first parameter (the phone number) is required for the `tapiRequestMakeCall` function. The other parameters are optional (dialing application, called party, and comment). You'll use those variables in the Visual Basic 4.0 project at the end of the chapter.

Save the form as `TAPI01.FRM`, the module as `TAPI01.BAS`, and the project as `TAPI01.VBP`. Now run the project. When you click on the `Get_Info` button, you'll see your country and city code. When you click on the `Place_Call` button, you'll be asked to enter a phone number to dial. Visual Basic will hand the number to the TAPI DLL, which will call the default dialer application (`DIALER.EXE`) which will then process the call. You'll hear the phone dialing and see the dialog asking you to pick up the phone and begin speaking.

Those are the basics of Assisted TAPI calls. Now you can use this knowledge to add dialing capabilities to an Excel spreadsheet.

Creating the `QikDial` Application Using Excel 95

It's really quite easy to add outbound dialing to any Excel spreadsheet. Since you only need one API call (`tapiRequestMakeCall`), you have very little code to deal with. All you need is a single declare statement to cover the API call and one subroutine to handle the details of gathering the phone number from the user and calling the API function.

For this chapter, you'll create a very simple phone book using Excel. The example here will allow users to create a two-column table within a worksheet that contains a name in one column and a phone number in the next column. Users can highlight a name and then press an on-screen command button that will then place the call for them.

> **NOTE**
>
> The example illustrated here was done using Excel 95, but the same general idea can be handled in Excel 5.0.

Start Excel and/or open a new workbook. Since you'll be doing a bit of coding, be sure that the Visual Basic toolbar and the Forms toolbar are visible. If not, select View | Toolbars and then place a check mark next to Visual Basic and Forms. Figure 29.2 shows you what your Excel spreadsheet should look like.

The first thing you need to do is add the TAPI function declaration. To do this you must first add a code module to the project. Select Insert | Macro | Module from the main menu or click on the Insert Module icon in the Visual Basic toolbar. Once the module has been added to the project, rename the tab to VBA Code. Now insert the code in Listing 29.4.

FIGURE 29.2.

Adding the Visual Basic and forms tools to Excel.

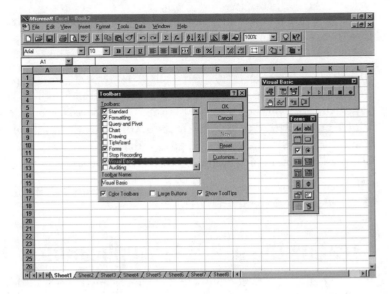

Listing 29.4. Adding the API declare to an Excel module.

```
'
' declare assisted-tapi function
'
Declare Function tapiRequestMakeCall Lib "TAPI32.DLL" (ByVal lpszDestAddress As
String, ByVal lpszAppName As String, ByVal lpszCalledParty As String, ByVal
lpszComment As String) As Long
```

> **WARNING**
>
> This example uses the 32-bit version of the API call. This code will not run under 16-bit Windows environments (Window 3.11 or Windows for Workgroups). If you are using Excel in a 16-bit environment, modify the declare statement to reference `TAPI.DLL` rather than `TAPI32.DLL`.

Now you need to add a small subroutine that will determine the cell selected by the user, locate the associated phone number and then place the call using the TAPI function declared in Listing 29.4. Listing 29.5 shows the code needed for this routine. Place this code in the same module that contains the API declare.

Listing 29.5. Adding the subroutine that makes the call.

```
'
' call number in active cell
'
Sub CallBtn()
    Dim x As Long ' for return
    Dim cPhone As String
    Dim cName As String
    '
    cName = ActiveCell
    cPhone = ActiveCell.Offset(0, 1)
    '
    x = tapiRequestMakeCall(cPhone, "", cName, "")
    '
End Sub
```

You'll notice that this routine passes empty strings for the second and fourth parameters of the API call. These are optional parameters and are not needed for our example. You'll use these extra parameters in the Visual Basic 4.0 example later in this chapter. Now all you need to do is lay out the worksheet page to contain the name/phone number pairs. Figure 29.3 shows one way to lay out the form.

FIGURE 29.3.

Laying out the QikDial *worksheet.*

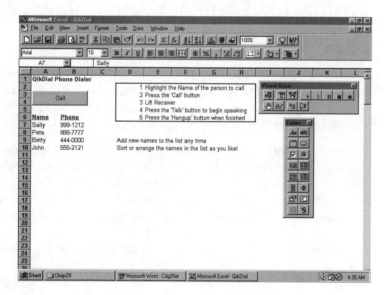

Notice that this worksheet contains a command button. Use the Create Button icon from the Forms toolbar to add the button to the worksheet. When you are prompted to enter the macro associated with this button, be sure to enter the name of the subroutine shown in Listing 29.5 (CallBtn). It doesn't matter where you place things on the form. Just be sure to arrange the Name and Phone columns next to each other. The CallBtn subroutine will only work if the two columns are arranged side-by-side in the proper order. This example also has some friendly instructions to help the first-time user.

Save the file as `QikDial.xls` and then highlight a name and press the `Call` button. You should hear the modem in your PC dialing the number and see a dialog box on your screen that looks like the one in Figure 29.4.

FIGURE 29.4.
Testing the `QikDial`
spreadsheet.

You now have a short set of code that can be added to any VBA-compatible program, including Microsoft Project and Microsoft Access. In the next section, you'll create a complete application in Visual Basic 4.0 that performs basically the same function.

Writing the `TeleBook` Application Using Visual Basic 4.0

`TeleBook` is a sample telephone dialing application that can be used to place voice calls using the modem attached to the PC. Once the phone number has been dialed, a dialog box will appear telling the user to pick up the handset and start talking. The user can then click on another button to hang up the call upon completion.

This project has three forms, one class module, and one basic code module. The main form contains a list box showing the list of all the people in the phone book and a set of pushbuttons that mimic the keys on a standard single-line phone. A set of command buttons appears at the bottom of the form to allow users to add, edit, delete, find, and dial numbers selected from the phone list. Figure 29.5 shows how the form will look when it is completed.

FIGURE 29.5.
Laying out the `TeleBook`
main form.

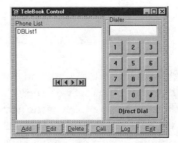

The second form in the project is the phone list entry form. This form appears when the user selects the add or edit buttons on the main form. This is where the user can add or edit `TeleBook` entries (see Figure 29.6).

FIGURE 29.6.

Laying out the phone list entry form.

The last form shows a log of all calls placed using the `TeleBook` application. `TeleBook` saves all call data in a Microsoft Access database for later use. The call history data can be shared with other programs that are capable of reading Microsoft Access files, including Excel, Microsoft Query, and several reporting tools. Figure 29.7 shows the `Call Log` form.

FIGURE 29.7.

Laying out the `Call Log` *form.*

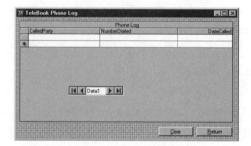

Before laying out the forms, you first need to create the basic code module that contains the TAPI declare statement and the support routines. You also need a class module to encapsulate the API call into an easy-to-use method that allows four property settings.

Creating the `TeleBook` Class Module

Start a new VB4 project and insert a new module. Add the code shown in Listing 29.6. This is the only Telephony API you need for the `TeleBook` application.

Listing 29.6. Adding the Telephony API call.

```
Option Explicit


'
' declare tapi-assist API
'
#If Win16 Then
    Declare Function tapiRequestMakeCall Lib "TAPI.DLL" (ByVal lpszDestAddress As
➥String, ByVal lpszAppName As String, ByVal lpszCalledParty As String, ByVal
➥lpszComment As String) As Long
#Else
    Declare Function tapiRequestMakeCall Lib "TAPI32.DLL" (ByVal lpszDestAddress As
➥String, ByVal lpszAppName As String, ByVal lpszCalledParty As String, ByVal
➥lpszComment As String) As Long
#End If
```

Notice that the code in Listing 29.3 uses the `#If...#Else...#End If` compiler directive. This is done to create a code piece that will compile properly for both 16-bit and 32-bit environments.

Before continuing, save this module as `TBOOK0.BAS` and save the project as `TELEBOOK.VBP`.

Now that the API declare is done, you are ready to build a class module that will encapsulate the API. By writing a class module as a "wrapper" for the API, you'll make your program easier to read and much easier to update in the future—especially if the syntax of the API declare changes in the future.

Insert a class module into your VB project, set its `Name` property to `clsPhoneCall`, and add the code shown in listing 29.7.

Listing 29.7. Coding the `clsPhoneCall` class module.

```
Option Explicit

Dim cDestAddress As String
Dim cAppName As String
Dim cCalledParty As String
Dim cComment As String
```

The code in Listing 29.7 declares four variables used within the class module to keep track of the property values set using the `Property Get` and `Property Let` routines. Next you need to add these routines.

WARNING

Be sure to use the Insert | Property menu option from the Visual Basic main menu. If you simply type Property Get and Property Let in the module, it will not work properly.

Listing 29.8 shows all four sets of Property Get/Property Let statement pairs. Use this listing to build your class module.

Listing 29.8. Coding the `clsPhoneCall` property routines.

```
Public Property Get DestAddress()
    DestAddress = cDestAddress
End Property

Public Property Let DestAddress(vNewValue)
    cDestAddress = vNewValue
End Property

Public Property Get AppName()
    AppName = cAppName
End Property

Public Property Let AppName(vNewValue)
    cAppName = vNewValue
End Property

Public Property Get CalledParty()
    CalledParty = cCalledParty
End Property

Public Property Let CalledParty(vNewValue)
    cCalledParty = vNewValue
End Property

Public Property Get Comment()
    Comment = cComment
End Property

Public Property Let Comment(vNewValue)
    cComment = vNewValue
End Property
```

The last routine you need to add to the class module is a function called RequestMakeCall. Since this function is built within a Visual Basic class module, it will act as a VB method. You'll call this method in the main program (see Listing 29.9).

Listing 29.9. Adding the `RequestMakeCall` function to the class module.

```
Public Function RequestMakeCall() As Long
    RequestMakeCall = tapiRequestMakeCall(cDestAddress, cAppName, cCalledParty,
cComment)
End Function
```

The function in Listing 29.9 calls the API declared in the `TBOOK0.BAS` module by using the four parameters set with the `Property Get`/`Property Let` routines defined in the `clsPhoneCall` class.

Coding the `TeleBook` Main Form

Now it's time to build the onscreen forms for the `TeleBook` application. Use the information in Table 29.1 and Figure 29.5 to build the main form.

There are a few things to be aware of as you build this form. It contains two command button arrays—`cmdKey(0-11)` and `cmdBtn(0-5)`. You can save typing by adding the first button and then using `Edit | Copy`, `Edit | Paste` from the Visual Basic main menu.

Also, be sure to place the `Frame` control on the form before you place any of the controls that appear within the frame. When you place controls in the frame, you must click the control from the toolbox and then *draw* the control within the frame.

Finally, be sure to set the `Data1.DatabaseName` property to point to the `TELEBOOK.MDB` database that ships with the CD-ROM. It can be found in the `CHAP29` directory.

> **NOTE**
>
> If you want to run the project, but don't want to do all the typing, you can find the source code in the `CHAP29` directory. Simply load this project (make sure the data control is set properly) and run it!

Table 29.1. Building the `TeleBook` main form.

Control	Property	Setting
Form	Name	frmTeleBook
	Caption	TeleBook Control
	Height	4515
	Left	1155
	MaxButton	0 - False
	Top	1155
	Width	5370

Control	Property	Setting
CommandButton	Name	cmdBtn
	Caption	&Add
	Font	Arial, 10pt
	Height	315
	Index	0
	Left	120
	Top	3660
	Width	750
CommandButton	Name	cmdBtn
	Caption	&Edit
	Font	Arial, 10pt
	Height	315
	Index	1
	Left	960
	Top	3660
	Width	750
CommandButton	Name	cmdBtn
	Caption	&Delete
	Font	Arial, 10pt
	Height	315
	Index	2
	Left	1800
	Top	3660
	Width	750
CommandButton	Name	cmdBtn
	Caption	&Call
	Font	Arial, 10pt
	Height	315
	Index	3
	Left	2640
	Top	3660
	Width	750

continues

Table 29.1. continued

Control	Property	Setting
CommandButton	Name	cmdBtn
	Caption	&Log
	Font	Arial, 10pt
	Height	315
	Index	4
	Left	3480
	Top	3660
	Width	750
CommandButton	Name	cmdBtn
	Caption	E&xit
	Font	Arial, 10pt
	Height	315
	Index	4
	Left	4320
	Top	3660
	Width	750
DataBound List	Name	DBList1
	Height	3180
	Left	120
	Top	360
	Width	2955
	Font	Arial, 10pt
	ListField	Name
	BoundColumn	Name
	DataSource	Data1
Data Control	Name	Data1
	DatabaseName	telebook.mdb
	RecordSource	MasterList
	Visible	False
Label Control	Name	Label1
	Caption	Phone List
	Font	Arial, 10pt

Control	Property	Setting
	Height	255
	Left	120
	Top	120
	Width	2955
Frame Control	Name	Frame1
	Caption	Dialer
	Font	Arial, 10pt
	Height	3555
	Left	3180
	Top	0
	Width	1935
TextBox Control	Name	txtDial
	Alignment	1 - Right Justify
	Font	Arial, 10pt
	Height	375
	Left	120
	Top	300
	Width	1635
CommandButton	Name	cmdKey
	Caption	1
	Font	MS Sans Serif, 10pt Bold
	Height	450
	Index	0
	Left	120
	Top	840
	Width	450
CommandButton	Name	cmdKey
	Font	MS Sans Serif, 10pt Bold
	Caption	2
	Height	450
	Index	1
	Left	720

continues

Table 29.1. continued

Control	Property	Setting
	Top	840
	Width	450
CommandButton	Name	cmdKey
	Font	MS Sans Serif, 10pt Bold
	Caption	3
	Height	450
	Index	2
	Left	1320
	Top	840
	Width	450
CommandButton	Name	cmdKey
	Caption	4
	Font	MS Sans Serif, 10pt Bold
	Height	450
	Index	3
	Left	120
	Top	1380
	Width	450
CommandButton	Name	cmdKey
	Font	MS Sans Serif, 10pt Bold
	Caption	5
	Height	450
	Index	1
	Left	720
	Top	1380
	Width	450
CommandButton	Name	cmdKey
	Font	MS Sans Serif, 10pt Bold
	Caption	6
	Height	450
	Index	5
	Left	1320

Control	Property	Setting
	Top	1380
	Width	450
CommandButton	Name	cmdKey
	Caption	7
	Font	MS Sans Serif, 10pt Bold
	Height	450
	Index	6
	Left	120
	Top	1920
	Width	450
CommandButton	Name	cmdKey
	Font	MS Sans Serif, 10pt Bold
	Caption	8
	Height	450
	Index	7
	Left	720
	Top	1920
	Width	450
CommandButton	Name	cmdKey
	Font	MS Sans Serif, 10pt Bold
	Caption	9
	Height	450
	Index	8
	Left	1320
	Top	1920
	Width	450
CommandButton	Name	cmdKey
	Caption	*
	Font	MS Sans Serif, 10pt Bold
	Height	450
	Index	9
	Left	120

continues

Table 29.1. continued

Control	Property	Setting
	Top	2460
	Width	450
CommandButton	Name	cmdKey
	Font	MS Sans Serif, 10pt Bold
	Caption	0
	Height	450
	Index	10
	Left	720
	Top	2460
	Width	450
CommandButton	Name	cmdKey
	Font	MS Sans Serif, 10pt Bold
	Caption	#
	Height	450
	Index	11
	Left	1320
	Top	2460
	Width	450
CommandButton	Name	cmdDial
	Caption	Direct Dial
	Font	Arial, 10pt Bold
	Height	450
	Left	120
	Top	3000
	Width	1635

Now that the form controls have been placed, there are six form events that need to be coded and two form-level variables that must be declared. Open the code window of the form and add the code in Listing 29.10 in the general declaration area.

Listing 29.10. Declaring the form-level variables for frmTeleBook.

```
Option Explicit
```

'

```
' form level vars
'
Dim nWidth As Integer
Dim nHeight As Integer
```

Next add the code for the Form_Load event of the form (see Listing 29.11). If you are not saving the code in the same directory that contains the TELEBOOK.MDB database, you need to modify the line that sets the Data1.DatabaseName property to point to the directory that contains the database.

Listing 29.11. Coding the Form_Load event.

```
Private Sub Form_Load()
    nWidth = Me.Width
    nHeight = Me.Height
    Data1.DatabaseName = App.Path + "\telebook.mdb"
    Data1.RecordSource = "MasterList"
    frmTBLog.Data1.DatabaseName = App.Path + "\telebook.mdb"
    frmTBLog.Data1.RecordSource = "PhoneLog"
End Sub
```

The first two lines of code in Listing 29.11 store the form's initial width and height. This will be used in the resize event to override users who attempt to resize the form. This could be done by setting the form's BorderStyle property to something other than 2 (Sizable). However, other styles do not allow the minimize button to appear. Because we want to allow users to minimize the TeleBook (to keep it handy!), we'll use this workaround to prevent users from resizing the form.

Listing 29.12 shows the code for the Form_Resize event that uses the variables we are talking about. Add this code to the main form.

Listing 29.12. Adding the Form_Resize event code.

```
Private Sub Form_Resize()
    '
    ' override resizing
    '
    If Me.WindowState <> vbMinimized Then
        Me.Width = nWidth
        Me.Height = nHeight
        '
        Me.Left = (Screen.Width - Me.Width) / 2
        Me.Top = (Screen.Height - Me.Height) / 2
        '
    End If
    '
End Sub
```

The main code for the TeleBook form is contained in the cmdBtn_Click event. This is where all the command button clicks are handled. Listing 29.13 shows the code needed to handle the Add, Edit, Delete, Call, Log, and Exit buttons for the form.

> **NOTE**
>
> This routine contains calls to four support routines (ClearRec, SaveRec, LoadRec, and CallRec). You'll build these routines as the last step in the project. If you attempt to run the program before you build these routines, you'll get an error message.

Listing 29.13. Coding the cmdBtn_Click event.

```
Private Sub cmdBtn_Click(Index As Integer)
    '
    ' handle button selection
    '
    Dim cName As String
    Dim nAns As Integer
    Dim lReturn As Boolean
    '
    Select Case Index
        Case Is = 0 ' add
            ClearRec ' clear input form
            frmTbMaster.Show vbModal
            If frmTbMaster.SaveFlag = True Then
                SaveRec frmTbMaster.txtFields(0), "ADD"
            End If
        Case Is = 1 ' edit
            cName = DBList1.BoundText
            If Len(Trim(cName)) = 0 Then
                MsgBox "Select a Name to Edit", vbExclamation, "Edit Error"
            Else
                If LoadRec(cName) Then
                    frmTbMaster.Show vbModal
                    If frmTbMaster.SaveFlag = True Then
                        SaveRec cName, "EDIT"
                    End If
                End If
            End If
        Case Is = 2 ' delete
            cName = DBList1.BoundText
            If Len(Trim(cName)) = 0 Then
                MsgBox "Select a Name to Delete", vbExclamation, "Delete Error"
            Else
                nAns = MsgBox("Remove [" + cName + "] from TeleBook?", vbYesNo +
➥vbInformation, "Delete Entry")
                If nAns = vbYes Then
                    Data1.Recordset.FindFirst "Name='" + cName + "'"
                    If Data1.Recordset.NoMatch = False Then
                        Data1.Recordset.Delete
                    End If
                End If
            End If
        Case Is = 3 ' call
```

```
            cName = DBList1.BoundText
            If Len(Trim(cName)) = 0 Then
                MsgBox "Select a Name to Call", vbExclamation, "Call Error"
            Else
                Data1.Recordset.FindFirst "Name='" + cName + "'"
                If Data1.Recordset.NoMatch = False Then
                    ' update master list
                    Data1.Recordset.Edit
                    Data1.Recordset.Fields("LastCalled") = Now
                    Data1.Recordset.Update
                    ' update phone log
                    frmTBLog.Data1.Recordset.AddNew
                    frmTBLog.Data1.Recordset.Fields("CalledParty") =
➥Data1.Recordset.Fields("Name")
                    frmTBLog.Data1.Recordset.Fields("NumberDialed") =
➥Data1.Recordset.Fields("Phone")
                    frmTBLog.Data1.Recordset.Fields("DateCalled") = Now
                    frmTBLog.Data1.Recordset.Update
                    ' now place call
                    CallRec
                End If
            End If
        Case Is = 4 ' show call log
            frmTBLog.Show vbModal
        Case Is = 5 ' exit
            Unload frmTbMaster
            Unload Me
            End
    End Select
    '
    Me.Data1.Refresh
    DBList1.Refresh
    '
End Sub
```

The code needed to handle the phone keypad buttons is much simpler than the code shown in Listing 29.13. Add the code shown in Listing 29.14 to the cmdKey_Click event.

Listing 29.14. Coding the cmdKey_Click event.

```
Private Sub cmdKey_Click(Index As Integer)
    '
    ' handle phone key presses
    '
    txtDial = Trim(txtDial) + Mid("123456789*0#", Index + 1, 1)
    '
End Sub
```

The code in Listing 29.14 takes the Index property of the cmdKey button and uses that as a pointer into a string that contains all the associated digits.

Another short code routine is the one in the DBList1_DblClick event. This code simply mimics the pressing of the Edit button whenever the user double-clicks a name in the phone list. Add the code shown in Listing 29.15.

Listing 29.15. Coding the `DBList1_DblClick` event.

```
Private Sub DBList1_DblClick()
    '
    cmdBtn_Click 1 ' send "Edit message"
    '
End Sub
```

The last bit of code for this form is the one that actually makes the phone call (finally!). Listing 29.16 shows the code needed for the `cmdDial_Click` event. This event reads the phone number entered into the `txtDial` control from the direct keypad and passes that to the properties of the new `clsPhoneCall` object. Once the properties are set, the `RequestMakeCall` method is invoked on the `clsPhoneCall` object.

Listing 29.16. Coding the `cmdDial_Click` event.

```
Private Sub cmdDial_Click()
    '
    ' handle direct dial from keypad
    '
    Dim lTapi As Long
    Dim TBCall As New ClsPhoneCall
    Dim cPhone As String
    '
    cPhone = Trim(txtDial.Text)
    If Len(cPhone) = 0 Then
        MsgBox "Enter a Number to Dial", vbExclamation, "Direct Dial Error"
    Else
        TBCall.DestAddress = cPhone
        TBCall.CalledParty = "Direct Dial"
        TBCall.AppName = "dialer.exe"
        '
        lTapi = TBCall.RequestMakeCall
    End If
    '
End Sub
```

That completes the code for the `frmTeleBook` form. Save the form as `TBOOK1.FRM` and save the project. You'll receive errors if you run the project now since there are four support routines called in the `cmdBtn_Click` event that will be defined in the following section.

Coding the `TeleBook` Phone Entry Form

The phone book entry form is used to add or edit phone entries. It contains two large control arrays—`txtFields(0-8)` and `lblLabels(0-8)`. These controls contain the data field contents and the data field names, respectively. Along with the `Save` and `Cancel` buttons, there is an additional invisible label control used as a flag value read from the main form. Use the information in Table 29.2 and Figure 29.6 to build the data table entry form.

Table 29.2. Controls for the `frmTbMaster` data entry form.

Control	Property	Setting
Form	Name	frmTbMaster
	BorderStyle	3 - Fixed Dialog
	Caption	TeleBook Entry
	Font	Arial, 10pt
	Height	5925
	Left	1785
	Top	1140
	Width	4590
CommandButton	Name	cmdBtn
	Caption	&Cancel
	Height	350
	Index	1
	Left	3180
	Top	5040
	Width	1200
CommandButton	Name	cmdBtn
	Caption	&Save
	Height	350
	Index	0
	Left	1860
	Top	5040
	Width	1200
Label Control	Name	lblLabels
	Caption	Name:
	Height	255
	Index	0
	Left	120
	Top	120
	Width	1200
Label Control	Name	lblLabels
	Caption	Address:

continues

Table 29.2. continued

Control	Property	Setting
	Height	600
	Index	1
	Left	120
	Top	540
	Width	1200
Label Control	Name	lblLabels
	Caption	City:
	Height	255
	Index	2
	Left	120
	Top	1200
	Width	1200
Label Control	Name	lblLabels
	Caption	StateProv:
	Height	255
	Index	3
	Left	120
	Top	1620
	Width	1200
Label Control	Name	lblLabels
	Caption	PostalCode:
	Height	255
	Index	4
	Left	120
	Top	2040
	Width	1200
Label Control	Name	lblLabels
	Caption	Country:
	Height	255
	Index	5
	Left	120

Control	Property	Setting
	Top	2505
	Width	1200
Label Control	Name	lblLabels
	Caption	Phone:
	Height	255
	Index	6
	Left	120
	Top	2940
	Width	1200
Label Control	Name	lblLabels
	Caption	Notes:
	Height	1110
	Index	7
	Left	120
	Top	3405
	Width	1200
Label Control	Name	lblLabels
	Caption	Last Called:
	Height	255
	Index	8
	Left	120
	Top	4560
	Width	1200
Text Box	Name	txtFields
	Height	360
	Index	0
	Left	1380
	Top	105
	Width	3000
Text Box	Name	txtFields
	Height	600
	Index	1

continues

Table 29.2. continued

Control	Property	Setting
	Left	1380
	MultiLine	-1 (True)
	ScrollBars	2 (Vertical)
	Top	540
	Width	3000
Text Box	Name	txtFields
	Height	360
	Index	2
	Left	1380
	Top	1200
	Width	3000
Text Box	Name	txtFields
	Height	360
	Index	3
	Left	1380
	Top	1620
	Width	3000
Text Box	Name	txtFields
	Height	360
	Index	4
	Left	1380
	Top	2040
	Width	3000
Text Box	Name	txtFields
	Height	360
	Index	5
	Left	1380
	Top	2475
	Width	3000
Text Box	Name	txtFields
	Height	360

Control	Property	Setting
	Index	6
	Left	1380
	Top	2925
	Width	3000
Text Box	Name	txtFields
	Height	1140
	Index	7
	Left	1380
	MultiLine	-1 (True)
	ScrollBars	2 (Vertical)
	Top	3360
	Width	3000
Text Box	Name	txtFields
	Height	360
	Index	8
	Left	1380
	Top	4560
	Width	3000
Label Control	Name	SaveFlag
	Visible	0 (False)

Once you complete the form design, save the form as `TBOOK2.FRM`.

Only two events need some code. Listing 29.17 shows the code needed for both the `Form_Load` event and the `cmdBtn_Click` event of the `frmTbMaster` form.

Listing 29.17. Adding the code for the `frmTbMaster` form.

```
Private Sub cmdBtn_Click(Index As Integer)
    '
    ' handle button select
    '
    If Index = 0 Then
        SaveFlag = True
    Else
        SaveFlag = False
    End If
    '
```

continues

Listing 29.17. continued

```
    Me.Hide
    '
End Sub


Private Sub Form_Load()
    '
    Me.Left = (Screen.Width - Me.Width) / 2
    Me.Top = (Screen.Height - Me.Height) / 2
    '
End Sub
```

After entering the code from Listing 29.17, save the form as TBOOK2.FRM and save the project before continuing.

Coding the Phone Log Form for TeleBook

The last form in the project is the Phone Log. This form shows a list of all the calls made using the TeleBook application. Use the data in Table 29.3 and Figure 29.7 to build the form.

Table 29.3. Controls for the frmTBLog form.

Control	Property	Setting
Form	Name	frmTBLog
	BorderStyle	3 - Fixed Dialog
	Caption	TeleBook Phone Log
	Height	4545
	Left	1065
	Top	1485
	Width	7650
CommandButton	Name	Command1
	Caption	&Clear
	Height	300
	Index	0
	Left	4860
	Top	3720
	Width	1200
CommandButton	Name	Command1
	Caption	&Return

Control	Property	Setting
	Height	300
	Index	1
	Left	4860
	Top	3720
	Width	1200
DBGrid	Name	DBGrid1
	Height	3435
	Left	120
	Top	120
	Width	7275
Data Control	Name	Data1
	Connect	Access
	DatabaseName	\CDG\CHAP29\TELEBOOK.MDB
	RecordSource	PhoneLog

NOTE

Be sure to change the DatabaseName property of the Data1 control to point to the directory on your workstation that holds the TELEBOOK.MDB file that was installed from the CD-ROM that ships with this book.

There are only two code routines needed for the frmTBLog form. The first just centers the form at load time. Add the code in Listing 29.18 to the Form_Load event.

Listing 29.18. Adding the code to the Form_Load event.

```
Private Sub Form_Load()
    '
    Me.Left = (Screen.Width - Me.Width) / 2
    Me.Top = (Screen.Height - Me.Height) / 2
    '
End Sub
```

Finally, add the code in Listing 29.19 behind the Command1_Click event of the two-button control array.

Listing 29.19. Adding code to the `click` event of the button array.

```
Private Sub Command1_Click(Index As Integer)
    '
    ' handle button press
    '
    Dim nCount As Integer
    Dim nLoop As Integer
    '
    Select Case Index
        Case Is = 0 ' clear log
            MousePointer = vbHourglass
            nCount = Data1.Recordset.RecordCount
            For nLoop = 1 To nCount
                Data1.Recordset.MoveFirst
                Data1.Recordset.Delete
            Next nLoop
            MousePointer = vbDefault
        Case Is = 1 ' exit form
            Unload Me
    End Select
    '
End Sub
```

The first case (`Case Is = 0`) handles the process of deleting all existing records in the log table. The second case exits the form.

Coding the Support Routines for the `TeleBook` Application

There are four support routines needed to complete the `TeleBook` project. Three of these routines deal with reading and writing phone book data records. The fourth routine uses the `clsPhoneCall` object to place a call.

Open the `TBOOK0.BAS` module and insert a new subroutine called `ClearRec`. This routine will be used to clear the data entry fields before adding a new record. Add the code in Listing 29.20.

Listing 29.20. Coding the `ClearRec` support routine.

```
Public Sub ClearRec()
    '
    ' clear input form
    '
    Dim nFlds As Integer
    Dim X As Integer
    '
    nFlds = frmTeleBook.Data1.Recordset.Fields.Count
    For X = 0 To nFlds - 1
        frmTbMaster.txtFields(X) = ""
    Next X
    '
End Sub
```

Next, add the routine needed to read an existing record from the database into the input form. Insert a new function called `LoadRec` and add the code in Listing 29.21. Be sure to modify the function declaration line to include the string parameter and the `As Boolean` return declaration.

Listing 29.21. Coding the `LoadRec` support function.

```
Public Function LoadRec(cTBName As String) As Boolean
    '
    ' load record data from
    ' frmTelebook to frmTbMaster
    '
    Dim nFlds As Integer
    Dim X As Integer
    Dim lReturn As Boolean

    frmTeleBook.Data1.Recordset.FindFirst "Name='" + cTBName + "'"
    If frmTeleBook.Data1.Recordset.NoMatch = False Then
        nFlds = frmTeleBook.Data1.Recordset.Fields.Count
        For X = 0 To nFlds - 1
            frmTbMaster.txtFields(X) = frmTeleBook.Data1.Recordset.Fields(X)
        Next X
        lReturn = True
    Else
        lReturn = False
    End If
    '
    LoadRec = lReturn
    '
End Function
```

The next routine needed is the one that writes the updated input data back to the data table. Insert the `SaveRec` subroutine and add the code shown in Listing 29.22. Be sure to add the two parameters to the declaration line.

Listing 29.22. Coding the `SaveRec` support routine.

```
Public Sub SaveRec(cTBName As String, cAction As String)
    '
    ' move data from frmTBMaster
    ' to frmTeleBook.data1
    '
    Dim nFlds As Integer
    Dim X As Integer
    '
    cAction = UCase(cAction)
    If cAction = "ADD" Then
        frmTeleBook.Data1.Recordset.AddNew
    Else
        frmTeleBook.Data1.Recordset.FindFirst "Name='" + cTBName + "'"
        If frmTeleBook.Data1.Recordset.NoMatch = False Then
```

continues

Listing 29.22. continued

```
            frmTeleBook.Data1.Recordset.Edit
        Else
            frmTeleBook.Data1.Recordset.AddNew
        End If
    End If
    '
    nFlds = frmTeleBook.Data1.Recordset.Fields.Count
    For X = 0 To nFlds - 1
        frmTeleBook.Data1.Recordset.Fields(X) = frmTbMaster.txtFields(X)
    Next X
    '
    frmTeleBook.Data1.Recordset.Update
    '
End Sub
```

The final routine of the project is used to place a call from the command button array on the main form. Insert a new subroutine called `CallRec` and add the code shown in Listing 29.23.

Listing 29.23. Coding the `CallRec` support routine.

```
Public Sub CallRec()
    '
    ' call the book entry
    '
    Dim lTapi As Long                   ' return value
    Dim TBCall As New ClsPhoneCall      ' declare new object
    '
    TBCall.DestAddress = frmTeleBook.Data1.Recordset.Fields("Phone")
    TBCall.CalledParty = frmTeleBook.Data1.Recordset.Fields("Name")
    TBCall.AppName = "Dialer.exe"        ' set service provider
    '
    lTapi = TBCall.RequestMakeCall       ' make the call
End Sub
```

After entering this routine, save the `TBOOK0.BAS` module and save the project. Run the project to check for errors and correct any problems before you create a compiled version of the `TeleBook` application.

Running the `TeleBook` TAPI Application

You are now ready to run the `TeleBook` application. When you first start the application, you'll see an empty phone list and the phone keypad. You can dial a number by clicking on the keypad, then click the `Direct Dial` button. Once you click the dialing button, you'll see the Windows `DIALER.EXE` program start and show you the number you are dialing along with the name of the person you are calling (see Figure 29.8).

FIGURE 29.8.

The TeleBook *application in action.*

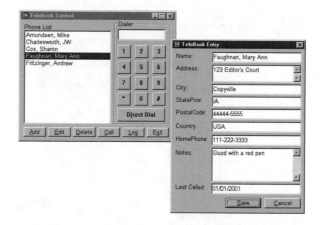

You can also click on the Add button at the bottom of the form to bring up the phone book entry form. When you fill out the form and click the Save button, you'll return to the main form and see the new phone book entry in the phone list. You can dial a name displayed on the phone list by highlighting the name (click once) and then clicking on the Call button.

The same code you used to build this form can be used to add dialing capabilities to all your VB applications.

Summary

In this chapter you learned how to use the Assisted TAPI function (tapiRequestMakeCall) to build outbound voice phone solutions in both Excel and Visual Basic 4.0.

A key point to remember is that the tapiRequestMakeCall function provides Windows applications with access to outbound dialing only.

You now have tools that allow you to add phone dialing to any VBA-compatible application. And you have a complete online phone book that will log all your calls into a Microsoft JET database that can be read, analyzed, and reported by other Windows programs.

This chapter covered the most rudimentary TAPI functions. In the next chapter, you'll learn how to write programs that use the API functions that belong to the Basic TAPI set.

30

Creating TAPI-Enabled Applications

In this chapter, you'll put together all the things you learned about TAPI in a single application. The TAPIFONE application is a complete single-line telephone device that runs on a Windows workstation. With a voice-data modem and sound card and this program up and running on your machine, you can completely eliminate the telephone handset from your desk.

In this program you'll add code for handling both inbound and outbound calls. You'll also give users access to the various TAPI dialog boxes and will maintain a set of configuration values for TAPIFONE in the Windows registry. You'll be able to write (and store) call notes on each outbound call made through TAPIFONE.

You'll use Data Access objects to maintain a simple phone book database and you'll also be able to keep track of outbound calls in a call log. This log can be exported to a comma-separated value (CSV) text file that can be loaded into Excel or Word.

When you complete this project you should have a full understanding of TAPI services and how you can use them to build full-featured telephone devices in Visual Basic.

> **NOTE**
>
> The best hardware configuration for this application is a voice-data modem and a sound card with external speakers and a microphone. You can also use this application with a standard modem and an attached telephone handset, but you'll only be able to make outbound calls.

Designing the TAPIFONE Application

The TAPIFONE application is designed to replace the telephone handset that appears on your desktop. As long as your Windows workstation has a voice-data modem or telephony card and an external microphone and speakers, you can use the TAPIFONE for all your in- and outbound voice call processing.

The TAPIFONE project has three forms and three code modules. The forms are:

- frmTAPI—This is the main form. It uses a tab layout with five tabs for dialing, a phone book, reviewing the call log, selecting a line device, and updating setup values.
- frmCall—This is a small dialog box that appears each time the user attempts to place a call. Users will be able to add call notes from this screen or, if needed, cancel the outbound call completely.
- frmVPhone—This is a simple About dialog box that lists the name of the application and its version number.

The three code modules in the project are:

- libTAPI—This BAS library contains a handful of support and helper routines used by the TAPIFONE project. These routines are called by one or more of the forms in the preceding list.

- TAPILine—This is the standard BAS module that contains all the structures, constants, and API routines needed to support the TAPILINE control.

- TAPICall—This is a standard BAS module that contains helper routines from the TAPILine module.

The TAPILine and TAPICall modules need not be keyed in since they are included on the CD-ROM that comes with this book. These are stock structures, constants, and API declares for the TAPILINE control covered earlier in this book (see Chapter 26, "TAPI Tools—Using the TAPILINE Control"). The libTAPI module will be built for this chapter.

> **TIP**
>
> If you do not want to enter all the code, you can locate and load the TAPIFONE project on the CD-ROM that ships with this book.

Along with the standard dial keypad, the TAPIFONE application has a Phone Book page that lists the person's name and phone number along with the last day and time that person was called using TAPIFONE. Users can select a name from this list and press the Dial button directly from the phonebook. As each call is placed, users will be asked to add call notes. These call notes are written to a log that can be viewed online or exported to a comma-delimited text file for further manipulation.

Users can set several TAPIFONE parameters to control the behavior of the application. These control values are stored in the Windows registry and recalled each time the program is run. Values are stored in the HKEY_CURRENT_USER\Software\Visual Basic and VBA Program Settings\TAPIFONE branch of the registry tree. Key values stored there are:

- MinimizeOnStart—When this is set to "1" the TAPIFONE application loads and immediately minimizes itself. Users can click on the application from the start bar to place calls. When a call comes in, the application automatically pops up on the user's workstation. The default is "0."

- Monitor—When this is set to "1" the application automatically opens the selected line device and waits for incoming calls. The default is "0."

- OutLog—When this is set to "1" all outbound calls are sent to the log table. The default is "1."

- ■ `OrigNumber`—This contains the telephone number from which calls are originating. The default is blank.
- ■ `StartPage`—When this is set to "1" the Phone Book page appears upon startup. When this is set to "0" the Dial Pad page appears. The default is "0."
- ■ `Selected`—This is set to the line device number that is used for all in- and outbound voice calls. The default value is "-1."

The `libTAPI` Module

The first step in building the `TAPIFONE` project is to start Visual Basic and create a new project. Load the `TAPILINE.BAS` and `TAPICALL.BAS` modules from a previous project (See Chapters 26 and 28 for more on these modules) by selecting `File | Add File` from the main menu. Once you've added these two BAS modules, save the project as `TAPIFONE.VBP`.

Next you need to add a new module to the project (`Insert | Module`). Set its `Name` property to `LibTAPIWrapper` and save it as `LIBTAPI.BAS`.

First, add some declaration code to the module. You need to declare a handful of public variables to handle flags and global values for the project. You'll also add two private (module-level) variables used to handle TAPI device information. Finally, you'll add a user-defined type to make it easy to place outbound calls. Open the declaration section of the form and enter the code shown in Listing 30.1.

Listing 30.1. Adding the declaration code to the `LIBTAPI` module.

```
'
Private udtLineDevCaps() As LINEDEVCAPS
Private cLineDevCapsExtra() As String * 2048
'
Public gDialString As String ' phone number to dial
Public gPlaceCall As Boolean ' ok to place call
Public gName As String ' name to call
Public gLineDev As Integer ' selected line device
'
Public gMinimize As Integer ' minimize at start
Public gMonitor As Integer ' monitor at startup
Public gOutLog As Integer ' log all outbound calls
Public gOrigNumber As String ' for calledID
Public gStartPage As Integer ' for default start page
'
Type DialParams
    DeviceNumber As Integer
    DialableString As String
    Privilege As Long
    MediaMode As Long
End Type
```

Next, add the routine to handle the initialization of TAPI services for the application. This routine will actually perform three things:

- Initialize TAPI services (calls `lineInitialize`)
- Verify the API version (calls `lineNegotiateAPIVersion`)
- Collect the line device capabilities (call `lineGetDevCaps`)

Add a new function called `initTAPI` to your project and enter the code shown in Listing 30.2.

Listing 30.2. Adding the `initTAPI` function.

```
Public Function InitTAPI(ctrl As Control, cAppName As String) As Long
    '
    ' perform initial startup of TAPI services
    '
    Dim lRtn As Long
    Dim iNumDev As Long
    Dim iLoop As Integer
    '
    TAPIClearHandles ctrl ' keep it clean!
    '
    ' start it up
    lRtn = ctrl.LineInitialize(cAppName)
    If lRtn < 0 Then
        GoTo TAPIErr
    End If
    '
    ' confirm devices
    iNumDev = ctrl.NumDevices
    For iLoop = 0 To iNumDev - 1
        lRtn = ctrl.LineNegotiateAPIVersion(iLoop, 65536, 65540)
        If lRtn < 0 Then
            GoTo TAPIErr
        End If
    Next
    '
    ' fill line device capabilities structures
    ReDim Preserve udtLineDevCaps(iNumDev)
    ReDim Preserve cLineDevCapsExtra(iNumDev)
    '
    For iLoop = 0 To iNumDev - 1
        lRtn = ctrl.LineGetDevCaps(iLoop)
        If lRtn = 0 Then
            LineDevCapsFunc TAPI_READ, udtLineDevCaps(iLoop),
➥cLineDevCapsExtra(iLoop)
            cLineDevCapsExtra(iLoop) = Clean(cLineDevCapsExtra(iLoop))
        End If
    Next
    '
    GoTo TAPIExit
    '
TAPIErr:
```

continues

Listing 30.2. continued

```
    MsgBox "Unable to Start TAPI Services", vbCritical, "InitTAPI"
    End
    '
TAPIExit:
    InitTAPI = lRtn
    '
End Function
```

You'll notice that there are two parameters for the function. The first is the TAPILINE control used on the main form. The second is the application name when initializing TAPI services. You'll also notice that this routine loads the capabilities of each device and stores that information in a private array. This array can be accessed using another function to be defined later in this section.

> **NOTE**
>
> You might be thinking this kind of code should be placed in a Visual Basic class module. And you'd be right—except for one little thing. Since the TAPILINE control must be placed on a form, we cannot use a class module to handle properties and methods on the control. Forms and controls cannot be encapsulated in class modules.

Next, you need to add the routine used to read the device capabilities stored in the udtLineDevCaps array. Add a new function to the project called ReadLineDevCaps and add the code shown in Listing 30.3.

Listing 30.3. Adding the ReadLineDevCaps function.

```
Public Function ReadLineDevCaps(iDevNum As Integer, udtLineDev As LINEDEVCAPS,
➥cExtra As String) As Long
    '
    ' return line caps
    '
    On Error GoTo LocalErr
    '
    Dim lRtn As Long
    '
    lRtn = 0
    udtLineDev = udtLineDevCaps(iDevNum)
    cExtra = Trim(cLineDevCapsExtra(iDevNum))
    '
    Exit Function
    '
LocalErr:
    lRtn = Err
    '
End Function
```

Next add the routine that will be called to place an outbound call. Add a new function called TAPIDial and enter the code from Listing 30.4.

Listing 30.4. Adding the TAPIDial function.

```
Public Function TAPIDial(ctrl As Control, dpType As DialParams) As Long
    '
    ' dial a selected number
    '
    Dim lRtn As Long
    '
    lRtn = ctrl.LineOpen(dpType.DeviceNumber, 0, dpType.Privilege,
➥dpType.MediaMode)
    If lRtn < 0 Then
        TAPIDial = lRtn
        Exit Function
    End If
    '
    SetCallParams dpType.MediaMode ' load defaults
    '
    ' place the call
    lRtn = ctrl.LineMakeCall(dpType.DialableString, 1)
    '
    TAPIDial = lRtn
    '
End Function
```

You'll notice that this routine uses the DialParams user-defined type. It also calls another custom routine—SetCallParams. You'll define this next. Add a new subroutine called SetCallParams to the project and enter the code shown in Listing 30.5.

Listing 30.5. Adding the SetCallParams routine.

```
Public Sub SetCallParams(lMode As Long)
    '
    ' set up call params data
    '
    Dim cp As LINECALLPARAMS
    Dim cpx As String
    '
    ' defaults for voice calls
    cp.dwBearerMode = LINEBEARERMODE_VOICE
    cp.dwMinRate = 9.6
    cp.dwMaxRate = 28.8
    cp.dwMediaMode = lMode
    cp.dwCallParamFlags = 0
    cp.dwAddressMode = lMode
    cp.DialParams.dwDialPause = 0
```

continues

Listing 30.5. continued

```
    cp.DialParams.dwDialSpeed = 0
    cp.DialParams.dwDigitDuration = 0
    cp.DialParams.dwWaitForDialtone = 0
    cp.dwOrigAddressSize = Len(Trim(gOrigNumber))
    cp.dwOrigAddressOffset = 0
    cp.dwCalledPartySize = 0
    cp.dwCommentSize = 0
    cp.dwUserUserInfoSize = 0
    cp.dwHighLevelCompSize = 0
    cp.dwLowLevelCompSize = 0
    cp.dwDevSpecificSize = 0
    '
    cpx = Trim(gOrigNumber)
    cp.dwTotalSize = Len(cp) + Len(cpx)
    LineCallParamsFunc TAPI_WRITE, cp, cpx
    '
End Sub
```

This routine sets an important TAPI structure. This structure contains information about the type of call that will be requested. Notice that the `gOrigNumber` variable is used to fill in the originating address. This will tell those who have caller ID who you are when they receive your calls.

There is one more high-level routine used when placing a call. This is the routine that will fill the `DialParams` structure with the actual number to dial and the type of call to make. Add a new subroutine called `TAPIPlaceCall` to the project and enter the code from Listing 30.6.

Listing 30.6. Adding the `TAPIPlaceCall` routine.

```
Public Sub TAPIPlaceCall(ctrl As Control, cdialtarget As String)
    '
    Dim lRtn As Long
    Dim cMsg As String
    Dim dpValue As DialParams
    '
    dpValue.DeviceNumber = gLineDev
    dpValue.Privilege = LINECALLPRIVILEGE_NONE
    dpValue.MediaMode = LINEMEDIAMODE_INTERACTIVEVOICE
    dpValue.DialableString = cdialtarget ' number to call
    '
    lRtn = TAPIDial(ctrl, dpValue)
    If lRtn < 0 Then
        cMsg = "TAPIDial - " & LineErr(lRtn)
        GoTo LocalErr
    End If
    '
    Exit Sub
    '
```

```
LocalErr:
    If Err <> 0 Then
        lRtn = Err
        cMsg = Error$
    End If
    '
    MsgBox cMsg, vbCritical, "Dialing Err[" & Hex(lRtn) & "]"
    '
End Sub
```

Only three support routines remain to be added. All three deal with the closing down of TAPI services. One, TAPIHangUp is used to gracefully end an active call. The TAPIClearHandles routine cleans up control properties after a call is completed. Finally, the TAPIShutdown routine closes down all TAPI services for the application. Add the three routines shown in Listing 30.7 to your project.

Listing 30.7. Adding TAPIHangUp, TAPIClearHandles, and TAPIShutdown.

```
Public Sub TAPIHangUp(ctrl As Control)
    '
    ' hang up any current call
    '
    ctrl.LineDrop "", 0
    ctrl.LineDeallocateCall
    ctrl.LineClose
    '
End Sub

Public Sub TAPIClearHandles(ctrl As Control)
    '
    ' clean up handles to a call
    '
    ctrl.HandleToCall = 0
    ctrl.LineHandle = 0
    ctrl.AddressID = 0
    '
End Sub

Public Sub TAPIShutdown(ctrl As Control)
    '
    ' close down TAPI services
    '
    ctrl.LineShutdown
    '
End Sub
```

Those are all the routines for the LIBTAPI.BAS module. Be sure to save the module and the project (TAPIFOINE.VBP) before you continue.

frmTAPI—The Main Form

The main form for the TAPIFONE project is the frmTAPI form. This form uses a tabbed dialog box to present five different services from one form:

- The *Dial Pad page* is used to place a call by pressing keys directly, as when using a physical telephone handset.

- The *Phone Book page* presents an online telephone book that users can update and edit. Users can also place outbound calls by selecting a name in the list and pressing the Dial button.

- The *Call Log page* shows a list of all calls made using TAPIFONE. Users can view the log, export it to a text file, or clear it.

- The *Lines page* shows all the TAPI devices recognized for this workstation. Users can select the line device that will be used for all TAPIFONE services.

- The *Setup page* contains a list of all the user configuration values stored in the Windows Registry.

The form also contains a menu that allows users to view information about the application (Help | About), exit the program (File | Exit), and access TAPI configuration dialog boxes (Configure...).

Laying Out the frmTAPI Form

The next few sections show you how to lay out the frmTAPI form. Since a tabbed dialog box is used, you are actually building five different dialog boxes in one. Refer to the figures in each section while adding the controls shown in the accompanying tables. Be sure to add the tab control first and to *draw* all the other controls on the tab control workspace. This will ensure that the other controls are child controls of the tab control.

Before building the details of each tab, you need to add the tab control itself along with a few command buttons. Refer to Table 30.1 and Figure 30.1 when adding these controls.

Table 30.1. Base controls for the frmTAPI form.

Control	Property	Settings
VB.Form	Name	frmTAPI
	Caption	"Form1"
	Left	1635
	LinkTopic	"Form1"
	MaxButton	0'False
	Top	1665
	Width	5685

Control	Property	Settings
VB.CommandButton	Name	cmdButtons
	Caption	"E&xit"
	Height	300
	Index	3
	Left	4140
	TabIndex	39
	Top	3480
	Width	1200
VB.CommandButton	Name	cmdButtons
	Caption	"&Start Monitor"
	Height	300
	Index	0
	Left	180
	TabIndex	33
	Top	3480
	Width	1200
VB.CommandButton	Name	cmdButtons
	Caption	"&Dial"
	Height	300
	Index	1
	Left	1500
	TabIndex	32
	Top	3480
	Width	1200
VB.CommandButton	Name	cmdButtons
	Caption	"&HangUp"
	Height	300
	Index	2
	Left	2820
	TabIndex	31
	Top	3480
	Width	1200

continues

Table 30.1. continued

Control	Property	Settings
TabDlg.SSTab	Name	SSTab1
	Height	3255
	Left	120
	TabIndex	17
	Top	120
	Width	5295
	TabsPerRow	5
	Tabs	5
	Style	1
	TabCaption(0)	"Dial Pad"
	TabCaption(1)	"Phone Book"
	TabCaption(2)	"Call Log"
	TabCaption(3)	"Lines"
	TabCaption(4)	"SetUp"
VB.Label	Name	lblStatus
	BorderStyle	1 'Fixed Single
	Caption	"Label1"
	Height	255
	Left	120
	TabIndex	16
	Top	3900
	Width	5295

After you've added the base controls, save the form as FRMTAPI.FRM before continuing.

The Dial Pad Tab

The first page of the dialog box is the Dial Pad. This provides the user with a keypad similar to that found on desktop phones. The user can also type the phone number directly into the text box, perform a redial on the last number dialed, clear the text box, or use its contents as the start of a new address listing.

Refer to Figure 30.2 and Table 30.2 when laying out this page.

FIGURE 30.1.

Adding the base controls to the frmTAPI *form.*

FIGURE 30.2.

Laying out the Dial Pad page.

WARNING

Be sure to place the Frame control on the dialog page first. Also, you'll want to add the small command buttons using the control array feature of Visual Basic 4.0.

Table 30.2. The Dial Pad page controls.

Control Name	Property	Settings
VB.Frame	Name	FraDial
	Height	2475
	Left	120
	TabIndex	18
	Top	480
	Width	2055
VB.CommandButton	Name	cmdKey
	Caption	"1"

continues

Table 30.2. continued

Control Name	Property	Settings
	Font	
		name="MS Serif"
		charset=0
		weight=700
		size=13.5
	Height	450
	Index	0
	Left	180
	TabIndex	30
	Top	240
	Width	450
VB.CommandButton	Name	cmdKey
	Caption	"2"
	Font	
		name="MS Serif"
		charset=0
		weight=700
		size=13.5
	Height	450
	Index	1
	Left	780
	TabIndex	29
	Top	240
	Width	450
VB.CommandButton	Name	cmdKey
	Caption	"3"
	Font	
		name="MS Serif"
		charset=0
		weight=700
		size=13.5

Control Name	Property	Settings
	Left	1380
	TabIndex	28
	Top	240
	Width	450
VB.CommandButton	Name	cmdKey
	Caption	"4"
	Font	
		name="MS Serif"
		charset=0
		weight=700
		size=13.5
	Height	450
	Index	3
	Left	180
	TabIndex	27
	Top	780
	Width	450
VB.CommandButton	Name	cmdKey
	Caption	"5"
	Font	
		name="MS Serif"
		charset=0
		weight=700
		size=13.5
	Height	450
	Index	4
	Left	780
	TabIndex	26
	Top	780
	Width	450

continues

Table 30.2. continued

Control Name	Property	Settings
VB.CommandButton	Name	cmdKey
	Caption	"6"
	Font	
		name="MS Serif"
		charset=0
		weight=700
		size=13.5
	Height	450
	Index	5
	Left	1380
	TabIndex	25
	Top	780
	Width	450
VB.CommandButton	Name	cmdKey
	Caption	"7"
	Font	
		name="MS Serif"
		charset=0
		weight=700
		size=13.5
	Height	450
	Index	6
	Left	180
	TabIndex	24
	Top	1320
	Width	450
VB.CommandButton	Name	cmdKey
	Caption	"8"
	Font	
		name="MS Serif"
		charset=0
		weight=700
		size=13.5

Control Name	Property	Settings
	Height	450
	Index	7
	Left	780
	TabIndex	23
	Top	1320
	Width	450
VB.CommandButton	Name	cmdKey
	Caption	"9"
	Font	
		name="MS Serif"
		charset=0
		weight=700
		size=13.5
	Height	450
	Index	8
	Left	1380
	TabIndex	22
	Top	1320
	Width	450
VB.CommandButton	Name	cmdKey
	Caption	"*"
	Font	
		name="MS Serif"
		charset=0
		weight=700
		size=13.5
	Height	450
	Index	9
	Left	180
	TabIndex	21
	Top	1860
	Width	450

continues

Table 30.2. continued

Control Name	Property	Settings
VB.CommandButton	Name	cmdKey
	Caption	"0"
	Font	
		name="MS Serif"
		charset=0
		weight=700
		size=13.5
	Height	450
	Index	10
	Left	780
	TabIndex	20
	Top	1860
	Width	450
VB.CommandButton	Name	cmdKey
	Caption	"#"
	Font	
		name="MS Serif"
		charset=0
		weight=700
		size=13.5
	Height	450
	Index	11
	Left	1380
	TabIndex	19
	Top	1860
	Width	450
VB.Label	Name	lblMonitor
	BackStyle	0 'Transparent
	Caption	"Monitoring Inbound Calls"

Control Name	Property	Settings
	Font	name="MS Sans Serif"
		charset=0
		weight=700
		size=8.25
	ForeColor	&H000000FF& (Red)
	Height	735
	Left	2460
	TabIndex	47
	Top	420
	Visible	0 'False
	Width	975
TapilineLib.Tapiline	Name	Tapiline1
	Left	2520
	Top	1080
VB.Image	Name	Image1
	Height	915
	Left	3000
	Stretch	-1 'True
	Top	480
	Width	2055

The Phone Book Tab

The next tab in the form is the Phone Book tab. This tab is a data entry form for the phone book. Users can also press the `Dial` button to place a call from this form. Use Figure 30.3 and Table 30.3 to place the controls on the form.

FIGURE 30.3.
Adding the Phone Book controls.

Table 30.3. The Phone Book page controls.

Control Name	Property	Settings
VB.Data	Name	Data2
	Caption	"Data2"
	Connect	"Access"
	DatabaseName	""
	Exclusive	0 'False
	Height	300
	Left	-72720
	Options	0
	ReadOnly	0 'False
	RecordsetType	1 'Dynaset
	RecordSource	""
	Top	1080
	Visible	0 'False
	Width	1140
VB.Data	Name	Data3
	Caption	"Data3"
	Connect	"Access"
	DatabaseName	""
	Exclusive	0 'False
	Height	300
	Left	-73980
	Options	0
	ReadOnly	0 'False
	RecordsetType	1 'Dynaset
	RecordSource	""
	Top	1800
	Visible	0 'False
	Width	2175
VB.TextBox	Name	txtName
	DataField	"Name"
	DataSource	"Data1"
	Height	300

Control Name	Property	Settings
	Left	-73440
	TabIndex	13
	Text	"Text2"
	Top	2100
	Width	3600
VB.CommandButton	Name	cmdDialPad
	Caption	"&Add to Phone Book"
	Height	300
	Index	2
	Left	2520
	TabIndex	37
	Top	2640
	Width	2400
VB.CommandButton	Name	cmdDialPad
	Caption	"&Clear Dial String"
	Height	300
	Index	1
	Left	2520
	TabIndex	36
	Top	2280
	Width	2400
VB.CommandButton	Name	cmdDialPad
	Caption	"&ReDial Number"
	Height	300
	Index	0
	Left	2520
	TabIndex	35
	Top	1920
	Width	2400
VB.CommandButton	Name	cmdData
	Caption	"R&estore"
	Height	300

continues

Table 30.3. continued

Control Name	Property	Settings
	Index	3
	Left	-74760
	TabIndex	8
	Top	1560
	Width	1200
VB.CommandButton	Name	cmdData
	Caption	"&Update"
	Height	300
	Index	2
	Left	-74760
	TabIndex	9
	Top	1200
	Width	1200
VB.TextBox	Name	txtDialString
	Alignment	1 'Right Justify
	Height	300
	Left	2520
	TabIndex	34
	Text	"Text6"
	Top	1500
	Width	2400
VB.CommandButton	Name	cmdData
	Caption	"&Remove"
	Height	300
	Index	1
	Left	-74760
	TabIndex	10
	Top	840
	Width	1200
VB.CommandButton	Name	cmdData
	Caption	"&Add"
	Height	300

Control Name	Property	Settings
	Index	0
	Left	-74760
	TabIndex	11
	Top	480
	Width	1200
VB.Data	Name	Data1
	Caption	"Data1"
	Connect	"Access"
	DatabaseName	""
	Exclusive	0 'False
	Height	315
	Left	-72600
	Options	0
	ReadOnly	0 'False
	RecordsetType	1 'Dynaset
	RecordSource	""
	Top	1980
	Visible	0 'False
	Width	1695
VB.TextBox	Name	txtLastCalled
	DataField	"Last Called"
	DataSource	"Data1"
	Height	300
	Left	-73440
	TabIndex	15
	Text	"Text2"
	Top	2820
	Width	3600
VB.TextBox	Name	txtPhoneNumber
	DataField	"PhoneNumber"
	DataSource	"Data1"
	Height	300

continues

Table 30.3. continued

Control Name	Property	Settings
	Left	-73440
	TabIndex	14
	Text	"Text2"
	Top	2460
	Width	3600
VB.Image	Name	Image2
	Height	1395
	Left	-71160
	Stretch	-1 'True
	Top	540
	Width	1275
MSDBGrid.DBGrid	Name	DBGrid1
	Bindings	"frmTAPI.frx":B60A
	Height	2295
	Left	-74940
	OleObjectBlob	"frmTAPI.frx":B618
	TabIndex	38
	Top	420
	Width	5115
MSDBCtls.DBList	Name	DBList1
	Bindings	"frmTAPI.frx":BD20
	Height	1425
	Left	-73440
	TabIndex	12
	Top	480
	Width	2175
	_Version	65536
	_ExtentX	3836
	_ExtentY	2514
	_StockProps	77
	ForeColor	-2147483640
	BackColor	-2147483643

Control Name	Property	Settings
	ListField	"Name"
	BoundColumn	"Name"
VB.Label	Name	Label3
	BorderStyle	1 'Fixed Single
	Caption	"Last Called:"
	Height	300
	Left	-74760
	TabIndex	5
	Top	2820
	Width	1200
VB.Label	Name	Label2
	BorderStyle	1 'Fixed Single
	Caption	"Phone Number:"
	Height	300
	Left	-74760
	TabIndex	6
	Top	2460
	Width	1200
VB.Label	Name	Label1
	BorderStyle	1 'Fixed Single
	Caption	"Name:"
	Height	300
	Left	-74760
	TabIndex	7
	Top	2100
	Width	1200

After you've built this page, be sure to save the project before continuing.

The Call Log Tab

The Call Log tab shows the user the list of all calls logged through the TAPIFONE application. Refer to Figure 30.4 and Table 30.4 when you build this page.

FIGURE 30.4.
Building the Call Log page.

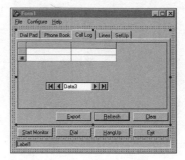

Table 30.4. The Call Log controls.

Control Name	Property	Settings
VB.CommandButton	Name	cmdLog
	Caption	"&Refesh"
	Default	-1 'True
	Height	300
	Index	1
	Left	-72300
	TabIndex	45
	Top	2820
	Width	1200
VB.CommandButton	Name	cmdLines
	Cancel	-1 'True
	Caption	"&Cancel"
	Height	300
	Index	1
	Left	-72300
	TabIndex	43
	Top	2820
	Width	1200
VB.CommandButton	Name	cmdLines
	Caption	"&Apply"
	Height	300
	Index	0

Control Name	Property	Settings
	Left	-70980
	TabIndex	42
	Top	2820
	Width	1200
VB.CommandButton	Name	cmdLog
	Caption	"&Clear"
	Height	300
	Index	0
	Left	-70980
	TabIndex	40
	Top	2820
	Width	1200
VB.Label	Name	Label4
	BackColor	&H00C0C0C0&
	Caption	"Originating Number"
	Height	315
	Left	-74700
	TabIndex	46
	Top	2400
	Width	2175
VB.Label	Name	lblLines
	Caption	"Select a Line Device:"
	Height	255
	Left	-74760
	TabIndex	44
	Top	480
	Width	3555
VB.Image	Name	Image3
	Height	1815
	Left	-71040
	Picture	"frmTAPI.frx":52E4
	Stretch	-1 'True

continues

Table 30.4. continued

Control Name	Property	Settings
	Top	720
	Width	1155
VB.CommandButton	Name	cmdLog
	Caption	"&Export"
	Height	300
	Index	2
	Left	-73620
	TabIndex	48
	Top	2820
	Width	1200

As a safety precaution, save this form before continuing.

The Line Tab

The Line tab allows user to select which line is active for the project. Refer to Figure 30.5 and Table 30.5 when building this page.

FIGURE 30.5.
Adding the Line page.

Table 30.5. The Line page controls.

Control Name	Property	Settings
VB.ListBox	Name	List1
	Height	1815
	Left	-74760
	TabIndex	41
	Top	720
	Width	3615

Control Name	Property	Settings
VB.CommandButton	Name	cmdLines
	Cancel	-1 'True
	Caption	"&Cancel"
	Height	300
	Index	1
	Left	-72300
	TabIndex	43
	Top	2820
	Width	1200
VB.CommandButton	Name	cmdLines
	Caption	"&Apply"
	Height	300
	Index	0
	Left	-70980
	TabIndex	42
	Top	2820
	Width	1200
VB.Label	Name	lblLines
	Caption	"Select a Line Device:"
	Height	255
	Left	-74760
	TabIndex	44
	Top	480
	Width	3555
VB.Image	Name	Image3
	Height	1815
	Left	-71040
	Stretch	-1 'True
	Top	720
	Width	1155

Before building the last tab for this form, save the form and project.

The Setup Tab

The Setup tab contains a small group of controls that are used to update registry settings. Refer to Figure 30.6 and Table 30.6 to build this last page of the form.

FIGURE 30.6.

Building the Setup page.

Table 30.6. The Setup page controls.

Control Name	Property	Settings
VB.Image	Name	Image4
	Height	1875
	Left	-71880
	Picture	"frmTAPI.frx":0442
	Stretch	-1 'True
	Top	420
	Width	1815
VB.CheckBox	Name	chkMinimize
	Alignment	1 'Right Justify
	Caption	"Minimize On StartUp"
	Height	300
	Left	-74700
	TabIndex	52
	Top	1440
	Width	2595
VB.Frame	Name	fraStartup
	Caption	"Startup Page"
	Height	915
	Left	-74700
	TabIndex	49

Control Name	Property	Settings
	Top	480
	Width	2595
VB.OptionButton	Name	optStartup
	Caption	"Phone Book"
	Height	255
	Index	1
	Left	180
	TabIndex	51
	Top	540
	Width	1275
VB.OptionButton	Name	optStartup
	Caption	"Dial Pad"
	Height	255
	Index	0
	Left	180
	TabIndex	50
	Top	240
	Width	1275
VB.CommandButton	Name	cmdStartUp
	Caption	"&Cancel"
	Height	300
	Index	1
	Left	-72300
	TabIndex	0
	Top	2820
	Width	1200
VB.CommandButton	Name	cmdStartUp
	Caption	"&Apply"
	Height	300
	Index	0
	Left	-70980
	TabIndex	1

continues

Table 30.6. continued

Control Name	Property	Settings
	Top	2820
	Width	1200
VB.TextBox	Name	txtOrigNumber
	Height	300
	Left	-72300
	TabIndex	4
	Text	"Text1"
	Top	2400
	Width	2475
VB.CheckBox	Name	chkOutLog
	Alignment	1 'Right Justify
	Caption	"Log all OutBound Calls"
	Height	300
	Left	-74700
	TabIndex	3
	Top	2040
	Width	2595
VB.CheckBox	Name	chkMonitor
	Alignment	1 'Right Justify
	Caption	"Monitor Calls At Start Up"
	Height	300
	Left	-74700
	TabIndex	2
	Top	1740
	Width	2595

This is the last of the dialog pages for the main form. Save the form as `FRMTAPI.FRM` and the project as `TAPIFONE.VBP`.

The `frmTAPI` Menu

The main form also has a set of menu options. These options allow the user to call up TAPI-generated dialog boxes to control communication between TAPI and your programs. Refer to Figure 30.7 and Table 30.7 when building the menu.

FIGURE 30.7.

Building the FRMTAPI *menu.*

Table 30.7. Adding menus to the FRMTAPI event.

Menu	Property	Value
VB.Menu	Name	mnuFile
	Caption	"&File"
VB.Menu	Name	mnuFileExit
	Caption	"E&xit"
VB.Menu	Name	mnuConf
	Caption	"Configure"
VB.Menu	Name	mnuConfItem
	Caption	"&Service Provider..."
	Index	0
VB.Menu	Name	mnuConfItem
	Caption	"&Line Device..."
	Index	1
VB.Menu	Name	mnuConfItem
	Caption	"&Dialing Properties..."
	Index	2
VB.Menu	Name	mnuHelp
	Caption	"&Help"
VB.Menu	Name	mnuHelpAbout
	Caption	"About &TAPILine"
	Index	0

continues

Table 30.7. continued

Menu	Property	Value
VB.Menu	Name	mnuHelpAbout
	Caption	"About &Virtual Phone"
	Index	1

Coding the `frmTAPI` Form

There are several code routines that need to be added to the `frmTAPI` form. These routines fall into four main groups:

- ■ *Form-level routines*—These routines execute when the form is loaded, and exit and act as support for the general form events.
- ■ *Menu-level routines*—These routines execute when a user selects a menu item.
- ■ *Page-level routines*—These routines execute based on user actions on one of the five pages of the Tab dialog box.
- ■ *The Support routines*—These routines are called by one or more other routines on the form.

Coding the Form-Level Routines

The first form-level code is the variable declaration code. Add the code shown in Listing 30.8 to the declaration section of the form.

Listing 30.8. Adding the form-level declarations.

```
Option Explicit
'
Dim lAdd As Boolean ' phonebook adding flag
Dim lMonitor As Boolean ' call monitoring flag
Dim lDevErr As Boolean ' line device select flag
'
Dim iWidth As Integer ' remember my size
Dim iHeight As Integer ' remember
'
Dim uLineDevCaps As LINEDEVCAPS ' line devices
Dim cLineDevCapsExtra As String ' extra data strings
```

Next, add the code for the `Form_Load` event. This code calls several support routines you'll add later. Enter the code from Listing 30.9 into the `Form_Load` event of the form.

Listing 30.9. Adding the `Form_Load` event code.

```
Private Sub Form_Load()
    '
    On Error GoTo LocalErr
    '
    Dim lRtn As Long
    Dim cMsg As String
    '
    ' save for later
    iWidth = Me.Width
    iHeight = Me.Height
    '
    ' initialize TAPI services
    lRtn = InitTAPI(Me.Tapiline1, App.EXEName)
    If lRtn < 0 Then
        cMsg = "InitTAPI - " & LineErr(lRtn)
        GoTo LocalErr
    End If
    '
    LoadImages ' fill in image controls
    InitDB ' set up data connections
    LoadDevices ' get device names
    ReadStartup ' get registry settings
    '
    ' check startup page
    If gLineDev = -1 Then
        SSTab1.Tab = 3 ' gotta select a device first
    Else
        SSTab1.Tab = gStartPage ' user selection
    End If
    '
    ' check monitor at startup
    If gMonitor And gLineDev <> -1 Then
        lblMonitor.Visible = True
        lMonitor = False ' pretend it's off
        cmdButtons_Click 0 ' start monitoring
    End If
    '
    ' check for minimize on startup
    If gMinimize And gLineDev <> -1 Then
        Me.WindowState = vbMinimized
    End If
    '
    ' clean up controls
    txtDialString = ""
    lblstatus = ""
    '
    ' setup this form
    Me.Icon = LoadPicture(App.Path & "\phone04.ico")
    Me.Caption = "TAPILine Virtual Phone"
    Me.Left = (Screen.Width - Me.Width) / 2
    Me.Top = (Screen.Height - Me.Height) / 2
    '
    Exit Sub
    '
```

continues

Listing 30.9. continued

```
LocalErr:
    If Err <> 0 Then
        lRtn = Err
        cMsg = Error$
    End If
    '
    MsgBox cMsg, vbCritical, "Form_Load Err[" & Hex(lRtn) & "]"
    TAPIShutdown Me.Tapiline1
    MousePointer = vbNormal
    End ' that's it!
    '
End Sub
```

Listing 30.10 shows the code for the Form_Resize and Form_Unload events. Add this to your project.

Listing 30.10. Adding the Form_Resize and Form_Unload event code.

```
Private Sub Form_Resize()
    '
    ' prevent resizing
    '
    If Me.WindowState <> vbMinimized _
       And Me.WindowState <> vbMaximized Then
         Me.Width = iWidth
         Me.Height = iHeight
    End If
    '
End Sub

Private Sub Form_Unload(Cancel As Integer)
    '
    TAPIHangUp Me.Tapiline1 ' hangup any open line
    TAPIShutdown Me.Tapiline1 ' close out TAPI Services
    '
End Sub
```

Listing 30.11 shows the code that belongs in the SSTab1_Click event. This is fired each time the user clicks to change a tab. This code will continue to remind the user to select a line device, if needed.

Listing 30.11. Coding the SSTab1_Click event.

```
Private Sub SSTab1_Click(PreviousTab As Integer)
    '
    ' force user to select a device, if needed
    If lDevErr = True Then
```

```
        MsgBox "You must select a Line Device!", vbCritical, "No Line Device"
        SSTab1.Tab = 3
    End If
    '
End Sub
```

The last bit of form-level code is the code for the `Tapiline1_TapiCallBack` event. This code is the same code you used in the TAPIANS project of Chapter 28. Add the code shown in Listing 30.12 to the `TAPICallBack` event of the `TAPILINE` control.

Listing 30.12. Coding the `TAPICallBack` event.

```
Private Sub Tapiline1_TapiCallBack(ByVal hDevice As Long, ByVal dwMessage As Long,
➥ByVal dwInstance As Long, ByVal dwParam1 As Long, ByVal dwParam2 As Long, ByVal
➥dwParam3 As Long)
    '
    ' handle TAPI messages
    '
    Dim cMsg As String
    '
    ' handle inbound call actions
    Select Case dwMessage
        Case LINE_CALLSTATE ' state of call on line changed
            Select Case dwParam1
                Case LINECALLSTATE_OFFERING ' get call handle
                    Tapiline1.HandleToCall = hDevice ' update handle to call
                    Beep ' tell user a call appeared
                    Me.WindowState = vbNormal ' pop up, if needed
                Case LINECALLSTATE_IDLE ' they hung up on me!
                    cmdButtons_Click 2 ' hangup process
                    TAPIClearHandles Me.Tapiline1
            End Select
        Case LINE_CLOSE ' line was closed
            cmdButtons_Click 2 ' force hangup
    End Select
    '
    ' report to status line
    lblstatus = TapiCallBackHandler(hDevice, dwMessage, dwInstance, dwParam1,
➥dwParam2, dwParam3)
    '
End Sub
```

That's it for the form-level code. Save the form and project before continuing.

Coding the Menu-Level Routines

There are three main menu branches. The first is the `File` menu. It has only one submenu—`Exit`. Listing 30.13 shows the code you need to add to the `mnuFileExit_Click` event.

Listing 30.13. Coding the `mnuFileExit_Click` event.

```
Private Sub mnuFileExit_Click()
    '
    Unload Me
    '
End Sub
```

The next branch in the menu tree is the `Configure` branch. This was built as a menu array with three elements. Listing 30.14 shows the code that should be added to the `mnuConfItem_Click` event.

Listing 30.14. Coding the `mnuConfItem_Click` event.

```
Private Sub mnuConfItem_Click(Index As Integer)
    '
    ' handle TAPI configuration dialogs
    '
    Select Case Index
        Case 0 ' service provider
            Tapiline1.PermanentProviderID = 1
            Tapiline1.LineConfigProvider Me.hWnd
        Case 1 ' line device
            Tapiline1.LineConfigDialog 5, Me.hWnd, "tapi/line"
        Case 2 ' dialing properties
            Tapiline1.LineTranslateDialog 5, Me.hWnd, ""
    End Select
    '
End Sub
```

The final menu routine is the one that handles the `Help` menu branch. This branch also contains a menu array for displaying the TAPILINE control About box and a custom About box for the application (you'll build it later). Add the code in Listing 30.15 to the `mnuHelpAbout_Click` event.

Listing 30.15. Coding the `mnuHelpAbout_Click` event.

```
Private Sub mnuHelpAbout_Click(Index As Integer)
    '
    ' handle about boxes
    '
    Select Case Index
        Case 0 ' tapiline
            Me.Tapiline1.AboutBox
        Case 1 ' virtual phone
            frmVPhone.Show vbModal
    End Select
    '
End Sub
```

That's the end of the menu-level routines. Save the form and project before continuing on to the page-level routines.

Coding the Page-Level Routines

There are ten page-level routines in the frmTAPI form. Most of these routines are for handling selections of button array commands. Listing 30.16 shows the code for the cmdButtons_Click event. This handles the button presses on the bottom of the form. Add this code to your project.

Listing 30.16. Coding the cmdButtons_Click event.

```
Private Sub cmdButtons_Click(Index As Integer)
    '
    ' handle user selections on main buttons
    '
    Select Case Index
        Case 0 ' start monitor
            If cmdButtons(0).Caption = "&Start Monitor" Then
                lMonitor = LineMonitor(Me.Tapiline1, True)
            Else
                lMonitor = LineMonitor(Me.Tapiline1, False)
            End If
            '
            If lMonitor = True Then
                cmdButtons(0).Caption = "&End Monitor"
                lblMonitor.Visible = True
            Else
                cmdButtons(0).Caption = "&Start Monitor"
                lblMonitor.Visible = False
            End If
        Case 1 ' Dial Number
            '
            ' check for call monitoring
            If lMonitor = True Then
                cmdButtons_Click 0 ' toggle off monitoring
            End If
            '
            Select Case SSTab1.Tab ' check selected tab
                Case 0 ' dialpad
                    gDialString = txtDialString
                    gName = "<Unknown>"
                    frmCall.Show vbModal
                    If gPlaceCall = True Then
                        TAPIPlaceCall frmTAPI.Tapiline1, gDialString
                    End If
                Case 1 ' phonebook
                    gDialString = txtPhoneNumber
                    gName = txtName
                    frmCall.Show vbModal
                    If gPlaceCall = True Then
                        TAPIPlaceCall frmTAPI.Tapiline1, gDialString
                    End If
```

continues

Listing 30.16. continued

```
                Case 2 ' call log
                    ' no action
                Case 3 ' properties
                    ' no action
            End Select
        Case 2 ' Hang Up
            '
            ' check call monitoring
            If lMonitor = True Then
                cmdButtons_Click 0 ' toggle monitoring off
            End If
            '
            TAPIHangUp Me.Tapiline1
            lblstatus = ""
        Case 3 ' exit
            Unload Me
    End Select
    '
End Sub
```

Next you need to add code to handle the command buttons on the Dial Pad itself. Enter the code from Listing 30.17 into the `cmdDialPad_Click` event.

Listing 30.17. Coding the `cmdDialPad_Click` event.

```
Private Sub cmdDialPad_Click(Index As Integer)
    '
    ' handle user selections on dial pad page
    '
    Select Case Index
        Case 0 ' redial last number
            cmdButtons_Click 1 ' press dial
        Case 1 ' clear dialstring
            txtDialString = ""
        Case 2 ' add a new record to the phone book
            cmdData_Click 0 ' add a new record
            txtPhoneNumber = txtDialString
            txtName.SetFocus
            SSTab1.Tab = 1 ' show page
    End Select
    '
End Sub
```

This same page has the array of command buttons that simulate the telephone handset key-pad. Listing 30.18 shows the code that should be copied into the `cmdKey_Click` event.

Listing 30.18. Coding the `cmdKey_Click` event.

```
Private Sub cmdKey_Click(Index As Integer)
    '
    ' handle user pressing keypad
    '
    Dim cDigit As String
    '
    cDigit = Mid("123456789*0#", Index + 1, 1)
    txtDialString = txtDialString & cDigit
    '
End Sub
```

The Phone Book page has two form-level routines. Listing 30.19 shows the code for handling the button array on the phone book page. Add this to your project.

Listing 30.19. Coding the `cmdData_Click` event.

```
Private Sub cmdData_Click(Index As Integer)
    '
    ' handle data stuff
    '
    Dim x As Integer
    '
    Select Case Index
        Case 0 ' add new
            Data1.Recordset.AddNew
            txtName.SetFocus
            lAdd = True
        Case 1 ' delete
            Data1.Recordset.Delete
            lAdd = False
        Case 2 ' update
            If Trim(txtName) <> "" Then
                Data1.UpdateRecord
            End If
            lAdd = False
        Case 3 ' refresh
            If lAdd = False Then
                Data1.Recordset.UpdateControls
            Else
                Data1.Recordset.CancelUpdate
            End If
            lAdd = False
    End Select
    '
    ' update the list and data table
    If lAdd = False Then
        Data1.Refresh
        Data2.Refresh
        DBList1.Refresh
    End If
    '
```

continues

Listing 30.19. continued

```
    ' enable all buttons
    For x = 0 To 3
        cmdData(x).Enabled = True
    Next x
    '
    ' turn of add/remove if add was pressed
    If lAdd = True Then
        cmdData(0).Enabled = False
        cmdData(1).Enabled = False
    End If
    '
End Sub
```

Listing 30.20 shows the code you need to add to the DBList1_DblClick event.

Listing 30.20. Coding the DbList1_DblClick event.

```
Private Sub DBList1_DblClick()
    '
    ' update data1 with this record
    '
    Dim cName As String
    '
    cName = DBList1.BoundText
    Data1.Recordset.FindFirst "Name='" & cName & "'"
    txtName.SetFocus
    '
End Sub
```

The Call Log page has one event routine—the cmdLog_Click event. Add the code shown in Listing 30.21 to your project.

Listing 30.21. Coding the cmdLog_Click event.

```
Private Sub cmdLog_Click(Index As Integer)
    '
    ' clear all records from the log
    '
    Dim iAns As Integer ' get user's answer
    '
    Select Case Index
        Case 0 ' clear log
            ClearLog
        Case 1 ' refresh dynaset
            Data3.Refresh
        Case 2 ' export data to text file
            ExportLog
    End Select
    '
End Sub
```

The Line page has a single event, too. Add the code from Listing 30.22 to the cmdLines_Click event of the form.

Listing 30.22. Coding the cmdLines_Click event.

```
Private Sub cmdLines_Click(Index As Integer)
    '
    ' handle user selection of line device
    '
    Select Case Index
        Case 0 ' apply
            If List1.ListIndex = -1 Then
                MsgBox "You must select a line device!", vbCritical, "No Line
Selected"
                lDevErr = True
            Else
                gLineDev = List1.ListIndex
                SaveSetting App.EXEName, "LineDevice", "Selected",
CStr(List1.ListIndex)
                lDevErr = False
            End If
        Case 1 ' cancel
            If List1.ListIndex = -1 Then
                MsgBox "You must select a line device!", vbCritical, "No Line
Selected"
                lDevErr = True
            End If
    End Select
    '
End Sub
```

The final page-level routine is the one that handles the Startup page. The code in Listing 30.23 shows what you should add to the cmdStartUp_Click event.

Listing 30.23. Coding the cmdStartUp_Click event.

```
Private Sub cmdStartUp_Click(Index As Integer)
    '
    ' review startup values for application
    '
    Select Case Index
        Case 0 ' apply
            gMinimize = chkminimize
            gMonitor = chkMonitor
            gOutLog = chkOutLog
            gOrigNumber = txtOrigNumber
            gStartPage = IIf(optStartup(0) = True, 0, 1)
            '
            SaveSetting App.EXEName, "Startup", "MinimizeOnStart", gMinimize
            SaveSetting App.EXEName, "Startup", "Monitor", gMonitor
            SaveSetting App.EXEName, "Startup", "OutLog", gOutLog
```

continues

Listing 30.23. Coding the `cmdStartUp_Click` event.

```
          SaveSetting App.EXEName, "Startup", "OrigNumber", gOrigNumber
          SaveSetting App.EXEName, "Startup", "StartPage", gStartPage
          '
      Case 1 ' Cancel
          ' na
    End Select
    '
End Sub
```

That is the end of the page-level routines for the `frmTAPI` form. Save the form and project before continuing.

Coding the Support Routines

There are eight support routines for the `frmTAPI` form. Half of these routines are called from the `Form_Load` event as initialization routines. The rest are called at various times throughout the project.

First, add a new subroutine called `LoadImages` to the form. Then add the code shown in Listing 30.24 to the project.

Listing 30.24. Adding the `LoadImages` routine.

```
Public Sub LoadImages()
    '
    ' fill in image controls
    ' on the pages
    '
    On Error GoTo LocalErr
    '
    ' page 0
    Image1.Picture = LoadPicture(App.Path & "\answmach.wmf")
    ' page 1
    Image2.Picture = LoadPicture(App.Path & "\rolodex.wmf")
    ' page 3
    Image3.Picture = LoadPicture(App.Path & "\clipbord.wmf")
    ' page 4
    Image4.Picture = LoadPicture(App.Path & "\phone.wmf")
    '
    Exit Sub
    '
LocalErr:
    MsgBox Error$, vbCritical, "LoadImages Err [" & CStr(Err) & "]"
    '
End Sub
```

Next, add the `LoadDevices` subroutine. This is the code that loads the device names into the list box on the Lines page. Enter the code from Listing 30.25.

Listing 30.25. Adding the `LoadDevices` routine.

```
Public Sub LoadDevices()
    '
    ' Load line devices into list box
    '
    Dim x As Integer
    Dim lRtn As Long
    '
    For x = 0 To Tapiline1.NumDevices - 1
        lRtn = ReadLineDevCaps(x, uLineDevCaps, cLineDevCapsExtra)
        If lRtn >= 0 Then
            List1.AddItem GetOffset(Len(uLineDevCaps) + 4,
uLineDevCaps.dwLineNameOffset, uLineDevCaps.dwLineNameSize, cLineDevCapsExtra)
        Else
            List1.AddItem "<BAD DEVICE> #" & CStr(x)
        End If
    Next
    '
    gLineDev = CStr(GetSetting(App.EXEName, "LineDevice", "Selected", "-1"))
    List1.ListIndex = gLineDev
    SaveSetting App.EXEName, "LineDevice", "Selected", CStr(List1.ListIndex)
    '
End Sub
```

Next add a new subroutine called `ReadStartUp` to the project and enter the code from Listing 30.26. This code loads the registry values at program startup.

Listing 30.26. Adding the `ReadStartUp` routine.

```
Public Sub ReadStartup()
    '
    ' load startup values
    '
    gMinimize = GetSetting(App.EXEName, "Startup", "MinimizeOnStart", 0)
    gMonitor = GetSetting(App.EXEName, "Startup", "Monitor", 0)
    gOutLog = GetSetting(App.EXEName, "Startup", "OutLog", 1)
    gOrigNumber = GetSetting(App.EXEName, "Startup", "OrigNumber", "")
    gStartPage = GetSetting(App.EXEName, "Startup", "StartPage", 0)
    '
    chkminimize = gMinimize
    chkMonitor = gMonitor
    chkOutLog = gOutLog
    txtOrigNumber = gOrigNumber
    '
    If gStartPage = 0 Then
        optStartup(0) = True
    Else
        optStartup(1) = True
    End If
    '
End Sub
```

The next two routines deal with loading or, if needed, creating the TAPI.MDB database file. First, create a subroutine called InitDB and enter the code from Listing 30.27.

Listing 30.27. Adding the InitDB routine.

```
Public Sub InitDB()
    '
    ' establish initial data connections
    '
    On Error Resume Next ' i'll handle this
    '
    ' see if db exists, if not - make it
    Open App.Path & "\tapi.mdb" For Input As 1
    If Err = 53 Then
        MakeDB ' must create the database!
    Else
        Close #1 ' fine, just checking
    End If
    '
    On Error GoTo LocalErr ' ok, pass them on...
    '
    ' the phone book
    Data1.DatabaseName = App.Path & "\tapi.mdb"
    Data1.RecordSource = "SELECT * FROM TAPI"
    Data1.Refresh
    '
    ' the lookup list
    Data2.DatabaseName = App.Path & "\tapi.mdb"
    Data2.RecordSource = "SELECT Name from TAPI ORDER BY Name"
    Data2.Refresh
    '
    ' the call log
    Data3.DatabaseName = App.Path & "\tapi.mdb"
    Data3.RecordSource = "SELECT Format(CallDate,'general date') AS DateCalled,
Name, NumberCalled, Comment FROM Log ORDER BY Name, CallDate"
    Data3.Refresh
    '
    Exit Sub
    '
LocalErr:
    MsgBox Error$, vbCritical, "InitDB Err [" & CStr(Err) & "]"
    End ' can't start without this!
    '
End Sub
```

The first thing the InitDB routine does is check for the existence of the TAPI.MDB data file. If it does not exist, the MakeDB routine is called to create the database. Add the MakeDB subroutine to the form and enter the code shown in Listing 30.28.

Listing 30.28. Adding the MakeDB routine.

```
Public Sub MakeDB()
    '
    ' create TAPIFONE database
    '
    Dim cMakeTAPI As String
    Dim cMakeLOG As String
    Dim cDBName As String
    Dim ws As Workspace
    Dim db As Database
    '
    ' set db name
    ' and SQL statements
    cDBName = App.Path & "\TAPI.MDB"
    cMakeTAPI = "CREATE TABLE TAPI (Name TEXT(30), PhoneNumber TEXT(20), [Last
Called] DATE)"
    cMakeLOG = "CREATE TABLE LOG (Name TEXT(30), CallDate DATE, NumberCalled
TEXT(20), Comment MEMO)"
    '
    ' create new database
    Set ws = Workspaces(0)
    Set db = ws.CreateDatabase(cDBName, dbLangGeneral)
    '
    ' execute SQL statements
    db.Execute cMakeTAPI, dbFailOnError
    db.Execute cMakeLOG, dbFailOnError
    '
    ' shut things down
    db.Close
    Set db = Nothing
    Set ws = Nothing
    '
    Exit Sub
    '
LocalErr:
    MsgBox Error$, vbCritical, "MakeDB Err [" & Str(Err) & "]"
    End ' gotta stop here!
    '
End Sub
```

The next two routines are called from the Call Log page of the form. Listing 30.29 shows the ClearLog routine. Add this to your project.

Listing 30.29. Adding the ClearLog routine.

```
Public Sub ClearLog()
    '
    ' clear all recs out of log
    '
    On Error GoTo LocalErr
    '
```

continues

Listing 30.29. continued

```
    Dim iAns As Integer
    '
    iAns = MsgBox("Ready to Erase All Log Entries", vbInformation + vbYesNo, "Clear
Call Log")
    If iAns = vbYes Then
        MousePointer = vbHourglass ' tell user you're busy
        '
        Data3.Recordset.MoveFirst ' start at the top
        '
        Do Until Data3.Recordset.EOF ' do until empty
            Data3.Recordset.Delete ' remove a rec
            Data3.Recordset.MoveNext ' go to next one
        Loop ' back to top
        '
        MousePointer = vbNormal ' ok, tell user you're done
        '
        MsgBox "Call Log Cleared", vbInformation ' alter user
    End If
    Exit Sub
    '
LocalErr:
    MsgBox Error$, vbCritical, "ClearLog Err [" & CStr(Err) & "]"
    '
End Sub
```

Listing 30.30 shows the ExportLog routine. This is used to create a text file version of the call log. Add this code to your project.

Listing 30.30. Adding the ExportLog routine.

```
Public Sub ExportLog()
    '
    ' write call log to text file
    '
    Dim cFldDelim As String
    Dim cLine As String
    Dim cFileName As String
    Dim cQuote As String
    '
    cFldDelim = Chr(44)
    cQuote = Chr(34)
    cFileName = App.Path & "\" & App.EXEName & ".log"
    '
    ' create new file
    Open cFileName For Output As 1
    '
    ' write header line
    cLine = "DateCalled,Name,NumberCalled,Comment"
    Print #1, cLine
    '
```

```
    ' export records
    Data3.Recordset.MoveFirst
    Do Until Data3.Recordset.EOF
        With Data3.Recordset
            cLine = cQuote & Trim(.Fields("DateCalled")) & cQuote & cFldDelim
            cLine = cLine & cQuote & Trim(.Fields("Name")) & cQuote & cFldDelim
            cLine = cLine & cQuote & Trim(.Fields("NumberCalled")) & cQuote &
➥cFldDelim
            cLine = cLine & cQuote & Trim(.Fields("Comment")) & cQuote
            Print #1, cLine
            .MoveNext
        End With
    Loop
    Close #1
    '
    MsgBox "Call Log Exported to [" & cFileName & "]", vbInformation, "Log Export"
    '
End Sub
```

The last support routine for the `frmTAPI` form is the `LineMonitor` function. This routine toggles on or off the TAPI call monitoring service. When monitoring is on, TAPIFONE answers the incoming call. Add the code in Listing 30.31 to your form.

Listing 30.31. Adding the `LineMonitor` function.

```
Public Function LineMonitor(ctrl As Control, lMonitor As Boolean) As Boolean
    '
    ' start/stop line monitoring
    '
    Dim lRtn As Long
    '
    If lMonitor = True Then
        lRtn = ctrl.LineOpen(gLineDev, 0, LINECALLPRIVILEGE_OWNER +
➥LINECALLPRIVILEGE_MONITOR, LINEMEDIAMODE_INTERACTIVEVOICE)
        If lRtn < 0 Then
            MsgBox LineErr(lRtn), vbCritical, "Line Monitor Error"
            LineMonitor = False
        Else
            LineMonitor = True
        End If
    Else
        TAPIHangUp ctrl
        LineMonitor = False
    End If
    '
End Function
```

That is all the coding needed for the `frmTAPI` form. Save this form and update the project before you add the Call and About dialog boxes.

The Call and About Dialog Boxes

The Call and About dialog boxes are two small forms that are used to support actions from the frmTAPI form. The Call dialog box appears just before an outbound call is placed. This allows the user to confirm the call and add any call notes if desired.

The About dialog box shows the name of the program, the current version, and other important information about the TAPIFONE application.

Laying Out and Coding the Call Dialog Box

Add a new form to your project and build the Call dialog box shown in Figure 30.8. You can also refer to Table 30.8 when laying out the frmCall form.

FIGURE 30.8.

Laying out the frmCall *form.*

Table 30.8. The frmCall form controls.

Control	Property	Settings
VB.Form	Name	frmCall
	BorderStyle	3 'Fixed Dialog
	Caption	"Ready to Place a Call"
	ClientHeight	3450
	ClientLeft	3090
	ClientTop	1770
	ClientWidth	3780
	Height	3855
	Icon	"frmCall.frx":0000
	Left	3030
	LinkTopic	"Form1"
	MaxButton	0 'False
	MinButton	0 'False
	ScaleHeight	3450

Control	Property	Settings
	ScaleWidth	3780
	ShowInTaskbar	0 'False
	Top	1425
	Width	3900
VB.TextBox	Name	txtNotes
	Height	1575
	Left	960
	MultiLine	-1 'True
	ScrollBars	2 'Vertical
	TabIndex	5
	Text	"frmCall.frx":0442
	Top	1320
	Width	2655
VB.Data	Name	Data1
	Caption	"Data1"
	Connect	"Access"
	DatabaseName	""
	Exclusive	0 'False
	Height	300
	Left	180
	Options	0
	ReadOnly	0 'False
	RecordsetType	1 'Dynaset
	RecordSource	""
	Top	3060
	Visible	0 'False
	Width	1140
VB.CommandButton	Name	cmdCall
	Caption	"&Cancel"
	Height	300
	Index	1
	Left	1080

continues

Table 30.8. continued

Control	Property	Settings
	TabIndex	3
	Top	3000
	Width	1200
VB.CommandButton	Name	cmdCall
	Caption	"&OK"
	Height	300
	Index	0
	Left	2400
	TabIndex	2
	Top	3000
	Width	1200
VB.Label	Name	Label3
	Caption	"Call Notes:"
	Height	195
	Left	1020
	TabIndex	6
	Top	1140
	Width	2595
VB.Label	Name	lblDialString
	Alignment	2 'Center
	Caption	"xxx-xxx-xxxx"
	Font	
		name="MS Sans Serif"
		charset=0
		weight=700
		size=8.25
		underline=0 'False
		italic=0 'False
		strikethrough=0 'False
	Height	300
	Left	0
	TabIndex	4

Control	Property	Settings
	Top	780
	Width	3795
VB.Image	Name	Image1
	Height	1575
	Left	-60
	Picture	"frmCall.frx":0448
	Stretch	-1 'True
	Top	1260
	Width	870
VB.Label	Name	lblName
	Alignment	2 'Center
	Caption	"name"
	Font	
		name="MS Sans Serif"
		charset=0
		weight=700
		size=8.25
		underline=0 'False
		italic=0 'False
		strikethrough=0 'False
	Height	300
	Left	0
	TabIndex	1
	Top	420
	Width	3795
VB.Label	Name	Label1
	Alignment	2 'Center
	Caption	"Placing Call to:"
	Font	
		name="MS Sans Serif"
		charset=0
		weight=700

continues

Table 30.8. continued

Control	Property	Settings
		size=8.25
		underline=0 'False
		italic=0 'False
		strikethrough=0 'False
	`Height`	300
	`Left`	0
	`TabIndex`	0
	`Top`	60
	`Width`	3795

After you finish laying out the `frmCall` form, you need to add three code routines. The first is the `Form_Load` event code. Listing 30.32 shows the code you need to add to the `frmCall` form.

Listing 30.32. Adding the `Form_Load` event code.

```
Private Sub Form_Load()
    '
    ' init stuff
    '
    lblDialString = Trim(gDialString)
    lblname = Trim(gName)
    txtNotes = ""
    Image1.Picture = LoadPicture(App.Path & "\payphone.wmf")
    '
    ' init form stuff
    Me.Caption = "Ready to Place a Call..."
    Me.Icon = LoadPicture(App.Path & "\phone04.ico")
    Me.Left = (Screen.Width - Me.Width) / 2
    Me.Top = (Screen.Height - Me.Height) / 2
    '
    ' handle db connections
    Data1.DatabaseName = App.Path & "\tapi.mdb"
    Data1.RecordSource = "Log"
    Data1.Refresh
    '
End Sub
```

Next you need to add the code shown in Listing 30.33 to the `cmdCall_Click` event of the form.

Listing 30.33. Coding the `cmdCall_Click` event.

```
Private Sub cmdCall_Click(Index As Integer)
    '
    ' handle user selection
    '
    Select Case Index
        Case 0 ' place call
            gPlaceCall = True ' ok to place call
            UpdateDB ' update tables
        Case 1 ' cancel call
            gPlaceCall = False ' no, skip it
    End Select
    '
    Unload Me
    '
End Sub
```

Finally, you need to add some code to support the `cmdCall_Click` event. Add a new subroutine called `UpdateDB` to the form and enter the code shown in Listing 30.34.

Listing 30.34. Adding the `UpdateDB` routine.

```
Public Sub UpdateDB()
    '
    ' update call log and master file
    '
    ' add call log record
    With frmCall.Data1.Recordset
        .AddNew
        .Fields("Name") = lblname
        .Fields("CallDate") = Now()
        .Fields("NumberCalled") = lblDialString
        .Fields("Comment") = txtNotes & " "
        .Update
    End With
    frmCall.Data1.Refresh
    '
    ' update master record
    frmTAPI.Data1.Recordset.FindFirst "Name='" & lblname & "'"
    If frmTAPI.Data1.Recordset.NoMatch = False Then
        With frmTAPI.Data1.Recordset
            .Edit
            .Fields("[Last Called]") = Now()
            .Update
        End With
    End If
    frmTAPI.Data1.Refresh
    '
End Sub
```

That is the end of the `frmCall` form. Save this form and update the project before you add the About dialog box.

Laying Out and Coding the About Dialog Box

The About dialog box is displayed when the user selects Help | About TAPIFONE. Add a new form to the project. Refer to Figure 30.9 and Table 30.9 when laying out the new form.

FIGURE 30.9.

Laying out the About dialog box.

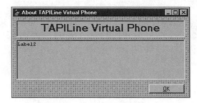

Table 30.9. The About dialog box controls.

Control	Property	Settings
VB.Form	Name	frmVPhone
	Caption	"About TAPILine Virtual Phone"
	ClientHeight	2670
	ClientLeft	2190
	ClientTop	2880
	ClientWidth	5955
	Height	3075
	Icon	"frmVPhon.frx":0000
	Left	2130
	LinkTopic	"Form1"
	ScaleHeight	2670
	ScaleWidth	5955
	Top	2535
	Width	6075
VB.CommandButton	Name	Command1
	Caption	"&OK"
	Height	300
	Left	4620
	TabIndex	2
	Top	2280
	Width	1200

Control	Property	Settings
VB.Label	Name	Label2
	BorderStyle	1 'Fixed Single
	Caption	"Label2"
	Font	
		name="MS LineDraw"
		charset=2
		weight=400
		size=8.25
		underline=0 'False
		italic=0 'False
		strikethrough=0 'False
	Height	1335
	Left	120
	TabIndex	1
	Top	780
	Width	5715
VB.Label	Name	Label1
	Alignment	2 'Center
	BorderStyle	1 'Fixed Single
	Caption	"TAPILine Virtual Phone"
	Font	name="MS Sans Serif"
		charset=0
		weight=700
		size=18
		underline=0 'False
		italic=0 'False
		strikethrough=0 'False
	Height	555
	Left	120
	TabIndex	0
	Top	120
	Width	5715

There are only two code routines needed for this form. Listing 30.35 shows the Form_Load event code. Add this to the form.

Listing 30.35. Adding the Form_Load event code.

```
Private Sub Form_Load()
    '
    ' fill in controls
    '
    Dim cAboutData
    Dim cVersion
    '
    cAboutData = ""
    cVersion = CStr(App.Major) & "." & CStr(App.Minor) & "." & CStr(App.Revision)
    '
    cAboutData = cAboutData & "Version......." & cVersion & Chr(13)
    cAboutData = cAboutData & "Title........." & App.Title & Chr(13)
    cAboutData = cAboutData & "Description..." & App.FileDescription & Chr(13)
    cAboutData = cAboutData & "Copyright....." & App.LegalCopyright
    '
    Label2 = cAboutData
    '
    Me.Left = (Screen.Width - Me.Width) / 2
    Me.Top = (Screen.Height - Me.Height) / 2
    '
End Sub
```

Listing 30.36 shows the line of code to add the Command1_Click event. This exits the About dialog box.

Listing 30.36. Adding the code to exit the dialog box.

```
Private Sub Command1_Click()
    Unload Me
End Sub
```

That's the end of the coding for the TAPIFONE project. Now save the form and the project. You are ready to test the application.

Testing TAPIFONE

When you first run TAPIFONE you'll be prompted to select a line device. This device will be used for all inbound and outbound calls (see Figure 30.10).

FIGURE 30.10.
TAPIFONE *requires you to*
select a line device.

Next, it's a good idea to select the Setup tab to review your startup configuration (see Figure 30.11).

FIGURE 30.11.
Adjusting the startup
configuration.

You can place a call using the keypad on the Dial Pad page (see Figure 30.12) or by selecting an entry in the phone book.

FIGURE 30.12.
Using the Dial Pad to place
a call.

In either case, when you press the Dial button, the Call dialog box appears asking you to confirm your call and enter any call notes (see Figure 30.13).

FIGURE 30.13.

Using the phone book to place a call.

Once your call is completed you can view the results on the log page and even export the log to a text file (see Figure 30.14).

FIGURE 30.14.

Exporting the log page to a text file.

Summary

In this chapter you applied all the information you have learned in the TAPI section to create a complete phone in software. You can use this device on any workstation that has TAPI services installed and has at least a voice-data modem. If the workstation has a speaker phone, you do not even need a telephone handset on your desk.

This chapter showed you what you can build in Visual Basic using the TAPILINE control. In the next chapter, you'll learn about three other TAPI tools that you can use to create TAPI-enabled applications. Two of the products are TAPI development tools. The third product is Microsoft Phone—Microsoft's e-mail-aware, telephone answering machine that can read text messages to you over the telephone.

31

Third-Party TAPI Tools

In the previous chapters you learned how the TAPI system works and how you can use Visual Basic and Microsoft C++ to build your own TAPI-compliant applications. In this chapter you'll learn how to use two of the most popular third-party development tools for TAPI services. Each of these tools has a unique approach to building TAPI-enabled applications. At the end of the chapter, you'll also get a look at Microsoft Phone, the new application from Microsoft that combines MAPI, SAPI, and TAPI services.

The first TAPI tool you'll review is the Visual Voice Telephony Toolkit for Windows from Stylus Innovation, Inc. This system includes a handful of OCX controls that you place on your Visual Basic forms to gain access to TAPI services. By setting control properties, invoking methods, and responding to defined events, you can build solid multiline telephony applications in a very short time.

> **NOTE**
>
> The Visual Voice system comes in several versions for both 16- and 32-bit Windows operating systems. Visual Voice also sells versions for TAPI- and MWAVE-based systems. The version covered here is the 32-bit TAPI system. It runs fine on both 16- and 32-bit Windows.

The second TAPI development tool you'll test is the VBVoice system from Pronexus. The VBVoice approach to TAPI design is quite different. Instead of placing controls on your form and using them to gain access to TAPI services, the VBVoice system allows you to visually build your telephony application by linking the controls in a flow diagram. Using this method, you can build complete telephony applications without writing a single line of Visual Basic code.

Finally, you'll get a peek at Microsoft Phone—the new application from Microsoft that combines MAPI, SAPI, and TAPI services into a single communication application. You'll learn how to install and configure Microsoft Phone and see how you can combine telephony, e-mail, and speech into a single system.

The Visual Voice Telephony Toolkit for Windows

The Visual Voice Telephony Toolkit is one of the most popular TAPI systems for Visual Basic development. The kit contains eight basic Visual Voice components. Three of these components are controls:

■ The Voice control—This is the main TAPI control. It gives you access to the standard TAPI events and methods.

■ The Test control—This control is used to simulate a live telephone line. With this control and a sound card, you can fully test your application without having to use live telephone lines.

■ The Vlink control—This control is used to create conversation links between separate Visual Basic applications on the same machine. This is similar to a Visual Basic OLE server.

There are also five valuable support applications you can use to build and manage your TAPI applications:

■ The *Voice Workbench*—This is a tool for creating and managing Visual Voice objects, including voice files, voice strings, voice queries, and code templates.

■ The *Voice Monitor*—This is a Visual Basic application that can be used to monitor line activity on a multiline TAPI workstation. You'll use this to keep track of telephony activity on your TAPI PC.

■ The *Virtual Phone*—This is a Visual Basic application that allows you to completely test your TAPI system without having to connect to and use live telephone lines. This application was built using the Test control mentioned above.

■ The *TAPI Examiner*—This is a Visual Basic program that allows you to test individual TAPI services. It is a helpful debugging tool.

■ *Stylus Trace*—This is a stand-alone program that you can use to trace all Visual Voice activity on your workstation. It is excellent for debugging and checking out your Visual Voice installation.

NOTE

You'll find a demonstration copy of the Visual Voice Toolkit on the CD-ROM that ships with this book. You can read this section of this chapter without installing the Visual Voice software, but you'll get more out of the material if you have Visual Voice up and running.

There are three Visual Voice controls. The Voice control is the main TAPI interface control. You'll use this control to gain access to TAPI services on your workstation. The Test control can be used to perform tests on your applications without the need for a live telephone line. The VLink control can be used to pass information between running Visual Basic Visual Voice applications.

The following sections review the controls and their methods, properties, and events more closely.

> **NOTE**
>
> The reviews of the methods, properties, and events of the Visual Voice components covers the OCX controls only. The Visual Voice Toolkit for Win32 also contains DLLs for use with C++ applications (or other programming languages that use DLLs). The descriptions of methods, properties, and events described for the Visual Basic controls are the same for the API calls in the DLL support files.

The Voice Control

The Voice control has 33 methods that you can invoke. Most of them correspond to methods found in the TAPILINE control and specific API functions defined within TAPI. For example, there is an AllocateLine method to open a line for voice output. There are also DeallocateLine and Stop methods for closing a line and shutting down TAPI services (see Figure 31.1).

FIGURE 31.1.

Viewing the Voice control properties page.

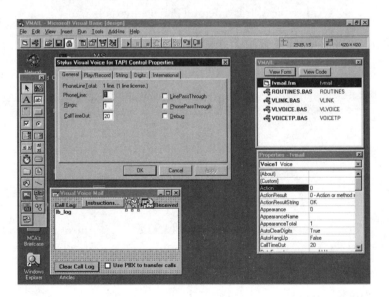

You can use the Voice control to place an outbound call by setting the Value property to "555-1212" and then invoking the Call method. When a call comes in to the line, the RingDetected event fires and you can use the PickUp method to answer the call.

The Voice control has several other unique, and very useful, methods. For example, the Voice control contains several Play... methods that can be used to play back numbers, dates, words, phrases, even complete sound files. There are also properties that identify the caller, including CallerID, ANI (*Automatic Number Identification*), and others.

> **TIP**
>
> There is also a Visual Basic BAS module called `VOICETP.BAS`. This module contains constant definitions and sample and helper functions and subroutines. This additional code is not required when using the `Voice` control, but it does come in quite handy. When you add the `Voice` control to your project, you should add the `VOICETP.BAS` module, too.

Table 31.1 lists all of the TAPI-related methods along with short descriptions of their use.

Table 31.1. The `Voice` control methods.

Method	Description
AbortTransfer	Aborts a transfer previously initiated through the `AttendedTransfer` method.
AllocateLine	Attempts to allocate the phone line specified in the `PhoneLine` property that will be used for all subsequent Visual Voice actions.
AttendedTransfer	Begins an attended transfer or conference to the extension specified in the `Value` property.
BlindTransfer	Blindly transfers the call to the number specified in the `Value` property and then hangs up.
Call	Dials the digits stored in the `Value` property and returns when call progress detection has completed. The `ActionResult` property will contain the status of the call.
CheckError	Generates an error condition if one has been set by way of the `SetError` method.
CompleteTransfer	Completes a transfer initiated through the `AttendedTransfer` method and disconnects from the call.
ConferenceTransfer	Completes a three-way conference with the calling party and a party called through the `AttendedTransfer` method.
DeallocateLine	Frees an allocated phone line.
Dial	Blind-dials the digits stored in the `Value` property and then returns immediately. This action can also be used to generate other telephony signals, including pulse dialing or a flash-hook.

continues

Table 31.1. continued

Method	Description
DisableIODevice	Disables the I/O terminal device specified in the Value property. This is used to switch between headsets and desktop phones, and so on.
EnableIODevice	Enables the I/O terminal device specified in the Value property. See the preceding description of DisableIODevice.
FlushDigitBuffer	Unconditionally retrieves all digits in the digit buffer, places them into the Digits property, and leaves the digit buffer empty.
GetDigits	Conditionally retrieves touch-tone digits from the digit buffer and places them into the Digits property. The number of digits retrieved is determined by the inputs to the action.
HangUp	Puts the line "on-hook" to conclude a call.
Hold	Places the current call on hold.
Park	Parks the current call to the phone number specified in the Value property.
PickUp	Takes the line "off-hook" to answer a ringing line or get a dial tone.
PlayCharacters	Plays the string stored in the Value property as a list of characters (for example, "a, b, c").
PlayDate	Plays the string stored in the Value property as a date and/or time in the format stored in the DateFormat property.
PlayFile	Plays the voice file named in the Value property.
PlayMoney	Plays the number stored in the Value property as money (dollars and cents).
PlayNumber	Plays the number stored in the Value property as a number, to the decimal precision stored in the Precision property.
PlayOrdinal	Plays the integer stored in the Value property as an ordinal number (1st, 2nd, 3rd, and so on).
PlayString	Plays the voice string stored in the Value property. A voice string is a collection of one or more values using various play methods, all played smoothly together. For example, "Order number [54321] was shipped on [Tuesday, October 2]."
PlayStringQ	Identical to the PlayString method but returns immediately so database or other processing can occur at the same time.

Method	*Description*
RecordFile	Records a voice file, using the file format specified in the FileFormat property, and saves it with the filename stored in the Value property.
SetError	Sets up an error condition so that the next Visual Voice action will return an error. The error number is specified in the Value property.
ShowConfigDialog	Displays the TAPI device driver's configuration dialog box.
Stop	Stops all Visual Voice activity, including all Play..., RecordFile..., Call, and GetDigits methods. It clears the entire queue of pending voice strings to be played (if any).
SwapHold	Swaps the active call, specified in the Appearance property, with the call in the TargetAppearance property, so that the active call is put on hold and the target call is taken off hold and becomes active.
Unhold	Retrieves a call on hold.
Unpark	Retrieves a call that has been parked via the Park method.

The Voice control sports 46 TAPI-related properties. Many of these properties are read-only and available only at run-time. Table 31.2 shows the list of properties for the Voice control.

Table 31.2. The Voice control properties.

Property	*Description*
Action	Initiates the specified Voice control action. This is a carryover from the 16-bit control and is not recommended. Instead, use the methods described in Table 31.1.
ActionResult	Stores status information about the result of the previous action. The default is VV_R_OK.
Appearance	Specifies the appearance on which subsequent Visual Voice actions will take effect. The default is 0 (for PBX systems).
AppearanceName	Returns, in an array, the names of the appearances at the current extension, specified in the PhoneLine property. This property is read-only. (PBX)
AppearanceTotal	Returns the total number of appearances at the current extension, specified in the PhoneLine property. This property is read-only. (PBX)

continues

Table 31.2. continued

Property	Description
AutoClearDigits	If this property is set to `False`, the digit buffer will not be cleared before each `Play...` or `RecordFile` method is initiated. The default is `True`.
CallTimeOut	Sets the maximum number of seconds to wait for a connection during the `Call` method. The default value is 20 seconds.
DateFormat	Specifies how a date and/or time is spoken when the `Play...` method is executed. The default is `mm/dd/yyyy`.
Debug	If this property is set to `True`, the `Debug` event executes at the start and finish of every Visual Voice action. The default is `False`.
Digits	Contains any touch-tone digits returned by the `GetDigits` or `FlushDigitBuffer` methods. This property is read-only. The default is "".
DigitsTimeOut	Sets the maximum number of seconds that the `GetDigits` method will wait for the specified digits before timing out. If this property is set to 0, there is no time-out. The default is 15 seconds.
DtermDigits	Specifies one or more touch-tone digits that will terminate the `GetDigits` method. The default is "#".
EndPosition	Returns the current position, in seconds, of the voice file specified in the `Value` property. This property is read-only.
ErrorLogString	Specifies a string to send to the Visual Voice `errorlog` text file. The default is "". (This is the error message body!)
FileFormat	The file format used when recording voice files. The default is the last file format specified at design time, or `0`.
FileLength	Returns the length, in seconds, of the voice file specified in the `Value` property.
hCall	Returns the TAPI call handle of the current Visual Voice connection. This property is read-only.
hLine	Returns the TAPI line handle of the current Visual Voice connection. This property is read-only.
hPhone	Returns the TAPI phone handle of the current Visual Voice connection. This property is read-only.
InterDigitTimeOut	Specifies the maximum number of seconds the `GetDigits` method will wait between digits before timing out. The default is `0`.

Property	Description
IODeviceName()	Returns the names of the I/O devices, if any, attached to terminals on the TAPI device. This property is read-only.
IODeviceTotal	Returns the total number of I/O devices attached to terminals on the TAPI device. This property is read-only.
LanguageDLL	Specifies the language DLL to use for speaking variable information. The default is VVLUSA16.DLL.
LanguageParams	Specifies any optional parameters to change the behavior of custom language DLLs. The default is "".
LinePassThrough	Specifies whether every low-level TAPI device event will be exposed through the LinePassThrough event. The default is False.
MaxDigits	Specifies the maximum number of digits to receive from the digit buffer before the GetDigits method returns. The default is 1.
PhoneLine	Sets the telephone line (port or channel) on which all of Visual Voice's actions will execute. The default is 1.
PhoneLineTotal	The total number of telephone lines (ports or channels) available to Visual Voice. This property is read-only.
PhonePassThrough	Specifies whether every low-level TAPI device phone event will be exposed through the PhonePassThrough event. The default is False.
Precision	The decimal precision to which any number or money value is played. The default is 6, general precision.
ProductInfo	Returns a string that contains version information for the Visual Voice for TAPI VBX, Visual Voice TAPI engine DLL, the TAPI API, and the TAPI drivers being used. This property is read-only.
Rate	Sets the speed voice files are played by any Play... method. The default is 0.
RecordBeep	Specifies whether a beep will be played before the RecordFile method records a voice file. The default is True.
RecordTimeOut	Sets the maximum length of any recording created by the RecordFile method. The default is 60 seconds.
Rings	Number of incoming rings before the RingDetected event is executed. The default is 1.

continues

Table 31.2. continued

Property	Description
StartPosition	Specifies the starting position, in seconds, at which subsequent Play... and RecordFile methods will play or record, respectively. The default is 0.
Status	Stores a value describing what is occurring over the line at any given time. This property is read-only.
StringItemSeparator	Specifies the character to be used to separate items in voice strings. The default is , (comma).
StringTokenSeparator	Specifies the character to be used to separate tokens in voice strings. The default is ¦ (vertical bar).
SystemError	The SystemError property contains additional information when an internal error occurs. This property is read-only.
SystemVoiceFile	Specifies the system file listing the voice files to use for speaking variable information. The default is VVSYSTEM.TXT. This file is the source of the most common words and phrases.
TargetAppearance	The second appearance that must be specified for the SwapHold and AttendedTransfer methods. The default is 0.
Value	Sets the value used for the RecordFile, Dial, Call, or any Play... method. The default is "".
Volume	Sets the volume at which voice files are played by any Play... method. The default is 0.
VtermDigits	Sets the terminating touch-tone digits that will stop any playing or recording (Play... and RecordFile methods).

Finally, there are eight TAPI-related events for the Voice control. Table 31.3 shows the events, along with descriptions of their use.

Table 31.3. The Voice control events.

Event	Description
CalledIDDetected	Triggers after DID (*Direct Inward Dialing*) or DNIS (*Dialed Number ID Service*) information is detected on the line. This is used to identify the exact line the caller used to enter your switch (PBX).
LineDropped	If the line is idle, this event executes whenever the line drops or the user hangs up.

Event	Description
PlayQueueDone	Triggers when all voice strings on the queue have completed playing. Place voice strings on the queue by way of the PlayStringQ method.
CallerIDDetected	Triggers after CallerID or ANI (Automatic Number Identification) information is detected on the line.
LinePassThrough	If the LinePassThrough property is set to True, this event triggers once for every line event returned by the TAPI device.
RingDetected	Executes after the number of rings in the Rings property have been detected on the line. The line must be allocated.
Debug	If the Debug property is set to True, this event triggers before every Voice control action starts and after every Voice control action finishes.
PhonePassThrough	If the PhonePassThrough property is set to True, this event triggers once for every phone event returned by the TAPI device.

The Test Control

The Test control simulates the existence of a live telephone line for your Visual Voice applications. When you are building and testing telephony applications, one of the hardest parts of the process is testing the application's response to inbound calls. The Test control solves this problem. Now, as you build your TAPI applications, you can test them without having to actually link your workstation to a live telephone line (see Figure 31.2).

The control works by communicating directly with the Voice control. Whenever the Voice control invokes a Call method, the Test control's VoiceCallInitiated event occurs. This simulates the receipt of an outbound call initiated by your application. You can also use the VoiceConnect method of the Test control to simulate the appearance of an inbound call for your TAPI application.

TIP

When you load the Test control into your Visual Basic projects, load the VVTEST.BAS module, too. This contains predefined constants that you can use to make it easier to program with the Test control.

FIGURE 31.2.
Viewing the Test *control properties page.*

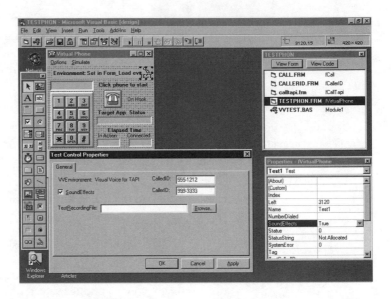

Table 31.4 shows the four methods of the Test control along with short descriptions of their use.

Table 31.4. Methods of the Test control.

Method	Description
Disconnect	Causes a line-dropped condition in the Voice control. This action simulates the caller hanging up.
SendLineDigits	Sends the string of digits specified in the Value property to the Voice control. This action simulates touch-tone digits being sent over the line, as though the digits were pressed on a telephone's keypad.
TimeOut	Immediately forces the current Visual Voice action to time out and terminate (if applicable). This action simulates a time-out.
VoiceConnect	Connects to the Voice control (if any) that has allocated the phone line. This action simulates a caller calling the Visual Voice application.

> **NOTE**
>
> There are five other methods listed in the `Test` control documentation, but they have no effect in the current version of Visual Voice for TAPI. These methods are `FaxConnect`, `HangUpHandset`, `PickUpHandset`, `SendCallProgress`, and `SendHandsetDigits`. These methods appear for backward compatibility with earlier versions of Visual Voice.

There are nine valid properties of the `Test` control. These properties are listed in Table 31.5 along with descriptions of their use.

Table 31.5. The `Test` control properties.

Property	Description
Action	Initiates the corresponding `Test` control action.
CalledID	Simulates a `CalledID` string sent to the `Voice` control.
CallerID	Simulates a `CallerID` string sent to the `Voice` control.
NumberDialed	Contains the number dialed after the `Voice` control's `Dial` or `Call` methods are initiated.
SoundEffects	Specifies whether sound effects are played over the speakers when `Test` control actions are initiated. The default is `True`.
Status	Indicates the status of the `Voice` control at any time.
TestRecordingFile	Specifies a WAV file that simulates a voice speaking over the phone line when the `Voice` control's `RecordFile` method is initiated. The default is "".
Value	Specifies the string used for the `SendLineDigits` method.
tVVEnvironment	Returns a value identifying the Visual Voice control with which the test control is working. This property is read-only. Possible values are `VISUAL_VOICE_PRO` `VISUAL_VOICE_MWAVE` `VISUAL_VOICE_TAPI`

> **NOTE**
>
> There are three properties of the `Test` control that are no longer valid: `FaxPageTotal`, `TestFaxFile`, and `TestStationID`. These are included for backward compatibility with other versions of Visual Voice, but have no effect in this version of the product.

It is important to comment on the `CalledID` and `CallerID` properties—don't confuse them. The `CalledID` value indicates the telephone number that the inbound caller dialed to reach you. In some PBX systems, this information is used to sort incoming calls for customized greetings (for example, calls coming in on line 1 might be answered "Welcome to Customer Service" and calls coming in on line 2 might be answered "Administration. May I help you?"). The `CallerID` value indicates the telephone number of the person who is placing the call. This can be used to automatically associate a name, address, or other account information with the calling party.

The `Test` control has three events. Table 31.6 lists these events along with a description.

Table 31.6. The `Test` control events.

Event	*Description*
ElapsedTime	Triggers periodically to keep track of how long a phone connection lasts and how long the current voice action has been executing. The counter starts for each `VoiceConnect`, `Dial`, or `Call` method of the `Voice` control event and is set to zero when the triggering method has completed.
VoiceCallInitiated	Triggers whenever the `Voice` control places a call with the `Call` method. Place code in this event to specify what type of response (for example, dial tone, busy, and so on) the `Voice` control will receive.
VoiceDialInitiated	Executes when the `Voice` control dials a number with the `Dial` method.

NOTE

There is also a `FaxSendInitiated` event that is no longer operable, but that is included for backward compatibility.

The `Vlink` Control

The `Vlink` control is used to send data between two Visual Basic programs running on the same workstation. This control was developed before Visual Basic 4 offered easy OLE server construction. Although you could accomplish the same tasks using OLE servers, the `Vlink` control is geared toward supporting Visual Voice services and should be used whenever you need to share telephony data between Visual Voice TAPI applications (see Figure 31.3).

FIGURE 31.3.
Viewing the Vlink
properties page.

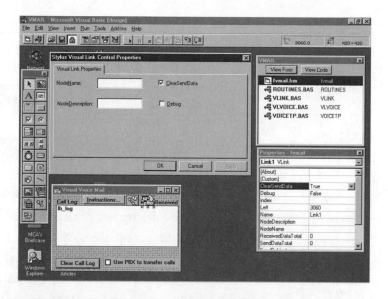

TIP

When you use the Vlink control, add the VLINK.BAS and VLVOICE.BAS modules to your project. These modules contain useful constants and helper functions that you can use to manipulate Vlink control events and data.

The Vlink control has only two methods. Table 31.7 lists and describes the methods.

Table 31.7. The methods of the Vlink control.

Method	Description
Request	Sends the contents of the SendData() property array to the node specified in the SendToNode property. This action waits for the target node to complete processing (and optionally return data) before returning.
Send	Sends the contents of the SendData() property array to the node specified in the SendToNode property, and returns immediately.

The Vlink control has 14 TAPI-related properties. Table 31.8 lists these properties and describes them.

Table 31.8. The properties of the Vlink control.

Property	Description
Action	Initiates the specified Visual Link action.
ClearSendData	Specifies whether the SendData() property array and the SendDataTotal property will be cleared after a Send or Request method is complete. Default is True.
Debug	If this property is set to True, the Debug event executes at the start and finish of every Vlink control action. The default is False.
NodeDescription	A string that describes the node. The default is null.
NodeDescriptionList	Returns the descriptions of all active nodes.
NodeName	Specifies the name of the node.
NodeNameList	Returns a list of node names for all active nodes.
NodeTotal	Returns the total number of active nodes in the system.
ReceivedData	Returns an array of strings sent from another node.
ReceivedDataTotal	Returns the number of items in the ReceivedData() property array when another node sends or returns data. This property is read-only.
SendData	Specifies an array of strings to send to another node.
SendDataTotal	Specifies the number of elements in the SendData() property array to send during a Send or Request method or when returning data in a RequestReceived event.
SendSubject	Specifies the subject of the data being sent.
SendToNode	Specifies which node will be the target of any subsequent Send or Request method.

There are three events defined for the Vlink control. Table 31.9 shows the three events and their meaning.

Table 31.9. The events of the Vlink control.

Event	Description
DataReceived	This event is triggered when another node has sent data by way of the Send method and the data is now available at this node.
Debug	If the Debug property is set to True, this event is triggered before every Visual Link action starts and after every Visual Link action finishes.
RequestReceived	This event is triggered when another node has sent a request by way of the Request method.

That completes the tour of the Visual Voice controls. Next you'll learn about the various support programs and development tools that are supplied with the Visual Voice Telephony TAPI Toolkit for Win32.

The Voice Workbench

The Voice Workbench is an essential tool for building Visual Voice TAPI applications. The Workbench allows you to create and maintain four key Visual Voice objects:

- Voice files
- Voice strings
- Voice queries
- Subroutine templates

Voice files are the actual WAV format recordings of human speech. The Voice Workbench allows you to record and catalog voice files for later reference in your Visual Basic project. Typical voice file objects would be "Welcome to Visual Voice," or "Press one to continue," and so on. Figure 31.4 shows the Voice Workbench while reviewing a set of voice files.

FIGURE 31.4.

Reviewing voice files with the Voice Workbench.

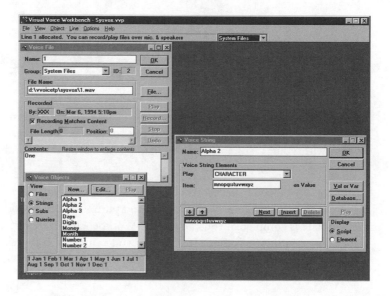

Voice strings are a collection of one or more voice files plus literal or variable values. The Workbench lets you link several prerecorded phrases along with fixed or variable data retrieved from a database or computed by your Visual Basic program. For example, you might create a voice string object that returns the total number of messages in your voice-mail inbox:

"There are" `MsgTable[MsgCount]` "new messages"

The phrase above links two voice files (possibly named `ThereAre.WAV` and `NewMsgs.WAV`) with a pointer to a field (`MsgCount`) in a database table (`MsgTable`). This is one of the most powerful aspects of the Workbench. You can very easily link your voice output to variables in your program or to data stored in a shared database. Figure 31.5 shows the Workbench building a voice string using a database link.

FIGURE 31.5.

Building a voice string using Voice Workbench.

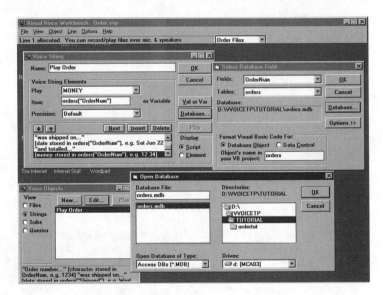

You can also build and maintain voice query objects with the Voice Workbench. *Voice queries* are just like voice strings except that they ask the user for a predetermined response in the form of keypad selections. You can build your queries to expect a set amount of input before continuing with your TAPI application. Figure 31.6 shows the Workbench editing an existing voice query.

Lastly, the Workbench also lets you create and store your own *subroutine templates.* These templates can link voice strings, voice queries, and pure Visual Basic code into a single unit. Once the template is completed, you can ask the Workbench to generate Visual Basic code for you to place into your application. In this way you can build complex telephony logic without spending a great deal of time writing Visual Basic code. Figure 31.7 shows an example of Workbench-generated code using a Visual Voice template object.

FIGURE 31.6.
Editing an existing voice query object.

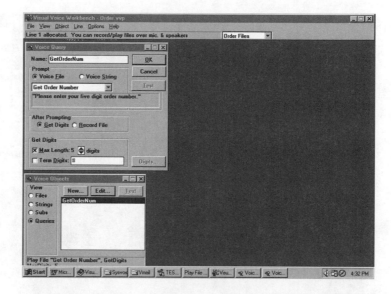

FIGURE 31.7.
Generating Visual Basic code using a Workbench template.

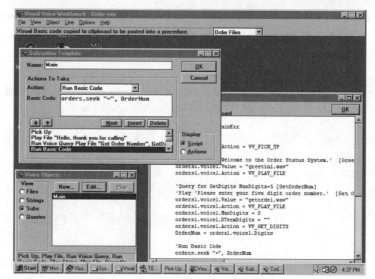

The Voice Monitor

The Voice Monitor is a Visual Basic application that can monitor activity on multiline phone installations (see Figure 31.8).

FIGURE 31.8.

Using Voice Monitor to track line activity.

This is very useful when you have a multiline telephony card in your TAPI workstation and are running one or more Visual Basic applications on each line.

The Virtual Phone

The Virtual Phone is a very handy testing tool. This tool simulates the appearance of a live telephone line for your Visual Voice applications (see Figure 31.9).

FIGURE 31.9.

Running the Virtual Phone.

The program is actually written in Visual Basic using Visual Voice's Test control, and the source code is included in the complete toolkit. The program works by talking directly to the Voice control rather than to a telephone line. For this reason, you cannot use the Virtual Phone for any other TAPI applications that do not use the Voice control.

You can set values for the CallerID and CalledID in the Virtual Phone and have these values passed into your Visual Basic application that uses the Voice control. In this way you can even test applications that require advanced telephony service features without having to use a live telephone line.

The TAPI Examiner and the Stylus Trace Applications

The TAPI Examiner is an excellent tool for testing your hardware's compatibility with TAPI services. The examiner runs through all the major service requests, including selecting and opening lines, placing outbound calls, receiving inbound calls, even testing advanced features such as transfer, park, and hold (see Figure 31.10).

FIGURE 31.10.

Using the TAPI Examiner.

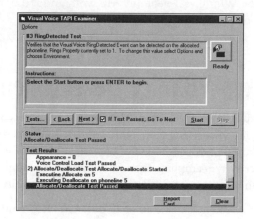

You also get the ability to log your test results to a text file for later reference. This is a very handy tool for testing new workstations and is a useful general diagnostic tool as well.

The Stylus Trace application provides an easy way to log and trace all activity involving Stylus controls. Listing 31.1 shows a sample of trace output.

Listing 31.1. Sample output from the Stylus Trace application.

```
Executing VV_VoiceInit
VVE ?: TAPI initialized 6 lines, 6 phones
VV_VoiceInit returned 0x00000000
VVE ?: 1 line license detected
Using profile C:\WINDOWS\VVOICETP.INI
Executing VV_SetSystemFileExtension(wav)
VV_SetSystemFileExtension returned 1
Executing VV_SetBeepFileName(C:\VVOICETP\TESTSNDS\BEEP.WAV, 0)
VV_SetBeepFileName returned 1
Executing VV_AllocateLine(PhoneLine = 1 Rings = 1)
VVE ?: Mapping VV PhoneLine 1 to TAPI device 5 [Windows Telephony Service Provider
for Universal Modem Driver - TeleCommander 2500 Voice]
```

continues

Listing 31.1. continued

```
VVE ?: line 5 - total appearances = 1
VVE 5: Appearance 0: [´]
VVE ?: lineOpen (OWNER, AUTOMATEDVOICE)
VVE ?: Allocated line ed0084.  Line handle = 372f1e3e
VV_AllocateLine returned 0
Allocated line 1.  1 appearances
```

> **NOTE**
>
> Since this product works by monitoring activity within the Stylus components, not within the Windows Telephony API, you cannot use the Stylus Trace to monitor non-Visual Voice telephony programs.

Pronexus' VBVoice Development Kit

The Pronexus VBVoice telephony development system is quite different from the Visual Voice toolkit. Each provides the same basic services, but in a very different way. While the Visual Voice toolkit emphasizes the use of custom controls linked together with Visual Basic code, the VBVoice system emphasizes the use of visual programming instead of Visual Basic code. In fact, you can build an entire VBVoice application without writing any Visual Basic code at all.

The VBVoice system is made up of 20 different OCX controls. These 20 controls represent all the major actions that can occur during a telephony session. You place these controls on your Visual Basic form and set their properties at design time. You then link them together in a call-flow diagram that visually defines your program.

After completing your call-flow diagram and setting the desired properties, you can test your VBVoice application by starting the application in TestMode. TestMode is similar to the Visual Voice Virtual Phone. VBVoice TestMode simulates call activity without the use of a live telephone line.

In the next few sections, you'll learn how the VBVoice controls work and how they can be used to develop Windows telephony programs.

> **NOTE**
>
> There is a demonstration version of the VBVoice development system on the CD-ROM that accompanies this book. You do not need a telephony card to use the demonstration version of the system. However, you do need a sound card to run the system in TestMode.

The VBFrame Control

Every VBVoice project contains at least one VBFrame control. This control is the "host" control for all other VBVoice controls in the project. The VBFrame acts as a visual workspace for your telephony project. Figure 31.11 shows a VBFrame control hosting several other VBVoice controls.

FIGURE 31.11.

Using VBFrame *to host other VBVoice controls.*

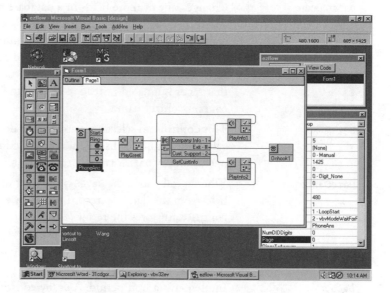

The VBVoice Controls

After you have placed a VBFrame control on a form, you are ready to add other VBVoice controls. Each VBVoice control handles a single typical event in a telephony application (playing a greeting, collecting digits, transferring a call, and so on). Along with the VBFrame control, there are another 19 VBVoice controls that you can use to build your telephony applications. Table 31.10 lists and describes the 19 VBVoice controls.

Table 31.10. The VBVoice controls.

Control	Description
Conference	The Conference control is used for merging individual voice lines together into a conference. This control is available as an option with VBVoice. Callers in a conference have the ability to verbally communicate to all other callers in the conference. Each instance of this control represents one unique conference.

continues

Table 31.10. continued

Control	Description
Count	This control maintains an internal counter which can be reset and incremented by call flow. It is useful for simple loops similar to the Visual Basic `for .. to .. step ..` construct.
DataChange	Changes one or more fields in a database record. The database and record to be changed are selected by a previous `DataFind` control. The field values of the record in the database selected by the `DataFind` control will be changed to the new values. If Add New Record is set, a new record is added and the fields in that record updated instead. The data to be inserted can contain control names.
DataFind	This control can select a record from a database for input validation and for subsequent data selection and update operations by `DataSwitch`, `DataChange`, and `Dial` controls.
DataSwitch	When a call enters the `DataSwitch` control, the control reads a field from the database record found by a previous `DataFind` control and stores the result in the `Result` property. The call is then passed to the control connected to one of the output nodes, based on a comparison operation performed on the field value obtained.
Delay	Implements a wait period. A `Delay` control can be used if your VB code has to perform a lengthy activity, and you want the caller to wait until it is complete, for instance to wait for a busy line to be free before re-attempting a transfer.
Dial	The `Dial` control can be used to go off-hook and start a call, or, on an existing call, it can perform a transfer to another extension or dial some digits to an automated system at the far end. If the number to dial is prefixed with the letter "S," call supervision is enabled to monitor the progress of the call until the result is determined—one of the outcomes listed in the Supervised Dial box. It does this by listening and analyzing the tones being returned from the telephone system after dialing. A built-in call-logging facility using a database is also provided.
GetDigits	The `GetDigits` control plays a greeting and waits for digits from the caller for a predetermined amount of time. Pattern matching is performed on the collected digits using as many exit conditions as required. `GetDigits` provides built-in invalid digit and time-out handling.

Control	Description
InConn	Used for connection from an output on one control to the input of another on a different form. Other controls cannot be connected across forms.
IniSwitch	Searches for an entry in a Windows initialization (.INI) file, and routes the call depending on the result found. You can set the filename, section name, and field name of the entry you wish to test. The Result property is set from the data found.
Language	The Language control is an optional control that performs several functions, including setting the language for each call using the graphical controls; overriding default phrase concatenation rules for the built-in system phrases with your own rules; and accepting a user-definable system phrase type.
LineGroup	This control "owns" a group of telephone lines, and can receive calls and initiate calls on these lines. The channels can be set using the property page at design time, or channels can be allocated at run-time by way of the AddChannel and RemoveChannel methods. LineGroup also contains handlers for global conditions on a channel: invalid and silence time-outs, call termination due to maximum call time or by the StopCall function, and global digit handlers.
Onhook	Plays a greeting, and hangs up the phone. Control of the line is returned to the LineGroup control that owns this channel, where a Disconnect event will occur. This event will allow termination code to run for this call.
OutConn	Used for connection from an output on one control to the input of another on a different form. Other controls cannot be connected across forms.
PlayGreeting	The PlayGreeting control plays a greeting and then passes the call to the next control. If the greeting plays to completion without any digits, the call will exit out of the Done node. The PlayGreeting control can also accept digits from the caller to pause, skip forward and backward in the greeting, or change the volume and speed of the playback. The volume and speed adjustments are reset to the default on entry and exit of the control.
PlayMsgs	Two types of messages are supported: New and Old. New messages are those that have not yet been heard, or have been saved as New. New messages are converted to Old once they

continues

Table 31.10. continued

Control	Description
	have been heard. When a call enters a `PlayMsgs` control, the control first plays the number of each type of message. (configurable in the `EntryGreeting`). It then plays the messages in sequence, starting with the new messages (oldest messages first), using the configurable `MsgGreeting`. The action after each message is configurable to either start playing the next message immediately, or to play the `OptionsGreeting`, allowing the caller to save, delete, forward, or skip the message, or exit. After both new and old messages have been played, the call exits the control.
Record	Records a wave file into the filename specified by either creating a new file or appending an existing one. Each message can be stored in a unique file name generated by the control. An options menu is provided to provide message review, re-record, and deletion.
TimeSwitch	Transfers the call to another control according to time of day and day of week. Several time zones can be set for each control. If the current time and day of week do not match any of the fields specified, the call continues by way of the default connection.
User	This control has no predetermined action. It allows Visual Basic to define all operations and provides complete control over the voice card.

The Process of Building a VBVoice Application

As mentioned earlier, you build VBVoice telephony applications by placing the various VBVoice controls into a VBFrame and then linking them together in a call diagram. Once they are linked together, you can set the properties of each control to alter the behavior of the system. Figure 31.12 shows the process of setting properties for the GetDigits control.

FIGURE 31.12.
Setting the properties of the `GetDigits` *control.*

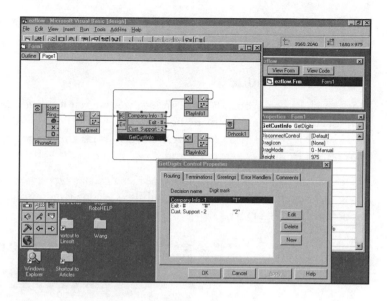

VBVoice and Voice Files

VBVoice allows you to build voice files using its own library of phrases or by recording your own phrases. You access the voice files through the VBVoice controls that use voice files. For example, you can call up the properties page of the `PlayGreeting` control, select `Properties` from the context menu (alternate mouse button), and then select the `Greetings` tab to gain access to the recorded voice library (see Figure 13.13).

FIGURE 13.13.
Accessing the Voice library files.

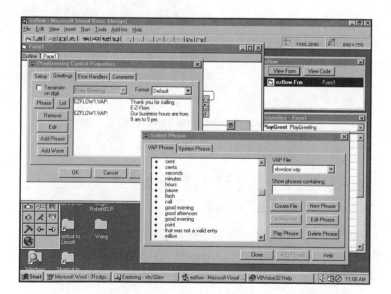

VBVoice allows you to record, playback, and store messages in a variety of file formats including the Windows standard WAV format.

VBVoice Test Mode

Once you have built your VBVoice project, you can test it by selecting the Start Test option from the context menu (alternate mouse button) of the control. All VBVoice controls can be started in this way. This makes it very easy to debug a telephony application. You can start your testing from anywhere in the call flow.

Once you start your application, you'll see a small dialog box appear asking you to start the test mode. While test mode is running, you'll also see a log window of all activity in the VBVoice application (see Figure 31.14).

FIGURE 31.14.

Running a VBVoice application in test mode.

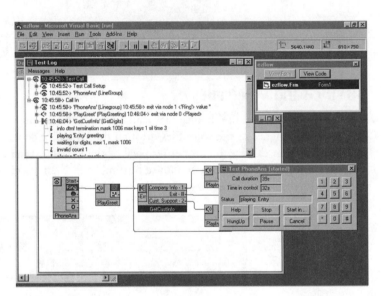

You can view the trace logs onscreen, send them to a printer, or save them to a disk file. Listing 31.2 shows sample output from a VBVoice log.

Listing 31.2. Sample output from a VBVoice log.

```
10:49:39-> Test Call
10:49:39-> Test Call Setup

10:49:39-> 'PhoneAns' (LineGroup)
10:49:40-> Call In  10:50:16->  call complete
10:49:40-> 'PhoneAns' (Linegroup) 10:49:40-> exit via node 1 <'Ring'> value ''
10:49:40-> exit via node 1 <'Ring'> value ''
10:49:41-> 'PlayGreet' (PlayGreeting) 10:49:47-> exit via node 0 <Played>
playing 'Entry' greeting
```

```
10:49:47-> exit via node 0 <Played>
10:49:47-> 'GetCustInfo' (GetDigits) 10:49:50-> exit via node 0 <'Company Info
info dtmf termination mask 1006 max keys 1 sil time 3
playing 'Entry' greeting
waiting for digits, max 1, mask 1006
10:49:50-> exit via node 0 <'Company Info - 1'> value '1'
10:49:50-> 'PlayInfo1' (PlayGreeting) 10:49:59-> exit via node 0 <Played>
playing 'Entry' greeting
10:49:59-> exit via node 0 <Played>
10:49:59-> 'GetCustInfo' (GetDigits) 10:50:02-> exit via node 2 <'Cust. Support
playing 'Entry' greeting
waiting for digits, max 1, mask 1006
10:50:02-> exit via node 2 <'Cust. Support - 2'> value '2'
10:50:02-> 'PlayInfo2' (PlayGreeting) 10:50:14-> exit via node 0 <Played>
playing 'Entry' greeting
10:50:14-> exit via node 0 <Played>
10:50:14-> 'GetCustInfo' (GetDigits) 10:50:15-> exit via node 1 <'Exit - #'> va
playing 'Entry' greeting
waiting for digits, max 1, mask 1006
10:50:15-> exit via node 1 <'Exit - #'> value '#'
10:50:15-> 'Onhook1' (OnHook) 10:50:16-> transfer to linegroup control (onhook)
playing 'Entry' greeting
10:50:16-> transfer to linegroup control (onhook)
```

Even though you can build complete telephony applications using only the VBFrame control and the visual call diagrams, you can also use the controls to build programs using traditional Visual Basic coding techniques. Each control has its own series of events, methods, and properties that can be accessed at run-time. You can read and set properties, invoke methods, and add code to the events just as you do with any other Visual Basic controls.

Microsoft Phone

Microsoft Phone is the first application released by Microsoft that combines the Messaging, Telephony, and Speech APIs into a single program (see Figure 31.15).

While Microsoft Phone is a very good PC phone and answering machine, it offers several other valuable features. First, you can use Microsoft Phone to designate several fax mailboxes. These mailboxes will send a selected fax back to the caller based on a telephone number left by the caller. You can also set up multiple message boxes that the caller can use to leave messages. Finally, you can build announcement-only mailboxes that can give the caller valuable information such as office hours, delivery directions, and so on.

The best part of all this is that you can link these three types of mailbox objects into a set of menu-driven options that provide callers with a full-featured auto-attendant system. All without writing a single line of code!

FIGURE 31.15.
Starting Microsoft Phone.

NOTE

NOTE

As of this writing, Microsoft Phone is not available as a stand-alone product. Microsoft Phone is to be included as the default telephony application for several voice-data modem products sold in stores. You cannot get a copy of Microsoft Phone unless you buy the voice-data modem hardware. The list of hardware vendors committed to shipping Microsoft Phone is constantly changing. To get the latest information, check the TAPI vendors list in Appendix C, "TAPI Resources." You can also check the Communications Developer's Guide Web site for more information on MAPI, SAPI, and TAPI tools.

Microsoft Phone can answer your telephone for you, record incoming messages, and send these recorded messages to your Microsoft Exchange inbox for your review at another time. You can call into Microsoft Phone from a remote location and have the program play your e-mail messages back to you. You can even ask Microsoft Phone to "read" your text e-mail to you over the phone!

You can also use Microsoft Phone to place outbound calls. You can dial calls directly using the Microsoft Phone keypad, you can use one of the speed dial buttons, or you can call up the Microsoft Exchange address book and select a user's phone number from the address book. Microsoft Phone even checks incoming caller ID information against your Exchange address book to see if you already have that person on file.

When you first install Microsoft Phone, you can configure it to record messages and place them in your Exchange mailbox. This is done using the Greeting Wizard (see Figure 31.16).

FIGURE 31.16.
Using the Microsoft Phone Greeting Wizard.

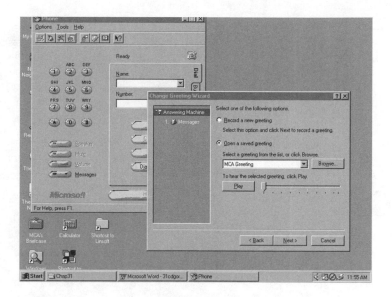

Adding Announcement, Message, and AutoFax Mailboxes

Microsoft Phone allows users to add several different mailboxes to handle incoming calls. Microsoft Phone recognizes three types of mailboxes:

- *Message mailboxes* allow callers to leave a recorded message.
- *Announcement mailboxes* play an announcement to the caller, but do not allow them to leave a message.
- *AutoFax mailboxes* send the caller a designated fax document.

You can set up your Microsoft Phone application to accept an incoming call, play a general message, and then allow the user to navigate between announcement, message, and fax mailboxes using his telephone keypad (see Figure 31.17).

Each message-type mailbox can be associated with a Microsoft Exchange mailbox. All messages sent to this Microsoft Phone mailbox will be delivered to the Microsoft Exchange box, too.

Each announcement-type mailbox can give the caller a complete message (for example, directions to the retail location, office hours, and so on) or can give the caller instructions on how to select a message box or receive a fax document.

Each AutoFax-type mailbox can send one (and only one) selected document to the user. The AutoFax box will ask the user for a telephone number as a destination address for the document and then send the document when the line is free.

FIGURE 31.17.
*Building additional
Microsoft Phone mailboxes.*

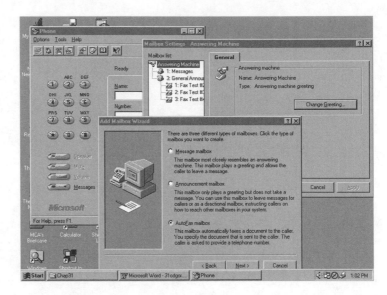

Configuring the Microsoft Phone Answering Machine

Once you install all the mailboxes, greetings, and fax documents you need, you can configure
the answering machine parameters (see Figure 31.18).

FIGURE 31.18.
*Configuring Microsoft
Phone.*

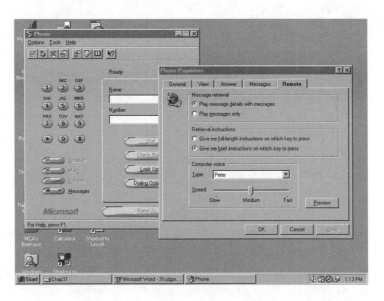

You can set parameters for several related groups of data:

- *General*—Use this page to control how Microsoft Phone handles incoming calls, including the use of caller ID and your Exchange address book, screening calls, and the use of Microsoft Voice to place speed-dial calls.

- *View*—Use this page to control how Microsoft Phone looks to the PC user. You can control the appearance of the toolbar, speed-dial buttons, and other onscreen displays.

- *Answer*—Use this page to control how Microsoft Phone behaves as an answering device. You can set the number of rings before Microsoft Phone picks up the call.

- *Message*—Use this page to control how long the recorded message will be and which Microsoft Exchange Profile is used to copy the messages from Microsoft Phone to Microsoft Exchange.

- *Remote*—Use this page to control how Microsoft Phone behaves when you call from a remote location to retrieve messages. You can direct Microsoft Phone to give either detailed or summary information about each message that is stored. You can also control which Microsoft Voice computer voice is used to read your text messages.

Summary

In this chapter you got a chance to review three tools that can help you develop end-user TAPI applications:

- *Visual Voice*—This is a set of OCX controls and support applications for creating telephony applications by using Visual Basic or C++ to place the Voice control on a form and then write Visual Basic code to set and get properties, invoke methods, and respond to TAPI events.

- *VBVoice*—This is a set of OCX controls that are used to create Visual Basic telephony applications without the use of Visual Basic code. You place a VBFrame control on a Visual Basic form, then place one of the other controls on the VBFrame. By setting control properties and linking the controls to each other, you can build a complete telephony application without writing Visual Basic code.

- *Microsoft Phone*—This is an end-user program that combines MAPI, SAPI, and TAPI services into a single virtual phone application. You can create message, announce-ment, and fax mailboxes and record menus and other greetings that instruct callers on how to leave messages and receive fax documents. Saved messages are placed in your Microsoft Exchange inbox and you can call Microsoft Phone from a remote location and direct it to use SAPI services to read your text e-mail messages over the phone.

32

Part IV Summary—The Telephony API

Chapter 22, "What Is TAPI?"

In the first chapter of this section you learned the general outline of the TAPI model including the use and meaning of two devices defined within the TAPI model:

- *Line devices* are used to model physical telephone lines.
- *Phone devices* are used to model physical telephone handsets.

You also discovered the relative advantages and disadvantages of the four main types of TAPI hardware configurations:

- *Phone-based*—for use in mostly voice-oriented calling
- *PC based*—for use in mostly PC-oriented calling
- *Shared* or *unified line*—for use when both voice and data share the phone use equally
- *Multiline*—for use as a voice server (for voice-mail) or as a PBX server (for computerized switchboards)

Finally, you learned how to identify the four main types of telephone service used to transmit voice and data signals:

- *Analog POTS* (*Plain Old Telephone Service*)—for general voice-grade transmissions and for data transmission up to 28.8kbps speed
- *Digital T1*—for dedicated high-speed voice and/or data services (56kbps and above)
- *ISDN* (*Integrated Services Digital Network*)—for high-speed multichannel simultaneous voice and data services
- *PBX* (*Private Branch Exchange*)—for use within proprietary switchboard hardware in an office setting

Chapter 23, "TAPI Architecture"

In Chapter 23 you learned how the TAPI service model is implemented as a set of API calls. You learned there are four levels of TAPI services:

- *Assisted Telephony* provides the simplest form of TAPI service.
- *Basic Telephony* provides basic in- and outbound telephony services for a single-line phone.
- *Supplemental Telephony* provides advanced telephone services such as hold, park, conference, and so on, to single and multiline phones.
- *Extended Telephony* provides a direct interface between Windows programs and vendor-specific TAPI services.

You also learned that the TAPI function set defines two different devices to handle telephony services:

- *Line devices* are used to control the connection between a data source and the physical telephone line.
- *Phone devices* are used to control the connection between a desktop handset and a line device.

Finally, you reviewed the API calls, data structures, and Windows messages defined for each level of TAPI service.

Chapter 24, "TAPI Basics"

In this chapter you learned how to build a simple TAPI dialer application in C using the Basic Telephony level of service. This application was used to highlight the basic operations required to build TAPI applications (in any language).

You learned how to perform line initialization, locate a usable outbound line, and open the line in preparation for dialing. You also learned how to place an outbound call and use the TAPI line callback function to monitor call progress. Finally, you learned how to close safely down a line after the call has been completed.

You learned the following key steps to placing outbound calls using Basic TAPI services:

- Call `lineInitialize` to start the TAPI session.
- Call `lineNegotiateAPIVersion` to make sure you can use the installed TAPI services.
- Call `lineOpen` to get a line that is appropriate for your needs (data, fax, voice, and so on).
- Use the `LINECALLPARAMS` structure to set up calling parameters before you place your call.
- Call `lineMakeCall` to actually attempt to place a TAPI call.

You also learned how to write a callback function to handle messages sent while the TAPI services are in action.

Chapter 25, "TAPI Hardware Considerations"

Chapter 25 showed you the differences between the three types of hardware options and how they rate in offering support for TAPI services on PC workstations.

- *Basic data modems* support Assisted Telephony services (outbound dialing) and can support only limited inbound call handling. Use this type of hardware if you are building simple outbound dialing applications.

- *Voice-data modems* are capable of supporting the Assisted Telephony and Basic Telephony services, and many of the Supplemental services. Use this type of hardware if you want to provide both inbound and outbound services on a single-line phone.

- *Telephony cards* support all of the Basic Telephony and all of the Supplemental Telephony services, including phone device control. Most telephony cards also offer multiple lines on a single card. This makes them ideal for supporting commercial-grade telephony applications.

You also got a quick review of modems and modem drivers. You learned that Win95 and WinNT rely on the UniModem or UniModemV modem drivers to communicate between the telephony hardware and your program. You also learned that, no matter what hardware you purchase, you will need a TAPI-compliant *TSPI* (*Telephony Service Provider Interface*) that matches the hardware you purchased. Hardware vendors can recognize the UniModem or UniModemV drivers, or ship their own TSPI drivers with their hardware.

Chapter 26, "TAPI Tools—Using the `TAPILINE` Control"

In this chapter you learned the properties, methods, and events of the `TAPILINE` control that ships on the CD-ROM that accompanies this book. You also learned how to use this control to gain access to TAPI services from within Visual Basic programs.

You learned how to perform the following TAPI service requests:

- Initialize a TAPI session.
- Confirm the TAPI version you are using.
- Get a list of device capabilities.
- Open a line for outbound calling.
- Place an outbound call.
- Drop an active call.
- De-allocate the idle call.
- Close an open line device.

You also learned how to monitor call progress using TAPI messages and the `lineGetCallInfo` and `lineGetAddress` methods. Finally, you learned how to call the four TAPI dialog boxes to gain access to configuration dialogs to customize your TAPI interface.

Chapter 27, "TAPI Behind the Scenes—The TELEPHON.INI File"

In Chapter 27 you learned that the TAPI system keeps track of vital information in the TELEPHON.INI file on the workstation. You learned there are four main sections in the TELEPHON.INI file:

- The *Service Provider section* holds information on all the Telephony service providers (TSPs) installed on the workstation.
- The *HandOff Priorities section* holds information about which line devices can support which media modes and the order in which the line devices should be called.
- The *Location section* holds information on the dialing locations of the workstation.
- The *Credit Card section* holds dialing instructions for using telephone service credit cards to control billing.

You learned the different predefined media modes that can be handled by registered TAPI applications in the [HandOffPriorities] section. You also learned the dialing codes that are used in the [Cards] section to tell TAPI how to place requested calls.

Finally, you built a small Visual Basic application that allowed you to gain direct access to the various TAPI line dialog boxes that can affect the TELEPHON.INI file.

Chapter 28, "Using TAPI to Handle Incoming Calls"

In Chapter 28 you learned how to use the TAPILINE control to create a Visual Basic application that can monitor a telephone line for incoming calls and allow users to answer those calls. In the process, you learned about the six steps needed to handle inbound calls using TAPI services:

- Initialize TAPI services on the workstation.
- Select and open valid line devices for incoming calls.
- Wait for an inbound call to appear on the line.
- When a call appears, accept the call and begin conversation.
- When the call ends, close the line and prepare for the next call.
- When the session is over, shut down TAPI services on the workstation.

You also learned the importance of the LINE_CALLSTATE message sent by TAPI whenever a new call appears on the line and when an active call becomes idle (the other party hangs up). You learned how to write code in the TapiCallBack event of the TAPILINE control to watch for and respond to LINE_CALLSTATE messages.

Finally, you learned the importance of getting the call handle from the LINECALLSTATE_OFFERING message and placing this value into the HandleToCall property of the TAPILINE control. This must be done before you can invoke the LineAnswer method to accept the incoming call.

Chapter 29, "Writing TAPI-Assisted Applications"

In this chapter you learned how to use the Assisted TAPI function (tapiRequestMakeCall) to build outbound voice-phone solutions in both Excel and Visual Basic 4.0. You developed tools that allow you to add phone dialing to any VBA-compatible application. You created a complete online phone book that can log all outbound calls into a Microsoft JET database that can be read, analyzed, and reported by other Windows programs.

You learned about the two API functions you can use to complete Assisted TAPI calls:

■ tapiGetLocationInfo returns the current country and city (area) codes set in the TELEPHON.INI file.

■ tapiRequestMakeCall initiates a voice-phone call by passing the dialing address (phone number) and other optional parameters including the dialing application to use, the name of the person you are calling, and a comment about the nature of the call.

You learned how to use these API calls to build a simple dialing routine in an Excel worksheet, and you used Visual Basic 4.0 to create an online telephone book that allows you to edit a phone list and place and track outbound calls.

Chapter 30, "Creating TAPI-Enabled Applications"

In Chapter 30 you applied all the information you have learned in the TAPI section to create a complete telephone in software. This "virtual phone" can be installed on any workstation that has TAPI services installed and at least a voice-data modem. If the workstation has a speaker phone, you do not even need a telephone handset on your desk.

You created the Visual Basic TapiFone project that used the TAPILINE control and contained code for handling both inbound and outbound calls. You also gave users access to the various TAPI dialog boxes and allowed them to maintain a set of configuration values for TAPIFONE in the Windows registry. TapiFone is also able to write and store call notes on each outbound call made through TapiFone.

Chapter 31, "Third-Party TAPI Tools"

Finally, in Chapter 31, you tested two third-party tools for developing TAPI solutions for Windows using Visual Basic 4.0. You learned how the Stylus Visual Voice Controls work with Visual Basic to provide a complete TAPI-compliant telephony solution.

You learned the Stylus Visual Voice kit contains eight basic Visual Voice components. Three of these components are controls:

- The Voice *control* is the main TAPI control. This gives you access to the standard TAPI events and methods.
- The Test *control* is used to simulate a live telephone line. With this control and a sound card, you can fully test your application without having to use live telephone lines.
- The VLink *control* is used to create conversation links between separate Visual Basic applications on the same machine. This is similar to a Visual Basic OLE server.

There are also five support applications that you can use to build and manage your TAPI applications:

- The *Voice Workbench* is a tool for creating and managing Visual Voice objects, including voice files, voice strings, voice queries, and code templates.
- The *Voice Monitor* is a Visual Basic application that can be used to monitor line activity on a multiline TAPI workstation. You'll use this to keep track of telephony activity on your TAPI PC.
- The *Virtual Phone* is a Visual Basic application that allows you to completely test your TAPI system without having to connect to and use live telephone lines. This application was built using the Test control mentioned earlier.
- The *TAPI Examiner* is a Visual Basic program that allows you to test individual TAPI services. This is a helpful debugging tool.
- *Stylus Trace* is a stand alone program that you can use to trace all Visual Voice activity on your workstation. It is excellent for debugging and checking out your Visual Voice installation.

You also learned how to use the VBVoice controls to create interactive telephony applications to handle all sorts of personal and commercial needs. The VBVoice system is made up of 21 different OCX controls. These controls represent all the major actions that can occur during a telephony session. You place these controls on your Visual Basic form and set their properties at design time. You then link them together in a call flow diagram that visually defines your program.

Finally, you got a quick tour of the Microsoft Phone system. This is a stand alone product that combines MAPI, SAPI, and TAPI services in a single package. With Microsoft Phone, you can create custom answering messages, have Microsoft Phone forward your messages to Microsoft Exchange, and have Microsoft Exchange read your text message back to you using the Speech API (SAPI).

The Future of Telephony and TAPI

The material covered here is just the tip of the iceberg for Windows telephony services. As the TAPI interface becomes more common, hardware prices will fall to levels that are affordable to almost anyone who purchases a PC. In the near future, the integration of e-mail, telephony, and speech services (such as Microsoft Phone) will become the norm instead of a unique occurrence.

As telephones become easier to program and operate from within PC workstations, it is quite possible that the telephone handset that adorns almost every desktop today will disappear. In its place will be a single workstation that can answer and place voice calls, transfer data between locations by way of e-mail and direct links, even read messages aloud to you both in the office and while you are away.

The next round of innovations will be the ability to switch between voice and data on the same line automatically. Some hardware is already available to handle such chores. In the not too distant future, users will be able to transfer voice and data at the same time over a single line—without switching modes at all.

In order to achieve the next level of telephony services, local loop service will need to improve to allow reliable data transfers at rates above 28.8Kbps. New data compression and correction technologies can help, but only to a point. The promised installation of high-speed ISDN lines that stretch from the local switch stations all the way to the home will do the most for improving the quality and capabilities of computerized telephony services in the future.

V

Creating Integrated
Applications

Now that you've learned how to develop applications that use messaging, speech, and telephony services, it's time to pull all your knowledge together. The chapters in this section show you how to use these related services to build tightly integrated applications that illustrate the power of using multiple service models in the same program.

As you've learned throughout this book, there are several places where these three API sets provide overlapping services. Chapter 33, "Design Considerations for Integrated Communications Applications," shows you how to determine when each of the three API sets covered in this book should be added to your program. You'll also learn how to best implement each of the services depending on the Windows operating system and programming tools available to you.

You'll use MAPI and TAPI to build a dial-up fax service in Chapter 34, "Building the FaxBack Application." Chapter 35, "Creating the Voice Phone Application," shows you how to use SAPI and TAPI to construct an application that allows callers to speak their requests to a telephony-enabled PC. In Chapter 36, "The Talk Mail Project," you'll build an application that combines all three services into a single system.

After working through the details of creating integrated applications, Chapter 37, "Integration Summary," will give you a concise review of the techniques covered in this section.

33

Design Considerations for Integrated Communications Applications

Introduction

Now that you have had experience with the three Windows communications extensions (MAPI, SAPI, and TAPI), you're ready to tackle the task of producing programs that integrate these API sets into a single application. But before you leap into the dark waters of multi-API application development, it's a good idea to take some time to test the depth of your ideas and review the pros and cons of using one or more of the API sets covered in this book.

As you've learned throughout this book, there are several places where these three API sets provide overlapping services. This chapter shows you how to determine when each of the three API sets covered in this book should be added to your program. You'll also learn how to best implement each of the services depending on the Windows operating system and programming tools available to you.

There are a number of things to consider when building an application that combines multiple services. This chapter will cover the following main points:

- *General considerations*—Some general rules of thumb regarding complexity, mixing of API sets, and the advantages and disadvantages of using native API calls vs. high-level third-party tools. This section wraps up with a discussion of the pros and cons of building standalone applications vs. creating extensions or add-ins for existing desktop applications.

- *MAPI versus Comm API*—This section covers some things to consider when building applications that will perform file transfers. Depending on the client and destination, it may be wise to use the Comm API to create a custom file transfer application instead of using MAPI services.

- *Assisted TAPI versus Full TAPI*—Much of Part IV was spent discussing the possibilities of full TAPI. Is it always needed? Often Assisted TAPI provides all the capability you need to implement TAPI services for your applications.

- *When to use the Speech API*—SAPI services are still quite new. Often you can use recorded WAV files to meet most of your human speech output needs. However, there are times when SAPI is the best answer. This section goes through some checklists to help you decide if the Speech API is the best route for your application.

When you finish this chapter, you should have a pretty good idea of how to evaluate your application needs and recognize how each of the Windows extension services fits into your application's design and implementation plans.

General Considerations

When first beginning the design phase of an application, ideas about what users need and how they will interact with the system are purposefully vague. The general flow of a software system and the interface needed to support that flow are only hinted at. Once it comes time to actually build the application, however, things are different. Now all the promises and hopes of the design group rest on the few brave souls who have the task of implementing the design.

As Windows services become more common and familiar to users, the minimum requirement for new applications is constantly being increased. A few years ago users were pleased to get friendly screens that beeped at the moment they entered invalid data instead of waiting until the batch was completed and the error report printed. Now users expect to see drop-down list boxes, context-sensitive help, and "wizards" and "assistants" that will tell them ahead of time what data they should be entering! And they often get just that.

It is very common for users to expect e-mail to be an integral part of every application. Now users are learning the possibilities of linking telephones to their systems, too. And where telephones appear, speech processing cannot be far behind. The hardest thing to keep in mind is that not all applications need all the extensions. And even the ones that do need extension services can often get by with less than a full plate of service options.

Adding features and services without taking the time to think about how they will interact can lead to major headaches. This section covers some general rules to keep in mind when designing and implementing multiservice apps.

Rules of Complexity

The first thing to keep in mind is that each new service you add to your system adds complexity. And this complexity increases by orders of magnitude. When you decide to add one of these services, think long and hard. And if you still want (or need) to add the service, prepare for additional time to redesign, code, and test your application. Despite what anyone tells you, adding e-mail or telephony or speech services to an application is no simple matter.

For example, adding e-mail to a system doesn't just mean you need to add a few menu items to the screens to allow users to send documents. You now have to deal with users attempting to format documents for printers *and* for e-mail messages. Now users will want to send multiple copies of the same message, possibly to someone halfway around the world. And that person probably uses a different e-mail format, too! While good e-mail service models (like MAPI) will mask much of this detail, you can still end up with requests for features that push the limits of your system.

Now consider adding telephony or speech services to the same program. While the possible applications of new technologies are exciting, the possible collisions of APIs can be daunting. For this reason, it is always a good idea to limit the feature sets you build into an application. While users will often ask for (and get) the latest technological breakthroughs, they don't often use them to their fullest potential. It is important to keep a clear head about just which "bells and whistles" are *required* and which are *desired.* Each new service extension adds a level of complexity to the system—for designers, programmers, and users. It is a good idea to do your best to limit the extension sets that are added to any single application. Usually this can be done without sacrificing features.

Native API versus High-Level Tools

Once you decide on just what services you will include in your application you need to decide on how you will deliver these services. Often the first inclination is to acquire the latest API/COM specification documents and begin coding function and class libraries to encapsulate the desired services. While this is good, it may be unnecessary. Often there is a very good high-level toolkit that you can use to gain access to the service. And these high-level tools come with support and documentation already built.

Visual Basic programmers tend to think first of third-party add-ons. This is because they usually live in a programming universe that is inundated with OLE, OCX, and VBX solutions to problems most of them never knew existed! But even C++ programmers can find more high-level tools on the market today—especially MFC libraries that encapsulate complex APIs. It pays to look around before you start any "deep coding" of the API set.

Of course, there are drawbacks to using high-level third-party tools. Sometimes they are limited in their performance. Sometimes, they even turn out to be buggy. While the latter is a rarity, the former is often the case. Most third-party tools are designed to solve a particular set of problems. If you attempt to use the tool to solve problems outside the original scope of the tool, you can easily become frustrated and disappointed. It's a good idea to thoroughly test controls and libraries before adding them to a production application.

Finally, using home-grown libraries or native API calls means that you will need to keep up with the latest bug lists and upgrades for the underlying API. This, too, can be a big job. Often, it is easier to spend the time shopping for a good tool and keep current on its upgrades. (Assuming, of course, that the product you purchase actually keeps up with the latest releases. Nothing is more annoying than discovering that the product you based your whole system upon is no longer in release!)

Standalone versus Extensions and Add-ins

The last thing to keep in mind when designing and implementing applications that take advantage of the new Windows services is the standalone versus extensions/add-ins debate. Is it better to write your own standalone voice-activated e-mail client or to create extensions or add-ins to existing clients already on the desktop (such as Windows Messaging or Microsoft Mail clients)?

Often it is easier to build your own standalone versions of common applications. It takes very little time to build a working e-mail client using the MAPI client interface. This allows you to add whatever features you need without concern for generating conflicts or confusion when adding features to existing products.

The advantage of extensions and add-ins is that you don't have to reinvent major portions of your application. Most of the primary desktop tools (e-mail, databases, spreadsheets, word-processors, and so on) are easier than ever to program. Most of the Microsoft Office applications are able to host the Visual Basic language, and even ones that do not will allow simple API calls into predefined "hooks" inside the target application. With a bit of reading and lot of experimentation, you can get your extensions to coexist comfortably with the desktop application.

The general rule to use in deciding whether to go the standalone or extensions/add-ins route is: Check your client base. If most clients have the targeted desktop application (and they are likely to keep it), then go the extension route. However, if most of your users have a mix of client applications, or no client applications at all, you would be better to build your own standalone application (based on the pertinent Windows extension service). Then you can deploy it among a wider collection of workstations without having to battle different hosting applications, and so on.

MAPI versus Comm API

A common dilemma for programmers is whether to use MAPI services or Comm API services to perform file transfers and retrievals. In the past almost all file transfers (such as daily payment batches, sales figures, and so on) were handled using dedicated applications. It sometimes took hours for these specialized transfer routines to perform their tasks and, instead of tying up existing systems, this kind of transfer work was off-loaded to dedicated machines.

With the maturing of e-mail and the expansion of the Internet, much of this activity is moving through electronic mail instead of direct dialup applications. For the most part this is good. But there are times when a simple dialup application can be a better solution than e-mail.

The advantage of e-mail is the widespread coverage that is so easy using a single protocol (MAPI). Also, the MAPI model has fairly good recovery in the cases of non-deliverable messages. While it is quite possible that an e-mail message will get routed to the wrong address or return to you marked "undeliverable," it's rare to actually *lose* a message sent via e-mail. Another plus for MAPI services is that there is a wealth of utilities and support software for both programmers and users. MAPI is the standard and almost any e-mail client supports MAPI services.

The disadvantage of MAPI is that this protocol can be quite limiting in the types and lengths of message formats that can be sent. The most reliable data format is an ASCII text file. If you plan to send binary data, you'll need to be sure your routing path to all points is able to handle the binary format. Also, large files tend to get garbled when sent using MAPI protocol. Many public mail servers even truncate messages to reduce bottlenecks in the system. This can lead to tedious conversions of binary data into multifile messages that must be reassembled and converted back to binary before they are usable for the recipient. While utilities exist for this type of arrangement (MIME encoders, for example), it's not always the best way to go.

The advantage of using a dedicated Comm API-based application is that you can write small, fast, and relatively simple file transfer programs using any one of several reliable and well-documented PC file transfer protocols (the X-, Y-, and Z-modem protocols are good examples).

By writing small, dedicated applications, you can focus on the things you need and leave out all the "headroom" required by MAPI e-mail systems.

One of the biggest headaches when using dedicated programs is file transfer scheduling. Usually both systems must be up and running at the exact same moment. This is often handled by establishing a fixed file transfer schedule. Each machine is expected to be available at a certain time of the day, week, or month to receive or send data files. Anyone who has nursed a system like this knows how troublesome this kind of scheduling can be. Unless the calls are timed correctly, sites that receive a lot of calls will send out frustrating busy signals. Also, if a receiving site goes down (due to power failure, for example) the whole system can grind to a halt in short order. As long as there are not a lot of sites involved in this kind of arrangement, dedicated binary transfers can often be faster and more reliable than ASCII text e-mail messaging.

So, to sum it up, if your application needs to distribute information to a wide number of locations on demand, mostly in ASCII text format, then e-mail and Internet/Intranet distribution is probably the best method. If you need to send binary data to just a few sites on a regular schedule (daily, weekly, and so on), then you should consider building a dedicated dialing application that uses the Comm API (or OCX) instead of MAPI services.

Assisted TAPI versus Full TAPI

As TAPI systems become more commonplace, it is more likely that creative minds will come up with a reason to use the new extensions for as yet undreamed-of applications. While the benefits of Full TAPI services are clear, most applications—especially client-side applications—do not need full use of the TAPI extension. For the most part, server systems tend to work with inbound calls and client systems usually handle outbound calling. If you are building a TAPI application, you need to determine if you are building a client- or a server-side application.

Of course, just what constitutes a server is hard to define. With the introduction of Win95 to the market, lots of end users have all the tools they need to act as a server in telephony or any other Windows extension service. But, despite changes in the operating systems, the rule still holds—clients place calls, servers answer them.

If you are designing a system for sales force automation, you may be able to provide solid support for key features using only Assisted (outbound) telephony services. In fact, some telemarketing shops do not want their employees handling any inbound calls at all. Keep in mind that you can still build serious "power-dialer" applications using only Assisted TAPI services. You can create applications that read phone number databases, automatically place calls, and present telemarketing staff with dialog boxes that contain customer-specific information without using Full TAPI services.

Another major advantage of using Assisted TAPI to meet your telephony needs is that almost any data modem is capable of successfully placing outbound calls. You will rarely need to purchase specialized hardware in order to allow users to call out using their workstations.

On the flip side, if you are in charge of building customer service center applications that can accept and route incoming calls based on ANI (Automatic Number Identification), caller ID, or other values such as an account number entered at the telephone keypad, you'll need the Full TAPI service model to reach your goals. If you decide you need to accept digits and other call-progress information from incoming calls, you should also consider using a third-party TAPI development tool. These are relatively inexpensive and usually provide excellent support and documentation. A good TAPI tool can make telephony programming relatively painless.

Of course, with the added capabilities comes the requirement for increased hardware features. TAPI applications that handle inbound calls will need to use at least a high-grade voice-data modem. If you are building an application that will get heavy use or one that uses multiple lines, you need to replace your modem with a telephony card. While these cost more, they mean a huge increase in capacity for your Windows TAPI applications.

So, again, if you are building client-side applications that will be used primarily for placing outbound calls, it is quite possible that you can solve your problems using Assisted TAPI services. If, however, you are building applications that will act as telephony server devices—answering and routing incoming calls—you'll need to use Full TAPI and you will probably need a full-featured telephony card, too.

When to Use the Speech API

Knowing when to use SAPI services can be a bit tricky, too. While speech systems for computers have been around for some time, the Microsoft SAPI model is still a newcomer. For the most part, SAPI works best as a text-to-speech engine instead of as a speech recognition system. Even as a TTS tool, the SAPI system has its limits.

Reading extensive amounts of text using SAPI's TTS engine can quickly tire the average user. This is because the computer-generated voice lacks the human prosody (speech patterns) to which users are accustomed. If you have material that is relatively stable (for example, directions to your office), it is a better idea to use a recorded WAV format file than to have SAPI "read" the text to users.

Another consideration is the amount of processing power needed for SAPI services. The SAPI system requires more memory and processor time than the other two services covered in this book—and for good reason. The amount of calculation needed to convert ASCII text into recognizable human speech is quite large. Converting speech into models that can be compared to registered voice menus is even more resource intensive. If you expect most (or even some) of your users to have less than 16MB of memory on their workstations, you'll have a hard time successfully deploying SAPI services within your applications.

Finally, the accuracy of SAPI speech recognition (SR) is highly variable. The current state of technology is only able to reliably handle single words or short phrases. SR systems are best used as an addition to keyboard or mouse controls within an application. It's frustrating to have to repeat the same phrase over and over again (getting ever louder each time) in an attempt to get your workstation to perform some simple task that could have been accomplished with a few clicks of the mouse or keyboard.

For the near term, save your users aggravation (and embarrassment) by providing speech recognition as an option in your programs, not a sole source of input. This will give users time to get used to the idea of talking to inanimate objects without feeling silly, and it will give the technology a bit more time to mature and improve its performance.

Summary

In this chapter you learned some of the advantages and disadvantages of deploying software that uses the MAPI, SAPI, and TAPI extension services for Windows operating systems. The general points discussed included:

- *The Rule of Complexity*—Where possible, try to limit the number and depth of service extensions used in a single application. With added services comes added complexity—both for the user and the programmer.

- *Native APIs versus High-Level Tools*—Consider the pros and cons of using native API calls vs. employing high-level third-party add-on tools to provide access to extension services. The Native API calls may be faster, but they will also require more coding and maintenance for you and your staff. Building applications with third-party tools can be more efficient as long as that tool is used correctly and it is well supported and documented by its authors.

- *Standalone versus Extensions and Add-Ins*—When adding new extensions to your applications consider the advantages of building simple standalone versions of the target application instead of adding features to existing applications. There are times when a standalone solution is most efficient. However, if you need to deploy MAPI, SAPI, or TAPI services to a large number of people who already have products they know and use often, it may be simpler to distribute add-ins or extensions instead of attempting to replace well-established user tools.

- *MAPI versus Comm API*—As a general rule, if your application needs to distribute information to a wide number of locations on demand, mostly in ASCII text format, your best bet is to use MAPI services. If, however, you need to send binary data to just a few sites on a regular schedule (daily, weekly, and so on) then you should consider building smaller, more focused, dedicated dialing applications that use the Comm API (or OCX).

- *Assisted TAPI versus Full TAPI*—Client-side applications usually need only outbound calling services. It is quite possible that you can meet client-side design goals using Assisted TAPI services and simple data/fax modems. If, however, you are building applications that will act as telephony server devices—answering and routing incoming calls—you'll need to use Full TAPI and you will probably need a full-featured telephony card, too.

■ *Using the Speech API*—Current speech technology is more consistent when delivering TTS (text to speech) services than SR (speech recognition) services. The SAPI system requires a hefty pool of memory (no less than 16MB is recommended on the workstation). Also, SR services are not always accurate. It is best to offer SAPI services as an additional service rather than as the primary service at this time. As the technology matures and users become more accustomed to hearing TTS output and speaking in a manner easily understood by SAPI systems, you can increase the use of speech services in your applications.

Now that you've got a handle on the ups and downs of mixing extension services, it's time to work through some sample applications that do just that. In the next three chapters you'll build applications that mix MAPI, SAPI, and/or TAPI services within the same application in order to fulfill a design goal.

34

Building the FaxBack Application

Introduction

In this chapter you'll build a Visual Basic 4.0 project that combines TAPI and MAPI services to create a dial-up FAX server. With this application running on a workstation, users could dial into the workstation, receive prompts for entering their own FAX telephone number, and select a document number. Then, when the user hangs up, the workstation will format and send the selected FAX document to the user's FAX address.

This example application will be a bit Spartan in construction. The caller prompts are simple and the error handling is very basic. This was done to focus on the details of putting together the larger pieces of the project. If you plan to implement a production version of this program, you'll need to spend a bit more time polishing it up. However, when you are done with this project, you'll have a working FAX server that you can install on any 32-bit Windows workstation.

> **NOTE**
>
> The evaluation version of VBVoice is not fully functional. You'll be able to complete a demonstration version of the project, but you will not be able to install a production version unless you purchase a licensed copy of VBVoice.

Project Resources

The VBVoice controls answer the incoming call and prompt the caller to enter a FAX number and the selected document number. Once this is done, the VBVoice controls turn the collected data over to the MAPI system for delivery of the selected FAX.

The following resources must be available on your workstation in order to build and run the FaxBack project:

- *Microsoft Exchange with FAX transport services installed*—The Microsoft Exchange Server and Workstation versions both come with FAX transport support built in. If you haven't installed FAX services for your Exchange profile, you should do it before you start this project. If you are running Microsoft Mail you can still complete this project if the Microsoft Mail server supports FAX transmissions.

- *FAX modem*—If you're running a stand-alone workstation, you'll need to have a FAX modem attached. If you are running as a client to a mail server that supports FAX transmissions, you may not need a FAX modem on your workstation.

- *Sound card and speakers*—This example program will use the sound card and speakers to simulate an incoming telephone call. The evaluation copy of VBVoice will not work with an installed telephony card.

The next few sections go into a bit more detail on the VBVoice controls and how they are used. You'll also get a quick review of the SMAPI interface and the support files you'll need to load in order to complete this project.

The VBVoice Controls

To gain access to the TAPI services, you'll use an evaluation version of the VBVoice control set from Pronexus, Inc. An evaluation version of the controls can be found on the CD-ROM that ships with this book. With this evaluation set, you'll be able to build and compile your Visual Basic 4.0 application and run it in test mode using your sound card and speakers.

> **NOTE**
>
> The VBVoice controls were briefly reviewed in Chapter 31, "Third-Party TAPI Tools." Refer to that chapter for more information on the VBVoice controls and how they are used to build telephony applications.

If you haven't already done so, install the evaluation copy of VBVoice32 from the CD-ROM that ships with this book.

> **WARNING**
>
> If you already own a working copy of VBVoice *do not* install the evaluation version because this may trash your working copy.

When you install VBVoice, you'll have a rich set of controls available for creating telephony applications. Be sure to add these controls to your FaxBack project before you begin coding (select Tools ¦ Custom Controls).

The FAX.VAP Voice Prompt File

The FaxBack project is based on a FAX demonstration project available from the Pronexus FTP site (ftp.pronexus.com). The demonstration program includes a *voice prompt file* (*VAP*) that has all the basic prompts you need to complete this project. Instead of going through the process of recording your own prompts for the FaxBack example, you'll use the FAX.VAP file that is provided by Pronexus. You'll find this on the CD-ROM that comes with this book, too.

> **NOTE**
>
> For those who are curious, the voice you'll hear in the VAP file is not mine (sorry!).

If you plan on putting a version of this application into production, you'll want to use the Pronexus voice recording tools to create your own set of prompts.

The SMAPI Support Modules

In this project you'll use the SMAPI interface to provide access to the message services of Windows. The SMAPI interface was chosen because it has a very small "footprint" in your project. While the MAPI.OCX controls and the OLE Messaging library would also work fine, the SMAPI provides all the MAPI access that is needed for this project.

> **TIP**
>
> The SMAPI interface was covered in depth in Chapter 6, "Creating MAPI-Aware Applications." You can refer to that chapter for more information on the SMAPI interface and how it works.

There are two support modules that you can add to your Visual Basic project to provide access to the SMAPI level of messaging services.

- VBMAPI32.DLL—This is the support DLL that sits between your Visual Basic calls and the MAPI subsystem. You can find this on the CD-ROM that ships with this book.

- VBAMAP32.BAS—This file contains type definitions, constants, and the API declarations needed to access Simple MAPI from any 32-bit platform. The API calls in this file go directly to the VBAMAP32.DLL mentioned above.

- MAPIERR.BAS—This file provides a handy function that translates the error codes returned by SMAPI into friendly strings. This project does not use this function, but it is a good idea to include it in all your SMAPI projects.

> **NOTE**
>
> All four files discussed here were covered in greater detail in Chapter 6, "Creating MAPI-Aware Applications." Refer to that chapter for more information on SMAPI services.

When you begin this project, you can add these BAS files (select File ¦ Add Files) instead of typing them in again.

Starting the FaxBack Project

So, here's a quick review—you'll need the following resources for this project:

- Access to a FAX modem.
- A sound card and speakers.
- A version of Microsoft Exchange or Microsoft Mail that supports FAX messaging.
- The evaluation version of VBVoice32 installed on your workstation.
- The FAX.VAP VBVoice prompt file installed in your project directory.
- The MAPI32.DLL installed in your WINDOWS\SYSTEM folder.
- The MAPIERR.BAS and VBAMAP32.BAS support files installed in your project directory.

Once you've assembled all these resources, you're ready to start your project. Start Visual Basic 4.0 and add the VBVoice controls to your toolbox (select Tools ¦ Custom Controls). Next add the two SMAPI support files (MAPIERR.BAS and VBAMAP32.BAS) to your project (select Files ¦ Add Files). It's a good idea to copy the support files to the sample directory that you'll be using to build the FaxBack project.

At this point your Visual Basic 4.0 design-mode environment should look something like the one in Figure 34.1.

FIGURE 34.1.

Visual Basic design-mode environment for the FaxBack project.

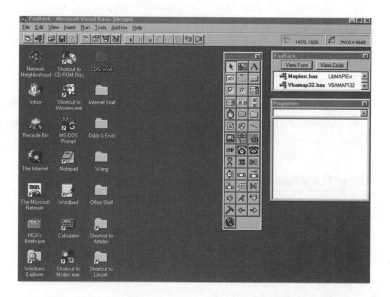

Notice the VBVoice controls in the toolbox and the two SMAPI support files in the project window. Now you're ready to start coding!

Coding the FaxBack Support Module

The FaxBack support module has five routines and several project-level variables. Add a new module to the project (Insert ¦ Module) and set its Name property to modFaxBack. Save the empty module as FAXBACK.BAS.

Now add the project-level variables. These will be used throughout the application. Listing 34.1 shows the code that you should place in the general declaration section of the module.

Listing 34.1. Adding the project-level variables.

```
Option Explicit
'
' fax variables
Public cFAXPrefix As String ' file prefix
Public cFAXSuffix As String ' file tail
Public cTestFAXAddr As String ' local FAX machine
Public cFAXFolder As String ' document folder
'
' SMAPI variables
Public lReturn As Long ' return flag
Public lSession As Long ' session handle
Public udtMessage As MapiMessage ' message object
Public udtRecip As MapiRecip ' recipient object
Public udtRecips() As MapiRecip ' recipient collection
Public udtFile As MapiFile ' attachment object
Public udtFiles() As MapiFile ' attachment collection
```

You can see there are two sets of variables. The first set will be used to keep track of FAX-related values. The second set of variables will be used to handle MAPI service requests.

The next routine you'll add to the project is a function to verify the existence of a file. Add a new function called FileExists to your project (Insert ¦ Procedure ¦ Function), then add the code shown in Listing 34.2.

Listing 34.2. Adding the FileExists function to the module.

```
Public Function FileExists(cFile As String) As Integer
    '
    ' return TRUE if found, FALSE if not
    '
    Dim x  As Integer
    x = FreeFile
    '
    On Error Resume Next
    Open cFile For Input As x
    If Err = 0 Then
        FileExists = True
    Else
        FileExists = False
    End If
```

```
      Close x
      '
End Function
```

This routine attempts to open a filename passed into the function. If the open is successful, the routine returns TRUE. If the open fails, it is assumed the file does not exist and the routine returns FALSE.

Now add a new subroutine called CenterForm. This will be used to center forms on the display. Listing 34.3 has the code you need to fill out this routine.

Listing 34.3. Adding the CenterForm routine.

```
Public Sub CenterForm(frm As Form)
    '
    ' place form in center of display
    '
    frm.Left = (Screen.Width - frm.Width) / 2
    frm.Top = (Screen.Height - frm.Height) / 2
    '
End Sub
```

The next two routines handle logging in and out of MAPI services. The first routine (SMAPIStart) initializes the workstation for MAPI services. Add the code shown in Listing 34.4 to your project.

Listing 34.4. Adding the SMAPIStart routine.

```
Public Sub SMAPIStart(lhWnd As Long, cLogID As String)
    '
    ' start an SMAPI session
    '
    lReturn = MAPILogon(lhWnd, cLogID, "", MAPI_LOGON_UI And MAPI_NEW_SESSION, 0, 
➥lSession)
    If lReturn <> SUCCESS_SUCCESS Then
        MsgBox MAPIErr(lReturn)
        End
    End If
    '
End Sub
```

The SMAPIStart routine attempts to log in with the profile name passed into the routine. If the profile name is invalid, a dialog box will appear to prompt you for a valid logon ID. The logon will result in a new MAPI session for this workstation. This way, any other open MAPI session you have on your station will not be affected by the FaxBack application.

Now add the SMAPIEnd routine to your project and enter the code from Listing 34.5.

Listing 34.5. Adding the SMAPIEnd routine.

```
Public Sub SMAPIEnd(lhWnd As Long)
    '
    ' end an SMAPI session
    '
    lReturn = MAPILogoff(lSession, lhWnd, 0, 0)
    '
End Sub
```

This routine simply logs off the current active MAPI session. You'll call this at the end of your program.

The only other support routine left is the routine that will actually compose and send the FAX by way of MAPI services. Add a new subroutine called SendSMAPIFax to the module and enter the code from listing 34.6.

Listing 34.6. Adding the SendSMAPIFax routine.

```
Public Sub SendSMAPIFax(lhWnd As Long, cFile As String, cRecipient As String)
    '
    ' queue up an smapi fax message
    '

    '
    ' get simple file name
    Dim cName As String
    cName = Mid(cFile, Len(cFAXFolder) + 2, 255)
    '
    ' make message
    udtMessage.Subject = "Requested FAX From FaxBack(tm)"
    udtMessage.NoteText = "Here's the FAX document you requested from FaxBack(tm)."
➥& Chr(13) & Chr(13) & " #"
    '
    ' make attachment
    ReDim udtFiles(1)
    udtFiles(0).Position = Len(udtMessage.NoteText) - 1
    udtFiles(0).PathName = cFile
    udtFiles(0).FileName = cName
    udtFiles(0).FileType = 0
    '
    ' make recipient
    udtRecip.Reserved = 0
    udtRecip.RecipClass = 1
    udtRecip.Name = "FAX:FaxBack_Request@" & cRecipient
    udtRecip.Address = "FAX:FAXBack_Request@" & cRecipient
    udtRecip.EIDSize = 100
    udtRecip.EntryID = ""
    '
    ' update message
    udtMessage.RecipCount = 1
    udtMessage.FileCount = 1
    '
    ' now call sendmail w/o dialog
```

```
    lReturn = MAPISendMail(lSession, lhWnd, udtMessage, udtRecip, udtFiles(0), &H0,
➥0)   '
End Sub
```

There's a lot going on in this routine. First, the routine accepts three parameters as input. The first parameter is the window handle used in all SMAPI calls. The second parameter is the file to be faxed. The third parameter is the phone number to use as the address for the MAPI fax. Once the routine has all the parameters, it's time to go to work.

The first step is to create a "simple" filename by stripping the folder name from the second parameter. This will be used as part of the attachment. Next, the routine builds a simple subject and message body for the MAPI message. The "#" at the end of the message marks the position where the attachment will be placed.

After building the message body, the attachment is created. Most of this should make sense. Setting the FileType property to "0" tells MAPI that this is an embedded data file instead of some type of OLE attachment.

Next comes the fun part—creating the recipient. Remember "one-off" addressing? That's where you use the actual MAPI transport name as part of the message. In this routine the .Name and .Address properties are both set to the internal complete MAPI address required for FAX messages. The FAX: tells MAPI to handle this message using the FAX transport provider. The stuff between the ":" and the "@" is just filler—MAPI ignores it. The last part of the address is the telephone number the FAX transport will use to deliver the message. The other property settings are default values used in all SMAPI recipient types.

Finally, after building the message, attaching the file, and creating the FAX address, the routine updates the recipient and file count and then calls the MAPISendMail function to place the message into the MAPI outbox.

What happens next depends on how your FAX transport is configured. If you have your FAX transport set to deliver faxes immediately, you'll see the FAX transport kick in, format the attachment, and send it out over the modem line. If you have your transport set to delay delivery for off-peak hours, you'll see the formatting, but the FAX will sit in a queue until later. Also, the cover sheet used for your FAX messages is established by settings for the FAX transport provider.

> **TIP**
>
> You can review your FAX transport settings from the Windows Messaging client by pressing the alternate mouse button on the Exchange inbox icon and selecting Properties from the context menu. Then select the FAX transport from the Services list and click the Properties button. You can even edit or invent new cover pages from this dialog box.

That's the end of the support routines. Save this module (FAXBACK.BAS) and the project (FAXBACK.VBP) before continuing with the next section.

The FaxBack Form

The FaxBack form is the main form of the project. Although there is not much code in the project, setting up the form takes quite a bit of doing. This is because most of the logic of the program is kept in the properties of the VBVoice controls on the form.

There are really three steps to building the FaxBack form:

- Laying out the controls on the form.
- Setting the VBVoice control properties.
- Coding the form.

The next three sections cover these three steps in greater detail.

Laying Out the FaxBack Form

Laying out the controls on the FaxBack form is more involved than doing the same for standard Visual Basic forms. This is because most of the controls on the form are VBVoice telephony controls. These controls require additional property settings and must be linked to one another to complete the call-flow diagram that will control each incoming call. You'll actually diagram the call progress and set the program properties at the same time. By the time you've diagrammed the call, you will have built almost all the logic needed to handle incoming fax requests.

First you need to lay out the controls on the form. Refer to Figure 34.2 and Table 34.1 for details on laying out the FaxBack form.

WARNING

Be sure to add the VBVFrame control to the form first. Then *draw* the VBVoice controls onto the VBVFrame control. If you do not draw them on (instead of double-clicking the control in the toolbox), you'll get error messages while you are trying to build your form.

FIGURE 34.2.
Laying out the FaxBack form.

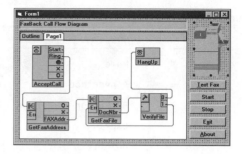

Table 34.1. The FaxBack form controls.

Control	Property	Setting
VB.Form	Name	frmFaxBack
	Caption	"Form1"
	Font	name="MS Sans Serif"
		charset=0
		weight=700
		size=8.25
	ForeColor	&H80000008&
	Height	4665
	Left	1470
	LinkTopic	"Form1"
	ScaleHeight	4260
	ScaleWidth	7290
	Top	1830
	Width	7410
VB.CommandButton	Name	cmdFax
	Appearance	0 'Flat
	BackColor	&H80000005&
	Caption	"&About"
	Height	300
	Index	4
	Left	6000
	TabIndex	11
	Top	3780
	Width	1200

continues

Table 34.1. continued

Control	Property	Setting
VB.CommandButton	Name	cmdFax
	Appearance	0 'Flat
	BackColor	&H80000005&
	Caption	"E&xit"
	Height	300
	Index	3
	Left	6000
	TabIndex	9
	Top	3360
	Width	1200
VB.CommandButton	Name	cmdFax
	Appearance	0 'Flat
	BackColor	&H80000005&
	Caption	"&Test Fax"
	Height	300
	Index	0
	Left	6000
	TabIndex	8
	Top	2100
	Width	1200
VB.CommandButton	Name	cmdFax
	Appearance	0 'Flat
	BackColor	&H80000005&
	Caption	"Start"
	Height	300
	Index	1
	Left	6000
	TabIndex	7
	Top	2520
	Width	1200
VB.CommandButton	Name	cmdFax
	Appearance	0 'Flat

Control	Property	Setting
	BackColor	&H80000005&
	Caption	"Stop"
	Height	300
	Index	2
	Left	6000
	TabIndex	6
	Top	2940
	Width	1200
VBVoiceLibCtl.VBVFrame	Name	VBVFrame1
	Height	3675
	Left	135
	TabIndex	0
	Top	435
	Width	5760
	CurrPage	0
	NumFields	0
	Playformat	3
	VoiceDir	"d:\sams\CDG\Chap34\"
	TimeFormat	0
	DateOrder	0
	LanguageId	0
	NumControls	5
VBVoiceLibCtl.User	Name	VerifyFile
	Height	900
	Left	4140
	TabIndex	1
	Top	2100
	Width	945
	ClearDigits	0 'False
	NumConditions	2
	Condition0.Name	"0"
	Condition0.Data	""

continues

Table 34.1. continued

Control	Property	Setting
	`Condition0.UseVB=`	'True
	`Condition1.Name`	"1"
	`Condition1.Data`	""
	`Condition1.UseVB=`	'True
	`FramePage`	0
	`NumNodes`	2
`VBVoiceLibCtl.Onhook`	`Name`	HangUp
	`Height`	600
	`Left`	3960
	`TabIndex`	2
	`Top`	540
	`Width`	855
	`EntryGreeting.` `Phrase0.Data=`	message has been sent"
	`EntryGreeting.` `Phrase0.Type=`	
	`FramePage`	0
	`NumNodes`	0
	`Comment`	""
`VBVoiceLibCtl.GetDigits`	`Name`	GetFaxFile
	`Height`	975
	`Left`	2340
	`TabIndex`	3
	`Top`	2160
	`Width`	1140
	`maxRetries`	2
	`EntryGreeting.` `Phrase0.Data=`	enter the number of the document you require."
	`ClearDigits`	0 'False
	`NumConditions`	1
	`Condition0.Name`	"DocNbr"
	`Condition0.Data`	"nnn"
	`Condition0.UseVB=`	'False

Control	Property	Setting
	FramePage	0
	NumNodes	3
	Dest2.Conn	-1 'True
	Comment	""
	MaxKeys	0
	MaxSil	5
	TermDtmf	4096
	RetryOnSilence	0 'False
	useDefaultError	0 'False
	DisableHelp	-1 'True
VBVoiceLibCtl.GetDigits	Name	GetFaxAddress
	Height	975
	Left	240
	TabIndex	4
	Top	2400
	Width	1440
	maxRetries	2
	EntryGreeting. Phrase0.Data=	enter the number of your fax machine followed by a pound sign"
	EntryGreeting. Phrase0.Type=	
	NumConditions	1
	Condition0.Name	"FAXAddr"
	Condition0.Data	"$"
	Condition0.UseVB=	'False
	FramePage	0
	NumNodes	3
	Dest2.Conn	-1 'True
	Comment	""
	MaxKeys	0
	MaxSil	5
	TermDtmf	4096

continues

Table 34.1. continued

Control	Property	Setting
	RetryOnSilence	0 'False
	useDefaultError	0 'False
	DisableHelp	-1 'True
VBVoiceLibCtl.LineGroup	Name	AcceptCall
	Height	1425
	Left	420
	TabIndex	5
	Top	480
	Width	1080
	FramePage	0
	NumNodes	5
	Comment	""
	DelayTime	5
	LineType	0
	Mode	2
	LinesInGroup	""
	Mode	2
VB.Image	Name	Image1
	Height	1815
	Left	6120
	Stretch	-1 'True
	Top	120
	Width	1155
VB.Label	Name	Label1
	BorderStyle	1 'Fixed Single
	Caption	"FaxBack Call Flow Diagram"
	Height	315
	Left	120
	TabIndex	10
	Top	60
	Width	5775

After you've placed the controls on the form, save it as FAXBACK.FRM and update the project (FAXBACK.VBP). Now you're ready to fine-tune the properties of the VBVoice controls.

Setting the VBVoice Control Properties

Setting the VBVoice controls is really the process of creating a telephony program. In this section you'll go through the process step by step. Two things must be accomplished in this part of the project. First, you must set the basic properties of each VBVoice control. This will determine the possible actions that can occur during a phone call. Next, you'll link each of the five controls together to form the call-flow diagram. This will complete the process by establishing a clear set of steps that each call can follow as it progresses through the conversation.

> **TIP**
>
> As you work through this part of the project, refer to Figure 34.2 to get an idea of what the finished product should look like.

The Frame Control

There is one property that must be set on the VBVFrame control. This property will tell all the other controls where to find the recorded prompts. Locate a blank spot on the frame and click the alternate mouse button to bring up the context menu, then select Properties to call up the custom properties box (see Figure 34.3).

FIGURE 34.3.
Editing the VBVFrame Properties.

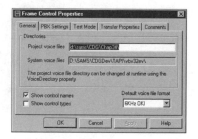

Make sure the Project Voice Files property is set to the folder that contains the FAX.VAP voice prompt file. All the other properties on this control can be left to their default values.

The AcceptCall LineGroup Control

The AcceptCall LineGroup control is where the incoming call will enter the program. You do not need to set any properties for this control. However, you need to connect the "Ring" node of the AcceptCall control to the input node of the GetFaxAddr GatherDigits control (see Figure 34.2).

The GetFaxAddress GatherDigits Control

The GetFaxAddress GatherDigits control will be used to get the destination FAX telephone address from the caller. You need to add a custom node to the control by adding an entry on the Routing page of the custom properties box. First, remove all the numerical entries from the routing page by highlighting each one and pressing the Delete button. Then press the New button on the Routing page and enter "$" for the digits and "FaxAddr" for the condition name (see Figure 34.4).

FIGURE 34.4.

Adding a new node to the GetFaxAddress *control.*

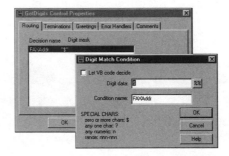

Next, you need to set the properties on the Terminations page. First, clear the Use Default Error Handler check box and make sure the Clear digits on entry and Disable global help boxes are checked. Next, set the Maximum Silence to "5," the retries on error to "2," and the Always terminate on to "#" (see Figure 34.5).

FIGURE 34.5.

Setting the termination properties of the GetFaxAddress *control.*

You also need to add a greeting to this control. Select the Greetings page in the custom properties dialog box and press Add Phrase to bring up the Select Phrase dialog box. Then find the FAX.VAP file in the VAP combo box. Select the first phrase in the file—"Enter the number of your fax machine followed by a pound sign" (see Figure 34.6).

Finally, connect the FaxAddr node of the GetFaxAddress control to the input node of the GetFaxFile control.

FIGURE 34.6.

Adding a new phrase to the
GetFaxAddress *control.*

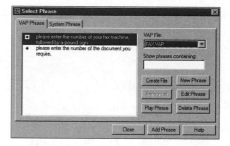

The GetFaxFile GatherDigits control

This second GatherDigits control will be used to collect the three-digit document number that the user wishes to receive. Erase the default routine options and add a custom node to the control by pressing the New button on the controls Routing page. Enter "nnn" in the Digits field (you'll accept three, and only three, digits) and enter DocNbr in the condition name field.

Set the termination values for the GetFaxFile control the same as you did for the GetFaxAddress control. The only difference is that you should leave the Clear Digits on Entry check box empty (unchecked). The rest of the termination settings are identical to those you used in the GetFaxAddress control.

Next, add a greeting for this control to tell the user to enter a document number. Press the Add Phrase button on the Greetings page, select the FAX.VAP prompt file, and pick the second prompt in the file—"Enter the number of the document you require."

Lastly, connect the DocNbr node of the GetFaxFile control to the input node of the VerifyFile control.

The VerifyFile User Control

The VerifyFile control is a VBVoice User control. The exact actions taken by this control are determined by the user, usually through the results of Visual Basic code. For this project, make sure there are only two possible options: "0" and "1" (press the Delete button to remove the rest). Next, click *off* the Clear digits on Entry check box.

Now connect the "0" node of the VerifyFile control to the input node of the HangUp control. Then connect the "1" node of the VerifyFile control to the back of the Err node of the GetFaxFile control.

The HangUp OnHook Control

The last control in the call-flow diagram is the HangUp OnHook control. This control's job is to hang up the phone to terminate the call. The only property you need to add to this control is a parting salutation. Call up the custom properties box and press the Add Phrase button to bring up the Select Phrase dialog box. Locate the RECORD.VAP prompt file (it was installed with VBVoice) and pick the last phrase in the list—"Your message has been sent."

That is the last of the property settings for the VBVoice controls. You now have defined the call-flow diagram for your FaxBack application. Be sure to save this form (FAXBACK.FRM) and update the project (FAXBACK.VBP) before you continue.

Coding the FaxBack Form

Since most of the logic is kept in the VBVoice controls, you only need to add a few code routines to the form itself. You'll add code to the Form_Load and Form_Unload events, code for the command button array, and code for the VerifyFile_Enter and AcceptCall_Disconnect events.

First, you need to declare three form-level variables. Enter the code from Listing 34.7 into the general declarations section of the form.

Listing 34.7. Declaring the form-level variables.

```
Option Explicit
'
Dim bFaxNbrCollected As Boolean
Dim bRunMode As Boolean
Dim cLogID As String
```

Next, add the code from Listing 34.8 to the Form_Load event of the form.

Listing 34.8. Coding the Form_Load event.

```
Private Sub Form_Load()
    '
    ' startup inits for system
    bRunMode = False
    bFaxNbrCollected = False
    cFAXFolder = App.Path
    cFAXPrefix = "\FAX"
    cFAXSuffix = ".DOC"
    '
    ' local values
    cLogID = "MCA" ' a valid MAPI ID for your system
    cTestFAXAddr = "999-9999" ' a valid target FAX machine
    '
    ' setup the form
    Me.Caption = "FaxBack SMAPI/TAPI Fax Handler"
    Image1.Stretch = True
    Image1.Picture = LoadPicture(App.Path & "\copymach.wmf")
    CenterForm Me
    '
    ' start up MAPI services
    SMAPIStart Me.hWnd, cLogID
    '
End Sub
```

This routine sets several variables for the fax handler, initializes form properties, and logs into MAPI services. Notice that this version of the program will be looking for FAX documents stored in the same directory as the application (App.Path) that have "FAX" as the first three letters of the filename and that have ".DOC" as the file tail. If you decide to put this project into production use, you may need to create a more flexible naming convention for your documents.

Also note that you need to set the cLogID variable to a valid MAPI profile name (one that has access to FAX services). You should also set the cTestFAXAddr variable to point to a FAX you can use to test the application.

The Form_Unload code is quite short. Listing 34.9 shows the line you need to add to log off the MAPI services before exiting the program.

Listing 34.9. Coding the Form_Unload event.

```
Private Sub Form_Unload(Cancel As Integer)
    '
    SMAPIEnd Me.hWnd
    '
End Sub
```

Now add the code to handle the user selections on the command button array. Add the code in Listing 34.10 to the cmdFax_Click event.

Listing 34.10. Coding the cmdFax_Click event.

```
Private Sub cmdFax_Click(Index As Integer)
    '
    ' handle user selections
    '
    Dim i As Integer
    Dim cFile As String
    '
    Select Case Index
        Case 0 ' test fax
            cFile = cFAXFolder & cFAXPrefix & "000" & cFAXSuffix
            SendSMAPIFax Me.hWnd, cFile, cTestFAXAddr
        Case 1 ' start run mode
            VBVFrame1.StartSystem True
            VBVFrame1.ShowLogWindow 1, True
            bRunMode = True
        Case 2 ' stop run mode
            i = VBVFrame1.StopSystem(False)
        Case 3 ' exit program
            Unload Me
            End
        Case 4 ' about box
            frmFBAbout.Show vbModal
    End Select
    '
End Sub
```

There's not much that's special in the code in Listing 34.10. The first command button sends a test fax, the second and third start and stop VBVoice in run mode, the fourth button ends the program, and the last button calls the About box.

> **NOTE**
>
> The evaluation copy of VBVoice will operate only in test mode. If you wish to be able to use VBVoice in run mode, you'll need to purchase a licensed copy of VBVoice from Pronexus.

There are only two remaining code events for this form. The first is the `Disconnect` event of the `AcceptCall` control. This event fires each time the `HangUp` control ends a call. This is where the program attempts to send the requested FAX document to the recipient's FAX number. Add the code from Listing 34.11 to the `AcceptCall_Disconnect` event.

Listing 34.11. Coding the `AcceptCall_Disconnect` event.

```
Private Sub AcceptCall_Disconnect(ByVal Channel As Integer, ByVal Reason As
Integer)
    '
    ' when the user hangs up, send the fax
    '
    ' NOTE ------------------------------------
    '        This routine does not run under
    '        TEST MODE - Only in RUN MODE.
    '        See the code in the VerifyFile_Enter
    '        event for details on TEST MODE
    '        behavior.
    ' ------------------------------------------
    '
    Dim cFile As String
    '
    If Not bFaxNbrCollected Then
        Exit Sub
    Else
        cFile = cFAXFolder & cFAXPrefix & CStr(GetFaxFile.Digits(Channel)) &
➥cFAXSuffix
        If FileExists(cFile) Then
            SendSMAPIFax Me.hWnd, cFile, GetFaxAddress.Digits(Channel)
        End If
    End If
    '
    bFaxNbrCollected = False ' for next time!
    '
End Sub
```

This routine first checks to make sure a document was selected, then confirms that it is on file, and then sends it out with a call to the `SendSMAPIFax` routine you coded at the start of this chapter. Once this is done, the program will wait for the next incoming call.

> **NOTE**
>
> You'll see from the comments, that this routine never executes in test mode. But if you have a licensed copy of VBVoice, you'll be able to run the code in this event.

The final code routine is the code for the VerifyFile_Enter event. This is the event tied to the User control. Under run mode, after a caller selects a document, this routine verifies it is on file and then passes the information on to the AcceptCall_Disconnect event. Under test mode, this routine verifies the file and then sends it out and exits the program. This exit is required in test mode since the program can never execute a disconnect in test mode.

Enter the code from Listing 34.12 into the VerifyFile_Enter event.

Listing 34.12. Coding the VerifyFile_Enter event.

```
Private Sub VerifyFile_Enter(ByVal Channel As Integer, ByVal Greeting As Object)
    '
    ' confirm valid fax selected
    '
    ' NOTE ---------------------------------------
    '         Under TEST MODE, this routine verifies
    '         the file name then sends it via the FAX
    '         transport and QUITS.
    '
    '         Under RUN MODE, this routine verfies
    '         the file name and then fires off the
    '         the HangUp control. At disconnect the
    '         the AcceptCall control ships the FAX
    '         document.
    ' ---------------------------------------
    '
    Dim cFile As String
    '
    cFile = cFAXFolder & cFAXPrefix & GetFaxFile.Digits(Channel) & cFAXSuffix
    '
    If FileExists(cFile) Then
        bFaxNbrCollected = True
        If bRunMode = True Then
            VerifyFile.GotoNode(Channel) = 0
        Else
            SendSMAPIFax Me.hWnd, cFile, GetFaxAddress.Digits(Channel)
            End ' have to do this in test mode
        End If
    Else
        bFaxNbrCollected = False
        If bRunMode = False Then
            MsgBox "File Is Missing!"
        Else
            VerifyFile.GotoNode(Channel) = 1 ' exit Error
        End If
    End If
    '
End Sub
```

Now that you've completed all the code for the FaxBack form, save the form (FAXBACK.FRM) and the project (FAXBACK.VBP) before moving on to the last coding section.

The About Dialog Box

The About dialog box is very simple. It displays a graphic, a label control that shows some basic information about the project, and an OK command button. Refer to Figure 34.7 and Table 34.2 for details on laying out the About dialog box.

FIGURE 34.7.

Laying out the About dialog box.

Table 34.2. The About box form controls.

Control	Property	Setting
VB.Form	Name	frmFBAbout
	BorderStyle	3 'Fixed Dialog
	Caption	"Form1"
	Height	2610
	Left	2685
	MaxButton	0 'False
	MinButton	0 'False
	ShowInTaskbar	0 'False
	Top	1890
	Width	4980
VB.CommandButton	Name	Command1
	Caption	"&OK"
	Height	300
	Left	3540
	TabIndex	1
	Top	1800
	Width	1200
VB.Image	Name	Image1
	Height	1455

Control	Property	Setting
	Left	120
	Top	180
	Width	1395
VB.Label	Name	Label1
	Caption	"Label1"
	Height	1455
	Left	1800
	TabIndex	0
	Top	180
	Width	2895

After laying out the form, you're ready to add code to the About box. You only need to add code to the Form_Load event and the Command1_Click event. Listing 34.13 shows all the code you need for the About form.

Listing 34.13. All the code for the About form.

```
Private Sub Command1_Click()
    Unload Me
End Sub

Private Sub Form_Load()
    '
    ' set up about dialog
    '
    Dim cVersion As String
    Me.Caption = "About " & App.ProductName
    Image1.Stretch = True
    Image1.Picture = LoadPicture(App.Path & "\copymach.wmf")
    '
    cVersion = "Version: " & CStr(App.Major) & "." & CStr(App.Minor) & "." &
➥CStr(App.Revision)
    Label1 = App.ProductName & Chr(13) & Chr(13)
    Label1 = Label1 & App.LegalCopyright & Chr(13) & Chr(13)
    Label1 = Label1 & App.FileDescription & Chr(13) & Chr(13)
    Label1 = Label1 & cVersion
    '
    CenterForm Me
    '
End Sub
```

Notice that most of the information displayed in the About box is drawn from the App object properties. You can set these properties using the File ¦ Make EXE File ¦ Options screen. Call up that screen now and enter the values from Table 34.3 into the dialog box.

Table 34.3. Setting the App object properties.

Property	Setting
Auto Increment	Checked ON
File Description	Demonstrates TAPI and SMAPI FAX
Legal Copyright	(c)1996 MCA/SAMS Publishing
Product Name	FaxBack FAX Server

That's the last code for this project. Save the form as FBABOUT.FRM and the project (FAXBACK.VBP).
Now is a good time to compile your project and check for bugs. Once you're sure you have all
the bugs worked out, you're ready to test your Visual Basic fax handler.

Testing the FaxBack Application

Testing the FaxBack application with the evaluation copy of VBVoice is a bit tricky, but not
impossible. First, start the program in design mode (not compiled). Your first screen should
look like the one in Figure 34.8.

FIGURE 34.8.
Starting the FaxBack
Application.

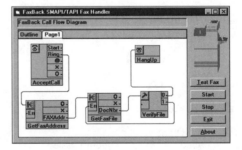

For a simple test, press the Test FAX button. This will test the SMAPI side of the program without
using any TAPI features. You should see the program locate the test document on your local
drive, format it for FAX transport, and, if you have immediate delivery turned on, the workstation will dial the address and send the FAX (see Figure 34.9).

FIGURE 34.9.
FaxBack sending a FAX.

> **TIP**
>
> If you are getting error messages telling you that Microsoft Exchange could not find a transport provider for your fax message, try moving the FAX service to the first service in the list of transports for your machine. You can do this from the Properties window of Microsoft Exchange.

Once you have the FAX portion of the system working, you're ready to add the TAPI side of the application. You'll test the telephony services using the test mode of VBVoice. Test mode uses your workstation's sound card and speakers to simulate an incoming call.

To start test mode, move your pointer over the AcceptCalls control, press the alternate mouse button, and select Start Test from the context menu. You'll then see a test dialog box appear. This dialog box will act as a caller's telephone handset. When you press the Start button, you'll see a debug screen and a "Ring or Call" dialog box appear. Now VBVoice is ready to start testing your application (see Figure 34.10).

FIGURE 34.10.
Starting VBVoice
in test mode.

Press the Ring button to start the test. This simulates a ringing phone for your application. You should see the debug window fill with tracking information and hear the prompts as they walk you through the process of entering a FAX address and selecting a document. Valid document numbers are "000," "100," and "200." These three Microsoft Word documents have been included in the same folder on the CD-ROM that has the FAX.VAP file and the other support files for this project. You can add other files if you wish.

Once the FAX document has been sent, the program exits to Visual Basic design mode. This is only true in test mode. If you were running a licensed copy of VBVoice in run mode, after sending the FAX, the program would wait for the next caller and start the process all over again.

Summary

In this chapter, you learned how to combine telephony and e-mail services to build a fax-on-demand server in Visual Basic 4.0, using VBVoice controls from Pronexus, and with the simple MAPI API declarations from Microsoft Exchange running the FAX transport.

This sample application does not contain all the bells and whistles needed to operate a production FAX server, but all the basics are here. If you wish, you can expand on this program by adding customized prompts and providing better error handling within the program and call flow. You should also consider writing a transaction log to keep track of all the calls you get and see what documents are being requested. With just a bit more work, you could have your very own FAX server up and running in no time!

35

Creating the Voice Phone Application

The example program in this chapter uses SAPI and TAPI services to create a true "hands-free" telephone. With this program and a PC speaker phone, you can lookup and dial telephone numbers by simply giving voice commands to your PC. You'll be able to initiate database adds, edits, and deletes; issue a voice command that will search the database for a name; and tell the program to *Dial Mike*. The Voice Phone will locate the record in the database, pull up the phone number, place the call, and then prompt you to begin speaking.

As an added bonus, this program gives audible responses to help requests and speaks the names and telephone numbers of selected records in the database. Even the About box is "read" to you! Figure 35.1 shows a completed version of Voice Phone in action.

FIGURE 35.1.
*The completed version
of Voice Phone.*

Project Resources

There is one main form for the project and three support forms:

- ■ *VPhone*—This is the main form. All primary operations are performed here, and it calls all other forms.
- ■ *VRec*—This is the form used to add and edit database records.
- ■ *VHelp*—This is a small help screen that displays and speaks help hints on using Voice Phone.
- ■ *VAbout*—This is the standard About box. It also speaks the application information to the user.

In addition to the forms, there are four support modules for the Voice Phone project:

- ■ VTAPI.BAS—This holds the Assisted TAPI API calls, two user-defined types, and two functions that are used to request Assisted TAPI services.
- ■ SRCBK.CLS—This is the speech recognition callback class module. This module will process the commands spoken to Voice Phone by users.
- ■ TTSCBK.CLS—This is the text-to-speech callback class module. The Voice Phone project does not use this module, but it is a good idea to include it in all projects that use the TTS engine.

■ VPHONE.BAS—This module contains the bulk of the project code. All supporting subroutines and functions are kept here.

Before you begin coding the project, you'll need to make sure you have the following resources loaded available on your workstation:

■ An Assisted TAPI compatible modem (almost any modem will do) with a telephone handset attached.

■ A sound card, a microphone, and speakers for speech recognition and text-to-speech services.

When you first start this project, you'll need to make sure you have loaded the proper support libraries for Visual Basic. Select Tools ¦ References and load the following:

■ Voice Command 1.0 type library

■ Voice Text 1.0 type library

■ Microsoft DAO 3.0 object library

NOTE

If you don't have these libraries available from your References dialog box, you'll need to use the Browse button to find them. Usually they can be found in the SYSTEM folder of the WINDOWS directory. The Voice libraries can also be found on the CD-ROM that ships with this book. You probably have other resources loaded for your programs. That's fine. Just be sure you have the three resources listed above.

Coding the Library Modules

The first step in the process of building the Voice Phone project is creating the library modules. Three of the modules exist to provide simple support for the Windows extension services (SAPI and TAPI). The fourth module holds most of the project code.

The AssistedTAPI Module

The AssistedTAPI module holds the Telephony API declarations, two type definitions, and two Visual Basic wrapper functions. With this one code module you can provide any Visual Basic or VBA-compatible program with basic TAPI services.

> **TIP**
>
> You might think it a better idea to implement Assisted TAPI support using a Visual Basic class module instead of a simple code module. However, the code module can be loaded into any VBA-compatible environment (including Visual Basic 3.0). The class module could only be used for Visual Basic 4.0.

Add a BAS module to your project (Insert ¦ Module) and set its Name property to AssistedTAPI. Save the module as VTAPI.BAS. Now you're ready to start coding.

The first things to add to this module are the Assisted TAPI API declarations. Listing 35.1 shows the code that imports the tapiRequestMakeCall and tapiGetLocationInfo API calls.

Listing 35.1. Adding the Assisted Telephony API Declarations.

```
'
' declare assisted tapi functions
'
#If Win32 Then
    Declare Function tapiRequestMakeCall Lib "TAPI32.DLL" (ByVal lpszDestAddress As
➥String, ByVal lpszAppName As String, ByVal lpszCalledParty As String, ByVal
➥lpszComment As String) As Long
    Declare Function tapiGetLocationInfo Lib "TAPI32.DLL" (ByVal lpszCountryCode As
➥String, ByVal lpszCityCode As String) As Long
#Else
    Declare Function tapiRequestMakeCall Lib "TAPI.DLL" (ByVal lpszDestAddress As
➥String, ByVal lpszAppName As String, ByVal lpszCalledParty As String, ByVal
➥lpszComment As String) As Long
    Declare Function tapiGetLocationInfo Lib "TAPI.DLL" (ByVal lpszCountryCode As
➥String, ByVal lpszCityCode As String) As Long
#End If
```

Notice that the code in Listing 35.1 uses the conditional compilation directives along with the code for both 16- and 32-bit Visual Basic 4.0. This ensures that the code will work in either version of Visual Basic 4.0 that you use.

Next you need to add two user-defined types to the module. These types encapsulate the parameters needed for the two TAPI calls. Using UDTs in this way reduces the complexity of your code and makes it easier to read. Add the code shown in Listing 35.2 to the general section of the module.

Listing 35.2. Adding the user-defined types.

```
'
' TAPILocation Type
Type TAPILocation
    Country As String * 1
    City As String * 3
```

```
End Type
'
' TAPIMakeCall Type
Type TAPICall
    Address As String
    AppName As String
    CalledParty As String
    Comment As String
End Type
```

After declaring the API routines and defining the type variables, you're ready to add the wrapper functions that will encapsulate the API calls. Listing 35.3 shows the function that supports the `tapiGetLocationInfo` API call. Add this to your module.

Listing 35.3. Adding the `TAPIGetLocation` function.

```
Public Function TAPIGetLocation() As TAPILocation
    '
    ' returns UDT w/ city and country
    '
    Dim lTapi As Long
    Dim cCountry As String * 1
    Dim cCity As String * 3
    '
    lTapi = tapiGetLocationInfo(cCountry, cCity)
    If lTapi >= 0 Then
        TAPIGetLocation.Country = cCountry
        TAPIGetLocation.City = cCity
    End If
    '
End Function
```

Notice that this function *returns* a UDT that contains both the country code and the city code for the workstation.

> **NOTE**
>
> The `TAPIGetLocation` function is not called in this project. It is included here for completeness. When you use this module for other TAPI projects, you'll have this function call already defined.

The second API wrapper function is the `TAPIMakeCall` function. This function accepts the `TAPICall` user-defined type as input and places an outbound call. Listing 35.4 shows the code for this function.

Listing 35.4. Adding the `TAPIMakeCall` function.

```
Public Function TAPIMakeCall(tapiRec As TAPICall) As Long
    '
    ' make an assisted TAPI call
    ' returns 0 if OK, <0 if error
    '
    TAPIMakeCall = tapiRequestMakeCall(tapiRec.Address, tapiRec.AppName,
➥tapiRec.CalledParty, tapiRec.Comment)
    '
End Function
```

This function returns a value that indicates the results of the TAPI request. If the value is less than 0, you've got an error condition. Only the first parameter is required (`Address`).

> **TIP**
>
> For a more detailed look at Assisted Telephony, refer to Chapter 29, "Writing TAPI-Assisted Applications."

That is the end of the Assisted TAPI support module. Save this module (`VTAPI.BAS`) and the project (`VPHONE.VBP`) before continuing.

The `CallBack` Modules

Since this project uses the SAPI Voice Command and Voice Text type libraries, you'll need to add a class module to your project for each of the two libraries. These classes were designed to allow high-level languages (like Visual Basic) to register services that require the use of notification callbacks. The callback module for the TTS engine will not be used in this project. However, you'll use the SR callback routines to trap and respond to spoken commands.

> **WARNING**
>
> The function names for these callbacks cannot be altered. The OLE libraries for SR and TTS services are looking for these specific function names. If you use some other names, the callbacks will not work and you will get an error report when you request TTS or SR services.

First add the TTS callback functions. In this project, the functions will be empty, but you'll need to register them anyway. Add a class module to your project (`Insert | Class Module`). Set the class name to `TTSCallBack`, set its `Instancing` property to `Creatable`, `MultiUse`, and its `Public` property to `TRUE`. Now add the two functions from Listing 35.5 to the class.

Listing 35.5. Adding functions to the `TTSCallBack` class.

```
Option Explicit

Public Function SpeakingDone()
    '
    ' this method will execute when the
    ' TTS engine stops speaking text
    '
End Function

Public Function SpeakingStarted()
    '
    ' this method will execute when the
    ' TTS engine starts speaking text
    '
End Function
```

When you've completed the functions, save the module as `TTSCBK.CLS`.

Now add a second class module to the project. Set its `Name` property to `SRCallBack`, its `Instancing` property to `Createable`, `MultiUse`, and its `Public` property to `TRUE`. Now add the code shown in Listing 35.6 to the class.

Listing 35.6. Adding functions to the `SRCallBack` class.

```
Option Explicit

Function CommandRecognize(szCommand As String, dwID As Long)
    '
    ' fires off each time a command goes by
    '
    Dim cToken As String
    Dim cContent As String
    Dim iSpace As Integer
    Dim cReturn As String
    '
    szCommand = Trim(szCommand) & " "
    iSpace = InStr(szCommand, " ")
    cToken = UCase(Left(szCommand, iSpace - 1))
    cContent = Mid(szCommand, iSpace + 1, 255)
    '
    Select Case cToken
        Case "NEW"
            AddRec 'frmVPhone.cmdPhone_Click 0
        Case "EDIT"
            EditRec cContent
        Case "DELETE"
            DeleteRec cContent
        Case "PLACE"
            PlaceCall frmVPhone.txtDial, ""
        Case "FIND"
            frmVPhone.txtDial = LookUp(cContent)
        Case "DIAL"
```

continues

Listing 35.6. continued

```
            cReturn = LookUp(cContent)
            frmVPhone.txtDial = cReturn
            PlaceCall cReturn, cContent
    End Select
    '
End Function

Function CommandOther(szCommand As String, szApp As String, szState As String)

End Function
```

You'll notice that the only routine used is the `CommandRecognize` function. This routine looks at each command that passes through the speech recognition engine, parses the input and, if it's a known command, executes the appropriate code.

The reason the command line must be parsed is that several of the voice commands will be in the form of lists. You may remember that you can register command lists with the SR engine without knowing the members of the list ahead of time. In your project, you'll fill these lists with the names of people in the user's phone directory at run-time.

After you've entered the code, save this module as `SRCBK.CLS` before continuing with the chapter.

Building the `LibVPhone` Module

The `LibVPhone` module contains most of the code for the project. It is here that you'll put the routines that initialize the speech engines, load the database engine, and handle the processes of adding, editing, and deleting records from the phone book.

First, add a code module to the project. Set its `Name` property to `LibVPhone` and save it as `VPHONE.BAS`. Next, add the project-level declarations shown in Listing 35.7 to the general declaration section of the module.

Listing 35.7. Adding the project-level declarations.

```
Option Explicit
'
' establish voice command objects
Public objVCmd As Object
Public objVMenu As Object
Public lVMenuIdx As Long
Public objVText As Object
Public iVType As Integer
Public cUserMsgs() As String
'
' spoken message handles
Public Const ttsHello = 0
```

```
Public Const ttsVPhone = 1
Public Const ttsList = 2
Public Const ttsExit = 3
Public Const ttsEdit = 4
'
' database objects
Public wsPhone As Workspace
Public dbPhone As Database
Public rsPhone As Recordset
```

The code here declares the required objects for SAPI and for database services. There are also several constants that will be used to point to text messages that will be spoken by the engine at requested times in the program.

Adding the Voice Command Routines

Next add the routine that will start the SAPI service initialization. Add a subroutine called `InitVCmd` to the project and enter the code from Listing 35.8.

Listing 35.8. Adding the `InitVCmd` routine.

```
Public Sub InitVCmd()
    '
    ' init voice command
    Set objVCmd = CreateObject("Speech.VoiceCommand")
    objVCmd.Register ""
    objVCmd.Awake = True
    objVCmd.Callback = App.EXEName & ".SRCallBack"
    '
    ' init voice menu
    BuildVMenu
    objVMenu.Active = True
    '
End Sub
```

This code initializes the voice command object that will be used to handle speech recognition services for the program. Notice the line that registers the `SRCallBack` class. The class name is prefixed with the application name. You must set this application name manually. To do this, select `Tools ¦ Options ¦ Project` and enter `VPHONE` in the `Project Name` field.

> **WARNING**
>
> You must update the `Project Name` field to match the `App.EXEName` value before you attempt to run the project. If you fail to do this, you will receive errors from the SR engine.

The InitVCmd routine calls another routine to handle the creation of the command menu. Add a new subroutine to the module called BuildVMenu and enter the code shown in Listing 35.9.

Listing 35.9. Adding the BuildVMenu routine.

```
Public Sub BuildVMenu()
    '
    ' build a voice menu
    '
    Dim iType As Integer
    Dim cState As String
    Dim lLangId As Long
    Dim cDialect As String
    Dim cAppName As String
    Dim cVMenu(3) As String
    Dim x As Integer
    '
    ' set params
    cAppName = App.EXEName
    cState = "Voice Phone"
    cDialect = ""
    lLangId = 1033
    iType = vcmdmc_CREATE_TEMP
    '
    ' set menu commands
    cVMenu(1) = "New Record"
    cVMenu(2) = "Place Call"
    cVMenu(3) = "Exit"
    '
    ' now instance menu
    Set objVMenu = objVCmd.MenuCreate( _
        cAppName, cState, lLangId, cDialect, iType)
    '
    ' add simple commands to menu
    For x = 1 To 3
        lVMenuIdx = lVMenuIdx + 1
        objVMenu.Add lVMenuIdx, cVMenu(x), "Voice Phone Commands", "Voice Phone
➡Commands"
    Next x

    '
    ' create list commands
    lVMenuIdx = lVMenuIdx + 1
    objVMenu.Add lVMenuIdx, "Edit <Name>", "Edit Name", "Edit Name"
    '
    lVMenuIdx = lVMenuIdx + 1
    objVMenu.Add lVMenuIdx, "Delete <Name>", "Delete Name", "Delete Name"
    '
    lVMenuIdx = lVMenuIdx + 1
    objVMenu.Add lVMenuIdx, "Dial <Name>", "Dial Name", "Dial Name"
    '
    lVMenuIdx = lVMenuIdx + 1
    objVMenu.Add lVMenuIdx, "Find <Name>", "Find Name", "Find Name"
    '
End Sub
```

There's a lot going on in this routine. First, internal variables are declared and set to their respective values. Next, the menu object is created using the MenuCreate method. After the menu object is created, the Add method of the menu object is used to add simple voice commands to the menu. Finally, the list commands are added to the menu (Edit, Delete, Dial, and Find). All these list commands refer to the Name list. This list will be filled in at run-time.

Now add the routine that will fill in the name list for the voice commands. Create a new subroutine called LoadNameList and enter the code you see in Listing 35.10.

Listing 35.10. Adding the LoadNameList routine.

```
Public Sub LoadNameList()
    '
    ' fill list of names for vCmd
    '
    Dim cNameList As String
    Dim iNameCount As String
    '
    cNameList = ""
    iNameCount = 0
    rsPhone.MoveFirst
    Do Until rsPhone.EOF
        cNameList = cNameList & rsPhone.Fields("Name") & Chr(0)
        iNameCount = iNameCount + 1
        rsPhone.MoveNext
    Loop
    '
    objVMenu.ListSet "Name", iNameCount, cNameList
    '
End Sub
```

As you can see, the LoadNameList routine reads each record in the open database table and adds the names, separated by chr(0), to a single string. This string is the list that is registered with the menu object using the ListSet method.

Adding the Voice Text Routines

Now you're ready to add the routines that will initialize the Voice Text object for TTS services. First, add a new subroutine called InitVTxt and enter the code shown in Listing 35.11.

Listing 35.11. Adding the InitVTxt routine.

```
Public Sub InitVTxt()
    '
    ' init voice text
    Set objVText = CreateObject("Speech.VoiceText")
    objVText.Register "", App.EXEName
    objVText.Enabled = True
    objVText.Callback = App.EXEName & ".TTSCallBack"
    '
End Sub
```

This looks a lot like the InitVCmd routine. Notice the callback registration here, too. Again, it is very important that the Project Title property (Tools ¦ Options ¦ Project ¦ Project Title) is set to the same value as the application executable filename. If not, you won't be able to use TTS services in your application.

The only other TTS support routine you'll need is the one that builds a set of messages that will be spoken by the TTS engine at different times in the program. Add a new subroutine called LoadMsgs to the module and enter the code from Listing 35.12.

Listing 35.12. Adding the LoadMsgs routine.

```
Public Sub LoadMsgs()
    '
    ' build a list of user messages
    '
    ReDim cUserMsgs(5)
    '
    cUserMsgs(0) = "Hello. Welcome to Voice Phone."
    cUserMsgs(1) = "Press New, Edit, or Delete to modify the phone list."
    cUserMsgs(2) = "Select a name from the list and press Place Call to dial the
➥phone."
    cUserMsgs(3) = "Press Exit to end this program."
    cUserMsgs(4) = "Enter name and phone number, then press OK or cancel."
    '
End Sub
```

The public constants declared at the top of this module will be used to point to each of these messages. This will make it easier to read the code.

Adding the Database Engine Routines

Next you need to add several routines to initialize and support database services. First, add the InitDB subroutine to your project and enter the code shown in Listing 35.13.

Listing 35.13. Adding the InitDB routine.

```
Public Sub InitDB()
    '
    ' set up db stuff
    '
    Dim cDBName As String
    cDBName = App.Path & "\VPHONE.MDB"
    On Error Resume Next
    Open cDBName For Input As 1
    If Err <> 0 Then
        Close 1
        BuildDatabase
    Else
        Close 1
    End If
```

```
    On Error GoTo 0
    '
    OpenDatabase
    '
End Sub
```

> **WARNING**
>
> Using the App.Path property to set the location of the MDB file assumes that you have created a project directory. If you attempt to place the project and the MDB files in the root directory of a drive, you'll receive error messages. It's recommended that you create a project directory and store the MDB in that directory.

The only real purpose of this routine is to check for the existence of the database file. If it is not found, the BuildDatabase routine is called before the OpenDatabase routine. Now add the BuildDatabase subroutine to your project as shown in Listing 35.14.

Listing 35.14. Adding the BuildDatabase routine.

```
Public Sub BuildDatabase()
    '
    ' build new database
    '
    On Error GoTo LocalErr
    '
    Dim ws As Workspace
    Dim db As Database
    Dim cSQL(3) As String
    Dim x As Integer
    '
    cSQL(1) = "CREATE TABLE VPHONE (Name TEXT(20),Phone TEXT(20));"
    cSQL(2) = "INSERT INTO VPHONE VALUES ('Information','1-555-1212');"
    cSQL(3) = "INSERT INTO VPHONE VALUES('SAMS Publishing','1-800-428-5331');"
    '
    Set ws = DBEngine.Workspaces(0)
    Set db = CreateDatabase(App.Path & "\VPHONE.MDB", dbLangGeneral)
    '
    For x = 1 To 3
        db.Execute cSQL(x), dbFailOnError
    Next x
    '
    db.Close
    Set db = Nothing
    Set ws = Nothing
    '
    Exit Sub
    '
LocalErr:
    MsgBox Err.Description & Chr(13) & Err.Source, vbCritical, "BuildDatabase"
    '
End Sub
```

The code here is quite handy. First, the database file is created. Then, three SQL statements are executed. The first one creates the new VPHONE table. The second two statements add two records to the new table.

> **TIP**
>
> This is a great technique for building databases upon installation of a new application. This way, users don't have to worry about copying data files, confusing older versions of the data, and so on. Even better, if you need to start the database from scratch, all you need to do is remove the database file and start the program—it will create the initial database for you!

After the BuildDatabase routine has been added, you need to add the code that will open the existing database and select the phone records. Create the OpenDatabase subroutine and enter the code from Listing 35.15.

Listing 35.15. Adding the OpenDatabase routine.

```
Public Sub OpenDatabase()
    '
    ' open phone database
    '
    On Error GoTo LocalErr
    '
    Dim cSelect As String
    '
    cSelect = "SELECT * FROM VPHONE"
    '
    Set wsPhone = DBEngine.Workspaces(0)
    Set dbPhone = wsPhone.OpenDatabase(App.Path & "\VPHONE.MDB")
    Set rsPhone = dbPhone.OpenRecordset(cSelect, dbOpenDynaset)
    '
    Exit Sub
    '
LocalErr:
    MsgBox Err.Description & Chr(13) & Err.Source, vbCritical, "OpenDatabase"
    '
End Sub
```

Nothing real fancy here. The database is opened and a single SQL SELECT statement is executed to create a Dynaset-type recordset for use in the program.

There are four remaining database service support routines:

■ AddRec

■ EditRec

- DeleteRec
- LookUp

The `AddRec` and `EditRec` routines use a secondary dialog form (`frmVRec`), which you'll build in the next section of this chapter.

Create a new subroutine called `AddRec` and enter the code from Listing 35.16.

Listing 35.16. Adding the `AddRec` routine.

```
Public Sub AddRec()
    '
    ' add a new record
    '
    Load frmVRec
    frmVRec.txtName = ""
    frmVRec.txtPhone = ""
    frmVRec.lblaction = "ADD"
    frmVRec.Show vbModal
    '
End Sub
```

Now add the `EditRec` subroutine and enter the code from Listing 35.17.

Listing 35.17. Adding the `EditRec` routine.

```
Public Sub EditRec(cName As String)
    '
    ' edit an existing record
    '
    Dim iAns As Integer
    '
    cName = Trim(cName)
    rsPhone.FindFirst "Name='" & cName & "'"
    If rsPhone.NoMatch = False Then
        Load frmVRec
        frmVRec.txtName = rsPhone.Fields("Name")
        frmVRec.txtPhone = rsPhone.Fields("Phone")
        frmVRec.lblaction = "EDIT"
        frmVRec.Show vbModal
    End If
    '
End Sub
```

The `DeleteRec` subroutine consists of a single message box confirmation and the delete action. Add the code in Listing 35.18 to the module.

Listing 35.18. Adding the DeleteRec routine.

```
Public Sub DeleteRec(cName As String)
    '
    ' delete record from table
    '
    Dim iAns As Integer
    '
    cName = Trim(cName)
    iAns = MsgBox(cName, vbExclamation + vbYesNo, "Delete Record")
    If iAns = vbYes Then
        rsPhone.FindFirst "Name = '" & cName & "'"
        If rsPhone.NoMatch = False Then
            rsPhone.Delete
            rsPhone.MoveNext
        End If
    End If
    '
End Sub
```

Finally, add a new function called LookUp to the module. This function takes one parameter (the Name) and returns the corresponding phone number. Enter the code from Listing 35.19.

Listing 35.19. Adding the LookUp function.

```
Public Function LookUp(cName As String) As String
    '
    ' lookup a name in the list
    ' return the phone number
    '
    Dim cRtn As String
    '
    cName = Trim(cName)
    rsPhone.FindFirst "Name = '" & cName & "'"
    If rsPhone.NoMatch = True Then
        cRtn = ""
    Else
        cRtn = rsPhone.Fields("Phone").Value
    End If
    '
    LookUp = cRtn
    '
End Function
```

Adding the TAPI and Form Support Routines

Only two support routines are left. The PlaceCall routine is used to perform the Assisted TAPI service request. Listing 35.20 shows you the code for this routine.

Listing 35.20. Adding the `PlaceCall` routine.

```
Public Sub PlaceCall(cPhone As String, cName As String)
    '
    Dim tCall As TAPICall
    Dim lRtn As Long
    '
    If Trim(cPhone) <> "" Then
        tCall.Address = cPhone
        tCall.AppName = App.EXEName
        tCall.CalledParty = cName
        tCall.Comment = ""
        lRtn = TAPIMakeCall(tCall)
        If lRtn < 0 Then
            MsgBox lRtn, vbcritical, "TAPI Error!"
        End If
    End If
    '
End Sub
```

The last routine is one that is used to center dialog boxes on the screen. Add the code from Listing 35.21 to your project.

Listing 35.21. Adding the `CenterForm` routine.

```
Public Sub CenterForm(frm As Form)
    '
    frm.Left = (Screen.Width - frm.Width) / 2
    frm.Top = (Screen.Height - frm.Height) / 2
    '
End Sub
```

That is the end of the LibVPhone module code. Save this module (VPHONE.BAS) and the project (VPHONE.VBP) before you move to the next section.

Laying Out the VPhone Form

The Vphone form is the main dialog box of the project. The first step is to lay out the controls on the form. Then you can add the menu and the code behind the form. Refer to Figure 35.2 and Table 35.1 for details on the size and position of the controls on the form.

FIGURE 35.2.
Laying out the
Vphone *form.*

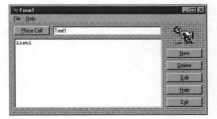

Table 35.1. Controls for the VPhone form.

Control	Property	Setting
VB.Form	Name	frmVPhone
	BorderStyle	3 'Fixed Dialog
	Caption	"Form1"
	Height	3795
	Icon	"VPHONE.ICO"
	Left	1755
	MaxButton	0 'False
	MinButton	0 'False
	ShowInTaskbar	-1 'True
	Top	2160
	Width	6720
VB.CommandButton	Name	cmdPhone
	Caption	"&Help"
	Height	300
	Index	4
	Left	5280
	TabIndex	7
	Top	2580
	Width	1200
VB.CommandButton	Name	cmdPhone
	Caption	"E&xit"
	Height	300
	Index	3
	Left	5280
	TabIndex	6

Control	Property	Setting
	Top	2160
	Width	1200
VB.CommandButton	Name	cmdPhone
	Caption	"&Edit"
	Height	300
	Index	2
	Left	5280
	TabIndex	5
	Top	1740
	Width	1200
VB.CommandButton	Name	cmdPhone
	Caption	"&Delete"
	Height	300
	Index	1
	Left	5280
	TabIndex	4
	Top	1320
	Width	1200
VB.CommandButton	Name	cmdPhone
	Caption	"&New"
	Height	300
	Index	0
	Left	5280
	TabIndex	3
	Top	900
	Width	1200
VB.ListBox	Name	List1
	Font	name="MS LineDraw"
		size=8.25
	Height	2370
	Left	120
	TabIndex	2

continues

Table 35.1. continued

Control	Property	Setting
	Top	540
	Width	4995
VB.CommandButton	Name	cmdDial
	Caption	"&Place Call"
	Height	300
	Left	120
	TabIndex	1
	Top	120
	Width	1200
VB.TextBox	Name	txtDial
	Height	300
	Left	1440
	TabIndex	0
	Text	"Text1"
	Top	120
	Width	3660
VB.Image	Name	Image1
	Height	615
	Left	5520
	Picture	"VPHONE.ICO"
	Stretch	-1 'True
	Top	120
	Width	675

> **NOTE**
>
> The VPHONE.ICO icon file that is used in this project can be found on the CD-ROM that ships with the book. Be sure to copy that file to the application directory before you start the project.

Along with the control layout, there is also a small menu that goes with the VPhone form. Refer to Figure 35.3 and Table 35.2 for details on laying out the Vphone menu.

FIGURE 35.3.

Laying out the
VPhone *menu.*

Table 35.2. The VPhone menu.

Level	Property	Setting
Top Level	Name	mnuFile
	Caption	"&File"
Level 2	Name	mnuFileItem
	Caption	"&New..."
	Index	0
Level 2	Name	mnuFileItem
	Caption	"&Edit..."
	Index	1
Level 2	Name	mnuFileItem
	Caption	"&Delete"
	Index	2
Level 2	Name	mnuFileItem
	Caption	"-"
	Index	3
Level 2	Name	mnuFileItem
	Caption	"&Place Call"
	Index	4
Level 2	Name	mnuFileItem
	Caption	"-"
	Index	5

continues

Table 35.2. continued

Level	Property	Setting
Level 2	Name	mnuFileItem
	Caption	"E&xit"
	Index	6
Top Level	Name	mnuHelp
	Caption	"&Help"
Level 2	Name	mnuHelpItem
	Caption	"Help..."
	Index	0
Level 2	Name	mnuHelpItem
	Caption	"&About..."
	Index	1

NOTE

Be sure to lay out the menu using menu arrays. You'll add code to the menu array in the next section.

After laying out the form, save it as VPHONE.FRM and the save the project as VPHONE.VBP before moving on to the next section.

Coding the VPhone Form

There's not a lot of code for the VPhone form. Most of the important stuff was built in the LibVPhone module. However, you'll need to add code to the control events that call the LibVPhone routines.

First, add the code from Listing 35.22 to the Form_Load event.

Listing 35.22. Coding the Form_Load event.

```
Private Sub Form_Load()
    '
    ' set form properties
    Me.Caption = "Voice Phone"
    Me.Icon = LoadPicture(App.Path & "\vphone.ico")
    Image1.Picture = LoadPicture(App.Path & "\vphone.ico")
    Image1.Stretch = True
```

```
        CenterForm Me
        '
        ' initialize objects
        InitVCmd ' start SR engine
        InitVTxt ' start TTS engine
        InitDB ' state DB engine
        LoadNameList ' fill SR list
        LoadList ' fill onscreen list
        LoadMsgs ' fill TTS list
        '
        ' set variables
        txtDial = ""
        iVType = vtxtst_READING + vtxtsp_NORMAL
        '
        objVText.Speak cUserMsgs(ttsHello), iVType
        '
End Sub
```

The code in Listing 35.22 sets up some basic form properties and then calls the initialization routines for the various services. Finally, the application sends out a greeting message to the user.

Next, add the code in Listing 35.23 to the Form_Unload event.

Listing 35.23. Coding the Form_Unload event.

```
Private Sub Form_Unload(Cancel As Integer)
    '
    ' destroy objects
    Set objVMenu = Nothing
    Set objVCmd = Nothing
    Set objVText = Nothing
    Set rsPhone = Nothing
    Set dbPhone = Nothing
    Set wsPhone = Nothing
    '
End Sub
```

This code destroys the programming objects created at startup. It's always a good idea to do this before exiting your application.

The Form_Load event calls a custom routine called LoadList. This subroutine fills the onscreen list box with the names and phone numbers from the database. Add the LoadList subroutine to your form and enter the code from Listing 35.24.

Listing 35.24. Adding the `LoadList` routine.

```
Public Sub LoadList()
    '
    ' fill onscreen list with name/phone
    '
    Dim cLine As String
    List1.Clear
    '
    ' add header line first
    List1.AddItem "NAME" & String(16, ".") & Space(5) & "PHONE" & String(15, ".")
    '
    ' now add database items
    rsPhone.MoveFirst
    Do Until rsPhone.EOF
        cLine = Space(50)
        Mid(cLine, 1, 20) = Left(rsPhone.Fields("Name"), 20)
        Mid(cLine, 26, 20) = Left(rsPhone.Fields("Phone"), 20)
        List1.AddItem cLine
        rsPhone.MoveNext
    Loop
    '
End Sub
```

Next, add the code from Listing 35.25 to handle the user selections on the main command button array (`cmdPhone`).

Listing 35.25. Coding the `cmdPhone_Click` event.

```
Private Sub cmdPhone_Click(Index As Integer)
    '
    ' handle user selections
    '
    Dim cName As String
    Dim iAns As Integer
    Dim x As Integer
    '
    Select Case Index
        Case 0 ' add a record
            AddRec
        Case 1 ' delete a record
            If List1.ListIndex > 0 Then ' skip first line!
                cName = Left(List1.List(List1.ListIndex), 20)
                DeleteRec cName
            End If
        Case 2 ' edit a record
            If List1.ListIndex > 0 Then
                cName = Left(List1.List(List1.ListIndex), 20)
                EditRec cName
            End If
        Case 3 ' help
            objVText.Speak cUserMsgs(ttsVPhone), iVType
            objVText.Speak cUserMsgs(ttsList), iVType
            objVText.Speak cUserMsgs(ttsExit), iVType
        Case 4 ' exit
```

```
            Unload Me
            End
    End Select
    '
    ' update lists
    LoadList
    LoadNameList
    '
End Sub
```

Notice that help is delivered in the form of three spoken messages to the user.

You also need to code the cmdDial_Click event. This code fires each time the user presses the Place Call command button. Enter the code from Listing 35.26.

Listing 35.26. Coding the cmdDial_Click event.

```
Private Sub cmdDial_Click()
    '
    ' try to place the call
    '
    If Trim(txtDial) <> "" Then
        PlaceCall txtDial, "" ' call dialer
    Else
        If List1.ListIndex > 0 Then
            List1_DblClick
            PlaceCall txtDial, ""
        Else
            MsgBox "Select a Name from the List", vbExclamation, "Place a Call"
        End If
    End If
    '
End Sub
```

The cmdDial_Click event will first check the txtDial control to see if a phone number is present. If it is, that number is used to place the call. If no number is present, the routine will see if the user has selected a name from the list box. If so, the routine first calls the List1_DblClick event to force the name into the txtDial text box, then calls the PlaceCall routine to make the call. Finally, if none of this works, a message is displayed telling the user to select a name from the list.

Now add code to the List1_DblClick event to move the phone number from the list box into the txtDial text box. Listing 35.27 shows how this is done.

Listing 35.27. Coding the `List1_DblClick` event.

```
Private Sub List1_DblClick()
    '
    ' select name from the list
    '
    Dim cReturn As String
    '
    If List1.ListIndex > 0 Then
        cReturn = Left(List1.List(List1.ListIndex), 20)
        txtDial = LookUp(cReturn)
    End If
    '
End Sub
```

The only code left to create is the code to handle the menu arrays. Listing 35.28 shows the code for both the `mnuFileItem_Click` and the `mnuHelpItem_Click` events. Add these two code modules to your form.

Listing 35.28. Coding the menu array events.

```
Private Sub mnuFileItem_Click(Index As Integer)
    '
    ' handle user clicks
    '
    Select Case Index
        Case 0 ' new
            cmdPhone_Click 0
        Case 1 ' edit
            cmdPhone_Click 1
        Case 2 ' delete
            cmdPhone_Click 2
        Case 4 ' place call
            cmdDial_Click
        Case 6 ' exit
            Unload Me
    End Select
    '
End Sub

Private Sub mnuHelpItem_Click(Index As Integer)
    '
    Select Case Index
        Case 0 ' help screen
            frmHelp.Show vbModal
        Case 1 ' about
            frmAbout.Show vbModal
    End Select
    '
End Sub
```

That's the end of the code for the VPhone form. Save the form (VPHONE.FRM) and the project (VPHONE.VBP) before continuing.

Laying Out the Support Forms

There are three small support forms for the VPhone project. The VRec form is used to handle adds and edits to the data table. The Vhelp form displays a set of help strings, and the VAbout dialog box just shows the standard program information.

The VRec Form

The VRec form is used to handle adding new records to the data table and editing existing records. There are two text boxes, three label controls, and three command buttons on the form. Add a new form to the project and lay out the controls on the form as shown in Figure 35.4 and Table 35.3.

FIGURE 35.4.

Laying out the VRec *form.*

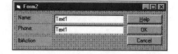

Table 35.3. The VRec form controls.

Control	Property	Setting
VB.Form	Name	frmVRec
	Caption	"Form2"
	Height	1680
	Left	1725
	Top	2445
	Width	5340
VB.CommandButton	Name	cmdRec
	Caption	"&Help"
	Height	300
	Index	2
	Left	3900
	TabIndex	7
	Top	120
	Width	1200
VB.CommandButton	Name	cmdRec
	Caption	"Cancel"
	Height	300

continues

Table 35.3. continued

Control	Property	Setting
	Index	1
	Left	3900
	TabIndex	5
	Top	840
	Width	1200
VB.CommandButton	Name	cmdRec
	Caption	"OK"
	Height	300
	Index	0
	Left	3900
	TabIndex	4
	Top	480
	Width	1200
VB.TextBox	Name	txtPhone
	Height	300
	Left	1380
	TabIndex	3
	Text	"Text1"
	Top	480
	Width	2400
VB.TextBox	Name	txtName
	Height	300
	Left	1380
	TabIndex	1
	Text	"Text1"
	Top	120
	Width	2400
VB.Label	Name	lblAction
	Caption	"lblAction"
	Height	255
	Left	120
	TabIndex	6

Control	Property	Setting
	Top	900
	Visible	0 'False
	Width	1155
VB.Label	Name	lblPhone
	Caption	"Phone:"
	Height	300
	Left	120
	TabIndex	2
	Top	480
	Width	1200
VB.Label	Name	lblName
	Caption	"Name:"
	Height	300
	Left	120
	TabIndex	0
	Top	120
	Width	1200

Notice that the lblAction label control is an invisible control. This control is used to pass information from the VPhone form to the VRec form, and is not used for direct display at run-time.

There is very little code needed for the VRec form. Listing 35.29 shows the code for the Form_Load and Form_Activate events. Add this code to your form.

Listing 35.29. Coding the Form_Load and Form_Activate events.

```
Private Sub Form_Activate()
    '
    ' tell them!
    '
    If Len(txtName.Text) <> 0 Then
        objVText.Speak txtName.Text, iVType
    End If
    If Len(txtPhone.Text) <> 0 Then
        objVText.Speak txtPhone.Text, iVType
    End If
    '
End Sub
```

continues

Listing 35.29. continued

```
Private Sub Form_Load()
    '
    Me.Caption = "Add/Edit a Record"
    CenterForm Me
    '
    txtName = "'"
    txtPhone = ""
    '
End Sub
```

Nothing fancy in the Form-Load event. The Form_Activate event contains code that will read the database record aloud to the user.

The only other code needed on the form is code for the cmdRec_Click event. Enter the code from Listing 35.30 into your project.

Listing 35.30. Coding the cmdRec_Click event.

```
Private Sub cmdRec_Click(Index As Integer)
    '
    ' handle user selections
    '
    Select Case Index
        Case 0 ' OK
            If Len(Trim(txtName)) <> 0 Then
                If lblaction = "ADD" Then
                    rsPhone.AddNew
                Else
                    rsPhone.Edit
                End If
                '
                rsPhone.Fields("Name") = txtName
                rsPhone.Fields("Phone") = txtPhone
                rsPhone.Update
            End If
            Unload Me
        Case 1 ' cancel
            Unload Me
        Case 2 ' help
            objVText.Speak cUserMsgs(ttsEdit), iVType
    End Select
    '
End Sub
```

You'll notice that this routine checks the contents of the invisible label control (lblAction) to see if this is an "add" or "edit" form. If this is an "add" form, the contents of the control are used to add a new record to the table.

That's it for this form. Save the form as VREC.FRM and update the project (VPHONE.VBP) before going on to the next section.

The VHelp Form

The VHelp form is a simple one-screen help box. This screen not only displays help tips on using the Voice Phone, it also speaks those tips to the user. Refer to Figure 35.5 and Table 35.4 for help in laying out the form.

FIGURE 35.5.

Laying out the VHelp form.

Table 35.4. The VHelp form controls.

Control	Property	Setting
VB.Form	Name	frmHelp
	BorderStyle	3 'Fixed Dialog
	Caption	"Help on Voice Phone"
	Height	3375
	Left	2745
	LinkTopic	"Form1"
	MaxButton	0 'False
	MinButton	0 'False
	Top	1875
	Width	4230
VB.CommandButton	Name	cmdOK
	Caption	"OK"
	Default	-1 'True
	Height	300
	Left	2760
	TabIndex	1
	Top	2520
	Width	1200
VB.Label	Name	Label1
	BorderStyle	1 'Fixed Single

continues

Table 35.4. controls

Control	Property	Setting
	Caption	"Label1"
	Height	2175
	Left	120
	TabIndex	0
	Top	180
	Width	3855

The only code needed for the form is the `Form_Load` event and the one-line `cmdOK_Click` event. Listing 35.31 shows both these routines. Add this code to your form.

Listing 35.31. Coding the `Form_Load` and `cmdOK_Click` events.

```
Private Sub cmdOK_Click()
    Unload Me
End Sub

Private Sub Form_Load()
    '
    ' setup help dialog
    '
    Dim x As Integer
    '
    Me.Caption = "Help on Voice Phone"
    Me.Icon = LoadPicture(App.Path & "\vphone.ico")
    CenterForm Me
    '
    Label1 = ""
    For x = ttsHello To ttsExit
        Label1 = Label1 & cUserMsgs(x) & Chr(13) & Chr(13)
    Next x
    '
    objVText.Speak Label1.Caption, iVType
    '
End Sub
```

That's it for the VHelp form. Save the form as VHELP.FRM and update the project (VPHONE.VBP) before moving on to the last coding section of the project.

The VAbout Form

The VAbout form shows the standard application information. This information is read from the properties of the App object. You set these properties using the File ¦ Make EXE ¦ Options menu selection. Table 35.5 shows the App object properties and their settings.

Table 35.5. The App object properties.

Property	Setting
Auto Increment	Checked ON
File Description	Demonstrates SAPI and TAPI
Legal Copyright	Copyright 1998 MCA/Sams Publishing
Product Name	Voice Phone

After setting these properties, you're ready to lay out the form and add the code. Refer to Figure 35.6 and Table 35.6 for the size and position of the controls on the form.

FIGURE 35.6.

Laying out the VAbout *form.*

Table 35.6. The VAbout form controls.

Control	Property	Setting
VB.Form	Name	frmAbout
	BorderStyle	3 'Fixed Dialog
	Caption	"Form1"
	Height	2610
	Left	2685
	MaxButton	0 'False
	MinButton	0 'False
	Top	1890
	Width	4980
VB.CommandButton	Name	Command1
	Caption	"&OK"
	Height	300
	Left	3540
	TabIndex	1
	Top	1800
	Width	1200

continues

Table 35.6. continued

Control	Property	Setting
VB.Image	Name	Image1
	Height	1455
	Left	120
	Top	180
	Width	1395
VB.Label	Name	Label1
	Caption	"Label1"
	Height	1455
	Left	1800
	TabIndex	0
	Top	180
	Width	2895

After laying out the form, you need to add code to the `Form_Load` and `Command1_Click` events. Listing 35.32 shows all the code you need for the form.

Listing 35.32. Coding the `Form_Load` and `Command1_Click` events.

```
Private Sub Command1_Click()
    Unload Me
End Sub

Private Sub Form_Load()
    '
    ' set up about dialog
    '
    Dim cVersion As String
    Me.Caption = "About " & App.ProductName
    Me.Icon = LoadPicture(App.Path & "\vphone.ico")
    Image1.Stretch = True
    Image1.Picture = LoadPicture(App.Path & "\vphone.ico")
    '
    cVersion = "Version: " & CStr(App.Major) & "." & CStr(App.Minor) & "." &
➥CStr(App.Revision)
    Label1 = App.ProductName & Chr(13) & Chr(13)
    Label1 = Label1 & App.LegalCopyright & Chr(13) & Chr(13)
    Label1 = Label1 & App.FileDescription & Chr(13) & Chr(13)
    Label1 = Label1 & cVersion
    '
    CenterForm Me
    '
    objVText.Speak Label1.Caption, iVType
    '
End Sub
```

Notice the use of the App object properties to fill in the Label control. This is a great way to provide up-to-date application version information for your projects.

Save the form as VABOUT.FRM and update the project file (VPHONE.VBP). That's the last of the coding for this project. Before moving on to the next section, compile the project and check for any errors. Once you're sure all the bugs have been ironed out, you're ready to test your Voice Phone.

Testing Voice Phone

When you first start Voice Phone, you'll get a short friendly greeting ("Hello. Welcome to Voice Phone."). Once the program has started, several voice commands have been registered with the Windows operating system. You can view these available commands by asking the workstation, *"What can I say?"* or by clicking the Microsoft Voice icon in the system tray and selecting "What can I say?" from the context menu. Figure 35.7 shows what your display should look like.

FIGURE 35.7.

Viewing the available Microsoft voice commands.

New data table records can be added by pressing the New button or by speaking the *New Record* command. You can also edit an existing record by selecting it from the list and pressing Edit or by speaking the command *Edit <Name>* where <Name> is the name of the person whose record you wish to edit (see Figure 35.8).

FIGURE 35.8.

Editing an existing Voice Phone record.

You can place a call by selecting a name from the list and pressing the `Place Call` button. Or you can simply tell Voice Phone to *Dial <Name>* where *<Name>* is the name of the person you wish to call. For example, if you wanted to call Susan, you'd speak the command *"Dial Susan."* Voice Phone will look up Susan's phone number, and place the call for you.

Since this project is using Assisted TAPI, the actual handling of the call is performed by the application on the workstation that is registered to handle Assisted TAPI requests. If you have Microsoft Phone installed on your workstation, you'll see Microsoft Phone appear and handle the call. If you have not installed any special telephony support applications, the default dialer, `DIALER.EXE`, will appear.

Finally, you can get help by pressing the `Help` button. This will force Voice Phone to speak helpful tips to you. If you want to view the help tips, select `Help ¦ Help` from the menu (see Figure 35.9).

FIGURE 35.9.

Viewing the Help screen.

Summary

In this chapter you built an application that combined SAPI and TAPI services to create a "hands-free" telephone interface. You learned how to register speech recognition and text-to-speech services, how to register Assisted TAPI services, and how to use both services to access database information and place telephone calls using the registered telephony application for handling Assisted TAPI service requests.

In the next chapter, you'll learn how to build an e-mail client that records audio messages instead of handling text messages.

36

The Talk Mail Project

The last integration project in the book combines MAPI services with audio recording. The Talk Mail project allows you to record messages and then send them to others via e-mail. It's a bit like an asynchronous telephone conversation.

You will need a sound card, a microphone, and speakers (or headphones) in order to run this project. You will be able to select one or more recipients, press the record button, record a message, and ship both the header data and the audio binary file to any other person in the MAPI directory.

NOTE

In this version of the Talk Mail project, all MAPI addresses are resolved against current names in your address book(s). You could add code to allow any user with a universal e-mail address (for example, yourname@internet.com) to receive the audio recordings. However, you'll need to ensure that the file is sent and received properly by Internet users before you add this feature.

You'll use the OLE Messaging library to implement the MAPI services. The audio recording will be handled using the Windows Media Control Interface (MCI). This project will make use of the new Windows 95 controls for Visual Basic, including the listview control, the toolbar control, and the statusbar control.

WARNING

Because this project makes extensive use of the Windows 95 controls, you will not be able to build it on a 16-bit Windows platform. You'll need to use the 32-bit version of Visual Basic and run it on Windows 95 or Windows NT.

Design Considerations

One of the advantages of the OLE Messaging library over the MAPI OCX tool is the added access to MAPI objects and properties. In this project we'll define a new message type (IPM.Note.TalkMail) for all messages generated by our Talk Mail application. The real benefit in this is that we'll be able to tell our Talk Mail client to pay attention only to the messages generated by other Talk Mail clients. This way, when our new voice-mail client checks the MAPI inbox for new messages, only the Talk Mail messages will appear on the screen.

The voice recordings, in the form of WAV files, will be shipped as an attachment with each MAPI message. The Talk Mail client will automatically load the WAV file into the MCI form control, ready for playback (or further recording). The Talk Mail client never tells the user that there is an attachment to the message. In fact, as far as the user is concerned, there is no attachment!

> **TIP**
>
> All Talk Mail messages can be viewed from the standard Windows Messaging or Microsoft Mail MAPI clients. When you use the standard MAPI clients, you'll see the WAV file appear as an attachment to the text message.

It may seem that we should use the SAPI services for the "talking" portion of the application. However, because the primary focus of this application is voice, it's a better idea to use the pure voice recording instead of rendering text into speech. Also, by using the MCI tool that ships with Visual Basic Professional and Enterprise Editions, you can provide full record and playback services with very little coding. Therefore, this application will take advantage of users' tendency to prefer actual voices over computer-generated sound.

Project Forms and Resources

The project has four forms and one code module. The code module holds routines for handling several OLE operations along with global variable declarations and other support routines. The four forms for the project are

- tmView—This is the main viewer form. When the application first starts, users will see this form. This is where the user performs MAPI logon and logoff, accesses the MAPI address book and creates new Talk Mail messages, and reads or deletes existing Talk Mail messages.
- tmNew—This is the form for creating new Talk Mail messages. The heart of the form is the MCI audio control. Users can manipulate the control like any other tape device (rewind, play, fast-forward, stop, and so on).
- tmRead—This form is almost identical to the tmNew form except that tmRead is for reading Talk Mail messages sent to you by others.
- tmAbout—This is a tiny form displaying the basic About box information for the project.

You'll need to make sure you have the following references and custom controls added to your project:

- Microsoft OLE/Messaging object library
- Microsoft Common Dialog control
- Microsoft MCI multimedia control
- Microsoft Windows Common controls (for Win95)

> **TIP**
>
> You load the object libraries using the `Tools | References` menu option. You load the OCX controls using the `Tools | Custom Controls` menu option.

Now that you have a good idea of how the project works, let's jump right into creating the BAS module that will hold the general support routines for the project.

Coding the `LibTalkMail` Module

The `LibTalkMail` module has seven subroutines and three functions. Most of these routines deal with MAPI service requests but others include error handling and simple helper functions to manage the Talk Mail messages. This module also has several public variables that are declared here and used throughout the program.

First, start a new Visual Basic project and make sure you have loaded the OLE Messaging library and the custom controls listed in the preceding section.

Next, add a module to the project (`Insert | Module`) and set its `Name` property to `LibTalkMail`. Now add the code in Listing 36.1 to the general declaration section of the module.

Listing 36.1. Public variables and objects for the Talk Mail project.

```
Option Explicit

'
' internal message pointer
Type MsgPtr
    ID As String
    Subject As String
End Type
'
' to track msgs
Public uMsgP() As MsgPtr
Public iMsgCount As Integer
Public cMsgID As String
'
' ole message libary objects
Public objSession As Object
Public objInBox As Object
Public objOutBox As Object
Public objMsgColl As Object
Public objAttach As Object
Public objAttachColl As Object
Public objRecipColl As Object
Public objRecip As Object
Public objMsg As Object
Public objAddrEntry As Object
'
```

```
' for MCI wav work
Public cWavFile As String
Public Const conInterval = 50
Public Const conIntervalPlus = 55
```

There are three sets of variables and objects in the code in Listing 36.1. First you see the creation of a user-defined type (UDT) that will hold the unique MAPI message ID and the MAPI subject. This UDT will be used to perform quick lookups of a selected record in the mail system. After defining the MsgPtr type, three variables are defined to hold information about the message pool. The next set of declarations defines the OLE message objects. These will be used (and re-used) throughout the program. Finally, the module contains a few variables for handling the MCI control.

Next you need to add the MAPI-related subroutines, the first of which is the MAPIStart routine. This routine is called to begin a MAPI session. Add a new subroutine called MAPIStart (select Insert ¦ Procedure) and enter the code shown in Listing 36.2.

Listing 36.2. Adding the MAPIStart routine.

```
Public Sub MAPIStart()
    '
    ' log into mapi
    '
    On Error GoTo LocalErr
    '
    Set objSession = CreateObject("MAPI.Session")
    objSession.Logon
    '
    Set objInBox = objSession.Inbox
    Set objOutBox = objSession.Outbox
    Exit Sub
    '
LocalErr:
    MsgBox ErrMsg(Err), vbCritical, "MAPIStart"
    '
End Sub
```

The MAPIEnd routine is called when the user wants to end the MAPI session completely. Most of the code in the MAPIEnd routine is required to free precious workstation memory.

TIP

It is always a good idea to set Visual Basic objects equal to Nothing when you are through with them. This frees workstation memory and can improve overall workstation performance.

Add a new subroutine (`MAPIEnd`) and enter the code from Listing 36.3.

Listing 36.3. Adding the `MAPIEnd` routine.

```
Public Sub MAPIEnd()
    '
    On Error Resume Next
    '
    objSession.Logoff
    Set objSession = Nothing
    Set objInBox = Nothing
    Set objOutBox = Nothing
    Set objMsgColl = Nothing
    Set objRecip = Nothing
    Set objMsg = Nothing
    '
End Sub
```

Two short MAPI routines are `MAPIAddrBook` and `MAPIDeleteMsg`. These two routines give the user access to the MAPI address book and delete a selected message, respectively. Add these two subroutines to your project from Listings 36.4 and 36.5.

Listing 36.4. Adding the `MAPIAddrBook` routine.

```
Public Sub MAPIAddrBook()
    '
    On Error GoTo LocalErr
    '
    objSession.AddressBook
    Exit Sub
    '
LocalErr:
    MsgBox ErrMsg(Err), vbCritical, "MAPIAddrBook"
    '
End Sub
```

The `MAPIDeleteMsg` routine will remove a selected message object from the collection. Add the code from Listing 36.5 to your project.

Listing 36.5. Adding the `MAPIDeleteMsg` routine.

```
Public Sub MAPIDeleteMsg(cMsgID As String)
    '
    ' delete selected message
    '
    On Error GoTo LocalErr
    '
    Dim iAns As Integer
    '
```

```
    Set objMsg = objSession.GetMessage(cMsgID)
    '
    iAns = MsgBox(objMsg.Subject, vbExclamation + vbYesNo, "Delete Talk Mail
➥Message")
    If iAns = vbYes Then
        objMsg.Delete
    End If
    '
    Exit Sub
    '
LocalErr:
    MsgBox ErrMsg(Err), vbCritical, "MAPIDeleteMsg"
    '
End Sub
```

Next you need to add two routines that call the `tmRead` and `tmNew` dialog boxes to read or create new messages. These two routines are almost identical. The only difference is the name of the form that is launched. Add the `MAPINewMsg` subroutine and enter the code form Listing 36.6.

Listing 36.6. Adding the MAPINewMsg routine.

```
Public Sub MAPINewMsg()
    '
    ' allow user to compose a message
    '
    frmTMView.CMDialog1.Filter = "WaveForm File (*.wav)¦*.wav"
    frmTMNew.MMControl1.DeviceType = "WaveAudio"
    frmTMNew.Show
    frmTMView.Hide
    '
End Sub
```

Note that this routine (and the `MAPIReadMsg` routine) both just hide the main form rather than unloading it. This is necessary because the project has some values that must be shared between forms. Now add the `MAPIReadMsg` routine shown in Listing 36.7.

Listing 36.7. Adding the MAPIReadMsg routine.

```
Public Sub MAPIReadMsg(cMsgID As String)
    '
    ' allow user to view a message
    '
    frmTMView.CMDialog1.Filter = "WaveForm File (*.wav)¦*.wav"
    frmTMRead.MMControl1.DeviceType = "WaveAudio"
    frmTMRead.Show
    frmTMView.Hide
    '
End Sub
```

The next routine is the largest one in the module. The MAPISendMsg routine is the one that builds the MAPI message object and makes sure it is sent off to the recipient(s). Add the MAPISendMsg subroutine to the project and enter the code from Listing 36.8.

Listing 36.8. Adding the MAPISendMsg routine.

```
Public Sub MAPISendMsg(objRecipList As Object, cSubject As String, cBody As String,
➥cWavFile As String)
    '
    ' construct a message and send it off
    '
    On Error GoTo LocalErr
    '
    Dim x As Integer
    '
    ' build new message
    Set objMsg = objOutBox.Messages.Add
    objMsg.Type = "IPM.Note.TalkMail"
    objMsg.Subject = cSubject
    objMsg.Text = " " & cBody
    '
    ' add wav file as attachment
    If Len(cWavFile) <> 0 Then
        Set objAttach = objMsg.Attachments.Add
        objAttach.Name = "Talk Mail.WAV" 'cWavFile
        objAttach.position = 0
        objAttach.Type = mapiFileData
        objAttach.Source = cWavFile
        objAttach.ReadFromFile cWavFile
    End If
    '
    ' load recipient(s)
    If objRecipList Is Nothing Then
        MsgBox "No Recipients!"
    Else
        For x = 1 To objRecipList.Count
            Set objRecip = objMsg.Recipients.Add
            objRecip.Name = objRecipList.Item(x).Name
        Next x
    End If
    '
    ' send it out quietly
    On Error Resume Next
    objMsg.Update ' update all the collections
    objMsg.Send showdialog:=False
    '
    ' let everyone know
    MsgBox "Message Sent", vbInformation, "Talk Mail"
    '
    Exit Sub
    '
LocalErr:
    MsgBox ErrMsg(Err), vbCritical, "MAPISendMsg"
    '
End Sub
```

There are four main tasks performed by this routine. First, the message body is assembled. Note the use of IPM.Note.TalkMail in the Type property. You'll use this value as a search criterion when you refresh the list of available Talk Mail messages.

Next, the recorded WAV audio file is added to the package as an attachment. There are a couple of important points to make here. First, it is important that you use ".WAV" as the suffix of the Name property of the attachment object. This will make sure you can click the object, and Windows will call up the audio player automatically. Also, when you are attaching data to the message (not just linking, but attaching), you need to invoke the ReadFromFile method to actually load the selected file into the message package. Unlike the OCX controls, OLE does not do this for you.

Third, you need to add the recipients from the collection returned by the address book into the collection for the message. This requires iterating through the source object and using the results to insert into the message's receipt object.

Lastly, the routine updates all its child objects and quietly sends the MAPI package to the MAPI spooler for delivery.

There are three general helper functions that need to be added to the LibTalkMail module. The first one is the FindSubject function. This is used to return a unique MAPI message ID using the UDT you built at the start of this section. Add the FindSubject function and enter the code shown in Listing 36.9.

Listing 36.9. Adding the FindSubject function.

```
Public Function FindSubject(cSubject As String) As String
    '
    ' takes subject line, returns MsgID
    '
    Dim x As Integer
    Dim cRtn As String
    '
    cRtn = "" ' start empty
    For x = 1 To iMsgCount
        If UCase(cSubject) = UCase(uMsgP(x).Subject) Then
            cRtn = uMsgP(x).ID
            Exit For
        End If
    Next x
    '
    FindSubject = cRtn
    '
End Function
```

Another very valuable helper function is the GetRecipients function. This routine accepts a collection of recipients and extracts the display name into a single string for producing an onscreen list of the message recipients. After adding the new `GetRecipients` function to the project, enter the code shown in Listing 36.10.

Listing 36.10. Adding the new `GetRecipients` function.

```
Public Function GetRecipients(objRecipColl As Object) As String
    '
    ' pull qualified recipients from object collection
    '
    Dim cRtn As String
    Dim x As Integer
    '
    cRtn = ""
    '
    If objRecipColl Is Nothing Then
        GoTo LeaveHere
    End If
    '
    For x = 1 To objRecipColl.Count
        Set objRecip = objRecipColl.Item(x)
        cRtn = cRtn & objRecip.Name & ";"
    Next x
    '
    If Len(cRtn) > 0 Then
        cRtn = Left(cRtn, Len(cRtn) - 1)
    End If
    '
LeaveHere:
    GetRecipients = cRtn
    '
End Function
```

The last helper function you need to add to the `LibTalkMail` module is the `ErrMsg` function. This routine uses the new Visual Basic 4.0 `Err` object to build an informative message concerning the name, type, and originator of the message. Add the code in Listing 36.11 to your project.

Listing 36.11. Add the `ErrMsg` function.

```
Public Function ErrMsg(ErrObj As Object) As String
    '
    ' return formatted message
    '
    Dim cMsg As String
    '
    cMsg = "ErrCode:" & Chr(9) & CStr(ErrObj.Number) & Chr(13)
    cMsg = cMsg & "ErrMsg:" & Chr(9) & ErrObj.Description & Chr(13)
    cMsg = cMsg & "Source:" & Chr(9) & ErrObj.Source
    '
    ErrMsg = cMsg
    '
End Function
```

That's all you need to add to the BAS module of the Talk Mail project. Be sure to save this file under the name `LIBTMAIL.BAS` and the project under the name `TALKMAIL.VBP` before continuing.

The `tmView` Form

The main form shows a list of all the Talk Mail messages in the user's inbox. It also has a set of toolbar buttons for performing the basic MAPI actions of logon, logoff, viewing the address book, creating a new Talk Mail message, reading an Existing Talk Mail message, and deleting a Talk Mail message. There are also buttons for adjusting the list view from large icon, small icon, list, and detail formats.

Laying Out `tmView`

The first step is to lay out the form's controls. Refer to Table 36.1 and Figure 36.1 for details on the layout of the `tmView` form.

FIGURE 36.1.

Laying out the `tmView` *form.*

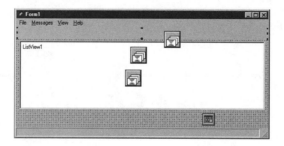

Table 36.1. The tmView form controls.

Control	Property	Setting
VB.Form	Name	frmTMView
	Caption	"Form1"
	Height	4410
	Left	1185
	Top	1665
	Width	8715
MSComDlg.CommonDialog	Name	CMDialog1
	Left	6360
	Top	2880

continues

Table 36.1. continued

Control	Property	Setting
ComctlLib.StatusBar	Name	StatusBar1
	Align	2 'Align Bottom
	Height	315
	Left	0
	TabIndex	2
	Top	3405
	Width	8595
	AlignSet	-1 'True
	SimpleText	""
ComctlLib.ImageList	Name	imglstSmall
	Left	3720
	Top	1440
ComctlLib.ImageList	Name	imglstBig
	Left	3900
	Top	660
ComctlLib.ImageList	Name	imglstToolBar
	Left	5040
	Top	120
	ImageWidth	16
	ImageHeight	16
ComctlLib.Toolbar	Name	tbrMain
	Align	1 'Align Top
	Height	390
	Left	0
	TabIndex	1
	Top	0
	Width	8595
	ImageList	""
	AlignSet	-1 'True
ComctlLib.ListView	Name	ListView1
	Height	2295
	Left	120

Control	Property	Setting
	TabIndex	0
	Top	480
	Width	8355
	Appearance	1
	Arrange	2
	Icons	"ImageList3"
	SmallIcons	"ImageList2"
	View	2

The form doesn't look like much at first, but you'll add all the fancy stuff (bitmaps, icons, and so on) at runtime. Once you get the controls onto the form, you need to build the menu. Figure 36.2 and Table 36.2 show you the details of the menu layout.

> **TIP**
>
> The menu layout makes extensive use of menu arrays. Be sure to pay close attention to the index number values when building the menu. You'll use these index values throughout the program.

FIGURE 36.2.

Laying out the tmView *menu.*

Table 36.2. The tmView form menu.

Menu Level	Properties	Settings
Top	Name	mnuFile
	Caption	"File"

continues

Table 36.2. continued

Menu Level	Properties	Settings
Level 2	Name	mnuFileItem
	Caption	"Log &In..."
	Index	0
Level 2	Name	mnuFileItem
	Caption	"Log &Out"
	Index	1
Level 2	Name	mnuFileItem
	Caption	"-"
	Index	2
Level 2	Name	mnuFileItem
	Caption	"&Scan Inbox"
	Index	3
Level 2	Name	mnuFileItem
	Caption	"&Address Book..."
	Index	4
Level 2	Name	mnuFileItem
	Caption	"-"
	Index	5
Level 2	Name	mnuFileItem
	Caption	"E&xit"
	Index	6
Top	Name	mnuMsgs
	Caption	"&Messages"
Level 2	Name	mnuMsgsItem
	Caption	"&New..."
	Index	0
Level 2	Name	mnuMsgsItem
	Caption	"&Read"
	Index	1
Level 2	Name	mnuMsgsItem
	Caption	"&Delete"
	Index	2

Menu Level	Properties	Settings
Top	Name	mnuView
	Caption	"&View"
Level 2	Name	mnuViewItem
	Caption	"Lar&ge Icons"
	Index	0
Level 2	Name	mnuViewItem
	Caption	"&Small Icons"
	Index	1
Level 2	Name	mnuViewItem
	Caption	"L&ist"
	Index	2
Level 2	Name	mnuViewItem
	Caption	"&Details"
	Index	3
Top	Name	mnuHelp
	Caption	"&Help"
Level 2	Name	mnuHelpItem
	Caption	"&About"
	Index	0

Once you have the form controls and menus in place, save the form as TMVIEW.FRM and save the project (TALKMAIL.VBP) before you go on to add the form code.

Coding tmView

Most of the code for the tmView form is needed to set up the toolbar, listview, and statusbar controls. There are also several code sections for handling the menu selections and the basic form events. There are a few short events for handling toolbar and list view clicks and there is one routine for requesting new messages from the MAPI service.

The code can be divided into the following related groups:

- The form event code
- The control-building code
- The menu-support routines
- The control event code

Coding the Form Events

The `Form_Load` event calls the routines to build the form controls and then set some properties of the form itself. Enter the code shown in Listing 36.12 into the `Form_Load` event.

Listing 36.12. Coding the `Form_Load` event.

```
Private Sub Form_Load()
    '
    BuildToolBar
    BuildListView
    BuildStatusBar
    '
    Me.Caption = "Talk Mail 95"
    Me.Left = (Screen.Width - Me.Width) / 2
    Me.Top = (Screen.Height - Me.Height) / 2
    Me.Icon = LoadPicture(App.Path & "\tmMsg32.ico")
    '
End Sub
```

> ### WARNING
>
> The code example above uses the `App.Path` property to locate the icon file. This will not work properly if you locate your project in a root directory of a drive. It is recommended that you place all project files in a single directory. If you place your files in a root directory, you'll need to modify the code that uses the `app.path` object.

You also need to add code to the `Form_Resize` event. This code will resize the `listview` control to make sure it fills the form. Enter the code from Listing 36.13 into your project.

Listing 36.13. Adding the `Form_Resize` event code.

```
Private Sub Form_Resize()
    '
    ' handle form resizing
    '
    If Me.WindowState <> vbMinimized Then
        ListView1.Left = 0
        ListView1.Top = tbrMain.Height
        ListView1.Width = Me.ScaleWidth
        ListView1.Height = Me.ScaleHeight - tbrMain.Height - StatusBar1.Height
    End If
    '
End Sub
```

The Control Building Code

Three of the controls (`listview`, `toolbar`, and `statusbar`) require extensive setup. While this could be done at design time using the custom property boxes, it is easier to modify the properties if you build the controls at run-time.

Add a new subroutine called `BuildStatusBar` and enter the code shown in Listing 36.14.

Listing 36.14. Adding the `BuildStatusBar` routine.

```
Public Sub BuildStatusBar()
    '
    ' create details of status bar display
    '
    Dim I As Integer
    '
    For I = 1 To 4
        StatusBar1.Panels.Add    ' Add Panel objects.
        StatusBar1.Panels(I).AutoSize = sbrContents
    Next I

    With StatusBar1.Panels
        .Item(1).Style = sbrText
        .Item(2).Style = sbrCaps ' Caps lock
        .Item(3).Style = sbrIns  ' insert
        .Item(4).Style = sbrDate ' date
        .Item(5).Style = sbrTime ' time
    End With
    '
    StatusBar1.Panels(1).Text = "Talk Mail" & Space(50)
    StatusBar1.Style = sbrNormal
    '
End Sub
```

The code in Listing 36.14 sets up a status bar that will show the status of the CAPS and INS buttons, the date and time, and reserve some space for a status message.

Next, add a new subroutine called `BuildListView` and enter the code shown in Listing 36.15.

Listing 36.15. Adding the `BuildListView` routine.

```
Public Sub BuildListView()
    '
    ' build list view
    '
    Dim clmX As ColumnHeader
    Dim ItmX As ListItem
    Dim ImgX As ListImage
    '
    ' set view properties
```

continues

Listing 36.15. continued

```
ListView1.BorderStyle = ccFixedSingle
ListView1.View = lvwReport
ListView1.Sorted = True
mnuViewItem(3).Checked = True ' show check on menu
'
' set column headers for detail view
Set clmX = ListView1.ColumnHeaders. _
    Add(, , "Subject", ListView1.Width * 0.25)
Set clmX = ListView1.ColumnHeaders. _
    Add(, , "RecvDate", ListView1.Width * 0.25)
Set clmX = ListView1.ColumnHeaders. _
    Add(, , "From", ListView1.Width * 0.25)
'
' set large image list control
imglstbig.ImageHeight = 32
imglstbig.ImageWidth = 32
Set ImgX = imglstbig.ListImages. _
    Add(, , LoadPicture(App.Path & "\tmMsg32.ico"))
Set ImgX = imglstbig.ListImages. _
    Add(, , LoadPicture(App.Path & "\note32.ico"))
'
' set small image control
imglstsmall.ImageHeight = 16
imglstsmall.ImageWidth = 16
Set ImgX = imglstsmall.ListImages. _
    Add(, , LoadPicture(App.Path & "\tmMsg16.ico"))
Set ImgX = imglstsmall.ListImages. _
    Add(, , LoadPicture(App.Path & "\note16.ico"))
'
' link image and listview
ListView1.Icons = imglstbig
ListView1.SmallIcons = imglstsmall
'
End Sub
```

The code in Listing 36.15 performs several tasks. First, columns are defined for the detail view. Next, two image controls are initialized for the large and small icon views. Finally, those two image controls are bound to the listview control so that the list view knows which icons to use when displaying the contents.

The last of the "build" routines is the BuildToolBar routine. This is the most involved of the three because it contains fourteen buttons (some of them separators) with all their icons, tooltips, and keys. Add the new subroutine (BuildToolBar) and enter the code shown in Listing 36.16.

Listing 36.16. Adding the BuildToolBar routine.

```
Public Sub BuildToolBar()
'
' set up win95 tool bar
'
```

```
Dim ImgX As ListImage
Dim BtnX As Button
Dim tlbrPics(14) As String
Dim tlbrKeys(14) As String
Dim tlbrTips(14) As String
Dim tlbrStyle(14) As Integer
Dim x As Integer
'
tlbrPics(1) = "tmStart.ico"
tlbrPics(2) = "tmEnd.ico"
tlbrPics(3) = "tmstart.ico"
tlbrPics(4) = "tmAdrBk.ico"
tlbrPics(5) = "tmScan.ico"
tlbrPics(6) = "tmstart.ico"
tlbrPics(7) = "tmMsg16.ico"
tlbrPics(8) = "tmRead.ico"
tlbrPics(9) = "tmTrash.ico"
tlbrPics(10) = "tmstart.ico"
tlbrPics(11) = "vw-lrgic.bmp"
tlbrPics(12) = "vw-smlic.bmp"
tlbrPics(13) = "vw-list.bmp"
tlbrPics(14) = "vw-dtls.bmp"
'
tlbrKeys(1) = "LOGIN"
tlbrKeys(2) = "LOGOUT"
tlbrKeys(3) = ""
tlbrKeys(4) = "ADDRBOOK"
tlbrKeys(5) = "SCANINBOX"
tlbrKeys(6) = ""
tlbrKeys(7) = "NEWMSG"
tlbrKeys(8) = "READMSG"
tlbrKeys(9) = "DELETE"
tlbrKeys(10) = ""
tlbrKeys(11) = "ICONS"
tlbrKeys(12) = "SMALLICONS"
tlbrKeys(13) = "LISTVIEW"
tlbrKeys(14) = "DETAILS"
'
tlbrTips(1) = "Log In"
tlbrTips(2) = "Log Out"
tlbrTips(3) = ""
tlbrTips(4) = "Address Book"
tlbrTips(5) = "Scan InBox"
tlbrTips(6) = ""
tlbrTips(7) = "New Msg"
tlbrTips(8) = "Read Msg"
tlbrTips(9) = "Delete Msg"
tlbrTips(10) = ""
tlbrTips(11) = "Icons"
tlbrTips(12) = "Small Icons"
tlbrTips(13) = "List View"
tlbrTips(14) = "Details"
'
imglstToolbar.ImageHeight = 16
imglstToolbar.ImageWidth = 16
'
' fill image list
```

continues

Listing 36.16. continued

```
    For x = 1 To 14
        Set ImgX = imglstToolbar.ListImages. _
          Add(, , LoadPicture(App.Path & "\" & tlbrPics(x)))
    Next x
    '
    ' fill toolbar
    tbrMain.ImageList = imglstToolbar
    For x = 1 To 14
        Set BtnX = tbrMain.Buttons.Add
        BtnX.Key = tlbrKeys(x)
        BtnX.ToolTipText = tlbrTips(x)
        If tlbrTips(x) <> "" Then
            BtnX.Style = tbrDefault
            BtnX.Image = x
        Else
            BtnX.Style = tbrSeparator
        End If
    Next x
End Sub
```

> **NOTE**
>
> This routine refers to several icon files. These icons can be found on the CD-ROM that ships with this book. They should have been copied to your local drive when you installed the CD-ROM. Make sure you copy them to your project directory before you run the project.

The Menu Support Routines

There are four main menu branches: File, Message, View, and Help. Each branch is built as a menu array. You need to add code to handle user selections for each menu branch.

First, add the code shown in Listing 36.17 to the mnuFileItem_Click event.

Listing 36.17. Adding the mnuFileItem_Click event code.

```
Private Sub mnuFileItem_Click(Index As Integer)
    '
    ' handle file menu stuff
    '
    Select Case Index
        Case 0 ' login
            MAPIStart
        Case 1 ' logout
            MAPIEnd
        Case 3 ' scan inbox
            MAPIScanInBox
```

```
            Case 4 ' addr book
                MAPIAddrBook
            Case 6 ' exit
                MAPIEnd
                Unload Me
        End Select
        '
End Sub
```

Next, add the code from Listing 36.18 to the `mnuMsgItem_Click` event.

Listing 36.18. Coding the `mnuMsgItem_Click` event.

```
Private Sub mnuMsgsItem_Click(Index As Integer)
    '
    ' handle msgs menu
    '
    Dim Itm As Object
    Dim x As Integer
    '
    Select Case Index
        Case 0 ' new
            MAPINewMsg
        Case 1 ' read
            If cMsgID <> "" Then
                MAPIReadMsg cMsgID
            End If
        Case 2 ' delete
            If cMsgID <> "" Then
                MAPIDeleteMsg cMsgID
                MAPIScanInBox ' update view
            End If
    End Select
    '
End Sub
```

The next code section deals with adjustments in the list view options. Add the code from Listing 36.19 to the `mnuViewItem_Click` event.

Listing 36.19. Coding the `mnuViewItem_Click` event.

```
Private Sub mnuViewItem_Click(Index As Integer)
    '
    ' handle views
    '
    Dim x As Integer
    '
    Select Case Index
        Case 0 ' large icon
            ListView1.View = lvwIcon
```

continues

Listing 36.19. continued

```
        Case 1 ' small icon
            ListView1.View = lvwSmallIcon
        Case 2 ' list view
            ListView1.View = lvwList
        Case 3 ' detail view
            ListView1.View = lvwReport
    End Select
    '
    For x = 0 To 3
        If x = Index Then
            mnuViewItem(x).Checked = True
        Else
            mnuViewItem(x).Checked = False
        End If
    Next x
    '
End Sub
```

The last menu code is for the mnuHelpItem_Click event. Enter the code from Listing 36.20 into your project.

Listing 36.20. Adding the mnuHelpItem_Click event code.

```
Private Sub mnuHelpItem_Click(Index As Integer)
    '
    ' handle help menu
    '
    Select Case Index
        Case 0 ' about
            frmAbout.Show vbModal
    End Select
    '
End Sub
```

The last control event code you need to add is the code that handles the toolbar selections. This code looks very similar to the menu event code. In this case, the user selection is determined by the value of the Button.Key property. Enter the code from Listing 36.21 into the tbrMain_ButtonClick event.

Listing 36.21. Coding the tbrMain_ButtonClick event.

```
Private Sub TbrMain_ButtonClick(ByVal Button As Button)
    '
    Select Case Button.Key
        Case "LOGIN"
            MAPIStart
            MAPIScanInBox
```

```
        Case "LOGOUT"
            MAPIEnd
            Unload Me
        Case "ADDRBOOK"
            MAPIAddrBook
        Case "NEWMSG"
            MAPINewMsg
        Case "READMSG"
            MAPIReadMsg cMsgID
        Case "DELETE"
            MAPIDeleteMsg cMsgID
            MAPIScanInBox
        Case "SCANINBOX"
            MAPIScanInBox
        Case "ICONS"
            mnuViewItem_Click 0
        Case "SMALLICONS"
            mnuViewItem_Click 1
        Case "LISTVIEW"
            mnuViewItem_Click 2
        Case "DETAILS"
            mnuViewItem_Click 3
    End Select
    '
End Sub
```

Coding the Control Events

The last set of code routines for the tmView form is the code that is executed for various control events. There are three events for the list control. These events adjust the sorting order, collect the subject of the selected item in the list, and launch the Talk Mail message reader. Add code for the three routines shown in Listing 36.22.

Listing 36.22. Coding the ListView events.

```
Private Sub ListView1_ColumnClick(ByVal ColumnHeader As ColumnHeader)
    ListView1.SortKey = ColumnHeader.Index - 1 ' change sort order
End Sub

Private Sub ListView1_DblClick()
    MAPIReadMsg cMsgID ' launch reader form
End Sub

Private Sub ListView1_ItemClick(ByVal Item As ListItem)
    cMsgID = FindSubject(Item.Text) ' get subject text
End Sub
```

There is only one more code routine for the tmView form—the MAPIScanInBox routine. This routine scans the MAPI inbox for any Talk Mail messages addressed to the user and fills the list view with the results. This routine also builds an array of message pointers that will be used to locate messages in the MAPI infostore whenever the user wishes to read a particular message. Add the MAPIScanInBox subroutine to the project and enter the code shown in Listing 36.23.

Listing 36.23. Adding the MAPIScanInBox code.

```
Private Sub MAPIScanInBox()
    '
    ' scan inbox for msgs
    '
    On Error Resume Next
    '
    Dim ItmX As ListItem
    '
    ' refresh collections
    Set objInBox = objSession.Inbox
    Set objMsgColl = objInBox.Messages
    '
    ListView1.ListItems.Clear
    iMsgCount = 0
    ReDim uMsgP(0)
    '
    ' only get talk mail records
    Set objMsg = objMsgColl.GetFirst("IPM.Note.TalkMail")
    Do Until objMsg Is Nothing
        Set ItmX = ListView1.ListItems.Add
        ItmX.Icon = 1
        ItmX.SmallIcon = 1
        If Trim(objMsg.Subject) = "" Then
            ItmX.Text = "<No Subject>"
        Else
            ItmX.Text = objMsg.Subject
        End If
        '
        ItmX.SubItems(1) = Format(objMsg.TimeReceived, "general date")
        '
        Set objAddrEntry = objMsg.Sender
        If objAddrEntry Is Nothing Then
            ItmX.SubItems(2) = "<No Sender>"
        Else
            ItmX.SubItems(2) = objAddrEntry.Name
        End If
        '
        ' store in pointer set
        iMsgCount = iMsgCount + 1
        ReDim Preserve uMsgP(iMsgCount)
        uMsgP(iMsgCount).ID = objMsg.ID
        uMsgP(iMsgCount).Subject = ItmX.Text
        '
        Set objMsg = objMsgColl.GetNext
```

```
    Loop
    '
    Set objMsg = Nothing
    Set objMsgColl = Nothing
    '
    StatusBar1.Panels(1).Text = CStr(iMsgCount) & " Talk Mail Message(s)" &
➡Space(40)
    '
    Exit Sub
    '
LocalErr:
    MsgBox ErrMsg(Err), vbCritical, "MAPIScanInBox"
    '
End Sub
```

That's the end of the code routines for the tmView form. Be sure to save the form (TMVIEW.FRM) and the project (TALKMAIL.VBP) before you continue.

The tmNew and tmRead Forms

The tmNew and tmRead forms are where the real action happens. These forms present the user with some input controls for selecting recipients, setting a subject line, and entering a supporting text message. The center of the form is the MCI control. This can be used for playback and recording of the audio WAV file.

Laying Out tmNew

First, refer to Figure 36.3 and Table 36.3 for the layout of the tmNew form.

FIGURE 36.3.

Laying out the tmNew *form.*

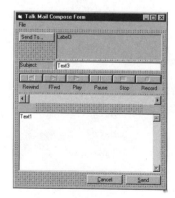

Table 36.3. The tmNew form controls.

Control	Property	Setting
VB.Form	Name	frmTMNew
	Caption	"Talk Mail Compose Form"
	Height	6030
	Left	2415
	Top	1455
	Width	5250
VB.HScrollBar	Name	HScroll1
	Height	300
	Left	120
	Max	100
	TabIndex	12
	Top	2220
	Width	4860
VB.CommandButton	Name	cmdNewMsg
	Cancel	-1 'True
	Caption	"&Cancel"
	Height	300
	Index	1
	Left	2460
	TabIndex	5
	Top	4920
	Width	1200
VB.CommandButton	Name	cmdAddrBook
	Caption	"Send To... "
	Height	300
	Left	120
	TabIndex	0
	Top	120
	Width	1200
VB.CommandButton	Name	cmdNewMsg
	Caption	"&Send"
	Height	300

Control	Property	Setting
	Index	0
	Left	3780
	TabIndex	4
	Top	4920
	Width	1200
VB.TextBox	Name	txtSubject
	Height	300
	Left	1380
	TabIndex	1
	Text	"Text3"
	Top	1080
	Width	3600
VB.TextBox	Name	txtBody
	Height	1995
	Left	120
	MultiLine	-1 'True
	ScrollBars	2 'Vertical
	TabIndex	3
	Top	2820
	Width	4860
VB.Label	Name	Label3
	Alignment	2 'Center
	Caption	"Pause"
	Height	300
	Left	2520
	TabIndex	16
	Top	1860
	Width	795
VB.Label	Name	lblFFwd
	Alignment	2 'Center
	Caption	"FFwd"
	Height	300

continues

Table 36.3. continued

Control	Property	Setting
	Left	960
	TabIndex	15
	Top	1860
	Width	735
VB.Label	Name	Label1
	Height	255
	Left	120
	TabIndex	14
	Top	2520
	Width	600
VB.Label	Name	Label2
	Height	255
	Left	4380
	TabIndex	13
	Top	2520
	Width	600
VB.Label	Name	lblRecord
	Alignment	2 'Center
	Caption	"Record"
	Height	300
	Left	4140
	TabIndex	11
	Top	1860
	Width	855
VB.Label	Name	lblStop
	Alignment	2 'Center
	Caption	"Stop"
	Height	300
	Left	3360
	TabIndex	10
	Top	1860
	Width	735

Control	Property	Setting
VB.Label	Name	lblPlay
	Alignment	2 'Center
	Caption	"Play"
	Height	300
	Left	1740
	TabIndex	9
	Top	1860
	Width	735
VB.Label	Name	lblRewind
	Alignment	2 'Center
	Caption	"Rewind"
	Height	300
	Left	120
	TabIndex	8
	Top	1860
	Width	795
MCI.MMControl	Name	MMControl1
	Height	315
	Left	120
	TabIndex	2
	Top	1500
	Width	4875
	BackVisible	0 'False
	StepVisible	0 'False
	EjectVisible	0 'False
	BorderStyle	1
VB.Label	Name	lblRecips
	BorderStyle	1 'Fixed Single
	Caption	"Label3"
	Height	900
	Left	1380
	TabIndex	7

continues

Table 36.3. continued

Control	Property	Setting
	Top	120
	Width	3615
VB.Label	Name	lblSubject
	BorderStyle	1 'Fixed Single
	Caption	"Subject:"
	Height	300
	Left	120
	TabIndex	6
	Top	1080
	Width	1200

The `tmNew` form also has a short menu. Refer to Figure 36.4 and Table 36.4 for laying out the form menu.

FIGURE 36.4.
Building the `tmNew` *form menu.*

Table 36.4. The `tmNew` form menu.

Level	Properties	Settings
Top	Name	mnuFile
	Caption	"File"
Level 2	Name	mnuFileItem
	Caption	"Save Wave File..."
	Index	0

Level	Properties	Settings
Level 2	Name	mnuFileItem
	Caption	"&Send Message"
	Index	1
Level 2	Name	mnuFileItem
	Caption	"-"
	Index	2
Level 2	Name	mnuFileItem
	Caption	"&Cancel && Exit"
	Index	3

Now is a good time to save the new form (TMNEW.FRM) and the project (TALKMAIL.VBP) before you add the code to the form.

Coding tmNew

Most of the code for the tmNew form is needed to handle MCI control events. However, there are also menu and button events that need to be addressed.

First, add the following lines to the general declaration area:

```
Option Explicit
'
Dim CurrentValue As Double
```

This variable is used to keep track of the progress of the audio playback.

Next, add the Form_Load event code shown in Listing 36.24. This code sets some basic form properties, creates a temporary filename for the audio file, and calls the HandleOpen routine to establish the audio WAV file.

Listing 36.24. Coding the Form_Load event.

```
Private Sub Form_Load()
    '
    ' first startup of form
    '
    MMControl1.Wait = True
    '
    txtSubject = "Talk Mail Message #" & Format(Now(), "DDHHmmss")
    txtBody = "Message Recorded at " & Format(Now, "general date")
    lblrecips = ""
    '
```

continues

Listing 36.24. continued

```
    Me.Icon = LoadPicture(App.Path & "\tmMsg32.ico")
    Me.Caption = "Talk Mail Compose Form"
    Me.Left = (Screen.Width - Me.Width) / 2
    Me.Top = (Screen.Height - Me.Height) / 2
    '
    cWavFile = App.Path & "\" & Format(Now(), "DDHHmmss") & ".wav"
    FileCopy App.Path & "\xxx.wav", cWavFile
    HandleOpen cWavFile
    '
End Sub
```

> **WARNING**
>
> The code in Listing 36.25 refers to a file called "xxx.wav." This is an empty WAV format audio file that is used as a "starter" file for each new message. This file can be found on the CD-ROM that ships with this book. If you cannot find the file, you can make a new one using the WAV audio applet that ships with Windows or the one that came with your sound card.

Listing 36.25 shows a short bit of code for the Form_Unload event. Add this to your project.

Listing 36.25. Coding the Form_Unload event.

```
Private Sub Form_Unload(Cancel As Integer)
    Me.Hide
    frmTMView.Show
End Sub
```

The next big chunk of code is for the HandleOpen subroutine. This routine initializes the MCI control and clears the scrollbar values. Add the code from Listing 36.26 to your form.

Listing 36.26. Adding the HandleOpen routine.

```
Private Sub HandleOpen(cWavFile As String)
    Dim msec As Double

    ' Set the number of milliseconds between successive
    ' StatusUpdate events.
    MMControl1.UpdateInterval = 0

    ' If the device is open, close it.
    If Not MMControl1.Mode = mciModeNotOpen Then
        MMControl1.Command = "Close"
    End If
```

```
    ' Open the device with the new filename.
    MMControl1.filename = cWavFile
    On Error GoTo MCI_ERROR
    MMControl1.Command = "Open"
    On Error GoTo 0
    '
    SetTiming
    '
    ' Set the scrollbar values.
    Hscroll1.value = 0
    CurrentValue = 0#
    '
    Exit Sub

MCI_ERROR:
    MsgBox ErrMsg(Err), vbCritical, "frmTMNew.HandleOpen"
    Resume MCI_EXIT

MCI_EXIT:
    Unload Me

End Sub
```

The `HandleOpen` routine calls another support routine—the `SetTiming` routine. This short routine establishes the total length of existing recordings and is used to set the start and stop limits of the scrollbar. Add the code from Listing 36.27 to your form.

Listing 36.27. Adding the `SetTiming` routine.

```
Public Sub SetTiming()
    '
    ' Set the timing labels on the form.
    Dim msec As Double
    '
    MMControl1.TimeFormat = mciFormatMilliseconds
    Label1.Caption = "0.0"
    msec = (CDbl(MMControl1.Length) / 1000)
    Label2.Caption = Format$(msec, "0.00")
    '
End Sub
```

Next you can add the code to handle the menu array. This code allows the user to save the recorded file to disk, send the message, and exit the form without sending the message. Add the code from Listing 36.28 to your form.

Listing 36.28. Coding the `mnuFileItem_Click` event.

```
Private Sub mnuFileItem_Click(Index As Integer)
    '
    ' handle user menu selections
    '
```

continues

Listing 36.28. continued

```
    Select Case Index
        Case 0 ' save as
            MMControl1.filename = cWavFile
            frmTMView.CMDialog1.ShowSave
            MMControl1.filename = frmTMView.CMDialog1.filename
            MMControl1.Command = "Save"
        Case 1 ' send
            cmdNewMsg_Click 0
        Case 2 ' na
        Case 3 ' close
            cmdNewMsg_Click 1
    End Select
End Sub
```

There are two command buttons on the form in a control array—Cancel and OK. The code in Listing 36.29 should be added to the cmdNewMsg_Click event.

Listing 36.29. Coding the cmdNewMsg_Click event.

```
Private Sub cmdNewMsg_Click(Index As Integer)
    '
    ' handle new msg buttons
    '
    Select Case Index
        Case 0 ' OK to send
            MMControl1.Command = "Save" ' save the wave file
            MMControl1.Command = "Close" ' close out and release
            MAPISendMsg objRecipColl, txtSubject, txtBody, cWavFile ' send message
        Case 1 ' cancel send
            ' na
    End Select
    '
    On Error Resume Next
    Kill cWavFile ' remove temp file
    Unload Me ' return to caller
    '
End Sub
```

Notice the call to the MAPISendMsg routine. You built this routine in the LibTalkMail module at the start of the chapter.

There is one other button on the form—the Send To... button. When the user presses this button, the MAPI address book appears. When the user is finished selecting addresses, a recipients collection is returned. This is the list of people who will receive the message.

> **NOTE**
>
> In this program users can send messages only if they use the To: option and not Cc: or Bcc: This was done to simplify the project. If you want, you can modify the project to address messages to courtesy copy and blind courtesy copy recipients.

Once the collection is returned, the GetRecipients function is used to pull the names out of the collection and insert them into the label control on the form. Add the code shown in Listing 36.30 to the cmdAddrBook_Click event.

Listing 36.30. Coding the cmdAddrBook_Click event.

```
Private Sub cmdAddrBook_Click()
    '
    ' get recipients from user
    '
    Dim x As Integer
    '
    Set objRecipColl = objSession.AddressBook(reciplists:=1, Title:="Select
➥TalkMail Recipient(s)")
    lblrecips = GetRecipients(objRecipColl)
    '
    '
End Sub
```

The last set of code routines for the tmNew form are for the MCI multimedia control. First, add the code in Listing 36.31 to the MMControl1_StatusUpdate event.

Listing 36.31. Coding the MMControl1_StatusUpdate event.

```
Private Sub MMControl1_StatusUpdate()
    Dim value As Integer

    ' If the device is not playing, reset to the beginning.
    If Not MMControl1.Mode = mciModePlay Then
        Hscroll1.value = Hscroll1.Max
        MMControl1.UpdateInterval = 0
        Exit Sub
    End If

    ' Determine how much of the file has played.  Set a
    ' value of the scrollbar between 0 and 100.
    CurrentValue = CurrentValue + conIntervalPlus
    value = CInt((CurrentValue / MMControl1.Length) * 100)
```

continues

Listing 36.31. continued

```
    If value > Hscroll1.Max Then
        value = 100
    End If

    Hscroll1.value = value
End Sub
```

This code is used to compute playback progress and update the scrollbar control on the form.

There are four other code events for the MCI control. These are executed whenever the user presses Pause, Play, Rewind, or Stop. Listing 36.32 shows the code for these four events.

Listing 36.32. Coding the MCI button events.

```
Private Sub MMControl1_PauseClick(Cancel As Integer)
    ' Set the number of milliseconds between successive
    ' StatusUpdate events.
    If MMControl1.UpdateInterval = 0 Then
        MMControl1.UpdateInterval = conInterval
    Else
        MMControl1.UpdateInterval = 0
    End If
End Sub

Private Sub MMControl1_PlayClick(Cancel As Integer)
    ' Set the number of milliseconds between successive
    ' StatusUpdate events.
    MMControl1.UpdateInterval = conInterval
End Sub

Private Sub MMControl1_PrevClick(Cancel As Integer)
    ' Set the number of milliseconds between successive
    ' StatusUpdate events.
    MMControl1.UpdateInterval = 0

    ' Reset the scrollbar values.
    Hscroll1.value = 0
    CurrentValue = 0#

    MMControl1.Command = "Prev"
End Sub

Private Sub MMControl1_StopClick(Cancel As Integer)
    '
    SetTiming ' compute any new value
    '
End Sub
```

That's the end of the code for the tmNew form. Save the form (TMNEW.FRM) and project (TALKMAIL.VBP) before coding the tmRead form.

Laying Out tmRead

The tmRead form is almost identical to the tmNew form. This form is used to read Talk Mail messages sent to the user. For this reason, most of the controls have been disabled and the form is basically in a "read-only" mode.

Normally, users would read a message and then generate a reply to the sender or forward the message to another party. For this example, no reply buttons have been placed on the form. This has been done to keep the project simple and to focus on the integration of MAPI and MCI services. You can add these options later if you wish.

Add a new form to the project and lay out the controls as shown in Figure 36.5 and in Table 36.5.

FIGURE 36.5.

Laying out the tmRead *form.*

Table 36.5. The tmRead controls.

Control	Property	Setting
VB.Form	Name	frmTMRead
	Caption	"Talk Mail Reader Form"
	Height	6030
	Left	2415
	Top	1455
	Width	5250
VB.HScrollBar	Name	HScroll1
	Height	300
	Left	120
	Max	100
	TabIndex	9

continues

Table 36.5. continued

Control	Property	Setting
	Top	2220
	Width	4860
VB.CommandButton	Name	cmdNewMsg
	Caption	"&Close"
	Height	300
	Index	0
	Left	3780
	TabIndex	2
	Top	4980
	Width	1200
VB.TextBox	Name	txtBody
	BackColor	&H00C0C0C0&
	Height	1995
	Left	120
	MultiLine	-1 'True
	ScrollBars	2 'Vertical
	TabIndex	1
	Top	2880
	Width	4860
VB.Label	Name	lblSubjLine
	BorderStyle	1 'Fixed Single
	Caption	"Label4"
	Height	315
	Left	1380
	TabIndex	15
	Top	1080
	Width	3615
VB.Label	Name	lblSender
	BorderStyle	1 'Fixed Single
	Caption	"Sent by:"
	Height	300
	Left	120

Control	Property	Setting
	TabIndex	14
	Top	120
	Width	1200
VB.Label	Name	Label3
	Alignment	2 'Center
	Caption	"Pause"
	Height	300
	Left	2520
	TabIndex	13
	Top	1860
	Width	795
VB.Label	Name	lblFFwd
	Alignment	2 'Center
	Caption	"FFwd"
	Height	300
	Left	960
	TabIndex	12
	Top	1860
	Width	735
VB.Label	Name	Label1
	Height	255
	Left	120
	TabIndex	11
	Top	2520
	Width	600
VB.Label	Name	Label2
	Height	255
	Left	4380
	TabIndex	10
	Top	2520
	Width	600

continues

Table 36.5. continued

Control	Property	Setting
VB.Label	Name	lblRecord
	Alignment	2 'Center
	Caption	"Record"
	Height	300
	Left	4140
	TabIndex	8
	Top	1860
	Width	855
VB.Label	Name	lblStop
	Alignment	2 'Center
	Caption	"Stop"
	Height	300
	Left	3360
	TabIndex	7
	Top	1860
	Width	735
VB.Label	Name	lblPlay
	Alignment	2 'Center
	Caption	"Play"
	Height	300
	Left	1740
	TabIndex	6
	Top	1860
	Width	735
VB.Label	Name	lblRewind
	Alignment	2 'Center
	Caption	"Rewind"
	Height	300
	Left	120
	TabIndex	5

Control	Property	Setting
	Top	1860
	Width	795
MCI.MMControl	Name	MMControl1
	Height	315
	Left	120
	TabIndex	0
	Top	1500
	Width	4875
	BackVisible	0 'False
	StepVisible	0 'False
	EjectVisible	0 'False
	BorderStyle	1
VB.Label	Name	lblRecips
	BorderStyle	1 'Fixed Single
	Caption	"Label3"
	Height	900
	Left	1380
	TabIndex	4
	Top	120
	Width	3615
VB.Label	Name	lblSubject
	BorderStyle	1 'Fixed Single
	Caption	"Subject:"
	Height	300
	Left	120
	TabIndex	3
	Top	1080
	Width	1200

After laying out the form controls, you can add the form menu. Refer to Figure 36.6 and Table 36.6 for details on the tmRead menu.

FIGURE 36.6.

Adding the tmRead *menu.*

Table 36.6. The tmRead menu levels and properties.

Level	Properties	Settings
Top	Name	mnuFile
	Caption	"File"
Level 2	Name	mnuFileItem
	Caption	"Save Wave File..."
	Index	0
Level 2	Name	mnuFileItem
	Caption	"-"
	Index	2
Level 2	Name	mnuFileItem
	Caption	"&Close"
	Index	3

After building the form, save it as TMREAD.FRM before you go on to add the code.

Coding tmRead

As mentioned earlier in the chapter, the tmNew and tmRead forms are very similar. In fact, the two largest sections of form code, the HandleOpen and the MMControl1... events, are the same in both projects. As long as you are careful, you can copy the code from the tmNew form onto the tmRead form. Do this by bringing up the tmNew form, highlighting all of the HandleOpen routine, select Edit ¦ Copy, and then move to the tmRead form and use Edit ¦ Paste to place the code in the general declarations section.

The following code sections from tmNew can be copied to tmRead using the same technique:

- OpenHandle()
- MMControl1_PauseClick()
- MMControl1_PlayClick()
- MMControl1_PrevClick()
- MMControl1_StatusUpdate()
- MMControl1_StopClick()
- SetTiming()

Once you've successfully copied these routines from tmNew to tmRead you need to add just a few more routines to the tmRead form.

First, add the following lines to the general declaration section of the form.

```
Option Explicit
'
Dim CurrentValue As Double
```

Next, add the Form_Load event code shown in Listing 36.33.

Listing 36.33. Adding the Form_Load event code.

```
Private Sub Form_Load()
    '
    ' first startup of form
    '
    On Error GoTo LocalErr
    '
    MMControl1.Wait = True
    '
    Dim cID As String
    Dim x As Integer
    '
    Set objMsg = objSession.GetMessage(cMsgID)
    '
    lblSubjLine = objMsg.Subject
    txtBody = objMsg.Text
    lblrecips = GetRecipients(objMsg.Recipients)
    '
    Me.Icon = LoadPicture(App.Path & "\tmMsg32.ico")
    Me.Caption = "Talk Mail Reader Form"
    Me.Left = (Screen.Width - Me.Width) / 2
    Me.Top = (Screen.Height - Me.Height) / 2
    '
    ' get attachment to read
    Set objAttachColl = objMsg.Attachments
    If objAttachColl Is Nothing Then Exit Sub
    For x = 1 To objAttachColl.Count
        Set objAttach = objAttachColl.Item(x)
        objAttach.WriteToFile "temp.wav"
        cWavFile = objAttach.Source
```

continues

Listing 36.33. continued

```
    Next x
    '
    ' go open it with the WAV device
    HandleOpen "temp.wav"
    '
    Exit Sub
    '
LocalErr:
    MsgBox ErrMsg(Err), vbCritical, "frmTMRead.Form_Load"
    '
End Sub
```

This code is slightly different from the code in the `Form_Load` event of `tmNew`. Here, you want to open the selected message object and extract the audio WAV attachment, save it to a temporary file, and then place that audio file into the MCI control for playback (using the `OpenHandle` routine).

Next, add the code for the `Form_Unload` event shown in Listing 36.34.

Listing 36.34. Coding the `Form_Unload` event.

```
Private Sub Form_Unload(Cancel As Integer)
    Me.Hide
    frmTMView.Show
End Sub
```

Because this form only has a `Close` button, you need to add one line of code to the `cmdNewmsg_Click` event:

```
Private Sub cmdNewMsg_Click(Index As Integer)
    Unload Me
End Sub
```

Next, you need to add a line of code to the `txtBody` control to prevent users from typing the read-only form.

```
Private Sub txtBody_KeyPress(KeyAscii As Integer)
    KeyAscii = 0 ' ignore any keystrokes here
End Sub
```

> **TIP**
>
> You may notice that the `txtBody` control's background color was set to light gray to make it look like a label control instead of an input control. Under the Windows GUI standards, "actionable" controls have a white background and read-only controls have a light gray background.

The only form code left is the code that handles the user's menu selections. Add the code shown in Listing 36.35 to your form.

Listing 36.35. Coding the mnuFileItem_Click event.

```
Private Sub mnuFileItem_Click(Index As Integer)
    '
    ' handle user menu selections
    '
    Select Case Index
        Case 0 ' save as
            MMControl1.filename = cWavFile
            frmTMView.CMDialog1.ShowSave
            MMControl1.filename = frmTMView.CMDialog1.filename
            MMControl1.Command = "Save"
        Case 2 ' close
            cmdNewMsg_Click 1
    End Select
End Sub
```

That's the end of coding for the tmRead form. Save the form (TMREAD.FRM) and the project (TALKMAIL.VBP) before you add the final About box to the application.

The tmAbout Box

The tmABout box is a simple About dialog box for the project. Figure 36.7 and Table 36.7 show the layout information for the form.

FIGURE 36.7.
Laying out the tmAbout *form.*

Table 36.7. The tmAbout controls.

Control	Property	Setting
VB.Form	Name	frmAbout
	BorderStyle	3 'Fixed Dialog
	Caption	"About Talk Mail"
	Height	2415
	Left	2955
	MaxButton	0 'False

continues

Table 36.7. continued

Control	Property	Setting
	MinButton	0 'False
	ShowInTaskbar	0 'False
	Top	2415
	Width	4230
VB.CommandButton	Name	cmdOK
	Caption	"OK"
	Height	300
	Left	2760
	TabIndex	0
	Top	1560
	Width	1200
VB.Label	Name	Label1
	Caption	"Label1"
	Height	1155
	Left	1320
	TabIndex	1
	Top	180
	Width	2595
VB.Image	Name	Image1
	Height	1215
	Left	180
	Top	120
	Width	915

You need to add just a little bit of code to the Form_Load event to complete the tmAbout form. Listing 36.36 shows the code you should add to the form.

Listing 36.36. Adding code to the Form_Load event.

```
Private Sub Form_Load()
    '
    ' build simple about box
    '
    Me.Icon = LoadPicture(App.Path & "\tmMsg32.ico")
    Me.Caption = "About " & App.Title
```

```
    Me.Left = (Screen.Width - Me.Width) / 2
    Me.Top = (Screen.Height - Me.Height) / 2
    '
    Image1.Stretch = True
    Image1.Picture = LoadPicture(App.Path & "\tmMsg32.ico")
    '
    Label1 = App.Title & Chr(13) & Chr(13)
    Label1 = Label1 & App.LegalCopyright & Chr(13) & Chr(13)
    Label1 = Label1 & App.FileDescription
    '
End Sub
```

The last bit of code is a single line in the cmdOK_Click event:

```
Private Sub cmdOK_Click()
    Unload Me
End Sub
```

Now save the form (TMABOUT.FRM) and the project (TALKMAIL.VBP). You are now finished coding and ready to test the program.

Testing Talk Mail

First, you need to compile Talk Mail and save it to disk, but before you compile it, you need to add a bit of information to the App object properties. These properties will be displayed in the application's About box.

Select File ¦ Make EXE ¦ Options to bring up the dialog box for setting the App objects properties. Refer to Table 36.8 and Figure 36.8 for setting the properties.

Table 36.8. Setting the App object properties.

Property	*Setting*
Title	Talk Mail
Comments	Demonstration of MAPI and MCI
Company	MCA/SAMS
File Description	E-mail Client for Voice Recording
Legal Copyright	(c)1996 MCA/SAMS Publishing
Auto Increment	Checked ON

Once you set these properties, press OK and then compile the project. When you are able to compile the project without errors, you're ready to start testing Talk Mail.

FIGURE 36.8.

The App *object properties dialog box.*

> It is a good idea to compile the Talk Mail project before running it. The process of compiling will point out any coding errors and the resulting program will run faster than in design mode.

When you first start Talk Mail, you see the populated button bar and an empty listview control. Press the green stoplight button (or select File ¦ Log In from the menu) to log into MAPI and collect any Talk Mail messages you have waiting in your inbox (see Figure 36.9).

FIGURE 36.9.

Logging into Talk Mail.

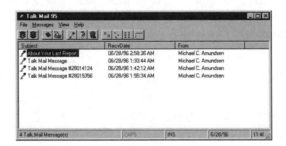

The first time you log into Talk Mail, you'll see no messages for you. You can fix this by using Talk Mail to send yourself the first message. To do this, press the microphone toolbar button or select Message ¦ New from the menu. You'll see the Talk Mail compose form ready to record your message (see Figure 36.10).

The form comes up with a default subject line and a notation in the text message area. You can press the record button to begin recording your message and press stop when you are finished. You can also press playback, pause, rewind, and fast-forward to review your message. You can even append additional information to the end of your message if you wish.

You must select at least one recipient before you can send your message. To address the Talk Mail message, press the Send To... button at the top left of the form. You'll see the MAPI address dialog box appear (see Figure 36.11).

FIGURE 36.10.

Adding a new Talk Mail message.

FIGURE 36.11.

Addressing the Talk Mail message.

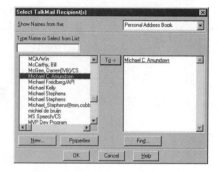

For your first message, address it to yourself. You can then "read" this message using Talk Mail. After addressing the message, press the Send button at the bottom of the form or select File ¦ Send Message from the menu. You'll receive notification that the message was sent and then you will be returned to the list view form.

Now you can select File ¦ Scan InBox from the menu or press the inbox button to re-read your inbox. Your message should now appear in the list view. You can listen to your message by selecting the item and pressing the read button (it's the ear!), or by selecting Message ¦ Read from the menu. You'll see the read form and be able to use the MCI control to play back the recording (see Figure 36.12).

To delete a Talk Mail message, simply highlight the message and press the trash can toolbar button or select Messages ¦ Delete from the menu. You'll see a confirmation message before you actually delete the item.

You can also use the toolbar to adjust the list view the same way you can adjust the Windows 95 Explorer views. Figure 36.13 shows the Talk Mail client in large icon view while showing the About box.

That's the end of the tour!

FIGURE 36.12.
Reading an incoming Talk Mail message.

FIGURE 36.13.
The Talk Mail About box.

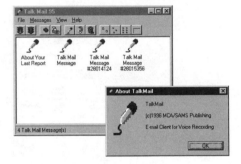

Summary

In this chapter, you learned how to combine the MAPI and Media Control Interface (MCI) services to create a voice-mail client. In the process you learned about declaring your own MAPI message type and about how to use the Windows 95 common controls.

This project is handy, but not quite complete. If you wish to use this application as more than a demonstration, you'll need to add the ability for users to reply to and forward received messages. You may also want to consider deploying this as a Microsoft Exchange form instead of as a standalone MAPI client. That way, all Microsoft Exchange users could install the form and use it throughout your organization.

37

Integration Summary

In this last part of the book, you've had the chance to build three sample applications that combine two or more of the Windows Extension services covered in this book. You also reviewed some of the common design issues that you'll face when building applications that require access to multiple extension services. The sections below briefly summarize the material covered in the last four chapters.

Design Issues

In Chapter 33, "Design Considerations for Integrated Communications Applications," you learned some of the advantages and disadvantages of deploying software that uses the MAPI, SAPI, and TAPI extension services for Windows operating systems. The following general points were discussed:

■ First, remember the Rule of Complexity. Where possible, try to limit the number and depth of service extensions used in a single application. With added services comes added complexity—both for the user and the programmer.

■ Consider the pros and cons of using native API calls versus employing high-level third-party add-on tools to provide access to extension services. The native API calls may be faster, but they will also require more coding and maintenance for you and your staff. Building applications with third-party tools can be more efficient as long as the tool is used correctly and is well supported and documented by its authors.

■ Also, when adding new extensions to your applications, consider the advantages of building simple stand-alone versions of the target application instead of adding features to existing applications. There are times when a stand-alone solution is most efficient. However, if you need to deploy MAPI, SAPI, or TAPI services to a large number of people who already have products they know and use often, it may be simpler to distribute add-ins or extensions instead of attempting to replace well-established user tools.

■ As a general rule, if your application needs to distribute information to a wide number of locations on demand, mostly in ASCII text format, your best bet is to use MAPI services. If, however, you need to send binary data to just a few sites on a regular schedule (daily or weekly, for example), you should consider building smaller, more focused dedicated dialing applications that use the Comm API (or OCX).

■ Client-side applications usually need only outbound calling services. It is quite possible that you can meet client-side design goals using Assisted TAPI services and simple data/fax modems. If, however, you are building applications that will act as telephony server devices—answering and routing incoming calls—you'll need to use Full TAPI, and you will probably need a full-featured telephony card, too.

■ Finally, current speech technology is more consistent when delivering TTS (text-to-speech) services than SR (speech recognition) services. The SAPI system requires a hefty pool of memory (no less than 16MB is recommended on the workstation). Also, SR services are not always accurate. It is best to offer SAPI services as an additional, rather than primary service at this time. As the technology matures and users become more accustomed to hearing TTS output and to speaking in a manner more easily understood by SAPI systems, you can increase the use of speech services in your applications.

If you keep these general rules in mind, you'll save yourself a lot of headaches when it comes time to deploy multiple-service applications.

The FaxBack Application

In Chapter 34, "Building the FaxBack Application," you built a Visual Basic 4.0 project that combined TAPI and MAPI services to create a dialup fax server. With this application running on a workstation, users can dial into the workstation, receive prompts for entering their own FAX telephone number, and select a document number. Then, when the user hangs up, the workstation formats and sends the selected FAX document to the user's FAX address.

This project used an evaluation version of Pronexus' VBVoice telephony control set. The VBVoice controls were used to answer the incoming call, and prompt the caller through entering their FAX number and the selected document number. Once this was done, the VBVoice controls turned the collected data over to the MAPI system for delivery of the selected FAX.

The Simple Mail API (SMAPI) interface was used to provide access to the message services of Windows. The SMAPI interface was chosen because it has a very small "footprint." While the MAPI.OCX controls and the OLE Messaging library would also work fine, the SMAPI provided all the MAPI access that was needed for the FaxBack project. This was a good example of how you can simplify programming and deployment by selecting the simplest implementation model that fulfills the project requirements.

The Voice Phone Application

In Chapter 35, "Creating the Voice Phone Application," you used SAPI and TAPI services to create a true "hands-free" telephone. With this program and a PC speaker phone, users can look up and dial telephone numbers by simply speaking voice commands to the workstation. Users are able to initiate database adds, edits, and deletes, or issue a voice command that will search the database for a name. Users can also tell the program to *Dial Mike* and Voice Phone will locate the record in the database, pull up the phone number, place the call, and prompt the user to begin speaking.

As an added bonus, this program has audible responses to help requests, and speaks the names and telephone numbers of selected records in the database. Even the About box is "read" to you.

Again, a simple TAPI interface was all that was needed for this project. Instead of adding Full TAPI services to the application, only Assisted TAPI was implemented. This provided all the power and features needed to implement a voice-activated outbound dialing program.

The Talk Mail Project

Chapter 36, "The Talk Mail Project," presented the last integration project in the book, in which you combined MAPI services with an audio recording. The Talk Mail project allows you to record messages, and then send them to others via e-mail. It's a bit like an asynchronous telephone conversation.

With Talk Mail you can select one or more recipients, press the record button, record a message, and ship both the header data and the audio binary file to any other person(s) in the MAPI directory.

The OLE Messaging library was used to implement the MAPI services for this program. This offered the ability to define a unique message class for audio e-mail. This way, the Talk Mail client can search incoming mail for audio messages, and present only those to the user for review.

The audio recording was handled using the Windows Media Control Interface (MCI). The Visual Basic 4.0 MCI control provided easy access to recording, storage, and playback facilities for WAV format audio files. Adding WAV support for an e-mail client is as easy as adding the MCI control to a project.

This project also made use of the new Windows 95 controls for Visual Basic, including the `listview` control, the `toolbar` control, and the `statusbar` control.

Some Final Remarks

The material in this book covers the multiple implementations of MAPI services, SAPI services, and TAPI services for 32-bit Windows operating systems. Even though this book is no quick read, it does not cover the three important Windows extension services completely. No single book could hope to accomplish that. The best way to learn about each of these API sets in detail is to work with them in your own programs. Only through constant experimentation and invention will you really learn the intricacies of these important Windows services.

It's also important to keep up with the latest developments regarding each of these API services. You can find lots of pointers to online and printed resources in the appendixes at the back of this book. You'll even find a Web site dedicated to supporting this book (`iac.net/ ~mamund/CDGPage.htm`).

I hope you'll find this book helpful in your quest to learn more about MAPI, SAPI, and TAPI implementations. I suspect many of you have already been struck with new ideas on how you can use these services to create new and valuable Windows applications. I also hope to hear from many of you as you discover new ways to bring speech, telephony, and e-mail services to the desktop. You can write me at my e-mail address (MikeAmundsen@msn.com), or visit the Web site. I look forward to hearing from you.

Good luck!

MCA

VI

Appendixes

The next several chapters contain resource pointers for MAPI, SAPI, and TAPI development. Each chapter contains lists of selected books, Web links to various sites around the world where you can find information on API-related hardware and software, and other online resources covering CompuServe forums, Internet news groups, and Microsoft Network links.

In addition to these references, the accompanying CD-ROM includes a set of HTML pages that can be loaded into any HTML-compliant Web browser and used as a launch document to link directly to sources on the World Wide Web.

There is also a directory that contains several MSN link files. If you are a subscriber to the Microsoft Network, you can double-click these links and your Microsoft Network software will take you directly to the related discussion group or topic.

Finally, there is an Access 2.0 format database on the CD-ROM called `CDGLIST.MDB`. This contains a more comprehensive version of the book lists, the Web pages, and other online resources. The tables list publisher and ISBN details for the books, and address, phone, and e-mail contacts for the vendors.

> **TIP**
>
> For the most recent lists of MAPI, SAPI, and TAPI resources, use your Web browser to connect to the *MAPI, SAPI, and TAPI Developer's Guide* home page at:
> `www.iac.net/~mamund/mstdg/index.htm`
> Note that this page is maintained by the author.

The CD-ROM also contains useful software utilities, product samples and demos, and information on API-related products and services. All the programming examples covered in this book are also included on the CD-ROM.

> **NOTE**
>
> Because the MAPI/SAPI/TAPI field is still young and changing, there may be additional information on the CD-ROM that did not make it into the printed book. Be sure to check the CD-ROM for late-breaking updates on communications API topics.

A

MAPI Resources

This chapter contains several listings of MAPI-related resources, including:

- Books
- Web links
- Other on-line resources

TIP

For the most recent list of MAPI-related resources, including updated books, Web links, other on-line resources, and MAPI software, use your Web browser to connect to the Communications Developer's Guide home page at:

`www.iac.net/~mamund/mstdg/index.htm`

Books

This is a sample list of books available at most large libraries. While this is not a definitive list, it is a good representation of writings on the subject.

Table A.1. MAPI-related books.

Title	Author	Notes
The Online User's Encyclopedia: Bulletin Boards and Beyond	Aboba, Bernard	Computer bulletin boards—Handbooks, manuals, etc.
		Internet (Computer network)—Handbooks, manuals, etc. Wide area networks (Computer networks)—Handbooks, manuals, etc.
Planning for Electronic Mail	Alan Simpson, Ed.	Electronic mail systems.
Introduction to X.400	Betanov, Cemil	Electronic mail systems. Computer networks—Standards.
The E-Mail Frontier: Emerging Markets and Evolving Technologies	Blum, Daniel J. Bracker, William E., Jr., Ed.	Electronic mail systems—United States. xx, 188 p. : ill. ; 24 cm.

Title	Author	Notes
Cases in Network Implementation: Enterprise Networking E-Mail	Caswell, Stephen A.	Electronic mail systems.
The Electronic Mail Handbook: A Revolution in Business Communications	Connell, Stephen	Electronic mail systems.
The Joy of Computer Communication	Cook, William J.	Data transmission systems. Computer networks. Electronic mail systems.
Networking: An Electronic Mail Handbook	Cross, Thomas B.	Electronic mail systems.
The Electric Mail Box, 1st Ed.	Davis, Steve	286 p. ; 23 cm.
The Internet Guide for New Users	Dern, Daniel P.	Internet (computer network) computer communication networks
LAN Times E-Mail Resource Guide	Drummond, Rik	334 p. : ill. ; 24 cm.
Electronic Mail Systems: A Network Manager's Guide	Fatah, Burhan	xviii, 380 p. : ill. ; 24 cm.
!%@:: A Directory of Electronic Mail Addressing & Networks	Frey, Donnalyn	Electronic mail systems—Directories.
		Computer networks—Directories.
E-Mail Addresses of the Rich & Famous	Godin, Seth	Celebrities—Directories. Electronic mail systems—Directories.
Zen and the Art of the Internet: A Beginner's Guide	Kehoe, Brendan P.	Subject: Internet (computer network)
Using E-mail Effectively, 1st Ed.	Lamb, Linda	xii, 146 p. : ill. ; 24 cm.
The Electronic Link: Using the IBM PC to Communicate	Magid, Lawrence J.	Data transmission systems. Electronic mail systems. IBM personal computer.
The Electronic Mailbox	Mayer, Ira	Electronic mail systems.

continues

Table A.1. continued

Title	Author	Notes
The Influence of Computer-Communications on Organizational Information Processing	McKenney, James L.	Electronic mail systems. Communication in organizations.
Computer Mediated Com-munications: Bulletin Boards, Computer Conferencing, Elec-tronic Mail, and Information Retrieval	Rapaport, Matthew	Computer conferencing.
The Internet Message: Closing the Book with Electronic Mail	Rose, Marshall T.	Electronic mail systems. Internet (Computer net-work). Computer network protocols.
The Internet by E-Mail	Shirky, Clay	xv, 220 p. : ill. ; 24 cm.
Connections: New Ways of Working in the Networked Organization	Sproull, Lee	Electronic mail systems. Communication in organ-izations. Decision-making.
Protect Your Privacy: The PGP User's Guide	Stallings, William	xvi, 302 p. : ill. ; 21 cm.
The Cultures of Computing	Start, Susan Leigh, Ed.	Communication—Social aspects. Electronic mail systems—Social aspects. Computer networks—Social aspects.
Crossing the Internet Threshold: an Instructional Handbook	Tennant, Roy	Internet (Computer net-work)—Handbooks, manuals, etc. Computer communication networks.
Internet Resources: a Subject Guide	Thompson, Hugh A.	Internet (Computer network)—Handbooks, manuals, etc. Library information networks. Electronic mail systems—Library applications.

Title	Author	Notes
E-Mail Essentials	Tittel, Ed	xx, 298 p. : ill. ; 24 cm.
Electronic Mail and Beyond: A User's Handbook of Personal Computer Communications	Townsend, Carl	xii, 323 p. : ill. ; 24 cm.
Options for Electronic Mail	Trudell, Libby	Electronic mail systems. Communication Information Systems. Online Systems
Computer Message Systems	Vallee, Jacques	Data transmission systems. Computer networks. Electronic mail systems. Teleconferencing. Videotex systems.
The Introduction of Electronic Mail: Perspectives for Telecommunication Managers	Vervest et al.	Electronic mail systems. Electronic mail equipment industry. Telecommunication.
Electronic Mail and Message Handling	Vervest, Peter	Electronic mail systems. Electronic mail equipment industry.
Innovation in Electronic Mail: Towards Open Information Networks: Perspectives on Innovation Policy	Vervest, Peter	Electronic mail systems. Telecommunication.
Introducing the Electronic Mailbox	Wilson, P.A.	Electronic mail systems.
Using Electronic Mail in an Educational Setting	Wishnietsky, Dan H.	Electronic mail systems in education.

NOTE

A more complete listing of books, including publisher data, can be found in the BOOKLIST table of the CDGLISTS.MDB database. You can use Microsoft Access, Microsoft Query, or any Access/Visual Basic database product to read this data file.

Web Links

This is a list of World Wide Web links on MAPI subjects. The list is constantly changing. An updated list is contained in the MAPIWEB.HTM data file on the companion CD-ROM. This file can be loaded into most Web browsers and used as a launch document to connect to the associated links.

Table A.2. PC-based e-mail links (MAPI).

Page Title	Web Address	Description
Access/Visual Basic Advisor	www.advisor.com/av.html	About developing applications with Microsoft Access, Visual Basic, Office (Excel, Word, Schedule+, PowerPoint), BackOffice, OLE, SQL Server, Exchange, and Internet Studio.
Aurora Communications Exchange	www.acemail.com/	Connect your LAN-based e-mail to the Internet. If you have Lotus Notes, cc:Mail, or Microsoft Mail, we can connect you to the Internet.
C2C Systems, Inc.	www.seanet.com/vendors/c2cusa/	Manufacturer of e-mail enhancement software for Microsoft Mail and cc:Mail.
Consensys Mail Net	www.consensys.com/	Mail Net is a 32-bit Windows NT service designed to provide a gateway between Microsoft Mail and SMTP mail.
Get Help With Windows 95	www.neosoft.com/~gregcms/helpme.html	Get help from a ClubWin member with Windows 95's Exchange. It's the universal inbox we've always wanted.
Homnick Systems	www.homnick.com	Microsoft Authorized training in NT, Windows 95, SQL Server 6.0, TCP/IP, Exchange Server, Visual Basic 4.0, Visual FoxPro 3.0, Access for Windows 95, and Systems Management Server.
Hype-It 1000	cykic.com/	Server software with HTML editor, built-in database, report generator, and SMTP e-mail connections.

Page Title	Web Address	Description
Infinite Technologies	`www.ihub.com/index.html`	Enterprise Messaging Solutions for LANs, including e-mail clients, high-performance message routers, and gateways to SMTP, Alpha Pagers, FAX, Microsoft Mail, cc:Mail, NetWare MHS.
In-Touch	`www.islandnet.com/ ~sword/win95.html`	A weekly e-mailed digest to keep you informed about the latest Windows 95 shareware available for download on the Internet.
L.R.Technologies	`www.lrt.be/`	E-mail specialist, Microsoft Solution Provider.
Microsoft Exchange Resource Page	`www.voicenet.com/ ~yakko/Exchange/ Exchange.html`	
netApp Systems	`www.netapps.com/`	SMTP/POP/USENET facilities for Microsoft Mail. Single and multiuser environments supported.
NetGain	`www.netgain.se/`	Developers of NetGain Mimetic SMTP-gateway for Microsoft Mail.
Queue Systems, Inc.	`www.queuesys.com/ software/ntmail/`	NT Mail—SMTP and POP3 Services for Microsoft Windows NT.
Spin mail	`www.cfw.com/~middletn/ spinmail.html`	A Microsoft Mail-to-Internet gateway.
Vision Computer Associates	`www.vca.net/`	Microsoft ATEC. Training in Windows NT, 95, VB, SQL, SNA, TCP/IP, Mail, C++, FCL, PowerBuilder, Delphi, Novell NetWare, FrameMaker, etc.
Windows NT in the Internet Environment	`www.neystadt.org/winnt/ winnt.htm`	NT Mailing List at Optimedia.
Winserve Windows Internet Server	`www.winserve.com/`	Bridging remote offices, and connecting mobile employees to the central office, Winserve uses Microsoft Windows NT Server 3.5 to provide virtual disk space and a Microsoft Mail post office.

> **NOTE**
>
> A more complete listing of these links can also be found in the WEBLIST table of the CDGLISTS.MDB database on the companion CD-ROM. You can use the database table to search for specific vendors, products, and so on.

Other Online Resources

Below is a list of MAPI-related topics that you can browse through on CompuServe.

Table A.3. MAPI-related CompuServe topics.

Forum or Topic Name
WinCim Forum
CompuServe Mail
Lotus cc:Mail Forum
Novell APP TID
Office Automation Forum
DaVinci Forum
Message Handling Service Hub
CS Mail for Microsoft Mail
CS Mail for Microsoft Exchange
Windows Comp C Forum
EDI Forum
Windows Extensions Forum

Below is a list of MAPI-related newsgroups maintained by Microsoft at their msnews.microsoft.com news server:

```
microsoft.public.exchange.admin
microsoft.public.exchange.applications
microsoft.public.exchange.clients
microsoft.public.exchange.connectivity
microsoft.public.exchange.misc
microsoft.public.exchange.setup
microsoft.public.mail.admin
```

```
microsoft.public.mail.connectivity
microsoft.public.mail.misc
microsoft.public.messaging.misc
```

An extensive list of topics for the Microsoft Network can be found in the MAPIMSN folder on the CD-ROM. This folder contains a list of MSN shortcuts. If you are an MSN subscriber, you can click these icons to connect directly to the topic area on MSN.

B

SAPI Resources

This appendix contains several listings of SAPI-related resources, including

■ Books

■ Web links

■ Other online resources

■ Software and hardware resources

TIP

For the most recent list of SAPI-related resources, including updated books, Web links, other online resources, and SAPI software and hardware, use your Web browser to connect to the Communications Developer's Guide home page at

`www.iac.net/~mamund/mstdg/index.htm`

Books

Table B.1 provides a sample list of books available at most large libraries. It is not a definitive list, but it is a good representation of writings on the subject of SAPI.

Table B.1. SAPI-related books.

Title	Author	Notes
Electronically Hearing: Computer Speech Recognition	Cater, John P.	Speech processing systems.
Electronically Speaking: Computer Speech Generation	Cater, John P.	Speech processing systems. Speech synthesis.
Computer Speech Processing	Fallside, Frank	Speech processing systems. Automatic speech recognition. Speech synthesis.
Hidden Markov Models for Speech Recognition	Huang, X. D.	Automatic speech recognition. Speech recognition by computer systems.

Title	Author	Notes
Designing with Speech Processing Chips	Jimenez, Ricardo.	Integrated circuits, design and construction, data processing. Speech processing systems. Computer-aided design.
Artificial Neural Networks for Speech and Vision, 1st Ed.	Mommone, Richard J.	Neural networks (computer science). Automatic speech recognition.
Neural Networks and Speech Processing	Morgan, David P.	
Principles of Computer Speech	Witten, Ian H.	Speech processing systems. Speech synthesis.

NOTE

A more complete listing of books, including publisher data, can be found in the BOOKLIST table of the CDGLISTS.MDB database. You can use Microsoft Access, Microsoft Query, or any Access/Visual Basic database product to read this data file.

Web Links

Table B.2 lists World Wide Web links related to SAPI. This list is constantly changing. An updated list is contained in the SAPIWEB.HTM data file in the RESOURCE folder on the companion CD-ROM. This file can be loaded into almost any Web browser and used as a launch document to connect to the associated links.

Table B.2. Computer speech links for SAPI.

Web Title	Web Address	Description
Access First	`www.inforamp.net/~access/af1.html`	We service the visually impaired and blind community in Canada. We deal with text-to-speech, screen-magnification, and voice-recognition systems. We also train in these areas.
AudioWav	`www.audiowav.com/`	Now you can create and publish audio files to any destination on the Net by simply using your touch-tone phone with RealAudio, IWave, and TrueSpeech.
Cobotyx	`www.cobotyx.com/`	PC-based systems for voice process-ing, computer telephony (CTI), voice mail, auto attendant, text to speech, voice networking, interac-tive voice response (IVR), and fax mail technologies.
Colibri	`colibri.let.ruu.nl`	An electronic newsletter and WWW service for people interested in the fields of language, speech, logic, and information.
Command Corp	`www.commandcorp.com/incube_welcome.html`	Speech recognition on the Web.
comp.speech WWW site [Australia]	`fortis.speech.su.oz.au/comp.speech/`	Information on speech technology products and software.
comp.speech WWW site [UK]	`svr-www.eng.cam.ac.uk/comp.speech/`	Information on speech technology products and software.

Web Title	Web Address	Description
Digital Dreams	emf.net/~dreams/	Offers speech-recognition plug-ins for multimedia developers. Current support for Macromedia Director and Hypercard. Demos available online.
Dragon Systems, Inc.	www.dragonsys.com/	DragonDictate for Windows and DOS. Discrete and continuous speech dictation and command/control products for the PC. Also links to other SR sites.
DragonDictate	www.waterw.com/~jkornit/	A speech-recognition software package that allows you to dictate directly into your DOS or Windows applications!
Eloquent Technology, Inc. (Eloquence)	www.fcinet.com/eti/index.html	Natural-sounding Text To Speech synthesis engine with Developer's Kit for several computer platforms.
First Byte	www.firstbyte.davd.com/	ProVoice Developers Tool Kit, Text To Speech synthesis for a wide variety of computers used in popular programs such as Monologue.
GT Technology, Inc.	www.portal.com/~gt-tech/	Provides consulting services in the field of error correction, image, and data and speech compression for computer and communication companies.

continues

Table B.2. continued

Web Title	Web Address	Description
Gus Communications, Inc.	`www.gusinc.com`	Speech disorders, augmentative communication.
Index - Speech Kolvox Communications Inc.	`mambo.ucsc.edu/psl/speech.html` `www.kolvox.com/`	Applications for speech input, recognition, and voice control, based on Kurzweil, IBM, Dragon, and other engines. Reseller inquiries welcome.
Kurzweil Applied Intelligence	`www.kurz-ai.com/`	Develops, markets, and supports automated speech-recognition systems used to create documents and interact with personal computers by voice.
Lakewood Desktop Publishing	`accessone.com/~mrbones/`	A licensed reseller of Kolvox Speech Systems. Control your Windows applications with your voice. Dictate up to 60 WPM.
MIT - Lyon Speech Transcript	`sap.mit.edu/projects/mit-lyon/project.html`	A multimedia collaborative project about communication between Lyon, France and MIT, Cambridge. Speech recognition, translation, speech synthesis, and video are parts of the exhibition.

Web Title	Web Address	Description
PureSpeech, Inc.	www.speech.com/	Speaker-independent recognition with natural language processing for personal computers and computer telephony applications.
Speech Systems, Inc.	www.speechsys.com/	Speech-recognition products, services, and technology.
Talk Technology, Inc.	www.usbusiness.com/talk/	Provides speech- and voice-recognition systems to doctors, lawyers, and people with repetitive strain injury. Wide range of software, including DragonDictate.
Toolz 2000	www.earthlink.net/~webwizard/toolz.html	Speech-recording software and pro audio sampler/hard disk recording software for Macintosh.
UltraMedia Systems International	www.infi.net/~ums/	Voice Recognition IBM VoiceType Dictation Technology.
Verbex Voice Systems	www.txdirect.net/verbex/	Download a freeware working demonstration of the continuous-speech voice-recognition system.
Voice Processing Corporation	www.vpro.com/	A speech-recognition company that provides voice engines for speech-enabling telephony and desktop applications.

> **NOTE**
>
> A more complete listing of these links can also be found in the WEBLIST table of the CDGLISTS.MDB database on the companion CD-ROM. You can use the database table to search for specific vendors, products, and so on.

Other Online Resources

The following is a list of SAPI-related topics that you can browse on CompuServe:

Forum or Topic Name
_____

WinCim Add-on – VOICE-MAIL
Disabilities Forum
IBM PSP A Product Forum
IBM VoiceType Forum
Windows Third-Party A Forum
Windows Third-Party App H Forum
Windows Extensions Forum

An extensive list of topics for The Microsoft Network can be found in the SAPIMSN folder on the CD-ROM. This contains a list of MSN shortcuts. If you are an MSN subscriber, you can click these icons to connect directly to the topic area on MSN.

Software and Hardware Resources

Table B.3 lists software and hardware vendors who are currently providing, or have pledged to provide, SAPI-compliant software and/or hardware products. A more complete list of vendors, including contact names, addresses, and phone numbers, can be found in the PRODUCTS table of the CDGLISTS.MDB database on the companion CD-ROM. You can use the data table to perform searches for selected products or vendors.

In the table there are three types of entries:

■ *SR*—Speech recognition products

■ *TTS*—Text-to-speech products

■ *API*—General SAPI products and contact names

Table B.3. SAPI-related software and hardware.

Type	Company	Products
SR	Advanced Recognition Technologies, Inc.	smARTspeakr for Windows—a compact speech-recognition engine suitable for command and control applications. Typical applications will be navigation of menus, phone and/or fax dialing, educational software, interactive games, and multimedia titles.
SR	AT&T	WATSON—Advanced Speech Applications Platform— Available for Beta release in 4Q95, WATSON incorporates AT&T- patented BLASR Speech Recognition and FlexTalk Speech Synthesis technologies in a software product running under Microsoft Windows 95.
SR	Cambridge Group Research, Ltd.	Cambridge Voice for Windows. The Cambridge Voice for Windows speech-recognition engine supports true speaker-independent recognition of continuous speech in real time. The engine does not require any speaker training.
SR	IBM Corporation	Source for IBM VoiceType technology information.
SR	Kurzweil Applied Intelligence, Inc.	Kurzweil VOICE for Windows Release 1.5 is the latest version of Kurzweil AI's award-winning voice-recognition system for Microsoft Windows.

continues

Table B.3. continued

Type	Company	Products
SR	Lernout & Hauspie Speech Products	ASR SDK for the L&H.asr1000M (computer/multimedia) and the L&H.1000T (telephony/telecommunications). L&H SDK for Automatic Speech Recognition is a speaker-independent recognizer that recognizes natural and fluently spoken words.
SR	PureSpeech, Inc.	PureSpeech 2.2 Recognizer. The PureSpeech engine permits speaker-independent, continuous speech recognition. No user training is required. Both microphones and recognition over telephone lines are supported.
SR	Speech Systems, Inc.	VoiceMatch System Development Kit (SDK) SpeechWizard. The VoiceMatch SDK is a suite of development tools for creating speech-aware applications in Microsoft Windows.
SR	Verbex Voice Systems, Inc.	VISE, FlexVISE. The Verbex Integrated Speech Engine (VISE) is a high-performance, speaker-independent, speaker-trainable, continuous speech-recognition engine widely used in industrial, home, and office environments.

Type	*Company*	*Products*
SR	Voice Control Systems, Inc.	
SR	Voice Processing Corporation	
TTS	AT&T	WATSON—Advanced Speech Applications Platform. Available for Beta release in 4Q95, WATSON incorporates AT&T-patented BLASR speech recognition and FlexTalk speech synthesis technologies in a software product running under Microsoft Windows 95
TTS	Berkeley Speech Technologies, Inc.	BeSTspeech T-T-S is text-to-speech conversion software. It creates computer-synthesized speech output in a wide variety of languages.
TTS	Cambridge Group Research, Ltd.	The Cambridge Voice for Windows text-to-speech engine provides synthetic speech with realistic, natural intonation. The engine uses linguistic rules and sentence analysis.
TTS	Centigram Communications Corporation	TruVoicer Text-to-Speech Converter is a premium-quality text-to-speech product that converts any written text into natural-sounding, intelligible, spoken American English, German, Spanish, Italian, or French.
TTS	Digital Equipment Corporation	DECtalk SDK for Windows 95. The DECtalk text-to-speech engine for Microsoft® Windows 95 provides highly intelligible, natural-sounding, synthesized speech from freeform text input.

continues

Table B.3. continued

Type	Company	Products
TTS	FirstByte	ProVoice Developers Kit for WIN 32. FirstByte, the OEM sales leader in text-to-speech software, offers development kits for the Microsoft Win32 Application Programming Interface (API), Microsoft Windows 3.1, Macintosh, OS/2, and embedded systems.
TTS	Lernout & Hauspie Speech Products	TTS SDK for telephony and desktop applications. L&H Text-To-Speech SDK is a multiple-language software-development package that converts any computer-readable text into natural-sounding synthetic speech.
TTS	SoftVoice, Inc.	SoftVoice, the developers of Apple Computer's original MacinTalk speech synthesizer and the Amiga's Narrator device, has developed a Windows version of its state-of-the-art, multilingual system.
TTS	Telefonica I+D	Spanish TTS engine for Windows 95. The Telefonica I+D text-to-speech engine for Windows 95 produces Spanish synthetic speech from unrestricted text. The synthetic output is of very high quality: highly intelligible and very natural.

Type	*Company*	*Products*
TTS	Telia Promotor AB	Infovox 230—State-of-the-art text-to-speech conversion software for Microsoft Windows 95. Available for British English, American English, German, French, Spanish, Italian, Norwegian, Swedish, Danish, Finnish, and Icelandic.
API	AT&T Microelectronics	
API	Berkeley Speech Technologies, Inc.	
API	Centigram Communications Corporation	
API	Creative Technology Ltd.	
API	Digital Equipment Corporation	
API	Dragon Systems, Inc.	
API	Eloquent Technology, Inc.	
API	First Byte	
API	Kolvox Communications	
API	Kurzweil Applied Intelligence, Inc.	
API	Lernout & Hauspie Speech Products	
API	Scott Instruments Corporation	
API	Speech Systems, Inc.	
API	S Systems, Inc.	
API	Telia Promotor Infovox AB	
API	Verbex Voice Systems	
API	Voice Processing Corporation	

C

TAPI Resources

This chapter contains several listings of TAPI-related resources including:

■ Books

■ Web links

■ Other online resources

■ Software and hardware resources

TIP

For the most recent list of TAPI-related resources, including updated books, Web links, other online resources, and SAPI software and hardware, use your Web browser to connect to the Communications Developer's Guide home page at:

www.iac.net/~mamund/mstdg/index.htm

Books

Table C.1 lists books on TAPI that are available at most large libraries. This is not a definitive list, but it is a good representation of writings on the subject.

Table C.1. TAPI-related books.

Title	Author	Notes
Telephony's Directory & Buyers' Guide For The Telecommunications Industry	(None)	Telephony's directory & buyers' guide for the telephone industry—Annual.
Toward Competition In Local Telephony	Baumol, William J.	Telephone—United States—Deregulation. Telephone companies—United States.
Digital Telephony	Bellamy, John	Digital telephone systems. Digital communications. Digital modulation. Telephone switching systems, Electronic.

Title	Author	Notes
LAN Times Guide To Telephony	Bezar, David D.	
Principles Of Telephony	Biswas, Nripendra Nath	
Telephony: Today And Tomorrow	Chorafas, Dimitris N.	Telecommunication—Technological innovations. Telephone—Technological innovations.
Telecom Basics	Dempsey, Jack L.	Telecommunication systems.
Modern Telephony	Harb, Mahmoud	Telephone. Telephone systems.
Data Transmission And Data Processing Dictionary	Holmes, James F.	Data transmission systems—Dictionaries.
A Compilation Of Terminology In The Fields Of Data Processing		Electronic data processing—Dictionaries.
Telephony's Dictionary: Defining 16,000 Telecommunication Words And Terms	Langley, Graham	Telecommunication—Dictionaries.
Computing System Architecture In Computer Telephony, 1st Ed.	Margulies, Edwin	
New Directions In Telecommunications Policy	Newburg, Paula	Telecommunication policy—United States.
Datacom Basics, 1st Ed.	Schatt, Stanley	Computer science. Computers.
The Telephone: An Historical Anthology	Shiers, George Shiers	Telephone—History—Addresses, essays, lectures.
Basic Carrier Telephony	Talley, David	Telephone, Carrier current.

> **NOTE**
>
> A more complete listing of books, including publisher data, can be found in the `BOOKLIST` table of the `CDGLISTS.MDB` database on the companion CD-ROM. You can use Microsoft Access, Microsoft Query, or any Access/Visual Basic database product to read this data file.

Web Links

Table C.2 provides a list of World Wide Web links on the subject of TAPI. This list is constantly changing. An updated list is contained in the `TAPIWEB.HTM` data file in the `RESOURCE` folder on the companion CD-ROM. This file can be loaded into almost any Web browser and used as a launch document to connect to the associated links.

Table C.2. Web links for TAPI.

Web Title	Web Address	Description
Access Superhighway	`www.super-hwy.com`	Specializes in Computer Telephony Integration (CTI).
Agile Communications	`www.spidermedia.com/agile.html`	Fiber-optic systems engineering for CATV, CCTV, telephony, and LAN applications. Simple advice via e-mail is free.
Allgon	`www.fti.se/allgon/eng`	Develops, manufactures, and markets products for radio signal transmission within mobile and personal telephony.
Alliance Systems	`www.asisys.com`	Computers, software, hardware, computer telephony, dialogic, fax-on-demand, interactive voice response, IVR, and Rhetorex.

Web Title	Web Address	Description
AMDEV Communications Corp.	www.amdevcomm.com	Products and services for voice processing, interactive voice response, voice mail, telephony, and automated voice attendant.
Ariel Corporation	www.ariel.com	Ariel Corporation's on-line guide to its Digital Signal Processing (DSP) and Computer Telephony Integration (CTI) products, newsletters, and technical information.
Big Island Communications	www.big-island.com	A new computer telephony company specializing in easy-to-use, full-featured computer telephony products for the small office/home office market.
Broadband Telephony Buyer's Guide	www.indra.com/unicom	More than 4,500 links to companies supplying transmission, switching, and power and distribution equipment and services.
Butler Telecom	www.fwi.com/butler/butler.html	Telephony catv idds drafting design technical staffing solutions.
Chromatic Research	www.mpact.com	Multimedia functions include: video, 2D graphics, 3D graphics, audio, FAX/modem, telephony, and videophone.

continues

Table C.2. continued

Web Title	Web Address	Description
Cobotyx	`www.cobotyx.com`	PC-based systems for voice processing, computer telephony (CTI), voice mail, auto attendant, text-to-speech, voice networking, interactive voice response (IVR), and fax mail technologies.
Computer Talk, Inc.	`www.gpl.net/itcb/cti`	Develops and maintains a suite of computerised voice processing telephony solutions for a diverse range of business sectors.
Computer Telephone Integrators, Inc.	`www.inforamp.net/mainstay/cti`	Guide to the latest in telephony technologies covering everything from IVR to fax-on-demand.
Cypress Research Corporation	`www.cypressr.com`	Desktop computer telephony applications. Cypress provides smart telephone software to small office and home users.
DAX Systems, Inc.	`www.daxsystems.com`	The definitive hardware source for computer telephony applications developers. Builds systems to meet a wide range of CT and IVR needs.
Dialogic	`www.dialogic.com`	Computer telephony industry's leading supplier of components for open systems signal computing.

Web Title	Web Address	Description
Dianatel Corporation	`www.dianatel.com`	Manufacturer of PC-based computer telephony components for digital telephone network interface, switching, and audio conferencing.
Digital Systems International, Inc.	`www.dgtl.com/index.html`	Computer-telephony systems, software, and services to the call center industry.
EMJ Data Systems, Limited	`www.emj.ca`	Publicly-owned distributor of computer products and peripherals, specializing in high performance products for Apple, CAD, Point of Sale, UNIX, and Telephony apps.
Explicit	`taz.hyperreal.com/ cyberia/explicit`	Innovative software development merging the worlds of computer telephony (CTI) and interactive multimedia.
F. F. Tronixs	`www.fftron.com/fftron`	A dealer and distributor specializing in products for surge protection, telephone, computer telephony, and teleconferencing; uniquely qualified to meet your home and corporate office needs.
Facilities Management Services	`web.hudsonet.com/enterprise`	ESS, Inc. specializes in Facilities and Assets Management systems, integrating client/server, CAD floorplans, and telephony systems.

continues

Table C.2. continued

Web Title	Web Address	Description
Genesys	`www.teleport.com/~genesys/index.shtml`	CallerEGO DX and other telephony products for Windows. Also RACom—Remote Agent Communicator for the ROLM CBX.
Helpdesk Response	`www.hr.com`	Providing knowledge-based expert systems through Internet and telephony interfaces for a more intelligent and responsive helpdesk.
Hongkong Telecom	`www.hkt.net`	Basic telephony, international calls, fax/data products, mobile telephones, satellite links, and turnkey telecommunications systems.
Index—Commercial Speech Recognition	`www.tiac.net/users/rwilcox/speech.html`	Gateway to voice recognition resources, with emphasis on commercial speech recognition engines for both PC and telephony use.
Information Technology and Communications Policy Forum of Japan	`ifrm.glocom.ac.jp/ipf/hp.html`	Comments on government-controlled debate and future of telephony monopoly under NTT.
Interactive Telephony, Ltd.	`www.business.co.uk`	
Interdisciplinary Telecommunications Program	`morse.colorado.edu`	Courses include ATM, ISDN, Wireless, Cable-TV, Telephony, Internet, and many more.

Web Title	Web Address	Description
Island Link Solutions	www.islandlink.com	Long Island–based Internet advertising company. Also offers a full range of business telephony solutions such as fax back and telemarketing.
Mwave Page at Watson	watson.mbb.sfu.ca	When combined with the mwaveOS (an onboard preemptive multitasking operating system), a variety of functions can be achieved. The Mwave technology can combine telephony and audio functions on a single card, for example, 14.4K data/fax modem, telephone answering machine (TAM), and 16-bit CD quality audio functions.
Networks Unlimited AG	ourworld.compuserve.com/ homepages/NUAG	Focuses on directory, messaging, workflow, and computer telephony technology.
Optelecom, Inc.	www.spidermedia.com/ optelecm.html	Fiber-optic equipment manufacturer for CCTV, CATV, telephony, and LAN applications.
Parity Software	www.paritysw.com	Software tools for building your own computer telephony applications, such as voice mail, fax-on-demand, and so on.

continues

Table C.2. continued

Web Title	Web Address	Description
Periphonics Corporation	www.peri.com	Makes some of the world's busiest Interactive Voice Response (IVR) systems. Learn about Voice Processing, IVR, and Computer-Telephony Integration (CTI).
PGPfone	web.mit.edu/network/pgpfone	PGPfone, aka Pretty Good Privacy Phone, is a desktop cryptogrphic telephony application available for download from MIT.
PhonetiCs, Inc.	www.phonetics.com/phonetics	IVR, voice mail, fax mail, audiotext, computer telephony, systems integrator, and software developer. Specializing in government and hospitality industries.
Pronexus, Inc.	www.pronexus.com	Computer telephony tools with the power of Visual Basic to enable Windows-based voice and fax processing.
PureSpeech, Inc.	www.speech.com	Speaker-independent recognition with natural language processing for personal computers and computer telephony applications.
Rhetorex, Inc.	www.rhetorex.com	Manufacturer of high-quality DSP-based multi-line computer telephony platforms.

Web Title	Web Address	Description
Sandman	www.sandman.com	Catalog of unique telecom products & cable installation tools with telephony history page.
SIM-phony—Home	www.sim-phony.com/~simphony	Providing technology in the field of computer-telephony integration.
SoftTalk, Inc.	www.softtalk.com	Vendor of computer telephony.
Stanford University's Applied Speech Technology Laboratory	www-csli.stanford.edu/users/bscott/ASTL.html	"To Humanize Speech Technology." The ASTL is devoted to applying speech recognition technology to user interfaces, the Internet, telephony, educational aides, and many other exciting areas.
Stylus Innovation, Inc.	northshore.shore.net/~stylus	Dedicated to the development of easy-to-use toolkits for computer telephony , voice processing, and faxing.
Technically Speaking, Inc.	www.techspk.com	Developer of software authoring tools and applications for enterprise computer telephony integration.
Tel-Com	www.tel-com.com	Utilizes modern telephony equipment and personable service to provide pagers, voice mail, answering service, and alpha dispatch.

continues

Table C.2. continued

Web Title	Web Address	Description
Teleconnect Magazine	`www.teleconnect.com`	Phones, voice mail, IVR, convergence technology, and computer telephony.
Tellabs Operations, Inc.	`www.tellabs.com`	Manufacturer of telecommunications equipment solutions for wireless, cable telephony, broadband, wideband, ATM, network management, and SONET/SDH transport and access.
Universal Interactive Systems	`www.primenet.com/~vladi`	Vendor of computer telephony software and services.
VISIT Computer Telephony Integration	`www.nortel.com/english/visit`	Neat computer telephony products (preview of a home page).
Visual Voice	`www.stylus.com`	Visual Voice is a telephony toolkit for MS Windows. Build sophisticated telephony applications such as IVR (e.g. touch-tone banking), fax-on-demand, voice mail systems.
Vive Synergies, Inc.	`www.vive.com`	Develop and market specialty telephony products for applications that enhance the

Web Title	Web Address	Description
		productivity of work operations through automated call processing and through taking advantage of the new services provided by the telephone company.
Voice Processing Corporation	www.vpro.com	A speech recognition company that provides voice engines for speech-enabling telephony and desktop applications.
Windows to Technology	www.kosone.com/wintech	A telecommunications and networking company established in 1989 to provide telephony peripherals such as headsets, interalia, board room conferencing units, and computer/LAN interfaces.

NOTE

A more complete listing of these links can also be found in the WEBLIST table of the CDGLISTS.MDB database on the companion CD-ROM. You can use the database table to search for specific vendors, products, and so on.

Other Online Resources

Table C.3 lists TAPI-related topics that you can browse on CompuServe.

Table C.3. TAPI-related CompuServe topics.

Forum or Topic Name
Office Automation Forum
Windows Components C Forum
EDI Forum
Windows Extensions Forum
Telecom Support Forum

An extensive list of topics for The Microsoft Network can be found in the TAPIMSN folder on the CD-ROM. This contains a list of MSN shortcuts. If you are an MSN subscriber, you can click on these icons to connect directly to the topic area on MSN.

Software and Hardware Resources

Table C.4 lists software and hardware vendors who are currently providing, or have pledged to provide, TAPI-compliant software and/or hardware products. A more complete list of vendors, including contact names, addresses, and phone numbers can be found in the PRODUCTS table of the CDGLISTS.MDB database on the companion CD-ROM. You can use the data table to perform searches for selected products or vendors.

There are six types of entries in the table:

- *API*—Client API products
- *SPI*—Server-side products
- *PBX*—PBX/Key system-related products
- *IDSN*—IDSN products
- *C/S*—Client/server products
- *CELL*—Cellular phone products

Table C.4. TAPI-related software and hardware.

Type	Company	Products
API	Active Voice	
API	Alcatel Business Systems	Alcatel PC-Tel Basic, Alcatel Proprietary PBX phone set adapter with Windows-based telephone manager including PBX feature access journal and phone books.
API	AlgoRhythms, Inc.	PhoneKits, Integrated Telephony with on-screen phone, call log, answering machine, address book, and fax.
API	AnswerSoft	
API	Aurora Systems, Inc.	FastCall (a middleware program that provides CTI for desktop call processing environments).
API	CCOM Information Systems	PhoneLine for Windows; PhoneLine is a fully configurable Computer Telephone Integrated (CTI), enterprise-wide directory manager providing online access to corporate and personal directory information.
API	Clearwave Communications, Inc.	Intellect, the telephone/PC link that organizes all your communication.
API	ConnectWare, Inc.	Cruiser (an intelligent communications integrator managing your mail and phone calls, allowing your correspondents to reach you wherever you are, organizing your calendar, and allowing you to focus on your work).
API	Delrina	WinFax PRO with Voice—The leading PC fax software now includes voice mail/messaging and telephony functionality.
API	Envision Telephony	SoundByte—record telephone conversations as they occur; play back and review via the computer screen.

continues

Table C.4. continued

Type	Company	Products
API	Ericsson Business Communications	
API	Executone Information Systems	Execudex—Rolodex-style TAPI application providing call control, call monitoring, and address book.
API	Exepos Software Solutions	EasySpeak.
API	Franklin Quest	Ascend 4.0 Personal Information Manager.
API	Global Communications Ltd.	WorldWindows—a personal telephony productivity tool to simplify access to telephony features.
API	Harris Digital Telephone Systems	Harris Telephone Services application—a TAPI-compliant Windows application which allows a user to access telephone services from a user configurable interface.
API	Intel Corporation	
API	Jensen-Jones	Commence 3.0 Personal Information Manager.
API	Logical Solutions	PhoneBar TAPI call control and personal voice mail application.
API	MediaTrends	Unified Messaging Systems (UMS), Integrated auto attendant and voice mail system for Windows 95.
API	MegaSoft GmbH	WinPhone—a very comfortable dialer that acts like an assistant.
API	Microsoft Corporation	TAZZ (beta) TAPI-compliant voice mail application.
API	NetManage	ECCO Professional—integrates personal and group information, including calendar, phonebook, project management, and group scheduling.
API	Northern Telecom, Inc.	VISIT Voice—A full-featured call management application for Windows. VISIT FastCall—PC-based solution

Type	Company	Products
		that provides call routing, screen-based telephony, and data screen population based on ANI or DNIS.
API	OCTuS, Inc.	PTA (Personal Telecommunications Assistant)—a communications control center for Windows, combining telephony control (even Centrex), Caller ID lookup, voice mail, and fax.
API	OKNA	DeskTop Set Professional—personal information manager.
API	PAGE TeleCOMPUTING	Sales Call Software—a telemarketing application for outbound power dialing of lists of prospects. LINK— utility software to take Caller-ID information and screen pop any PIM, contact manager, or database.
API	Parsons Technology	Address Book 2.0 for Windows— keeps your most important names, addresses, and phone numbers close at hand.
API	The Periscope Company, Inc.	WinScope—Windows API debugging, discovery, and reverse engineering tool with TAPI support.
API	Pronexus	TAPISTRY—an object-oriented VBX custom control TAPI software development kit. TAPISTRY for Windows 95—a 32-bit OCX control version of TAPISTRY. VBVoice for Visual Basic.
API	Q.Sys International, Inc.	CallManager—Personal PhoneWare, Group PhoneWare.
API	Siemens ROLM	ComManager—personal productivity tool providing immediate access to information such as corporate directories, notes, call logs, reminders, and telephone features such as conferencing.

continues

Table C.4. continued

Type	Company	Products
API	SoftTalk, Inc.	Phonetastic for TAPI—graphical desktop call center software.
API	Stylus Innovation, Inc.	Visual Voice—a Visual Basic custom control and graphical workbench that allows developers to build voice mail, fax-on-demand, and interactive voice response (e.g. TouchTone banking) type applications.
API	Symantec Corporation	ACT! 2.0 for Windows—manage your business relationships more productively with ACT!, the top-rated, best-selling contact manager.
API	Synchro Development	Multimedia Connect—provides the look, feel, and function of a desktop telephone/fax right on your computer screen.
API	TEDAS	Phoneware—sophisticated voice mail system for individual users, featuring voice recognition for password access and full interaction with analog phones.
API	VoiceMark Corporation (Pty) Ltd.	Creation—generates custom telephony solutions, using OLE custom controls in a drag-and-drop fashion, so even novice developers can quickly assemble voice mail, fax services, call routing, and voice recognition applications.
API	Voysys	VoysAccess 1.0—a telephony applications toolkit that enables developers to embed telephone access and control into their Microsoft FoxPro databases.
SPI	America Megatrends, Inc.	Media-Tel—a concurrent, multi-function fax/modem, voice mail, and sound card.
SPI	C-T Link	C-T Link 1000.

Type	*Company*	*Products*
SPI	Clearwave Communications, Inc.	Intellect-ID—complete Caller-ID and intelligent telephone control for your PC.
SPI	Columbia Communications	The M4—a Multimedia Messaging Modem.
SPI	Comdial	PATI—PC and Telephony Interface.
SPI	ConnectWare	PhoneWorks—an integrated PC-based communications solution that supplies advanced voice and data features through the analog telephone network with single or dual versions.
SPI	Dialogic	Multi-line computer telephony add-in cards.
SPI	Global Communications Ltd.	WorldWindows.
SPI	Microsoft	UNIMODEM/V—Windows 95 universal modem driver supports a wide variety of voice modems.
SPI	Miro	
SPI	Momentum Data Systems	Eagle-56—a DSP add-in card with Motorola DSP56002 and TAPI service provider.
SPI	Motorola, Inc.	PC Media—Telephony Developers Kit.
SPI	Rhetorex	
SPI	SDX	SPOT 1 (Smart Plain Ordinary Telephone)—an analog hands-free telephone that can be totally controlled from your PC via the serial port.
SPI	SounDesigns Multimedia Communications Systems, Ltd.	SoundModem—turns your existing SoundBlaster board into an affordable, plug and play, professional computer telephony platform.
SPI	Spectrum Signal Processing	Solo—combines telephony, fax, and data capabilities with professional quality 16-bit stereo sound all on a single PC plug-in card.

continues

Table C.4. continued

Type	Company	Products
SPI	Staria, Ltd.	ST32—single line telephony card, DSP-based, TAPI-compliant.
SPI	Xinex Labs	MindSet mS1201 XC—a PC integrated telephone that is bundled with contact management software.
PBX	Alcatel Business Systems	Alcatel TAPI Interface Kit—Alcatel proprietary PBX phone set adapter with link to PC COMM port, TSPI, and TAPI-based clipboard dialer.
PBX	AT&T Global Business Communications Systems	PassageWay Direct Connect.
PBX	Bosch Telecom	
PBX	Comdial	
PBX	Executone Information Systems	M160 TAPI Service Provider—TAPI service provider that connects through the serial port of the Executone M160 model phone.
PBX	Fujitsu Business Communications Systems	PC-DT—a TAPI-compliant card for Fujitsu's digital telephone.
PBX	Harris Digital Telephone Systems	Harris Optic Service Provider—a TAPI-compliant service provider for use with Harris telephone switching systems.
PBX	InteCom	
PBX	Inter-Tel	Axxessory Connect—TAPI service provider and PC phone for the Inter-Tel Axxess hybrid/PBX phone system.
PBX	Iwatsu America	
PBX	Lexical	PowerPhone/N—provides easily accessible desktop telephony services for connection to a Northern Telecom Norstar or Meridian PBX.
PBX	Matra Communication	MC6500-TAPI-TSPI—telephony service provider interface for MC6500 PBXs.

Type	*Company*	*Products*
PBX	MCK Telecommunications	Telebridge—service provider allowing access to all features of a Northern Telecom feature set.
PBX	Mitel	TalkTo/TAPI—PC phone card and TAPI service provider for Mitel PBXs.
PBX	National Semiconductor	IsoEthernet PC ISA Bus Adapter—provides multiple independent data channels and software stacks enabling data network, telephone, and real time multimedia applications.
PBX	NEC America	PC Telephony Adapter—adapter for the Dterm Series III telephone. Provides a serial connection to the PC and a TAPI SPI. Dterm PC—ISA Bus PC card that connects to a Dterm Series III phone line. Has a headset connection and a connection for a Dterm s.
PBX	Northern Telecom, Inc.	TAPI Service Provider Toolkit—developer's toolkit for customizable interfaces to Northern Telecom switching platforms.
PBX	Panasonic DBS	DBS TAPI Box—DBS CTI interface for software applications.
PBX	Siemens ROLM	CallBridge for Desktop—TAPI extends telephone control from a ROLMphone with a data module to any TAPI-compliant application.
PBX	Toshiba America Information Systems, Inc.	Toshiba TSPI—for DK280, Perception e/ex, Perception 4000 switches.
PBX	Voice Technologies Group	Scorpion—TAPI card for digital phone systems.
ISDN	ISDN Systems Corporation	SecureLink ISDN Adapter—low-cost ISDN voice and data solution that has state of the art data interoperability (PPP/MPP) and TAPI support.

continues

Table C.4. continued

Type	Company	Products
ISDN	Oxus Research	Oxus PC/SO ISDN Board—ISDN BRI PC board.
C/S	Dialogic	CT-Connect—a Windows NT–based CTI link server which supports most popular PBXs and ACDs and supports TAPI clients.
C/S	Genesys Labs	Genesys T-Server—TAPI-compliant CTI middleware.
C/S	Northern Telecom, Inc.	
CELL	Nokia Mobile Phones, Ltd.	Nokia TAPI Development Toolkit— the TAPI interface to integrate Nokia cellular phones and personal computers.

D

The CD-ROM Contents

The CD-ROM that ships with this book has a wealth of information that will be useful to you when you begin developing your own applications using MAPI, SAPI, and TAPI services. Along with the source code from the book, the CD-ROM contains pointers to additional developer resources and copies of Microsoft files that can be redistributed with your applications. There are also a number of third-party tools and demos for you to test.

> **TIP**
>
> Even if you don't plan on working through all the code examples, it is a good idea to run the installation routine on the CD-ROM. This routine will alert you to any late-breaking news regarding the book or any related software.

The CD-ROM that ships with this book is divided into four main sections:

■ *Source code libraries*—This section contains folders that correspond to the chapters in the book. Each chapter that contains source code exercises is represented here. If you are interested in a particular set of code, but don't want to have to type it in from scratch, look in this portion of the CD-ROM for the code you need.

■ *Developer resources*—This section contains folders for each API set (MAPI, SAPI, and TAPI). In turn, these folders contain information on third-party vendors (including e-mail addresses), available development tools, and even pointers to Internet Web sites and other online resources. Although much of this material is covered in the book's appendixes, check here for the most recent version of the resource lists. There is even an Access database that contains names, phone numbers, and addresses of third-party vendors that provide tools for MAPI, SAPI, and TAPI developers.

■ *Microsoft redistribution libraries*—This section of the CD-ROM contains a set of Microsoft files that can be redistributed with your API applications. You will need to have access to the MSDN Professional Level CD-ROM in order to develop some of the projects in this book, but you do not need MSDN to distribute completed API applications.

■ *Third-party tools and product demos*—This section contains a wealth of product demos, shareware, and freeware tools that can be handy when developing your applications. Some of the material here is free for your use, other material is for evaluation only. Please be sure to honor the copyrights on all material on the CD-ROM.

I

Index

A

**About dialog box,
438-440, 698-701**
  coding, 305-307,
    834-836, 919-920
  Command1_Click
    event, 836
  controls, 305-307
  designing, 834-836
  *FaxBack project,
    918-920*
  form controls,
    834-836, 918-920
  Form_Load event
    code, 836
  frmTAPI, 828-836
  laying out, 305-307
  properties, setting,
    919-920
**AcceptCall Linegroup
  Control, setting VBVoice
  control properties, 911**
**AcceptCall_Disconnect
  event (FaxBack
  form), 916**
**Access Superhighway
  Web site, 1044**
accessing
  AddressEntry Details
    dialog box, 206-207
  MAPI
    MAPI 1.0 API set, 7
    *MAPI OCX controls,
      7-8*
    *OLE Message Library,
      7-8*
  MAPI Address Book,
    165-167
  SMAPI API calls, MAPI
    services, 97-100
  storage folders (MAPI
    Client), 46-47

Acemail Web site, 1022
**ACT! 2.0 for
  Windows, 1058**
**Action property
  (MAPISession control),
  132-134**
**active calls, dropping
  TAPI, 694-696**
**Active property (OLE
  Voice Menu object), 450**
**Add (Attachments collec-
  tion object method), 209**
**Add (Messages collection
  object method), 181**
**Add (Recipients collection
  object method), 195**
Add method
  OLE Voice Menu
    object, 450
  parameters, 494-497
Add Mode button, 508
Add Phrase button, 913
Add Rule form
  building MAPI Email
    Agent, 327-332
  control arrays (MAPI
    Email Agent), 327-332
**AddAction routine,
  adding, 354**
adding
  AddAction routine, 354
  AddrDetails routine,
    111, 207-208
  AddressBook routine,
    106-107
  AddrProps routine,
    205-206
  AddRule routine, 355
  AddTest routine,
    352-353
  ArchEdit routine, 234
  AssistedTAPI module
    *Assisted TAPI declara-
      tions, 925-926*

  *TAPIGetLocation
    function, 927*
  *TAPIMakeCall
    function, 928*
AttachAdd routine, 216
AttachColl routine, 211
AttachProps routine,
  214-215
AttachSave routine,
  218-219
CallBack module
  functions, 928-931
CheckMsgSignature
  routine, 403-405
CheckPriority routine,
  362-363
CheckRule routine,
  359-360
CheckSender function,
  360-361
CheckSubject routine,
  361-362
class module
  SR callbacks, 499-500
  *TTS callbacks,
    486-489*
CloseDown routine,
  350-351
CollectFolders
  routine, 269
ControlsEdit
  routine, 230
ControlsLoad
  routine, 228-229
DeleteRule routine, 356
DoAction routine,
  363-364
Emp tag for word
  emphasis, 512
ErrMsgBox routine,
  403-405
Excel
  *MAPI services,
    121-123*

outbound dialing,
749-752
TAPI declarations,
750-752
FaxBack module
CenterForm routine,
901
FileExists function,
900-901
project-level variables,
900
SendSMAPIFax
routine, 902-903
SMAPIStart routine,
901
faxBack module, 902
FillList routine, 351-352
FillOutline routine,
274-275
FindArc routine, 252
FolderProps routine,
179-180
FoldersColl routine,
176-177
forms
designer notes, 75
field-level help, 76
form-level help, 75
online help, 75-76
windows-level help,
75-76
Forms Designer Wizard,
fields to forms, 65-66
frmTAPI menus,
810-812
GetFolderRec function,
271-279
GetMsgRec function, 274
InfoStoreProps
routine, 174
INIActions routine,
349-350
INIGeneral routine,
346-347

INIRegSetting function,
347-348
INIRules routine, 349
INITests routine,
349-350
InitStuff routine, 344
libTAPI module
declaration code, 782
initTAPI function,
783-784
ReadLineDevCaps
function, 784
SetCallParams routine,
785-786
TAPIClearHandles
routine, 787
TAPIDial function,
785
TAPIHangUp
routine, 787
TAPIPlaceCall routine,
786-787
TAPIShutdown
routine, 787
LibVPhone module,
project-level declara-
tions, 930-931
LoadFolders routine, 270
LoadLists routine, 351
LoadMsgRec
routine, 288
LoadStrings routine, 345
LogWrite routine, 357
MakeRule routine,
355-356
MakeTimeStamp
routine, 275
MAPI Email Agent
codes, 316-341
Form_Load code, 324
Form_Resize
event, 324
rules, 370-371
MAPI services to existing
applications, 121-123

MAPIAddrBook
routine, 166
MAPIEnd routine,
165, 236
MAPIStart routine,
164-165, 235-236
MDIForm_Activate
routine, 285-286
MDIForm_Load
routine, 285
MDIForm_Resize
routine, 285-286
MDIForm_Unload
routine, 286
message attachments,
215-216
Message objects,
191-194
MessageAdd routine,
192-194
MessageMake routine,
193-194
MessageProps
routine, 190
MessagesColl
routine, 183
Microsoft Phone
announcement
mailboxes, 871
AutoFax mailboxes,
871
message mailboxes, 871
MLM subscribers,
243-246
MsgFwdReply
routine, 365
MsgIndex function, 273
MsgMoveCopy routine,
366-367
MsgNotify routine, 364
MsgPtr function, 273
NerwMsgRec
routine, 287
OLE Voice Text Object,
Visual Basic, 470-489

OLEMAPIEnd
  routine, 268
OLEMAPIGetMsgs
  routine, 271-273
OLEMAPIPostMsg
  routine, 276-277
OLEMAPIReplyMsg
  routine, 277-278
OLEMAPIStart
  routine, 268
Pau tag, text pauses,
  512-513
ProcessInbox routine,
  241-242
ProcessInboxMsg
  routine, 243
ProcessInboxMsgArcGet
  routine, 251
ProcessInboxMsgArcList
  routine, 249-250
ProcessInboxMsgNewSub
  routine, 244
ProcessInboxMsgUnSub
  routine, 247
ProcessSubList routine,
  237-238
ProcessSubListMsg
  routine, 238-239
ReadInbox routine,
  241-242
ReadMail routine,
  119-121
RecipAdd routine, 202
RecipColl routine, 197
Recipient objects,
  201-202
RecipProps routine,
  200-201
ResolveName subroutine,
  108-109
SaveValues routine, 346
ScanMsgs routine,
  358-359
SendDialog routine, 116

SendDocs routine, 113
SendMail routine, 236
SessionInfoStoreColl
  routine, 172
SetupPageLoad
  routine, 339
SetupPageSave
  routine, 340
SkedEdit routine, 233
SMAPIEnd routine, 104
SMAPIStart routine, 104
SR services to Windows
  95, 565
StatusUpdate
  routine, 297
SubBye routine, 248-249
SubDelete routine,
  247-248
SubEdit routine, 232
SubGreet routine, 246
SubWrite routine, 245
TAPI Dialog Utility
  option buttons,
  705-707
TAPIANS project,
  support routines,
  733-736
TAPILINE controls to
  tool box, 665-666
TAPILINE form
  button event code,
  689-702
  form event code,
  688-689
  support routines,
  685-687
TTS engine
  callback controls,
  487-488
  playback controls,
  483-485
Visual Basic 4.0 MAPI
  services, 123-127
Voice Menu object
  commands, 494-497

Voice Phone project
  AddRec routine, 937
  BuildDatabase
  routine, 935
  BuildVMenu
  routine, 932
  CenterForm
  routine, 939
  database engine
  routines, 934-938
  DeleteRec routine, 938
  EditRec routine, 937
  InitDB routine,
  934-935
  InitVCmd routine, 931
  InitVTxt routine,
  933-934
  LoadMsgs routine, 934
  LoadNameList
  routine, 933
  LookUp function, 938
  OpenDatabase
  routine, 936
  PlaceCall routine, 939
  voice command
  routines, 931-933
  voice text routines,
  933-934
WriteArcGet routine,
  253-254
WriteArcList routine,
  250-251
**ADDRBOOK, context
  maps, 377**
**AddrDetails routine,
  adding, 111, 207-208**
**AddRec routine (Voice
  Phone project), 937**
Address (MAPIRecip), 95
**Address (Recipient object
  property), 198-199**
**Address Book 2.0 for
  Windows, 1057**

address books
MAPI Server, 52-54
modifying entries in
MAPIAddress,
105-107
ResolveName service,
52-54
storage formats, 52-54
address status, viewing
(TAPI), 696-697
AddressBook (Session
Object method),
162-163
AddressBook routine,
adding, 106-107
AddressCaption property
(MAPIMessage control),
138-141
AddressEditFieldCount
property (MAPIMessage
control), 138-141
AddressEntry (Recipient
object property), 199
AddressEntry Details
dialog box, accessing,
206-207
AddressEntry object
methods
Delete, 203
Details, 203
Update, 203-204
properties
Application, 203-204
Class, 204
DisplayType, 204
Fields, 204
ID, 204
Name, 204
Type, 204-209
addresses, MAPI Client,
47-48
AddressID
(TAPILINE.OCX
properties), 668

AddressLabel property
(MAPIMessage control),
138-141
AddressModifiable
property (MAPIMessage
control), 138-141
AddressResolveUI property
(MAPIMessage control),
139-141
AddrProps routine,
adding, 205-206
AddRule routine,
adding, 355
AddTest routine, inserting,
352-353
AdjustForm routine,
coding, 148-149
adjusting
audio playback speed,
480-482
Vol tag volume, 514
AdjustReader()
(MAPIREAD.FRM),
155-156
Advanced Filter dialog
box, 85
ADVANCEDCRITERIA,
context maps, 377
Advisor Web site, 1022
Agile Communications
Web site, 1044
Alcatel PC-Tel Basic, 1055
Alcatel Proprietary
PBX, 1055
Alcatel TAPI Interface
Kit, 1060
Allgon Web site, 1044
Alliance Systems Web
site, 1044
alt() rule
overview, 518
utilizing context free
grammars, 518
AMDEV Web site, 1045

analog lines, 602
Plain Old Telephone
Service (POTS),
603-604
announcement mailboxes,
adding (Microsoft
Phone), 871
answering machine,
configuring (Microsoft
Phone), 872-873
API calls
Basic Telephony,
611-613
Extended Telephony, 630
Supplemental Telephony,
622-627
API development tools
Microsoft Access 95, 6-7
Microsoft Excel 95, 6-7
Microsoft FoxPro, 6-7
Microsoft Visual Basic
4.0 Professional
Edition, 6-7
API line device structures,
Basic Telephony,
614-616
API phone device struc-
ture, Supplemental
Telephony, 627-628
API/SPI interface, WOSA
components, 13
Application (AddressEntry
object property),
203-204
Application (Attachments
collection object
property), 209
Application (Folder object
property), 177-178
Application (Folders
collection object prop-
erty), 175
Application (InfoStore
Collection property), 171

Application (InfoStore Object property), 173-174
Application (Message object property), 185-189
Application (Messages collection object property), 181
Application (Recipient object property), 199
Application Design command (Tools menu), 60
Application Design menu commands (Forms Design Wizard), 60-61
applications
Assisted TAPI versus Full TAPI, designing, 890-891
building VBVoice, 866
design considerations, 886-889
designing
SR interfaces, 464-465
TTS interfaces, 466-467
electronic mail clients, MAPI, 31-32
leveraging WOSA, 19-20
MAPI versus Comm API services, designing, 889-890
message aware MAPI, 32
message-enabled MAPI, 32-33
native API versus third party tools, designing, 888
notification callbacks, establishing, 438-439
rules of complexity, designing, 887

SAPI services, designing, 891-892
standalone versus extensions, laying out, 888-889
Voice Text Callbacks, establishing, 452-453
ArchEdit routine, adding, 234
architecture
client layer in MAPI, 27-28
High-level SAPI, 436
Low-level SAPI, 440-446
MAPI consistency, 28
MAPI DLL, 27-28
MAPI flexbility, 27-28
MAPI overview, 26
MAPI portability, 28-29
MAPI service layer, 27-28
TAPI, 608-631
archives
editing MLM, 234
listing MLM, 249-251
sending MLM, 251-254
subscribers, receiving, 251-254
Ariel Corporation Web site, 1045
Ascend 4.0 Personal Information Manager, 1056-1057
ASCII text, controlling, 228-229
Assisted TAPI
functions, testing, 747-749
tapiGetLocationInfo function, 746
tapiRequestMakeCall function, 746
Assisted TAPI declarations, adding, 925-926

Assisted TAPI versus Full TAPI, designing applications, 890-891
Assisted Telephony
calls, 608-609
overview, 608-609
TAPI model, 608-609
AssistedTAPI module
adding Assisted TAPI declarations, 925-926
TAPIGetLocation function, adding, 927
TAPIMakeCall function, adding, 928
AT & T WATSON, 1035
AttachAdd routine, 216
AttachColl routine, 211
attached files (MAPIFile), 96-97
attaching text messages to graphics, 30
Attachment object
methods
Delete, 212
ReadFromFile, 212
WriteToFile, 212-213
properties
Class, 213-220
Index, 213
Name, 213
Position, 213
Source, 213
AttachmentIndex property (MAPIMessage control), 139-141
AttachmentName property (MAPIMessage control), 139-142
AttachmentPathName property (MAPIMessage control), 139-142
AttachmentPosition property (MAPIMessage control), 139-142

attachments, adding
messages, 215-216
Attachments collection
object
  methods
    Add, 209
    Delete, 209
  properties
    Application, 209
    Class, 209
    Count, 209
    Item, 209-212
AttachmentType property
(MAPIMessage control),
139-142
AttachProps routine,
adding, 214-215
AttachSave routine,
adding, 218-219
attributes command
interface, 437-438
Attributes interface (Voice
Text object), 439-440
audio
  Awake property, process-
    ing, 491
  modifying speed (Spd
    tag), 513-514
  speed, adjusting,
    480-482
  SR engines, interpreting,
    516-517
  TTS engine control tags,
    506-508
  TTS technology, 463
AudioFastForward method
(Voice Text object),
452-454
AudioWav Web site, 1030
AutoFax mailboxes
(Microsoft Phone), 871
automating session (Logon
method), 167-168
AutoPause method (Voice
Text object), 452

AutoResume method
(Voice Text object), 452
AutoRewind method
(Voice Text object), 452
Awake property
  OLE Voice Command
    object properties, 448
  setting SR engine, 491
Aztech Systems, 658

B

base controls (frmTAPI),
788-790
basic data modems
  cost, 656-657
  speed, 656-657
  supporting TAPI services,
    656-657
Basic Rate Interface,
604-605
Basic Telephony
  API calls, 611-613
  API line device structures,
    614-616
  call groups, 611-613
  line device messages,
    616-620
  overview, 610-620
  POTS lines, 610-620
  TAPI model, 610-620
benefits of WOSA
  isolated development,
    18-19
  multivendor support,
    19-20
  upgrade protection, 19
BeSTspeech T-T-S, 1037
Big Island Communica-
tions Web site, 1045
binary files, MAPI message
types, 30

books
  MAPI reference re-
    sources, 1018-1021
  SAPI reference resources,
    1028-1029
  TAPI reference resources,
    1042-1044
Broadband Telephony
Buyers Guide Web
site, 1045
BuildDatabase routine,
adding (Voice Phone
project), 935
building
  Forms Designer Wizard
    initiating forms, 62
    response forms, 62
  MAPI Client application,
    143-159
  MAPI E-Mail Agent
    Add Rule form,
      327-332
    Main form, 316-327
    Setup form, 332-341
  Message Signing exten-
    sion, initial header file,
    387-390
  MLM subscriber
    files, 232
  OLE Messaging library
    discussion tools,
    265-266
  ProcessSubListMsg
    routine, messages,
    239-242
  VBVoice applications, 866
  Visual Basic
    SR services, 564-581
    TTS services, 564-581
  Voice Workbench voice
    queries, 858
BuildListView routine
(tmView form), 975-976

BuildStatusBar routine (tmView form), 975

BuildToolBar routine (tmView form), 976-978

BuildVMenu routine, adding (Voice Phone project), 932

Butler Telecom Web site, 1045

button event code
adding to TAPILINE form, 689-702
cmdLineClose code, 694-696
cmdLineDealloc, 694-696
cmdLineDrop, 694-696
cmdLineGetDevCaps_Click code, 690-696
cmdLineInit_Click code, 689-696
cmdLineMakeCall_Click event code, 693-696
cmdLineNegAPI_Click code, 689-696
cmdLineOpen_Click event code, 691-696

buttons
Add Mode, 508
Add Phrase, 913
cmdAdd, 492
cmdAwake, 491
cmdCreate, 492
cmdDisable, 473
cmdEnable, 473
cmdSleep, 491
Line Translate Dialog option, 719
Register, 508
Speed, 481
Test FAX, 920
TextData, 510

C

C++
SR applications, creating, 541-561
TTS applications, building, 534-541

Call dialog box
cmdCall_Click event, 833
coding, 828-833
designing, 828-833
form controls, 828-833
Form_Load event code, 832
frmTAPI, 828-836
UpdateDB routine, 833

call information, displaying (TAPI), 696-697

Call Log page
controls, placing, 803-806
frmTAPI
designing, 803-806
tabbed dialog boxes, 788

call parameters, setting, 635

callback controls, adding to TTS, 487-488

CallBack modules, adding functions, 928-931

CallBack property
OLE Voice Command object properties, 448
Voice Text object, 451-452

CallBridge for Desktop, 1061-1062

calling cards
Location section, 720-721
settings, testing, 722-723

CallRec support routine, TeleBook application, 776

CallState message function
code listing, 677-678
TAPICALL.BAS, 677-678

Cambridge Voice for Windows, 1035

CenterForm routine, adding
FaxBack module, 901
Voice Phone project, 939

checking TTS engine status, 485-486

CheckMsgSignature routine, 403-405

CheckPriority routine, 362-363

CheckRule routine, 359-360

CheckSender function, 360-361

CheckSubject routine, 361-362

child object
SR Engine Enumerator object (Speech Recognition object), 441
SR Sharing object (Speech Recognition object), 441
Voice Menu object (Voice Command object), 438

Chr tag
voice character, setting, 509
voice character tags, 509

Chromatic Research Web site, 1045

Cirrus Logic, 658

Class (AddressEntry object property), 204
Class (Attachment object property), 213
Class (Attachments collection object property), 209
Class (Folder object property), 177-178
Class (Folders collection object property), 175
Class (InfoStore Collection property), 171
Class (InfoStore Object property), 173-174
Class (Message object property), 185-189
Class (Messages collection object property), 181
Class (Recipient object property), 199
Class (Recipients collection object property), 195
Class (Session Object property), 168-170
class module
  clsPhoneCall, 754-756
  creating for TeleBook application, 753-756
  SR callbacks, adding, 499-500
  TTS callbacks, adding, 486-489
Class Module command (Insert menu), 499, 928
Clean function
  code, 678-679
  TAPICALL.BAS, 678-679
ClearHandles routine
  TAPIANS project, 735-736
  TAPILINE form, 686

ClearLog routine (frmTAPI), 825-826
ClearRec support routine, TeleBook application, 774-776
Client API
  dynamic link library (DLL), 15-21
  responding requests toServer SPI, 14-15
  services, requesting, 13-14
  WOSA components, 13
clients
  electronic mail services, MAPI, 31-32
  interchangeability of MAPI, 27-28
CloseDown routine, 350-351
closing open lines (TAPI), 694-696
clsPhoneCall class module, 754-756
  PropertyGet routine, coding, 755-756
  PropertyLet routine, coding, 755-756
cmdAdd button, 492
cmdAddrBook_Click event (tmNew form), 993
cmdAudio_Click method, coding, 484-485
cmdAwake button, 491
cmdBtn_Click event, TeleBook application, 764-766
cmdButton Array, coding, 737-741
cmdButtons_Click event (frmTAPI), 817-818
cmdCall_Click event (Call dialog box), 833

cmdCreate button, 492
cmdData_Click event (frmTAPI), 819-820
cmdDial_Click event
  TeleBook application,766
  VPhone form, 947
cmdDialPad_Click event (frmTAPI), 818
cmdDisable button, 473
cmdEnable button, 473
cmdFax_Click event (Faxback form), 915
cmdKey_Click event, TeleBook application, 765-766
cmdLineClose code (button event code), 694-696
cmdLineDealloc (button event code), 694-696
cmdLineDrop (button event code), 694-696
cmdLineGetAddrStatus code (TAPILINE form), 696-697
cmdLineGetCallInfo method (TAPILINE form), 696-697
cmdLineGetDevCaps_Click code (button event code), 690-696
cmdLineInit_Click code (button event code), 689-696
cmdLineMakeCall_Click event code (button event code), 693-696
cmdLineNegAPI_Click code (button event code), 689-696
cmdLineOpen_Click event code (button event code), 691-696
cmdList_Click method, coding, 500-502

**cmdNewMsg_Click event
(tmNew form), 992**
**cmdOK_Click event
(VHelp form), 954**
**cmdPhone_Click event
(VPhone form), 946-947**
**cmdRec_Click event (Vrec
form), 952**
**cmdRemove_Click
method, coding, 503**
cmdSleep button, 491
**cmdSpeak_Click method,
coding, 479-480**
**cmdSpeed_Click method,
coding, 480-481**
**Cobotyx Web site,
1030, 1046**
coding
About dialog box,
305-307, 834-836,
919-920
Call dialog box, 828-833
clsPhoneCall class
module
*PropertyGet routine,
755-756*
*PropertyLet routine,
755-756*
cmdAudio_Click
method, 484-485
cmdList_Click method,
500-502
cmdRemove_Click
method, 503
cmdSpeak_Click method,
479-480
cmdSpeed_Click method,
480-481
CommandSpoken
property, 498
FaxBack form, 914-918
frmTAPI, 812-828
*form-level routines,
812-815*

*menu-level routines,
815-817*
*page-level routines,
817-822*
*support routines,
822-827*
global variables
SR services, 565
TTS services, 565
Inbox routines, 240-243
MAPI Email Agent
support routines, 341
MAPIMAIN.FRM
*AdjustForm routine,
148-149*
*Command1_Click
event, 153-154*
Form_Load(), 152
Form_Resize(), 152
Form_Unload, 152
List1_DblClick(), 152
*MAPIFetch
routine, 150*
*MAPISave routine,
151*
*MAPIStart
routine, 149*
MAPIREAD.FRM
*AdjustReader(),
155-156*
Form_Load(), 156
LoadReader(), 156
MDI Discuss form,
285-288
MDI frmNote, 291-298
MDI Msgs form,
289-291
MDI Options form,
298-304
Message Signing exten-
sions
*Main DLL routines,
390-405*
*Property Sheet dialog
box, 405-409*

MLM forms, edit
routines, 230-235
Talk Mail project,
LibTalkMail module,
962-969
TAPI dialog boxes,
700-701
TAPI Dialog Utility,
707-711
TAPIANS form,
731-741
TAPIANS PROJECT,
cmdButton Array,
737-741
TAPILINE form,
685-701
TeleBook application
*phone entry form,
766-772*
*phone log form,
772-774*
*support routines,
774-776*
TeleBook application
main form, 756-766
tmNew form, 989-990
tmRead form,
1000-1008
tmView form, 973-983
*control events,
981-983*
form events, 974
*menu support routines,
978-981*
Voice Phone project,
library modules,
925-930
VPhone form, 944-948
Colibri Web site, 1030
**CollectFolders routine,
adding, 269**
Columns dialog box, 83
**Com tag, low-level TTS
control tags, 514-516**

Comm API versus MAPI services, designing applications, 889-890
ComManager, 1057
command button arrays, TeleBook application, 756-766
Command Corp Web site, 1030
Command Verification dialog boxes, 438
Command1_Click event
About dialog box, 836
coding MAPIMAIN.FRM, 153-154
CommandOther (Voice Command Callback), 448-449
CommandRecognize (Voice Command Callback), 448-449
commands
adding to Voice Menu object, 494-497
Application Design menu, Forms Design Wizard, 60-61
Compose menu
New Forms, 78, 87
New Post in this Folder, 85
Reply, 79
Edit menu
Copy, 103
Paste, 103
File menu
Install, 77
Properties, 82
Scan InBox, 1007
Send Messages, 1007
Help menu, Designer Notes, 75

Insert menu
Class Module, 499, 928
Module, 267, 747
Microsoft Exchange menu, Microsoft Exchange Forms Designer, 60-61
Programs menu, Microsoft Exchange, 60
removing from Voice Menu object, 502-503
Tools menu
Application Design, 60
Custom Controls, 132, 665
Deliver Now Using, 79
Reference, 266, 470, 925
View menu
Form Properties, 74
Show Scroll Bars, 68
Window Properties, 68
CommandSpoken property
coding, 498
memo commands, responding, 497-499
OLE Voice Command object properties, 448
Commence 3.0 Personal Information Manager, 1056-1057
Common Application Services, 16-17
Communication Services, 16-17
Microsoft RPC (remote procedure calls), 17
overview, 17
Windows SNA Application Program Interface, 17-18
Windows Sockets, 17

compiling
context-free grammars, 521-527
TAPIOUT project, 651
Component Object Model, *see* COM
Compose menu commands
New Forms, 78, 87
New Post in this Folder, 85
Reply, 79
Compose method (MAPIMessage control), 135-138
composing e-mail (MAPISendMail), 113-116
CompuServe
MAPI forums, reference resources, 1024
SAPI forums, reference resources, 1034
TAPI forums, reference resources, 1054
Computer Talk, Inc. Web site, 1046
configuring
MAPI Email Agent folders, 369
Microsoft Phone answering machine, 872-873
TAPI applications, 597-598
Voice Command Callback, 448-449
Voice Text Callback, 452-453
confirming TAPI versions, 689-696

connecting
lineMakeCall function, phones, 636
Register method, TTS engine, 472-473
SR engine, Register method, 490
Consensys Web site, 1022
consonants, International Phonetic Alphabet (IPA), 528-530
context-free grammars, 516
alt() rule, utilizing, 518
compiling, 521-527
creating, 521-527
elements
lists, 432-433
rules, 432-433
words, 432-433
loading, 526
opt() rule, utilizing, 519
overview, 516-517
rep() rule, utilizing, 519-520
rules, defining, 432-433, 518
run-time lists, 520-521
seq() rule, 518-519
speech recognition, grammar rules, 431-432
testing, 526
words, defining, 517
context maps (Exchange Client extensions)
ADDRBOOK, 377
ADVANCED CRITERIA, 377
PROPERTY SHEETS, 377
READNOTE MESSAGE, 377

READPOST MESSAGE, 377
READREPORT MESSAGE, 377
REMOTE VIEWER, 377
SEARCHVIEWER, 377
SENDNOTE MESSAGE, 377
SENDREPOST MESSAGE, 377
SENDRESEND MESSAGE, 377
SESSION, 377
TASK, 376
VIEWER, 377
continuous speech
word selection, 460-462
word separation methods, 425-426
control arrays
MAPI Email Agent
Add Rule form, 327-332
Main form, 316-327
Setup form, 332-341
TeleBook application, 766-772
control buttons
placing in TAPILINE form, 680-685
TAPIANS form, 729-731
control events (tmView form), 981-983
control messages, MAPI message types, 30-31
control parameters, modifying (TAPIFONE application), 781-782
control tags
audio output in TTS engines, 506-508

low-level TTS tags, 507-508
phrase modification tags, 507-508
voice character tags, 507-508
controlling
MAPIMessage control, e-mail, 134-143
message stores, properties, 51-52
MLM, ASCII text, 228-229
SendMail routine, schedule control file, 236
ControlsEdit routine, 230
ControlsLoad routine, 228-229
ConversationID (MAPIMessage), 94
ConversationIndex (Message object property), 185-189
ConversationIndex property, 262-263
ConversationTopic (Message object property), 186-189
ConversationTopic property, 262-263
Copy command (Edit menu), 103
Count (Attachments collection object property), 209
Count (InfoStore Collection property), 171
Count (Recipients collection object property), 195-196

creating
  C++
    SR applications,
    541-561
    TTS applications,
    534-541
  context free grammars,
    521-527
  EFD
    Post forms, 58
    Send forms, 58
  Exchange Client property
    pages, 382
  Exchange Client exten-
    sions, 375-376
  folders, 81-82
  Forms Designer Wizard
    forms, 61
    Post form, 61
    Send form, 61
  frmTAPI base controls,
    788-790
  mail-aware applications,
    121
  MAPI Email Agent
    control file, 314-315
    initialization routines,
    341-351
    list-handling routines,
    351-358
    message processing
    routines, 358-369
  MAPIMessage control,
    e-mail attachments,
    141-142
  Message Signing exten-
    sion, 387
  message stores, folders,
    51-52
  posts, folders, 85-86
  QikDial application in
    Excel, 749-752
  SR engine, menu object,
    491-494

TAPI dialer, 636-650
TAPI Dialog Utility,
  704-711
TAPIANS project,
  728-743
TeleBook application,
  class module, 753-756
VBVoice, voice files,
  867-868
Voice Command object,
  489-490
Voice Menu object list
  commands, 500-502
Voice Workbench
  subroutine templates,
  858-859
Creative Labs Phone
Blaster, 658
Credit Card section
  calling card settings,
    testing, 722-723
  card entry parameters,
    721-723
  TELEPHON.INI,
    720-723
  telephone credit cards,
    storing, 720-723
Cruiser, 1055
Ctx tag
  message context, setting,
    509-510
  parameters, 509-510
  voice character tags,
    509-510
CurrentUser (Session
Object property),
168-170
Custom Controls com-
mand (Tools menu),
132, 665
Cypress Research Corp.
Web site, 1046

D

database engine routines
(Voice Phone project),
934-938
database search tools,
34-35
databases, attaching text
messages, 30
DateReceived
(MAPIMessage), 94
DAX Systems, Inc. Web
site, 1046
DbList1_DblClick event
(frmTAPI), 820
DBS TAPI Box, 1061
deallocating idle calls
(TAPI), 694-696
declaration code, adding to
libTAPI module, 782
declaring
  DLL functions,
    TAPILINE controls,
    669-670
  FaxBack form, form-level
    variables, 914-918
  TeleBook application,
    form-level variables,
    762-766
DECtalk SDK for
Win 95, 1037
defining
  context free grammars
    rules, 518
    words, 517
  SR engine rules, 518
Delete (AddressEntry
object method), 203
Delete (Attachment object
method), 212
Delete (Attachments
collection object
method), 209

Delete (Message object method), 184-185

Delete (Messages collection object method), 181

Delete (Recipient object method), 198

Delete (Recipients collection object method), 195

Delete method (MAPIMessage control), 137-138

Deleted (MAPI storage folders), 45-47

DeleteRec routine (Voice Phone project), 938

DeleteRule routine, 356

deleting
  MLM subscribers, 247
  Talk Mail project messages, 1007

Deliver Now Using command (Tools menu), 79

delivering message attachments, 44-45

DeliveryReceipt (Message object property), 186-189

designer notes, adding to forms, 75

Designer Notes command (Help menu), 75

designing
  About dialog box, 834-836
  applications, 886-889
    Assisted TAPI versus Full TAPI, 890-891
    MAPI versus Comm API services, 889-890
    native API versus third-party tools, 888
    rules of complexity, 887

SAPI services, 891-892
standalone versus extensions, 888-889

Call dialog box, 828-833

Call Log page (frmTAPI), 803-806

Dial Pad page (frmTAPI), 790-797

EFD folder views, 58

FaxBack form, 904-910

FaxBack project, About dialog box, 918-920

folders overview, 80-81

Lines page (frmTAPI), 806-807

MAPI Client application forms, 143-147

MAPI Email Agent, 312-313

Phone Book page (frmTAPI), 797-803

Setup page (frmTAPI), 808-810

SR interfaces, 464-465

Talk Mail project, considerations, 960-961

TAPIFONE application, 780-782

TAPILINE form, 680-685

tmNew form, 983-988

tmRead form, 995-1000

tmView form, 969-971

TTS interfaces, 466-467

VAbout form, 954-955

VHelp form, 953-954

voice command menus, 465-466

Vphone form, 939-942

VPhone project, 949-951

Details (AddressEntry object method), 203

developing
  MAPI applications, 58
  MLM schedule, 233
  speech recognition, 424-425

Dial Pad page
  controls, placing, 790-797
  frmTAPI
    designing, 790-797
    tabbed dialog boxes, 788

Dialing Properties dialog box, 699-701, 719

dialing rules
  dialable digits, 721-723
  insertion codes, 721-723
  Location section, 716-720
  pauses, 721-723

dialog boxes
  About, 698-701
  About Box, 438, 440
  AddressEntry Details, 206
  Advanced Filter, 85
  coding TAPI, 700-701
  Columns, 83
  Command Verification, 438-439
  Dialing Properties, 699-701, 719
  displaying TAPI, 697-701
  Field Properties, 66-67
  Folder Properties, 85
  Forms Manager, 87
  General Dialog, 438, 440
  Group By, 83
  Lexicon Dialog, 438, 440
  Line Configuration, 698-701
  MAPI Send, 191

Microsoft Exchange
  compose, 157
  Provider Configuration,
  698-701
  References, 925
  Select Phrase, 912
  Send Note, 116
  Set Library To, 87
  TAPIANS, 743
  Translate Dialog, 440
  Views, 83
  Window Properties, 75
dialogs command interface,
437-438
Dialogs interface, Voice
Text object, 439-440
Diamond Telecommander
658, 2500
Dianatel Corporation Web
site, 1047
dictation grammars, 516
  elements
    common, 433
    group, 433
    sample, 433
    topic, 433
  importance of vocabulary
    database, 433
  speech recognition,
    grammar rules,
    431-432
Digital lines, 602
  E1 lines, 604
  ISDN, 602
  T1, 602
    dedicated data
      tramissions, 604
    telephone line
      services, 604
Digital Systems Interna-
tional Web Site, 1047
diphone concatenation
  overview, 431
  TTS technology, 463

discrete speech
  word selection, 460-462
  word separation methods,
    425-426
discussion groups
  ConversationIndex
    property, 262-263
  ConversationTopic
    property, 262-263
  MAPIPost Code Library
    module, 266-279
  message destinations,
    folders, 261
  topics, tracking, 261-263
  Update method,
    263-265
  versus e-mail, 260-261
discussion tools
  building OLE Messaging
    library (OML),
    265-266
  loading, 307-308
  testing, 307-308
disks, saving message
attachments, 217-218
displaying TAPI
  call information,
    696-697
  dialog boxes, 697-701
DisplayType
(AddressEntry object
property), 204
DisplayType (Recipient
object property), 199
DLL functions, declaring,
669-670
DoAction routine,
363-364
DownloadMail property
(MAPISession control),
132-134
Dragonsys Web site, 1031
dropping active call
(TAPI), 694-696

DSP (digital signal
processor) card, 459-460
Dynamic Link Libraries
(DLLs), creating,
375-376
dynamic link library
(DLL)
  Client API, 15-16
  Server SPI, 15-16

E

e-mail
  accounts processing,
    254-258
  BCC (blind courtesy
    copies), 32
  CC (courtesy copies), 32
  client services, 31-32
  controlling, 134-143
  creating attachments,
    141-142
  EFD overview, 58-60
  MAPI client applications,
    31-32
  MAPIFindNext, search-
    ing, 116-121
  MAPIReadMail, reading,
    116-121
  MAPISendDocuments,
    sending, 111-113
  MAPISendMail, compos-
    ing, 113-116
  send method, 263-265
  versus discussion groups,
    260-261
Earthlink Web site, 1033
EasySpeak, 1056
Edit menu commands
  Copy, 103
  Paste, 103
edit routines, coding MLM
forms, 230-235

editing MLM archives, 234

EditRec routine (Voice Phone project), 937

EFD (Exchange Forms Designer)
folder views, designing, 58-59
forms, installing, 77-78
interaction with Visual Basic, 59-60
launching, 60-61
MAPI applications, developing, 58
overview, 58-60
Post forms, creating, 58
QuickHelp feature, 59
Send forms, creating, 58

EIDSize (MAPIRecip), 95

electronic forms applications, message-enabled, 33-35

EMJ Data Systems Web site, 1047

Emp tag
phrase modification tag, 512
word emphasis, adding, 512-513

Enabled property
setting TTS engine, 473
Voice Text object, 451-452

enabling TTS engine (Speak method), 474-480

Encrypted (Message object property), 186-189

Eng tag, low-level TTS control tags, 515-516

EntryID (MAPIRecip), 95

ErrMsg function, LibTalkMail module, 968-969

ErrMsgBox routine, 403-405

ESS technology sound cards, 459-460

establishing
applications, Voice Text Callbacks, 452-453
context-free grammar rules, 432-433
Visual Basic
links with server, 131
SR callback, 499-500
TTS callback, 486-489
Voice Command object, notification callback, 438-439

Excel
creating QikDial application, 749-752
MAPI services, adding, 121-123
outbound dialing, adding, 749-752
TAPI declarations, adding, 750-752
tapiRequestMakeCall, 750-752

Exchange Client extensions
advantages
coding, 376
compatibility of extensions, 376
portability of extensions, 376
context maps
ADDRBOOK, 377
ADVANCED CRITERIA, 377
PROPERTY SHEETS, 377
READNOTE MESSAGE, 377
READPOST MESSAGE, 377
READREPORT MESSAGE, 377
REMOTE VIEWER, 377
SEARCH VIEWER, 377
SENDNOTE MESSAGE, 377
SENDPOST MESSAGE, 377
SENDRESEND MESSAGE, 377
SESSION, 377
TASK, 376
VIEWER, 377
defined, 374-375
Dynamic Link Libraries (DLLs), creating, 375-376
process overview, 375-376
registering, 383-386
registration parameters, 384-386

Exchange COM interfaces
IExchExt:Iunknown, 378
IExchExtAdvanced Criteria, 378
IExchExtAttachedFile Events, 378
IExchExtCallBack, 378
IExchExtCommands, 378
IExchExtMessage Events, 379
IExchExtProperty Sheets, 379
IExchExtSession Event, 379
IExchExtUserEvents, 379
mapping Exchange Client contexts, 379-381

Exchange Forms Designer, *see* **EFD**

Execudex, 1056

existing applications, adding MAPI services, 121-123

ExportLog routine (frmTAPI), 826-827

Extended Telephony
API calls, 630
overview, 630
TAPI model, 630

extensions
registering(Exchange Client), 383-386
registration parameters (Exchange Client), 384-386
versus standalones, 888-889

F

F. F. Tronixs Web site, 1047

fast-forwarding method, TTS engine, 483-485

FastCall, 1055

FaxBack form
AcceptCall_Disconnect event, 916
cmdFax_Click event, 915
coding, 914-918
designing, 904-910
form controls, 904-910
form-level variables, declaring, 914-918
Form_Load event, 914
Form_Unload event, 915
VerifyFile_Enter event, 917

FaxBack module
CenterForm routine, 901
FileExists function, 900-901

project-level variables, adding, 900

SendSMAPIFax routine, 902-903

SMAPIEnd routine, 902

SMAPIStart routine, 901

FaxBack project
About dialog box, designing, 918-920
launching, 899
project resources, 896-898
testing, 920-921
VBVoice control properties, setting, 911-914

Fetch method (MAPIMessage control), 137-138

FetchMsgType property (MAPIMessage control), 139-141

FetchSorted property (MAPIMessage control), 139-141

FetchUnreadOnly property (MAPIMessage control), 139-141

Field Properties dialog box, 66-67

field-level help, adding to forms, 76

fields, adding to forms (Forms Designer Wizard), 65-66

Fields (AddressEntry object property), 204

Fields (Folder object property), 178

Fields (Message object property), 186-189

File menu commands
Install, 77
Properties, 82

Scan InBox, 1007

Send Messages, 1007

file transfer routines, 34-35

FileCount (MAPI Message), 94

FileExists function, adding (FaxBack module), 900-901

FileName (MAPIFile), 97

FileType (MAPIFile), 97

FillCallParams routine (TAPILINE form), 687

FillList routine, 351-352

FillOutline routine, 274-275

filtering criteria, setting for messages, 84-85

FindArc routine, 252

FindSubject function, LibTalkMail module, 967

Firstbyte Web site, 1031

Flags (MAPIFile), 96

Flags (MAPIMessage), 94

flat-table discussion tools, 261-263

FlexVISE, 1036

Folder objects
InBox, 180
OutBox, 180
properties
Application, 177-178
Class, 177-178
Fields, 178
FolderID, 178
Folders, 178
ID, 178
Messages, 178
Name, 178
StoreID, 178-181

Folder Properties dialog box, 85

FolderID (Folder object property), 46-47, 178

FolderID (Message object property), 186-189
FolderProps routine, 179-180
folders
configuring MAPI
Email Agent, 369
creating, 81-82
message stores, 51-52
posts, 85-86
design overview, 80-81
designing views with
EFD, 58
discussion groups,
message destinations,
261-262
installing forms, 87-89
message destinations,
261-262
Update method, mes-
sages, 263-265
views
setting, 82-85
testing, 85-86
**Folders (Folder object
property), 178**
Folders collection object
methods
GetFirst, 175
GetLast, 175
GetNext, 175
GetPrevious, 175-178
properties
Application, 175
Class, 175
**FoldersColl routine,
176-177**
form event code
adding to TAPILINE
form, 688-689
Form_Load event code,
688-689
Form_Unload event
code, 688-689
tmView form, 974

**form-level help,
adding, 75**
**form-level routines, coding
(frmTAPI), 812-815**
**form-level variables,
declaring**
FaxBack form, 914-918
TeleBook application,
762-766
**Form_Activate event (VRec
form), 951-952**
**Form_Load code, adding
(MAPI E-Mail Agent),
324**
Form_Load event
Faxback form, 914
TAPIANS form,
732-741
TeleBook application,
763-766
tmNew form, 989-990
tmRead form,
1001-1002
tmView form, 974
VHelp form, 954
VPhone form, 944-945
VRec form, 951-952
Form_Load event code
About dialog box, 836
Call dialog box, 832
form event code,
688-689
MAPIMAIN.FRM, 152
MAPIREAD.FRM, 156
Form_Resize event
adding MAPI E-Mail
Agent, 324
MAPIMAIN.FRM, 152
TeleBook application,
763-766
tmView form, 974
Form_Unload event
FaxBack form, 915
MAPIMAIN.FRM, 152

TAPIANS form,
732-741
tmNew form, 990
tmRead form, 1002
VPhone form, 945
**Format tab (Field Proper-
ties dialog box), 66**
**formatted documents,
MAPI message types, 30**
forms
creating with Forms
Designer Wizard, 61
designer notes,
adding, 75
designing MAPI Client
applications, 143-147
field-level help,
adding, 76
folders, installing, 87-89
form-level help,
adding, 75
installing EFD, 77-78
naming with Forms
Designer Wizard,
63-64
online help, adding,
75-76
selecting, 78-80
sending, 78-80
support routines,
228-230
window properties,
setting, 68-75
windows-level help,
adding, 75-76
**Forms Design Wizard
command (Application
Design menu), 60-61**
Forms Designer Wizard
forms
adding fields, 65-66
creating, 61
naming, 63-64

initiating forms,
building, 62
Post form, creating, 61
response forms, building,
62-63
Send form, creating, 61
single-window forms,
selecting, 63
two-window forms,
selecting, 63
**Forms Manager dialog
box, 87**
**Forms Properties com-
mand (View menu), 74**
**Forward method
(MAPIMessage control),
136-138**
FreePages, 383-385
**frmNote controls,
291-298**
frmTAPI
About dialog box,
828-836
base controls, creating,
788-790
Call dialog box, 828-836
coding, 812-828
designing
Call Log page,
803-806
Dial Pad page,
790-797
Lines page, 806-807
Phone Book page,
797-803
Setup page, 808-810
form-level routines,
coding, 812-815
laying out, 788-810
menu-level routines
coding, 815-817
mnuConfItem_Click
event, 816

mnuFileExit_Click
event, 816
mnuHelpAbout_Click
event, 816
menus, adding, 810-812
page-level routines
cmdButtons_Click
event, 817-818
cmdData_Click event,
819-820
cmdDialPad_Click
event, 818
coding, 817-822
DbList1_DblClick
event, 820
support routines
ClearLog routine,
825-826
coding, 822-827
ExportLog routine,
826-827
InitDB routine, 824
LineMonitor
function, 827
LoadDevices
routine, 823
LoadImages
routine, 822
MakeDB routine, 825
ReadStartUp
routine, 823
tabbed dialog boxes
Call Log page, 788
Dial Pad page, 788
Lines page, 788
Phone Book page, 788
Setup page, 788
TAPIFONE application,
780-782, 788
**frmVPhone (TAPIFONE
application), 780-782**
**Full TAPI versus Assisted
TAPI, designing applica-
tions, 890-891**

functions
adding CallBack mod-
ules, 928-931
CallState message,
677-678
Clean, 678-679
ErrMsg, 968-969
FileExists, 900-901
FindSubject, 967
GetOffset, 679
GetRecipients, 968
initTAPI, 783-784
lineMakeCall, 636
LineMonitor, 827
lineNegotiateAPI
Version, 635
LookUp, 938
MAPIAddress, 105-107
MAPIDetails, 109-111
MAPIErr, 100-102
MAPIFindNext,
116-121
MAPILogOff, 102-104
MAPILogon, 102-104
MAPIReadMail,
116-121
MAPIResolveName,
107-109
MAPISendDocuments,
111-113
MAPISendMail,
113-116
PlaceCall, 644-645
ReadLineDevCaps, 784
TAPICallBackHandler,
676-677
TAPIDial, 785
TAPIGetLocation, 927
tapiGetLocation
Info, 746
TAPIMakeCall, 928
tapiRequestMake
Call, 746

G

GatheredDigits
(TAPILINE.OCX
properties), 668
General Dialog dialog box,
438-440
General tab (Field Proper-
ties dialog box), 66
Genesys T-Server, 1062
Genesys Web site, 1048
GET YYMMDD com-
mand, 240-243
GetAddressEntry (Session
Object method), 163
GetFaxAddress
GatherDigits control,
setting (VBVoice control
properties), 912
GetFaxFile GatherDigits
control, setting (VBVoice
control properties), 913
GetFirst (Folders collection
object method), 175
GetFirst (Messages
collection object
method), 181
GetFolder (Session Object
method), 163
GetFolderRec function,
271-279
GetInfoStore (Session
Object method), 163
GetLast (Folders collection
object method), 175
GetLast (Messages collec-
tion object method), 181
GetMaxPageCount, 383
GetMessage (Session
Object method)s, 163
GetMsgRec function, 274
GetNext (Folders collec-
tion object method), 175

GetNext (Messages
collection object
method), 181
GetOffset function
code, 679
TAPICALL.BAS, 679
GetPages, 383
GetPrevious (Folders
collection object
method), 175-178
GetPrevious (Messages
collection object
method), 181
GetRecipients function,
LibTalkMail module, 968
GetVarInfo routine
(TAPILINE form), 686
global constants (SMAPI),
99-100
global variables
SR services, coding, 565
TTS services, coding,
565
Grammar object interfaces
ISRGramCFG, 443-444
ISRGramCommon,
443-444
ISRGramDictation,
443-444
grammar rules
context-free grammars,
516-517
speech recognition,
431-432
dictation grammars, 516
speech recognition,
431-432
limited domain gram-
mars, 516
speech recognition,
431-432
SR engine, 516
graphics, attaching to text
messages, 30
Group By dialog box, 83

H

HandleOpen routine
(tmNew form), 990-991
HandleToCall
(TAPILINE.OCX
properties), 668
HandleToConfCall
(TAPILINE.OCX
properties), 668
HandleToConsultCall
(TAPILINE.OCX
properties), 668
handling
Inbox routines, messages,
240-243
TAPI inbound calls,
726-728
HandOffPriorities
automatedvoice,
714-715
datamodem, 714-715
interactivevoice, 714-715
RequestMakeCall,
714-715
TELEPHON.INI file,
714-715
handshaking,
modems, 655
HangUp OnHook control,
setting (VBVoice control
properties), 913-914
hardware
DSP (digital signal
processor) card,
459-460
microphones, 459-460
multifunction cards,
459-460
prerequisites
FaxBack project,
896-898
Talk Mail project, 960
Voice Phone
project, 925

SAPI overview, 456
SAPI requirements, 457
SAPI resources,
    1034-1039
sound cards, 459-460
speakers, 459-460
system requirements, 7-8
TAPI resources,
    1054-1062
telephony overview, 654
**Harris Optic Service
Provider, 1060**
**Help menu commands,
Designer Notes, 75**
High-level SAPI
architecture, 436
OLE automation,
    446-447
overview, 436
Voice Command object
    overview, 437
Voice Text object,
    439-440
High-level SAPI, *see also*
SAPI
Homnick Web site, 1022
**Hongkong Telecom Web
site, 1048**
**hWndMenu property
(OLE Voice Menu
object), 450**

I

**ID (AddressEntry object
property), 204**
**ID (Folder object prop-
erty), 178**
**ID (InfoStore Object
property), 173-174**
**ID (Message object
property), 186-189**

**idle calls, deallocating,
694-696**
IExchExt:Iunknown, 378
**IExchExtAdvanced
Criteria, 378**
**IExchExtAttachedFile
Events, 378**
IExchExtCallBack, 378
IExchExtCommands, 378
**IExchExtMessage
Events, 379**
methods
    OnCheckNames, 381
    *OnCheckNames
        Complete, 381*
    OnRead, 381
    OnReadComplete, 381
    OnSubmit, 381
    *OnSubmit
        Complete, 381*
    OnWrite, 381
    *OnWriteComplete,
        381-382*
**IExchExtProperty
Sheets, 379**
methods
    FreePages, 383-385
    *GetMaxPageCount,
        383-384*
    GetPages, 383
**IExchExtSession
Event, 379**
IExchExtUserEvents, 379
**Importance (Message
object property),
187-189**
inbound calls
handling TAPI, 726-728
TAPIANS project,
    728-743
    testing, 741-743
**Inbox (MAPI storage
folders), 45-47**
**Inbox (Session Object
property), 168-170**

Inbox routines
coding, 240-243
GET YYMMDD
    command, 240-243
LIST command,
    240-243
messages, handling,
    240-243
SUB command, 240-243
UNSUB command,
    240-243
**Index (Attachment object
property), 213**
**Index (InfoStore Object
property), 173-174**
**Index (Recipient object
property), 199**
Inforamp Web site, 1030
InfoStore Collection
properties, 170-171
    Application, 171
    Class, 171
    Count, 171
    Item, 171
**InfoStore Object proper-
ties**
Application, 173-174
Class, 173-174
ID, 173-174
Index, 173-174
ProviderName, 173-174
RootFolder, 173-174
**InfoStoreProps
routine, 174**
**InfoStores (Session Object
property), 168-170**
**INIActions routine,
adding, 349-350**
**initiating forms, building
(Forms Designer Wiz-
ard), 62**
**INIGeneral routine,
adding, 346-347**
**INIRegSetting function,
adding, 347-348**

INIRules routine, 349
InitDB routine
    adding to Voice Phone
        project, 934-935
    frmTAPI support
        routines, 824
INITests routine, adding,
    349-350
initial declarations,
    TAPIOUT project,
    637-638
initial header file
    building, Message
        Signing extension,
        387-390
    CDGEXT32.H,
        387-390
Initial Value tab (Field
    Properties dialog
    box), 67
initialization routines,
    creating (MAPI E-Mail
    Agent), 341-351
initializing TAPI sessions,
    688-689
InitSAPI routine, 567
InitStuff routine, 344
initTAPI function, adding
    (libTAPI module),
    783-784
InitVCmd routine, adding
    (Voice Phone project),
    931-932
InitVoice routine, 568
InitVText routine, 569
InitVTxt routine, adding
    (Voice Phone project),
    933-934
input recognition, SR
    technology limitations,
    462-463
Insert menu commands
    Class Module, 499, 928
    Module, 267, 747

Insert Module icon, 749
inserting libTAPI module,
    782-787
insertion codes, TAPI
    dialing rules, 721-723
Install command (File
    menu), 77
installing
    EFD forms, 77-78
    forms to folders, 87-89
    MAPI E-mail Agent, 369
    Message Signing exten-
        sion, 408-409
    TAPILINE control,
        664-666
Integrated Services Digital
    Network, see ISDN
Intellect, 1055
International Phonetic
    Alphabet (IPA)
    phonemes, 430
    Pulmonic obstruents,
        530
    Pulmonic resonants, 530
    rounded vowels, 530
    unicode values, 528-530
    unrounded vowels, 530
interpreting audio with SR
    engines, 516
ISDN (Integrated Services
    Digital Network)
    Basic Rate Interface,
        604-605
    Primary Rate Interface,
        605
    TAPI functions, 602
    telephone line services,
        604-605
Islandnet Web site, 1023
IsoEthernet PC ISA Bus
    Adapter, 1061
ISRAttributes interface (SR
    Engine Object), 443
ISRCentral interface (SR
    Engine Object), 442-443

ISRDialogs interface (SR
    Engine Object), 443
ISREnum interface (SR
    Engine Enumerator
    object), 442
ISRFind interface (SR
    Engine Enumerator
    object), 442
ISRGramCFG interface
    (Grammar object),
    443-444
ISRGramCommon
    interfaces (Grammar
    object), 443-444
ISRGramDictation
    interface (Grammar
    object), 443-444
ISRLexPronounce interface
    (SR Engine Object), 443
ISRResAudio interface
    (Results object), 444-445
ISRResBasic interface (SR
    Results object), 444-445
ISRResCorrection interface
    (Results object), 444-445
ISRResEval interfaces
    (Results object) 444-445
ISRResGraph interface
    (Results object), 444-445
ISRResMemory interface
    (Results object), 445
ISRResMerge interface
    (Result object), 445
ISRResModifyGUI
    interface (Results
    object), 445
ISRResSpeaker interface
    (Results object), 444-445
ISRSharing interface (SR
    Sharing object), 442
ISRSpeaker interface (SR
    Engine Object), 443
IsSpeaking property
    TTS status reports,
        obtaining, 485-486
    Voice Text object, 452

Item (Attachments collection object property), 209-212

Item (InfoStore Collection property), 171

Item (Recipients collection object property), 195

ITTSAttributes interface (TTS Engine object), 446

ITTSBufNotifysink (TTS Engine object), 446

ITTSCentral interface (TTS Engine object), 446

ITTSDialogs interface (TTS Engine object), 446

ITTSEnum interface (TTS Engine Enumerator object), 445-446

ITTSFind interface (TTS Engine Enumerator object), 445-446

ITTSNotifySink (TTS Engine object), 446

J - K

Kolvax Web site, 1032
Kurzweil VOICE for Windows, 1035

L

L R Technologies Web site, 1023

language constants, setting (SR engines), 492-494

launching
EFD, 60-61
FaxBack project, 899
MAPI Client application, 157-158

MAPI Email Agent, 371

Message Signing extension, 409-410

Talk Mail project, 1005-1007

TAPI lineInitialize routine, 634-635

TAPIFONE application, 836-838

TeleBook application, 776-777

Voice Phone project, 957-958

laying out
About dialog box, 305-307
frmTAPI, 788-810
MAPIMAIN.FRM, 144-147
MAPIREAD.FRM, 147-148
MDI Discuss form, 279-285
MDI frmNote, 291-298
MDI Msgs form, 289-291
MDI Options form, 298-304
Message Signing extensions, 405-409
MLM form, 222-225
TAPI Dialog Utility, 704-707
TAPIANS form, 729-731
VPhone form, 943-944

leveraging WOSA applications, 19-20

Lexicon Dialog dialog box, 438-440

library modules, coding (Voice Phone project), 925-930

LibTalkMail module
coding Talk Mail project, 962-969
ErrMsg function, 968-969
FindSubject function, 967
GetRecipients function, 968
MAPIAddrBook routine, 964
MAPIDeleteMsg routine, 964-965
MAPIEnd routine, 964
MAPINewMsg routine, 965
MAPIReadMsg routine, 965
MAPISendMsg routine, 966
MAPIStart routine, 963

libTAPI module
declaration code, adding, 782
initTAPI function, 783-784
inserting, 782-787
ReadLineDevCaps function, 784
SetCallParams routine, 785-786
TAPIClearHandles routine, 787
TAPIDial function, 785
TAPIFONE application, 781-782
TAPIHangUp routine, 787
TAPIPlaceCall routine, 786-787
TAPIShutdown routine, 787

LibVPhone module, project-level declarations, 930-931

License Service Application
Program Interface
(LSAPI), 17
limited domain grammars,
516-517
elements
group, 434
sample, 434
words, 434
speech recognition,
grammar rules,
431-432
Line Configuration dialog
box, 698-701
line devices
datalinks, 595-596
fax, 595-596
HandOffPriorities section
(TELEPHON.INI),
714-715
obtaining TAPI,
690-696
voice, 595-596
Line Translate Dialog
option button, 719
LINE_CALLSTATE
messages (TAPIANS
project), 743
LineApp (TAPILINE.OCX
properties), 668
lineCallBackProc routine
(TAPIOUT project),
647-651
LINECALLSTATE_
CONNECTED messages
(TAPIANS project), 743
LineHandle
(TAPILINE.OCX
properties), 668
lineInitialize routine,
starting TAPI, 634-635
lineMakeCall function,
phones, connecting, 636
LineMonitor function
(frmTAPI), 827

lineNegotiateAPIVersion
function, verifying
TAPI, 635
lineOpen function
lines, locating, 635
locating line for
TAPI, 635
Lines page
controls, placing,
806-807
frmTAPI
designing, 806-807
tabbed dialog
boxes, 788
linking voice strings (Voice
Workbench), 857-858
LIST command, Inbox
routines, 240-243
list commands, creating
(Voice Menu object),
500-502
list-handling routines
(MAPI E-Mail Agent),
351-358
List1_DblClick event
(VPhone form), 948
listing MLM archives,
249-251
ListSet method (OLE
Voice Menu object), 450
LoadDevices routine
(frmTAPI), 823
LoadFolders routine
(frmTAPI), 270
LoadImages routine
(frmTAPI), 822
loading
context free
grammars, 526
discussion tools, 307-308
Visual Basic Voice
Command object,
489-490
Visual Basic Object
browser, 470-472

LoadList routine (VPhone
form), 946
LoadLists routine, 351
LoadMsgRec routine, 288
LoadMsgs routine, adding
(Voice Phone
project), 934
LoadNameList routine,
adding (Voice Phone
project), 933
LoadReader routine,
coding
(MAPIREAD.FRM), 156
LoadRec support routine
(TeleBook application),
775-776
LoadStrings routine, 345
LocalGetLineInfo routine
(TAPILINE form), 687
locating
lineOpen function,
lines, 635
SMAPI directory, 92-93
TAPI line, lineOpen
function, 635
Location section
entry parameters,
717-720
modifying, 718-720
TELEPHON.INI file,
716-720
workstation dialing rules,
716-720
logging off MAPI,
102-104
logging on MAPI,
102-104
Logicode 14.4 PCM
CIA, 658
Logoff (Session Object
method), 163-165
Logon (Session Object
method), 163-165
Logon method, session
automation, 167-168

LogonUI property (MAPISession control), 133-134
LogWrite routine, 357
LookUp function, adding (Voice Phone project), 938
Low-level SAPI
architecture, 440-446
overview, 436, 440-441
Speech Recognition object, 441
TTS Engine object, 445
see also SAPI
low-level TTS control tags
Com tag, 514-516
Eng tag, 515-516
Mrk tag, 515-516
Prn tag, 515-516
Pro tag, 515-516
Prt tag, 515-516
low-level TTS tags, 507-508

M

mail-aware applications, creating, 121
Mailing List Manager, *see* **MLM**
mailing lists, subscribers, deleting, 247-249
Main DLL routines
CDGEXT32.CPP, 390-405
coding Message Signing extensions, 390-405
Main form
building MAPI Email Agent, 316-327
control arrays, MAPI Email Agent, 316-327

MainDialog
TAPI messages, posting, 643-644
TAPI messages, responding, 642-644
TAPI project, 639-644
MakeDB routine (frmTAPI), 825
MakeRule routine, 355-356
MakeTimeStamp routine, 275
MAPI (Messaging Application Programming Interface)
accessing services, SMAPI API calls, 97-100
adding services, SMAPI, 92-93
applications
electronic mail clients, 31-32
message aware, 32
message-enabled, 32-33
architectural overview, 26
architecture
client layer, 27-28
consistency, 28
flexbility, 27-28
MAPI DLL, 27-28
portability, 28-29
service layer, 27-28
availability on all Windows platforms, 28-29
clients, interchangeability of, 27-28
developer tools, 7-8
errors (MAPIErr function), 100-102
integration summary, 1010-1013
MAPI 1.0 API set, accessing, 7

MAPI OCX controls, accessing, 7-8
MAPILogOff, logging off, 102-104
MAPILogon, logging on, 102-104
message types
binary files, 30
control, 30-31
formatted documents, 30
text, 30
OLE Message Library, accessing, 7-8
overview, 4-9
primary functions, 29
reference resources
books, 1018-1021
CompuServe forums, 1024
Microsoft newsgroups, 1024-1025
Web, 1022-1024
servers, interchangeability of, 27-28
SMAPI API calls, 97-100
summary review, 412-420
text messages
ASCII text, 30
rich text format, 30
versus Comm API services, 889-890
MAPI 1.0 API set, 7
MAPI Address Book
accessing, 165-167
appearance, modifying, 167-168
MAPI addresses
properties
Address, 47-48
DisplayType, 47-48
Name, 47-48
Type, 47-48

MAPI Client
accessing storage folders, 46-47
addresses, 47-48
applications
building, 143-159
forms, designing, 143-147
implementing, 157-158
message object components, 39-45
Microsoft Exchange, 39
Microsoft Mail, 39
overview, 39-48
storage folders, 45-47
MAPI DLL architecture, 27-28
MAPI Email Agent
actions, 313-314
Add Rule form
building, 327-332
control arrays, 327-332
automatic forwarding, 313-314
automatic message copying, 313-314
automatic replies, 313-314
codes, adding, 316-341
comparisons, 313-314
control file, creating, 314-315
designing, 312-313
folders, configuring, 369
Form_Load code, adding, 324
Form_Resize event, adding, 324
initialization routines, creating, 341-351
installing, 369
launching, 371
list-handling routines, creating, 351-358

Main form
building, 316-327
control arrays, 316-327
message notification, 313-314
message processing routines, creating, 358-369
rules, adding, 370-371
Setup form
building, 332-341
control arrays, 332-341
support routines
coding, 341
Initialization, 341-351
List-Handling, 351-358
message processing, 358-369
testing, 369
tests, 313-314
timed scanning, 313-314
MAPI OCX controls, 7
MAPI Send dialog box, 191
MAPI Server
address books, 52-54
message stores, 51-52
message transport, 50
Microsoft Exchange Server, 48-50
Microsoft Mail Server, 48-50
overview, 48-54
peer-to-peer message servers, 49-50
MAPI services, adding
Excel, 121-123
existing applications, 121-123
Visual Basic 4.0, 123-127

MAPI Spooler
functional overview, 54-55
messages
retrieving, 54-55
routing, 54-55
MAPIAddrBook routine
adding, 166
LibTalkMail module, 964
MAPIAddress, address book entries, 105-107
MAPIAddress function, 105-107
MAPIDeleteMsg routine (LibTalkMail module), 964-965
MAPIDetails, recipients, inspecting, 109-111
MAPIDetails function, 109-111
MAPIEnd routine
adding, 165, 236
LibTalkMail module, 964
messages, processing, 236
MAPIErr function, 100-102
MAPIFetch routine, coding (MAPIMAIN.FRM), 150
MAPIFile
attached files, 96-97
FileName, 97
FileType, 97
Flags, 96
PathName, 97
Position, 96
structure, 96-97
MAPIFindNext, searching e-mail, 116-121
MAPIFindNext function, 116-121
MAPILogOff function, 102-104

MAPILogon function, 102-104

MAPIMAIN.FRM
AdjustForm routine, 148-149
Command1_Click event, 153-154
Form_Load(), 152
Form_Resize(), 152
Form_Unload, 152
laying out, 144-147
List1_DblClick(), 152
MAPIFetch routine, 150
MAPISave routine, 151
MAPIStart routine, 149

MAPIMessage
ConversationID, 94
DateReceived, 94
FileCount, 94
Flags, 94
message packets, 93-95
MessageType, 94
NoteText, 94
RecipCount, 94
structure, 93-95
Subject, 93

MAPIMessage control
AddressCaption property, 138-141
AddressEditFieldCount property, 138-141
AddressLabel property, 138-141
AddressModifiable property, 138-141
AddressResolveUI property, 139-141
AttachmentIndex property, 139-141
AttachmentName property, 139-141
AttachmentPathName property, 139-141
AttachmentPosition property, 139-141

AttachmentType property, 139-141
Compose method, 135-138
Delete method, 137-138
e-mail, controlling, 134-143
e-mail attachments, creating, 141-142
Fetch method, 137-138
FetchMsgType property, 139-141
FetchSorted property, 139-141
FetchUnreadOnly property, 139-141
Forward method, 136-138
methods, 134-135
MsgConversationID property, 139-141
MsgCount property, 139-141
MsgIndex property, 140-141
MsgNoteText property, 140-141
MsgOrigAddress property, 140-141
MsgOrigDisplayName property, 140-141
MsgRead property, 140-141
MsgReceiptRequested property, 140-141
MsgSent property, 140-141
MsgSubject property, 140-141
MsgType property, 140-141
properties, 138-141
RecipDisplayName property, 140-141

RecipIndex property, 140-141
RecipType property, 140-141
Reply method, 136-138
ReplyAll method, 136-138
Send method, 135-138
Show method, 138
Visual Basic, 134-143

MAPINewMsg routine (LibTalkMail module), 965

MAPIPost Code Library module, folder routines, 266-279

MAPIREAD.FRM
AdjustReader(), 155-156
Form_Load() 156
laying out, 147-148
LoadReader(), 156

MAPIReadMail function, 116-121

MAPIReadMsg routine (LibTalkMail module), 965

MAPIRecip
Address, 95
EIDSize, 95
EntryID, 95
message recipients, 95-96
RecipClass, 95
structure, 95-96

MAPIResolveName, recepients validation, 107-109

MAPIResolveName function, 107-109

MAPISave routine, coding (MAPIMAIN.FRM), 151

MAPIScanInBox code (tmView form), 982-983

MAPISendDocuments
exisiting applications,
adding MAPI services,
121-123
sending e-mail, 111-113
**MAPISendDocuments
function, 111-113**
**MAPISendMail function,
113-116**
**MAPISendMsg routine
(LibTalkMail
module), 966**
MAPISession control
Action property,
132-134
DownloadMail property,
132-134
LogonUI property,
133-134
methods
SignOff, 131-132
SignOn, 131-132
NewSession property,
133-134
Password property,
133-134
SessionID property, 134
UserName property,
133-134
Visual Basic, 131
MAPIStart routine
adding, 164-165,
235-236
coding
MAPIMAIN.FRM, 149
LibTalkMail
module, 963
messages, processing,
235-236
**mapping Exchange COM
interfaces, 379-381**
MCF40.DLL, 665-666

**MCIStart routine
(TAPIANS project),
735-736**
MDI Discuss form
coding, 285-288
controls, 279-285
laying out, 279-285
MDI frmNote
coding, 291-298
laying out, 291-298
MDI Msgs form
coding, 289-291
controls, 289-291
laying out, 289-291
MDI Options form
coding, 298-304
controls, 298-304
laying out, 298-304
**MDIForm_Activate
routine, 285-286**
**MDIForm_Load
routine, 285**
**MDIForm_Resize routine,
285-286**
**MDIForm_Unload
routine 286**
**Media Vision sound cards,
459-460**
Media-Tel, 1058
memory
SR requirements, 457
TTS requirements, 458
menu commands
recognizing SR engine,
497-499
responding,
CommandSpoken
property, 497-499
**menu objects, creating,
491-494**
**menu support routines,
coding (tmView form),
978-981**

menu-level routines
coding frmTAPI,
815-817
mnuConfItem_Click
event (frmTAPI), 816
mnuFileExit_Click event
(frmTAPI), 816
mnuHelpAbout_Click
event (frmTAPI), 816
**MenuCreate method
properties, 448**
menus
adding frmTAPI,
810-812
voice commands,
designing, 465-466
message attachments
delivery protocols, 44-45
disk, saving to , 217-218
Index, 44-45
Name, 44-45
Position, 44-45
Source, 44-45
Type, 44-45
**message aware applications
(MAPI), 32**
message body
ASCII text, 41-43
MAPI message objects,
41-43
rich text format, 41-43
**message filtering agents,
34-35**
message headers
DeliveryReceipt, 41
Importance, 41
MAPI message objects,
40-41
Recipients, 40
Sender, 40
Sent, 41
Signed, 41
Subject, 40
Submitted, 41

MAPI types
  binary files, 30
  control, 30-31
  formatted docu-
    ments, 30
  text, 30
phone devices (Supple-
  mental Telephony),
  628-629
processing
  MAPIEnd routine, 236
  MAPIStart routine,
    235-236
retrieving with MAPI
  Spooler, 54-55
rich text format, 30
routing with MAPI
  Spooler, 54-55
sending in Talk Mail
  project, 1006-1007
setting context, Ctx tag,
  509-510
Messages (Folder object
property), 178
Messages collection object
  methods
    Add, 181
    Delete, 181
    GetFirst, 181
    GetLast, 181
    GetNext, 181
    GetPrevious, 181
    Sort, 181-185
  properties
    Application, 181
    Class, 181
MessagesColl routine, 183
MessageType
(MAPIMessage), 94
Messaging Application
Programming Interface,
see **MAPI**

microphones
  directional, 459-460
  headset, 459-460
  lavaliered, 459-460
Microsoft Access 95, API
  development tools, 6-7
Microsoft Excel 95, API
  development tools, 6-7
Microsoft Exchange
  command (Programs
  menu), 60
Microsoft Exchange
  compose dialog box, 157
Microsoft Exchange Forms
  Designer, *see* **EFD**
Microsoft Exchange Forms
  Designer command,
  60-61
Microsoft Exchange menu
  commands, Microsoft
  Exchange Forms De-
  signer, 60-61
Microsoft Exchange
  Server, 7-8
Microsoft FoxPro, API
  development tools, 6-7
Microsoft Mail Server, 7
Microsoft Multimedia
  Communications Inter-
  face (MMCI), 5
Microsoft Phone
  announcement mail-
    boxes, adding, 871
  answering machine,
    configuring, 872-873
  AutoFax mailboxes,
    adding, 871
  combines MAPI, SAPI,
    TAPI, 869-870
  features, 869-870
  message mailboxes,
    adding, 871
Microsoft RPC (remote
  procedure calls), 17

Microsoft Visual Basic 4.0
  Professional Edition, API
  development tools, 6-7
Microsoft Web site, MAPI
  newsgroups, 1024
MLM (Mailing List
Manager)
  archives
    editing, 234
    listing, 249-251
    sending, 251-254
  ASCII text, controlling,
    228-229
  features, 222
  form, laying out,
    222-225
  forms, support routines,
    228-230
  requests, processing,
    254-258
  schedule, developing, 233
  subscriber files, build-
    ing, 232
  subscribers
    adding, 243-246
    deleting, 247
MLM forms, coding,
  230-235
MMControl1_StatusUpdate
  event (tmNew form),
  993-994
mnuConfItem_Click event
  (frmTAPI), 816
mnuFileExit_Click event
  (frmTAPI), 816
mnuFileItem_Click event
  tmNew form, 991-992
  tmRead form, 1003
  tmView form, 978-979
  VPhone form, 948
mnuHelpAbout_Click
  event (frmTAPI), 816
mnuHelpItem_Click event
  tmView form, 980
  VPhone form, 948

TimeReceived, 40
TimeSent, 40
Unread, 41
**message mailboxes, adding
(Microsoft Phone), 871**
Message objects
messages, adding,
191-194
attachments, 43-45
body, 41-43
components of MAPI
Client, 39-45
headers, 40-41
methods
Delete, 184-185
Options, 184-185
Send, 185
Update, 185-189
properties
Application, 185-189
Class, 185-189
*ConversationIndex,
185-189*
*ConversationTopic,
186-189*
*DeliveryReceipt,
186-189*
Encrypted, 186-189
Fields, 186-189
FolderID, 186-189
ID, 186-189
Importance, 187-189
ReadReceipt, 187-189
Recipients, 187-189
Sender, 187-189
Sent, 187-189
Signed, 188-189
Size, 188-189
StoreID, 188-189
Subject, 188-189
Submitted, 188-189
Text, 188-189
*TimeReceived,
188-189*

TimeSent, 188-189
Type, 188-189
Unread, 189-195
message packets, 93-95
**message processing
routines**
creating for MAPI Email
Agent, 358-369
MAPI Email Agent
support routines,
358-369
Message Signing extensions
creating, 387
initial header file,
building, 387-390
installing, 408-409
launching, 409-410
Main DLL routines,
coding, 390-405
Property Sheet dialog box
coding, 405-409
laying out, 405-409
testing, 408-409
message stores
folders, creating, 51-52
MAPI Server, 51-52
properties, controlling,
51-52
message transport
MAPI Server, 50
multiple formats, 50
**message-driven applica-
tions**
database search tools,
34-35
file transfer routines,
34-35
message filtering agents,
34-35
message-enabled, 33-35
**message-enabled applica-
tions**
electronic forms, 33-35
MAPI, 32-33
message-driven, 33-35

**MessageAdd routine,
192-194**
**MessageMake routine,
193-194**
**MessageProps routine,
190-191**
messages
adding asMessage objects,
191-194
attachments, adding,
215-216
BCC (blind courtesy
copies), 32
building
(ProcessSubListMsg
routine), 239-242
CC (courtesy copies), 32
deleting in Talk Mail
project, 1007
EFD overview, 58-60
events, monitoring,
381-382
filtering criteria, setting,
84-85
folder as destinations, 261
folders (Update method),
263-265
handling, Inbox routines,
240-243
line devices (Basic
Telephony), 616-620
MAPI consistency, 28
MAPI Email Agent
*automatic forwarding,
313-314*
*automatic message
copying, 313-314*
control file, 314-315
*message notification,
313-314*
tests, 313-314
*timed scanning,
313-314*

mnuMsgItem_Click event (tmView form), 979
mnuViewItem_Click event (tmView form), 979-980
modems
basic data, 656-657
handshaking, 655
processing data, TAPI, 655
Telephony Service Provider Interface (TSPI)
UniModem Driver, 655-656
UniModemV Driver, 655-656
voice data, 657-659
modifying
Location section, entry parameters, 718-720
MAPI Address Book appearance, 167
MAPIAddress, address book entries, 105-107
Pit tag, voice pitch, 513
Spd tag, audio playback speed, 513-514
TAPIFONE application control parameters, 781-782
TELEPHON.INI, 711-712
Module command (Insert menu), 267, 747
modules
libTAPI, 781-782
MAPIPost Code Library, 266-279
TAPICall, 781-782
TAPILine, 781-782
monitoring
messages, 381-382
TTS engine status, 485-486

Mrk tag, low-level TTS control tags, 515-516
MsgConversationID property (MAPIMessage control), 139-141
MsgCount property (MAPIMessage control), 139-141
MsgFwdReply routine, 365
MsgIndex function, 273
MsgIndex property (MAPIMessage control), 140-141
MsgMoveCopy routine, 366-367
MsgNoteText property (MAPIMessage control), 140-141
MsgNotify routine, 364
MsgOrigAddress property (MAPIMessage control), 140-141
MsgOrigDisplayName property (MAPIMessage control), 140-141
MsgPtr function, 273
MsgRead property (MAPIMessage control), 140-141
MsgReceiptRequested property (MAPIMessage control), 140-141
MsgSent property (MAPIMessage control), 140-141
MsgSubject property (MAPIMessage control), 140-141
MsgType property (MAPIMessage control), 140-141
MSVCRT40.DLL, 665-666

multifunction cards, 459-460
Multimedia Connect, 1058
multiple message transports, 50

N

Name
MAPI addresses properties, 47-48
storage folders properties, 46-47
Name (AddressEntry object property), 204
Name (Attachment object property), 213
Name (Folder object property), 178
Name (Recipient object property), 199
naming forms, 63-64
native API versus third-party tools, designing applications, 888
Neosoft Web site, 1022
NerwMsgRec routine, 287
netApp Systems Web site, 1023
Netgain Web site, 1023
New Forms command (Compose menu), 78, 87
New Post in this Folder command (compose menu), 85
NewSession property (MAPISession control), 133-134
Nokia TAPI Development Toolkit, 1062

non-threaded discussion tools, 261-263
NoteText (MAPI Message), 94
notification callbacks
establishing Voice Command object, 438-439
ITTSBufNotifysink (TTS Engine object), 446
ITTSNotifySink (TTS Engine object), 446
NumberOfRings (TAPILINE.OCX properties), 668
NumDevices (TAPILINE.OCX properties), 668

O

Object Linking and Embedding, *see* **OLE**
obtaining
IsSpeaking property, TTS status reports, 485-486
TAPI line devices, 690-696
OLE Automation
High-level SAPI, 446-447
OLE Voice Command object, 447-448
OLE Voice Menu object, 447-448
OLE Messaging Library, 7
discussion tools, building, 265-266
Session Object methods, 162-163
storage folder properties, 46-47

OLE Voice Command object
properties
Awake property, 448
CallBack property, 448
CommandSpoken property, 448
MenuCreate method, 448
Register method, 448
OLE Voice Command Object Library, 489
OLE Voice Menu object
properties
Active property, 450
Add method, 450
hWndMenu property, 450
ListSet method, 450
Remove method, 450
OLE Voice Text Library, 470
OLE Voice Text Object
loading Visual Basic Object browser, 470-472
Visual Basic, adding, 470-489
OLEMAPIEnd routine, 268
OLEMAPIGetMsgs routine, 271-273
OLEMAPIPostMsg routine, 276-277
OLEMAPIReplyMsg routine, 277-278
OLEMAPIStart routine, 268
OnCheckNames (IExchExtMessage Events), 381
OnCheckNamesComplete (IExchExtMessage Events), 381
online help, adding, 75-76

OnRead (IExchExtMessage Events), 381
OnReadComplete (IExchExtMessage Events), 381
OnSubmit (IExchExtMessage Events), 381
OnSubmitComplete (IExchExtMessage Events), 381
OnWrite (IExchExtMessage Events), 381
OnWriteComplete (IExchExtMessage Events), 381-382
Open Database Connectivity (ODBC), 14-17
open lines, closing, 694-696
OpenDatabase routine, adding (Voice Phone project), 936
opening ProcessSubList routine, 238-239
operating system, SR requirements, 458-459
OperatingSystem (Session Object property), 168-170
opt() rule
overview, 518
utilizing context free grammars, 519
Optelecom, Inc. Web site, 1049
option buttons, adding to TAPI Dialog Utility, 705-707
Options (Message object method), 184-185
outbound calls placing, 691-696

outbound dialing, adding to Excel, 749-752

OutBox Folder objects, 180

Outbox (MAPI storage folders), 45-47

Outbox (Session Object property), 168-170

Oxus PC/SO ISDN Board, 1062

P

page-level routines (frmTAPI)
  cmdButtons_Click event, 817-818
  cmdData_Click event, 819-820
  cmdDialPad_Click event, 818
  coding, 817-822
  DbList1_DblClick event, 820

parameters, TAPIFONE application, 781-782

Parent storage folders, 46-47

Parity Software Web site, 1049

Password property (MAPISession control), 133-134

Paste command (Edit menu), 103

PathName (MAPIFile), 97

Pau tag
  phrase modification tags, 512-513
  text pauses, adding, 512-513

PBX (Private Branch Exchange) lines
  Private protocol lines, 602
  proprietary office settings, 605
  telephone line services, 605

PC Telephony Adapter, 1061

peer-to-peer message servers, 49-50

PermanentProviderID (TAPILINE.OCX properties), 668

Phone Book page
  controls, placing, 797-803
  frmTAPI
    designing, 797-803
    tabbed dialog boxes, 788

phone devices
  data structure (Supplemental Telephony), 627-628
  function calls (Supplemental Telephony), 624-627
  TAPI emulation, 596
  virtual phones, 596

phone dialer, creating, 636-650

phone entry forms, coding (TeleBook application), 766-772

phone log forms, coding (TeleBook application), 772-774

PhoneBar, 1056

PhoneKits, 1055

PhoneLine for Windows, 1055

phonemes
  International Phonetic Alphabet (IPA), 430
  storage, 461-462
  sub-word matching, 461-462
  TTS fundamentals, 428-429
  word matching methods, 427-428

phones
  connecting, lineMakeCall function, 636
  TAPI configurations, 598

Phonetastic for TAPI, 1058

PhonetiCs, Inc. Web site, 1050

Phoneware, 1058

PhoneWorks, 1059

phrase modification tags, 507-508
  Emp tag, 512
  Pau tag, 512-513
  Pit tag, 512-513
  Spd tag, 512-514
  Vol tag, 512-514

Pit tag
  maximum pitch, 513
  minimum pitch, 513
  phrase modification tags, 513
  voice pitch, modifying, 513

PlaceCall function (TAPI project), 644-645

PlaceCall routine, adding (Voice Phone project), 939

placing
  TAPI outbound calls, 691-696
  TAPILINE form, control buttons, 680-685

Plain Old Telephone Service (POTS), 603-604
playback controls, adding to TTS engine, 483-485
portability, MAPI architecture, 28-29
Position (Attachment object property), 213
Position (MAPIFile), 96
Post forms, creating
　EFD, 58
　Forms Designer Wizard, 61
posting TAPI messages, 643-644
posts, creating, 85-86
Primary Rate Interface, 605
Priority (TAPILINE.OCX properties), 668
priority levels, setting TTS engine, 475-480
Private Branch Exchange, *see* PBX
Private protocol lines, 602
Prn tag, 515-516
Pro tag, 515-516
ProcessInbox routine, 241-242
ProcessInboxMsg routine, 243
ProcessInboxMsgArcGet routine, 251
ProcessInboxMsgArcList routine, 249-250
ProcessInboxMsgNewSub routine, 244
ProcessInboxMsgUnSub routine, 247
processing
　audio (Awake property), 491
　MAPIEnd routine messages, 236

MAPIStart routine messages, 235-236
MLM requests, 254-258
TAPI inbound calls, 726-728
processors
　SR requirements, 457
　TTS requirements, 458
ProcessSubList routine
　adding, 237-238
　schedule control file, opening, 238-239
ProcessSubListMsg routine
　adding, 238-239
　messages, building, 239-242
Programs menu commands, Microsoft Exchange, 60
project-level declarations, adding (LibVPhone module), 930-931
project-level variables, adding (FaxBack module), 900
Pronexus, Inc. Web site, 1050
Pronexus VBVoice Telephony Development Kit
　OCX controls, 862
　VBVoice controls, 863-866
　visual programming versus Visual Basic code, 862
pronunciation anomalies, voice quality, 429-430
properties
　setting for Field Properties dialog box, 66-67
　viewing in Voice Command object, 489

Properties command (File menu), 82
property pages, creating (Exchange Client), 382
Property Sheet dialog box
　CDGEXT32.RC, 406-409
　coding, 405-409
　laying out, 405-409
PropertyGet routine, coding (clsPhoneCall class module), 755-756
PropertyLet routine, coding (clsPhoneCall class module), 755-756
PROPERTYSHEETS, context maps, 377
prosody
　speech quality, 429-430
　TTS technology limitations, 463-464
Provider Configuration dialog box, 698-701
ProviderName (InfoStore Object property), 173-174
ProVoice Developers Kit for WIN 32, 1038
Prt tag, 515-516
PSTAPIDLL32 DLL, 665-666
　declarations in TAPILINE.BAS, 671-673
Pulmonic obstruents, 530
Pulmonic resonants, 530
PureSpeech 2.2 Recognizer, 1036
PureSpeech Web site, 1033, 1050

Q - R

QikDial application, creating (Excel), 749-752
Queuesys Web site, 1023
QuickHelp (EFD), 59

RAM (Random Access Memory)
    SR requirements, 457
    TTS requirements, 458
ReadFromFile (Attachment object method), 212
ReadInbox routine, 241-242
reading e-mail (MAPIReadMail), 116-121
ReadLineDevCaps function, adding (libTAPI module), 784
ReadMail routine, 119-121
READNOTEMESSAGE, context maps, 377
READPOSTMESSAGE, context maps, 377
ReadReceipt (Message object property), 187-189
READREPORTMESSAGE, context maps, 377
ReadStartUp routine (frmTAPI), 823
receiving subscriber archives, 251-254
RecipAdd routine, 202
RecipClass (MAPI Recip), 95
RecipColl routine, 197
RecipCount (MAPIMessage), 94
RecipCount property (MAPIMessage control), 140-141

RecipDisplayName property (MAPIMessage control), 140-141
Recipient collection, adding Recipient objects, 201-202
Recipient objects
    adding, 201-202
    methods
        Delete, 198
        Resolve, 198-199
    properties
        Address, 198-199
        AddressEntry, 199
        Application, 199
        Class, 199
        DisplayType, 199
        Index, 199
        Name, 199
        Type, 199-203
Recipients (Message object property), 187-189
Recipients collection object
    methods
        Add, 195
        Delete, 195
        Resolve, 195
    properties
        Class, 195
        Count, 195
        Item, 195
        Resolved, 195-198
RecipIndex property (MAPIMessage control), 140-141
RecipProps routine, 200-201
RecipType property (MAPIMessage control), 140-141
recognition accuracy
    ambient noise levels, 463
    regional dialects, 463
    SR technology limitations, 462-463

recognizing SR engine menu commands, 497-499
recording
    VBVoice voice files, 867-868
    Voice Workbench voice files, 857-858
Reference command (Tools menu), 266, 470, 925
reference resources
    CompuServe SAPI forums, 1034
    CompuServe TAPI forums, 1054
    MAPI books, 1018-1021
    MAPI CompuServe forums, 1024
    MAPI Web sites, 1022-1024
    Microsoft MAPI newsgroups, 1024
    SAPI books, 1028-1029
    SAPI Web sites, 1029-1034
    TAPI books, 1042-1044
    TAPI Web sites, 1044-1053
References dialog box, 925
Register button, 508
Register method
    connecting to SR engine, 490
    OLE Voice Command object properties, 448
    parameters, 472-473
    TTS engine, connecting, 472-473
    Voice Text object, 451-452
registering extensions (Exchange Client), 383-386

registration parameters, Exchange Client extensions, 384-386

REMOTEVIEWER, context maps, 377

Remove method (OLE Voice Menu object), 450

removing Voice Menu object commands, 502-503

rep() rule
overview, 518
utilizing context free grammars, 519-520

Reply command (Compose menu), 79

Reply method (MAPIMessage control), 136-138

ReplyAll method (MAPIMessage control), 136-138

requesting Client API services, 13-14

requests, processing with MLM, 254-258

requirements
system hardware, 7-8
system software, 7-8

Resolve (Recipient object method), 198-199

Resolve (Recipients collection object method), 195

Resolved (Recipients collection object property), 195-198

ResolveName service, 52-54

ResolveName subroutine, 108-109

responding
CommandSpoken property, memo commands, 497-499
MainDialog code, TAPI messages, 642-644
Server SPI requests from Client API, 14-15

response forms, building (Forms Designer Wizard), 62

retrieving messages (MAPI Spooler), 54-55

rewinding method (TTS engine), 483-485

Rhetorex, Inc. Web site, 1050

rich text format, MAPI messages, 30

RootFolder (InfoStore Object property), 173-174

rounded vowels, 530

routing messages (MAPI Spooler), 54-55

rules
adding for MAPI Email Agent, 370-371
defining
context-free grammars, 518
SR engine, 518
designing applications, 887
establishing context-free grammars, 432-433
MAPI Email Agent, storing, 314-315

run-time lists, context-free grammars, 520-521

S

Sandman Web site, 1051

SAPI (Speech Application Programming Interface)
architecture, 436-454
design considerations for applications, 891-892
developer tools, 7-8
hardware overview, 456
hardware requirements, 457
hardware resources, 1034-1039
integration summary, 1010-1013
overview, 5-9
reference resources
books, 1028-1029
CompuServe forums, 1034
Web, 1029-1034
software overview, 456
software resources, 1034-1039

SAPI, *see also* **High-level SAPI**

SAPI, *see also* **Low-level SAPI**

SaveRec support routine (TeleBook application), 775-776

SaveValues routine, 346

saving message attachments to disk, 217-218

Scan InBox command (File menu), 1007

ScanMsgs routine, 358-359

schedule, developing with MLM, 233

schedule control file
   controlling with
      SendMail routine, 236
   opening with
      ProcessSubList routine,
      238-239
Seanet Web site, 1022
searching e-mail
   (MAPIFindNext),
   116-121
SEARCHVIEWER, context
   maps, 377
SecureLink ISDN
   Adapter, 1061
Select Phrase dialog
   box, 912
selecting
   forms, 78-80
   Forms Designer Wizard
      single-window
         forms, 63
      two-window forms, 63
Send (Message object
   method), 185
Send forms, creating
   EFD, 58
   Forms Designer
      Wizard, 61
Send Messages command
   (File menu), 1007
Send method
   e-mail messages,
      263-265
   versus Update method,
      263-265
Send method
   (MAPIMessage control),
   135-138
Send Note dialog box, 116
SendDialog routine, 116
SendDocs routine, 113
Sender (Message object
   property), 187-189

sending
   e-mail
      (MAPISendDocuments),
      111-113
   forms, 78-80
   MLM archives, 251-254
   Talk Mail project
      messages, 1006-1007
SendMail routine
   adding, 236
   schedule control file,
      controlling, 236
SENDNOTEMESSAGE,
   context maps, 377
SENDREPOSTMESSAGE,
   context maps, 377
SENDRESENDMESSAGE,
   context maps, 377
SendSMAPIFax routine,
   adding (FaxBack mod-
   ule), 902-903
Sent (MAPI storage
   folders), 45-47
Sent (Message object
   property), 187-189
seq() rule
   overview, 518
   utilizing context free
      grammars, 518-519
Server SPI
   dynamic link library
      (DLL), 15-21
   Open Database Connec-
      tivity (ODBC), 14-15
   requests from Client API,
      responding, 14-15
   WOSA components, 13
servers, MAPI, 27-28
service layer, MAPI
   architecture, 27-28
Service Provider section
   TELEPHON.INI,
      712-714
   Telephony Service
      Providers (TSPs),
      712-714

session, automating with
   Logon method, 167-168
SESSION, context
   maps, 377
Session Object
   properties, 168-170
      Class, 168-170
      CurrentUser, 168-170
      Inbox, 168-170
      InfoStores, 168-170
      OperatingSystem,
         168-170
      Outbox, 168-170
      Version, 168-170
Session Object methods
   AddressBook, 162-163
   GetAddressEntry, 163
   GetFolder, 163
   GetInfoStore, 163
   GetMessage, 163
   Logoff, 163-165
   Logon, 163-165
   OLE Messaging Library,
      162-163
SessionID property
   (MAPISession
   control), 134
SessionInfoStoreColl
   routine, 172
Set Library To dialog
   box, 87
SetCallParams routine,
   adding (libTAPI mod-
   ule), 785-786
SetTiming routine (tmNew
   form), 991
setting
   About dialog box
      properties, 919-920
   Chr tag, voice
      character, 509
   Ctx tag, message context,
      509-510
   Faxback project, VBVoice
      control properties,
      911-914

Field Properties dialog box properties, 66-67
folder views, 82-85
forms, window properties, 68-75
LINECALLPARAMS, 635-636
messages, filtering criteria, 84-85
SR engines, language constants, 492-494
Talk Mail project properties, 1005-1007
TTS engine
  Enable property, 473
  priority levels, 475-480
  Speed property, 480-482
VAbout form properties, 954-955
VBVoice control properties
  AcceptCall LineGroup control, 911
  GetFaxAddress GatherDigits control, 912
  GetFaxFile GatherDigits control, 913
  HangUp OnHook control, 913-914
  VBVFrame control, 911
  VerifyFile control, 913
Vce tag, 510-512
see also configuring
Setup form (MAPI Email Agent)
building, 332-341
control arrays 332-341

Setup page
controls, placing, 808-810
frmTAPI
  designing, 808-810
  tabbed dialog boxes, 788
SetupPageLoad routine, 339
SetupPageSave routine, 340
SetVarProps routine (TAPI project), 646
shared lines, TAPI configurations, 600
Show method (MAPIMessage control), 138
Show Scroll Bars command (View menu), 68
ShowHandles routine (TAPILINE form), 686-687
ShowProgress routine (TAPIOUT project), 646
Signed (Message object property), 188-189
SignOff (MAPISession control), 131-132
SignOn (MAPISession control), 131-132
SIM-phony—Home Web site, 1051
Simple MAPI, *see* **SMAPI**
single-window forms, selecting (Forms Designer Wizard), 63
sites
Access Superhighway, 1044
Acemail, 1022
Advisor, 1022
Agile Communications, 1044

Allgon, 1044
Alliance Systems, 1044
AMDEV, 1045
Ariel Corporation, 1045
AudioWav, 1030
Big Island Communications, 1045
Broadband Telephony Buyers Guide, 1045
Butler Telecom, 1045
Chromatic Research, 1045
Cobotyx, 1030, 1046
Colibri, 1030
Command Corp, 1030
Computer Talk, Inc., 1046
Consensys, 1022
Cypress Research Corp., 1046
DAX Systems, Inc, 1046
Dianatel Corporation, 1047
Digital Systems International, 1047
Dragonsys, 1031
Earthlink, 1033
EMJ Data Systems, 1047
F. F. Tronixs, 1047
Firstbyte, 1031
Genesys, 1048
Homnick, 1022
Hongkong Telecom, 1048
Inforamp, 1030
Islandnet, 1023
Kolvax, 1032
L R Technologies, 1023
Neosoft, 1022
netApp Systems, 1023
Netgain, 1023
Optelecom, Inc., 1049
Parity Software, 1049
PhonetiCs, Inc., 1050

50
3
c., 1050
23
c., 1050
1051
1022
SIM phony—Home,
1051
SoftTalk, Inc., 1051
Speech Systems, 1033
Stanford University
Applied Speech
Technology Lab, 1051
Tel-Com, 1051
Teleconnect Magazine,
1052
Tellabs Operations,
1052
Vision Computer
Associates, 1023
VISIT Computer, 1052
Visual Voice, 1052
Vive Synergies, Inc.,
1052
Voice Processing Corp,
1033
Voice Processing Corp.,
1053
Winserve, 1023
**Size (Message object
property), 188-189**
SkedEdit routine, 233
**SMAPI (Simple Messaging
Application Program-
ming Interface)**
components, 93
directory, locating, 92-93
global constants, 99-100
MAPI services, adding,
92-93
VBAMAP32.DLL,
92-93

SMAPI API calls
function declarations,
97-100
MAPI services, accessing,
97-100
MAPIAddress, 105-107
MAPIDetails, 109-111
MAPIErr, 100-102
MAPIFindNext,
116-121
MAPILogOff, 102-104
MAPILogon, 102-104
MAPIReadMail,
116-121
MAPIResolveName,
107-109
MAPISendDocuments,
111-113
MAPISendMail,
113-116
VBAMAP32.BAS
module, 98-100
SMAPIEnd routine
adding, 104
faxBack module, 902
SMAPIStart routine, 104
FaxBack module, 901
**smARTspeakr for Win-
dows, 1035**
**SoftTalk, Inc. Web site,
1051**
SoftVoice, 1038
software
prerequisites
*FaxBack project,
896-898*
*Talk Mail project,
961-962*
*Voice Phone project,
925*
SAPI overview, 456
SAPI resources,
1034-1039

system requirements, 7-8
TAPI resources,
1054-1062
**Sort (Messages collection
object method), 181-185**
**Sound Blaster sound cards,
459-460**
sound cards
ESS technology,
459-460
Media Vision, 459-460
Sound Blaster, 459-460
SoundByte, 1055
sounds
Pulmonic obstruents, 530
Pulmonic resonants, 530
rounded vowels, 530
unrounded vowels, 530
**Source (Attachment object
property), 213**
Spd tag
audio playback speed,
modifying, 513-514
phrase modification tags,
513-514
Speak method
enabling TTS engine,
474-480
parameters, 474-480
text, playing, 474-480
Voice Text object, 452
speaker dependence
drawbacks, 461-464
methods
*speaker adaptive,
426-427*
*speaker dependent,
426-427*
*speaker independent,
426-427*
speech recognition
fundamentals, 426-427

speaker identification
multiple speakers,
462-463
SR technology limita-
tions, 462-463
SpeakingDone (Voice Text Callback), 453
SpeakingStarted (Voice Text Callback), 453
Speech Application Programming Interface, *see* **SAPI**
speech engines, SR requirements, 458-459
speech recognition
developing, 424-425
fundamentals, 424-425
speaker dependence,
426-427
vocabulary, 428
word matching,
427-428
word separation,
425-426
grammar rules
context-free, 431-432
dictation grammars,
431-432
limited domain
grammars, 431-432
Speech Recognition object
child object
SR Engine Enumerator
object, 441
SR Sharing object, 441
Low-level SAPI, 441
speech recognition, *see* **SR**
Speech SDK
VCAUTO.TLB, 447
VTXTAUTO.TLB, 447
Speech Systems Web site, 1033

speed, adjusting audio playback, 480-482
Speed button, 481
Speed property
setting TTS engine,
480-482
voice playback, adjusting,
480-482
Voice Text object,
451-452
SR (Speech Recognition)
building services with
Visual Basic, 564-581
creating applications with
C++, 541-561
operating system require-
ments, 458-459
processor and memory
requirements, 457
technology
speaker dependence,
460-462
word analysis,
460-462
word selection,
460-462
technology limitations
input recognition,
462-463
recognition accuracy,
462-463
speaker identification,
462-463
SR callbacks
adding class module,
499-500
establishing Visual Basic,
499-500
SR engine
alt() rule, 518
Awake property,
setting, 491
context-free grammars,
516-517

compiling, 521-527
creating, 521-527
loading, 526
testing, 526
dictation grammars, 516
grammar rules, 516
interpreting audio, 516
language constants,
setting, 492-494
limited domian gram-
mars, 516
menu commands,
recognizing, 497-499
menu object, creating,
491-494
opt() rule, 519
Register method,
connecting, 490
rep() rule, 519-520
rules, defining, 518
seq() rule, 518-519
words, defining, 517
SR Engine Enumerator object
interfaces
ISREnum, 442
ISRFind, 442
Speech Recognition
object, child object, 441
SR Engine Object
interfaces
ISRAttributes, 443
ISRCentral, 442-443
ISRDialogs, 443
ISRLexPronounce, 443
ISRSpeaker, 443
SR Results object
interfaces
ISRResAudio,
444-445
ISRResBasic, 444-445
ISRResCorrection,
444-445
ISRResEval, 444-445

ISRResGraph,
444-445
ISRResMemory, 445
ISRResMerge, 445
ISRResModifyGUI,
444-445
ISRResSpeaker,
444-445
SR services
coding global
variables, 565
Windows 95, adding, 565
SR Sharing object
interfaces, ISR
Sharing, 442
Speech Recognition
object, child
object, 441
**SRCBK.CLS module
(Voice Phone project),
924-925**
**standalone programs
versus extensions,
designing applications,
888-889**
**Stanford University
Applied Speech Technol-
ogy Lab, 1051**
**StartTAPI routine (TAPI
Dialog Utility), 708-711**
**status, monitoring TTS
engine, 485-486**
StatusUpdate routine, 297
**StopSpeaking method
(Voice Text object), 452**
storage folders
Deleted, 45-47
Inbox, 45-47
MAPI Client, 45-47
accessing, 46-47
OLE Messaging Library,
identifying properties,
46-47

organization of, 47
Outbox, 45-47
properties
FolderID, 46-47
Folders, 46-47
Messages, 46-47
Name, 46-47
Parent, 46-47
Sent, 45-47
User-defined, 45-47
**StoreID (Folder object
property), 178-181**
**StoreID (Message object
property), 188-189**
storing
attached files (MAPIFile),
96-97
Credit Card section,
telephone credit cards,
720-723
message packets
(MAPIMessage), 93-95
message recipient
(MAPIRecip), 95-96
rules (MAPI Email
Agent), 314-315
Stylus Trace
sample output, 861-862
Visual Voice Telephony
Toolkit, 861-862
components, 843-844
**SUB command, Inbox
routines, 240-243**
sub-word matching
phonemes, 461-462
word analysis, 461-462
SubBye routine, 248-249
**SubDelete routine,
247-248**
SubEdit routine, 232
SubGreet routine, 246
**Subject (MAPI
Message), 93**

**Subject (Message object
property), 188-189**
**Submitted (Message object
property), 188-189**
**subroutine templates,
creating (Voice Work-
bench), 858**
subscribers
adding to MLM,
243-246
archives, receiving,
251-254
building in MLM, 232
deleting from MLM, 247
SubWrite routine, 245
Supplemental Telephony
advanced device handling
features, 620-621
API calls, 622-627
API phone device
structure, 627-628
functions, 621-622
overview, 620-629
phone device messages,
628-629
TAPI model, 620-629
support routines
adding
TAPIANS project,
733-736
TAPILINE form,
685-687
ClearLog routine
(frmTAPI), 825-826
coding
frmTAPI, 822-827
MAPI Email
Agent, 341
TeleBook application,
774-776
ExportLog routine
(frmTAPI), 826-827
InitDB routine
(frmTAPI), 824

Initialization (MAPI Email Agent), 341-351
LineMonitor function (frmTAPI), 827
List-Handling (MAPI Email Agent), 351-358
LoadDevices routine (frmTAPI), 823
LoadImages routine (frmTAPI), 822
MakeDB routine (frmTAPI), 825
message processing (MAPI E-Mail Agent), 358-369
MLM forms, 228-230
ReadStartUp routine (frmTAPI), 823

T

T1 lines, TAPI functions, 602
tabs
Format (Field Properties dialog box), 66-67
General (Field Properties dialog box), 66
Initial Value (Field Properties dialog box), 67
Talk Mail project
design considerations, 960-961
hardware resources, 960
launching, 1005-1007
LibTalkMail module, coding, 962-969
messages
deleting, 1007
sending, 1006-1007

properties, setting, 1005-1007
software resources, 961-962
testing, 1005-1007
tmAbout box, 1003-1004
tmAbout form, 961-962
tmNew form, 961-962
tmRead form, 961-962
tmView form, 961-962
TAPI (Telephony Application Programming Interface)
active call, dropping, 694-696
adding declarations to Excel, 750-752
address status, viewing, 696-697
architecture, 608-631
Assisted Telephony, 608-609
basic data modems, 656-657
Basic Telephony, 610-620
call information, displaying, 696-697
configurations, 597-598
developer tools, 7-8
devices
lines, 594-595
phones, 594-595
dialer, creating, 636-650
dialing rules
dialable digits, 721-723
insertion codes, 721-723
pauses, 721-723
dialog boxes
coding, 700-701
displaying, 697-701

Extended Telephony, 630-631
hardware resources, 1054-1062
idle calls, deallocating, 694-696
inbound calls, handling, 726-728
integration summary, 1010-1013
line devices, 595-596
obtaining, 690-696
LINECALLPARAMS, 635-636
lineInitialize routine, starting, 634-635
lineMakeCall function, 636
lineNegotiateAPIVersion function, verifying, 635
lineOpen function, locating line, 635
modem processing, 655
multiple configurations
PBX server, 601-602
voice server, 601-602
open lines, closing, 694-696
outbound calls, placing, 691-696
overview, 4-9, 594-595
PC-based configurations, 598-599
phone devices, 596
phone-based configurations, 598
posting messages (MainDialog), 643-644
reference resources
books, 1042-1044
CompuServe forums, 1054
Web, 1044-1053
responding to messages, 642-644

sessions, initializing,
688-689
shared line configurations, 600
software resources,
1054-1062
summary, 876-882
Supplemental Telephony,
620-629
TeleBook application,
class module declarations, 753-756
TELEPHON.INI
overview, 711-712
telephone line
services, 602
telephony cards,
659-660
Telephony Service
Provider Interface
(TSPI), 655-656
unified line configurations, 600
versions, confirming,
689-696
voice data modems, 657
WOSA compliance,
596-597
TAPI Dialog Utility
coding, 707-711
creating, 704-711
laying out, 704-707
option buttons, adding,
705-707
StartTAPI routine,
708-711
TAPI Examiner
compatibility testing,
861-862
Visual Voice Telephony
Toolkit, 861-862
components, 843-844
**TAPI Service Provider
Toolkit, 1061**

**TAPI v1.4 for Windows
95, 7-8**
TAPIANS dialog box, 743
TAPIANS form
coding, 731-741
control buttons, 729-731
Form_Load event,
732-741
Form_Unload event,
732-741
laying out, 729-731
TAPIANS project
ClearHandles routine,
735-736
cmdButton Array,
coding, 737-741
creating, 728-743
LINE_CALLSTATE
messages, 743
LINECALLSTATE_
CONNECTED
messages, 743
MCIStart routine,
735-736
support routines, adding,
733-736
TapiCallBack event,
736-737
TapiGetDevCaps
routine, 734-736
TAPIStart routine,
733-736
testing, 741-743
**TAPICall module,
781-782**
TAPICALL.BAS
CallState message
function, 677-678
Clean function, 678-679
GetOffset function, 679
TAPICallBackHandler
function, 676-677
TAPILINE controls,
support modules, 671

TapiCallBack event
message IDs, 673
message names, 666-667
TAPIANS project,
736-737
TAPILINE.OCX control,
666-667
**TAPICallBackHandler
function**
code listing, 676-677
TAPICALL.BAS,
676-677
**TAPIClearHandles
routine, adding (libTAPI
module), 787**
**TAPIDial function, adding
(libTAPI module), 785**
TAPIFONE application
control parameters,
modifying, 781-782
designing, 780-782
frmCall, 780-782
frmTAPI, 780-782, 788
frmVPhone, 780-782
launching, 836-838
libTAPI module,
781-782
TAPICall module,
781-782
TAPILine module,
781-782
testing, 836-838
**TapiGetDevCaps routine
(TAPIANS project),
734-736**
**TAPIGetLocation function, adding
(AssistedTAPI
module), 927**
**tapiGetLocationInfo
function, 746**
testing, 747-749
**TAPIHangUp routine,
adding (libTAPI module), 787**

TAPILINE controls
About dialog box,
698-701
constants, 673-675
Dialing Properties dialog
box, 699-701
DLL functions, 669-670
files
MCF40.DLL,
665-666
MSVCRT40.DLL,
665-666
PSTAPIDLL32.DLL,
665-666
TAPILINE.LIC,
665-666
TAPILINE.OCA,
665-666
TAPILINE.OCX,
665-666
TAPILINE.TLB,
665-666
installing, 664-666
Line Configuration dialog
box, 698-701
line structures, 673-675
Provider Configuration
dialog box, 698-701
support modules
TAPICALL.BAS, 671
TAPILINE.BAS, 671
TAPIPHON.BAS,
671-672
TapiCallBack event, 673
tool box, adding,
665-666
TAPILINE form
button event code,
adding, 689-702
cmdLineGetAddrStatus
code, 696-697
cmdLineGetCallInfo
method, 696-697
coding, 685-701

control buttons, placing,
680-685
designing, 680-685
form event code, adding,
688-689
support routines
adding, 685-687
ClearHandles, 686
FillCallParams, 687
GetVarInfo, 686
LocalGetLineInfo, 687
ShowHandles, 686
TAPILine module,
781-782
TAPILINE.BAS
error values, 672-673
PSTAPIDLL32 DLL
declarations, 671-673
TAPILINE controls,
support modules, 671
TAPILINE.LIC, 665-666
TAPILINE.OCA, 665-666
TAPILINE.OCX, 665-666
methods, 668-669
properties
AddressID, 668
APIVersion, 668
CompletionID, 668
GatheredDigits, 668
HandleToCall, 668
HandleToConf
Call, 668
HandleToConsult
Call, 668
LineApp, 668
LineHandle, 668
NumberOfRings, 668
NumDevices, 668
PermanentProvider
ID, 668
Priority, 668
TAPILINE.OCX control,
666-667
TAPILINE.TLB, 665-666

TAPIMakeCall function,
adding (AssistedTAPI
module), 928
TAPIOUT project
coding overview,
636-650
compiling, 651
initial declarations,
637-638
lineCallBackProc routine,
647-651
MainDialog code,
639-644
PlaceCall function,
644-645
SetVarProps
routine, 646
ShowProgress
routine, 646
WinMain routine,
638-644
TAPIPHON.BAS, 671
TAPIPlaceCall routine,
adding (libTAPI mod-
ule), 786-787
tapiRequestMakeCall
function, 746-749
TAPIShutdown routine,
adding (libTAPI mod-
ule), 787
TAPIStart routine
(TAPIANS project),
733-736
TAPISTRY for Windows
95, 1057
TASK, context maps, 376
tbrMain_ButtonClick
event (tmView form),
980-981
Tel-Com Web site, 1051
TeleBook application
class module
creating, 753-756
TAPI declarations,
753-756

clsPhoneCall class
module, 754-756
cmdBtn_Click event,
764-766
cmdDial_Click
event, 766
cmdKey_Click event,
765-766
command button arrays,
756-766
control arrays, 766-772
form-level variables,
declaring, 762-766
Form_Load event,
763-766
Form_Resize event code,
763-766
launching, 776-777
main form, coding,
756-766
phone entry form,
coding, 766-772
phone log form, coding,
772-774
support routines
*CallRec support
routine, 776*
*ClearRec support
routine, 774-776*
coding, 774-776
*LoadRec support
routine, 775-776*
*SaveRec support
routine, 775-776*
Visual Basic, writing,
752-777
**Teleconnect Magazine
Web site, 1052**
TELEPHON.INI
calling card settings,
722-723
components, 712-714
Credit Card section,
711-712

HandOff Priorities
section, 711-712
Location section,
711-712
*entry parameters,
717-720*
modifying, 711-712
Service Provider section,
711-712
**telephone credit cards,
storing, 720-723**
telephone line services
ISDN lines, 604-605
PBX lines, 605
Plain Old Telephone
Service (POTS),
603-604
T1 lines, 604
TAPI functions, 602
**Telephony Application
Programming Interface,
see TAPI**
telephony cards
commercial grade
applications, 659-660
cost, 659-660
multiple line capabilities,
659-660
**telephony hardware
overview, 654**
**Telephony Service Pro-
vider Interface (TSPI),
655-656**
UniModem Driver,
655-656
**Telephony Service Provid-
ers (TSPs), 712-714**
**Tellabs Operations Web
site, 1052**
**Test control (Visual Voice
Telephony Toolkit)**
components, 842-844
events, 854
methods, 851-854
properties, 853

Test FAX button, 920
testing
Assisted TAPI functions,
747-749
calling card settings,
722-723
context-free grammars,
526-527
discussion tools, 307-308
Faxback application,
920-921
folder views, 85-86
MAPI E-Mail
Agent, 369
Message Signing exten-
sion, 408-409
Talk Mail project,
1005-1007
TAPI Examiner compat-
ibility, 861-862
TAPIANS project,
741-743
TAPIFONE application,
836-838
VBVoice application,
868-869
Voice Phone project,
957-958
text
adding pauses (Pau tag),
512-513
playing (Speak method),
474-480
**Text (Message object
property), 188-189**
text messages
graphics, attaching, 30
MAPI message types, 30
text-to-speech, *see* TTS
TextData button, 510
**third-party tools versus
native API tools, design-
ing applications, 888**

TimeReceived (Message object property), 188-189

TimeSent (Message object property), 188-189

tmAbout box
form controls, 1003-1004
Talk Mail project, 1003-1004

tmNew form
cmdAddrBook_Click event, 993
cmdNewMsg_Click event, 992
coding, 989-990
designing, 983-988
form controls, 983-988
Form_Load event, 989-990
Form_Unload event, 990
HandleOpen routine, 990-991
menu properties, 988-989
MMControl1_StatusUpdate event, 993-994
mnuFileItem_Click event, 991-992
SetTiming routine, 991

tmRead form
coding, 1000-1008
designing, 995-1000
form controls, 995-1000
Form_Load event, 1001-1002
Form_Unload event, 1002-1003
menu properties, 1000
mnuFileItem_Click event, 1003

tmView form
BuildListView routine, 975-976
BuildStatusBar routine, 975
BuildToolBar routine, 976-978
coding, 973-983
control building codes, 975-978
control events, coding, 981-983
designing, 969-971
form controls, 969-971
form events, coding, 974
Form_Load event, 974
Form_Resize event, 974
MAPIScanInBox code, 982-983
menu properties, 971-973
menu support routines, coding, 978-981
mnuFileItem_Click event, 978-979
mnuHelpItem_Click event, 980
mnuMsgItem_Click event, 979
mnuViewItem_Click event, 979-980
tbrMain_ButtonClick event, 980-981

tool box, adding TAPILINE controls, 665-666

Tools menu commands
Application Design, 60
Custom Controls, 132, 665
Deliver Now Using, 79
Reference, 266, 470, 925

tracking discussion groups topics, 261-263

Translate Dialog dialog box, 440

TruVoicer, 1037

TTS (Text To Speech)
adding callbacks, 486-489
building services in Visual Basic, 564-581
callback controls, adding, 487-488
creating applications with C++, 534-541
establishing callback in Visual Basic, 486-489
fundamentals
phonemes, 428-429
TTS diphone concatenation, 428-429
TTS synthesis, 428-429
voice quality, 428-429
processor and memory requirements, 458
technology
audio-output synthesis, 463
diphone concatenation, 463
technology limitations
individualized voices, 463-464
prosody of speech, 463-464

TTS diphone concatenation, 428-429

TTS engine
connecting viaRegister method, 472-473
control tags, audio output, 506-508
Enable property, setting, 473

fast-forwarding method, 483-485

IsSpeaking property, 485-486

playback controls, adding, 483-485

priority levels, setting, 475-480

rewinding method, 483-485

Speak method, enabling, 474-480

Speed property, setting, 480-482

status, monitoring, 485-486

TTS Engine Enumerator object
interfaces
ITTSEnum, 445-446
ITTSFind, 445-446

TTS Engine object
interfaces
ITTSAttributes, 446
ITTSCentral, 446
ITTSDialogs, 446
Low-level SAPI, 445
notification callbacks
ITTSBufNotify sink, 446
ITTSNotifySink, 446

TTS services, coding global variables, 565

TTS synthesis, 428-429
methods
diphone concatenation, 430-431
synthesis, 430-431

TTS systems, design issues, 466-467

TTSCBK.CLS module (Voice Phone project), 924-925

two-window forms, selecting (Forms Designer Wizard), 63

Type (MAPI addresses properties), 47-48

Type (AddressEntry object property), 204-209

Type (Attachment object property), 213-220

Type (Message object property), 188-189

Type (Recipient object property), 199-203

U

unicode values, International Phonetic Alphabet (IPA), 528-530

unified lines, TAPI configurations, 600

Unified Messaging Systems (UMS), 1056

UniModem Driver, Telephony Service Provider Interface (TSPI), 655-656

UNIMODEM/V— Windows 95, 1059

UniModemV Driver, Telephony Service Provider Interface (TSPI), 655-656

UnInitSAPI routine, 567

Unread (Message object property), 189-195

unrounded vowels, 530

UNSUB command, Inbox routines, 240-243

Update (AddressEntry object method), 203-204

Update (Message object method), 185-189

Update method
messages in folders, 263-265
versus Send method, 263-265

UpdateDB routine (Call dialog box), 833

User-defined (MAPI storage folders), 45-47

UserName property (MAPISession control), 133-134

utilizing
context-free grammars
alt() rule, 518
opt() rule, 519
rep() rule, 519-520
run-time lists, 520-521
seq() rule, 518-519

V

VAbout form
designing, 954-955
form controls, 954-955
properties, setting, 954-955

validating recipients (MAPIResolveName), 107-109

VBAMAP32.BAS module, 98-100

VBAMAP32.DLL, SMAPI calls, 92-93

VBVFrame control, setting, 911

VBVoice
applications, building,
866-867
Start test option,
868-869
voice files
creating, 867-868
recording, 867-868
VBVoice control properties
AcceptCall LineGroup
control, 911
GetFaxAddress
GatherDigits
control, 912
GetFaxFile GatherDigits
control, 913
HangUp OnHook
control, 913-914
setting Faxback project,
911-914
VBVFrame control, 911
VerifyFile control, 913
**VBVoice controls,
863-866**
**VCAUTO.TLB (Speech
SDK), 447**
Vce tag
parameters, 510-512
setting, 510-512
voice character tags,
510-512
**Verbex Integrated Speech
Engine (VISE), 1036**
**VerifyFile control,
setting, 913**
**VerifyFile_Enter event
(FaxBack form), 917**
**verifying TAPI
(lineNegotiateAPIVersion
function), 635**
**Version (Session Object
property), 168-170**

**Vertical Market
Services, 17**
overview, 17-18
WOSA Extensions for
Financial Services, 18
WOSA Extensions for
Real-Time Market
Data, 18
VHelp form
cmdOK_Click
event, 954
designing, 953-954
form controls, 953-954
Form_Load event, 954
View menu commands
Forms Properties, 74
Show Scroll Bars, 68
Window Properties, 68
**VIEWER, context
maps, 377**
viewing
TAPI address status,
696-697
Voice Command object
properties, 489
views
setting in folders, 82-85
testing in folders, 85-86
Views dialog box, 83
**Virtual Phone (Visual
Voice Telephony
Toolkit), 860-861**
components, 843-844
**Vision Computer Associ-
ates Web site, 1023**
**VISIT Computer Web site,
1052**
VISIT Voice, 1056
Visual Basic
adding MAPI services,
123-127
adding OLE Voice Text
Object, 470-489

building MAPI Client
application, 143-159
InitSAPI routine, 567
InitVoice routine, 568
InitVText routine, 569
interaction with EFD,
59-60
language constants,
492-493
links, establishing with
server, 131
MAPIMessage control,
134-143
MAPISession
control, 131
SR callback, establishing,
499-500
SR services, building,
564-581
TTS callback, establish-
ing, 486-489
TTS services, building,
564-581
UnInitSAPI routine, 567
Voice Command object
adding, 489
loading, 489-490
VTextAction routine,
570-571
writing TeleBook
application, 752-777
**Visual Basic Object
browser, loading,
470-472**
Visual Voice, 1058
**Visual Voice Telephony
Toolkit**
CD demo copy, 842-844
components
Stylus Trace, 843-844
*TAPI Examiner,
843-844*
Test control, 842-844
*Virtual Phone,
843-844*

Vlink control,
  843-844
Voice control, 842-844
Voice Monitor,
  843-844
Voice Workbench,
  843-844
Stylus Trace, 861-862
TAPI Examiner,
  861-862
Test control
  events, 854
  methods, 851-854
  properties, 853
Virtual Phone, 860-861
Vlink control
  events, 856-857
  methods, 854-855
  properties, 856
Voice control
  events, 850-851
  methods, 844-847
  properties, 847-850
Voice Monitor, 859-860
Voice Workbench,
  857-858
**Visual Voice Web
  site, 1052**
**Vive Synergies, Inc. Web
  site, 1052**
**Vlink control (Visual Voice
  Telephony Toolkit)**
  components, 843-844
  events, 856-857
  methods, 854-855
  properties, 856
vocabulary
  dictation grammars, 433
  issues
    accuracy, 428
    size, 428
  speech recognition
    fundamentals, 428

voice
  maximum pitch, 513
  minimum pitch, 513
  modifying pitch
    (Pit tag), 513
  setting character (Chr
    tag), 509
**voice character tags,
  507-508**
  Chr tag, 509
  Ctx tag, 509-510
  types
    Chr, 509
    Ctx, 509
    Vce, 509
  Vce tag, 510-512
Voice Command Callback
  CommandOther,
    448-449
  CommandRecognize,
    448-449
  configuring, 448-449
**Voice Command dialog
  boxes, 437-438**
**voice command menus,
  designing, 465-466**
Voice Command object
  adding with Visual
    Basic, 489
  child object (Voice Menu
    object), 438
  creating, 489-490
  interfaces
    attributes, 437-438
    dialogs, 437-438
    voice command,
      437-438
  loading in Visual Basic,
    489-490
  notification callback,
    establishing, 438-439
  overview of High-level
    SAPI, 437
  properties, viewing, 489

**voice command routines,
  adding (Voice Phone
  project), 931-933**
**Voice control (Visual Voice
  Telephony Toolkit)**
  components, 842-844
  events, 850-851
  methods, 844-847
  properties, 847-850
voice data modems
  Aztech Systems, 658
  caution concerning TAPI
    compliance, 657-659
  Cirrus Logic, 658
  Compaq Presario
    Systems, 658-659
  cost, 657-659
  Creative Labs Phone
    Blaster, 658, 658-659
  Diamond
    Telecommander
    2500, 658
  Logicode 14.4 PCM
    CIA, 658
  UniModemV driver,
    657-659
voice files
  creating (VBVoice),
    867-868
  recording
    VBVoice, 867-868
    Voice Workbench,
      857-858
Voice Menu object
  Add method, 494-497
  commands
    adding, 494-497
    removing, 502-503
  list commands, creating,
    500-502

Voice Monitor
  multiphone installations,
    859-860
  Visual Voice Telephony
    Toolkit, 859-860
    components, 843-844
Voice Phone project
  AddRec routine, 937
  BuildDatabase
    routine, 935
  BuildVMenu
    routine, 932
  CenterForm
    routine, 939
  database engine routines,
    934-938
  DeleteRec routine, 938
  EditRec routine, 937
  hardware resources, 925
  InitDB routine, 934-935
  InitVCmd routine, 931
  InitVTxt routine,
    933-934
  launching, 957-958
  library modules, coding,
    925-930
  LoadMsgs routine, 934
  LoadNameList
    routine, 933
  LookUp function, 938
  OpenDatabase
    routine, 936
  PlaceCall routine, 939
  software resources, 925
  SRCBK.CLS module,
    924-925
  testing, 957-958
  TTSCBK.CLS module,
    924-925
  VAbout form, 924-925
  VHelp form, 924-925
  voice command routines,
    adding, 931-933

voice text routines,
    adding, 933-934
  VPhone form, 924-925
  VPHONE.BAS
    module, 925
  VRec form, 924-925
  VTAPI.BAS module,
    924-925
**Voice Processing Corp
Web site, 1033, 1053**
voice quality
  factors
    emotion, 429-430
    *pronunciation anoma-
      lies, 429-430*
    prosody, 429-430
  TTS fundamentals,
    428-429
**voice queries, building
(Voice Workbench), 858**
**voice server, TAPI configu-
rations, 601-602**
**voice strings, linking
(Voice Workbench),
857-858**
Voice Text Callbacks
  configuring, 452-453
  establishing applications,
    452-453
  SpeakingDone, 453
  SpeakingStarted, 453
**Voice Text dialog
boxes, 440**
Voice Text object
  interfaces
    Attributes, 439-440
    Dialogs, 439-440
    Voice Text, 439-440
  properties
    *AutoFastForward
      method, 452-454*
    *AutoPause
      method, 452*
    *AutoResume
      method, 452*

*AutoRewind
      method, 452*
    *Callback property,
      451-452*
    *Enabled property,
      451-452*
    *IsSpeaking property,
      451-452*
    *Register method,
      451-452*
    Speak method, 452
    *Speed property,
      451-452*
    *StopSpeaking
      method, 452*
**voice text routines, adding
(Voice Phone project),
933-934**
Voice Workbench
  subroutine templates,
    creating, 858
  Visual Voice Telephony
    Toolkit, 857-858
    components, 843-844
  voice files, recording,
    857-858
  voice queries, building,
    858
  voice strings, linking,
    857-858
**VoiceMatch System
Development Kit, 1036**
Vol tag
  phrase modification
    tags, 514
  volume, adjusting, 514
**volume, adjusting (Vol
tag), 514**
**vowels, International
Phonetic Alphabet (IPA),
528-530**
VoysAccess 1.0, 1058
VPhone form
  cmdDial_Click
    event, 947

cmdPhone_Click event, 946-947

coding, 944-948

designing, 939-942

form controls, 939-942

Form_Load event, 944-945

Form_Unload event, 945

List1_DblClick event, 948

LoadList routine, 946

mnuFileItem_Click event, 948

mnuHelpItem_Click event, 948

VPhone menu, laying out, 943-944

VPhone menu

laying out, 943-944

property settings, 943-944

VPhone project

Vrec form, designing, 949-951

VPHONE.BAS module, 925

Vrec form

cmdRec_Click event, 952

designing VPhone project, 949-951

form controls, 949-951

Form_Activate event, 951-952

Form_Load event, 951-952

VTAPI.BAS module, 924-925

VTextAction routine, 570-571

VTXTAUTO.TLB (Speech SDK), 447

W-Z

Web

sites

Access Superhighway, 1044

Acemail, 1022

Advisor, 1022

Agile Communications, 1044

Allgon, 1044

Alliance Systems, 1044

AMDEV, 1045

Ariel Corporation, 1045

AudioWav, 1030

Big Island Communications, 1045

Broadband Telephony Buyers Guide, 1045

Butler Telecom, 1045

Chromatic Research, 1045

Cobotyx, 1030, 1046

Colibri, 1030

Command Corp, 1030

Computer Talk, Inc., 1046

Consensys, 1022

Cypress Research Corp., 1046

DAX Systems, Inc, 1046

Dianatel Corporation, 1047

Digital Systems International, 1047

Dragonsys, 1031

Earthlink, 1033

EMJ Data Systems, 1047

F. F. Tronixs, 1047

Firstbyte, 1031

Genesys, 1048

Homnick, 1022

Hongkong Telecom, 1048

Inforamp, 1030

Islandnet, 1023

Kolvax, 1032

L R Technologies, 1023

MAPI reference resources, 1022-1024

Neosoft, 1022

netApp Systems, 1023

Netgain, 1023

Optelecom, Inc., 1049

Parity Software, 1049

PhonetiCs, Inc., 1050

Pronexus, Inc., 1050

PureSpeech, 1033

PureSpeech, Inc., 1050

Queuesys, 1023

Rhetorex, Inc., 1050

Sandman, 1051

SAPI reference resources, 1029-1034

Seanet, 1022

SIM-phony—Home, 1051

SoftTalk, Inc., 1051

Speech Systems, 1033

Stanford University Applied Speech Technology Lab, 1051

TAPI reference resources, 1044-1053

Tel-Com, 1051

Teleconnect Magazine, 1052

Tellabs Operations, 1052

Vision Computer Associates, 1023

VISIT Computer,
1052
Visual Voice, 1052
Vive Synergies, Inc.,
1052
Voice Processing Corp,
1033, 1053
Winserve, 1023
whole-word matching
word analysis, 461-462
word matching methods,
427-428
Window Properties
command (View
menu), 68
Window Properties dialog
box, 75
windows, setting properties
in forms, 68-75
Windows 3.11, MAPI
portability, 28-29
Windows 95
adding SR services, 565
MAPI portability, 28-29
Windows Messaging Client
for Windows 95, 49-50
Windows NT, MAPI
portability, 28-29
Windows Open Services
Architecture, *see* WOSA
Windows Registry,
TAPIFONE parameters,
781-782
Windows SNA Application
Program Interface, 17
Windows Sockets, 17
windows-level help, adding
to forms, 75-76
WinFax PRO with
Voice, 1055
WinMain routine
(TAPIOUT project),
638-644
WinPhone, 1056

WinScope, 1057
Winserve Web site, 1023
word analysis
sub-word matching,
461-462
whole-word matching,
461-462
word matching
methods
phoneme matching,
427-428
whole-word matching,
427-428
speech recognition
fundamentals, 427-428
word selection
continuous speech,
460-462
discrete speech, 460-462
word spotting, 460-462
word separation
methods
continuous speech,
425-426
discrete speech,
425-426
word spotting,
425-426
speech recognition
fundamentals, 425-426
word spotting
word selection, 460-462
word separation methods,
425-426
words
adding emphasis (Emp
tag), 512
defining context-free
grammars, 517
WorkGroup Post Office
for Windows, 49-50
workstations, dialing rules,
TAPI, 716-720
WorldWindows, 1056

WOSA (Windows Open
Services Architecture)
applications, leveraging,
19-20
benefits
isolated development,
18-19
multivendor
support, 19
upgrade protection, 19
Communication Services
Microsoft RPC (remote
procedure calls), 17
Windows SNA
Application Program
Interface, 17
Windows Sockets, 17
components
API/SPI interface, 13
Client API, 13
Server SPI, 13
models
License Service
Application Program
Interface
(LSAPI), 17
Messaging Application
Programming
Interface (MAPI), 17
Open Database
Connectivity
(ODBC), 17
Speech Application
Program Interface
(SAPI), 17
Telephony Application
Program Interface
(TAPI), 17
overview, 12-13
services
Common Application
Services, 16-17
Communication
Services, 17
Vertical Market
Services, 17-18

TAPI compatibility,
596-597
Vertical Market Services
*WOSA Extensions for
Financial
Services, 18*
*WOSA Extensions for
Real-Time Market
Data, 18*
**WOSA Extensions for
Financial Services, 18**
**WOSA Extensions for
Real-Time Market
Data, 18**
**WriteArcGet routine,
253-254**
**WriteArcList routine,
250-251**
**WriteToFile (Attachment
object method), 212-213**
**writing TeleBook applica-
tion (Visual Basic),
752-777**

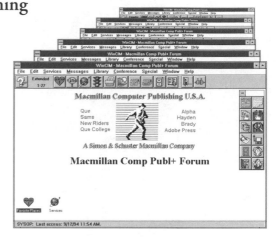

CGI Developer's Guide

Eugene Eric Kim

This book is one of the first books to provide comprehensive information on developing with CGI (the Common Gateway Interface). It covers many of the aspects of CGI, including interactivity, performance, portability, and security. After reading this book, the reader will be able to write robust, secure, and efficient CGI programs.

CD-ROM includes source code, sample utilities, and Internet tools

Covers client/server programming, working with gateways, and using Netscape

Readers will master forms, image maps, dynamic displays, database manipulation, and animation

Price: $45.00 USA/$63.95 CDN   User Level: Accomplished – Expert
ISBN: 1-57521-087-8   600 pp.   06/01/96   Internet, Programming

Tricks of the Visual Basic 4 Gurus

James Bettone, et al.

Microsoft is betting that the new release of Visual Basic 4 will create a mass migration from other compilers including its own Visual Basic 3 compiler. In expectation of that migration, *Tricks of the Visual Basic 4 Gurus* presents tips and secrets from programmers who work inside Microsoft, giving developers the "inside scoop" on the latest shortcuts and techniques to VB programming. Both 16-bit and 32-bit development is covered, in addition to tips on OLE and OCX programming.

CD-ROM contains source code from the book and the complete referenced applications

Covers Windows 32-bit programming for Windows 95

Teaches about OLE and the Win32 API

Programmers learn to port between 16-bit OCX controls and 32-bit OLE controls

Price: $49.99 USA/$67.99 CDN   User Level: Accomplished – Expert
ISBN: 0-672-30929-7   744 pp.   06/01/96   Programming

Windows NT 4 Server Unleashed

Jason Garms

The Windows NT server has been gaining tremendous market share over Novell, and the new upgrade—which includes a Windows 95 interface—is sure to add momentum to its market drive. To that end, *Windows NT 4 Server Unleashed* is written to meet that growing market. It provides information on disk and file management, integrated networking, BackOffice integration, and TCP/IP protocols.

CD-ROM includes source code from the book and valuable utilities

Focuses on using Windows NT as an Internet server

Covers security issues and Macintosh support

Price: $59.99 USA/$84.95 CDN   User Level: Accomplished – Expert
ISBN: 0-672-30933-5   1,100 pp.   07/01/96   Networking

Microsoft Exchange Server Survival Guide

Pete McPhedran—Aurora Communications Exchange

Readers will learn the difference between Exchange and other groupware, such as Lotus Notes and everything about the Exchange Server, including troubleshooting, development, and how to interact with other BackOffice components.

Includes everything operators need to run an Exchange server

Teaches how to prepare, plan, and install the Exchange server

Explores ways to migrate from other mail apps, such as Microsoft Mail and cc:Mail

Covers Microsoft Exchange

Price: $49.99 USA/$70.95 CDN   User Level: New – Advanced
ISBN: 0-672-30890-8   800 pp.   09/01/96   Groupware

Teach Yourself CGI Programming
with Perl in a Week

Eric Herrmann

This book is a step-by-step tutorial of how to create, use, and maintain a Common Gateway Interface (CGI). It describes effective ways of using CGI as an integral part of Web development.

Adds interactivity and flexibility to the information that can be provided through your Web site

Includes references to major protocols such as NCSA HTTP, CERN HTTP, and SHTTP

Covers PERL 4.0 and 5.0, and CGI

Price: $39.99 USA/$53.99 CDN　　　*User Level: Casual – Accomplished*
ISBN: 1-57521-009-6　　544 pp.　　　*01/01/96*　　　*Internet, Programming*

Paul McFedries' Windows 95 Unleashed,
Premier Edition

Paul McFedries

Completely updated and revised, this is bestselling author Paul McFedries' Windows 95 masterpiece. And in the traditional style of the Unleashed series, every new feature is discussed in detail so that the reader is fully informed and prepared to work with the new operating system. This book also includes coverage of soon-to-be-released Microsoft Internet products, such as Visual Basic Script, Internet Studio, and Microsoft Exchange—coverage not found anywhere else.

CD-ROM contains an easy-to-search online chapter on troubleshooting for Windows 95

Covers Internet topics, including the Microsoft Network

Discusses multimedia topics, internetworking, and communication issues

Price: $59.99 USA/$84.95 CDN　　　*User Level: Accomplished – Expert*
ISBN: 0-672-30932-7　　1,376 pp.　　　*07/01/96*　　　*Programming*

Programming Windows NT 4 Unleashed

David Hamilton, Mickey Williams, & Griffith Kadnier

Readers get a clear understanding of the modes of operation and architecture for Windows NT. Everything—including execution models, processes, threads, DLLs, memory, controls, security, and more—is covered with precise detail.

CD-ROM contains source code and completed sample programs from the book

Teaches OLE, DDE, drag and drop, OCX development, and the Component Gallery

Explores Microsoft BackOffice programming

Price: $59.99 USA/$84.95 CDN　　　*User Level: Accomplished – Expert*
ISBN: 0-672-30905-X　1,200 pp.　　　*07/01/96*　　　*Programming*

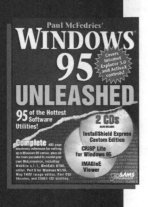

Add to Your Sams Library Today with the Best Books for Programming, Operating Systems, and New Technologies

The easiest way to order is to pick up the phone and call

1-800-428-5331

between 9:00 a.m. and 5:00 p.m. EST.
For faster service please have your credit card available.

ISBN	Quantity	Description of Item	Unit Cost	Total Cost
1-57521-087-8		CGI Developer's Guide (Book/CD-ROM)	$45.00	
0-672-30929-7		Tricks of the Visual Basic 4 Gurus (Book/CD-ROM)	$49.99	
0-672-30933-5		Windows NT 4 Server Unleashed (Book/CD-ROM)	$59.99	
0-672-30890-8		Microsoft Exchange Server Survival Guide (Book/CD-ROM)	$49.99	
0-672-30953-X		BackOffice Survival Kit (3 Books/4 CD-ROMs)	$149.99	
1-57521-009-6		Teach Yourself CGI Programming with Perl in a Week (Book/CD-ROM)	$39.99	
0-672-30932-7		Paul McFedries' Windows 95 Unleashed, Premier Edition (Book/CD-ROM)	$59.99	
0-672-30905-X		Programming Windows NT 4 Unleashed (Book/CD-ROM)	$59.99	
❏ 3 ½" Disk		Shipping and Handling: See information below.		
❏ 5 ¼" Disk		TOTAL		

Shipping and Handling: $4.00 for the first book, and $1.75 for each additional book. Floppy disk: add $1.75 for shipping and handling. If you need to have it NOW, we can ship product to you in 24 hours for an additional charge of approximately $18.00, and you will receive your item overnight or in two days. Overseas shipping and handling adds $2.00 per book and $8.00 for up to three disks. Prices subject to change. Call for availability and pricing information on latest editions.

201 W. 103rd Street, Indianapolis, Indiana 46290

1-800-428-5331 — Orders   1-800-835-3202 — FAX   1-800-858-7674 — Customer Service

Book ISBN 0-672-30928-9